The Leo Burnett Worldwide
Advertising
and
Media Fact Book

The Leo Burnett Worldwide
Advertising
and
Media Fact Book

───────

TRIUMPH BOOKS
CHICAGO

This book is available in quantity at special discounts for your group or organization. For further information contact:

Triumph Books, Inc.
644 South Clark Street
Suite 2000
Chicago, IL 60605
Tel: (312) 939-3330, Fax: (312) 663-3557

Design and Typography: Marilyn Justman

For each country within this book, statistics for total area, population and GDP were reproduced from information available in *The World Factbook, 1993*, produced by the Central Intelligence Agency (CIA).

Library of Congress Cataloging-in-Publication Data

The Leo Burnett worldwide advertising and media factbook : the international sourcebook of media conditions, facts and statistics/ Leo Burnett Company : [edited by Brian Jacobs].
    p.   cm.
    ISBN 1-880-141-57-4 : $250.00
    1. Advertising media planning–Directories. 2. Advertising–Directories. 3. Mass media–Directories.
I. Jacobs, Brian. II. Leo Burnett Company.

    HF5826.5.L46 1993   93-33593
    659.1'025–dc20   CIP

Acknowledgements

We hope that as a user of this book, you find it useful as a source of basic media information country-by-country throughout the world. Our aim has been to provide you with an overview of the media available, and to include sufficient detail so that you are able to consider your media and advertising needs within a context of what is realistic and possible within each market.

It is important to understand that, while the information presented here is the latest available, media markets around the world are changing fast in light of technological and governmental developments. We have used our best efforts to be as up-to-date as possible, but there is inevitably a gap between what is current today and what was current at time of publication.

Those who work in media will understand how important it is to use only the very latest information when proposing a budget, preparing a media plan or executing a buy. This book does not purport to be a substitute for many and detailed research sources used locally for such specific tasks. Rather, it should be seen as one of the many resources in approaching such tasks; certainly it has been our experience over the seven years that we have published this volume as an internal resource that the information contained within it has been extremely helpful in constructing international strategies and researching new markets.

A compilation such as this inevitably requires many hands, and sources. We wish to thank the members of the Leo Burnett media departments around the world, whose hard work has made this book possible.

We also want to thank the world's media research data suppliers, whose statistics have been referenced throughout the book.

While we have made every attempt to ensure the accuracy of the Fact Book, we do not warrant that it is error free as there may be errors and/or typographical errors contained in this book. We apologize for any oversights—and we welcome any suggestions for improving future editions.

Preface

Welcome to the *The Leo Burnett Worldwide Advertising and Media Fact Book.*

In 1993, advertisers around the world spent an estimated US$ 312.3 billion promoting their products through the major media. Managing the majority of this huge sum and ensuring that the money was spent in the most efficient and effective way possible is the job of the media departments of the world's advertising agencies.

Leo Burnett is one of the biggest agency networks in the world, with 55 offices in 49 countries handling over US$ 4 billion on behalf of their clients. To help us provide our advertisers with an unrivaled service in media planning and buying, we have, for the past seven years, published a worldwide media fact book, for our own internal use.

This year we have expanded the scope of the book, both in terms of the content of the material and by offering it as a service to the industry as a whole. We have been encouraged to do this by the ever-increasing demand for a comprehensive, and global, look at the world of advertising and media today.

This fact book has been compiled by the media departments of the Leo Burnett network of agencies. Such a source book is more relevant today than ever as more and more companies begin to think regionally, or even globally, about their advertising campaigns. We intend for this book to be a thorough reference to which companies may turn as they consider their advertising investments in markets with which they may be unfamiliar.

The information found in this book is useful to people of all levels working on global business. Executives of global companies will find the book a quick, easy reference for information regarding the advertising climate in countries in which they currently operate or which they are seeking to enter. International media planners will find the book an invaluable reference for media costs and coverage, and will also find it useful in drafting initial regional or global plans.

We hope *The Leo Burnett Worldwide Advertising and Media Fact Book* will become an invaluable part of your reference library. We have tried to incorporate information useful to anyone involved or interested in the global arena. At the same time, we are certain that the book can be improved and welcome any comments as we strive to make the next edition even more comprehensive and useful than this one.

Brian Jacobs
Senior Vice President and
International Media Director

Contents

Middle East   275

Latin America   331

North America   469

Leo Burnett Offices   ix

Structure of the Fact Book

How it can help

The Leo Burnett Worldwide Advertising and Media Fact Book provides comprehensive media information about 57 countries around the world. The Fact Book is divided into five parts—Asia/Pacific, Europe, the Middle East, Latin America and North America. Each section is prefaced by an introduction that outlines trends and changes that are developing in that region's marketplace. Those who plan to enter international media or advertising will find this book invaluable due to the immense data resources it contains, everything from population information to CPM's to regulations.

Each chapter provides an in-depth look at each country from a media standpoint. To provide the most information in the most efficient manner, each chapter is broken into sections. A representational outline of a section within a country is listed here:

> **Television**
> > **Overview**
> > **Percentage of households with TV's**
> > **Opportunities**
> > **Historic and Primetime Costs**
> > **Average audience profile**
> > **CPMs**
> > **Viewing statistics**
> > **Languages used for broadcasts**
> > **Commercial lengths**
> > **Restrictions on commercial timing**
> > **Regional/Local vs. national advertising**
> > **Children's advertising**

Profile

Here the reader will find country-specific demographic information such as the number of households, population by sex, age group and socio-economic status, GNP distribution by industry and inflation and exchange rates. A listing of federal and school holidays is also included in this section.

Major Influences and Trends

This section should give the reader a sense of the overall media environments in each country. It provides a brief description of main influences as well as media trends. The specifics vary from country-to-country, depending on the market and what information is available. Main vehicles, buying clubs, media ownership, changing media structure and any other relevant data is discussed.

Spending Analysis

In addition to an advertising expenditure overview of the market, this section provides 1991 and 1992 historical national spending by medium as well as a brief synopsis describing the negotiation practices for each medium. A list of top advertisers by product and by category is also provided. This spending analysis section not only gives the reader an indication of how advertisers are reacting to the economic climate compared to years past, but also in which media the majority of spending falls.

After the overview of the country, the chapter discusses each media type available in the country. The information presents the medium first, which is then followed by market data about the medium. The chapter finishes with information about trends, outlooks and percent change in costs versus previous years.

The next sections discuss media that may be relatively new in many countries. All available information about these media is provided under the countries where it exists.

Television

Here the reader will find a listing of commercial channels, primary and secondary languages spoken and television coverage. This section also specifies household penetration, available commercial lengths, Cost per Thousand (CPM's) by station and dayparts, impressions by dayparts and percent change in primetime costs from 1989-1992. For those interested in the children's market, a listing of channels that accept children's programming is included, as well as children's dayparts and average impressions.

Radio

Here the reader will be provided with the languages of programs, commercial availability, percent change in costs versus previous years and CPM's by dayparts.

Cable/Satellite

This section gives current and projected cable and satellite penetration along with the languages used for broadcast. The cable and satellite network cost and type of programming available is also outlined. These sections will vary as cable and satellite are still fairly underdeveloped in some countries.

Video Cassettes

This section provides an overview of the video cassette recorder market and its penetration. Where applicable, information about commercial advertising on pre-recorded video cassette tapes is provided.

Cinema

In addition to an overview of the cinematic scene as it pertains to advertising, number of theaters, available commercial lengths and costs are also furnished.

Magazines/Newspapers

Names of major daily newspapers and magazines, their circulation, costs and average daily readerships are supplied in this section.

Outdoor/Transit

Detailed information about size, availability, costs and lead time needed to reserve these types of advertising can be found in this section.

Direct Marketing

Names of direct mail consumer list brokers, as well as the top telemarketing companies in the country, where available, are listed in this section.

Non-traditional Media

This section will vary for each country, depending on the types of innovative media used. Some examples might include hot air balloon or grocery cart advertising.

Research Sources

This section provides a listing of research companies that provide media data in that country. This list is not all inclusive, but will, in some cases, be quite detailed.

Advertising Regulations

Here the advertising regulations are listed by subject matter and by medium. This section will give the reader an indication of the advertising regulatory environment of each country. The section will also list those products, if any, for which advertising is banned altogether.

Sources Consulted

Found here is a listing of the organizations and publications that have been used as sources of information for each country.

Asia/Pacific

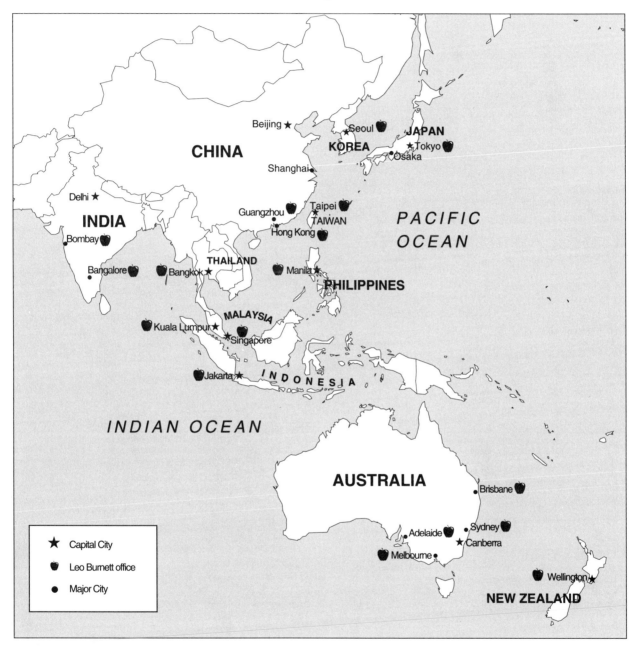

Asia/Pacific

Regional Summary

Satellite and Cable Television

Satellite TV is broadcast across Asia from two satellites–Asiasat and Palapa. Asiasat has the highest household penetration at 11.2 million (January 1993) and carries the five STAR TV channels. Palapa, with 1.8 million households, is currently home to CNN International, ESPN, Australia Television International (ATVI) and HBO, with Asian Business Network (ABN) planned for late 1993.

STAR TV has taken the lead in driving satellite distribution in Asia, going from 3 million homes in June 1992 to 11.2 million homes in January 1993. This meteoric growth is predicted to continue, with 18.8 million homes anticipated by December 1993.

China is now STAR's largest single market at 4.8 million homes, followed by India and Taiwan. Hong Kong will become a more significant market for STAR TV when 800,000 public housing units are brought on-line in late 1993.

STAR TV introduced four subscription channels in October 1993, with more likely to follow. The purchase of a controlling interest in STAR by Rupert Murdoch's News Corporation in July 1993 will also open new programming avenues for STAR TV, such as an open university channel, the first education channel in Asia.

In the face of stiff competition from STAR, ESPN, HBO, CNN International and ATVI from Palapa, plus TVBI, have formed a consortium with the primary aim of building distribution. As yet there are no details of any joint marketing operations.

The launching of the Asiasat II and Apstar II satellites in late 1994 will increase the potential footprints to 70 percent of the world's population. The new technology that these advanced satellites will bring will have the capacity for a hundred plus channels on each satellite. Confirmation as to future satellite usage is awaited from stations.

Cable is playing an increasingly important role in many Asian countries and is expected to continue to grow. One example is the launch of Wharf Cable in Hong Kong in October 1993. The growth of cable is significant, not only in its own right, but also for satellite, as much of the future satellite stations' growth in homes is expected to come via cable networks. For example, cable is already important to STAR TV in India, Taiwan, Hong Kong and soon China.

Print

All major international titles are available in Asia Pacific. There are also a number of regional titles, primarily focusing on news and business. Asia Magazine has the highest circulation across Asia. This is due to its role as a magazine supplement to a number of leading local English language newspapers (e.g., Hong Kong with South China Morning Post, Thailand with Bangkok Post). Apart from Asia Magazine, Reader's Digest and National Geographic, circulation is primarily by subscription.

The majority of available titles are English language. This means that readership tends to be the highest where English is widely used-particularly in Singapore, Malaysia, Indonesia, Hong Kong and the Philippines. There has been a trend in Korea and Japan towards more local language editions of international titles such as *Newsweek*, but the costs of launching local language editions are high. *Time Magazine* recently set up on office in Japan to publish a local edition but pulled out when the costs were too high in light of the current recession. Local language titles effectively become local titles, evaluated on a local basis. If Korea, Japan, Taiwan or China are important markets, then the regional schedule needs supplementing with local titles to achieve good coverage levels.

International/regional titles play an important role in reaching an upscale audience across Asia, offering an international and, more importantly, largely unbiased and uncensored perspective. This is particularly important in markets such as Singapore and Malaysia, with Singapore still posing a problem for a number of titles in either gazetting or restricting the circulation.

Gary Brown
Regional Media Director

Australia

Area	7,686,850 km^2
Population (1992)	17,576,354
Population growth rate (1992)	1.4%
GDP	US$ 280.8 billion
GDP/per capita	US$ 16,200
Real growth rate (1991)	0.6%
Capital	Canberra

Population Breakdown

By Sex		*By Age Group*		*By Socio-Economic Status*	
Male	49.8%	Children	18.1%	A&B	23%
Female	50.2%	Teens	7.2%	C	22%
		Adults	74.7%	D	19%
				E&F	36%

Source (Sex, Age Group): Australian Bureau of Statistics (1991)

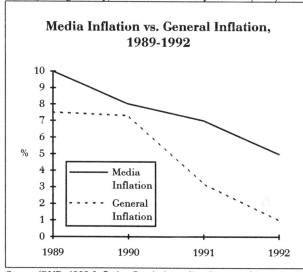

Media Inflation vs. General Inflation, 1989-1992

Legend:
— Media Inflation
⋯ General Inflation

Number of Households	5,400,000

Ownership of household durables
- Car 98%
- Phone 94.4%
- Washers 86.5%
- *(purchasing power equivalent)*

GNP distribution by industry
- Agriculture.................... 9%
- Industry...................... 21%
- Services...................... 70%

Exchange rates (US$ to local currency)
- 1991.........................0.7577
- 1992.........................0.6747

Source (GNP, 1992 Inflation Rate): Australian Bureau of Statistics (1993)

National Holidays

Holiday	*1993 Date*
New Years Day	January 3
Australia Day	January 26
Easter	April 1-4
Anzac Day	April 25
Labor Day	October 3
Queens Birthday	June 13
Christmas Day	December 25
Boxing Day	December 26

School Holidays *

Holiday	*1993 Date*
Summer Vacation	December 20, 1993 - January 28, 1994
Easter Vacation	April 1, 1994 - April 8, 1994
Winter Vacation	June 27, 1994 - July 8, 1994
Spring Vacation	September 26, 1994 - October 7, 1994
Summer Vacation	December 19, 1994 - January 27, 1995

Dates vary by state.

Major Influences and Trends

Television
The Nine Network is operating successfully under ACP Ltd. (Kerry Packer), while the Ten Network is now controlled by a consortium headed by Canwest Communications. The Seven Network is undergoing public ownership in late 1993. All regional independent market stations were aggregated in 1991/92 to provide a choice of three commercial services in all major markets.

Pay TV
Two commercial Satellite TV licenses have been awarded to independent groups, however there will be a complete restriction on advertising until 1997.
Microwave (MDS) TV has been banned from broadcasting until the start of 1995, by which time satellite pay TV should be operational.

Press
Dominated by Murdoch-owned News Limited. *Conrad Black* controls *John Fairfax*, the other significant newspaper player. The industry is currently stable and profitable.

Radio
Continued flight of AM music stations to FM. Advertising sales declining. FM profitable - AM marginal.

Magazines
Successful introduction of *Who Weekly* in 1992 with a variety of new titles emerging in 1993/94 including SHE magazine.

Media Buying Groups
Equmedia, commissioned in 1991, is the largest media rate negotiation group. Equmedia is composed of Leo Burnett Connaghan & May, Young & Rubicam, Grey Advertising , DMB&B, Total, and AIS.

Spending Analysis

National advertising spending by medium
based on appropriate year's exchange rate

	1989 US$ MM	1990 US$ MM	1991 US$ MM	1992 US$ MM
TV	1,324.6	1,355.6	1,222.9	1,207
Cinema	53.6	63.2	62.9	53
Radio	335.7	334.6	318.2	289
Newspaper	1,711.5	1,560.8	1,494.2	1,409
Magazine	264.8	305	262.9	219
Direct Response	451.5	537.4	468.3	461
Outdoor	269.5	221.5	201.5	177
Total	**4,411.2**	**4,378.1**	**4,030.9**	**3,815**

Source: Commercial Economic Advisory Service of Australia (1992)

Media Buying

Television
Rates applied to large agencies are negotiated annually, based on total agency billings. Smaller agencies negotiate on a client specific basis as needed.

Other Media
Published rate card rates are subject to negotiation for most media.

Current Media Environment
Current economic conditions are conducive to off rate card deals. Buying services handle approximately 30% of total advertising dollars.
Additionally, a number of consortia exist for the negotiation of rates only.

Proportionate spending among media 1991-92

1991
Direct Response 12%
Outdoor 5%
Magazine 6%
TV 30%
Newspaper 37%
Radio 8%
Cinema 2%

1992
Direct Response 12%
Outdoor 4.6%
Magazine 5.7%
TV 31.7%
Newspaper 37%
Cinema 1.4%
Radio 7.6%

Source: Commercial Economic Advisory Service of Australia (1992)

Buying Sevices with 1992 Billings

Buying Service	Parent Company	US$ M
AIS Media	Dentsu	151.5
Media Decisions	George Patterson (BSBW)	118
Merchant & Partners	Interpublic	264.5
Total Media	Mattingly & Partners (Dentsu,Y&R)	187
Mitchell & Partners (Ind.)	Private	N/A

Source: Adnews, Feb 26, 1993

Consortia for Rate Negotiations

Consortium	US$ M	Affiliates
Equmedia	675	LBC&M,Y&R, Grey,Total,AIS, DMB&B
Interpublic	472	Lintas, McCann, Merchant & Ptnrs
Omnicom	506	Clemmenger, DDB Needham
George Pattersons Group	576	George Pattsrson, Saatchi & Saatchi, Media Decisions
Mitchell & Partners Group	472	Includes 37 agencies

Source: Adnews, Feb 26, 1993

Top advertisers (1992 spending)

Expenditure figures are estimates and exclude sponsorships.

By Company

Parent Company	Product Category	US$ MM
Coles Myer	Retailing	59.2
Unilever	Packaged Goods	36.8
Telecom	Government Telecommunications Service	35.7
Kellogg's	Cereals	25.3
Woolworth's	Retailing	23.5
Mitsubishi	Automotive	22.3
Nestle	Food	22.0
Toyota	Automotive	21.8
Pacific Dunlop	Manufactured Goods	20.4
Effem Foods	Food	19.7

Source: AIM Data (1993)

By Product

Product Category	Advertiser	US$ MM
Automotive	Mitsubishi	22.3
Retailing	Coles Myer	59.2
Telecommuni-cations	Telecom	35.7
Packaged Goods	Unilever	36.8
Beverages	Coca Cola Amatil	19.6
Food	Nestle	22.0

Source: AIM Data (1993)

Television

Adult Reach	
at 250 GRPs	75%
at 500 GRPs	84%
at 1000 GRPs	90%

Overview

- Television sets are owned by 97% of Australian households.
- Cost increases are consistant with Consumer Price Index increases. Negotiable market due to recession. Highly competitive in non-metropolitan markets.

Opportunities

Network	Number of Stations	Ownership	Station Profile	Commercial Min/Hr	Coverage	Broadcast Hours (Sign-On/Off)
METRO						
Seven	5	Receivership	General	11-13	Metro	24 hours
Nine	5	Kerry Packer (A.C.P.)	General	11-13	Metro	24 hours
Ten	5	Canwest	General	11-13	Metro	24 hours
SBS	5	Government	Ethnic	5	Metro	approx 12 hours / day
REGIONAL						
Prime Television (Seven)	4	Independent	General	11-13	Regional Aggregated Markets	24 hours
Nine Affiliates (Nine)	4	Independent	General	11-13	Regional Aggregated Markets	24 hours
Media Sales Network (Ten)	4	Independent	General	11-13	Regional Aggregated Markets	24 hours
Independent	12	Independent	General	11-13	Local Market Coverage	24 hours

Costs

Prime Time TV Costs for :30 in US$			
1989	*1990*	*1991*	*1992*
2,820	2,930	2,990	2,800

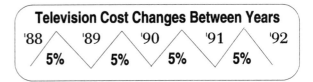

Audiences/CPM's

Average Cost, Audience and CPM's by Daypart
(Top 3 Stations, :30, in Sydney, Target=Adults 18+ 32% of population, May 23 '93–June 19 '93)

Hours	Morning 09:00-12:00	Daytime 12:00-18:00	Prime Time 18:00-22:30	Late Night 22:30-24:00	Weekend	Children
Station: Seven						
US$	394	398	2,639	674	N/A	N/A
Avg. Aud. (000)	31	110	316	131	N/A	N/A
CPM	12.71	3.62	8.35	5.15	N/A	N/A
Station: Nine						
US$	311	635	3,812	783	N/A	N/A
Avg. Aud. (000)	52	120	417	168	N/A	N/A
CPM	6.0	5.30	9.14	4.66	N/A	N/A
Station: Ten						
US$	201	391	1,929	567	N/A	N/A
Avg. Aud. (000)	31	77	243	81	N/A	N/A
CPM	6.48	5.08	7.94	7.00	N/A	N/A

Source (Ratings only): A. C. Nielsen 1993

Audiences/Ratings by Dayart (Target=Adults 18+; Sydney 32% of National Metro Population)

Daypart	Hours	Household				Adult		
		Universe (000)	Hut Levels	Household Rating	Impressions (000)	Universe (000)	Adult Rating	Impressions (000)
Morning	09:00-12:00	1,263	N/A	3.9	50	2,822	1.3	38
Daytime	12:00-18:00	1,263	N/A	7.4	93	2,822	3.6	102
Primetime	18:00-22:30	1,263	N/A	18.2	230	2,822	11.5	325
Late Night	22:30-24:00	1,263	N/A	7.8	98	2,822	4.5	126
Weekend	N/A	N/A	N/A	N/A	N/A	N/A	N/A	N/A
Children's	N/A	N/A	N/A	N/A	N/A	N/A	N/A	N/A

Source: A.C. Nielsen 1993

Scheduling

- The primary broadcasting language is English; 5% of programs are broadcast in various other languages.
- About 80% of all commercials are :30; other commercial lengths available are :15, :45, :60, :90, :120 and :180.

Children's Advertising

ADULT PROGRAMMING			Kids'		
Station	Hours	Days	Universe (000)	Ratings	Impressions (000)
Seven*	18:00-20:30	Sun - Fri	420	15.7	66
Nine*	18:00-20:30	Sun - Fri	420	8.3	33
Ten*	18:00-20:30	Sun - Fri	420	9.4	40

| CHILDREN'S PROGRAMMING | | | | Kids' | |
Station	Hours	Days	Universe (000)	Ratings	Impressions (000)
Seven*	07:00 - 09:00	Mon - Fri	420	9.7	41
	16:00 - 17:00	Mon - Fri	420	7.5	32
	07:00 - 09:00	Sat & Sun	420	10.8	46
Nine*	07:00 - 12:00	Sat	420	5.5	23
Ten*	07:00 - 09:00	Mon - Fri	420	3.5	15
	07:00 - 12:00	Sun	420	5.8	25

*Based on Sydney (Period 23.5.93-19.6.93) Children 5-12   Source: A. C. Nielsen 1993

Radio

Overview

- There are 386 radio stations in Australia, of which 197 are commercial. Sydney has 14 major stations.
- Virtually all households and 97% of automobiles have radios; the estimated household penetration is 5,400,000.
- The primary broadcasting language is English; other languages are also used.
- No premiums are required. The most popular program types are Classic Rock, Talk Back and Sports.
- Prime Time is breakfast time: 05:30-09:00.
- Available lengths include :15, :30, :45, :60 and :120.

Costs

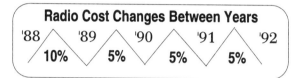

Averages By Daypart

(Top 3 Sydney stations, Target=18+, Universe 2,816,000)

Daypart	Local Time	Avg.Cost :30 US$	Audience (000)	CPM (US$)
Breakfast	05:30 - 09:00	360	154	2.34
Morning	09:00 - 12:00	303	126	2.40
Afternoon	12:00 - 16:00	248	83	2.98
Drivetime	16:00 - 19:00	285	67	4.25
Late Night	19:00 - 24:00	147	30	4.90

Source (Ratings): AGB McNair (1993)

Cable

No information is available about cable in Australia.

Satellite

- Satellite market is undeveloped. Currently only Sky Channel is available, however, it broadcasts exclusively to clubs and hotels. Licenses have been awarded for two commercial pay TV stations with broadcast to begin in 1995.
- Satellite penetration is expected to reach 10%, approximately 525,000 households, within 5 years.

Satellite Channel	Country of Origin	Language	Programming
Sky Channel	Australia	English	Sport, Music

Video Cassettes

Roughly 71% of TV households have video cassette recorders (VCRs). The use of commercials in pre-recorded tapes is limited and tapes average one sponsor per tape. There is no predictable fee structure. A. C. Nielsen people meters measure VCR usage.

Cinema

- There are 1,800 cinemas in Australia, all of which offer commercial time.
- Potential reach over 4 weeks, for a buy of 600 cinemas is about 26%. (*Source (Potential reach): Roy Morgan Research (1992).*)
- Commercials are available in :30, :60, :90 and :120 lengths.
- The average cost of a four-week cinema schedule for a :30 commercial at 140

cinemas is US$ 45,000 (US$ 81 each). No information is available about cinema cost changes.
- Increases in multi-cinema complexes are expected. Cinema attendance in 1992 was 20% higher than in 1988. (*Source: Motion Picture Distributors Association of Australia, Sydney (1992)*)

Newspapers

There are 2 national daily papers which accept advertising. Combined circulation is 225,000 The literacy rate in English is 95%.
Source: ABC Audit (1993)

Newspaper Cost Changes Between Years

'88	'89	'90	'91	'92
10%	10%	10%	5%	

Newspaper	Market	Size	Circ. (000)	Avg. Daily Aud. (000)	1 page/B&W Cost (US$)	Accept Color?
The Australian	National	Broadsheet	150	400	8,690	Yes**
Aust. Financial Review	National	Tabloid	74	279	4,775	Yes**
Sydney Morning Herald	Sydney	Broadsheet	267	913	16,885	Yes**
Daily Telegraph Mirror	Sydney	Tabloid	438	1,374	9,835	Yes**
The Age	Melbourne	Broadsheet	237	729	11,785	Yes**
Herald Sun	Melbourne	Tabloid	575	1,658	11,920	Yes**
Courier Mail	Brisbane	Broadsheet	251	705	8,650	Yes**
Advertiser	Adelaide	Broadsheet	218	621	7,045	Yes**
West Australian	Perth	Tabloid	258	696	4,060	Yes**
Canberra Times	Canberra	Broadsheet	47	137	4,470	Yes**

*Circulation Figures: ABC Audit: Mon-Sat, (1.10.92-31.3.93)
Readership Figures: Roy Morgan Research, Mon-Fri, (1.4.92-30.3.93) (1993)
**Run of Press, spot and four color plus pre-printed four color inserts available in all newspapers.

Magazines

There are 600 national consumer magazines which accept advertising in Australia, and another 700 trade and technical magazines.

Magazine Cost Changes Between Years

'88	'89	'90	'91	'92
10%	10%	10%	5%	

Magazine	Type	Frequency	Circ.* (000)	Audited?	Avg. Issue Aud (000)	1 page/4/C Cost (US$)
Australian Womens Weekly	Womens	Monthly	1152	Yes	3,571	14,900
New Idea	Womens	Weekly	1,044	Yes	2,694	11,720
Womens Day	Womens	Weekly	1,102	Yes	2,643	11,060
Cleo	Womens	Monthly	322	Yes	1,125	7,020
Cosmopolitan	Womens	Monthly	316	Yes	1,025	6,620
Business Review Weekly	Business	Weekly	72	Yes	332	5,370
Australian Business Monthly	Business	Monthly	36	Yes	122	3,345
Bulletin w/ Newsweek	Business	Weekly	107	Yes	460	5,835
Time	General	Weekly	110	Yes	448	5,110
Readers Digest	General	Monthly	480	Yes	1,402	6,280
Who Weekly	Entertainment	Weekly	182	Yes	679	4,040
TV Week	Entertainment	Weekly	625	Yes	2,066	8,935

*Circulation Figures ABC Audit (1.4.92-30.9.92)
Readership Figures (1.4.92-30.3.93)

Outdoor/Transit

Billboard	**Transit**
Sites available ....48,000 Lead Time to reserve ....8-12 weeks max. Exposure (prime, metro sites).........85%	Boards available..............................9,000 Exposure (metro)..............................60%

Costs
Average, 1 billboard/month
    6 sheets (10 ft x 15 ft)....................US$ 101
    24 sheets (20 ft x 10 ft)..................US$ 303
    Supersites (40 ft x 10 ft)...............US$ 2940
 	
Billboard Cost Changes Between Years
'88 / '89 / '90 / '91 / '92
10% / 5% / 5% / 5%
	Costs
	Average, 1 board/month
	    10 ft ....US$ 108
	
	Transit Cost Changes Between Years
	'88 / '89 / '90 / '91 / '92
	10% / 10% / 5% / 5%

Sizes 5 ft x 3 ft, 10ft x 5 ft, 20 ft x 10 ft, 40 ft x 10 ft	**Sizes** 6 ft x 2 ft, 8 ft x 2 ft, 10 ft x 2 ft, 24 ft x 2 ft

Direct Marketing

Very active and increasing volume of advertising dollars

List Broker	*Information Provided*
Logos Drake List Management Dun & Bradstreet International List Brokers The Mailing List Centre	Varies from list to list. Can be as little as personal name and postcode selection or as much as title, income level, occupation, interests, products bought, etc...
Top Telemarketing Companies	**Direct Marketing Association**
Key Direct Response/Levita Group Apple Telemarketing (Melbourne) Camco Communications	The Australian Direct Marketing Association Ltd. Level 7, 22-30 Bridge Street, Sydney 2000

Non-Traditional Media

- There has been an increase in point-of-purchase media.
- Types currently available:
    - Ad Trolley - US$ 1.47 per trolley/week (3 month rate)
    - In-store Radio - US$ 8,500/week (1 x :30 sec per 1/2 hour)
    - All major supermarkets (National Coverage)

Research Sources

Medium covered	*Research company*	*Information provided*

TV (Metro)	A.C. Nielsen
	  85 Epping Road
	  North Ryde
	  NSW 2113
		Ratings, Reach and Frequency

Continued on following page

Research Sources, continued

Medium Covered	*Research Company*	*Information Provided*
Radio & TV (Regional)	AGB McNair 168 Walker Street North Sydney NSW 2060	Ratings, Reach and Frequency
Press/Magazines	Roy Morgan Research 2nd Floor 232 Sussex Street Sydney NSW 2000	Demographic and Lifestyle Readership Data
Cinema	Roy Morgan Research	Demographic Data

Television Research Currently Available

Research Method	*Frequency*
(Metro TV) people meters	Daily, Weekly or Monthly
(Regional TV) Diary	Monthly (8 times per year for aggregated markets)

Advertising Regulations

By Product

Beverages/Alcohol
Advertising restricted to after 20:30 on
Television. Strict copy limitations.

Cigarettes
Total media advertising ban. Sponsorships
currently in phase-out situation.

Pharmaceuticals/Drugs
Strict copy limitations. Restricted from
children's programming.

Advertising To Children
Strict copy limitations during children's television time.

Commercial Production
Generally limited to in-country production.
However, 20% of foreign footage can be used in a
television commercial.

Australian ghost crews and talent can be used to
shoot a television commercial overseas for use in
Australia.

By Medium

Television
Commercial content
    13 minutes/hour during peak time.
    16 minutes/hour during off-peak time.
    Maximum 20% foreign commercials.
    Censorship classifications apply.

Outdoor
Some local council restrictions may apply.

China

Area	9,596,960 km²
Population (1992)	1,171,710,000
Population growth rate (1992)	1.6%
GDP	US$ 45 billion
GDP/per capita	US$ 1,300
Real growth rate (1991)	3.7%
Capital	Beijing

Population Breakdown

By Sex		By Age Group	
Male	51.5%	Under 15	28%
Female	48.5%	15+	82%

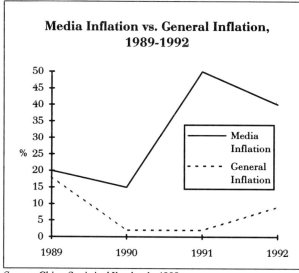

Media Inflation vs. General Inflation, 1989-1992

Number of Households	288,812,000

Ownership of household durables
- Car .... N/A
- Phone 5.2%
- Washers 11.74%
- *(purchasing power equivalent)*

GNP distribution by industry
- Agriculture.................. 27%
- Industry 46%
- Services 27%

Exchange rates (US$ to local currency)
- 1991............................0.19
- 1992............................0.19
- 1993............................0.17

Source: China Statistical Yearbook, 1992.

National Holidays

Holiday	1993 Date
New Year's	January 1
Chinese New Year	January 23-26
Woman's Day	March 8 (half day for females only)
Labor Day	May 1
National Day	October 1
Children's Day	June 1 (half day for parents only)

School Holidays

Holiday	1993 Date
New Year's	January 1
Chinese New Year	January 17-February 14
Woman's Day	March 8 (half day for females only)
Labor Day	May 1
Youth Day	May 4 (half day for young students)
Children's Day	June 1 (for children only)
Summer Holiday	Mid-July to end of August
National Day	October 1

Major Influences and Trends

Under new advertising regulations issued by the State Administration of Industry & Commerce, all advertisers must schedule advertising space or time through an advertising agency instead of dealing directly with media suppliers. As a result, most media suppliers set up their own advertising agencies to handle media bookings.

Media costs have increased drastically, especially for joint venture advertisers (50%–100% rate increase 1993).

More and more new TV and radio stations are coming on-air. These stations are more flexible in terms of administration, programming, and trade, because they are now responsible for their own profit or loss following the removal of many state subsidies.

A number of international publications have joint ventures with local publications to launch Chinese language editions of existing publications, i.e., Businessweek, Executive, World Executive Digest, Walt Disney Magazines, etc. Many more such arrangements are predicted in the near future.

Spending Analysis

National advertising spending by medium
based on appropriate year's exchange rate

	1989 US$ MM	1990 US$ MM	1991 US$ MM	1992 US$ MM
TV	70	109	197	N/A
Radio	18	17	27	N/A
Newspaper	122	132	184	N/A
Magazine	16	17	21	N/A
Direct Response	165	210	252	N/A
Total	391	485	681	1,188

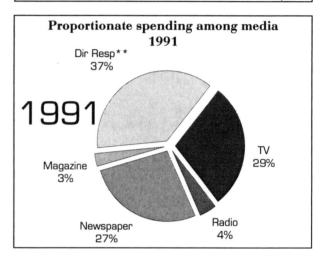

Proportionate spending among media 1991

Dir Resp** 37%
Magazine 3%
Newspaper 27%
Radio 4%
TV 29%
1991

*Breakdowns for 1992 are not available. Spending based on appropriate year's exchange rate
**Figures for Direct Response include outdoor, cinema, direct marketing and others. All billings shown at historical exchange rates.

Media Buying

In China, media is monopolized and controlled by government institutions. There are 3 basic levels:
- Central
- Provincial
- Local/City

Media pricing is negotiable. The 3-tier rate structure is:
- Foreign Advertiser
- Joint Venture Advertiser
- Local Advertiser

10% agency commission rebate to local/joint venture advertisers (although an increase to 15% has been discussed in line with attempts to standardize pricing along international lines).

15% agency commission rebate to foreign advertisers. There are no buying services.

Only local and international advertising agencies who have a joint venture partner in China are allowed to execute media placements directly with media.

Television

Overview

TV HH Penetration		
1989	*1990*	*1991*
51.47%	59.04%	68.41%
163,005,000	186,979,000	190,603,000

Source: China Statistical Yearbook, 1992

- A number of new TV stations or channels have been launched in China with improved programming (more lively and innovative).
- Foreign program suppliers (primarily from Hong Kong, Taiwan, and the U.S.) are now supplying programs to TV stations in exchange for commercial air-time allocations which are then re-sold to foreign advertisers.
- There is an increasing usage of satellite to live broadcast foreign events, especially "live" sports.
- The last year has seen significant rate increases for both local and joint venture advertisers, thus bringing advertising costs more in line with foreign rates.
- Advance payment is mandatory (one month prior to on-air date) for local and joint venture advertisers. This advance payment does not apply to foreign advertisers.
- In 1991, household TV penetration was 68.41%.

Opportunities

Network	Number of Stations	Ownership	Station Profile	Commercial Minutes/Day	Coverage	Broadcast Hours (Sign-On/Off)
CCTV	1	Central Government	Channel 1 General, News, Varieties	60	585MM	08:30-24:00
CCTV	(same as above)	Central Government	Channel 2 Drama, Imported Programs	60	250MM	08:30-24:00

Source: CCTV Station

Costs

Prime Time TV Costs for :30 in US$			
	1991	*1992*	*Cost Change, 1991-1992*
BJTV	1,300	1,600	23%
GZTV	840	885	5%
SHTV	1,300	1,800	38%

Audiences/CPM's

Average Cost, Audience, and CPMs by Daypart
(Top three stations, :30, national audience, Target=Adults, 15+)

Hours	Morning 07:00-11:59	Daytime 12:00-18:00	Prime Time 18:00-22:59	Late Night After 23:00	Weekend 18:00-22:59	Children 17:31-18:30
Station: Beijing TV 1						
US$	500	500	2,500	2,500	3,000	2,500
Avg. Aud. (000)	42	39	609	166	853	N/A
CPM	11.90	12.82	4.10	15.10	3.50	
Station: Guangzhou TV						
US$	N/A	170	1,020	850	1,326	820
Avg. Aud. (000)	N/A	9	352	32	310	N/A
CPM	N/A	18.90	2.90	26.60	4.30	
Station: Shanghai TV 1						
US$	500	800	2,340	1,900	2,808	800
Avg. Aud. (000)	46	43	1,143	80	1,046	N/A
CPM	10.90	18.60	2.00	23.80	2.70	

Source: SRG China 1993

Audiences/Ratings by Daypart (CCTV - Ch 1, Target = Persons 4+)

	Hours	Household				Adult		
		Universe (000)	Hut Levels	Household Rating	Impressions (000)	Universe (000)	Adult Rating	Impressions (000)
Morning	9:00-12:00	N/A	N/A	N/A	N/A	585,000	0.8	4,680
Daytime	12:00-19:00	N/A	N/A	N/A	N/A	585,000	3.0	17,550
Primetime	19:00-23:00	N/A	N/A	N/A	N/A	585,000	17.0	99,450
Late Night	22:30-24:00	N/A	N/A	N/A	N/A	585,000	18.0	17,550
Weekend	19:00-22:30	N/A	N/A	N/A	N/A	585,000	18.0	105,300
Children's	18:30-19:00	N/A	N/A	N/A	N/A	585,000	3.5	20,475

Source: CCTV Research Dept.

Scheduling/Regional/Languages

LANGUAGES	Programming	Commercials
Primary	Manadarin 100% Except Guangdong, Cantonese	Mandarin
Secondary	Local dialect	Cantonese in Guangdong only

- Commercials are available in :05, :10, :15, :45 and :60 spots; 80% of all commercial time sold is :30 in length.

- Commercials are aired throughout the day for all stations, usually at the beginning and end of programs.
- Provincial level stations in each province sell commercial time in dayparts. The cost is approximately 163% of national time.

Children's Advertising

Every program accepts advertising targeted at children. (*Source: China Statistical Yearbook, 1992*)

Radio

Overview

Radio Cost Changes Between Years

'88	'89	'90	'91	'92
N/A	100%	-25%	67%	

- There are 724 stations; in China, all are commercial. 2 are in Guangdong, 2 are in Shanghai, and 3 are in Beijing. (*Source: China Statistical Yearbook, 1992*)
- Approximately 81% of all households have radios; the estimated number is 257,160,000.
- The primary broadcasting language is Mandarin, however, English and local dialects, e.g. Cantonese, are also used.
- The most popular programs are News and Weather Reports.
- Commercial lengths available are :15, :30, :45 and :60.

Ratings

Prime/Peak Time for Radio	Daypart	Adult Rating	Adult (000)
Beijing	07:00-07:29	12	629
Shanghai	06:00-06:29	31	2172
Guangzhou	10:00-12:00	11	321

Source: SRG China, 1993

Costs

Daypart Costs/CPMs (Beijing Radio, Target=15+)

Daypart	Local Time	Avg. Cost :30 US$	Adult Rating	Audience (000)	CPM (US$)
Prime Time	6:00-8:00	307	8	414	0.74
Daytime	8:00-14:00	53	1	45	1.17
Late Night	23:00-24:00	53	N/A	19	3.00

Source (Ratings): SRG China, 1993

Cable

- Cable TV has been established in some local cities, such as Beijing, Shanghai, Wuhan, Chengdu, Zhongshan, etc.
- The subscription is limited in some districts to the greater city.
- The monthly subscription rate is approximately RMB 5.00–10.00.
- Cable channels broadcast programs produced by national, provincial and local TV stations, as well as their own programs.
- Cable channels primarily broadcast foreign movies and drama series.
- Under current advertising regulations, cable TV is not allowed to accept commercials. However, stations continue to sell commercial air-time to advertisers.

Satellite

- Some provincial stations transmitted by satellite due to the geographic barriers, especially in remote areas.

- About 4.8 million households in China can receive Hong Kong's Star TV.
- Many provincial stations plan to broadcast their programs via satellite in order to cover outside areas.

Satellite Channel			
	Country of Origin	Language	Programming
CCTV-Ch. 2	China	Mandarin	General
CCTV-Ch. 4	China	Mandarin	General
Yunnan TV-1	China	Mandarin	General
Guizhou TV-1	China	Mandarin	General
STAR TV	Hong Kong	Mandarin and English	General, Entertainment, Music, News, Sports

Video Cassettes

Although video cassette recorders (VCRs) are available in most cities in China, there is no information available regarding video cassette advertising.

Cinema

- There are 139,639 cinemas in China, of which all offer commercial time.
- Most theaters have been renovated with air-conditioning and better facilities.
- Mini cinemas are now becoming very popular, screening foreign movies by using video tapes and laser discs. Smaller audiences, approx. 150 per screening.
- An average 4-week cinema schedule for a foreign advertiser costs about US$ 1,350.
- Rates have not increased in the last 5 years.

Newspapers

There are 10 national daily papers in China which accept advertising. Their combined circulation is 17,200,000.

Newspaper	Market	Size	Circ. (000)	Avg. Daily Aud. (000)	1 page/B&W Cost (US$)	Accept Color?
People Daily	National	Broadsheet	4,500	N/A	80,000	N/A
Economic Daily	National	Broadsheet	1,000	N/A	30,720	N/A
Beijing Daily	Beijing	Broadsheet	700	N/A	38,000	N/A
Beijing Evening News	Beijing	Tabloid	800	N/A	21,420	N/A
Ximin Wan Bao	Shanghai	Tabloid	1,450	N/A	16,320	N/A
Jiefang Daily	Shanghai	Broadsheet	850	N/A	24,960	N/A
Yangcheng Evening News	Guangdong	Broadsheet	1,000	N/A	34,000	N/A
Guangzhou Daily	Guangzhou	Broadsheet	600	N/A	21,169	N/A
Nanfang Daily	Guangzhou	Broadsheet	500	N/A	18,708	N/A

Source (All newspaper data): China Statistical Yearbook, 1992

Magazines

There are 250 national consumer magazines, and 5,800 trade and technical magazines published in China.

Rate changes are not available.

Magazine	Type	Frequency	Circ. (000)	Audited?	Avg.Issue Aud. (000)	1 page 4/C Cost (US$)
Popular Cinema	Entertainment	Monthly	1,000	No	N/A	3,000
Chinese Youth	General	Monthly	1,300	No	N/A	4,000
Family Doctor	General	Monthly	1,730	No	N/A	8,400
Golden Age	General	Monthly	870	No	N/A	2,250
Family Periodical	General	Monthly	2,000	No	N/A	13,500

Source (All magazine data): China Statistical Yearbook, 1992

Outdoor/Transit

Billboard	**Transit**
Sites available ....N/A	Boards available
Lead Time to reserve ....N/A	Bus ....N/A
Exposure ....N/A	Exposure ....N/A
Costs	**Costs**
Average, 1 billboard/month	Average, 1 board/month:
3 m x 5.6 m ....US$ 1,000	Double-decker.................US$ 2,560/month
	Bus shelter panel...........US$ 1,500/month
	Subway............................US$ 1,950/month

- Minimum booking is a 1-year contract.
- Other outdoor opportunities include: Moving trucks, taxi top light-boxes, video walls, hot-air balloons, and LED display panels.

There are currently no restrictions for advertisements on outdoor media.

Direct Marketing

Direct marketing is in its beginning stage, and only foreign advertisers have shown interest. The most common method is to drop the DM material into the household's mailbox. Sampling or handing out leaflets at high traffic areas or close to the promoter's outlet is also a method widely used.
There are no list brokers, telemarketing companies or direct marketing associations.

Non-Traditional Media

Recently, many new media opportunities have been introduced in the market such as moving trucks, hot-air balloons, air-ship, video-wall, etc. More and more event marketing activities such as concerts, sports, and exhibitions are sponsored by both local and foreign marketers.

Research Sources

Medium Covered	Research Company	Information Provided
TV, Radio, Newspaper, Magazine Cinema	Survey Research Group	Media Index Annual Report (Beijing/Shanghai/Guangzhou)
TV, Print	Survey Research Group	Media spending by category/brand (Beijing/ Shanghai/Guangzhou)
Major TV/Print	Beijing Ad Corp.	Media spending on major joint venture/ Foreign Advertisers

Television Research Currently Available
Diary information available weekly.

Advertising Regulations

By Product

Beverages/Alcohol
Drinks with over 39% alcohol must obtain prior permission from the Administration for Industry & Commerce. Under 39% must state alcohol percentage.

Food/Restaurants
Provide media with a "Food Advertising Permission Form" issued by the Food Hygiene Supervisor Institutions.

Cigarettes
Cigarette advertising is prohibited in broadcast media and print. Other media have to get permission from provincial, autonomous, regional or municipal industry and commerce.

Pharmaceuticals/Drugs
Provide media with "Medicine Advertising Permit" issued by the appropriate public health departments. Veterinary medicines should provide a certificate of inspection and permission by department of agriculture, animal husbandry and fisheries.

Advertising To Children
No restrictions

Commercial Production
Prior censorship of advertising content by media. No restriction on commercial production origin.

By Medium

Television

All advertisements must be censored and approved by the Administration for Industry and Commerce.

Print

All advertisements must be censored and approved by the Administration for Industry and Commerce.

Outdoor

All advertisements must be censored and approved by both the City Planning Department and the Administration for Industry and Commerce.

Hong Kong

Area	1,040 km²
Population (1992)	5,902,100
Population growth rate (1992)	0.6%
GDP	US$ 80.9 billion
GDP/per capita	US$ 13,800
Real growth rate (1991)	3.8%

Population Breakdown

By Sex		By Age Group		By Socio-Economic Status	
Male	51.6%	Children, 0-9	16.3%	A, under US$ 770	7%
Female	48.4%	Teens, 10-19	14.0%	B, US$ 771-1,282	20%
		Adults, 20-24	26.7%	C, US 1,283-1,923	33%
		Adults, 35-44	16.8%	D, US$ 1,924+	37%
		Adults, 45-54	8.9%		
		Adults, 55+	17.3%		

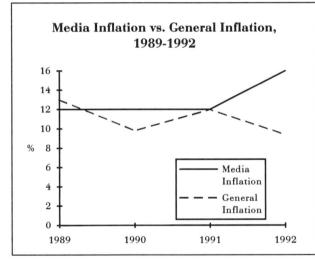

Media Inflation vs. General Inflation, 1989-1992

Media Inflation / General Inflation

Number of Households 1,636,000
Ownership of household durables
Car 7.3%
Phone 99.2%
Washers 76.4%
(purchasing power equivalent)
GNP distribution by industry
Agriculture 0.2%
Industry 23%
Services 76.8%
Exchange rates (US$ to local currency)
1991 .... 0.128
1992 .... 0.128

National Holidays

Holiday	1993 Date
Every Sunday	
First weekday in January	January 1
Lunar New Year's Day	February 10
Second Day of Lunar New Year	February 11
Third Day of Lunar New Year	February 12
Good Friday	April 1
Day following Good Friday	April 2
Easter Sunday	April 3
Easter Monday	April 4
Ching Ming Festival	April 5
Birthday of Her Majesty the Queen	June 11
Monday following Queen's Birthday	June 13
Tuen Ng Festival	June 14
Saturday preceding last Monday in Aug.	August 27

Holiday	1993 Date
Liberation Day, last Monday in Aug.	August 29
Day following Chinese Mid-Autumn Festival	September 21
Chung Yeung Festival	October 13
Christmas Day	December 25
First weekday after Christmas Day	December 26
Second weekday after Christmas	December 27

School Holidays

School holidays are basically the same as the federal holidays but depend upon the schedules of the individual schools. Chinese New Year, Easter and Christmas holidays extend over one week, plus there are summer holidays and term breaks.

Major Influences and Trends

- Satellite (STAR) TV, with its introduction of Cantonese programming and subscription channels, and Cable TV (to be launched by the end of 1993) will increase TV programming choices to local audience.
- The magazine market has been quite soft. Except for the life-style weeklies, there has been a decline in both readership and advertisers.
- On the whole, the media scene remains quite static, and unless Satellite and Cable are able to build up a strong audience base, the challenge to local existing media is yet to be seen.

Spending Analysis

National advertising spending by medium
based on appropriate year's exchange rate

	1989 US$ MM	1990 US$ MM	1991 US$ MM	1992 US$ MM
TV	280.7	317.2	343.2	386.5
Cinema	7.6	8.3	4.7	2.8
Radio	20.9	28.4	13.4	16.4
Newspaper	158.8	185.6	194.9	188.7
Magazine	71.6	87.2	136.8	149.5
Outdoor	14.0	18.8	44.3	40.5
Other	1.2	1.5	12.8	8.7
Total	554.8	647	750.1	793.1

Source: HK Adex

Media Buying

- Almost all media pricing is negotiable in Hong Kong, more so for print medium than TV.
- In some cases clients will deal with media directly, but generally they will refer media buying to agencies.
- In Hong Kong, there are 9 TV channels and 6 commercial radio channels accepting advertising, and they are controlled by five private owners.
- Buying services are emerging and will become a feature of the local/regional scene in the future. It will be tough for them

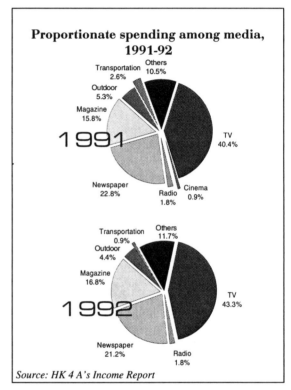

Proportionate spending among media, 1991-92

1991
- Transportation 2.6%
- Others 10.5%
- Outdoor 5.3%
- Magazine 15.8%
- TV 40.4%
- Newspaper 22.8%
- Radio 1.8%
- Cinema 0.9%

1992
- Transportation 0.9%
- Others 11.7%
- Outdoor 4.4%
- Magazine 16.8%
- TV 43.3%
- Newspaper 21.2%
- Radio 1.8%

Source: HK 4 A's Income Report

to enter the market profitably, but potential exists for those companies prepared to trade at a loss for the first 2-3 years.

Top Advertisers

By Company

Parent Company	Product Categories	US$ MM
Sharp (Roxy) Co. Ltd.	Household Appliances	14.29
Kao Co. Ltd.	Household Items	14.06
McDonald's	Fast Food	11.52
National Products	Household Appliances	9.75
Marlboro Cig. & Related Products	Cigarettes	9.36
Hong Tai Travel	Travel Services	7.79
Hutchison Comm. Eqpt.	Telecommunication	7.49
Johnson & Johnson Prod.	Household Items	6.84
Citibank	Bank	6.80
Sunflower Travel	Travel Services	6.56

By Product

Product Category	Advertiser	US$ MM
Electical Appliances	Sharp Products	14.29
Toiletries	Kao Co. Ltd.	14.06
Travel Services	Hong Tai Travel	7.79
Industrial/Offices	Hutchison Comm. Eqpt.	7.49
Finance/Investment/Banking	Citibank	6.80
Personal Items	Universal Geneve Watch	5.54
Foodstuffs	Nestle Products	4.14
Retail	Seiyu Dept. Store	3.48
Clothing	Giordano Products	2.93
Real Estates	South Horizons	N/A

Television

Overview

TV HH Penetration			
1989	*1990*	*1991*	*1992*
98.3%	98.5%	98%	97.5%
1,545,000	1,556,000	1,550,000	1,596,000

Source: AGB Establishment Survey

Hong Kong is a TV-dominated market with 2 commercial stations, TVB and ATV, each with Chinese and English channels. Coverage is territory wide, including HK Island, Kowloon and the New Territories, the outlying islands and the southern region of China. STAR TV, the new satellite TV, went on-air in September 1991 and its 5 channels are now in full operation.

Opportunities

Networks	Number of Stations	Ownership	Station Profile	Commercial Minutes/Hr	Coverage	Broadcast Hours (Sign-On/Off)
Television Broadcast Ltd.	2	Private	General	10, max. 10% of broadcast time	80%	06:00-03:00
Asia Television	2	Private	General	Same as above	20%	060:0-03:00
Satellite Television Asia Region (STAR)	5	Private	Sports, Music, News, Mandarin Chinese, Entertainment	10	6%	00:00-24:00

Costs

Prime Time TV Costs for :30 in US$			
1989	*1990*	*1991*	*1992*
4,586.2	5,090.6	5,701.1	6,384.6

Television Cost Changes Between Years
'88   '89   '90   '91   '92
13%   13%   15%   12%

Audiences/CPM's

Average Cost, Audience, and CPMs by Daypart
(Top 2 stations; :30, national audience, Target=Adults, 15+)

Hours	Morning 07:00 - 09:00	Daytime 14:30-16:00	Prime Time 19:00-22:00	Late Night 23:45-00:30	Weekend 19:00-22:00	Children 16:30-17:30
Station: TVB Jade						
US$	917	917	7418	3858	6191	994
Avg. Aud. (000)	206	302	1689	344	1270	537
CPM	4.45	3.04	4.39	11.22	4.88	1.85
Station: ATV Home						
US$	141	299	1626	876	1128	487
Avg. Aud. (000)	163	86	377	146	456	88
CPM	0.87	3.48	4.31	6.00	2.47	5.53

Source: SRG Research Services (HK) Ltd.

Audience/Ratings by Daypart

Daypart	Hours	Household				Adult		
		Universe (000)	Hut Levels	Household Rating	Impressions (000)	Universe (000)	Adult Rating	Impressions (000)
Morning	07:00-09:00	1596	7%	7	111.72	3603	3	108.09
Daytime	14:30-16:30	1596	10%	10	159.60	3603	5	180.15
Primetime	19:00-22:00	1596	30%	31	494.76	3603	27	972.81
Late Night	23:45-00:30	1596	9%	9	143.64	3603	10	360.30
Weekend	19:00-22:00	1596	26%	27	430.92	3603	23	829.38
Children's	16:30-17:30	1596	13%	13	207.48	3603	4	144.12

Source: SRG Research Services (HK) Ltd.

Scheduling and Regional/Local Buying

LANGUAGES	Programming		Commercials
Primary	Chinese channels	Cantonese 99%	Cantonese
	English channels	English 96%	Cantonese
Secondary	Chinese channels	English 1%	English & Mandarin
	English channels	Putonghua (Mandarin) 4%	English & Mandarin

- The most common commercial length is :30; lengths from :05 to :120 are also available.
- Commercials are aired throughout the day and only in specific time blocks. Ads for alcohol, feminine hygienc products, and video games with violent content are not allowed between 16:30 and 20:30 for all stations, usually at the beginning and end of programs.
- Hong Kong is too small geographically to have regions.

Children's Advertising

Every program in Hong Kong accepts advertising directed at children, but the advertising content has to be censored against violence and sex.

ADULT PROGRAMMING (Target=4-14)				Kids'	
Station	Hours	Days	Universe (000)	Ratings	Impressions (000)
TVB Jade	19:00-22:00	Mon-Sun	844	30	253
ATV Home	19:00-22:00	Mon-Sun	844	7	59

CHILDREN'S PROGRAMMING (Target=4-14)				Kids'	
Station	Hours	Days	Universe (000)	Ratings	Impressions (000)
TVB Jade	16:30-17:30	Mon-Fri	844	25	211
ATV Home	16:00-18:00	Mon-Fri	844	3	25

Source (Children's Advertising): SRG Research Services (HK) Ltd.

Radio

Overview

- There are 3 stations in Hong Kong, of which 2 are commercial.
- All households have radios; the estimated number is 1,281,000. About 97% of automobiles have radios.
- The primary broadcasting language is Cantonese, however, English and Mandarin are also used.
- The most most popular programs are News, Current Affairs and Music. Prime/Peak Time is 09:00-12:00.
- Commercial lengths available are :15 through :60. Longer lengths are negotiable.

Ratings

Daypart	Adult Rating	Adults (000)
Primetime	33	392
Daytime	14	166
Late Night	20	238

Source: SRH Media Index

Costs

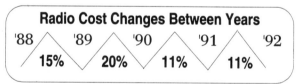

Radio Cost Changes Between Years

'88 /\ '89 /\ '90 /\ '91 /\ '92

15%   20%   11%   11%

Source: SRH Media Index

Daypart Costs/CPMs (Target=All people 9+)

Daypart	Local Time	Avg.Cost :30 US$	Audience (000)	CPM (US$)
Prime Time	09:00-12:00	321	358	0.90
Daytime	03:00-06:00	282	175	1.61
Late Night	06:00-11:00	141	241	0.59

Source: SRH Media Index

Cable

- Cable TV was not available in Hong Kong until October 1993.

Satellite

- STAR TV was launched Sept. '91. Household penetration has increased from 117,000 in Jan '92 to 154,000 in June '92 to 305,000 in Jan. '93.
- Satellite is a dominant player in regional broadcast media. Household penetration is expected to continue with the rising trend.

Satellite Channel	Country of Origin	Language	Programming
STAR TV	Hong Kong	English	Sports, News, Music, Entertainment, Mandarin

Video Cassettes

Roughly 71% of TV households have video cassette recorders (VCRs). Video cassettes in Hong Kong do carry commercials–the average is 2-3 sponsors per tape. The average cost of VCR advertising is US$ 7,050 per title. People Meter measures VCR usage.

Cinema

- All cinemas in Hong Kong offer commercial time. Over 4 weeks, the reach is 27% of people over 9.
- Commercial lengths available range from :15 to :60. Longer lengths are negotiable.
- An average 4 week buy costs US$ 3,038.

Cinema Cost Changes Between Years

'88	'89	'90	'91	'92
	12%	0%	0%	0%

Newspapers

There are 18 national daily papers which accept advertising. Combined circulation is 2,006,000.

Newspaper Cost Changes Between Years

'88	'89	'90	'91	'92
	10%	15%	15%	15%

Newspaper	Market	Size	Circ. (000)	Avg. Daily Aud. (000)	1 page. B&W Cost (US$)	Accept Color?
Oriental Daily News	N/A	FP,B/W	450	1871	6,321	Yes
Sing Pao Daily News	N/A	FP,B/W	233*	756	5,340	Yes
Ming Pao Daily News	N/A	FP,B/W	118*	427	3,694	Yes
Hong Kong Daily News	N/A	FP,B/W	100*	229	2,833	Yes
Tin Tin Daily News	N/A	FP,B/W	195*	670	6,282	Yes
Sing Tao Daily	N/A	FP,B/W	52*	177	3,335	Yes
Sing Pao Evening Post	N/A	FP,B/W	31*	53	3,215	Yes
Express	N/A	FP,B/W	70	96	2,808	Yes
HK Economic Journal	N/A	FP,B/W	69	85	3,029	Yes
HK Economic Times	N/A	FP,B/W	55	--	2,964	Yes
South China Morning Post	N/A	FP,B/W	110*	288	6,667	
The Standard	N/A	FP,B/W	48*	--	2,243	Yes
Wah Kiu Yat Pao	N/A	FP,B/W	50	52	3,269	Yes
Wen Wai Pao	N/A	FP,B/W	120	--	3,335	Yes
Ta Kung Pao	N/A	FP,B/W	125	--	3,038	Yes
HK Commerical Daily	N/A	FP,B/W	70	51	3,590	Yes
Huanan Jingji Journal	N/A	FP,B/W	50	--	2,594	Yes
United Daily	N/A	FP,B/W	70	--	981	Yes

*ABC Audited

Source: SRH Media Index Interim Report 1993

Magazines

There are 614 consumer magazines published in Hong Kong, and an unknown number of trade and technical magazines.

Magazine Cost Changes Between Years

'88	'89	'90	'91	'92
10%	10%	10%	10%	

Magazine	Type	Frequency	Circ.* (000)	Audited?	Avg. Issue Aud. (000)	1 page 4/C Cost (US$)
Next Magazine	Lifestyle	Weekly	129	Yes	402	3,269
B-International	Lifestyle	Monthly	32	No	--	5,769
City Magazine	Lifestyle	Monthly	33	No	--	3,205
Hong Kong Tatler	Lifestyle	Monthly	22	No	--	4,255
The Peak	Lifestyle	Monthly	14	Yes	--	3,462
Cosmopolitan	Women's	Monthly	40	No	--	3,846
Mode	Women's	Monthly	32	No	--	3,161
Elegance	Women's	Monthly	75	No	--	3,205
Marie Claire	Women's	Monthly	40	No	--	3,269
Elle (HK)	Women's	Monthly	45	No	--	3,295
Eve	Women's	Monthly	31	No	--	3,074
Eve in Mode	Women's	Half-yearly	32	No	--	3,063
Harper's Bazaar	Women's	Monthly	31	No	--	3,590
Style	Women's	Monthly	35	No	--	2,962
Sister's Pictorial	Women's	Monthly	61	Yes	82	2,038
Esquire	Men's	Monthly	22	No	--	3,205
Golden Age	Men's	Monthly	45	No	--	2,410
Hong Kong Business	Business	Monthly	21	No	--	2,729
Capital	Business	Monthly	22	Yes	--	2,821
The Executive	Business	Monthly	20	Yes	-	3,603
Beautiful Home	Home Dec.	Monthly	32	No	--	5,769
Dimensions	Home Dec.	Monthly	30	No	--	1,927
Elle Decoration	Home Dec.	Quarterly	30	No	--	3,295
Home Journal	Home Dec.	Monthly	33	No	--	2,744
Ming Pao Weekly	Entertain.	Weekly	120	No	303	3,321
Metropolitan Weekly	Entertain.	Weekly	80	No	76	2,564
Fresh Weekly	Entertain.	Weekly	50	No	52	2,282
TV Week	Entertain.	Weekly	64	Yes	247	2,692
Yuk Long TV Week	Entertain.	Weekly	64	Yes	203	2,282
Oriental Sunday Week	Entertain.	Weekly	120	Yes	390	2,795
Car & Driver	Car	Monthly	65	No	--	3,397
Automobile	Car	Monthly	31	No	--	1,538
Champion	Sports	Bi-Monthly	30	No	--	1,179
Racing World	Sports	Monthly	15	Yes	--	2,538
Lisa Yam's World	Food	Bi-Weekly	50	No	--	1,769
Men Mode	Men's	Monthly	21	No	--	3,161

*All claimed circulation
Source: SRH Media Index Interim Report 1993

Outdoor/Transit

Billboard	**Transit**
Sites available ....N/A Lead Time to reserve ....6 months Exposure 40%	Boards available ....N/A Exposure 3%

Costs
 	
Average, 1 billboard/month
  80 ft (W) x 50 ft (H).......................US$ 23,490
Billboard Cost Changes Between Years
'88 / '89 / '90 / '91 / '92
15% / 30% / 30% / 30%
	Costs
	
	Average, 1 board/month:
	  ....US$ 930
	Transit Cost Changes Between Years
	'88 / '89 / '90 / '91 / '92
	25% / 25% / 25% / 25%

Sizes From 458 mm (W) to 205 mm (H)	**Sizes** to 4,128 (W) mm x 1,499 (H) mm

Product/category restrictions for outdoor advertising
Cigarette advertising should carry a 'Health Warning.'

Direct Marketing

Direct marketing is growing in importance. It is currently not very well developed but there is a high level of sophistication in direct mail package design.

List Broker	*Information Provided*
Times	List of business in different fields that can be selected by geographical area, staff size, sales figures and functional title of prospects.
Datatrade Ad Post Mailing List Asia Dun & Bradstreet	*See above* *See above* *See above* *See above*

Telemarketing Companies	*Direct Marketing Association*
Times Datatrade Ad Post Mailing List Asia Dun & Bradstreet	Hong Kong Direct Marketing Association

Product/category restrictions for direct marketing
Cigarette sampling is not permitted.

Non-Traditional Media

A wide variety of non-traditional media forms are available and being used in Hong Kong.

Research Sources

Medium Covered	Research Company	Information Provided
TV	AGB Research Services HK Ltd. 7/F., Warwick House, West Wing 28 Tong Chong St., Quarry Bay Hong Kong	Home rating Individual rating
Magazine/ Newspaper	Survey Research HK Ltd. 7/F., Warwick House, West Wing 28 Tong Chong St., Quarry Bay Hong Kong	Readership profile Net reach and duplication with media
Radio	Survey Research HK Ltd.	Listenership by day of week and break
Cinema	Survey Research HK Ltd.	Cinema goers in past week and month
MTR/KCR	Survey Research HK Ltd.	Travellers' profile Travellers' in past week/month

Television Research Currently Available

Research method	Frequency
People Meter	Daily

Advertising Regulations

By Product

Beverages/Alcohol
Such advertisements should not be aired in proximity to children's programs. Not permissible on TV from 16:30 to 20:30.

Cigarettes
Total ban on electronic media effective August 1992. There is an "industry agreement" on limits of outdoor sites.

Pharmaceuticals/Drugs
Copy has to be cleared through the Broadcasting Authority.
No endorsement claims from medical practitioners.
No overclaims.

Advertising To Children
Restrictions mentioned earlier.

By Medium

Television
All broadcast material has to be cleared through the TV stations which are guided by the Broadcast Authority which enforces the advertising standard code of practice.

Print
The publisher has the final clearance authority.

Outdoor
The outdoor operation has the final clearance authority.

Sources Consulted

Hong Kong American Association of Advertising
  Agencies Income Report
Hong Kong Adex
AGB Establishment Survey

SRG Research Services (Hong Kong), Ltd.
SRH Media Index
Media Index Interim Report 1993

India

Area	3,287,590 km^2
Population (1992)	860,000,000
Population growth rate (1992)	1.9%
GDP	US$ 328 billion
GDP/per capita	US$ 380
Real growth rate (1992 est.)	2.5%
Capital	Delhi

Population Breakdown

By Sex		*By Age Group*		*By Socio-Economic Status*	
Male	52%	Children, 0-4	13%	A	9%
Female	48%	Children, 5-14	27%	B	16%
		Teens, 15-19	10%	C	19%
		Tenns, 20-24	9%	D	22%
		Adults, 25+	41%	E	34%

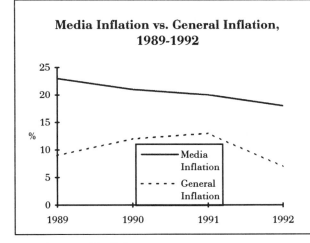

Media Inflation vs. General Inflation, 1989-1992

Media Inflation / General Inflation

Number of Households	169,000,000

Ownership of household durables
Car	3%
Phone	2%
Washers	3%

(purchasing power equivalent)

GNP distribution by industry
Agriculture	34%
Industry	26%
Services	40%

Exchange rates (US$ to local currency)
1991	0.03515
1992	0.03213

National Holidays

Holiday	1993 Date		Holiday	1993 Date
New Year's Day	January 1		Parsi New Year Day	August 23
Makar Sankranti/Pongal/Magha Bihu	January 14		Independence Day	August 15
Republic Day	January 26		Id e Miland	August 31
Basant Panchami/Shri-Panchami	January 28		Ganesh Chaturthi	September 19
Mahashivratri	February 19		Gandhi Jayanti	October 2
Holi	March 8th		Dussehra/Durga Puja	October 24
Gudi Padwa	March 24		Deepawali/Lazmi Puja	November 13
Ramsan Id	March 25		Bhaubeej	November 15
Ramanavami	April 1		Guru Nanak Javanti	November 29
Mahavir Javanti	April 5		Christmas Day	December 25
Good Friday	April 9			
Baisakhi	April 13			
Dr. Babasaheb Ambedkar Jayanti	April 14			
Buddha Pournima	May 6			
Bakri Id	June 1			
Moharrum	July 1			
Janamashtmi	August 11			

School Holidays

Same as federal holidays, plus:

Summer vacations	Apr. 15-Jun. 15
Diwali	Oct. 15-Nov. 15 (Total, 3 weeks)
Christmas (convent schools only)	Dec. 24-Jan. 1

Major Influences and Trends

Satellite TV, with its 24-hour programming featuring sports, music, soaps & current affairs, has been the one major influence in the last one and a half years. Not only have the satellite channels changed viewer behavior, they have also affected their lifestyles. Doordarshan, the government body controlling Indian television, plans to counteract the satellite move by adding 4 more channels by the end of the year. The Indian viewer will have more than 15 channels to choose from by the end of the year.

For the media planner, this multiplicity of channels will mean an opportunity to target niche audiences (though these viewers can only be reached at higher CPMs). Increased numbers of channels will open the doors for negotiations. Given the current scenario and the emerging trends, the job of the media planner and researcher is sure to become more challenging than ever before.

Spending Analysis

National advertising spending by medium
based on appropriate year's exchange rate

	1990 US$ MM	1991 US$ MM	1992 US$ MM
TV	123.0	89.5	128.5
Cinema	3.7	1.8	1.3
Radio	14.1	14.1	20.8
Newspaper/ Magazine	421.8	369.0	433.7
Direct Response	-	3.7	
Outdoor	26.4	52.7	-
Other	3.7	-	70.6
Total	**592.7**	**530.8**	**654.9**

Media Buying

Media price negotiation in India can be divided into three categories:

Entirely negotiable: Outdoor
Outdoor media is owned by various private contractors. Negotiations depend on volume (number of boardings booked), duration of contract, payment policy, future prospects, and the Agency-Contractor relationship. The negotiation can be between Contractor-Agency (on behalf of the client) or directly with the client.

Fixed discount on bulk bookings: Radio (government owned).
Special concessions/incentives have been introduced for bulk bookings over a number of stations.

Part Negotiations: Press
Three basic components:
1. Discount:
    a. Discounts mentioned in the rate card.
    b. Discounts mentioned in the rate card but still given to the agency due to volume booked or future prospects.

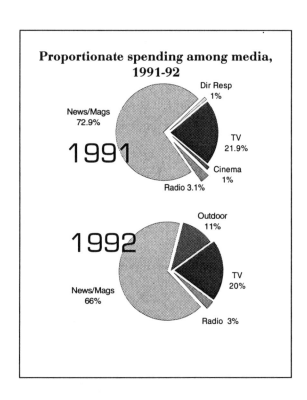

Proportionate spending among media, 1991-92

2. Guaranteed Position:
    a. Guaranteed position at no extra cost, even though a premium is specified for the same in the rate card.
    b. Guaranteed position even though there is no clause in the rate card charging a premium for a specific position. Here is a case of implied discount.
3. Surcharge Waiver
    a. Surcharge/premium for special ads (other than display ads), corporate ads, financial ads, tender ads, etc., waived.

Sponsored programs over television (government-owned medium): No negotiations are possible for spot rates, but one can negotiate production costs of serials produced for Doordarshan (the body controlling TV in India).

Satellite TV:
This medium offers opportunities for negotiation. Negotiations basically depend on the buying strength of the agency and/or the client.

Top Advertisers

By Company

Parent Company	Product Categories	US$MM
Hindustan Levers	Unilever	14.39
ITC	British & American Tobacco	9.95
Godfrey Philips	Philip Morris	7.38
Brook Bond	Brook Bond	6.78
Nestle	Nestle	6.43
Colgate	Colgate Palmolive	5.59
Shaw Wallace	Shaw Wallace	5.20
Godrej	Procter & Gamble	4.89
P&G	Procter & Gamble	4.88
Philips	Philips	4.84

By Product

Product Category	Advertiser	US$ MM
Washing Soaps	Ariel	3.9
Toilet Soaps	Lifebuoy	.7
Toothpaste	CloseUp	1.1
Tea	Tata Tea	.6
Two-Wheelers	Bajaj	.5

Television

Overview

	TV HH Penetration			Adult Reach	
1989	*1990*	*1991*	*1992*	at 250 GRPs	70%
15%	22%	24%	27%	at 500 GRPs	85%
20,000	30,000	36,000	40,000	at 1,000 GRPs	95%

Due to its sheer reach (67% of urban adults watch TV at least once a week), Doordarshan TV is still the primary medium for all mass national brands. With 3.3 million HHs owning satellite TV, this medium is the ideal vehicle to reach the upper strata of society.

Opportunities

Networks	Number of Stations	Ownership	Station Profile	Commercial Minutes/Day	Coverage	Broadcast Hours (Sign-On/Off)
National	1*	Government	General	30	India	07:00-08:45 Wk 07:00-08:30 Sun 09:00-12:00 Sat 13:00-16:00 Wk 13:00-17:00 Sun, Sat 20:30-23:30 Wk 17:00-23:30 Sat
Regional Delhi	1	Government	General	10	North India/ East India except W. Bengal	08:30-09:00 Sun 12:00-00:30 17:00-20:30 Wk 19:30-19:45 Sat 17:15-20:30 Sun
Bombay	1	Government	General	15	Maharashtra	
Maharashtra	1	Government	General	10	Gujarat	
Ahmedabad	1	Government	General			
Bangalore	1	Government	General	10	Karnataka	
Trivandrum	1	Government	General	10	Kerala	
Hyderabad	1	Government	General	10	Andhra Pradesh	
Madras	1	Government	General	15	Tamil Nadu	
Calcutta	1	Government	General	15	West Bengal	
Guwahati	1	Government	General	2	Parts of Assam	
Lucknow	1	Government	General	5	Parts of UP	

Continued on following page

Opportunities, continued

Networks	Number of Stations	Ownership	Station Profile	Commercial Minutes/Day	Coverage	Broadcast Hours (Sign-On/Off)
Jallandhar	1	Government	General	5	Parts of Punjab	
Bhopal	1	Government	General	2	Parts of Madhya Pradesh	
4 Metro Channels	(Bombay, Delhi, Calcutta, Madras)					

Relayed from Delhi

Costs

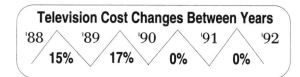

Television Cost Changes Between Years

'88 15% '89 17% '90 0% '91 0% '92

Prime Time TV Costs for :30 in US$			
1989	1990	1991	1992
7,711	8,675	8,675	8,675

Since Nov. 1991 there has been no price increase and it is unlikely that there will be one before the end of the year. This status quo is primarily due to the increased audience for various satellite channels (a chunk of advertising has moved to these channels from terrestrial TV).

Audiences/CPM's

Average cost, Audience, and CPMs by Daypart
(Top three Stations :30, national audience, Target=Adults 15+)

Hours	Morning 07:35-07:55	Daytime 13:00-13:45	Prime Time 21:00-21:30	Late Night 22:40-23:15	Weekend 18:00-20:30	Children
Station: National						
US$	4,820	1,446	8,675	1,446	9,639	N/A
Avg. Aud. (000)	40,345	10,086	40,345	5,043	50,431	N/A
CPM	0.12	0.14	0.22	0.29	0.19	N/A
	08:00-08:30		19:00-20:30		19:00-20:30	
Station: Bombay						
US$	N/A	N/A	1,735	N/A	2,313	N/A
Avg. Aud. (000)	N/A	N/A	6,061	N/A	6,927	N/A
CPM	N/A	N/A	0.29	N/A	0.33	N/A
Station: Madras						
US$	N/A	N/A	2,313	N/A	2,313	N/A
Avg. Aud. (000)	N/A	N/A	7,185	N/A	7,185	N/A
CPM	N/A	N/A	0.32	N/A	0.32	N/A

Audiences/Ratings by Daypart

Daypart	Hours	Household				Adult		
		Universe (000)	Hut Levels	Household Rating	Impressions (000)	Universe (000)	Adult Rating	Impressions (000)
Morning	07:35-08:00	36	-	0.3	10,800	129	30	38,880
Daytime	13:00-16:00	36	-	0.2	7,200	129	20	25,920
Primetime	20;45-21:45	36	-	0.3	10,8000	129	30	38,880
Late Night	22:30-24:00	36	-	.01	360	129	10	1,296
Weekend	17:00-20:30	36	-	0.5	18,000	129	50	64,800
Children's								

Languages

LANGUAGES		*Programming*		*Commercials*	
Primary	National network	Hindi	90%	Hindi	90%
	Regional network	Local languages, (*see chart*)		Local languages, (*see chart*)	
Secondary	National network	English, Tamil, Kannada, Malayalam, Telugu, Marathi, Bengali, Gujarat		English, Tamil, Kannada, Malayalam, Telugu, Marathi, Bengali, Gujarat	
	Regional network	Local languages, (*see chart*)		Local languages, (*see chart*)	

Regional Languages

Region	*Language*	*Region*	*Language*
Madras	Tamil	Calcutta	Bengali
Hyderabad	Telugu	Ahmedabad	Gujarati
Bangalore	Kannada	Jallandhar	Punjabi
Trivandrum	Malayalam	Guwahati	Assamese
Bombay	Marathi		

Scheduling/Regional

- The most common commercial length is :20; multiples of :05 and :10 are also available. The :20 length is used for 46% of national commercials and 49% of regional commercials.
- Commercials are aired throughout the day, only at the beginning and end of programs.
- Forty-one percent of all advertising is aired regionally, amounting to US$ 40,763 out of US$ 70,692 overall.

Network	Station	Region	Hours	Cost Index	US$ (:30)
National	Delhi	India	17:30-24:00 Saturday 20:30-24:00 Other days	100	11,567
Regional	Delhi	N. India and E. India	17:30-20:30 All days except Saturday	42	4,820
Regional	Bombay	Maharashtra	17:30-20:30 All days except Saturday	20	2,313
Regional	Ahmedabad	Gujarat	17:30-20:30 All days except Saturday	8	964
Regional	Bangalore	Karnataka	17:30-20:30 All days except Saturday	10	1,157
Regional	Trivandrum	Kerala	17:30-20:30 All days except Saturday	8	964
Regional	Hyderabad	Andhra Pradesh	17:30-20:30 All days except Saturday	13	1,542
Regional	Madras	Tamil Nadu	17:30-20:30 All days except Saturday	20	2,313
Regional	Calcutta	West Bengal	17:30-20:30 All days except Saturday	13	1,446
Regional	Guwahati	Parts of Assam	17:30-20:30 All days except Saturday	3	386
Regional	Lucknow	Parts of Uttar Prasesh	17:30-20:30 All days except Saturday	5	578
Regional	Jallandhar	Parts of Punjab	17:30-20:30 All days except Saturday	5	578
Regional	Bhopal	Parts of Madhya Pradesh	17:30-20:30 All days except Saturday	5	578
Regional	Metro Ch. 4 (Bom, Mad, Cal, Del)	Local Metro	17:30-22:30 All days	4	482

Children's Advertising

All programs accept commercials targeted at children. However, there is no regular research conducted to measure viewership among children. Research conducted for the following viewership figures for programs like movies, film songs, etc. Limited children's programming is available.

Programming which accepts advertising directed to children (Target=Children 4-14)

ADULT PROGRAMMING			Kids'		
Station	Hours	Days	Universe (000)	Rating	Impressions (000)
Bombay	17:30-20:30	Saturday	1,046	80	837
Delhi	17:30-20:30	Saturday	1,146	85	974
Calcutta	17:30-20:30	Saturday	531	90	478
Madras	17:30-20:30	Sunday	302	90	272
Bangalore	17:30-20:30	Sunday	384	85	326
Ahmedabad	17:30-20:30	Saturday	482	85	410
Hyderabad	17:30-20:30	Sunday	397	86	341

CHILDREN'S PROGRAMMING			Kids'		
Station	Hours	Days	Universe (000)	Rating	Impressions (000)
Bombay	N/A	N/A	1,046	62	649
Delhi	N/A	N/A	1,146	85	974
Madras	N/A	N/A	302	70	211
Calcutta	N/A	N/A	531	45	238
Bangalore	N/A	N/A	384	70	268
Hyderabad	N/A	N/A	397	73	290
Ahmedabad	N/A	N/A	482	65	313

Radio

- There are 2 channels. The Primary channel has 92 stations, of which 56 are commercial; the Vivdh Bharati has 29 stations, all of which are commercial.
- Household penetration of radios is 57% or 97,000,000.
- The top 20 states all have at least one commercial Primary Channel/Vividh Bharati station. Similarly, the top 50 cities can be reached by a Primary Channel or Vividh Bharati station.
- Language varies by region. Vividh Bharati - Hindi (except for 4 states in south where local language is used). The secondary language in the South is Hindi.
- The most most popular programs are film songs and movie reviews.
- Commercial lengths available are :10, :15 and multiples of :10.
- An average :30 buy targeting adults 15+ varies from US$ 6 to US$ 62, with a CPM of US$ 0.21.

Note: The government of India started FM transmission from Bombay and Delhi on August 1, 1993. There is one channel in each city broadcasting 8 hours of programming which consists of talk shows, film, music and other popular music. Rates for a :30 is around US$ 30. Time on FM channel is sold to private bodies who then procure/produce programs and commercial support.

After having no increase in rates for 3 years, radio rates increased in 1991 by an average of 30% (Primary channel) and 43% (Vividh Bharati). In 1993 the rates have increased by an average of 56% (Primary channel) and 41% (Vividh Bharati)

Prime/Peak Time for Radio:
Radio is most popular in the mornings between 07:00-09:00. People listen to radio in the morning as they get ready to work/school, etc. With the introduction of FM transmission from August 1, the afternoon daypart is likely to become more popular.

Cable

Cable HH Penetration			
1989	*1990*	*1991*	*1992*
0.33%	1%	1.05%	2.3%
500,000	1,500,000	1,602,000	4,125,000

- Cable TV connection has seen a spurt in growth after the satellite invasion. Unlike in the U.S., we do not have cable networks. As a result, there is a cable operator for every 300-400 household. Therefore there is no way one can ensure that our ads are not zapped. Zapping depends on the whims of cable operators. Various surveys have shown that over 75% of cable operators zap ads. As a result National advertisers stay away from this medium.
- Unlike in the US, there are cable operators who transmit signals to 200-300 HHs each. Hence the airing of advertisements is in their hands.
- About 2.3% or 4,125,000 households have cable reception. Within 2 years, 12 million more households are expected to receive cable.
- The primary languages used for broadcasting are Hindu in the North, West & East; Tamil in Tamilnadue; Kannada in Karnataka; Telugu in Andhra Pradesh and Malayalam in Kerala. Secondary languages are: Hindu in Tamilnadu, Karnataka, Andhrapradesh and Kerala.

Satellite

- Satellite TV, through 24-hour programming, has altered the lifestyles of the Indian viewer. With less than 2 channels to choose from in October '91, the Indian viewer will have a choice of over 15 channels by the end of the year. (Currently, there are 9 channels, all commercial.)
- While satellite TV is still a far cry in terms of reach when compared to terrestrial television, the introduction of language channels through satellite is bound to increase HH penetration.
- Reach of satellite TV approximates the upper class of the society and therefore offers advertisers a chance to reach them at low absolute costs.
- Household penetration of satellite is 1.9%, or 3,300,000 households. Within the next 5 years, satellite is expected to reach 12,000,000 households.
- Satellite TV has already led to fragmented audiences and challenges media planners to predict and plan viewership ratings accurately.
- The Indian government as of date has not spelled out any restrictions for Indian products and their advertising over satellite channels. Satellite channels, however, follow their own rules and regulations as far as products/advertising allowed over their channels are concerned. As far as the two controversial product categories, tobacco advertising is banned while alcohol advertising is allowed.

Satellite Channel	*Country of Origin*	*Language*	*Programming*
STAR			
Star Plus	Hong Kong	English	Soaps, talk shows
Prime Sports	Hong Kong	English	Sports
MTV	Hong Kong	English	Popular Music
BBC	Hong Kong	English	Current affairs, news
Chinese Channel	Hong Kong	Chinese	Soaps, talk shows, music
ZEE TV	Hong Kong	Hindi	Films, talk shows, soaps
ATN	Moscow	Hindu	Films, songs, soaps
SUN TV	Moscow	Tamil	Films, songs, soaps
CNN	USA	English	Current affairs, news

Video Cassettes

- Though the Indian market saw a spate of video magazines in the late 80's, with the advent of satellite channels and therefore multiple advertising options, it's unlikely that video as a medium will thrive.
- Of TV-owning households, 7% have video cassette recorders (VCRs).
- Pre-recorded cassettes may carry 10 minutes (on a 3-hr cassette) of advertising.
- The average cost of a :30 commercial is US$ 500-US$ 1,500.

Cinema

Overview

- There are over 10,000 cinemas in India, with a potential reach of 95 million people. Most sell commercial time.
- Commercial lengths available include :30, :60, :90, :120, and :150. Costs vary, and they have been increasing at a rate of 10-15% per year in recent years.
- Cinema has been losing its position versus other media since the emergence of TV, video, cable and now satellite channels. As its viewership levels keep falling, it is no longer of interest to national level advertisers.

Costs

Major Cinema Halls	US$ 17–$28 (100 ft commercial or one minute run per week)
Category A Cinema Halls	US$ 12–$17
Category B Cinema Halls	US$ 10–$12
Category C Cinema Halls	US$ 8–$10

Over 1 million population towns:		Below 100,000 population towns:	
Major Cinema Halls	US$ 12–$14	Major Cinema Halls	US$ 10–$12
Category A Cinema Halls	US$ 10–$12	Category A Cinema Halls	US$ 6–$8
Category B Cinema Halls	US$ 7–$9	Category B Cinema Halls	US$ 4–$6

Newspapers

Newspaper Cost Changes Between Years

'88	'89	'90	'91	'92
	20%	20%	20%	16%

- There are 350 national daily papers with a combined circulation of 19 million. Each state has one or more mainline English and/or national daily.
- The literacy rate in English is 5%.

Newspaper	Market	Language	Size	Circ. (000)	Avg. Daily Aud. (000)	1 page/B&W Cost (US$)	Accept Color?
The Hindi	Tamil Nadu	English	54x8	470	2,082	7,980	Yes
Daily Thanthi	Tamil Nadu	Tamil	53x8	323	3,460	4,685	Yes
Malayala Manorama	Kerala	Malayalan	53x8	673	2,230	4,223	Yes
Mathrubhumi	Kerala	Malayalan	63x8	442	1,776	3,883	Yes
Eenadu	Andhra Pradesh	Telugu	52x8	360	2,083	5,012	Yes
Dectan Chronicle	Andhra Pradesh	English	51x8	74	445	2,360	Yes
Prajavani	Karnataka	Kannada	52x8	212	2,010	2,740	Yes
Deccan Herald	Karnataka	English	53x8	135	1,021	2,657	Yes
Bajaret Samachar	Bujarat	Bujarati	54x8	551	1,786	6,246	Yes
Sandesh	Bujarat	Bujarati	54x8	443	1,420	4,511	Yes
Times of India	Maharashtra	English	52x8	631	2,536	16,039	Yes
Loksatta	Naharashtra	Marathi	53x8	251	2,095	6,471	Yes
Dainik Bhaskar	Madhya Pradesh	Hindi	55x8	129	1,360	4,241	Yes
Navabharat	Madhya Pradesh	Hindi	54x8	186	2,229	4,164	Yes

Continued on following page

Newspapers, continued

Newspaper	Market	Language	Size	Circ. (000)	Avg. Daily Aud. (000)	1 page/B&W Cost (US$)	Accept Color?
Rajasthan Patrika	Rajasthan	Hindi	54x8	283	1,873	3,054	Yes
Daily Jagran	Uttar Pradesh	Hindi	54x8	343	2,957	8,328	Yes
Amar Ujala	Uttar Pradesh	Hindi	54x8	263	1,709	4,580	Yes
Aaj	Uttar Pradesh	Hindi	55x8	400	2,248	9,896	Yes
Panjab Kesari	Punjab	Hindi	52x8	563	2,127	3,676	Yes
Tribune	Punjab	English	53x8	158	240	2,997	Yes
Hindustan Times	Delhi	English	55x8	358	1,041	7,422	Yes
Navgharat Times	Delhi	Hindi	57x8	428	3,584	7,326	Yes
The Statesman	West Bengal	English	55x8	147	718	3,676	Yes
Ananda Bazar	West Bengal	Bengali	55x8	436	2,905	5,655	Yes
Samaj	Orissa	Uriya	50x8	110	630	1,285	Yes
Assan Tribune	Assam	English	53x8	33	165	1,362	Yes
Danik Assam	Assam	Assami	53x8	30	259	1,362	Yes
Gomantak	Goa	Gomantaki	53x8	16		545	Yes
FINANCIAL							
Economic Times	National	English	54x8	175	290	10,826	Yes
Financial Express	Natonal	English	53x8	36		3,678	Yes

Magazines

There are 20,000 consumer magazines published in India, of which 500 carry advertising on a regular basis. There are 375+ trade and technical magazines.

Magazine Cost Changes Between Years

'88	'89	'90	'91	'92
25%	23%	20%	18%	

Magazine	Language	Type	Frequency	Circ. (000)	Audited?	Avg. Issue Aud. (000)	1 page 4/C Cost (US$)
National:							
India Today	English	General	2x/month	340	Yes	4,987	4,820
Reader's Digest	English	General	Monthly	363	Yes	3,525	3,791
Competition Success Review	English	Career Advancement	Monthly	245	Yes	3,689	1,928
Stardust	English	Film	Monthly	180	Yes	1,327	2,008
Sunday	English	Political	Weekly	76	Yes	659	1,767
Sportstar	English	Sports	Weekly	32	Yes	1,953	771
Business India	English	Business	2x/month	97	Yes	583	2,153
Femina	English	Women's	Monthly	77	Yes	327	1,670
Regional:							
Sarita	Hindi	Family	Monthly	214	Yes	3,809	1,414
Chitralekha	Gojarati	General	Weekly	300	Yes	1,791	2,570
Sudha	Kannada	General	Weekly	151	Yes	1,783	559
Mangalam	Malayalan	Family	Weekly	340	Yes	4,987	4,820
Malayala Manorama	Malayalan	Family	Weekly	1,148	Yes	2,206	2,313
Kumudam	Tamil	Family	Weekly	406	Yes	3,220	1,125
Anand Viketan	Tamil	Family	Weekly	227	Yes	1,996	514

Outdoor/Transit

Billboard	**Transit**
Sites available ....N/A Lead Time to reserve ....varies Exposure 50%	**Boards available** ....N/A Exposure 3%
Costs **Average, 1 billboard/month** Rates for billboards vary from area to area in the same city and from city to city. The rates in Bombay vary from US\$ 600 to US\$ 7,000 for one billboard per month. In other cities rates vary from US\$ 150 to US\$ 3,000 per month. Billboard Cost Changes Between Years '88 '89 '90 '91 '92 35% 17% 20% 20%	**Costs** **Average, 1 board/month:** Bombay, full bus..........................US\$ 850 Side panel ....US\$ 15 Back panel ....US\$ 20 Delhi, full bus ....US\$ 350 Side panel ....US\$ 12 Back panel ....US\$ 20 Though rates keep increasing every year, they are negotiable.
Sizes 20 ft x 15 ft, 10 ft x 5 ft, and other sizes	**Sizes** Full Bus, side panel (2 ft x 10 ft), back panel (3 ft x 3ft)

Alcohol advertising is not permitted though boarding contractors accept surrogate advertising from alcohol manufacturers, i.e., beer mugs are shown but not the actual beer.

Direct Marketing

As mass media costs soar, more and more marketers are turning to direct marketing tools. While many agencies profess to have a 'Direct Marketing Cell,' there are very few agencies which have a fully functional DM cell. Two established Direct Cells are O&M Direct and Trikaya Grey Direct.

Few organizations offer a choice as far as segmented consumer lists are concerned. Most of the companies/agencies have compiled their own lists over the years. The following two organizations have an exhaustive consumer list.

List Broker	*Information Provided*
Datamatics Direct	Consumer by location (zip), sex, occupation and profession
Reader's Digest	Consumer by location, sex and income

Telemarketing Companies
Telemarketing is a new concept in India. There are a lot of small marketing services outfits which provide telemarketing services. While there is no telemarketing industry as such, many companies, especially multinationals like Citibank, have opted for telemarketing.

Non-Traditional Media

Event Marketing has come a long way in the last couple of years. As product differentiation through advertisements becomes tougher, marketers prefer to sell lifestyles through their advertising and back it up with relevant event sponsorship. The regularly available events are rock shows, fashion shows, car/bike rallies, cricket matches.

Research Sources

Medium Covered	Research Company	Information Provided
Press	Operations Research Group (ORG) Dr. Vikram Sarabhai Rd. Baroda 390007	National Readership survey in the age groups 15-24, 25-34, 35-44 45+, in the income group up to Rs 750, 751 to 1500, 1501 to 2500, 2501 to 4000+, across cities and states in the country for men and women and total adults in rural and urban areas. Also gives exposure to other media viz cinema, TV, radio, and duplication between media
	ORG (see above)	Press audit monitoring of press ads - monthly and annual reports
	Indian Market Research Bureau (IMRB) Esplanade Mansion M.G. Road Bombay 400001	National Readership surveys in the age group 15-19, 20-24, 25-34, 35-44 and 45+ across cities and states in the country for men, women and total adults. Reports out so far: 1) NRS II jointly w/ORG 2) NRS III 1983-84 3) NRV IV 1991
	IMRB (see above)	Businessmen's readership survey among a select target group comprising of businessmen, company executives, government officials and self-employed professionals
	Audit Bureau of Circulation Wakefield House 4th Fl., Ballard Estate Bombay	Audit of press circulation, conducted semi-annually
TV	Indian Market Research Bureau (IMRB) Esplanade Mansion M.G. Road Bombay 400001	Weekly, monthly and quarterly TV programming for Delhi, Calcutta & Madras, and 5 mini-metros viz Kanpur, Bangalore, adults 25-34, 35-44, 45+ Weekly satellite program ratings for Bombay only soon to extended to remaining 8 cities mentioned above
	IMRB (see above)	TRP clutter index giving impact of clutter on advertising viewership
	Operations Research Group (ORG) Dr. Vikram Sarabhai Rd. Baroda 390007	TV audit: monitoring of TV ads appearing in the Doordashan Kendras for all product categories. Analysis according to nature of advertisements (whether :10 or :20 spot, etc) and analysis according to program before which the advertisement appears (monthly and annual reports)
	Super Services 7 Koyalgeet Vallabhai Road Bombay 400007	Monitoring of TV spots advertisements with respect to product advertised, station, date, day, program, duration, language etc of the advertisements
	MRAS/BURKE 803 Embassy Center Nariman Point Bombay 400021	NTS I,II,III,IV.A report on households with Rs 500+ monthly income in 50,000+ towns. Reports carried out so far: National Television Survey IV-1992 III-1988, II-1986, I-1985
	MRAS/BURKE (see above)	TV clutter report: research to study the relationship between clutter and viewership. Children in the 6-14 age group and adults in the 15+ age group in the 4 metros, Bangalore & Hyderabad considered.
	Audience Research DD Doordarshan Bhavan Copernicus Marg. New Delhi 110 001	Annual report on TV coverage in Directorate General India. Gives basic information like 1) existing TV transmitters and proposed TV transmitters, 2) existing and proposed production centers, 3) Television coverage by population and area, 4) total TV sets and TV advertising revenue
Radio	Audience Research Unit All India Radio Central Sales Unit Bombay	Radio reach and coverage, 1988. Gives data regarding radio ownership and listnership in the country for the Primary Channel

Continued on following page

Research Sources /continued

Medium Covered	Research Company	Information Provided
Video	Pathfinders, India (A Lintas Group) Manek Mahal, V Floor Veer Nariman Road Bombay 400 020	Video viewing habits of males and females in the age group 15-18, 19-25, 26-35, 36-45 and 46-55 and in the income group Rs. 750-1500, Rs. 1501-2500 and Rs. 2501+ in metros and mini-metros
Media Habits	Pathfinders, India (see above)	P: CSNAP: Media habits of Children P: SNAP: Media habits of housewives with reference to children
	MARG Marketing & Research Group, Ltd. World Trade Ctr. Complex 30th Floor Bombay 400 005	Children Media Survey, 1989. Studies the media habits of children 5-10 in 1-5 lakhs and towns
	MARG (see above)	Businessmen's Readership Survey - studies the media habits of businessmen and professionals in the top 10 cities - 1992
	MARG (see above)	Demographics II - studies the demographics, urbanographics - 91 census highlights and market potential of India - 1993

Television Research Currently Available

Research Method	Frequency
Diary	Weekly and monthly rating points reports for TV programs for the top 9 cities
Satellite	Weekly rating points report for STAR and Cable channel for Bombay Ahmedabad and Delhi only

Advertising Regulations

By Product

Beverages/Alcohol
Advertising is strictly prohibited on Doordarshan television and all other national and local mass media. Press and outdoor, however, indulge in indirect advertising for alcoholic beverages. However, STAR TV accepts advertising which sells alcohol directly.

Cigarettes
Advertising is not allowed on Doordarshan television and radio. STAR TV channels also do not accept cigarette advertising. Some leading magazines like the Reader's Digest do not accept cigarette advertising as a matter of principle.

Pharmaceuticals/Drugs
1. **Cure:** No advertisement should contain a claim to cure any ailment or symptoms of ill-health. Nor should an advertisement contain a word or expression used in such a form or context as to mean in the positive sense the expiration of any ailment illness or disease.
2. **Illness etc., properly requiring medical attention:** No advertisement should contain any matter which can be regarded as an offer of medicine or product for or advice relating to the treatment of serious diseases, complaints, conditions, indications or symptoms which should rightly receive the attention of a registered medical practitioner.
3. **Misleading or exaggerated claims:** No advertisement should contain any matter which directly or by implication misleads or departs from the truth as to the composition, character or action of the medicine or treatment advertised or as to its suitability for the purpose for which it is recommended.
4. **Appeals to fear:** No advertisement should be calculated to induce fear on the part of the reader that he is suffering or may without treatment suffer from an ailment, illness or disease.
5. **Diagnosis or treatment by correspondence:** No advertisement should offer to diagnose by correspondence, diseases, conditions or any symptoms of ill-health in a human being or request from any person or a statement of his or any other person's symptoms of ill-health with a view to advertising as to or providing for treatment of such conditions of ill-health by correspondence. Nor should any advertisement offer to treat by correspondence any ailment, illness, disease or symptoms thereof in a human being.

6. **Disparaging references:** No advertisement should directly or by implication disparage the products, medicines or treatments of another advertiser and/or manufacturer or registered medical practitioner or the medical profession.

7. **College, clinic, institute, laboratory:** No advertisement should contain these or similar terms unless an establishment corresponding with the description used does in fact exist.

8. **Doctors, hospitals, etc.:** No advertisement should contain any reference to doctors or hospitals whether Indian or foreign unless such reference can be substantiated by independent evidence and can properly be used in the manner proposed.

9. **Products offered particularly to women:** No advertisement of products, medicines or treatments of disorders or irregularities peculiar to women should contain expressions which may imply that the product, medicine or treatment advertised can be effective in inducing miscarriage.

10. **Family Planning:** Advertisement for measures or apparatus concerning family planning would be permissible in so far as they conform to the generally accepted national policy in this behalf.

11. **Illustrations:** No advertisement should contain any illustration which by itself or in combination with other words used in connection therewith is likely to convey a misleading impression or if the reasonable inference to be drawn from such advertisement infringes any of the provisions of this code.

12. **Exaggerated copy:** No advertisement should contain copy which is exaggerated by reason of improper use of words, phrases or methods of presentation, e.g. the use of the words "magic, magical, miracle, miraculous."

13. **Natural remedies:** No advertisement should claim or suggest contrary to the fact that the article advertised is in the form in which it occurs in the nature or that its value lies in its being a "natural" product.

14. **Special claims:** No advertisement should contain any reference which is calculated to lead the public to assume that the article product, medicine or treatment advertised has some special property or quality which is in fact unknown or unrecognized.

15. **Sexual weakness, premature aging, loss of virility:** No advertisement should claim that the product, medicine or treatment advertised will promote sexual virility or be effective in treating sexual weakness or habits associated with sexual excess or indulgence or any ailment, illness or disease associated with those habits. In particular, such terms as "premature aging, loss of virility" will be regarded as conditions for which medicines, products, appliances or treatment may not be advertised.

16. **Slimming, weight reduction or limitation or figure control:** No advertisement should offer any medical product for the purpose of slimming, weight reduction or limitation or figure control. Medical products intended to reduce appetite will usually be regarded as for slimming purposes.

17. **Tonics:** The use of this expression in advertisements should not imply that the product or medicine can be used in the treatment of sexual weakness.

18. **Hypnosis:** No advertisement should contain any offer to diagnose or treat complaints or conditions by hypnosis.

19. **Materials to students**: Materials meant for distribution in educational institutions must not carry advertisements of things other than those of value to students.

20. **Rule 106 of the Drug Rules, 1945,** provides that:

    a. No drug may purport or claim to prevent or cure or may convey to the intending user thereof any idea that it may prevent or cure one or more of the diseases or ailments specified in schedule 'J.'

    Schedule 'J'

Blindness	Bright's disease	Cancer
Cataract	Deafness	Delayed Menstruation
Diabetes	Epilepsy	Hydroceles
Infantile Paralysis	Leprosy	Leucoderma
Lockjaw	Locomotor Ataxia	Insanity
Tuberculosis	Tumors	Venereal Diseases
Female Diseases (in general)	Fevers	Fits
Glaucoma	Goitre	Gonorrhea
Heart Disease	Soft Cancer	Syphilis
Obesity	Paralysis	Lupus
Rupture	High Blood Pressure	Plague
	Sexual impotence	Small pox

    b. No drug may purport or claim to procure or assist to procure or convey to the intending user thereof any idea that it may procure or assist to procure miscarriage in women.

Advertising To Children

1.   No advertisement for a product or a service shall be accepted if it suggests in any way that unless the children themselves buy or encourage other people to buy the products or services, they will be failing in their duty or loyalty to any person or organization.
2.   No advertisement shall be accepted which leads children to believe that if they do not own or use the advertised product, they will be inferior in some way to other children or that they are liable to be condemned or ridiculed for not owning or using it.
3   Any advertisement which endangers the safety of the children or creates in them any interest in unhealthy practices, shall not be accepted, e.g playing in the middle of the road, leaning dangerously out of a window, playing with match boxes and other goods which can cause accidents.

Commercial Production

There is no objection whatsoever to advertisements produced outside India. Advertisements produced outside India can be telecast in Doordarshan and can be released in Press.

By Medium

Television

Alcohol and Tobacco related advertising is banned. Each storyboard and film is to be approved by Doordarshan's Controller of Sales before the film is to be aired.

Print

Alcohol advertising is banned by the Government, though companies' resort to indirect alcohol advertising. Some publications refuse tobacco related advertising.

Outdoor

Alcohol advertising is banned by the government, though companies resort to indirect alcohol advertising.

Cable

Alcohol advertising is banned by the government but companies resort to indirect advertising.

Direct Marketing

Direct Marketing in the form of mailers, personal interviews, telephone interviews etc. even for products like tobacco and alcohol are allowed.

Non-traditional

Event sponsorships like international sporting events, rock shows and fashion shows can be sponsored by tobacco/alcohol companies though they cannot indulge in direct advertising.

Sources Consulted

1991 Census
Tata's Statistical Outline of India 1991-1992
IMRB's NRS IV 1991
MARG's Demographics 1992
Economic Times Research Bureau
The Hindu, 28 March 1993.
ORG's TV Adspend 1992
IMRB's NRS & IMRB's TRP Reports

Children's Media Survey 1990
IENS 1992
F.S. & A, Feb., 1993
Indian Society of Advertisers
ORG Adspender 1992
ABC- July-Dec. 1992
IMRB's NRS IV

Indonesia

Area	1,919,440 km²
Population (1992)	195,683,531
Population growth rate (1992)	1.7%
GDP (1992)	US$ 122 billion
GDP/per capita (1992)	US$ 650
Real growth rate (1991)	6.0%
Capital	Jakarta

Population Breakdown

By Sex
Male 49.9%
Female 50.1%

By Age Group
Children 34.7%
Teens 11.0%
Adults 54.3%

By Socio-Economic Status
A 16%
B 23%
C 38%
D 23%

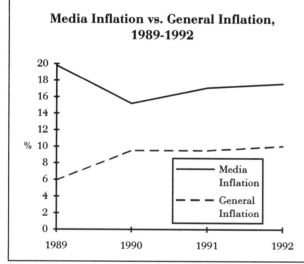

Media Inflation vs. General Inflation, 1989-1992

Media Inflation — General Inflation

Number of Households   2,772,800
(in 9 major cities)
Ownership of household durables
Car 16%
Phone 14%
Washers 9%
(purchasing power equivalent)
GNP distribution by industry
Agriculture 19.6%
Industry 20.8%
Services 59.6%
Exchange rates (US$ to local currency)
1991 .... 0.0005007
1992 .... 0.0004810

Sources (All demographic and Economic): Central Bureau of Statistics, the Indonesian People, 1990 Census, Jakarta, Indonesia, Jan. 1991. Survey Research Indonesia, "Printscope", Jakarta, Indonesia, 1992.

National Holidays

Holiday	1993 Date
New Year	January 1
Ascension Day of Prophet Muhammad SAW	January 10*
Idul Fitri/The End of Fasting Period (2 days)	March 14-15*
Good Friday	April 1*
Caka New Year (Hindu)	April 12*
Ascension Day of Jesus Christ	May 12*
Idul Adha/The Feast of Sacrifice (Moslem)	May 21*
Waisak/The Birthday of Buddha	May 25*
1 Muharam/Moslem New Year	June 11*
Independence Day of the Republic of Indonesia	August 17
The Birthday of Prophet Muhammad SAW	August 20*

Holiday	1993 Date
Christmas Day	December 25
Ascension Day of Prophet Muhammad SAW	December 30*

Non-Christian holiday dates vary each year on Christian calendar.

School Holidays

Private and Government schools have different holiday periods.

Generally, holidays occur four times in a year (i.e.- in early February [one week], at the end of June until mid-August [six weeks], mid-October [one week], and at the end of December [one week]).
Source (Holidays): Ministry of Religion, 1993.

Major Influences and Trends

In July 1993, the government awarded nationwide television broadcast licenses to five private stations (RCTI, TPI, SCTV, AN-teve, IVM) and five other private stations to broadcast locally in Yogyakarta, Semarang, Batam, Palembang and Lampung.

RCTI now can be received in Jakarta, Bandung, Surabaya, Denpasar and its surrounding areas. SCTV is another private TV station which broadcasted as a network with RCTI to cover Surabaya and Denpasar.
'

On August 25, 1993, RCTI and SCTV started operating independently of each other. Both cover the same 7 cities (Jakarta, Bandung, Solo, Semarang, Yogyakarta, Surabaya, Denpasar) and two different cities in East Indonesia: Dili and Ampenan/Mataram (SCTV), Ambon and Jayapura (RCTI). Throughout September-December both stations gradually broadened their coverage into 18 cities. RCTI retains the current programming while SCTV offers a completely new set of programs.

TPI (Educational Television of Indonesia) was the first nationwide station to be launched in early 1991. On air from 5:30 to 13:30 on weekdays, starting November 1992. TPI expanded its broadcast into the evening (16:00 to 21:00) and the morning hours on holiday with the coverage of Greater Jakarta only. Due to inadequate transmission power, the reception was not very good until June 1993 when the building of a second tower was finished near RCTI. The evening programs provide more entertainment than the morning broadcast.

In February 1993, AN-teve started broadcasting in Lampung (South Sumatra) and Jakarta. Like TPI's evening broadcast, reception had not been very good, but AN-teve built new tower locations in September, and now broadcasts to Lampung, Jakarta, and Surabaya. They have selected programming skewed towards the middle-to-upper income groups. They will cover 9 cities (Jakarta, Surabaya Bandung, Semarang, Denpasar, Jogyakarta, Medan, Ujung Pandang and Greater Lampung) by January 1994.

A host of provincial newspapers under the auspices of major publishers in Jakarta and Surabaya have also been relaunched.

Spending Analysis

National advertising spending by medium based on appropriate year's exchange rate

	1989 US$ MM	1990 US$ MM	1991 US$ MM	1992 US$ MM
TV	16	26	105	186
Cinema	4	4	4	5
Radio	42	54	52	47
Newspaper	137	132	177	180
Magazine	41	42	45	45
Outdoor	32	31	29	26
Total	**272**	**289**	**412**	**489**

Source: Media Scene 1992-1993, Indonesia

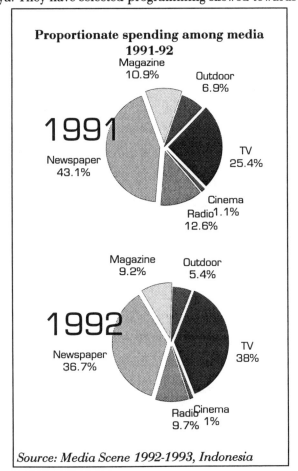

Proportionate spending among media 1991-92

1991
Magazine 10.9%
Outdoor 6.9%
Newspaper 43.1%
TV 25.4%
Cinema 1.1%
Radio 12.6%

1992
Magazine 9.2%
Outdoor 5.4%
Newspaper 36.7%
TV 38%
Radio 9.7%
Cinema 1%

Source: Media Scene 1992-1993, Indonesia

Media Buying

All media pricing is negotiable, except for leading media such as Kompas (newspaper). Agencies or clients can deal directly with the media. At the moment, buying services are becoming a part of the environment, and handle 5% of all advertising expenditures. Media are mostly not controlled by one or two monopolies of ownerships. Volume commitments and history of prompt payment are the most important factors in facilitating negotiations with the media.

Buying Services with 1992 Billings

Buying Service	Members	US$ MM
Pelita Alembana	Fortune Adv.	5.0
Wahana Adimedia	BSB Indonesia	4.0
Sentra Media	Independent	3.5
Duta Media Internusa	Matari Inc.	1.5
Transito	Gramedia	4.0
Others (smaller companies)		15

Top Advertisers (1992 spending)

Product Category	US$ MM
Pharmaceuticals	56.3
Bank & Insurance	23.8
Beverages	22.0
Vehicles & Spare Parts	21.2
Cigarettes	16.5
Food	16.0
Toiletries	14.9
Tours & Travel	13.8
Media	13.4
Household Cleaner	9.7

Source: A&M, April 1993

Television

Overview

Prior to August 1993, there were four commercial stations in addition to one owned by the government (non-commercial); three of them broadcast locally and the fourth with nationwide coverage. Five new private stations have government's license to broadcast nationally starting July 1993.

TV HH Penetration				Adult Reach	
1989	1990	1991	1992	at 250 GRPs	75%
70%	74%	76%	78%*	at 500 GRPs	95%
3,069,000	3,344,000	4,296,000	9,070,000	at 1,000 GRPs	95%

*Eleven major cities

Sources (HH Penetration): Central Bureau of Statistics, The Indonesian People, 1990, Jakarta, Indonisia, Jan. 1991. Survey Research Indonesia, "Printscope", Jakarta, Indonesia, 1992.
Source (Adult Reach): "TV Audience Measurement, weeks 9330-33", Jakarta, Indonesia, 1992.

The TV stations currently broadcasting as of Aug. 1993 are:

- TVRI-1 (Government owned - Nationwide)
- TVRI-2 (Government owned - Local Jakarta)
- RCTI - Jakarta (covers 18 cities)
- SCTV - Surabaya (cover 18 cities)
- TPI (Nationwide)
- AN-teve - Jakarta (covers 10 cities)
- IVM - Jakarta (will broadcast in 1994)

Coverage

RCTI (18 cities)	SCTV (18 cities)
- Java/Bali: (Jakarta, Bandung, Surabaya, Denpasar, Semarang, Yogyakarta, Solo, Malang)	Same as RCTI
- East Indonesia: Ambon, Jayapura	East Indonesia: Dili, Ampenan/Mataram
- Sumatra: (Medan, Palembang, Batam)	Same as RCTI
- Kalimantan:(Balikpapan, Pontianak,Banjarmasin)	Same as RCTI
- Sulawesi: (Menado, Ujung Pandang)	Same as RCTI
AN-teve Lampung, Jakarta, Surabaya, Bandung, Semarang, Medan, Ujung Pandang, Bali, Yogjakarta and Greater Lampung	

Opportunities

Network	Ownership	Station Profile	Commercial Minutes/Day	Coverage	Broadcast Hours (Sign-On/Off)
Televisi Republik Ind. Jkt (TVRI 1)	Government	General	None	National	14:30-24:00
TVRI 2 -Jakarta	Government	General	None	Local	16:30-21:00
Televisi Pendidikan Indonesia–Jakarta	Private	Educational	96	National	05:30-01:30
			60	Local	16:00-21:00 (Jakarta and surrounding areas)
RCTI- Jakarta	Private	General	240	National (18 cities)	06:00-02:00 (Weekdays & Sunday) 06:00-03:00 (Saturdays/Holidays)
			255		
SCTV- Surabaya	Private	General	216	National (18 cities)	06:00-24:00 (Everyday)
AN-teve	Private	General	96	National (9 cities)	16:00-24:00 (Weekdays)

Sources: Central Bureau of Statistics, The Indonesian People, 1990, Jakarta, Indonisia, Jan. 1991.

Prime Time TV Costs for :30 in US$			
1989	*1990*	*1991*	*1992*
1,293	1,293	4,618	4,535

Source: "TV Audience Measurement, weeks 9330-33", Jakarta, Indonesia, 1992.

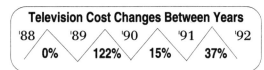

Television Cost Changes Between Years

'88	'89	'90	'91	'92
0%	122%	15%	37%	

Source: "TV Audience Measurement, weeks 9330-33", Jakarta, Indonesia, 1992.

Audiences/CPM's

Average Cost, Audience, and CPM's by Daypart
(Top three stations, :30, national audience, Target=Adults 15+)

Hours	Morning 06:00-13:00	Daytime 13:00-19:30	Prime Time 19:30-22:30	Late Night 22:30-02:00	Weekend 06:00-03:00	Children 13:00-17:30
Station: RCTI						
US$	1,363	1,759	3,928	838	1,632	1,858
Avg. Aud. (000)	675	1,075	2,245	386	836	951
CPM	2.02	1.64	1.75	2.15	1.95	1.95
Station: SCTV						
US$	690	822	2,886	722	981	539
Avg. Aud. (000)	644	853	1,851	184	668	820
CPM	1.07	0.96	156	3.92	1,47	.66

Hours		Morning		Daytime	Evening	
	05:30-07:30	07:30-09:30	09:30-12:00	12:00-13:00	04:00-21:00	
Station: TPI Jakarta						
US$	3,848	2,405	6,731	722	630	N/A
Avg. Aud. (000)	5,158	2,021	8,460	173	93	N/A
CPM	.75	1.19	.80	4.17	6.8	N/A

Source: SRI PC TV Diary Analysis System (weeks 9330-9333)

Audiences/Ratings by Daypart

Daypart	Hours	Household				Adult		
		Universe (000)	Hut Levels	Household Rating	Impressions (000)	Universe (000)	Adult Rating	Impressions (000)
RCTI								
(18 cities)								
Morning	06:00-13:00	2,543	78	8	203.4	9,178	6	550
Daytime	13:00-19:30	2,543	78	12	305.2	9,178	10	918
Primetime	19:30-22:30	2,543	78	21	534.0	9,178	22	2,019
Late Night	22:30-02:00	2,543	78	1	25.4	9,178	4	367
Weekend	06:00-03:00	2,543	78	8	203.4	9,178	8	734
Children's	06:00-18:00	2,543	78	7	178.0	9,178	9	826
SCTV								
(18 cities)								
Morning	06:00-13:00	2,543	78	7	178.0	5,723	6	343
Daytime	13:00-19:30	2,543	78	9	228.9	5,723	8	458
Primetime	19:30-22:30	2,543	78	17	432.3	5,723	18	1,030
Late Night	22:30-24:00	2,543	78	1	25.4	5,723	2	114
Weekend	06:00-24:00	2,543	78	6	152.6	5,723	6	343
Children's	13:00-17:00	2,543	78	5	127.2	5,723	8	458
TPI								
(Nationwide coverage)								
Morning	05:30-07:30	11,605	78	14	1,624	44,528	12	5,343
	07:30-09:30	11,605	78	7	812	44,528	5	2,226
	09:30-11:30	11,605	78	29	3,365	44,528	19	8,460
Daytime	12:00-13:30	11,605	78	1	116	44,528	0	445
Evening	04:00-21:00	1,842	78	1	18	7,068	1	71

Source: SRI "TV Audience Measurement, weeks 9330-33", Jakarta, Indonesia, 1992.

Languages

LANGUAGES	Programming	Commercials
Primary	TVRI1, TVRI2,...Indonesian (95%)	
	TPI.....................Indonesian (80%)	TPI .... Indonesian
	RCTI....................... English (75%)	RCTI .... Indonesian
	SCTV .... English (75%)	SCTV .... Indonesian
	AN-teve .... English (75%)	AN-teve:....................... Indonesian
Secondary	TVRI1, TVRI2,	
	TPI .... English (20%)	TPI .... English
	RCTI.................Indonesian (25%)	RCTI .... English
	SCTV ....Indonesian (25%)	SCTV .... English
	AN-teve ....Indonesian (25%)	AN-teve............................. English

Scheduling/Regional/Local

- Commercials are aired throughout the day for all stations.
- Commercials are aired only at the beginning and end of religious, educational and news programs on TPI.

Commercial Lengths

Most Popular	Also Available
TPI........................ 47.7% are :30	TPI...............:10, :15, :45 and :60
RCTI .... 51.4% are :30	RCTI...................:15, :45 and :60
SCTV .... 53.3% are :30	
AN-teve................................. N/A	

Regional airing is available. About 35% of all TV expenditures are spent on regional advertising, which averages about 30% of the cost of national.

Network	Station	Region	Hours
TPI Evening	TPI	Jakarta	16:00-21:00
RCTI	RCTI	Jakarta, Bandung, Surabaya 15 cities	06:00-02:00
SCTV	SCTV	Jakarta. Surabaya, Denpasar, Other cities	06:00-24:00

Children's Advertising

Programming which accepts advertising directed to children

ADULT PROGRAMMING				Kids'	
Station	Hours	Days	Universe (000)	Ratings	Universe (000)
RCTI	20:00-02:00	Monday	3,280	6%	197
(18 cities)	20:00-02:00	Tuesday	3,280	8%	262
	20:00-02:00	Wednesday	3,280	14%	459
	20:00-02:00	Thursday	3,280	17%	558
	20:00-02:00	Friday	3,280	13%	426
	20:00-02:00	Saturday	3,280	3%	98
	20:00-02:00	Sunday	3,280	7%	230
SCTV	20:00-24:00	Monday	1,833	10%	183
(18 cities)	20:00-24:00	Tuesday	1,833	8%	147
	20:00-24:00	Wednesday	1,833	13%	238
	20:00-24:00	Thursday	1,833	17%	312
	20:00-24:00	Friday	1,833	14%	257
	20:00-24:00	Saturday	1,833	4%	73
	20:00-24:00	Sunday	1,833	7%	128
TPI	05:30-07:00	Monday	15,895	8%	1,272
(nationwide)	05:30-07:00	Tuesday	15,895	7%	1,113
	05:30-07:00	Wednesday	15,895	9%	1,431
	05:30-07:00	Thursday	15,895	9%	1,431
	05:30-07:00	Friday	15,895	9%	1,431
	05:30-07:00	Saturday	15,895	8%	1,272
	05:30-07:00	Sunday	15,895	1%	159

CHILDREN'S PROGRAMMING				Kids'	
Station	Hours	Days	Universe (000)	Ratings	Universe (000)
RCTI	06:00-20:00	Monday	3,280	11%	361
(18 cities)	06:00-20:00	Tuesday	3,280	14%	459
	06:00-20:00	Wednesday	3,280	20%	656
	06:00-20:00	Thursday	3,280	14%	459
	06:00-20:00	Friday	3,280	23%	754
	06:00-20:00	Saturday	3,280	9%	295
	06:00-20:00	Sunday	3,280	18%	590
SCTV	12:30-20:00	Monday	1,833	7%	128
(18 cities)	12:30-20:00	Tuesday	1,833	10%	183
	12:30-20:00	Wednesday	1,833	11%	202
	12:30-20:00	Thursday	1,833	8%	146
	12:30-20:00	Friday	1,833	16	293
	12:00-20:00	Saturday	1,833	7%	128
	08:30-20:00	Sunday	1,833	15%	274
TPI	07:30-13:30	Monday	15,895	15%	2,384
(nationwide)	07:30-13:30	Tuesday	15,895	18%	2,861
	07:30-13:30	Wednesday	15,895	14%	2,225
	07:30-13:30	Thursday	15,895	20%	3,179
	07:30-13:30	Friday	15,895	13%	2,066
	07:30-13:30	Saturday	15,895	16%	2,543
	07:30-13:30	Sunday	15,895	3%	477

Sourc (Children's Advertising): SRI "TV Audience Measurement, weeks 9330-33", Jakarta, Indonesia, 1992.

Radio

Overview

- There are 627 privately owned stations and 196 government stations.
- Approximately 65% of all households have radios; the estimated number is 1,796,400 (in 9 major cities) nationwide; of these, 48% are in Jakarta.
- The primary broadcasting language is Indonesian (Malay); however local languages (Sundanese-West Java, Javanese-Central and East Java, Padangese -West Sumatra, and others) are also used.
- Commercial lengths available are :30, :45, :60. Prime/Peak Time is 05:30-09:30.

Ratings for 9 major cities

Daypart	Prime Time	Adult Rating	Adult (000)
Morning	05:30-09:30	69	9,566
Daytime	14:00-17:30	50	6,932
Evening	07:30-22:00	48	6,655
Late Night	22:00-02:00	15	2,080

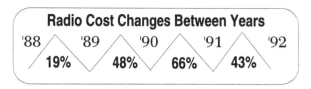

Radio Cost Changes Between Years
'88 19% '89 48% '90 66% '91 43% '92

Most Popular Program Types
Indonesian Pop Music
Dangdut Music
Contemporary Pop Music
News
Religious Sermons
Traditional Arts
Plays/Comedy

Costs

Daypart Costs/CPMs
(Jakarta, :30, Target=Adults 15+)

Daypart	Local Time	Cost :30 US$	Audience (000)	CPM (US$)
Prime time	05:30-09:30	6.26	76	0.090
Other time	10:00-14:00	5.22	88	0.075

Sources (All Radio): SRI, Printscope. Indonesian Association of Advertising Agencies, "Media Scene 1992-1993 Indonesia", Jakarta, Indonesia, 1993.

Cable

No data is available on Cable TV in Indonesia.

Satellite

Indonesian satellite 'PALAPA' is rented by most of ASEAN countries for commercial and non-commercial purposes (e.g., Malaysia uses it for television penetration). This means that we can receive RTM programs (including commercials) here in Indonesia by using Parabolic Antenna. Since July 1, 1991 RCTI and SCTV have used one of Palapa's transmitters, so every household with a parabolic antenna in Indonesia can receive RCTI's signal. The new TV stations, AN-teve and TPI, are also utilizing Palapa to broadcast their programs in the evening. There are currently 4 satellites in operation: PALAPA B2P, PALAPA B2R, PALAPA B4, PALAPA Pacific 1.

Because of clearance from the Government for private TV stations to air nationally, satellite is becoming important. There are good prospects in the satellite business due to the emergence of new TV stations. Bimantara Group is the first company which will have its own satellite by next year. This group owns RCTI.

Satellite Household Penetration (in 9 major cities)

	% of Total HH		(000) Satellite HH	
	Jakarta	*Others*	*Jakarta*	*Others*
Domestic programs	17.3	82.7	9	45
Palapa	17.3	82.7	9	43
Int. programs	17.3	82.7	9	45
Others	N/A	N/A	N/A	N/A

Households Expected To Receive Satellite Within The Next Five Years	Domestic (commercial):	5% (RCTI)
		80% (TVRI non-commercial)
	International:	5%

Satellite Channel	Country of Origin	Language Used	Programming
RTM 1	Malaysia	English & Malay	General
RTM 2	Malaysia	English & Malay	General
TV 3	Malaysia	English & Malay	General
ARMY 5	Thailand	Thailand	General
BBTV	Thailand	Thailand	General
China	PRC	Chinese	General
CNN	USA	English	General
ESPN	USA	English	General
CFI	France	French	General
STAR TV 1	Hong Kong	English	Music Video
STAR TV 2	Hong Kong	English	Sports
STAR TV 3	Hong Kong	Mandarin	Entertainment
STAR TV 4	Hong Kong	English	News/BBC

Video Cassettes

Roughly 15.9% of TV households have video cassette recorders (VCRs). However, video cassettes in Indenesia do not carry commercials. There is no service to measure usage, and the situation is not expected to change.

Cinema

Cinema has been used for very selective products. Since the beginning, cinema usage has been the lowest among the above-the-line media. Its popularity has further decreased since the advent of commercial TV in early 1990. Its penetration is highest among young, middle to upper class people.

- There are 2,700 cinemas in Indonesia. About 80% of these offer commercial time.
- Commercial media include slides (:05 and :10), Sound slides (:60), and trailer film (:60).
- An average one-week buy of slides costs between US$ 36 - 192, of sound slides costs US$ 144 - 240 and of trailer film costs US$ 1,250.
- Potential cinema reach over 4 weeks is 19% of adults over 15.

Newspapers

There are 18 national daily papers which accept advertising. Combined circulation is 3,100,000 copies.

Newspaper Cost Changes Between Years
'88 / 18% \ '89 / 20% \ '90 / 13% \ '91 / 15% \ '92

Newspaper	Market	Size	Circ. (000)	Avg. Daily Aud. (000)	1 page/B&W Cost (US$)	Accept Color?
Kompas	National	Broadsheet	550	1,794	23,377	Yes
Suara Pembaruan	National	Broadsheet	342	554	18,701	Yes
Suara Karya	National	Broadsheet	135	306	9,351	Yes
Merdeka	National	Broadsheet	125	65	7,013	Yes
Berita Buana	National	Broadsheet	150	N/A	9,351	Yes
Jakarta Post (English)	National	Broadsheet	25	45	7,013	Yes
Indonesia Times (Eng)	National	Broadsheet	25	25	5,844	Yes
Ind. Observer (Eng)	National	Broadsheet	15	20	5,844	Yes
Pos Kota	Local Jak.	Broadsheet	600	2,189	15,194	Yes
Sinar Pagi	Local Jak.	Broadsheet	250	243	9,350	Yes
Pelita	Local Jak.	Broadsheet	125	82	7,013	Yes
Berita Yudha	Lcal Jak.	Broadsheet	45	N/A	7,013	Yes
Jayakarta	Local Jak.	Broadsheet	40	188	8,182	Yes
Harian Terbit	Local Jak.	Broadsheet	200	97	7,013	Yes
Pikiran Rakyat	West Java	Broadsheet	180	570	10,519	Yes
Gala	West Java	Broadsheet	50	61	9,551	Yes
Suara Merdeka	Cen. Java	Broadsheet	262	365	9,351	Yes
Wawasan	Cen. Java	Broadsheet	65	50	3,507	Yes
Kedaulatan Rakyat	Cen. Java	Broadsheet	143	147	7,013	Yes
Jawa Post	East Java	Broadsheet	450	655	12,857	Yes
Surabaya Post	East Java	Broadsheet	170	221	8,766	Yes
Memorandum	East Java	Broadsheet	75	N/A	3,506	Yes
Analisa	N. Sumatra	Broadsheet	85	169	8,182	Yes
Sinar Ind. Baru	N. Sumatra	Broadsheet	60	148	5,844	Yes
Waspada	N. Sumatra	Broadsheet	95	289	5,844	Yes
Haluan	W. Sumatra	Broadsheet	50	152	4,675	Yes
Singgalang	W. Sumatra	Broadsheet	50	56	4,675	Yes
Semangat	W. Sumatra	Broadsheet	35	N/A	3,273	Yes
Sriwijaya Post	S .Sumatra	Broadsheet	45	N/A	4,675	Yes
Lampung Post	S. Sumatra	Broadsheet	48	N/A	4,675	Yes
Sumatra Express	S. Sumatra	Broadsheet	35	N/A	4,675	Yes
Mando Post	N. Sulawesi	Broadsheet	15	N/A	3,506	Accept
Cahaya Siang	N. Sulawesi	Broadsheet	18	N/A	2,338	Yes
Pedoman Rakyat	S Sulawesi	Broadsheet	25	218	4,675	Yes
Harian Fajar	S. Sulawesi	Broadsheet	30	N/A	4,675	Yes
Banjarmasin Post	Cen. Kalimantan	Broadsheet	40	109	4,675	Yes
Dinamika Berita	Cen. Kalimantan	Broadsheet	30	27	3,272	Yes
Manuntung	East Kalimantan	Broadsheet	25	N/A	4,675	Yes
Akcaya	West Kalimantan	Broadsheet	69	81	4,675	Yes

Sources (Newspapers): SRI, Printscope. Indonesian Association of Advertising Agencies, "Media Scene 1992-1993 Indonesia", Jakarta, Indonesia, 1993.

Magazines

There are 116 national consumer magazines, and 11 trade and technical magazines published in Indonesia.

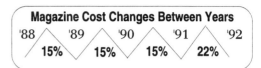

Magazine Cost Changes Between Years

'88	'89	'90	'91	'92
15%	15%	15%	22%	

Magazine	Type	Frequency	Circ. (000)	Audited?	Avg. Issue Aud. (000)	1 page 4/C Cost (US$)
Tempo	News	Weekly	150	Yes	907	4,954
Kartini	Women's	Bi-monthly	190	No	899	3,367
Femina	Women's	Weekly	140	No	602	2,982
Sarinah	Women's	Bi-monthly	140	No	466	2,308
Editor	News	Weekly	73	No	180	3,318
Eksekutif	Business	Monthly	25	No	52	1,924
Mode	Teens	Bi-monthly	100	No	476	1,443
Gadis	Young Women's	Every 10 days	98	No	710	1,683
Bola	Sports	Weekly	436	Yes	1,510	6,333
Swa	Business	Monthly	45	Yes	90	3,126
Matra	Gen. Interest	Monthly	100	Yes	311	2,645
Jakarta-Jakarta	Gen. Interest	Weekly	85	Yes	314	1,924
Hai	Young Men's	Weekly	75	Yes	637	1,443
Intisari	Digest	Monthly	147	Yes	850	2,020
Nova	Women's	Weekly	270	Yes	740	2,405
Warta Ekonomi	Business	Bi-monthly	40	No	81	2,164
Info Bank	Business	Monthly	40	No	110	2,405

Sources (Magazines): SRI, Printscope. Indonesian Association of Advertising Agencies, "Media Scene 1992-1993 Indonesia", Jakarta, Indonesia, 1993.

Outdoor/Transit

Billboard

Sites available	300,000
Lead Time to reserve	12 weeks
Exposure	N/A

Costs

Average, 1 billboard/year
8 x 4 m² .... US$ 14,430

Billboard Cost Changes Between Years

'88	'89	'90	'91	'92
30%	30%	39%	10%	

Sizes

Giant 150 m²; Standard 32 m²
Minimum 2-4 m²

Transit

Boards available
Bus 1,200
Taxis 2,000
Exposure .... N/A

Costs

Average, 1 board/month:
Bus back panel .... US$ 842/year
Bus left side .... US$ 1,684/year
Bus right side .... US$ 1,443/year
Metro US$ 84,175-144,300/5 years

Transit Cost Changes Between Years

'88	'89	'90	'91	'92
0%	0%	33%	35%	

Sizes

Bus back panel 0.8 m², left side 3.7 m²
Bus right side 5.7 m², Taxi 104 cm² x35 cm²

There are currently no restrictions for advertisements on outdoor media.

Source: P3, Media Scene

Direct Marketing

Direct Marketing is now in its infancy. Some of the few companies that have helped developed this area are credit card companies, banks, airlines, etc.

There are no telemarketing companies, nor any direct marketing association.

List Broker	Information Provided
Target	Names/Addresses
Adyapaket Internusa	Names/Addresses

Non-Traditional Media

These media have always been quite popular among advertisers, particularly prior to the advent of commercial TV. Cigarette and personal care products often sponsor events such as motor-car rallies and races, beauty pageants, music shows, seminars, etc., usually combined with marketing PR.

Sales promotions for consumers are usually in the forms of rebates, sampling, gifts with purchase, sweepstakes.

This group of non-traditional media is expected to become increasingly popular as manufacturers seek more direct contact points with their consumers.

Currently, there are events marketing, sales promotions, and PR.

Research Sources

Medium Covered	Research Company	Information Provided
Newspaper, Magazine, Television, Radio	Survey Research Indonesia Wisma Bank Dharmala I5/F Jl. Jend. Sudirman Kav.28 Jakarta 12910	General Report on media index Telescope/PC Diary Analysis on TV Printscope/PC Analysis on print Adex
Print, TV, Radio, Magazine	Surindo Utama Wisma SURINDO Jl. Raya Pasar Minggu No. 5 Jakarta Selatan	Adex for print, radio, television Copy ad/TVCs

Television Research Currently Available

Research method	Frequency
Diary System	Weekly

Advertising Regulations

By Product

Beverages/Alcohol

Advertisements should not influence or encourage the public to begin consumption of alcoholic beverages.

Advertisements should not portray consumption of alcohol in activities needing concentration, as its use may endanger safety.

Advertisements should not be directed at children under age of 16 and/or pregnant women, or portray them in any such advertisement.

Cigarettes

Advertisements should not suggest that smoking is conducive to good health and/or free from health hazards.

Advertisements should not be aimed at children below age of 16 and/or pregnant women, or portray them in any such advertising.

Pharmaceuticals/Drugs

Advertisements should be in accordance with indications of the drug as approved by the Indonesian Department of Health.

Advertisements should not use copy/terminology/illustrations promising a cure for a disease, but may only state assistance in alleviating symptoms.

Doctors, nurses, medical professionals, pharmacists, and other professional persons or institutions including hospitals should not give any audio or visual presentation to portray or give impression of giving advice, information or recommendation in usage of an advertised drug.

Advertisements should fully take into consideration the safety of the drugs advertised, particularly those directed at children.

Advertisements should not encourage over-usage of drugs.

Advertisements should not suggest certain drugs are essential for physical health.

Advertisements should not induce fear of certain diseases or imply that non-usage of an advertised drug may increase possibility of contracting such a disease.

Advertisements should not use exaggerated words such as 'safe', 'not dangerous or hazardous', 'no risk,' etc. without a full explanation.

Advertising To Children

Advertisements directed at or possibly seen by children should not portray elements considered to be disturbing or damaging to their physical and mental growth, or take advantage of their guilelessness, lack of experience and innocence.

Advertisements should not portray a child in danger, act out scenes unseemly for children, or lead them astray.

Children should not be used to advertise products not fit for child consumption.

Commercial Production

Foreign models or locations are not allowed except for international non-consumer products.

All TVCs must be of local production or a joint venture and must have a production permit before shooting.

By Medium

Television

A maximum of 20% of broadcasting time can be commercial breaks.

Print

A maximum of 30% of print space can be allocated to ads. Advertisements may not be pornographic, and should be polite.

Outdoor

Outdoor advertising requires local government approval and payment of a full municipality tax prior to installation.

Outdoor advertisements must use Indonesian copy. Foreign languages, where necessary, may be used in smaller letters under the Indonesian text. Script other than Latin is permitted only for trademarks.

Cable

No cable stations.

Direct Marketing

No regulation yet.

Non-traditional

Under goverment control. Permits are needed before execution.

Japan

Area	377,750 km²
Population (1992)	123,587,297
Population growth rate (1992)	0.4%
GDP (1992)	US$ 3,949.7 billion
GDP/per capita (1992)	US$ 31,960
Real growth rate (1992)	1.3%
Capital	Tokyo

Population Breakdown

By Sex
Male 49.2%
Female.............................. 50.8%

By Age Group
Children, 5-12..................... 10.4%
Teens, 13-19 .... 10.7%
Adults, 20+ 73.7%

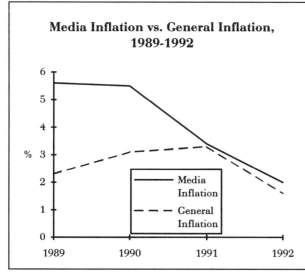

Media Inflation vs. General Inflation, 1989-1992

Number of Households   42,457,975
Ownership of household durables
  Car.............................81.4%
  Phone........................91.8%
  Washers.....................99.8%
  (purchasing power equivalent)
GNP distribution by industry
  Agriculture................. 2.2%
  Industry 37.2%
  Services 60.6%
Exchange rates (US$ to local currency)
  1991 .... 0.007955
  1992 .... 0.009394

National Holidays

Holiday	1993 Date
New Year's Day	January 1
Adult's Day	January 15
National Foundation Day	February 11
Vernal Day	March 20
Green Day	April 29
Constitution Memorial Day	May 3
National Holiday	May 4
Children's Day	May 5
Respect For The Aged Day	September 15
Autumnal Equinox	September 23
Physical Education Day	October 10
Culture Day	November 3
Labor Thanksgiving Day	November 23
Emperor's Birthday	December 23

School Holidays

Holiday	1993 Date
Spring Break	Approx. 2 weeks; (End of Mar.—Beginning of Apr.)
Summer Break	Approx. 5 weeks; (End of Jul.—End of Aug.)
Winter Break	Approx. 2 weeks; (End of Dec—Beginning of Jan.)

Major Influences and Trends

- Advertising expenditure in each medium has fallen below the level of the previous year due to recession in the Japanese economy.
- By medium, TV advertising expenditure in 1992 was 98.4% of that in 1991. This downward trend is predicted to continue for a couple of years and, therefore, cost setting tends to be softening.
- As with TV, radio expenditure dropped in 1992 as compared to 1991. Ad expenditure related to promotional activities especially decreased as compared to the previous year.
- The number of new magazines decreased and suspending publication increased in 1992.
- Decrease of newspaper ad expenditure in 1992 was the biggest of the four media. It was 90.5% of the 1991 expenditure. In each newspaper, a reduction the number of pages was caused by the ad expenditure decrease.
- Substantial recovery in the ad expenditure situation is hard to predict until spring of 1994.

Spending Analysis

National advertising spending by medium
based on appropriate year's exchange rate

	1989 US$ MM	1990 US$ MM	1991 US$ MM	1992 US$ MM
TV	10,658.7	11,043.7	13,358.8	15,524.5
Radio	1,518.8	1,610.9	1,914.0	2,207.6
Newspaper	9,272.7	9,377.1	10,695.5	11,434.4
Magazine	2,444.0	2,580.9	3,075.4	3,468.3
Direct Response	1,332.0	1,359.7	1,645.1	2,087.3
Outdoor	2,562.9	2,632.0	3,143.8	3,526.5
Other	9,167.1	9,762.7	11,718.5	13,053.0
Total	**36,956.2**	**38,367.0**	**45,511.1**	**51,301.6**

All billings shown at historical exchange rates

Media Buying

- Advertising agencies in Japan buy media directly from media owners since there are no buying service companies there.
- In principle, media owners sell their media to advertisers through agencies; therefore, it is very rare that advertisers negotiate with media owners directly, skipping the agencies as intermediaries.
- There are no tight media groups in Japan; media owners run independently of each other. Consequently, there is little opportunity to enjoy advantages of 'bulk buying,' which is one of the reasons there are no media service companies thus far.

Top Advertisers (1992 spending)

By Company

Parent Company	Product Categories	US$ MM
Matsushita	Electrical/Electronics	510.6
Toyota	Automobiles	441.5
NEC	Electrical/Electronics	427.4
Kao	Toiletries/Cosmetics	426.5
Suntory	Alcoholic Beverage/Soft Drinks	350.3
Mitsubishi Motors	Automobiles	346.6
Asahi Beer	Alcoholic Beverage	322.9
Hitachi	Electrical/Electronics	321.6
Toshiba	Electrical/Electronics	303.6
Shiseido	Cosmetics	303.3

By Product

Product Category	Advertiser	US$ MM
Electrical/Electronics	Matsushita	510.6
Automobiles	Toyota	441.5
Toiletries/Cosmetics	Kao	426.5
Alcoholic Beverage/Soft Drinks	Suntory	350.3
Service/Leisure	NTT	299.3
Wholesale/Retail	Takashimaya	274.9
Chemical	Fuji Film	226.6
Food	Ajinomoto	215.3
Electric Power	Tokyo Denryoku	214.8
Housing/Construction	Daiwa House	170.5

Source: Nikkei Advertising Institute, Advertising expenses of companies listed on stock exchanges, Tokyo, Japan, 1992

Television

Overview

TV HH Penetration				Adult Reach	
1989	*1990*	*1991*	*1992*	at 250 GRPs	70%
99.9%	99.9%	99.9%	99.9%	at 500 GRPs	83%
40,520,000	41,115,000	41,756,000	42,416,000	at 1,000 GRPs	90%

Source (TV Viewing): Video Research Ltd., Tokyo, Japan, 1992.

TV is the number one medium in Japan. It covers virtually every household; it is preferred to any other medium for a wide range of audiences. It is, in general, the second most cost-efficient medium next to radio.

TV will enjoy this leading position for a good while. Audiences' viewing habits are/will be stable, while cable and satellite are growing so slowly that they have not yet become threats to TV.

Opportunities

Networks	Number of Stations	Ownership	Station Profile	Commercial Minutes/Day	Coverage	Broadcast Hours (Sign-On/Off)
NNN	27 (30*)	Yomiuri Shimbun	General	240+/-	99%	Weekday All day / Saturday All day / Sunday 5:00-2:00
JNN	28 (28*)	Mainichi Shimbun	General	240+/-	97%	Weekday 5:00-4:00 / Saturday 5:00-4:00 / Sunday 5:00-2:00
FNN	23 (26*)	Sankei Shimbun	General	240+/-	97%	Weekday All day / Saturday All day / Sunday 5:30-3:00
ANN	19 (21*)	Asahi Shimbun	General	240+/-	91%	Weekday 5:30-4:30 / Saturday 6:00-5:00 / Sunday 6:00-2:00
TXN	6 (6*)	Nihon Keizai Shimbun	General	240+/-	61%	Weekday 5:30-4:00 / Saturday All day / Sunday 5:00-1:30
NHK		Public	General & Education	None	100%	5:00/6:00-24:00

Includes cross-over stations

Costs

Prime Time TV Costs for :30 in US$			
1989	*1990*	*1991*	*1992*
45,560	46,970	42,273	42,743

Television Cost Changes Between Years

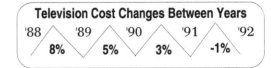

'88	'89	'90	'91	'92
	8%	5%	3%	-1%

Audiences/CPM's

Average Cost, Audience, and CPMs by Daypart
(for the primary three stations; :30, national audience, Target=Households)

Hours	Morning 6:00-12:00	Daytime 12:00-18:00	Prime Time 19:00-23:00	Late Night 23:00-24:00	Weekend 12:00-18:00	Children
Station: NTV/NNN						Children's
US$	11,743	10,991	42,743	17,850	31,940	programs
Avg. Aud. (000)	4,287	3,068	7,230	4,414	3,026	are
CPM	2.74	3.58	5.91	4.04	10.56	scattered
Station: TBS/JNN						throughout
US$	11,743	11,743	42,743	17,850	32,880	various
Avg. Aud. (000)	2,759	2,759	5,683	3,583	3,088	dayparts
CPM	4.26	4.26	7.52	4.98	10.65	
Station: CX/FNN						
US$	11,743	11,743	42,743	17,850	32,880	
Avg. Aud. (000)	2,183	3,418	6,589	2,512	3,212	
CPM	5.38	3.44	6.49	7.11	10.24	

Audiences/Ratings by Daypart (Target=Adults 20-49)

Daypart	Hours	Household				Adult		
		Universe (000)	Hut Levels	Household Rating	Impressions (000)	Universe (000)	Adult Rating	Impressions (000)
Morning	06:00-12:00	42,458	25.5	5.1	2,165	53,339	2.1	1,120
Daytime	12:00-18:00	42,458	31.0	6.2	2,632	53,339	1.9	1,013
Night Fringe	18:00-19:00	42,458	47.1	7.4	4,000	53,339	3.7	1,974
Primetime	19:00-23:00	42,458	59.0	11.8	5,010	53,339	7.3	3,894
Late Night	23:00-24:00	42,458	34.5	6.9	2,930	53,339	4.6	2,454
Weekend	12:00-18:00	42,458	36.5	7.3	3,099	53,339	3.1	1,653

Source (TV Viewing): Video Research Ltd., Tokyo, Japan, 1992.

Scheduling/Regional/Languages

- Commercials are aired throughout the day, at the beginning, end and within programs.
- 75% of commercials are :15, another 24% are :30. Other lengths available include :60, :120, and :180.
- The primary programming language is Japanese. Occasionally, on multiple broadcasts, news, movies, etc., English is also used. The primary commercial language is Japanese.
- Regional and local buys account for 80% of the TV advertising expenditures. The average cost is about 220% that of national advertising.

Children's Programming

All adult and children's programs on commercial stations accept advertising targeted at children.

Radio

Overview

- There are 89 stations in Japan, of which 87 are commercial. Seven of these are in Tokyo.
- Everyone in Japan has radios, in homes and in cars. The approximate number of radio households is 42,458,000.
- Japanese is the only language used in radio broadcasting.
- Commercial lengths available are :20, :30, :40; :60, :80 and up.
- The most popular program types are News, Music Variety, Traffic Information and Pro Baseball.
- Prime/Peak Time for teens (13-19) is 20:00-24:00, for males 35-49 is 12:00-18:00, and for housewives is 06:00-12:00.

Ratings

Daypart	Hours	Adult Rating (20-49)	Adult (000)
Morning	5:00-12:00	1.8	190
Daytime	12:00-19:00	1.9	200
Nighttime	19:00-02:00	0.6	63
Weekend	12:00-19:00	1.4	147

Costs

Daypart Costs/CPMs

Location	Local Time	Cost :30 US$	Audience (000)	CPM (US$)
Tokyo	All day	658	25	26.32
Osaka	All day	338	18	18.78

Radio Cost Changes Between Years

'88   '89   '90   '91   '92

3%   3%   2%   0%

Source (Radio Rating): Video Research Ltd., Tokyo, Japan, 1992.

Cable

Overview

In Japan, cable TV started as a community of receiving systems in poor TV reception areas. The number of subscribing households reached 7,430,000 at the end of 1992. Today, it is turning into a so-called urban-type cable TV: a new communication. The penetration of this urban-type TV remains very low, at 3.1% of total households.

Programs supplied by communication satellite have been available on cable television (CATV) since August 1989. However, they have not increased subscription of CATV.

Cable TV Penetration			
1989	*1990*	*1991*	*1992*
1.6%	1.8%	2.5%	3.1%
640,000	752,000	1,030,000	1,337,000

Currently, a multi-channel CATV station has 30 channels on average. The contents of the programs of each channel are as follows:

- Re-transmission of terrestrial wave
- Re-transmission of broadcast satellite programming
- Local programs produced by own station, local information programs
- Programs provided by program suppliers (via communication satellite)

Advertising space is sold directly by the program suppliers. As of December 1992, there were 16 program suppliers which broadcast advertising.

The CATV penetration projection by the Ministry of Posts and Telecommunications in 1987 was 3,000,000 households in 1992, but the penetration level remained low. However, as the number of households equipped with HOMEBUS, the cable infrastructure has already reached 6,120,000 and quite a few new stations are planning to open, its future looks promising.

- The penetration of cable has increased from 1.6% in 1989 to 3.1% in 1992. Over the next 5 years, another 3,000,000 households are expected to receive cable.
- Japanese is the only language used for cable broadcasts.

- There are 22 cable channels, of which 15 are commercial.

Cable Networks	HH Circulation (000)
Nippon Network Service	100
LVC	60
ACCS	40
TV Matsumoto Cable Vision	35
Ueda Cable Vision	30
Nagasaki Cable Television	28
Sapporo Cable Vision	25
Sida Cable Media	25
Tokyu Cable Television	24
Izukyu Cable Network	23

Source: CAB Japan, Tokyo, Japan, 1992.

Top Cable Channels	Cost (US$)	Rating	Commercial Min/Hr
JCTV (CNN)	112.7	N/A	6
Satellite Channel	112.7	N/A	6
SVN	112.7	N/A	6
Star Channel	Non-Commercial	N/A	Non-Commercial
CSN	112.7	N/A	6

Satellite

- Practical non-commercial direct broadcast satellite (DBS) in Japan began in July 1987.
- The number of households owning a receiving system reportedly reached around 6,000,000 as of December 1992. Thus, penetration is 14% of total households. Within five years, the total is expected to reach 24%, or 10,000,000 households.
- Private sector DBS, started in April 1991, does not accept advertising.
- DBS Television is broadcast by BS-3 satellite which has 3 channels (2 public, 1 private)
- Program supply using communication satellite (CS), started August 1989. It currently reaches households mainly via CATV or by direct transmission.
- CS Television is broadcast by 2 communication satellites called 'Super Bird' and 'JC-SAT.'
- Nine out of 22 CS channels are also directly received with dishes.
- The penetration of BS Television will reach 10,000,000 households in 1997-1998.
- The Ministry of Posts and Telecommunications is planning a new satellite (BS-4), which has 8 channels, to start in 1998.
- As of December 1992, the number of CS Television direct subscribing households (Super-Bird-affiliated and JC-SAT-affiliated) were 2,000 and 5,000 respectively, which are very low numbers.

- In the long term, it is predicted that there will be a reasonable increase in subscribers but in the short term, the most that can be done is to generate public interest by trying to make receiving systems inexpensive with cooperation from electronics manufacturers and by widening channel choices on satellite.

Satellite HH Penetration

	% of Total HH	*(000) Satellite HH*
DBS	14%	6,000
CS (Vi CATV)	1.9%	800
CS (Direct)	0.06%	25

Satellite Channels Available

Satellite Channel	*Country of Origin*	*Language*	*Programming*
Direct Broadcast Channel			
NHK Channel 1	Japan	Japanese	General
NHK Channel 2	Japan	Japanese	General
JSB	Japan	Japanese	Movie, Sports, Music
Program Supply To CATV			
Channel NECO	Japan	Japanese	Movie, Documentary
NSN News	Japan	Japanese	Economic News
Japan Sports Channel	Japan	Japanese	Sports (ESPN)
CSN	Japan	Japanese	Movie (Japanese/Foreign)
Satellite Channel	Japan	Japanese	News, Culture
Canday	Japan	Japanese	Kid's program
SVN	Japan	Japanese	Sports, Variety
NCN News	Japan	Japanese	News
Super Channel	Japan	Japanese	Overseas Drama
Space Shower TV	Japan	Japanese	Music
JCTV	Japan/US	Japanese/English	CNN News
Channel O	Japan	Japanese	Variety Show
Let's Try	Japan	Japanese	Lectures
Satellite Theater	Japan	Japanese	Japanese Movie, Stages
Star Channel	Japan	Japanese	Movie
The Weekend Theater	Japan	Japanese	Movie
OIC	Japan	Japanese	Korean Programs
Igo/Shogi Channel	Japan	Japanese	Games, Lectures
Rainbow Channel	Japan	Japanese	Adults
Fantasy Channel	Japan	Japanese	Adults
MTV	Japan	Japanese	MTV
Weather Channel	Japan	Japanese	Weather Forecasts

Video Cassettes

- Of TV households, 80.2% own a video cassette recorder (VCR).
- Prerecorded tapes may carry 6-10 sponsors per tape, at a cost of US$ 6,890 to US$ 8,275 for a :30 commercial.
- The Video Research/Chuo Chosa-Sha service measures VCR usage.

Cinema

- There are 1,744 cinemas in Japan, all of which offer commercial time.
- Lengths available include :15, :30, :60.
- An average 4 week buy of :30 spots costs US$ 2,255 to US$ 4,855 per theater.
- Potential cinema reach is not available.

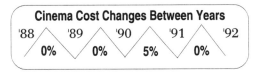

Cinema Cost Changes Between Years

'88	'89	'90	'91	'92
0%	0%	5%	0%	

Newspapers

There are 5 national daily papers which accept advertising. Combined circulation for morning (M) papers is 26,799,207; for evening (E) papers it is 13,826,388.

Newspaper Cost Changes Between Years

'88	'89	'90	'91	'92
3%	6%	4%	-5%	

Newspaper	Market	Size	Circ. (000)	Avg. Daily Aud. (000)	1 page B&W Cost (US$)	Accept Color?
Yomiuri	National	Broadsheet –M	9,764	31,268	419,066	Yes
		Broadsheet –E	4,521	23,605	321,698	Yes
Asahi	National	Broadsheet –M	8,218	31,020	374,680	Yes
		Broadsheet –E	4,609	24,223	288,866	Yes
Mainichi	National	Broadsheet –M	4,006	10,258	243,492	Yes
		Broadsheet –E	1,989	7,910	171,065	Yes
Sankei	National	Broadsheet –M	1,901	7,044	131,046	Yes
		Broadsheet –E	989	5,561	104,978	Yes
Nihon Keizai Economic	National	Broadsheet –M	2,910	9,269	172,474	Yes
		Broadsheet –E	1,718	5,809	112,164	Yes
Hokkaido	Hokkaido	Broadsheet –M	1,170	1,929	67,637	Yes
		Broadsheet –E	783	1,471	62,141	Yes
Kahoku	Miyagi	Broadsheet –M	475	1,149	31,282	Yes
		Broadsheet –E	172	971	19,586	Yes
Shizuoka	Shizuoka	Broadsheet –M	702	1,778	17,614	Yes
		Broadsheet –E	702	989	17,614	Yes
Chunichi	Nagoya	Broadsheet –M	2,232	11,761	126,396	Yes
		Broadsheet –E	840	5,293	88,491	Yes
Kyoto	Kyoto	Broadsheet –M	474	2,098	31,000	Yes
		Broadsheet –E	340	1,753	25,364	Yes
Chugoku	Hiroshima	Broadsheet –M	702	1,492	34,664	Yes
		Broadsheet –E	101	353	8,314	Yes
Nishinihon	N. Kyushu	Broadsheet –M	806	1,460	53,405	Yes
		Broadsheet –E	200	698	28,605	Yes

Source (Daily newspapers, combined circulation): Japan Audit Bureau of Circulations, Tokyo, Japan, 1992.

Magazines

There are over 2,000 consumer magazines, and over 1,500 trade and technical magazines published in Japan.

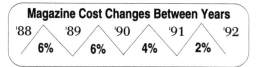

Magazine Cost Changes Between Years

'88	'89	'90	'91	'92
6%	6%	4%	2%	

Magazine	Type	Frequency	Circ. (000)	Audited?	Avg. Issue Aud. (000)	1 page 4/C Cost (US$)
Weekly Post	General	Weekly	686	Yes	2,934	17,379
Weekly Shincho	General	Weekly	533	Yes	1,333	15,970
Weekly Asahi	General	Weekly	450	Yes	1,387	15,030
Focus	General/Photo	Weekly	850	N/A	4,960	20,667
Nikkei Business	Business	Weekly	288	Yes	800	19,821
PIA	Information	Weekly	400	N/A	1,013	15,030
Josei Jishin	Women's	Weekly	825	Yes	4,694	22,546
Hanako	Young Women's	Weekly	350	N/A	587	12,682
Weekly Shonen Jump	Comic	Weekly	6,100	N/A	7,894	28,182
Popeye	Young Men's	Bi-Weekly	580	N/A	800	16,909
Non no	Young Women's	Bi-Weekly	1,600	N/A	1,707	23,485
Orange Page	Home	Bi-Weekly	1,200	N/A	3,307	23,485
Big Comic	Comic	Bi-Weekly	1,500	N/A	3,414	13,621
Playboy	Men's	Monthly	450	N/A	693	16,909
More	Women's	Monthly	800	N/A	1,867	23,485

Source (Major magazines): Japan Audit Bureau of Circulations, Tokyo, Japan, 1992.

Outdoor/Transit

Billboard	**Transit**
Sites available .... 14,000 Lead Time to reserve .... 24 weeks Exposure .... N/A	Boards available ....Numerous (No reliable data available) Exposure ....N/A
Costs Average, 1 billboard/month Large ....5,343 Poster Boards (3mx 4m) .... 1,672 Billboard costs increase about 3% every year. Initial contract for a billboard requires a deposit, of about US$ 121,302.	**Costs** Average, 1 board/month: ....US$ 578 Transit costs usually increase about 7% every year.
Sizes 6 m x 18 m, 6 m x 12 m, 6 m x 8 m, 3 m x 8 m, 3 m x 4 m	**Sizes** 3 m x 4 m, 1.5 m x 2.2 m, 1.7 m x 2.3 m, 1.7 m x 4.5 m, 1.8 m x12 m

Tobacco advertising is subject to certain restrictions in outdoor advertising. Also, non-bank money-lending advertising is limited in transit ads.

Direct Marketing

Although Japanese economic growth has been flat the past several years, direct marketing has averaged 15% growth every year from 1986 through 1990. According to the Japan Direct Marketing Association (JADMA), direct marketing sales grew 7.3% in 1991 to 1.76 trillion yen (US$ 14.1 billion). Direct Marketing sales in FY '92 (April '92 - March '93) are reported at 1.85 trillion Yen (US$ 17.1 billion), an increase of 5% vs. a year ago. Direct Marketing continues to grow despite a 1993 decrease in total advertising expenditures of 4.6% vs. a year ago to 5.5 trillion Yen (US$ 51.6 billion).

List Broker	*Information Provided*
Fuji TV Direct Marketing	DM 'Fan' list of consumers who respond to TV/radio quizzes or giveaway programs - approximately 2MM names.
Nikkei BP Sha	Subscribes to Nikkei business publications – approximately 1.2MM names.
Kozuka Shoko	Compiled lists from local government sources. Can include age, gender, occupation – approximately 10MM names.
Pan World	Compiled list from local government and private sources. Can include age, gender, occupation – approximately 10MM names.
Teikoku Data Bank	Compiled list of high level business executives. Can include title, company type, etc. – approximately 850 M names.

Lists cannot be merged and duplicated between brokers. Standard formats have not been established. About half of Japan's 2,000+ lists are computerized. More than 80% are compiled, not response lists. Cost are high, averaging 20,000 yen per thousand (US$ 185/ per thousand), and can go up to US$ 300/per thousand. Lists are cleaned about 1x/year or less, depending upon use. Bad addresses run from 3 to 10% within one list. Brokers will refund money for bad addresses, but will not sell on a net name basis, nor discount the cost. Most likely, you will also have to use the broker's computer processing and lettershop. Census overlays, value-added demographics are not available. Credit card and department store lists (response lists) are available as co-op only.

Telemarketing Companies

Bell system K.K.	2,000 operators Inbound : order/inquiry complaints etc. Outbound: Sales follow-up, Market research
NTT Telemarketing	900 operators Inbound: Teleconferencing Business support, order/inquiry, complaints. Outbound: Survey, Business follow-up
Dai Ichi Ad Systems	700 operators Inbound: Business support, order/inquiry, complaints. Outbound: Survey, Business follow-up
Moshi-Moshi Hotline	450 operators Inbound: Customer Service, order/inquiry, complaints. Outbound: Survey, Business /Sales follow-up, market research
K.K. Active	100 operators Inbound: order/inquiry, Outbound: Business/Sales follow-up, market research

Outbound telemarketing is not used for sales in Japan. There's still a great deal of importance placed on 'face-to-face' sales. Toll-free (Free Dial) calling is new, and used in very specific industries, thus most consumers have not been exposed to it. Local calls are still inexpensive, about ¥ 10 (9 cents). 900 numbers are associated with the steamy side of life.

Direct Marketing Associations

Japan Direct Marketing Association (JADMA).	Official business association organized in 1983 under the Ministry of International Trade and Industry (MITI). There are about 250 member businesses all merchandise sellers; and 140 associate (non-voting) members in the services sector. This is a closed association where you must prove your credentials in order to gain entry.
Japan Direct Mail Association (JDMA).	Official services association organized in 1984 under the Ministry of Posts and Telecommunications (MPT). There are about 310 members, all sellers of direct marketing services.
Japan Telemarketing Association (JTA).	A private (no official sanction) association of telemarketing related companies. Established in 1987, about 160 members.
Nihon Direct Marketing Association (MOBA).	Formerly the Mail Order Business Association. A private (no official sanction) association of primarily direct mail merchandise sellers. Established in 1976, approximately 210 members.
American Chamber of Commerce in Japan's Direct Marketing Committee (ACCJ).	A private association of direct marketer merchandisers and services companies are among the membership of the ACCJ. Primarily educational based.
Japan Chamber of Commerce and Industry	
Tokyo Chamber of Commerce and Industry	

Non-Traditional Media

There has been little development of non-traditional media in Japan.

Research Sources

Medium covered	Research Company	Information Provided
TV, Radio	Video Research Ltd. 2-16-7, Ginza Chuo-ku, Tokyo 104	HH Rating/Target Rating Advertising Statistics
Newspaper, Magazine	Japan Audit Bureau of Circulation 1-3, Hibiyakoen, Chiyoda-ku, Tokyo 106	Circulation
	MRS 1-2-2, Sarugakucho, Chiyoda-ku, Tokyo 106	Advertising Statistics Readership
	Video Research Ltd.	

Television Research Currently Available

Research method	Frequency
Meter System	Daily –HH Rating
Diary Method	Monthly–Target Rating

Advertising Regulations

By Product

Cigarettes

1. Advertising Media
   a. Advertising on TV and radio for a tobacco product shall be conducted only during the first three years after the start of that product's nationwide distribution in Japan.
      > **Note:** The product distributed in an area with a population of over 5% of the national total shall be regarded as being 'distributed nationally.'
   b. The household GRP ceiling limits on TV and radio are as follows.
      > TV: 1 month maximum: 933 GRP's–fiscal year (April - March): 2,800 GRP's
      > Radio:1 month maximum: 900 GRP's–fiscal year (April - March): 2,700 GRP's
   c. Advertisements in newspapers shall not exceed 1/3 page of broadsheet type and 1 page of tabloid type newspaper per issue and per brand.
   d. Advertisements in magazines shall not exceed 2 consecutive page per issue and per brand in size.
2. No advertising shall be targeted at minors.
   a. Popular personalities or models known to appeal primarily to minors shall not be used in the advertising of tobacco products.
   b. Advertising through TV, newspapers, and magazines shall contain a warning notice concerning the prohibition of smoking by minors as well as a health warning.
   c. Advertising on TV during the time periods when minors primarily watch shall not be done.
   Note: Duration of time for which minors primarily watch shall be defined as 'from 5:00 to 22:54 for each day.'
3. Reflecting the current social environment, no advertising shall be conducted to encourage females to smoke.
   a. Advertising image of females smoking on tobacco products shall not be used.
   b. Advertising through newspapers and/or magazines which appeal mainly to females shall not be done.
   Note: Publications with over 50% female readership shall be defined as 'mainly appealing to females.'

Pharmaceutical/Drugs

1. Advertising Media
   a. Advertisement in newspapers shall not exceed 7 full columns (about a half page) per issue and per advertiser
   b. TV/radio programs shown below can not be sponsored.
      - Nightly prime time program 15 minutes or longer.
      - Regular prime time program 1 hour or longer
2. Advertising Copy
   Medicine requiring cautions include medicine for cold anodyne including antipy razolon drugs, medicine for external application including antihistamine, insecticide, eye lotion including nafazoline.
   a. TV : Must include the message 'Read instructions of this medicine carefully' written in clear letters at a stationary position for more than three seconds.
      In this case, a sound is used simultaneously which calls the attention of the audience to the message.
   b. Radio Must include the line 'Read instructions of this medicine carefully' for more than three seconds.
   c. Newspaper Must carry a line 'Read instructions of this medicine carefully and use it properly' in Gothic type face and in bold print that is larger than 12 points in size. The message must be clear and placed where it can be easily read.
   d. Magazine Must include the line 'Read instructions of this medicine carefully and use it properly' in Gothic type face in bold print that is larger than 9 points in size. The message must be clear and placed where it can be easily read.

By Medium

Television

Total amount of commercial time should be:
- 18% or less vs. total broadcasting hours on a weekly basis.
- In terms of prime time, 10% or less vs. total on a daily basis.

Print

Total advertising pages in an issue should be 50% or less of total volume.

Outdoor

Various regulations are posed administratively area by area.

Direct Marketing

Advertising restrictions that apply to direct marketing
- The 'Door to Door' Sales Law enacted by MITI covers all aspects of mail order sales and fulfillment, including a suggestion for appropriate lag time between order receipt and merchandise delivery (1 week).
- The Unjustifiable Premiums and Misleading Representation Act, enacted by the Japan Fair Trade Commission (JFTC), attempts to regulate closed lotteries (purchase required), premium sales and advertising games of chance.
- Anti-monopoly laws (JFTC) restrict the value and volume of prizes awarded in open lotteries (sweepstakes) to a percent of the revenue generated by the program. This is thought to create a 'level playing field' for all competitors in a given product category.
- Regulations of Fair Competition Agreement
- 'Gentlemen's Agreements' within a particular product category

    Note: Although these agreements prescribe the rules within the respective industries, with few exceptions, most are vaguely written and are open to interpretation. For example, there are 'Gentlemen's Agreements that one can only send a sample of a tobacco product to an individual once. However, the size of the sample and the frequency with which you can sample are left unsaid.

Korea

Area	120,540 km²
Population (1992)	22,227,303
Population Growth Rate (1992)	1.9%
GDP	US$ 8.75 billion
GDP/per capita	US$ 6,200
Real growth rate (1992)	4.7%
Capital	Seoul

Population Breakdown

By Sex		*By Age Group*		*By Socio-Economic Status*	
Male	50.2%	Children	16%	A	5%
Female	49.8%	Teens	20%	B	25%
		Adults	64%	C	45%
				D	25%

Source (Population Breakdown): Bank of Korea Annual

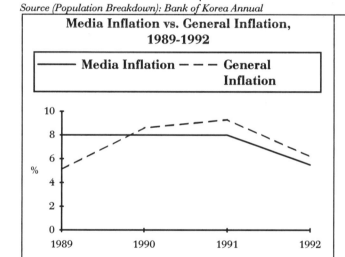

Media Inflation vs. General Inflation, 1989-1992

—— Media Inflation   – – General Inflation

Source (General and Media Inflation Rates): Leo Burnett Media.

Number of households   12,253,000

Ownership of household durables
Car (passenger only) 74.9%
Phone 138.1%*
Washers 76.6%
(purchasing power equivalent)

GNP distribution by industry
Agriculture: 8.1%
Industry: 48.9%
Services: 43.0%

Exchange rate (US$ to local currency)
1991 .... 0.0012655
1992 .... 0.0012455

official use included

Source (Household durables): Daewoo Securities Research 1993. Electron Communication Annual; (GNP by Industry and Number of Households): Bank of Korea Annual

National Holidays

Holiday	1993 Date	Holiday	1993 Date
New Year's	January 1-2	Independence Day	August 15
Lunar New Year's (Lunar calendar Dec. 31-Jan. 2)	January 22-24	Chusuk Holiday (Thanksgiving) (Lunar Calendar August 14-16)	September 29-October 1
Independence Movement Day	March 1	Foundation Day	October 3
Arbor Day	April 5	Christmas	December 25
Children's	May 5		
Buddhist Day	May 28 (Lunar Calendar April 8)		
Memorial Day	June 6		
Constitution Day	July 17		

School Holidays

Holiday	1993 Date
Summer Vacation	Mid July - August
Winter Vacation	Mid December - February

Major Influences and Trends

Despite the establishment of a fourth TV station (SBS), which has lead to more commercial air time availabilities, the Korean broadcasting market still remains a seller's market. Currently, all broadcast commercials are booked through KOBACO (Korean Broadcasting Advertising Corp.).

The growth rate of the four major media seemed to have leveled off. However, in the case of print media, competition among newspapers and magazines has intensified due to the 1987 Liberalization Act which increased the number of newspapers. Despite increased competition, the total spending in print media is stagnant (excluding the natural inflation rate).

Spending Analysis

National advertising spending by medium
based on appropriate year's exchange rate

	1989 US$ MM	1990 US$ MM	1991 US$ MM	1992 US$ MM
TV	665.6	757.0	817.1	1,049.9
Radio	79.2	120.6	152.9	161.4
Newspaper	776.8	1,079.9	1,290.3	1,420.8
Magazine	104.6	147.9	158.6	151.2
Other	353.4	426.6	529.3	590.9
Total	**1,979.7**	**2,532.0**	**2,948.3**	**3,374.2**

Source: Korean Broadcasting Advertising Corporation, "Ad Information", 1993.

Media Buying

- Broadcasting media must be bought through KOBACO.
- Print/Other media can be brought directly.
- Newspaper and magazine rate cards are negotiable.

Buying Services—1992 Billings

Buying services represent less than 1% of the market's total expenditures. Some inflight magazines should be bought through buying services.

Buying Service	Parent Company	US$
Kaya Ad	None	700,000
Doobee Int'l	None	300,000

Source: Leo Burnett Media.

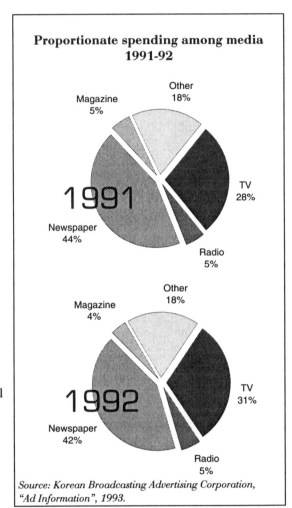

Proportionate spending among media 1991-92

1991: Other 18%, Magazine 5%, TV 28%, Radio 5%, Newspaper 44%

1992: Other 18%, Magazine 4%, TV 31%, Radio 5%, Newspaper 42%

Source: Korean Broadcasting Advertising Corporation, "Ad Information", 1993.

Top Advertisers (1992 Spending)

By Company

Parent Company	Product Category	US$ MM
Samsung Electronics	Electronics	41.65
Lucky Chemicals	Consumer goods	35.33
Pacific Chemicals	Cosmetics	33.61
Gold Star	Electronics	32.16
Daewoo Electronics	Electronics	31.20
Lotte Confectionery	Confectionery	25.26
Cheil foods	Sugar, food, etc.	25.22
Hyundai Motors	Automobiles	25.11
Daewoo Motors	Automobiles	23.92
Lotte-Chilsung	Beverage	23.76

Source: KOBACO, "Ad Information", Jan. 1993.

By Product

Product Category	Advertiser	US$ MM
Food/Drinks	Lotte Confectionery	22.26
Pharmaceutical	Dae Woong	22.04
Electronics	Samsung Electronics	41.64
Automobiles	Hyundai Motors	25.11
Cosmetics	Pacific chemicals	33.61
Distribution	Lotte Department store	18.13
HH Consumer goods	Lucky chemicals	35.33

Source: KOBACO, "Ad Information", Jan. 1993.

Television

Overview

TV HH Penetration				Adult Reach	
1989	*1990*	*1991*	*1992*	at 250 GRPs	45 (3+)
99%	99%	99.4%	99.4%	at 500 GRPs	65 (3+)
9,884,000	9,894,000	11,017,.000	12,179,.000	at 1,000 GRPs	82 (3+)

Source (HH Penetration): Electronic Communications Annual   *Source (Adult Reach): Leo Burnett Media*

- TV household penetration is 99.4%, or 12,179,000 HH.
- Booked through KOBACO only. Commercial airtime is limited to 8% of program length.
- There is no mid-program commercial break. Commercial lengths include :15, :20 and :30, with :15 and :30 being the most often used.
- AGB's People Meter recently incepted.
- Korean is the only language used on TV.

Opportunities

Network	Number of Stations	Ownership	Station Profile	Commercial Minutes/Day	Coverage	Broadcast Hours (Sign-On/Off)
KBS-1	20	Government	Public interest/ Commercial	6 blocks/week	Nationwide	06:00-10:00 17:30-24:00
KBS-2	20	Government	Commercial	8% of program length	Nationwide	'
MBC	20	Semi-government	'	'	'	'
SBS	1	Private	'	'	Seoul	'
EBS	16	Government	Educational (Non-Commercial)	-	Nationwide	'

Source: Leo Burnett Media.

Costs

Prime Time TV Costs for :30 in US$			
1989	*1990*	*1991*	*1992*
6,082	7,012	7,228	7,589

Source: Leo Burnett Media

Television Cost Changes Between Years

'88 '89 '90 '91 '92
7%   8%   8%   4%

Source: Leo Burnett Media

Audiences/CPM's

Average Cost, Audience, and CPMs by Daypart
(Top 3 stations , :30, national TV, Target=People 4+)

Hours	Morning 07:00-10:00	Early Evening 9:00-20:00	Prime Time 20:00-22:30	Late Night 23:00-24:00	Weekend 10:00-18:00	Children 17:30-19:00
Station: KBS-2TV						
US$	1,935	5,063	7,983	5,063	2,655	1,935
Avg. Aud. (000)	824	2,430	3,428	1,301	2,046	1,996
CPM	2.34	2.08	2.33	3.89	1.30	1.00
Station: MBC						
US$	1,948	5,095	8,038	5,095	2,839	1,948
Avg. Aud. (000)	1,996	3,298	4,469	3,861	2,367	1,562
CPM	0.98	1.54	1.80	1.32	1.20	1.25
Station: SBS (Seoul Area)						
US$	343	1,184	2,031	1,184	763	343
Avg. Aud. (000)	441	441	581	771	391	260
CPM	0.78	2.67	3.50	1.53	1.95	1.32

Source: Media Service Korea People Meter and Leo Burnett Media

Audiences/Ratings by Daypart

Daypart	Hours	Household				Adult		
		Universe (000)	Hut Levels	Household Rating	Impressions (000)	Universe (000)	Adult Rating	Impressions (000)
Morning	06:30-10:00	12,253	36.0	36.2	4,436	14,481	N/A	N/A
Daytime	19:00-20:00	12,253	51.6	51.9	6,359	14,481	N/A	N/A
Primetime	20:00-22:30	12,253	65.8	66.2	8,111	14,481	N/A	N/A
Late Night	23:00-24:00	12,253	45.0	45.3	5,551	14,481	N/A	N/A
Weekend	10:00-18:00	12,253	41.9	42.2	5,171	14,481	N/A	N/A
Children's	17:30-19:00	12,253	37.3	37.5	4,594	14,481	N/A	N/A

Source: MSK People Meter and Leo Burnett.

Scheduling/Regional/Languages

- Most stations air commercials throughout the entire time the networks are on the air, although commercials are limited to the beginning and end of programs.

- KBS-1 airs commercials only in specific time blocks (6/week).

Network	Station	Region	Hours
KBS	KBS subsidiaries	7 major cities	20 spots/day
MBC	MBC subsidiaries	7 major cities	18 spots/day

Children's Advertising

All adult programming accepts advertising targeted at children. There are no formal restrictions regarding advertising which targets children.

CHILDREN'S PROGRAMMING			Kids'		
Station	Hours	Days	Universe (000)	Ratings	Impressions (000)
K-2	17:30-19:00	Mon-Fri	7,854	N/A	N/A
MBC	17:30-19:00	Mon-Fri	7,854	N/A	N/A
SBS	17:30-19:00	Mon-Fri	7,854	N/A	N/A

Source: Leo Burnett Media

Radio

Overview

- There are 11 radio stations in Korea (all in Seoul), of which seven are commercial.
- Korean is the only language used to broadcast.
- All commercials are :20 long.
- Regional/local buys are possible, and no premium is charged for them.
- The most popular program types are: women's morning, late night, FM music for teenagers and traffic guide.

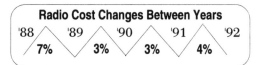

Radio Cost Changes Between Years

'88 — '89 — '90 — '91 — '92
7%   3%   3%   4%

Costs

Daypart	Local Time	Avg. Cost :20 US$	Audience (000)	CPM (US$)
Prime Time	07:00-13:00	435	N/A	N/A
Daytime	13:00-19:00	266	N/A	N/A
Late Night	19:00-24:00	154	N/A	N/A

Cable

Overview

Cable TV is now being tested, airing in 2 large apartment complexes in Seoul. It is expected to start in early 1995. Up to two million households are expected to receive cable within the next five years.
Source: Leo Burnett Media

Satellite

- Japan (NHK) and Hong Kong (Star TV) programs are receivable. There are seven satellite channels, of which 5 (Star TV's) are commercial. (*Source: Leo Burnett Media*). The Japanese NHK programs are non-commercial.
- The penetration is continuously increasing and the number of households owning satellite receivers are reportedly over 100,000. (*Source: Leo Burnett Media*). Satellite receiver ownership is still illegal but nevertheless is becoming widespread.
- Two Korean satellites will be launched in 1995. One million households are expected to receive satellite signals when that happens.

Satellite Channel	Country of Origin	Language	Programming
NHK	Japan	Japanese	2 channels
Star TV	Hong Kong	English/Mandarin	5 channels

Video Cassettes

- 52% of TV households have video cassette recorders (VCRs). (*Source: Electronic Communication Annual*).
- AGB People Meter measures VCR usage.
- Pre-recorded tapes carry commercials, but thus far, they are being used primarily by the tape manufacturers, at 1 ad per tape and are not sold to general advertisers. There are therefore no precedents for costs.

Cinema

- Commercials are available at 99% of all cinemas. They are sold at lengths of :30 and :60.
- The total number of cinemas in Korea is not available, nor is the potential reach.
- A 4-week cinema schedule for a first-run movie shown once a day would cost approximately US$ 380. (*Source: Leo Burnett Media*)
- Cinema advertising costs rise an average of 3% each year. (*Source: Leo Burnett Media*)
- The situation is expected to stay as it is.

Newspapers

There are 19 national daily newspapers which accept advertising. No reliable circulation or rate information is available. (*Source: Leo Burnett Media*)

Newspaper Cost Changes Between Years

'88	'89	'90	'91	'92
4%	10%	10%	7%	

Source: Leo Burnett Media

Newspaper	Market	Size	Circ. (000)	Avg. Daily Aud. (000)	1 page B&W Cost (US$)	Accept Color?
Chosun Ilbo	Nationwide	37x51 cm	N/A	N/A	69,115	Yes
Dong-A Ilbo	Nationwide	37x51 cm	N/A	N/A	69,115	Yes
Chung Ang Ilbo	Nationwide	37x51 cm	N/A	N/A	69,115	Yes
Hankook Ilbo	Nationwide	37x51 cm	N/A	N/A	69,115	Yes
Kyunghyang Shinmun	Nationwide	37x51 cm	N/A	N/A	44,925	Yes
Seoul Shinmun	Nationwide	37x51 cm	N/A	N/A	44,925	Yes
Hankyoreh Shinmun	Nationwide	37x51 cm	N/A	N/A	69,115	Yes
Kookmin Ilbo	Nationwide	37x51 cm	N/A	N/A	44,925	Yes
Segye Ilbo	Nationwide	37x51 cm	N/A	N/A	44,925	Yes
Munwha Ilbo	Nationwide	37x51 cm	N/A	N/A	44,925	Yes
Hankook Economic	Nationwide	37x51 cm	N/A	N/A	24,191	Yes
Daily Economic	Nationwide	37x51 cm	N/A	N/A	24,191	Yes
Chung-Ang Economic	Nationwide	37x51 cm	N/A	N/A	24,191	Yes
Seoul Economic	Nationwide	37x51 cm	N/A	N/A	24,191	Yes
Naewoi Economic	Nationwide	37x51 cm	N/A	N/A	20,562	Yes
Cheil Economic	Nationwide	37x51 cm	N/A	N/A	17,478	Yes
Daily Sports	Nationwide	37x51 cm	N/A	N/A	23,310	Yes
Sports Seoul	Nationwide	37x51 cm	N/A	N/A	23,310	Yes
Sports Chosun	Nationwide	37x51 cm	N/A	N/A	23,310	Yes

Source: Leo Burnett Media

Magazines

There are over 2,500 consumer magazines, and over 40 trade and technical magazines in Korea.

Source: Leo Burnett Media

Magazine	Type	Frequency	Circ.	Audited?	Avg. Issue Aud. (000)	1 page 4/C Cost (US$)
Yosung Dong-A	Women's	Monthly	N/A	No	N/A	2,428
Gajung Chosun	Women's	Monthly	N/A	No	N/A	2,428
Women Sense	Women's	Monthly	N/A	No	N/A	2,428
Better Homes & Garden's	Women's	Monthly	N/A	No	N/A	1,868
Labelle	Women's	Monthly	N/A	No	N/A	1,868
Bride	Women's	Monthly	N/A	No	N/A	1,494
Young Lady	Women's	Monthly	N/A	No	N/A	1,494
Shin Dong-A	General interest	Monthly	N/A	No	N/A	1,993
Monthly Chosun	General interest	Monthly	N/A	No	N/A	2,242
Sisa Journal	General interest	Monthly	N/A	No	N/A	1,518
Business Korea	Economic	Weekly	N/A	No	N/A	1,494
Economist	Economic	Monthly	N/A	No	N/A	1,245
Maekyung Business	Economic	Monthly	N/A	No	N/A	1,245
Sonyon Chungang	Children's	Monthly	N/A	No	N/A	1,245
IQ Jump	Children's	Monthly	N/A	No	N/A	1,245
Cartoon Kingdom	Hobby	Monthly	N/A	No	N/A	1,245
Monthly Screen	Hobby	Monthly	N/A	No	N/A	1,245
Road Show	Hobby	Monthly	N/A	No	N/A	1,245
Eumak Dong-A	Leisure	Monthly	N/A	No	N/A	996
Monthly Auto	Leisure	Monthly	N/A	No	N/A	996
Fishing Seasons	Leisure	N/A	N/A	No	N/A	996

Source: Leo Burnett Media

Outdoor/Transit

Billboards

- Many outdoor sites are available, although finite numbers are not available. Costs vary by site and size, and increase by an average of 5% per year.
  Source: Leo Burnett Media
- At least 4 weeks' lead time is needed to reserve an outdoor billboard.
  Source: Leo Burnett Media

Transit

There are many opportunities to place advertising on transit boards. An average cost for a 400 cm x 225 cm transit board for 1 month is US$ 1,000. Transit board costs tend to increase by an average of 5% per year. Cigarette advertising is prohibited.

Source: Leo Burnett Media

Direct Marketing

- Direct marketing is still emerging and the agencies are not professional.
- There are no telemarketing companies, nor a direct marketing association.

List Broker	Information
Cheil Direct	*All provide lists*
Doo wool	*compiled by age,*
Duck Sung	*sex, occupation,*
Cheil Express	*etc.*
Yon Hee	

Source: Leo Burnett Media.

Non-Traditional Media

There is no evidence of non-traditional media being used for advertising in Korea.

Research Sources

Medium Covered	Research Company	Information Provided

TV	MSK (AGB)
	  Gsung Bd. 54 Dohwa-Dong
	  Mapo-Ku, Seoul, Korea
	
	Gallup Korea
	  221 Sajick-Dong, Jongno-Ku,
	  Seoul, Korea
		TV audience data.

TV, Radio, Newspaper, Magazines	Lee's RP/SMS
	  Samduck Bd. 131 Da-Dong,
	  Chung-Ku, Seoul, Korea
		Audience/ Readership data

Source: Leo Burnett Media

Television Research Currently Available

Research Method	Frequency
People Meter	Daily/Weekly/Quarterly/Annually
Questionnaire	Daily/Weekly/Quarterly/Annually/Monthly

Advertising Regulations

By Product

Alcohol
Aired late night only (after 10:00 pm).
Over 17% spirit unaccepted.
See following section for details.

Food/Restaurants
See following section for details.

Cigarettes
Magazine is the only medium allowed for cigarettes, with 120 insertions per brand per year. Health warning required.

Pharmaceuticals/Drugs
Prohibited from 17:30 to 20:00 on TV.
See following section for details.

Advertising To Children
See following section for details.

Commercial Production
No foreigners are allowed to be portrayed as heroes.
Pre-censorship by KBC (Korea Broadcasting Committee)

By Medium

Television
Pre-censorship by KBC (Korea Broadcasting Committee); booked through KOBACO (Korea Broadcasting Advertising Corporation).

Outdoor
Some regulations are posed by the authorities, area by area.

Source: Korean Broadcasting Advertising Corporation and Korean Broadcasting Committee.

KOREAN ADVERTISING REGULATIONS

Alcohol

(1) Particular attention should be paid to alcohol and liquor advertising, considering its influences on juveniles and society as a whole.

(2) Alcohol and liquor advertising should not contain the following :

(a) Commercial songs.

(b) Depiction of a drinking mood, such as a scene or the sound of drinking.

(c) Models who are minors.

(d) Presentations that imply that drinking is sociable and indicative of success.

(e) Presentations showing drinking as masculine or a sign of strength

(f) Presentations that might encourage excessive drinking, such as a scene showing a liquor in any container form being passed from person to person

(g) Presentations that suggest drinking is good for one's health or that connect drinking with health.

(h) Presentations that imply that drinking eliminates worries and troubles.

(i) Presentations that associate drinking with a dangerous action, such as driving, exercising, climbing, operating machinery, etc.

Food

(1) Food advertising should not contain exaggerated statements and visual presentations.

(a) Different or exaggerated presentations of ingredients and content.

(b) Misleading medical claims, including those portraying a product as an effective medical treatment or way to prevent disease.

(c) ndications or presentations of health improvement, longevity and youth maintenance capabilities.

(d) Presentations about beautifying capabilities.

(e) Portrayal of product as a natural food rather than an artificial food.

(2) Presentations of food being consumed in an unrefined manner of being handled.

Medicine

(1) Medicine (insecticide, agricultural medicine, veterinary medicine) advertisements must be prudent and consider the effects on public health.

(2) Medicine advertising should not contain statements or visual presentations that misuse or exaggerate the effects of medicine.

(a) Expressions such as "safe", "non-reaction"

(b) Expressions that imply the medicine will cure the user's ailment or lead to complete recovery.

(c) Expressions that the medicine will have miraculous, marvelous or wonderful effects.

(d) Expressions that quote testimonials, recommendations, or personal recollection attesting to the medicine's benefits.

(e) Expressions that may overstate the efficacy of the medicine, quoting clinical results, related literature of statistical data.

(f) Expressions that exaggerate the efficacy of a drug as it was approved.

(g) Expressions that name domestic or foreign hospitals and institutions and imply that these institutions recommend the medicine or reveal experimental results.

(h) Expressions regarded as direct advertising in which the efficacy and capacity of a medicine is testified to, recommended, specified or encouraged by medical persons including surgeons, physicians, dentists, herb doctors and pharmacists, as well as models represented as medical persons or the professionals in the medical care and medicines.

(i) Expressing a diagnosis, prescription or medical treatment through advertising.

Children

(1) In advertising for children, manners and self-morals should be treated as important, increasing respectfulness to the society and other people.

(2) Expressions that could hurt a child's character and sentiment will not be allowed.

(a) Direct communication of the commercial sentence by a child.

(b) Commercial songs sung by a child.

(c) Expressions stirring up a speculative spirit.

(d) Expressions making children feel inferior if they do not have the (advertised) product or expressions giving the impression that being without the product is to be ridiculed or despised.

(e) Expressions that show a child in a dangerous position or stimulate a child to engage in dangerous behavior.

3) Medicine advertising should not contain any visual presentations that could possibly disgust or offend an audience as outlined in the previous article including:

(a) Use of commercial song

(b) Presentations that give an excessive feeling of uneasiness and dreadfulness about disease.

(c) Presentations that describe or dramatize in too much detail the suffering caused by disease or a scene descriptive of such.

(d) Presentation that would make members of the audience believe that they are seriously diseased.

(e) Presentations that hold patients up to ridicule or treat disease in a callous man

(4) Advertising for contraceptives should be treated delicately, and should not contain presentations that are likely to misrepresent the purpose of family planning.

Malaysia

Area	329,750 km^2
Population (1992)	18,410,920
Population growth rate (1992)	2.4%
GDP	US$ 48.0 billion
GDP/per capita	US$ 2,670
Real growth rate (1991)	8.6%
Capital	Kuala Lumpur

Population Breakdown

By Sex
Male 50%
Female 50%

By Age Group
Children, 1-12 .... 31%
Teens, 13-19 .... 18%
Adults, 20+ 51%

By Socio-Economic Status
A, US$ 780* 19%
B, US$ 390 .... 28%
C, US$ 200 .... 30%
D, US$ 200 and below 23%
monthly household income

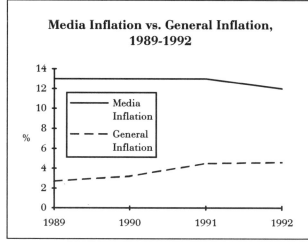

Media Inflation vs. General Inflation, 1989-1992

— Media Inflation
- - - General Inflation

Number of Households 3,160,000
Ownership of household durables
  Car 42%
  Phone 44%
  Washers 47%
  (purchasing power equivalent)
GNP distribution by industry
  Agriculture 24%
  Industry 32%
  Services 44%
  Source: Economic Report 1992, 1993
Exchange rates (US$ to local currency)
  1991 .... 0.3991
  1992 .... 0.3912

National Holidays

Holiday	1993 Date
New Year	January 1
Chinese New Year	January 23-January 24
Hari Raya Puasa	March 26-March 27
Labour Day	May 1
Wasak Day	May 6
Hari Raya Haji	June 1
King's Birthday	June 5
Prophet Muhammad's Birthday	August 30
National day	August 31
Deepavali	November 13
Christmas	December 25

School Holidays

Holiday	1993 Date
1st Term Breaks	January 23-January 31
2nd Term Breaks	March 20-March 30
3rd Term Breaks	May 29-June 20
4th Term Breaks	August 21-August 29
5th Term Breaks	October 30-November 30

Major Influences and Trends

Two new networks—TV4, a private channel, and SNS (Subscription News Service), a government controlled network—are expected to be operational in 1994. A change in TV audience research from diary system to people meters is also expected in 1994. These developments will impact buying patterns and rate structures because of audience fragmentation and more up-to-date audience data.

A new English daily, *The Sun*, was launched on June 1st 1993 and another, *The Leader*, is expected towards thc fourth quarter of 1993. At present, their entry does not pose a threat to the established English dailies.

An anticipated total ban on cigarette parallel advertising has not materialized but tighter restrictions for this category may be expected in the coming years.

Spending Analysis

National advertising spending by medium
based on appropriate year's exchange rate

	1989 US$ MM	1990 US$ MM	1991 US$ MM	1992 US$ MM
TV	112.4	130.8	163.8	174.8
Cinema	0.3	1.2	2.0	1.7
Radio	N/A	2.9	8.4	10.4
Newspaper	97.6	133.5	177.2	187.3
Magazine	18.5	20.1	35.3	44.1
Outdoor	5.1	9.6	7.0	8.5
Other	4.9	4.6	11.2	14.4
Total	**238.8**	**302.7**	**404.9**	**441.2**

Source: SRM Adex Report

Media Buying

Most media pricing is negotiable, mainly negotiated by the Media Department, but occasionally some major advertisers do get involved in the negotiations.

The media market is not controlled or monopolized by any one media owner.

The 'intended media buying service' has turned out to be another agency and was rejected in its application to be a 4A's member, as it is still not a full-service ad agency. This agency is currently offering planning and buying services to the smaller agencies.

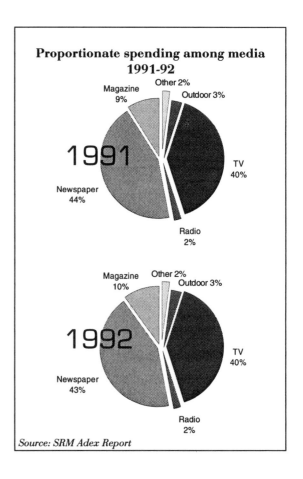

Proportionate spending among media 1991-92

1991: Magazine 9%, Other 2%, Outdoor 3%, TV 40%, Radio 2%, Newspaper 44%

1992: Magazine 10%, Other 2%, Outdoor 3%, TV 40%, Radio 2%, Newspaper 43%

Source: SRM Adex Report

Top Advertisers (1992 Spending)

By Company

Parent Company	Product Categories	US$ MM
CID	Tobacco/Trademark	29.5
Nestle	Consumer Products	12.6
MTC	Tobacco/Trademark	12.3
Colgate/Palmolive	Consumer Products	9.9
Lever Brothers	Toiletries/House Supplies	8.3
RJR	Tobacco/Trademark	7.9
Matsushita	Electrical Appliances	3.9
Godfrey Philips	Tobacco/Trademark	3.9
Tohtonku	Toiletries	3.4
MAS	Airlines	3.3

Source: SRM Adex Report

By Product

Product Category	US$ MM
Cigarette, Trademark, Parallel Products/Services	59.1
Toiletries & Toilet Goods	31.7
Automotive	28.2
Apparel/Departmental Store	26.7
Non-alcoholic Beverages	24.8
Household Supplies	23.5
Household Equipment Appliances	23.5
Food	22.8
Industrial	18.9
Communication, Publishing & Media Exhibitions	18.2

Source: SRM Adex Report

Television

Overview

	TV HH Penetration			Adult Reach	
1989	*1990*	*1991*	*1992*	at 250 GRPs	75%
86%	86%	87%	88%	at 500 GRPs	85%
2,407	2,479	2,575	2,728	at 1000 GRPs	93%

Opportunities

There are three channels: TV1 and TV2, which are government-controlled, and TV3, a privatized network.

Networks	Number of Stations	Ownership	Station Profile	Commercial Minutes/Hr	Weekly Coverage	Broadcast Hours (Sign-On/Off)
RTM (Radio TV Malaysia)	TV1	Government Owned	Malay Dominated Programming Malay (85%) Audience	10	79%	M-W 16:00-00:15 Thu 13:00-00:15 F-Su 08:30-00:15
	TV2	Government Owned	Skewed Chinese/English Programming	10	89%	M-Th 17:00-24:00 F-Su 08:00-00:15
STMB (System TV Malaysia Berhad)	TV3	Privately Owned	More News/ Entertainment Skewed	13	87%	M-W 16:20-00:25 Thu 13:00-00:25 F-Su 09:00-00:45

Source: SRM TV Scope.

Costs

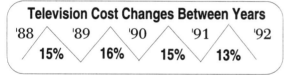

Television Cost Changes Between Years

'88	'89	'90	'91	'92
	15%	16%	15%	13%

Source: TV Station rate card

Prime Time TV Costs for :30 in US$			
1989	*1990*	*1991*	*1992*
2,163	2,333	2,350	2,380

Since Nov. 1991 there has been no price increase and it is unlikely that there will be one before the end of the year. This status quo is primarily due to the bargaining audience for various satellite channels (a chunk of advertising has moved to these channels from terrestrial TV).

Audiences/CPM's

Average Cost, Audience, and CPMs by Daypart
(Top 3 stations, :30, national audience; Target=15+)

Hours	Morning 08:00-12:00	Daytime 12:00-18:00	Prime Time 18:00-22:00	Late Night 22:00-24:00	Weekend 13:00-22:00	Children 08:00-18:00
Station: TV1						
US$	321	385	2,050	1,050	1,032	365
Avg. Aud. (000)	140	351	1,302	887	855	267
CPM	2.29	1.10	1.57	1.18	1.21	1.37
Station: TV2						
US$	412	788	1,619	812	1,291	305
Avg. Aud. (000)	39	317	800	494	665	206
CPM	10.56	2.49	2.02	1.64	1.94	1.48
Station: TV3						
US$	513	541	1,701	757	1,169	248
Avg. Aud. (000)	166	290	1,236	422	908	241
CPM	3.09	1.87	1.38	1.79	1.29	1.03

Source: SRM TV Scope and Media owners rate card

Television, continued

Audiences/Ratings by Daypart (Target=Adults 15+)

Daypart	Hours	Household				Adult		
		Universe (000)	Hut Levels	Household Rating	Impressions (000)	Universe (000)	Adult Rating	Impressions (000)
Morning	08:00-12:00	N/A	N/A	N/A	N/A	8,708	1.3	113
Daytime	12:00-18:00	N/A	N/A	N/A	N/A	8,708	3.7	322
Primetime	18:00-22:00	N/A	N/A	N/A	N/A	8,708	12.8	1115
Late Night	22:00-24:00	N/A	N/A	N/A	N/A	8,708	6.9	601
Weekend	13:00-22:00	N/A	N/A	N/A	N/A	8,708	9.3	810
Children's	08:00-18:00	N/A	N/A	N/A	N/A	8,708	2.7	235

Source: SRM TV Scope.

Scheduling/Regional/Languages

- The most common commercial length is :30; lengths of :07, :10, :15, :20, :30, :40, :60 are also available.
- Commercials are aired throughout the day, both at the beginning and end of programs, and within programs.
- There is no regional advertising in Malaysia.

LANGUAGES	*Programming*	*Commercials*
Primary	Bahasa Malaysia....................45%	Bahasa Malaysia 45%
Secondary	English.................................42%	English 42%
	Chinese 10%	Chinese..................................10%
	Tamil....................................3%	Tamil 3%

Children's Advertising

Both adult and children's programs accept commercials targeted at children.

ADULT PROGRAMMING (Target=6-14)				Kids'	
Station	Hours	Days	Universe (000)	Ratings	Impressions (000)
TV1	20:30-21:30	Mon-Sun	2,966	26	771
TV2	20:30-21:30	Mon-Sun	2,966	6	178
TV3	20:30-21:30	Mon-Sun	2,966	15	445

Source: SRM TV Scope.

CHILDREN'S PROGRAMMING (Target=6-14)				Kids'	
Station	Hours	Days	Universe (000)	Ratings	Impressions (000)
TV1	17:30-18:00	Mon-Sun	2,966	6	178
	16:30-17:30	Thu-Fri	2,966	7	208
	19:00-19:30	Mon-Sun	2,966	6	178
	09:00-12:00	Sat	2,966	4	119
TV3	09:00-13:00	Sat	2,966	10	297
TV3	20:30-21:30	Mon-Sun	2,966	15	445

Source: SRM TV Scope.

Radio

Overview

- There are 6 stations, all commercial, in Malaysia.
- Ninety-three percent of all households have radios; the estimated number is 2,883,000. About 80% of automobiles have radios.

- The primary broadcasting language is Bahasa Malaysia; however, English, Mandarin, Chinese dialects, Tamil and other indigenous languages are used.

- The most popular programs are Music. Prime/Peak Time is 07:00-09:00 and 17:00-19:00.
- Commercial lengths available are :10, :15, :20, :30, :40 and :60.

- The average Cost/CPM of a :30 radio commercial is US$ 63/US$ 0.45 CPM.

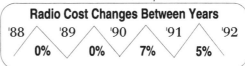

Radio Cost Changes Between Years

'88 / '89 / '90 / '91 / '92
0% 0% 7% 5%

Costs

Daypart Costs/CPMs
(Jakarta, :30, Target=Adults 15+)

Daypart	Local Time	Avg. Cost :30 US$	Audience (000)	CPM (US$)
RADIO 1 (Malay Nat'l)				
Primetime	06:00-12:00	94	480	0.20
Daytime	12:00-20:00	70	284	0.25
Latenight	20:00-24:00	47	237	0.20
RADIO 4 (English Nat'l)				
Primetime	06:00-09:00	123	91	1.35
Daytime	12:00-20:00	72	49	1.47
Latenight	20:00-24:00	53	64	0.83
RADIO 5 (Mandarin Nat'l)				
Primetime	06:00-09:00	82	307	0.27
Daytime	12:00-20:00	53	305	0.17
Latenight	20:00-24:00	41	305	0.13
RADIO 6 (Tamil Nat'l)				
Primetime	06:00-09:00	47	397	0.12
Daytime	12:00-20:00	38	329	0.12
Latenight	20:00-24:00	35	205	0.17

Source: SRM Radioscope and radio stations' rate cards

Cable

No data is available on cable in Malaysia.

Satellite

No data is available on satellite reception/advertising in Malaysia.

Video Cassettes

- Roughly 50% of TV households have video cassette recorders (VCRs). Video cassettes in Malaysia do carry commercials–the average is one sponsor per tape. The average cost of VCR advertising is US$ 1,428 per title. Ad Hoc VCR Audience Research measures VCR usage.
- In the past few years, a slow and steady increase in viewership was observed. The trend can be expected to continue as the cost of video recorders is further reduced. However, this growth may not be signficant, especially with the revival of cinema and the appearance of cineplexes.

Cinema

- All cinemas in Malaysia offer commercial time. Over 4 weeks, the reach is 12%.
- Commercial lengths available include :30, :40, :60, :90, and :120.
- An average 4 week buy of :60 spots in 80 halls costs US$ 4,000.

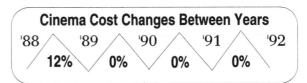

Cinema Cost Changes Between Years

'88 / '89 / '90 / '91 / '92
12% 0% 0% 0%

Newspapers

There are 12 national daily papers which accept advertising. Combined circulation is 1,540,000. Literacy rate in English is 47%.

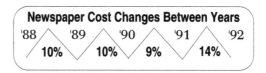

Newspaper	Market	Size	Circ. (000)	Avg. Daily Aud. (000)	1 page B&W Cost (US$)	Accept Color?
English						
New Strait Times	National	54 cm x 8 cm	172	663	4,225	Yes
The Star	National	37 cm x 7 cm	166	674	1,804	Yes
Business Times	Central	54 cm x 8 cm	12	62	1,352	Yes
Malay Mail	Central	33 cm x 6 cm	65	299	1,046	Yes
The Sun	Central	33 cm x 7 cm	50	200	497	Yes
Malay						
Berita Harian	National	54 cm x 8 cm	286	1,772	4,225	Yes
Utusan Malaysia	National	54 cm x 8 cm	231	1,485	2,662	Yes
Utusan Melayu	National	54 cm x 8 cm	18	73	879	Yes
Harian metro	Central	33 cm x 6 cm	30	93	542	Yes
Chinese						
Tong Bao	Central	53 cm x 10 cm	32	97	1,037	Yes
Nanyang Siang Pau	National	53 cm x 10 cm	190	649	2,695	Yes
Sin Chew Jit Pao	National	53 cm x 10 cm	196	680	2,861	Yes
Shin Min	National	53 cm x 10 cm	36	170	1,203	Yes
China Press	National	53 cm x 10 cm	98	327	1,659	Yes
Kwong Wah	Northern	35.5 cm x 20 cm	70	300	1,389	Yes
Tamil						
Tamil Nesan	National	52 cm x 8 cm	25	135	814	Yes

Source: SRM Readership Data and media owners' rate cards

Magazines

There are 210 consumer magazines published in Malaysia, and 15 trade and technical magazines.

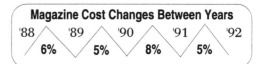

Magazine	Type	Frequency	Circ. (000)	Audited?	Avg. Issue Aud. (000)	1 page 4/C Cost (US$)
Asia Magazine(Malaysia Ed.)	Regional	Weekly	130	Yes	N/A	3,987
Asia Week	Regional	Weekly	74	Yes	N/A	9,260
Expression	Credit Card	Bimonthly	90	Yes	N/A	4,831
Wanita	Women	Monthly	118	Yes	N/A	1,735
Fu Ni	Women	Monthly	65	Yes	N/A	900
Bacaria	Children/ Educational	Biweekly	100	Yes	N/A	2,155
Dewan Pelajar	Children/ Educational	Monthly	98	No	N/A	479
Gila-Gila	Entertainment	Fortnightly	153	No	N/A	1,397
Utusan Radio & TV	Entertainment	Fortnightly	127	No	N/A	755
Malaysian Business	Business	Fortnightly	16	No	N/A	822
Female	Women	Monthly	35	Yes	N/A	1,314
Destination	Credit Card	Quarterly	80	No	N/A	2,543
Her World	Women	Monthly	35	Yes	N/A	1,487
Jelita	Women	Monthly	80	Yes	N/A	1,643
Visage	Credit Card	Monthly	60	No	N/A	3,012
Business World	Business	Monthly	20	No	N/A	587

Source: Media owners' rate cards

Outdoor/Transit

Billboard	**Transit**
Sites available 3,000	Boards available.........................N/A
Lead Time to reserve .... 3 months	

Outdoor sizes/costs

Costs have been increasing at between 5% and 10% annually.

Type	Size	Avg. Adv. Rate in US $
Supersites		
Backlit Stretched FYC	3.0 m x 11.0 m	1,400/site per month
Hoardings	6.0 m x 123 m	3,200/site per month
Three-sided Pillar	2.7 m x 1.4 m	3,200/site per month
Unipole "V" shaped	6.1 m x 18.3 m	120,300 perannum (2 sided)
Standard Poster		
4-Sheet	1.5 m x 1.0 m	120/poster per month
12-Sheet	2.0 m x 1.5 m	235/panel per month
48-sheet	3.0 m x 6.1 m	370/panel per month
96-sheet	3.0 m x 12.2 m	640/panel per month
Overhead Bridges	L: 30 ft, 50 ft W: 3 ft	20,800/year for 2 panels
Directional Road Signs	14 ft x 10 ft	8,400 for 10 units perannum
Backlit Lightbox	20 ft x 60 ft	48,000 perannum
Nettlefold Electronic Box	3.2m x 7.6m	14,000/hour (daily for 1 year)
Eagle Electronic Board	17 ft x 33 ft	1,600 per month, 120 spots daily
Backlit lightbox w/uniflex face	12 ft x 30 ft	32,000 for 2 years
Megasites	10 ft x 30 ft	35,000 for 6 months
Pillar	12 ft x 60 ft	48,000/annum
Superscam		18,000/annum
Superflex	14 ft x 45 ft	22,000/annum
Retail Adv. Panels (Rural Areas)	Height: 6 ft /Width: 2 ft	310 for 26 weeks
Revolving Stands	2 ft x 3 ft	233/panel per month for 5 panels
Airport Poster Suspended Panel	82 cm x 105 cm	1,500/panel per month
Baggage Reclaim		
Column mounted	102 cm x 152 cm	300/panel per month
Free standing	297 cm x 105 cm	790/panel per month
Travelator	292 cm x 82 cm	790/panel per month
Wall mounted	282 cm x 105 cm	1,290/panel per month
Rotating drum	60 ft x 40 ft	24,000/month (3 panels)
Tri-signs	786mm x 766mm	20,000/annum (3 panels)
Transit		
Bus stop shelters	6.1m x 3m x 0.8m	300-360/site per month
Bus back panels	6 ft x 2 ft	40/panel per month
Bus side	11 ft x 2 ft	80-100/side
Interior bus panels	18 ft x 4 ft	18/panel per month
Train posters	50.6 cm x 76.2 cm	7/poste per month
Ferry panel	173.3 cm x 40.55 cm	36/double sided panel
(Penang/PW)	312 cm x 40.5 cm	
Taxitop	91.4 cm x 30.5 cm	50/taxi per month
Airport Trolleys	50.8 cm x 35.0 cm	72/panel per month

Source: Media owners' rate cards

Product/Category Restrictions   See further, under Alcohol and Cigarettes.

Direct Marketing

Some major international agencies offer direct marketing services and Direct Marketing specialty shops have also entered the scene, notably Kobbs & Draft, Union 2000, and Direct Marketing Asia.

List Broker	*Information Provided*
DMA	Banking/Profession/Industry
Times (formerly DM&M)	Banking/Profession/Industry
Target	Banking/Profession/Industry
List Marketing Asia	Banking/Profession/Industry
Oh's International	Banking/Profession/Industry
All Major Credit Cards	Banking/Profession/Industry

Telemarketing Companies	*Direct Marketing Association*
Times Business Communications Centre (Singapore based)	Currently being established

Non-Traditional Media

Demand for non-traditional media is expected to grow if the government ban on "cigarette parallel advertising" (non-tobacco products or services bearing cigarette brand names) over traditional media is enforced.

Non-traditional media currently available	
Vision Four	A closed circuit hotel video network, covering about 100 up-market hotels. :30 cost = US$ 2,760 per month
Rail Channel	An on-train video service. :30 cost = US$ 782 per month
Inflight Video	Provided aboard all MAS international flights. Average :30 cost = US$ 5,430 per month
Beriteks	An electronic newspaper broadcasting through RTM and TV3. Cost = US$ 60 per full page
Sound Ads	An audio medium played through the public address system in about 140 supermarket/department store outlets. :30 cost = US$ 1,012 per week

Research Sources

Medium covered	Research Company	Information Provided
TV, Radio, Print, Cinema, VCR	Survey Research Malaysia 19th Floor, Menara MPPJ, Jalan Tengah 46000, P.J. Selangor Malaysia	General mass media audiences Readership data-Weekly Adults 15+ and Kids (6-14 yrs.) TV ratings based on a diary method Target Group Index Adex
TV, Radio, Print, Cinema, VCR	Frank Small & Associates 32nd Floor, UBN Tower Letter Box 63, No. 10 Jalan P. Ramlee, 50250 Kuala Lumpur, Malaysia	General mass media audiences Readership data Weekly Adults 15+ and Kids (6-14 yrs.)

Television Research Currently Available

Research method	Frequency
Diary method, based on a panel of TV population	Weekly

Advertising Regulations

By Product

Beverages/Alcohol

Not permitted in TV, Radio, Outdoor, Rediffusion (cable radio).

Food/Restaurants

All food products must comply with the Trade Description Act. Advertisements for pork or pork products are not allowed in government-owned media.

Cigarettes

Not permitted in TV, Radio, Outdoor, Rediffusion (cable radio). However, housename or parallel trademark advertising permitted.

Pharmaceuticals/Drugs

All advertisements containing health claims must be approved by the medical board.

Advertising To Children

No product or service which might result in harm to children physically, mentally or morally may be advertised.

Commercial Production

Commercials must reflect the multi-racial nature of Malaysia.

All actors, actresses, narrators and singers must be Malaysian projecting the Malaysian identity.

No scene or shot that can be done in Malaysia should be shot overseas. If foreign footage is deemed necessary, only 20% of the total commercial footage is allowed to be foreign and prior approval from the Ministry of Information must be obtained.

All filmlets other than in Bahasa Malaysia must have subtitles or super titles in Bahasa Malaysian.

End supertitle must be descriptive and in Bahasa Malaysian.

By Medium

Television

Alcohol and cigarettes product advertising is not permitted. All forms of gambling (e.g., lottery tickets) and consumer contests are not allowed on government-owned media, i.e., television and radio.

Print

Alcohol advertising is not allowed in national language (Malay) publications.

Outdoor

Alcohol and cigarette product advertising are not permitted.

Non-traditional

Vision Four (Hotel In-House Video System) & Home Video

Alcoholic advertising is allowed.

Others (Government Service Tax)

As of January 1, 1992, all advertising production, media and other agency services are subject to a 5% government service tax.

New Zealand

Area	268,680 km^2
Population (1992)	3,347,369
Population growth rate (1992)	0.7%
GDP	US$ 46.2 billion
GDP/per capita	US$ 14,000
Real growth rate (1991)	0.4%
Capital	Wellington

Population Breakdown

By Sex		*By Age Group*		*By Socio-Economic Status*	
Male	49.2%	Children, 0-9	15.7%	Level 1	6.8%
Female	50.8%	Teens, 10-19	16.0%	Level 2	10.7%
		Adults, 20-39	31.8%	Level 3	18.5%
		Adults, 40-59	21.7%	Level 4	22.3%
		Adults, 60+	14.8%	Level 5	10.1%
				Level 6	5.8%
				Other	25.8%

Source: Department of Statistics, 1993 Yearbook.

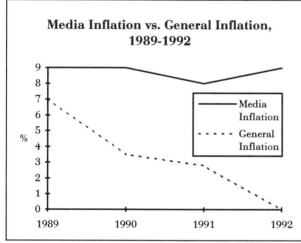

Media Inflation vs. General Inflation, 1989-1992

Source: Department of Statistics, 1993 Yearbook.

Number of Households   1,780,000

Ownership of household durables

Car	87.6%
Phone	93.6%
Washers	96.2%

(purchasing power equivalent)

GNP distribution by industry

Agriculture	9.2%
Industry	32.4%
Services	49.3%
Other	9.1%

Exchange rates (US$ to local currency)

1991	0.5443
1992	0.5428

National Holidays

Holiday	1993 Date
New Years Day	January 1 (observed)
Waitangi Day	February 6
Good Friday	April 9
Easter Monday	April 12
Anzac Day	April 25
Queen's Birthday	June 7
Labor Day	October 25
Christmas Day	December 25 (observed 27th)
Boxing Day	December 26 (observed 28th)

School Holidays

Holiday	1993 Date
Christmas	
- Primary	December 15 - February 1
- Secondary	December 10 - February 1
May Holidays	
- Primary	May 8 - May 23
- Secondary	May 8 - May 23
Mid-term Break	
- Primary	July 3 - July 11
- Secondary	July 3 - July 11
August Holidays	
- Primary	August 28 - September 12
- Secondary	August 21 - September 12

Major Influences and Trends

To date there are no recognized buying clubs in New Zealand and the media deal based on client size, not necessarily agency size. These deals are negotiated through the agency with occasional involvement from the client.

Media ownership of television networks:
> **TVNZ** (2 channels) - state owned enterprise - 80% audience share
> **TV3** - non state owned - 20% audience share
> **Sky** - privately owned (108,000 subscribers or approx 6% of households)

One radio representation group - New Zealand Radio Sales - represents approx 95% of all radio stations.

Spending Analysis

National advertising spending by medium
based on appropriate year's exchange rate

	1989 US$ MM	1990 US$ MM	1991 US$ MM	1992 US$ MM
TV	155	189	190	213
Radio	66	73	75	76
Newspaper	206	219	204	191
Magazine	48	51	49	44
Other	39	42	44	45
Total	**514**	**574**	**562**	**569**

Source: The Association of Accredited Advertising Agencies.

Media Buying

Although pricing is still largely negotiable in New Zealand, the TV market place has in 1991 and more so in 1992, seen a controlling of negotiation by the networks. Discounts have been fixed against certain buying criteria i.e., 10% for airtime purchased 3 months from airdate and 15% for 5 months before transmission. The networks work on added value rather than additional discounts. Examples of added value are bonus airtime, fixed placements, one off sponsorship opportunities etc.

Media buying specialists do not publish their billings, but a reasonable estimate of 15% of total revenue is placed through Buying Services.

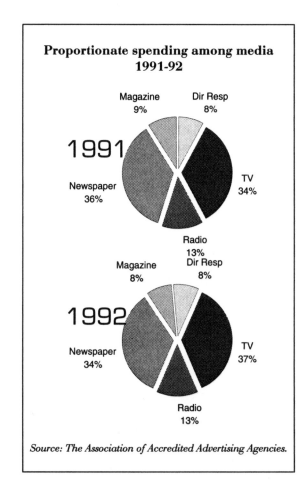

Proportionate spending among media 1991-92

1991
Magazine 9%
Dir Resp 8%
Newspaper 36%
TV 34%
Radio 13%

1992
Magazine 8%
Dir Resp 8%
Newspaper 34%
TV 37%
Radio 13%

Source: The Association of Accredited Advertising Agencies.

Buying Services

Buying Services	Parent Company
Total Media	
Media Buying Services	
Strategic Media	
Media Decision (BSB)	BSB
M for Media	
Outside the Square	

Top Advertisers

By Company

Parent Company	Product Categories	US$ MM
Unilever NZ Ltd	Household/personal products/foodstuffs	15.4
NZ Government	Public admin/community services	12.2
Telecom Corporation	Telecommunications	10.6
Foodstuffs NZ Ltd	Supermarkets	9.8
Deka-Farmers	Retail	8.8
Wattie Foods Group	Foodstuffs	8.6
Britannia Brands NZ Ltd	Foodstuffs	7.9
Cadbury Schweppes	Foodstuffs	7.8
Lion Nation	Breweries	7.7
The Warehouse Ltd	Retail	7.1

By Product

Product	Advertiser	US$ MM
Supermarket chains	Foodstuffs NZ Ltd	9.8
Telephone Services	Telecom Corp of NZ Ltd	10.6
Banking/Finance	Bank of New Zealand	4.4
Department Store/Chain	Deka//Farmers	8.8
Fast-food chain	McDonald's Corp	4.2
Lottery Commission	NZ Lotteries Commission	4.5
Appliance	Fisher & Paykel Ind Ltd	2.9
Automotive	Toyota NZ Ltd	3.5
Foodstuffs	Wattie Foods Groupo	8.6
Insurance	AMP Society	1.9

Television

Overview

Adult Reach	
at 250 GRPs	78%
at 500 GRPs	85%
at 1,000 GRPs	96%

- The household penetration level for TV has remained at 99% since 1989; the reach is 1,762,000 households.
- New Zealand has three television networks: TV1 and Channel 2, both operated by State Owned Enterprise Television NZ Ltd., provide national coverage with option of networking or regionalizing commercials. TV3 is privately owned and also offers national as well as regional commercial breaks.
- Recent introduction of local TV in Christchurch and Racing TV (TAB) channels.

Opportunities

Network	Number of Stations	Ownership	Station Profile	Commercial Minutes/Hr	Coverage	Broadcast Hours (Sign-On/Off)
TV1	1	TVNZ (state)	General	12	99%	06:30-26:00 Sat/Sun 12:00-26:00
Channel 2	1	TVNZ (state)	General	12	99%	Mon-Fri 06:30-26:00 Sat/Sun 12:00-26:00
TV3	1	30% Westpac 50% Receivers 20% Canwest	General	14	89%*	Mon-Fri 06:30-24:00 Sat/Sun 06:30-26:00

Coverage is expected to increase to 93% in the next 12 month period

Costs

Television Cost Changes Between Years

'88	'89	'90	'91	'92
20%	28%	3%	9%	

Prime Time TV Costs for :30 in US$			
1989	1990	1991	1992
2,180	2,789	2,903	3,143

Audiences/CPM's

Average Cost, Audience, and CPMs
(Top 3 Stations, :30, national audience, Target=Adults 20+)

Hours	Morning 06:30 - 12:00	Daytime 12:00-18:00	Prime Time 18:00-22:00	Late Night 22:00-26:00	Weekend 06:30-26:00	Children 15:30-18:00
Station: TV1						
US$	108	317	2,963	664	1,168	N/A
Avg. Aud. (000)	22	156	558	179	268	223
CPM	4.91	2.03	5.31	3.71	4.36	N/A
Station: Channel2						
US$	122	466	2,988	731	1,198	473
Avg. Aud. (000)	22	67	290	156	134	89
CPM	5.55	6.94	10.30	4.69	8.94	5.32
Station: TV3						
US4	135	255	1,564	687	800	285
Avg. Aud. (000)	22	45	156	67	89	45
CPM	6.14	5.66	10.02	10.25	8.99	6.30

Source (Audience): AGB: McNair.

Audience/Rating by Day part (Target Adults 20+)

Daypart	Hours	Household				Adult		
		Universe (000)	Hut Levels	Household Rating	Impressions (000)	Universe (000)	Adult Rating	Impressions (000)
Morning	06:00-12:00	1780	N/A	N/A	N/A	2232	1%	22
Daytime	12:00-18:00	1780	N/A	N/A	N/A	2232	4%	89
Primetime	12:00-22:00	1780	N/A	N/A	N/A	2232	15%	335
Late Night	22:00-26:00	1780	N/A	N/A	N/A	2232	6%	134
Weekend	06:30-26:00	1780	N/A	N/A	N/A	2232	5%	112
Children's	15:30-18:00	1780	N/A	N/A	N/A	2232	7%	156

Source (Audience): AGB: McNair.

Scheduling/Regional/Languages

LANGUAGES	Programming		Commercials
Primary	English	99%	English
Secondary	Maori	1%	None

- The most common commercial length is :30; air time is available in multiples of :15 up to :180.
- Commercials are aired throughout the day, except Sunday morning, which is non-commercial. Commercials are aired only within programs.
- 16% of all commercials are aired regionally. The cost is approximately 120% of national advertising.

Regional Networks

Network	Station	Region	Hours
TVNZ	TV1	Northern, Central, Southern	M-F 10:00-24:00 S-S 12:00-24:00
TVNZ	Ch2	Auckland, Hamilton, Palmerston North, Wellington, Christchurch, Dunedin	M-F 06:30-08:30 M-F 11:00-24:00 S-S 18:00-24:00
TV3	TV3	Northern, Central, Southern	M-F 06:30-15:00 M-F 16:30-24:00 S-S 12:00-24:00

Children's Advertising

Advertising targeted at children can air anytime during commercial time. Target=Children 4-14

CHILDREN'S PROGRAMMING			Kids'		
Station	Hours	Days	Universe (000)	Ratings	Impressions(000)
TV2	15:30-18:00	Mon-Sun	512	15	77
TV3	15:30-18:00	Mon-Fri	512	5	26

Radio

- There are 90 stations in New Zealand, of which 86 are commercial. Sixteen of these are in Auckland.
- 99% of all households have radios; the estimated number is 1,115,000.
- The primary broadcasting language is English, however, Maori is also used.
- The most popular programs are Adult Contemporary, Classic Hits, Talkback and Rock/Dance.
- Commercial lengths available are :15, :30, :45, :60, :90 and :120.
- An average :30 buy costs US$ 21, or CPM of US$ 0.71.

- Cost changes are dictated by survey results. Some may increase while others decrease so, in effect, there is no change.
- Radio generally does not have a primetime rotation. Most stations are bought by "run-of-station" spots during a 06:00 - 20:00 rotation.

Daypart Costs/CPMs (Target=Adults 20+)

Daypart	Local Time	Cost :30 US$	Audience (000)	CPM (US$)
Prime time	06:00-20:00	24	36.1	0.66
Daytime	06:00-19:00	25	37.9	0.66
Late Night	20:00-24:00	11	13.4	0.82

Source (Audience): Research International Radio Surveys.

Cable

No information is available on cable in New Zealand.

Satellite

- Sky TV - subscriber UHF channels sourced from satellite feed.
- 3 UHF channels. Movies, sport, news.
- Continued growth is predicted for Sky TV.

Satellite Channel	Country of Origin	Language	Programming
Sky Movies	Around the World	English	Movies HBO
Sky News	CNN - US	English	News
	BBC - UK		
Sky Sports	NZ and around the World	English	Sports - ESPN

Video Cassettes

Roughly 67% of TV households have video cassette recorders (VCRs). Usage is monitored by AGB McNair. However, video cassettes in New Zealand do not carry commercials and there is no immediate likelihood of that situation changing.

Cinema

- There are 143 theaters in New Zealand, with a potential reach of 50% of the population over 4 weeks. All offer commercial time.
- Val Morgan offers commercial lengths as follows: :15, :30, :45, :60, :90. Everard offers the same, except no :45 and adds :120.

Cinema Cost Changes Between Years

'88	'89	'90	'91	'92
14.2%	0%	0%	0%	

- Continued growth is expected with the growth in multiplex cinemas. Takings for 1st Qtr 1993 are 62% greater than those for the same period of 1992.
- An average :30 4 week buy at all 143 cinemas costs US$ 10,800.

Newspapers

There are no national daily papers, but 6 regional ones. English language literacy is 99%.

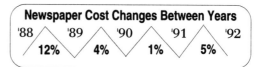

Newspaper	Market	Size	Circ. (000)	Avg. Daily Aud. (000)	1 page/B&W Cost (US$)	Accept Color?
NZ Herald	Auckland/Northland	560 mm x 395 mm	243.2	396.2	6,026	Yes
Dominion	Wellington/ Central	560 mm x 395 mm	67.0	111.7	3,671	Yes
Evening Post	Wellington	560 mm x 395 mm	72.5	159.6	3,671	Yes
The Press	Christchurch/ Canterbury	560 mm x 395 mm	100.0	159.8	2,449	Yes
Otago Daily Times	Dunedin/Otago	560 mm x 395 mm	49.0	60.0	1,996	Yes
Waikato Times	Hamilton/Waikato	560 mm x 395 mm	41.9	54.3	2,280	Yes

Magazines

There are 15 consumer magazines published in New Zealand, and about 200 trade and technical magazines.

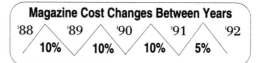

Magazine	Type	Frequency	Circ. (000)	Audited?	Avg. Issue Aud. (000)	1 page 4/C Cost (US$)
Aust. Woman's Weekly	Women's	Monthly	120.8	Yes	776	4,709
More	Women's	Monthly	37.8	Yes	259	2,970
New Idea	Women's	Weekly	91.8	Yes	494	2,155
NZ Woman's Weekly	Women's	Weekly	156.6	Yes	870	3,672
Woman's Day	Women's	Weekly	195.1	Yes	658	3,132
Metro	Lifestyle	Monthly	28.7	Yes	259	2,997
North & South	Lifestyle	Monthly	38.1	Yes	329	2,754
Reader's Digest	General	Monthly	151.9	Yes	564	3,591
Listener	Entertainment	Weekly	120.6	Yes	423	3,510
TV Guide	Entertainment	Weekly	229.5	Yes	658	1,566
Time	General	Weekly	42.8	Yes	235	3,116
Pacific Way	Inflight	Monthly	70.0	Yes	165	2,840
Next	General	Monthly	37.3	Yes	117	2,052

Outdoor/Transit

Billboard

Sites available 1,000
Lead Time to reserve .... 4–6 wks
Exposure 40%

Costs

Average, 1 billboard/month
   Minimum size US$ 675
   6 m x 3 m (Metro)......................... US$ 810
   6 m x 3 m (Provincial) .... US$ 540
Billboard cost changes have been steady at 2% for the last 4 years.

Transit

Boards available
   on Buses 1,000
Exposure .... N/A

Costs

Average, 1 board/month:
   .... US$ 85

No tobacco advertising allowed by law.

Direct Marketing

Direct marketing is growing in importance. It is currently not very well developed but there is a high level of sophistication in direct mail package design.

List Broker	Information Provided
Rod Spence Ltd. Holbrook List Services Moore Business Forms NZ Post	Consumer lists, existing lists from direct mail retailers. Largely demographic information. Product usage lists becoming more readily available.
Telemarketing Companies	*Direct Marketing Association*

Startel
Insight
	Direct Marketing Association
	  P O Box 33432
	  Takapuna, Auckland
	  NEW ZEALAND (ph) 09 489 9329

Non-Traditional Media

Currently, there are shopping carts in supermarkets. Costs are negotiable.

Research Sources

Medium covered	Research company	Information provided
Television, News- paper, Magazine, Cinema	AGB McNair	Audience research by demographic, psychographic, product, category, competitive data.
Radio	Research Int.	Audience research by demographics

Television Research Currently Available

Research method	Frequency
People Meter	Weekly in hard copy book. Daily downloaded via online PC link.

Advertising Regulations

By Product

Beverages/Alcohol
No alcohol advertising can be broadcast outside the hours of 21:00 - 06:00.

Food/Restaurants
No specific restrictions.

Cigarettes
Prohibited by law.

Pharmaceuticals/Drugs
Must comply with the Medicine Act as administered by the Department of Health.

Advertising To Children
The ASA Code of Advertising states that ads should clearly not portray violence or aggression, should not encourage anti-social behavior and should not urge children to ask their parents to buy particular products for them.

Commercial Production
No restrictions as to local content.

By Medium

Television
No tobacco advertising.
No alcohol advertising until 21:00.
Restrictions on adult advertising during kids time.

Print
No tobacco advertising.

Outdoor
No tobacco advertising.

Direct Marketing
No specific restrictions.

Non-traditional
No specific restrictions.

Philippines

Area	300,000 km^2
Population (1992)	64,300,000
Population growth rate (1992)	2.3%
GNP	US$ 48.4 billion
GNP/per capita	US$ 259.35
Real growth rate (1991)	5.9%
Capital	Manila

Population Breakdown

By Sex		*By Age Group*		*By Socio-Economic Status*	
Male	50%	Children	27%	A&B	0-4%
Female	50%	Teens	23%	C	19%
		Adults	50%	D&E	77%

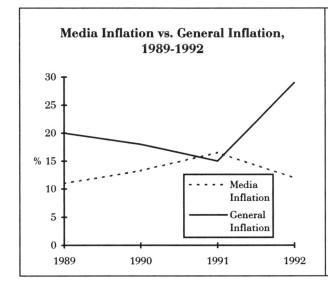

Media Inflation vs. General Inflation, 1989-1992

- - - - Media Inflation
——— General Inflation

Number of Households	11,600,000

Ownership of household durables

Car	9%
Phone	6%
Washers	3%

(purchasing power equivalent)

GNP distribution by industry

Agriculture	68%
Industry	N/A
Services	32%

Exchange rates (US$ to local currency)

1991	0.04032
1992	0.03745

National Holidays

Holiday	1993 Date
New Year's	January 1
Maundy Thursday	April 8
Good Friday	April 9
Labor Day	May 1
Independence Day	June 12
All Saints Day	November 1
Bonifacio Day	November 30
Christmas Day	December 25
Rizal Day	December 30

School Holidays

Holiday	1993 Date
Linggo ng Wika (National Language Week)	August 16-22
United Nation	October 24
Christ the King	October 25
Immaculate Conception	December 8

Major Influences and Trends

Television

There is a proliferation of cable TV companies throughout the country. However, it is projected that the emergence of these will not affect TV viewing on free television (VHF) for a number of years.

Radio

Radio will continue to be a dominant medium in provincial areas due to the geographic situation.

Print

With the current number of publications available, especially the daily newspapers, the industry's demand for audited circulation becomes firmer through the various advertising associations' efforts.

Spending Analysis

National advertising spending by medium
based on appropriate year's exchange rate

	1989 US$ MM	1990 US$ MM	1991 US$ MM	1992 US$ MM
TV	82.2	98.0	118.9	154.4
Radio	21.9	25.2	28.7	37
Newspaper/ Magazine	32.9	36.6	35.3	43.6
Direct Response/ Outdoor/ Other	1.8	1.9	2.0	2.1
Total	**138.8**	**161.7**	**184.9**	**237.1**

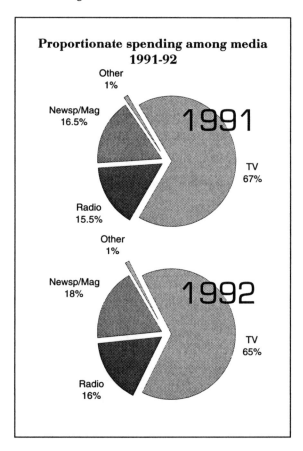

Proportionate spending among media 1991-92

1991
Other 1%
Newsp/Mag 16.5%
Radio 15.5%
TV 67%

1992
Other 1%
Newsp/Mag 18%
Radio 16%
TV 65%

Media Buying

- The industry follows the standard spot buying principle on broadcast with the uniform 15% agency commission, except for Procter & Gamble which initiated the Agency of Record system in 1992 among its four agencies.
- There are no buying services in the Philippines.

Television

Overview

- Television is the primary medium in Metro Manila and in five major cities in the Philippines.
- TV household penetration is 57% nationwide; 91% in Metro Manila (1,456 households).

	TV HH Penetration		
1989	1990	1991	1992
51%	51%	53%	57%

Opportunities

Network	Number of Stations	Ownership	Station Profile	Commercial Mins/Hr	Coverage	Broadcast Hours (Sign-On/Off)
Ch. 2	6	Private	Various	15-17	CEBU, Bacolod, Davao, Zamboanga	Metro Manila: 18 hours daily
Ch. 4	7	Government	Various	15-17	CEBU, Bacolod, Iloilo, Davao, Cagayan de Oro	Provincial: 12 hours daily
Ch. 5	1	Private	Various	15-17	Luzon	12 hours daily
Ch. 7	21	Private	Various	15-17	CEBU, Bacolod, Iloilo, Cag. de Oro, Davao, Zamboanga, Ozamis, Cotabato, Iligan, Legaspi	Provincial: 12 hours daily
Ch. 9	20	*	Various	15-17	CEBU, Bacolod, Iloilo, Davao, Cag. de Oro, Zamboanga, Legaspi	Provincial: 12 hours daily
Ch. 13	12	*	Various	15-17	CEBU, Bacolod, Iloilo, Davao, Cotabato	Provincial: 12 hours daily

Government controlled since 1986.

Costs

Prime Time TV Costs for :30 in US$			
1989	1990	1991	1992
725	797	775	866

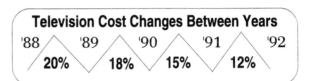

Television Cost Changes Between Years

'88 20% '89 18% '90 15% '91 12% '92

Audiences/CPM's

Average Cost, Audience, and CPMs by Daypart
(Top 3 Stations, :30, national audience, Target=Adults 18+)

Hours	Morning 07:00-11:00	Daytime 11:00-16:00	Prime Time 19:00-22:30	Late Night 23:00-01:00	Weekend 07:00-01:00	Children 07:00-01:00
Station: Ch. 2						
US$	186	494	1,173	598	488	298
Avg. Aud. (000)	13	160	195	53	187	19
CPM	14.31	3.09	6.02	11.28	2.61	15.68
Station: Ch. 7						
US$	178	285	1,125	500	339	232
Avg. Aud. (000)	6	55	89	27	97	10
CPM	29.67	5.18	12.64	18.52	3.49	23.20
Station: 9						
US$	143	244	1,053	500	285	250
Avg. Aud. (000)	8	27	50	27	40	5
CPM	17.88	9.04	21.06	18.52	7.13	50.00

Audiences/Rating by Daypart (:30 commercial, national TV, Target=Adults 18-49)

Daypart	Hours	Household Universe (000)	Hut Levels	Household Rating	Impressions (000)	Adult Universe (000)	Adult Rating	Impressions (000)
Morning	07:00-08:00	34	5	4.2	1.4	17	2	.34
Daytime	11:00-16:00	288	52	34.3	98.8	117	16	18.7
Primetime	19:30-22:30	443	35	51.4	227.7	212	30	63.6
Late Night	23:00-01:00	144	18	1.4	2.0	45	6	2.7
Weekend	07:00-01:00	363	1	11.5	41.7	48	7	3.36
Children's	08:00-10:00	45	6	1.0	4.5	10	1	1

Television, continued

Scheduling/Regional/Languages

LANGUAGES	Programming		Commercials
Primary	Tagalog	60%	Tagalog
Secondary	English	38%	English
	Chinese	2%	

- Commercials are aired throughout the day, both at the beginning and end of programs.

- Regional buys are available, but they get only 3% of the total TV advertising expenditures.
- Commercial lengths available include :15, :45 and :60, in addition to :30, which accounts for 80% of the commercials sold.

Children's Advertising

ADULT PROGRAMMING			Kids'		
Station	Hours	Days	Universe (000)	Ratings	Impressions (000)
Ch. 2	20:00-21:00	Friday	18	11.0	1.98
Ch. 7	19:00-20:00	Saturday	16	7.8	1.25
Ch. 9	19:00-20:00	Saturday	59	12.6	7.43
Ch. 13	19:30-22:00	Wednesday	66	14.1	9.31

CHILDREN'S PROGRAMMING			Kids'		
Station	Hours	Days	Universe (000)	Ratings	Impressions (000)
Ch. 2	16:30-17:00	Daily	61	7	4.27
Ch. 4	16:00-16:30	M-Sat	22	3	.66
Ch. 5	16:00-16:30	M-Sat	22	3	.66
Ch. 7	16:30-17:00	M-Fri	94	11	10.34
Ch. 9	08:30-10:30	Saturday	19	5	.95
Ch. 13	13:30-14:30	Daily	44	5	2.2

Radio

Overview

- There are 386 radio stations in the Philippines; of which 355 are commercial. Of the latter, 42 are in Manila.
- There is no national radio. All radio spot buys are on per area basis.
- Approximately 93% of the households in Metro Manila have radios; for the entire Philippines, the total is 84%, or 94,744 households.
- The primary broadcasting language is English. Tagalog is also used.

Radio Cost Changes Between Years

'88		'89		'90		'91		'92
	25%		30%		25%		20%	

- The most popular program types are news, commentary programs and soap operas.
- Commercial lengths sold include :15, :30, :45, :60.
- Prime Times are 06:00-09:00, 11:00-12:00 and 15:00-18:00.

Costs

Daypart Costs/CPMs (Target=Adults)

Daypart	Local Time	Cost :30 US$	Audience (000)	CPM (US$)
Prime Time	N/A	40	73	0.55
Daytime	N/A	35	83	0.42
Late Night	N/A	25	64	0.39

Cable

- More cable companies opened in 1992 throughout the country. In Metro Manila, 4 cable companies operate, but only 1 major company is currently open to commercial advertising.
- Subscriptions are still limited due to the limited number of existing cable lines. It is very upscale since cable lines are only available in class A areas. Penetration is currently estimated at 12% of TV households.
- Cable should gain popularity in Metro Manila, particularly in upscale homes. In Metro Manila, 150,000 households are expected to get cable by 1997.
- There are 34 channels available, of which 5 are commercial. The primary broadcast language is English; Chinese is also used.
- Approximately an average of 3 to 4 cable companies are operating in every locality/area outside metro Manila, with an average cable subscriber of 800 HH.

Top Cable Channels	Cost in US$	Commercial Min/ Hr
Sky Entertainment Channel	125	2
ESPN Sports	220	2
Sky Sports Channel	125	2
Sky Community Channel	75	2
HBO (Home Box Office)	N/A	N/A

Cable Networks	HH Circulation (000)	Programming
147 cable companies	Manila: 70M	News
Privately owned	Provincial: 20M	Sports
3 cable companies are	Total: 90M	Movie entertainment
operating in Manila		MTV
		Local video karaoke

Satellite

- Satellite signals originate from Hong Kong, Japan, Australia, and the U.S. There are about 16 channels.
- Signals are received through Cable TV and some private dish operators.
- There are currently no restrictions specifically for satellite imported programs and commercials, nor any research on audiences.

Satellite Channels Available

Channel	Country of Origin	Language	Programming
STAR TV	Hong Kong	English/Chinese	Various
CNN	U.S.	English	News
ESPN	U.S.	English	Sports

Video Cassettes

Roughly 35% of TV households in Metro Manila and 56% of TV households Philppines-wide have video cassette recorders (VCRs). However, VCR cassettes don't carry commercials. There is also no service to measure usage. It will take a couple of years for VCR advertising to start due to film piracy.

Cinema

- The total number of theaters in the Philippines is over 1,200.

- Commercials are available in :30 and :60 lengths at all cinemas (35 mm material).

- The average cost of a four-week cinema schedule for a :30 commercial at 4 selected cinemas is US$ 630.

- No cost change data is available.

Newspapers

There are 25 national daily papers which accept advertising. Combined circulation is 2,700,000.

Newspaper	Market	Size	Circ. (000)	Avg. Daily Aud. (000)	1 page B&W Cost (US$)	Accept Color?
Manila Bulletin	National	9 x 54 cm	239.6	N/A	2,351	Yes
Phil. Daily Inquirer	National	9 x 54 cm	204.0	N/A	2,351	Yes
Malaya	National	9 x 54 cm	140.1	N/A	1,665	Yes
Philippine Star	National	9 x 52 cm	192.5	N/A	2,264	Yes
Manila Times	National	9 x 54 cm	117.0	N/A	1,909	Yes
Manila Chronicle	National	9 x 54 cm	108.2	N/A	1,763	Yes
Manila Standard	National	7 x 35 cm	120.0	N/A	875	Yes
Business World	National	9 x 54 cm	57.8	N/A	2,449	Yes
Phil. Times Journal	National	9 x 54 cm	110.0	N/A	2,155	Yes
Business Star	National	9 x 52 cm	77.4	N/A	2,340	Yes

Magazines

There are 33 national consumer magazines which accept advertising, and 20 trade and technical magazines published in the Philippines.

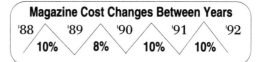

Magazine	Type	Frequency	Circ. (000)	Audited?	Avg. Issue Aud. (000)	1 page 4/C Cost (US$)
MOD Filipina	Women's	N/A	131.0	N/A	N/A	559
Woman's Home Companion	Women's	N/A	131.0	N/A	N/A	449
Women's Journal	Women's	N/A	111.0	N/A	N/A	486
Woman Today	Women's	N/A	103.6	N/A	N/A	479
Mr. & Ms.	General	N/A	135.5	N/A	N/A	477
Miscellaneous	General	N/A	82.9	N/A	N/A	504
Liwayway	Vernacular	N/A	141.9	N/A	N/A	264
Visaya	Vernacular	N/A	49.3	N/A	N/A	176
Bannawag	Vernacular	N/A	46.0	N/A	N/A	157
Yuhum	Vernacular	N/A	52.5	N/A	N/A	170
Youngster	Children's	N/A	90.0	N/A	N/A	N/A
Sports Weekly	Sports	N/A	96.2	N/A	N/A	254
Sports Flash	Sports	N/A	46.0	N/A	N/A	241

Outdoor/Transit

Billboard		Transit	
Sites available ....Upon request Lead Time to reserve ....4 weeks Exposure ....N/A		Boards available ....150 Exposure ....N/A	
Costs Average, 1 billboard/month 20 ft x 20 ft ....US$ 370 Billboard Cost Changes Between Years '88 /\ '89 /\ '90 /\ '91 /\ '92 N/A 15% 10% 0%		**Costs** Average, 1 board/month: Bus ....US$ 140 Taxi ....US$ 100	
Sizes 11 ft x 23 ft, 14 ft x 23 ft, 16 ft x 29 ft, 18 ft x 39 ft		**Sizes** 2 ft x 8 ft (bus); 2 ft x 4 ft (bus); 12 ft x 36 ft in (taxi)	

Direct Marketing

Still in the infancy stage. Banks, hotels and credit cards have active efforts, but these efforts are not done through direct marketing companies or agencies.

Non-Traditional Media

Non-traditional media are used for tactical efforts especially in areas not adequately covered by television and radio.

Research Sources

Medium Covered	Research Company	Information Provided
TV	Phil. Survey Research Ctr. (PSRC)	Qualitative Analysis
	Media Pulse, Inc.	Qualitative Analysis
Radio	Radio Research Council	Qualitative Analysis
Print	Asia Research Organization (ARO)	Qualitative Analysis
	Phil. Survey & Research Center (PSRC)	

Television Research Currently Available

Research Method	Frequency
People meter	Monthly
Coincidental (House to House)	Monthly

Advertising Regulations

By Product

Beverages/Alcohol

Drinking of liquor is strictly prohibited in television commercials and ads should clearly carry the disclaimer 'Drink Moderately.'

Food/Restaurants

There are no specific restriction on food and restaurant advertising.

Cigarettes

Ad material should not depict actual act of smoking.

Pharmaceuticals/Drugs

Precautionary measures is tagged after 'If symptoms persist, consult a doctor.' Generic name should also be reflected or mentioned in the ad material.

Advertising To Children

Ads and promo activities for proprietary drugs, medicine, devices and treatment should not be directed to children. Ads must not show children taking drugs or medicine without the supervision of a responsible adult.

Ads should not encourage reckless, improper or anti-social behavior.

Commercial Production

Advertising regulations are being implemented and enforced by the Advertising Board of the Philippines (Adboard). Regulations are thoroughly screened by this body.

By Medium

Television

AdBoard clearance is required by stations.

Contracted commercial length placement should be strictly followed.

Ad material should be in the station 48 hours before telecast.

Maximum commercial loading per hour is 18 minutes.

Spot reservation is by first come first serve basis.

A written 15-day notice of cancellation/suspension of spot placement is required.

Ad material for :05 and :10 will be charged at 60% of the cost of :30's.

Print (deadlines based on working days)

Medium	Newspapers	Magazines
BW Cancellation	2 days	30 days
Material deadline	1 day	30 days
FC Cancell	5 days	30 days
Material deadline	4 days	25 days
Min. ad size	3 x 9 (27 cm)	1/4 sq (26 cm)
Material accepted	positives	–
Color surcharge	80%	

Outdoor

Minimum contract is one year rental.

Exposure of lighted billboard/neon light is up to 9 PM only.

Sources Consulted

Phillipine Survey & Research Center, Inc.
Print Media Organization
Kapisanan NG MGA Brodkaster SA Philipinas
Marketing and Opinion Research Society of the Phillipines
Adboard Data Center
4-A's Media Fact Book

Singapore

Area	632.6 km^2
Population (1992)	2,792,092
Population growth rate (1992)	1.3%
GDP	US$ 38.3 billion
GDP/per capita	US$ 13,900
Real growth rate (1991)	6.5%
Capital	Singapore

Population Breakdown

By Sex
Male 51%
Female................................... 49%

By Age Group
Children, 0-14......................23.1%
Adults , 15+.........................76.9%

By Socio-Economic Status
A 18.6%
B...24.7%
C...16.3%
D...16.6%
E 23.8%

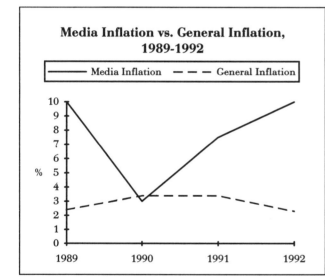

Media Inflation vs. General Inflation, 1989-1992

—— Media Inflation   – – – General Inflation

Number of Households   686,000
Ownership of household durables
   Car................................ 35%
   Phone........................... 80%
   Washers....................... 87%
      (purchasing power equivalent)
   Source: SRS Media Index 1992
GNP distribution by industry
   Agriculture................. 0.2%
   Industry 35.0%
   Services 64.8%
Exchange rates (US$ to local currency)
   1991 ....0.6181
   1992 ....0.6211

National Holidays

Holiday	1993 Date
New Year's Day	Jan 1 (Wed)
Chinese New Year	4 February (Tues)
Chinese New Year	5 February (Wed)
Hari Raya Puaasa	5 March (Sun) **
Good Friday	17 April (Fri)
Labor Day	1 May (Fri)
Vesak Day	17 May (Sun) **
Hari Raya Haji	11 June (Thurs)
National Day	9 August (Sun) **
Deepaveli	24 October (Sat)
Christmas	25 December (Fri)

*** The following Monday is a public holiday*

School Holidays

Holiday	1993 Date
Term 1	13-21 March
Term 2	19 May - 22 June
Term 3	4 Sept - 12 Sept
Term 4	20 Nov - 31 Dec
Youth Day	9 July
Teacher's Day	1 Sept
Children's Day	1 October

Major Influences and Trends

After management restructuring at the Singapore Broadcasting Corporation (SBC) in 1991 and the launch of Singapore CableVision (SCV) in 1992, very little has changed in the Singapore media scene. It is still dominated by two huge monopolies, SBC and Singapore Press Holdings (SPH), who control the broadcast and press markets respectively. Since there is no intra-media competition they battle each other, and frequently sales policies seem designed to steal share from the competition rather than benefit loyal advertisers.

1992 saw an apparent shift of revenue from press to TV, but in reality it may well have been a reflection of the inadequacy of the research methodology. SBC had introduced a sales policy which awarded free spots to certain advertisers, but the advertising expenditure report continued to count all spots as fully paid. This had the effect of inflating TV revenue estimates. As long as SBC continues to adopt this sales policy the actual shares of revenue will be impossible to determine.

Generally, however, 1992 was a year of anticipation. AC Nielsen was awarded a contract to conduct TV audience measurement using electronic people meters. This system will replace the current diary method in January 1994. The first ever quarter-hourly radio audience research was conducted in May and June 1993. Despite heavy promotional activity by SBC radio stations intending to inflate audience numbers during the period of the sweep, the data will be the most accurate ever available, and will allow for more sophisticated and quantifiable radio planning in the future. Finally, SBC is preparing for privatization, but details are still unconfirmed.

Spending Analysis

National advertising spending by medium
based on appropriate year's exchange rate

	1989 US$ MM	1990 US$ MM	1991 US$ MM	1992 US$ MM
TV	140.8	173.6	119.3	150.0
Cinema	2.7	3.7	2.9	3.7
Radio	11.7	11.9	9.7	15.7
Newspaper	243.0	299.7	211.9	233.5
Magazine	41.9	63.0	37.4	38.6
Direct Response	-	-	-	-
Outdoor	10.6	26.3	18.3	16.0
Other	13.8	3.8	2.3	2.1
Total	**464.5**	**582**	**401.8**	**459.6**

Source: SRS Adex

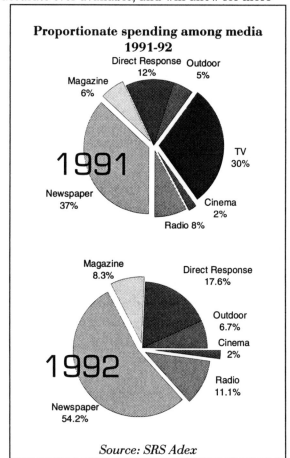

Proportionate spending among media 1991-92

1991: Direct Response 12%, Outdoor 5%, TV 30%, Cinema 2%, Radio 8%, Newspaper 37%, Magazine 6%

1992: Magazine 8.3%, Direct Response 17.6%, Outdoor 6.7%, Cinema 2%, Radio 11.1%, Newspaper 54.2%

Source: SRS Adex

Media Buying

In essence there are two media monopolies in Singapore: Singapore Broadcasting Corporation (SBC) for TV and Singapore Press Holdings (SPH) for press. TV spots are bought at fixed rates but costs can be adjusted with discounts, and discretionary bonus airtime can be awarded to those who sign a contract committing funds to TV for the year, and who are seen to be supporting the medium. The same policies are adopted by SBC Radio. No discounts are given for press, but positional loadings are reduced or waived for high spenders. Media owners continue to deal directly with clients, but rarely sell the media on their merits, instead choosing to frame deals in terms of discounts which give little indication of true value. There is no way of establishing average market prices to compare buying performance between agencies.

Top Advertisers (1992 Spending)

Expenditure figures are estimates and exclude sponsorships.

By Company

Parent Company	Product Category	US$ MM
McDonald's	Quick Service Restaurant	4.11
Courts	Retail	3.02
Metro	Retail	2.85
Shaw Organisation	Cinema	2.49
KFC	Quick Service Restaurant	2.42
Yaohan	Retail	2.37
American Express	Financial	2.26
Tiger Beer	Alcohol	2.26
Singapore Airlines	Travel	2.21
Cathay	Cinema	2.15

Source: SRS Adex

By Product

Product	Advertiser	US$ MM
Retail	Courts	3.02
Entertainment	Shaw Organisation	2.49
Watches	Rolex	1.69
Leisure/Travel	Singapore Airlines	2.21
Credit/Charge Card	American Express	2.26
Banking/Finance	CitiBank	1.66
Government	Family Life Education	1.93

Source: SRS Adex

Television

Overview

TV HH Penetration				Adult Reach	
1989	1990	1991	1992	at 250 GRPs	75%
99%	99%	99%	99%	at 500 GRPs	85%
618,000	618,000	665,000	679,000	at 1,000 GRPs	95%

There are three major channels; all are owned by the Singapore Broadcast Corporation. Three new 'cable' (actually encoded UHF broadcast) channels were launched in 1992 but have low penetration and are unlikely to become major advertising vehicles. Since these are partly owned by SBC, the monopoly in the TV market has been maintained. Although satellite dishes are still not allowed in Singapore, SBC is clearly worried that outside competition is inevitable. To shore up their defenses, they have been investing in programming with a strong local content and flavor. This has resulted in a string of hit shows which are giving Channel 5 its best ratings ever. Current events programming has also been given a cash injection, but further efforts are necessary to give it the credibility and prestige of international competition like CNN.

Opportunities

Network	Number of Stations	Ownership	Station Profile	Commercial Minutes/Hr	Coverage	Broadcast Hours (Sign-On/Off)
SBC	5	Singapore Broadcasting Corp.	General (English)	2	79%	15:00 - 24:00 (M-F) 09:00 - 24:00 (W/E)
SBC	8		General (Mandarin)	2	90%	15:00 - 24:00 (M-F) 09:00 - 24:00 (W/E)
SBC	12		Cultural/Sports (English/Mandarin)	12	44%	19:00 - 24:00 (M-S) 09:00 - 24:00 (Sun)

Source: SRS Media Index

Costs

Prime Time TV Costs for :30 in US$				
	1989	*1990*	*1991*	*1992*
SBC 5	1,428	1,995	1,545	1,500
SBC 8	1,752	2,205	2,935	3,100

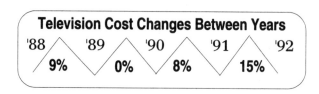

Audiences/CPM's

Average Cost, Audience, and CPMs by Daypart (Top 3 stations, :30, national audience)

Hours	Morning N/A	Daytime 15:00-17:00	Prime Time 19:00-22:30	Late Night 22:30-24:00	Weekend	Children 18:30-19:00
Station: SBC 5						
US$	N/A	215	1,500	2,235	Same	1,118
Avg. Aud. (000)	N/A	34	125	142	as	79
CPM	N/A	6.32	12.00	15.74	Weekday	14.15
Station: SBC 8						
US$	N/A	370	3,100	2,100		
Avg. Aud. (000)	N/A	92	705	404		
CPM	N/A	4.02	4.39	5.20		N/A
Station: SBC 12						
US$	N/A	N/A	185	185		N/A
Avg. Aud. (000)	N/A	N/A	15	17		N/A
CPM	N/A	N/A	12.33	10.88		N/A

Source: SRS TV Diary

Audiences/Ratings by Daypart (Target='Households' represented by housewives)

Daypart	Hours	Household Universe (000)	Hut Levels	Household Rating	Impressions (000)	Adult Universe (000)	Adult Rating	Impressions (000)
Morning								
Daytime	15:00-14:00	686	N/A	6	41	2357	4	94
Primetime	19:00-22:30	686	N/A	36	247	2357	30	707
Late Night	22:30-24:00	686	N/A	19	130	2357	18	424
Weekend	Same pattern as weekdays							
Children's	18:30-19:00	686	N/A	2	14	2357	2	47

Source: SRS TV Diary

Scheduling/Regional/Languages

LANGUAGES	Programming		Commercials
Primary Language	English	62%	English
Secondary Language	Mandarin	30%	Mandarin

- Half of the commercials bought are :30s but any multiple of :05 is available.
- Commercials are aired throughout the day at the beginning and end of programs.
- There is no regional buying in Singapore.

Children's Advertising

All programs accept advertising targeted at children. The example below shows the high ratings that can be achieved by using local drama series.

ADULT PROGRAMMING			Kids'		
Station	Hours	Days	Universe (000)	Ratings	Impressions (000)
SBC 8	19:00-20:00	Weekdays	491		186

Source: SRS TV Diary

Children's programming runs Weekdays from 15:00–19:00 and weekend mornings. The following example is the most popular segment.

CHILDREN'S PROGRAMMING			Kids'		
Station	Hours	Days	Universe (000)	Ratings	Impressions (000)
SBC5	18:30-19:00	M-F	491	16	79

Source: SRS TV Diary

Radio

- There are 11 radio stations in Singapore, all of which are commercial.
- Ninety-six percent of households have radios.
- The primary broadcasting language is English; Mandarin is also used.

- The most popular program types are Easy Listening, magazine format (talk shows, music, documentaries).
- The first quarter-hour listening survey was conducted in August, 1993.
- Available lengths include :15, :30, :45, :60 and :120 and any multiple of :05.

Radio Cost Changes Between Years

'88 — 0% — '89 — 0% — '90 — -7% — '91 — 2% — '92

Daypart Costs

Daypart	Local Time	Cost :30 US$	Audience (000)	CPM (US$)
Prime Time	07:00-09.30	130	N/A	N/A
Daytime	09:30-17:00	65	N/A	N/A
Late Night	20:00-24:00	65	N/A	N/A

Cable

Singapore CableVision (SCV) was launched in 1992, but its name is a misnomer since the service is broadcast on conventional UHF channels. Its launch was seen by many as a tactical move, a stop-gap measure to stifle demand for STAR-TV, which could steal audience from SBC, thereby jeopardizing its revenues.

One news channel (sourced primarily from CNN), a Mandarin variety channel similar to the existing SBC 8, and a movie channel, HBO Asia, which is like HBO USA but with the interesting bits (or more risque programs) taken out.

Penetration of SCV is low (2%), and over half of its subscriptions come from corporations and hotels. The TV market in Asia is changing rapidly, and the influx of pan-regional channels into Singapore is inevitable. There is still concern that such channels may represent external interference with internal affairs and the simplest solution to the problem is for the new stations to be provided via a relay service rather than direct-to-home. To that end, SBC and Singapore have undertaken a study on the feasibility of introducing a sophisticated fiber-optic communications network throughout the island. It is likely that this will happen before the end of the decade, and it therefore seems that the future of broadcasting rests in cable rather than satellite.

- Primary language used to broadcast cable is English (67%). Secondary language is Mandarin (33%).
- Ownership of Singapore CableVision is 65% Temasek Holdings, 35% Singapore Broadcasting Corp. (Both are government regulated).

Satellite

Overview

Satellite dishes are not allowed to the general public. The government is cautious about allowing a facility which could be abused, particularly in the area of external comment on internal affairs. Furthermore, it could jeopardize SBC's revenue base. Nevertheless, there is a demand for more (and better) TV options and this has been tackled in a number of ways, from the creation of Singapore CableVision to the programming of selections from ESPN sports and MTV in off-peak hours.

It is probable that satellite TV stations will gain access to the Singapore market in a few year's time, but probably in the form of a signal relayed by SBC or SVC. In that way the broadcast material can still be regulated to Singapore's standards, and revenues can be protected through subscriptions.

Video Cassettes

Roughly 84% of TV households have video cassette recorders (VCRs). Current indications are that no VCR advertising will be allowed, possibly to protect SBC's revenues. Recent censorship changes will result in any film classified for exhibition only to people over the age of 16 not being made available for hire or purchase in the country, so opportunities are becoming more limited anyway. SRS TV Diary/Media INDEX measures VCR usage.

Cinema

- There are 92 cinemas in Singapore, all of which offer commercial time.
- Potential reach over 4 weeks, for a buy of all cinemas is about 24%.
- The average cost of a four-week cinema schedule for a :30 commercial at all 92 cinemas is US$. 12,200. Costs rose 5% last year after remaining steady for a while.
- Commercials are available in virtually any length.

Multi-screen cineplexes have just started to sprout up in Singapore and are attracting large audiences. The quality of commercial presentation has been appalling: reels last almost half an hour, and are shown at reduced sound levels, with house lights on. The newer cinemas are recognizing the needs of advertisers and correcting these problems. With a limited set of entertainment options available in Singapore, cinema will continue to thrive.

Newspapers

There are 8 national daily papers which accept advertising. Combined circulation is 912,141

Newspaper Cost Changes Between Years

'88	'89	'90	'91	'92
10%	0%	7%	0%	

Newspaper	Market	Size	Circ. (000)	Avg. Daily Aud. (000)	1 page B&W Cost (US$)	Accept Color?
The Straits Times	English	Broadsheet	340	1,115	8,720	Yes
Business Times	English	Broadsheet	25	136	2,725	Yes
Lianhe Zaobao	Chinese	Broadsheet	199	723	6,530	Yes
Lianhe Wanbao	Chinese	Broadsheet	112	379	2,304	Yes
Shin Min Daily News	Chinese	Broadsheet	101	328	2,304	Yes
Berita Harian	Malay	Broadsheet	52	206	2,259	Yes
The New Paper	English	Tabloid	83	345	1,448	Yes
Tamil Murasu	Tamil	Broadsheet	15	N/A	1,530	Yes

Magazines

There are 100 national consumer magazines which accept advertising in Singapore, and another 50 trade and technical magazines.

Magazine	Type	Frequency	Circ. (000)	Audited?	Avg. Issue Au.d (000)	1 page 4/C Cost (US$)
8 Days	Entertainment	Weekly	75	Yes	234	1,366
Beauty	Women's	Monthly	20	Yes	32	1,478
Female	Women's	Monthly	26	Yes	196	1,863
Go	Women's	Monthly	24	Yes	119	1,075
Golf	Sport	Monthly	15	Yes	N/A	1,863
Her World	Women's	Monthly	59	Yes	258	2,050
Home & Decor	Home	Bi-monthly	15	Yes	106	1,118
Motherhood	Family	Monthly	22	Yes	49	1,677
Motoring	Automobile	Monthly	18	Yes	101	1,429
NTUC Lifestyle	General	Bi-Monthly	217	Yes	295	2,435
RTV Times	Entertainment	Weekly	131	Yes	380	1,553

Continued on following page

Magazines, continued

Magazine	Type	Frequency	Circ. (000)	Audited?	Avg. Issue Aud. (000)	1 page 4/C Cost (US$)
Reader's Digest (E&C)	General	Monthly	67	Yes	284	4,770
Signature	General	Bi-Monthly	30	Yes	50	2,422
Singapore Business	Bus/ Finance	Monthly	9	Yes	55	1,242
Teenage	Teen Interest	Monthly	37	Yes	N/A	1,553
Teens	Teen Interest	Monthly	32	Yes	97	1,491
The Reservist	Men's Lifestyle	Bi-Monthly	88	Yes	N/A	1,429
Young Parents	Family	Quarterly	14	Yes	N/A	1,366

Outdoor/Transit

There are no static outdoor sites. Limited back-illuminated sites are available within the Rapid Transit System (MRT) and shopping malls.

Billboard	**Transit**
Lead time to reserve Quality sites tied up on t/c basis. Packages available at three-month notice **Exposure** (prime, metro sites) 55%	**Exposure** (metro) 55%
Costs	**Costs**
Average, 1 back-illuminated "sitei" in Rapid Transit system (MRT) and shopping malls/ month: 1.5 m x 1.0 m .... US$ 400 1.5 m x 1.0 m .... US$ 370 1.5 m x 3.0 m .... US$ 480	**Average, 1 board/month:** US$ 1500.........fully painted double-decker bus US$ 600 ....surrounded panels on bus US$ 90 .... taxi-top panels

Source (Exposure): SRS Media Index

Direct Marketing

Singapore is a very small market with a highly developed IT (Information Technology) database sophistication. With an advertising industry in love with lucky draws and promotions, and a society where social standing is judged by credit card ownership and club membership, the number of companies with customer databases is huge. Since these databases are frequently sold, the average Singaporean is inundated by direct mailings. In short the market is saturated. Therefore, the quality of the direct mailers has to be high, so as to capture the immediate attention of its audience. Unfortunately, mailpieces of a high standard are in the minority.

Top Direct Mail Consumer List Brokers

List Broker	*Information Provided*
Ampex	Demographic
Datapool	Demographic
Dun & Bradstreet	Demographic
Mardev	Demographic
Top Telemarketing Companies	*Direct Marketing Association*
MMS Consultancy Singapore Press Holdings (Audiotext) Singapore Telecom (Call tracking)	Direct Marketing Association of Singapore #27-06 Shaw Towers 100 Beach Road Singapore 0718 Contact: Joseph Telephone: (65) 297-0438

Non-Traditional Media

- Not likely to become a major force; even the outdoor industry is unable to grow. Nevertheless, though small, there are many interesting opportunities.
- Types currently available include video walls, TVs for shopping/post office lines, admission tickets.

Research Sources

Medium	Research Company	Information Provided
TV	Survey Research Singapore 51 Newton Road, #04-01-12 Goldhill Plaza Singapore 1130 Tel: 252 8695	TV Diary On-line/PC TV log of all transmissions
Radio	SRS (Radio Diary)	Began August 1993
Print	SRS (Media Index/Printscope)	Reach & Frequency models, readership by demographic sub-groups

Television Research Currently Available

A.C. Nielsen produces weekly minute-by-minute ratings using electronic metering system, which began January 1994 (Household and people meters).

Research Method	Frequency
Quarter-hour, self completion diary	Weekly
Meters	Weekly

Advertising Regulations

By Product

Beverages/Alcohol
Cannot be advertised in children's programs.
Cigarettes
Absolute ban right down to point of sale. Foreign or international magazines carrying tobacco advertising will have their Singapore circulation restricted to 10,000.
Pharmaceuticals/Drugs
All advertising must be approved by The Ministry of Health.

By Product

Television
All commercials must be approved by SBC prior to transmission.

Taiwan

Area	35,980km^2
Population (1992)	20,878,556
Population growth rate (1992)	1.0%
GDP	US$ 150.8 billion
GDP/per capita	US$ 7,380
Real growth rate (1991)	5.2%
Capital	Taipei

Population Breakdown

By Sex		*By Age Group*		*By Socio-Economic Status*	
Male	52%	Children	17%	A, US$ 38,913+	18%
Female	48%	Teens	19%	B, US$ 19,661-38,913	47%
		Adults	64%	C, US$ 11,059-19,661	25%
				D, Under US $ 11,059	10%
				(Annual income)	

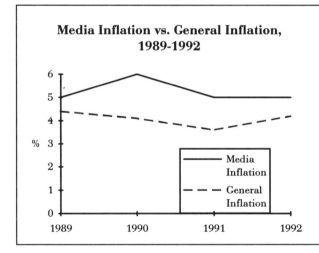

Media Inflation vs. General Inflation, 1989-1992

Number of Households	5,382,314

Ownership of household durables

Car	33.7%
Phone	94.8%
Washers	89.5%

(purchasing power equivalent)

GNP distribution by industry

Agriculture	3.5%
Industry	41.4%
Services	55.1%

Exchange rates (US$ to local currency)

1991	0.040961
1992	0.038640

National Holidays

Holiday	1993 Date
New Year	January 1-2
Chinese Lunar New Year	February 9-13
Youth Day	March 29
Grave Sweeping Festival	April 5
Dragon Boat Festival	June 13
Mid Autumn Festival	September 20
Teacher Day	September 28
Double Tenth Day	October 10
Taiwan Retrocession Day	October 25
Chang Kai-Shek's Birthday	October 31
Dr. Sun Yat-Sen's Birthday	November 12
Constitution Day	December 25

School Holidays

Holiday	1993 Date
Spring Vacation	March 29 - April 5
Summer Vacation	July - August
Winter Vacation	January - February
Summer Holiday	July 1 - August 31

Major Influences and Trends

- Rapid growth of Star TV; by January 1993, total Star TV households reached 1.98 million or 41% of total TV households.
- Legalization of Cable TV operators in July 1993; official operation begins in the middle of 1994.
- Government Information Office (G.I.O.) has opened two more TV stations which should be in operation by 1995.
- G.I.O. has forced the current three government-owned TV stations to be listed on the stock market which hopefully will diminish the monopoly situation manipulated by the government.
- G.I.O. has opened 28 regional FM radio channels which should be operational in 1994.
- SRT People Meter is expected to launch in August 1993 which will affect the ratings significantly. Currently, Redwood's diary-based ratings are used.

Spending Analysis

National advertising spending by medium
based on appropriate year's exchange rate

	1989 US$ MM	1990 US$ MM	1991 US$ MM	1992 US$ MM
TV	531.72	597.18	733.24	882.08
Cinema	5.60	5.62	-	-
Radio	85.58	92.79	109.25	105.11
Newspaper	783.77	742.82	870.48	1,071.70
Magazine	115.55	121.83	145.30	168.24
Direct Response	33.76	33.93	40.97	52.29
Outdoor	37.55	41.42	53.29	53.91
Other	211.97	238.80	286.36	381.44
Total	1,805.50	1874.39	2,238.89	2,714.77

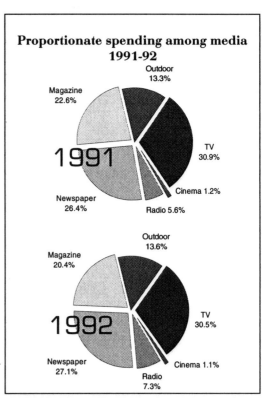

Proportionate spending among media 1991-92

1991: Outdoor 13.3%, Magazine 22.6%, TV 30.9%, Cinema 1.2%, Radio 5.6%, Newspaper 26.4%

1992: Outdoor 13.6%, Magazine 20.4%, TV 30.5%, Cinema 1.1%, Radio 7.3%, Newspaper 27.1%

Media Buying

In general, most clients allow their agencies to negotiate with the media vendors directly. There are no buying services. However, because of the kickbacks and lucrative deals in TV buying, it is not unheard of for clients to get involved in negotiations. The three local TV networks are all government-controlled. Air time is sold by their respective reps as wells as by outside reps.

Pricing is very firm with negotiation only possible for reducing compulsory package buys. Other media (i.e., magazines, newspapers, radio, alternative) are negotiable in rates.

Top Advertisers

By Company

Parent Company	Product Categories	US$ MM
President Enterprise	Food	22.9
Ho-Tai Automotive	Automotive	22.5
P&G	Consumer Products	20.5
Unilever	Consumer Products	13.7
Kao	Consumer Products	13.4
King Car Soft Drink	Soft Drink	13.1
Nan-Yang Automotive	Automotive	12.9
Yu-Loong Automotive	Automotive	12.5
Ford Automotive	Automotive	12.2
Anchor	Daily Product	10.0

By Product

Product Category	Advertiser	US$ MM
Automotive	Nan-Yang Automotive	5.9
Dairy Product	Anchor	4.6
Air Conditioner	Hitachi	2.9
Drink/Canned Coffee	Tiger Coffee	2.7
Motorcycle	Yamaha	2.4
Detergent	Unilever	2.2
Airline	China Airline	2.0
Tea	Kai-Shi Wu Loong Tea	1.9

Television

Overview

- Three nationwide TV stations in Taiwan: monopoly situation; no dominant station; competition controlled by government.
- Compulsory package buys for high rating programs:
  - One high rating program packaged with at least one low rating program.
  - Costs are same regardless of performance of programs.
  - Cannot buy more than 50% prime time program due to package buys.
  - TV stations sub-contract commercial air time out to production houses to help with sales.
- Prime time program costs decreased in 1992, while rest of rates went up.

TV HH Penetration				Adult Reach	
1989	*1990*	*1991*	*1992*	at 250 GRPs	80%
				at 500 GRPs	87%
97.8%	98.26%	99.16%	99.16%	at 1,000 GRPs	90%

Opportunities

Network	Ownership	Station Profile	Commercial Minutes/Hr	Coverage	Broadcast Hours (Sign-On/Off)
TTV	Taiwan Provincial Government	General	10	95%	WD 06:10-01:30 WE 06:10-02:30
CTV	KMT	General	10	95%	WD 06:30-01:30 WE 06:30-02:30
CTS	Ministry of National Defense	General	10	95%	WD 7:00-02:00 WE 7:00-02:30

WD=Weekday; WE=Weekends

Costs

Prime Time TV Costs for :30 in US$			
1989	*1990*	*1991*	*1992*
3,478	3,478	3,825	3,825

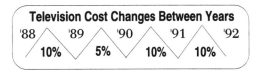

Television Cost Changes Between Years

'88 / '89 / '90 / '91 / '92
10% / 5% / 10% / 10%

Audiences/CPM's

Average Cost, Audience, and CPMs by Daypart
(Top 3 stations;Target=Adults 15+)

Hours	Morning 06:00-09:00	Daytime 09:00-16:00	Prime Time 19:00-21:00	Late Night 21:00+	Weekend 19:00-21:00 (Prime)	Early Fringe 16:00-19:00	Children 04:30-06:00 (Cartoon time)
Station TTV							
US$	1,294	2,574	3,777	1,241	3,810	2,583	2,317
Avg. Aud. (000)	181	742	3,277	1,234	4,190	460	259
CPM:	7.15	3.47	1.15	1.00	0.91	5.62	8.95
Station CTV							
US$	1,449	2,586	3,686	1,556	3,810	2,604	2,317
Avg. Aud. (000)	112	533	2,953	1,147	3,241	621	248
CPM	12.94	4.85	1.25	1.36	1.18	4.19	9.34
Station CTS							
US$	1,068	2,559	3,710	1,271	3,810	2,550	2,317
Avg. Aud. (000)	170	449	3,598	1,318	2,570	453	274
CPM	6.28	5.70	1.03	.96	1.48	5.63	8.46

Audiences/Ratings by Daypart (Target=Adults 15+)

Daypart	Hours	Household				Adult		
		Universe (000)	Hut Levels	Household Rating	Impressions (000)	Universe (000)	Adult Rating	Impressions (000)
Morning	06:00-09:00	5,338	N/A	N/A	N/A	14,712	4.1	603
Daytime	09:00-16:00	5,338	N/A	40.5	2,162	14,712	8.4	1,236
Primetime	19:00-21:00	5,338	N/A	76.5	4,083	14,712	57.8	8,504
Late Night	21:00-24:00	5,338	N/A	63.3	3,379	14,712	25.8	3,796
E. Fringe	16:00-19:00	5,338	N/A	44.1	2,354	14,712	21.0	3,090
Weekend	19:00-21:00	5,338	N/A	75.6	4,036	14,712	57.6	8,474
Children's								

Scheduling/Regional/Languages

LANGUAGE	Programming		Commercials
Primary	Mandarin	87.5%	Mandarin
Secondary	Taiwanese Dialect	6.6%	Taiwanese
	English	6.8%	

- The most common commercial lengths are :20 and :30. Lengths of :10 and greater, at :05 increments, are also available.
- Commercials are aired in blocks throughout the day, both at the beginning and end of programs, and within programs.

Children's Advertising

Both adult and children's programs accept commercials targeted at children.

Radio

Overview

- There are 33 stations; 21 of which are commercial, in Taiwan.
- The primary broadcasting language is Mandarin; however, Taiwanese dialect and English are also used.
- The most most popular programs are pop music. Prime/Peak Times are 09:00-11:00 and 15:00-17:00.
- Commercial lengths available are :20, :30, or multiples of :10.
- Among the radio stations in Taiwan, BCC-Broadcast Company China (FM) is the most popular station and has the widest coverage.
- Audience information is not available.

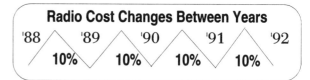

Radio Cost Changes Between Years

'88	'89	'90	'91	'92
10%	10%	10%	10%	

Costs

Costs By Daypart (BCC-FM)

Local Time	Cost:30 US$	Local Time	Cost:30 US$
08:00-09:00	12,738	17:00-18:00	12,738
09:00-10:00	11,773	18:10-19:00	12,738
10:10-12:00	12,738	19:00-20:00	11,001
12:15-13:00	9,341	20:00-22:00	11,001
13:00-14:00	9,766	22:00-23:00	11,387
14:00-15:00	10,615	23:00-24:00	11,001
15:10-17:00	10,615	00:00-01:00	8,878
		01:00-05:00	3,774

Cable

CABLE HH PENETRATION				
1989	*1990*	*1991*	*1992*	*1997*
0%	14%	23.4	39.1%	50%

- Based on an unofficial survey there are approximately 350 companies that offer Community Antenna Television (CATV) and cable TV. Together, these companies cover an estimated one million households. Up until recently, cable had been illegal in Taiwan, so there could be even more households who received cable.
- Cable TV can be divided into two types:
  (1) Community Antenna Television. These are legally operated and simply transmit the three channels' programs.
  (2) 'The 4th TV station,' or cable TV. These are illegally operated and the source of their programming is primarily video tapes and satellite programs.
- Most cable TV companies offer 10 to 30 channels with various programming content.

The Government passed the 'Laws for Cable Television' on July 18, 1993, making it legal for cable operators to set up their systems. Programming is in Mandarin, Taiwanese and English.

Satellite

- The viewership of satellite TV represents a skew toward an educated audience, aged 20-44. It is estimated that 40% of total households can receive satellite TV through Direct Broadcast System of Cable TV for reception of CNN, WOWOW and STAR TV.
- The viewership of satellite TV will continue to grow during 1994.
- Cigarette advertising is not allowed.

Satellite Channel	*Country of Origin*	*Language*	*Programming*
STAR TV	Hong Kong	English, Mandarin	Sports, MTV, News, Entertainment, Drama, Cartoons
WOWOW	Japan	English. Japanese	Movie, Music, Entertainment
NHK	Japan	English, Japanese	Drama, Kids programs, Music, News, Sports

Video Cassettes

- Roughly 87% of TV households have video cassette recorders (VCRs). Video cassettes in Taiwan do carry commercials–the average is 1 sponsor per tape. SRT (Survey Research Taiwan) measures VCR usage.
- Videotape rental is getting popular in Taiwan. Advertising is only available at the end of the film, which reduces the chance to be seen by the viewers. Though carrying commercials in videotapes is legal in Taiwan, due to poor reaction from viewers, all production companies have stopped carrying them. Thus, the cost of VCR advertising is not available.

Cinema

- There are 500+ cinemas in Taiwan, 90% of which offer commercial time. Over 4 weeks, the reach is 6.8%. Due to the ticket price increase and the recession of the film production industry, the viewership of cinema continues to drop.
- Commercial lengths available include :30, :40, :60, and :120.
- There have been no cost changes in the last four years.
- An average 4 week buy of a :60 commercial at one cinema costs US$ 1,458.

Newspapers

- There were 296 newspapers registered in Taiwan at the end of 1992. Currently about 30 newspapers are National Daily papers which accept advertising. Literacy rate in English is 3%.
- Four-color is standard for newspaper advertising.

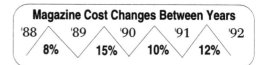

Newspaper Cost Changes Between Years

'88		'89		'90		'91		'92
	19%		10%		10%		8%	

- The following newspapers always run in split run editions: (1) United Daily News (2) China Times.

Newspaper	Market	Size	Claimed Circ. (000)	Avg. Daily Aud. (000)	1 page B&W Cost (US$)	Accept Color?
United Daily	National	Broadsheet	1200	3,815	14,606	Yes
China Times	National	Broadsheet	1200	3,269	15,336	Yes
Min Sheng Pao	National	Broadsheet	550	1,785	15,147	Yes
Taiwan Times	Central/South	Broadsheet	600	768	10,046	Yes
Min Chung	South	Broadsheet	540	713	12,056	Yes
China Times Express	National	Broadsheet	450	487	9,737	Yes
Liberty Times	Central/North	Broadsheet	550	797	14,042	Yes
China Daily News	South	Broadsheet	500	319	13,060	Yes
Econ. Daily News	National	Broadsheet	300	283	11,679	Yes
Commercial Times	National	Broadsheet	250	205	10,451	Yes

Magazines

About 4,667 magazine were registered in Taiwan at the end of 1992. There are 300 to 500 active magazines available for advertising. There are about 60-70 trade and technical publications

Magazine Cost Changes Between Years

'88		'89		'90		'91		'92
	8%		15%		10%		12%	

Magazine	Type	Frequency	Circ. (000)	Audited?	Avg. Issue Aud. (000)	1 page 4/C Cost (US$)
Reader's Digest	Gen. Interest	Monthly	217	Audited	1,280	8,655
China Times Weekly	Gen. Interest	Weekly	76	Claimed	1,707	6,955
Scoop	Gen. Interest	Weekly	45	Claimed	660	5,023
Mei-Hwa	Gen. Interest	Bi-Weekly	40	Claimed	423	5,023
Commonwealth	Business	Montly	90	Claimed	621	8,114
Money	Business	Monthly	40	Claimed	426	4,637
Global View	Business	Monthly	41	Claimed	365	4,830
Wealth	Business	Monthly	50	Claimed	334	4,637
The Journalist	Current Events	Weekly	35	Claimed	144	3,091
New Woman	Female	Monthly	32	Claimed	282	2,115
Non Non	Female	Monthly	30	Claimed	599	3,478

Outdoor/Transit

Billboard	**Transit**
Sites available ....20,000+ Lead Time to reserve ....4 weeks	Boards available.........................8,000
Cost	**Cost**
Avg. for 10 ft x 20 ft billboard/month US$ 1,739	Average for one transit board/month US$ 250
Sizes	**Sizes**
10 ft x 20 ft, others available upon request	4 ft x 30 ft, 3 ft x 30 ft , 3 ft x 20 ft, 3 ft x 10 ft, 3 ft x 6 ft, 55 cm x 80 cm

Product/Category Restrictions for Outdoor/Transit Advertising   Cigarettes and alcoholic beverages are not permitted. POS (point-of-sale) is allowed at licensed outlets.

Direct Marketing

Direct Marketing showed prosperous growth in Taiwan, and advertising agencies such as O&M started establishing direct marketing companies. No direct marketing association has yet been formed.

List Broker	*Information Provided*
Response Company	List rental, database, management, lettershop, telemarketing, fulfillment, sampling
Auto-Mail Company	List rental, database, management, lettershop, telemarketing, fulfillment, sampling
Sk-Mail Company	List Rental,database, management, lettershop, fullfilment, delivery
Showlin Company	List Rental, database, management, lettershop, telemarketing, fulfillment, sampling
Universal Company (Billing is not available)	Lettershop

Telemarketing Companies
Response Company
Auto-Mail Company
Showlin Company

Non-Traditional Media

- Non-traditional media are becoming more and more available in Taiwan.
- Types currently available include: L.E.D. Boards, Q-Boards, Receipts, Shopping Carts.
- Costs:
    L.E.D. Board US$ 8,000 (per month)
    Receipt US$ 0.93 (per 200 receipts)
    Shopping Cart US$ 1,500 (200 carts per month)

Research Sources

Medium Covered	Research Company	Information Provided
All (except outdoor)	SRT-Survey Research Taiwan 2F, 77, Nanking E. Rd., Sec 4, Taipei, Taiwan	Islandwide - Print readership - STAR TV Penetration - TV Watching Habit - Radio Listening Habit - Household/Durable Product Penetration - Durable Products Ownership
TV	Redwood Market Research Center 7F, 31, Lane 341 Chung-Jing Road, Taipei, Taiwan	Islandwide - Daily Ad Monitoring - Ad. Expenditure & TV Performance - Commercial Recordings
	Rainmaker Industrial Inc., 2F, 20, Alley 16, Lane 2, Kuang Fu ST. Yung Ho, Taipei, Taiwan	Greater Taipei Only Same as above

Television Research Currently Available

Research method	Frequency
Diary (Redwood)	Daily, Weekly, Monthly
Telephone (Rainmaker)	Daily, Weekly, Monthly

Advertising Regulations

By Product

Beverages/Alcohol

No liquor commercials can be aired on TV. Brandy and whisky are allowed to advertise in magazines for a one year period; wine or beer are allowed to advertise in newspapers and magazines with no time restrictions.

Food/Restaurants

Food advertising can not explicitly or implicitly claim that they possess any medical benefits or contain exaggarated claims. No restrictions for restaurants.

Cigarettes

Cigarette advertising is only allowed in magazines.

Pharmaceuticals/Drugs

All advertising of pharmaceuticals/drugs needs approval from Bureau of Health.

Advertising To Children

No regulations. All TV commercials are required to be reviewed and approved by the TV and Radio Broadcasting Board before first airing. Food ads with premiums targeting children should not feature the premium for over half of the commercial length.

Commercial Production

All TV commercials must be censored by the Government Information Office. Commercial lengths vary
from 10 seconds to 2 minutes (in 5 second increments).

Comparative claims must be validated and substantiated by an independent authority.

Endorsement ads must be supported by the usage evidence of endorser.

By Medium

Television

All TV commercials must be sponsored by the Government Information Office (G.I.O.) before being
broadcast.

Food, medicine and cosmetics TVC must be approved by Bureau of Health before sending to G.I.O. for
censorship.

Comparative advertising is required to provide independent product tests to prove its authenticity during
the censorship.

Cigarette and liquor advertising are not allowed on TV.

Print

Cigarette advertising should include a 'Health Warning'

Cosmetic and medicine ads should include the approval number provided by Bureau of Health after the
censorship

Outdoor

Cigarette and alchoholic beverages ads are allowed only at licensed outlets.

Sources Consulted

Billboard: More O'Ferall Co., Taipei, Taiwan, July 1993. (Telephone survey by Leo Burnett/TPE Media
Department consulting More O'Ferall Co.)

Brain Magazine, Taipei, Taiwan, Oct., 1992.

Breakthrough Magazine, Taipei, Taiwan, April, 1993.

Broadcast Company China (BCC), Taiwan, 1993

Commercial Times, Taipei, Taiwan, July, 1993

Directorale-General of Budget, Accounting and Statistics, Executive Yuan, Republic of China, 1993.

Fan-Mei Advertising Co., Taipei, July, 1993. (Telephone survey by Leo Burnett/TPE, Media Consulting
Fan-Mei Advertising Co.)

Frank Small & Associates, Feb., 1993

Government Information Office, Republic of China, 1992.

Leo Burnett Co., Ltd., Taipei, 1993

Magazine Committee Taipei, Taiwan, July, 1993

Magazines Rate Card, Taipei, Taiwan, July, 1993

Newspaper Committee, Taiwan, Taipei, July, 1993

Newspaper Rate Card, Taipei, Taiwan, July, 1993

Newspaper claimed circulation, Taiwan, July, 1993

Reader's Digest, claimed, Taipei, Taiwan, Feb., 1993

Redwood Media Research, Taiwan, 1993

SRT Media Index 1993, Taipei, Taiwan, July, 1993

SRT Media Index 1992 Data, Taipei, Taiwan

SRT Media Habit Research Jan.-June 1993, Survey Research Taiwan Co., Taipei, Taiwan, July, 1993.

Taipei Advertising Agency Association

Telephone survey by Leo Burnett/Taipei Research Department, July, 1993

Transit Board-Tai-Yu, Bus Panel Advertising, Taipei, Taiwan, July, 1993. (Telephone survey by Leo
Burnett/TPE Media Department Consulting Tai-Yu Co.)

TTV, CTV, CTS, Taiwan, 1993

Thailand

Area	514,000 km²
Population (1992)	57,624,180
Population growth rate (1992)	1.4%
GDP	US$ 198 billion
GDP/per capita	US$ 3,400
Real growth rate (1991)	1.5%
Capital	Bangkok

Population Breakdown

By Sex		*By Age Group*		*By Socio-Economic Status*	
Male	49%	Children, 0-9	17%	Under US$ 115	35%
Female	51%	Teens, 10-14	11%	US$ 115-192	27%
		Adults, 15+	72%	US$ 192-385	22%
				US$ 385-577	6%
				US$ 577-769	5%
				US$ 962+	4%

Source (Population Breakdown): Deemar Media Index, Bangkok, Thailand 1992

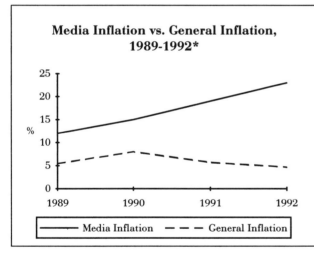

Media Inflation vs. General Inflation, 1989-1992*

— Media Inflation   – – – General Inflation

Number of Households	12,311,000

Ownership of household durables*

Car	14%
Phone	13%
Washers	11%

(purchasing power equivalent)

GNP distribution by industry*

Agriculture	13%
Industry	26%
Services	13%
Others	48%

Exchange rates (US$ to local currency)*

1991	0.039
1992	0.039

National Holidays

Holiday	1993 Date
New Year's Day	January 1
Chinese New Year	February 4
Makabucha Day	February 18
Chakri Day	April 6
Songkran Day	April 13
National Labour Day	May 1
Coronation Day	May 5
Visakabucha Day	May 18
Khao Pansa Day	July 15
H.M. The Queen's Birthday	August 12
Chulalongkorn Day	October 23
H.M. The King's Birthday	December 7
Constitution Day	December 10
Christmas Day	December 25
New Year's Eve	December 31

School Holidays

Holiday	1993 Date
Summer Holiday	March 15 - May 1
Term Break	October 1 - November 1

*Sources:

(Media Inflation): Leo Burnett, Bangkok, Thailand
(General Inflation and GNP): National Economic and Social Development Board, Bangkok, Thailand, 1993
(Household Durables): Deemar Media Index, Bangkok, Thailand, 1992.
(Exchange Rates): Bank of Thailand, 1992

Major Influences and Trends

Television is still the most popular medium, controlling half of the total ad expenditures. Newspaper is second at 27%. Among the four major media, newspaper saw the highest growth in ad revenue in 1992, followed by television, magazine, and radio. The high growth in ad revenue is mostly enjoyed by two major TV stations, channel 3 and channel 7. Their primetime news and drama series must be booked a year in advance. They are thus in a position to dictate a yearly rate increase from 20-33%. *Thai Rath*, a leading Thai language newspaper, also benefits from these increases. Payment to the newspaper is made in cash with a 5-10% commission given to agencies.

The Thai media scene will also see some new media options. It is expected that outdoor media will be used even more in 1994. This includes the new laser, electronic and moving billboards, as well as airborne inflatables. In addition, one of Hong Kong's media start-ups (regional satellite service STAR TV) will likely have far-reaching effects on broadcast media in Asia, Thailand included.

Spending Analysis

National advertising spending by medium
based on appropriate year's exchange rate

	1989 US$ MM	1990 US$ MM	1991 US$ MM	1992 US$ MM
TV	195.0	244.0	323.3	390.6
Cinema	-	1.0	1.1	1.5
Radio	50.0	108.0	73.9	30.5
Newspaper	104.0	124.0	182.0	219.4
Magazine	32.0	43.0	59.6	65.2
Outdoor	-	-	27.9	1.9
Total	**381.0**	**520.0**	**667.8**	**709.1**

Sources: Media Data Resources, Bangkok, Thailand, 1989, 1990, 1991;
Media Focus, Bangkok, Thailand, 1989, 1990, 1991

Media Buying

For print, space is bought directly from the publisher. For television, Channel 3, 7, and 9 mostly produce and sell their own program airtime. Channel 5 sells all airtime to independent program producers who resell the time to advertisers. Radio stations mostly sell airtime to independent program producers then sell it to advertisers.

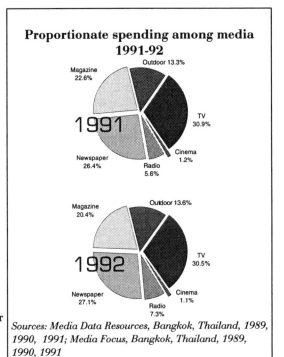

Proportionate spending among media 1991-92

1991
Magazine 22.6%
Outdoor 13.3%
TV 30.9%
Cinema 1.2%
Radio 5.6%
Newspaper 26.4%

1992
Magazine 20.4%
Outdoor 13.6%
TV 30.5%
Cinema 1.1%
Radio 7.3%
Newspaper 27.1%

Sources: Media Data Resources, Bangkok, Thailand, 1989, 1990, 1991; Media Focus, Bangkok, Thailand, 1989, 1990, 1991

All media pricing is negotiable, except for television, which is a sellers' market. Agencies deal with the media but some clients deal directly with the media as well. There are no buying services but there are media brokers who buy a certain amout of airtime for certain programs and re-sell them to advertisers and agencies. The Thai media market is not controlled or monopolized.

Top Advertisers

By Company

Parent Company	Product Categories	US$MM
Muang Thong Thani	Residential Condos	5.8
Pailin Square	Residential Condos	2.8
Lever Brothers	Powder Detergent	2.7
Fuji Foto Film	Color Film	2.5
Robinson	Department Store	2.5
Bank of Ayudhaya	Banking	2.4
Muang Thong Bang-na	Corporate	2.4
Kodak Thailand	Color Film	2.4
T.C. Mycin	Energy Drink	2.3
Thai Pure Drink	Coca-Cola	2.3

Sources: Media Data Resources, Bangkok, Thailand, 1991;
Media Focus , Bangkok, Thailand, 1991

By Product

Product Category	Advertiser	US$MM
Housing Proj./Real Estate	Muang Thong Thani	2.4
Department Store/Trade Cntr	The Mall Department Store	2.3
Pharmaceutical Products	Nutacold Med	1.5
Office Machines/Equipment	Nokia Mobil Telephone	1.6
Alcoholic Beverage	Singha Beer	3.1
Shampoo/Hair Conditioners	Sunsilk Shampoo	2.8
Milk/Dairy Products	Milo	1.6
Skin-Care Cosmetics	Oil Of Ulan	.9
Petroleum Products	Esso Gasoline	1.1
Building Materials	Elephant Tile Roof	1.3

Sources: Media Data Resources, Bangkok, Thailand, 1991;
Media Focus , Bangkok, Thailand, 1991

Television

Overview

There are a total of five TV stations in Thailand (3,5,7,9 and 11), all of which are headquartered in Bangkok. The first four channels accept advertising, while Channel 11 is non-commercial.

Television HH Penetration				Adult Reach	
				at 250 GRPs	70%
1989	*1990*	*1991*	*1992*	at 500 GRPs	79%
64%	70%	75%	81%	at 1000 GRPs	84%

Source: Deemar Media Index, Bangkok, Thailand: 1989, 1990, 1991, 1992

Source: Deemar's Telescope, Bangkok, Thailand, 1992

Opportunities

	Number of Stations	Ownership	Station Profile	Commercial Minutes/Hr	Coverage	Broadcast Hours (Sign-On/Off)
Thai TV Ch. 3	1	The Mass Communication Organization of Thailand (MOT)	General	10	95%	06:00-00:45
Army TV Ch. 5	1	Army	General	10	80%	06:00-01:00
Army TV Ch. 7	1	Army	General	10	95%	05:30-01:15
Thai TV Ch. 9	1	MOT	General	10	95%	06:00-01:20
Television of Thailand Ch. 11	7	The Government Public Relation Department	Education/ News/General	Non-commercial Bangkok Station	70%	05:30-09:15 16:00-24:00 Weekday 05:30-24:00 Weekend

Source: Individual TV stations provided 1992 data

Costs

Prime Time TV Costs for :30 in US$			
1989	*1990*	*1991*	*1992*
1,190	1,309	1,904	2,307

Source: Deemar's Telescope, Bangkok, Thailand, 1992

Television Cost Changes Between Years

Source: Deemar's Telescope, Bangkok, Thailand, 1992

Television, continued

Audiences/CPM's

Average Cost, Audience, and CPMs by Daypart (Top 3 stations; Target=Adults 15+)

Hours	Morning 06:00-10:00	Daytime 06:00-19:00	Prime Time 19:00-22:00	Late Night 22:00-24:00	Weekend 06:00-18:00	Children 17:00-19:00
Ch.3						
US$	893	1,488	2,678	1,984	1,488	1,290
Avg. Aud. (000)	198	295	619	419	399	420
CPM	4.51	5.04	4.33	4.74	3.73	3.07
Ch.5						
US$	893	1,548	2,232	1,885	1,548	1,290
Avg. Aud. (000)	227	248	558	499	237	195
CPM	3.93	6.24	4.00	3.77	6.53	6.62
Ch.7						
US$	853	1,687	3,175	2,480	2,182	1,290
Avg. Aud. (000)	292	377	1,504	1,123	702	625
CPM	2.92	4.47	2.11	2.21	3.11	2.06
Ch.9						
US$	853	1,190	1,806	1,786	1,389	992
Avg. Aud. (000)	64	188	563	230	368	415
CPM	13.33	6.33	3.21	7.77	3.77	2.39

Audience/Ratings by Daypart (Target=Adults 15+)

	Hours	Household				Adult		
		Universe (000)	Hut Levels	Household Rating	Impressions (000)	Universe (000)	Adult Rating	Impressions (000)
Morning	06:00-10:00	12,311	81	1.2	147	14,129	1.4	198
Daytime	06:00-19:00	12,311	81	1.7	209	14,129	2.0	283
Primetime	19:00-22:00	12,311	81	4.7	579	14,129	5.7	805
Late Night	22:00-24:00	12,311	81	3.2	394	14,129	4.0	565
Weekend	06:00-18:00	12,311	81	2.6	320	14,129	3.0	424
Children's	17:00-19:00	12,311	81	2.6	320	14,129	2.9	410

Source:Deemar's Telescope, Bangkok, Thailand, 1992

Scheduling and Regional/Local

LANGUAGE	Programming	Commercials
Primary	Thai 95%	Thai
Secondary	English 5%	English

- The most common commercial lengths are :15 and :30.
- Commercials are aired throughout the day, during program time rather than before or after.
- Regional scheduling is available. About 5% of all commercials are aired regionally, where the cost is 30% that of national time.

Source: Leo Burnett, Bangkok, Thailand, 1992

REGIONAL PROGRAMMING

Network	Station	Region	Hours
Channel 11	Khon Kaen Ch. 4	Northeast	16:00-24:00
	Ubon Ch. 4	Northeast	16:00-24:00
	Lampang Ch. 8	Lampang	16:00-24:00
	Pisanuloke Ch.7	Lampang	16:00-24:00
	Surat Ch.7	South	16:00-24:00
	Haddyai Ch. 10	South	16:00-24:00

Source: The Government Public Relations Department, Bangkok, Thailand, 1992

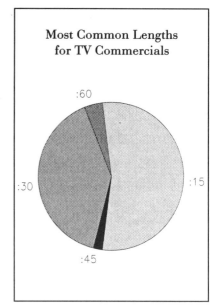

Most Common Lengths for TV Commercials

Children's Advertising

Both adult and children's programs accept commercials targeted at children.

ADULT PROGRAMMING				Kids'	
Station	Hours	Days	Universe (000)	Ratings	Impressions (000)
All Commercial Stations :	06:00-24:00 07:00-10:00	Mon.-Fri. Sat.-Sun.	3,423 3,423	2.1 4.6	72 157

Source:Deemar's Telescope, Bangkok, Thailand, 1992

CHILDREN'S PROGRAMMING				Kids'	
Station	Hours	Days	Universe (000)	Ratings	Impressions (000)
All Commercial Stations :	18:00-19:00 07:00-10:00	Mon.-Fri. Sat.-Sun.	3,423 3,423	3.6 4.6	124 159

Source:Deemar's Telescope, Bangkok, Thailand, 1992

Radio

- There are 357 stations, all of which are commercial, in Thailand. Sixty-two of these are in Bangkok.
- The primary broadcasting language is Thai; however, English is also used.
- The most most popular program type is Thai modern music.
- Commercial lengths available are :30 and :60.

Source:Deemar Media Index, Bangkok, Thailand, 1992

Daypart Costs/CPMs (Target=Adults, 15+)

Daypart	Local Time	Avg. Cost :30 US$	Avg. Audience (000)		CPM	
			BKK	Up-c	BKK.	Up-c
Prime Time	06:00-10:00 AM	3.17	162	2,322	0.02	0.001
	06:00-10.00 FM	59.5	839	3,442	0.07	0.017
Daytime	06:00-18:00 AM	3.17	110	1,994	0.03	0.029
	06:00-18:00 FM	59.5	778	4,952	0.08	0.012
Late Night	22:00-24:00 AM	3.17	61	314	0.05	0.010
	22:00-24:00 FM	59.5	689	1,890	0.09	0.031

Source:Deemar Media Index, Bangkok, Thailand, 1992

Cable

The International Broadcast Corporation (IBC) was awarded a concession by the government's Mass Communication Organization of Thailand (MOT) to operate a cable television service as of September 1989. Under the contract, IBC has received five bans of frequencies for use in its cable programs for home subscribers. MOT, in mid-1989, awarded another concession to Siam Broadcast & Communication Co., Ltd. (SBC) to operate a cable television service scheduled for August 1991. SBC also operates 3 channels. IBC and SBC now operate Bangkok cable TV with 24 hour broadcasting and no commercials.

There are a total of eight cable channels. The primary language used to broadcast on cable is English; Thai is also used. The system is publicly owned but operated under the government's supervision by the Mass Communications Organizatiaon of Thailand. Less than 1% of the TV households have cable presently, but 250,000 are projected within 5 years.

No commercials are broadcast on cable TV.

Cable, continued

Cable Networks	HH Circulation (000)	Programming
International Broadcasting Corporation (IBC)	215	IBC 1 (News Channel) IBC 2 (English Entertainment) IBC 3 (Thai Variety) IBC 4 (Sports Channel) IBC 5 (English Movie)
Siam Broadcasting & Communications (TST)	23	TST 1 (Documentary) TST 2 (Music) TST3 (Movie Channel)

Source (All cable information): 1) The International Broadcast Corporation (IBC), Bangkok, Thailand, 1992;
2) Siam Broadcast and Communication, Bangkok, Thailand, 1992

Satellite

Due to national security, satellite antennas are restricted to residents with specific qualifications such as international business operations and government officials of higher than C-8 rank. People who live outside the range of locally transmitted television signals are also eligible. After Star TV launched the BBs 24-hour world television news service in November 1991, the Thai government is expected to remove the ownership restrictions of satellite receiving antennas to allow more Thais and foreigners to use the service.

Satellite Channel	Country of Origin	Language	Programming
RCTs	Indonesia	English	Entertainment
STMB-TV3	Malaysia	English	Entertainment
RTM-1	Malaysia	English	Entertainment
Pacific Network	Thailand	English	News, Documentaries, Entertainment
CETV1	China	English	Documentaries
CETV2	China	English	Documentaries
CCTV1	China	English	Documentaries
CCTV2	China	English	Documentaries
CCTV3	China	English	Documentaries
VTR1	Indonesia	English	Entertainment, Documentaries, Music VDO,
Myanmar TV	Myanmar	English	Documentaries
Moscow TV 1	Russia	English	Documentaries, Entertainment
Moscow TV 2	Russia	English	Entertainment, Documentaries
Vietnam TV	Vietnam	English	Entertainment, Documentaries
CNN International	USA	English	Entertainment, Documentaries
STAR TV	Hong Kong	English	Entertainment, News, Sport, Music VDO, Entertainment

Video Cassettes

- Roughly 65% of TV households have video cassette recorders. Video cassettes in Thailand do carry commercials–the average is one sponsor per tape. The Deemar Co., Ltd (affiliated with AGB) measures VCR usage. An average cost is US$ 32 per minute.
- TVB Hong Kong entered a joint venture with a Thai media company and launched a new VCR advertising campaign in early 1993. With Hong Kong's TVB experience and vast supply of TVB VCR ownerships, this makes VCR advertising in the Thai market more exciting.

Cinema

- There are 247 cinemas in Thailand, most of which offer commercial time. Over 4 weeks, the reach is 5%. Due to the ticket price increase and the recession of film production industry, the viewership of cinema continues to drop.
- Commercial lengths available include :30, :45, :60.

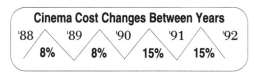

- An average 4 week buy of a :60 commercial at one cinema costs US$ 476.

Source: Apex Ad, Wiwatpong and Associate, Wellfilm, Cine Ad., Bangkok, Thailand: 1989, 1990, 1991, 1992

Newspapers

- There are 40 newspapers in Thailand, with a combined circulation of 4,930,000.

Newspaper	Market	Size	Circ. (000)	Avg. Daily Aud. (000)	1page B&W Cost (US$)	Accept Color?
BAHN MUANG	National	12 x 20"	160	236	3,333	yes
DAILY MIRROR	National	12 x 20"	80	104	3,333	yes
DAILY NEWS	National	12 x 20"	400	5,667	6,857	yes
DAO SIAM	National	12 x 20"	80	64	2,857	yes
GOLF EXPRESS	National	12 x 20"	20	N/A	4,762	yes
KHAO SUD	National	12 x 20"	40	260	3,048	yes
KRUNGTHEP TURAKIJ	National	12 x 20"	70	199	5,524	yes
LOKE KEE-LARAIWAN	National	12 x 20"	80	93	3,333	yes
MA-TI CHON	National	12 x 20"	90	1,519	4,952	yes
NAEW NAH	National	12 x 20"	80	195	2,857	yes
PHOO JAD KARN	National	12 x 20"	70	302	6,000	yes
SIAM KEE-LA	National	12 x 20"	80	936	4,286	yes
SIAM RATH	National	12 x 20"	80	374	4,000	yes
THAI RATH	National	12 x 20"	800	11,172	9,048	yes
WATA JAK	National	12 x 20"	60	151	4,762	yes
BANGKOK POST	National	9 x 21"	45	132	990	yes
STUDENT TIME	National	10 x 13"	60	53	1,548	yes
STUDENT WEEKLY	National	10 x 13"	150	109	1,754	yes
THE NATION	National	9 x 21"	44	108	810	yes
KIA HUA TONG	National	20 x14"	50	12	1,222	yes
SIN SIAN	National	20 x14"	30	22	1,556	yes
TONG HUA	National	20 x14"	40	28	3,889	yes

Source: Deemar Media Index, Bangkok, Thailand, 1992

Magazines

There are 258 consumer magazines published in Thailand, and an unknown number of trade and technical magazines.

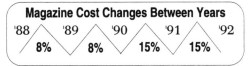

Source: Leo Burnett, Ltd., Bangkok, Thailand: 1989, 1990, 1991, 1992

Magazine	Type	Frequency	Circ. (000)	Audited?	Avg. Issue Aud. (000)	1 page 4/C Cost (US$)
Dichan	Women	Bi-Monthly	40	No	690	1,230
Image	Women	Monthly	30	No	208	1,071
Kwan Ruen	Women	Bi-Monthly	150	No	1,450	1,429
Kullasatri	Women	Bi-Monthly	180	No	1,067	1,389
Lalana	Women	Bi-Monthly	40	No	279	992

Continued on next page

Magazines, continued

Magazine	Type	Frequency	Circ. (000)	Audited?	Avg. Issue Aud. (000)	1 page 4/C Cost (US$)
Mae Lae Dek	Women	Monthly	30	No	395	952
Praew	Women	Bi-Monthly	50	No	642	1,349
Sakul Thai	Women	Weekly	180	No	652	1,786
Wai Nar Rak	Women	Bi-Monthly	50	No	769	952
Dok Bia	Business	Monthly	30	No	185	1,032
Money & Banking	Business	Monthly	40	No	149	1,230
Koo Kaeng	Business	Monthly	45	No	238	1,548
Poo Jad Karn	Business	Monthly	40	No	543	1,548
Matichon	Business	Weekly	40	No	391	1,270
Siam Rath	Business	Weekly	40	No	205	1,190
Bahn Lae Suan	Home	Monthly	60	No	868	1,389
Star's Soccer	Sport	Weekly	60	No	396	754
Phuen Dern Tang	Travel	Monthly	40	No	185	952
T.O.T	Travel	Monthly	80	No	460	873
Grand Prix	Vehicle	Monthly	40	No	198	873
Nak Leng Rot	Vehicle	Monthly	40	No	545	635
Praew Weekly	Women	Bi-Monthly	45	No	358	1,190

Outdoor/Transit

Billboard

Sites available	N/A
Exposure	80%
Lead Time to reserve	12 weeks

Cost

10 m x 24 m .... US$ 3,846–7,692

Costs have been increasing at 20% annually since 1990.

Sizes

10 m x 24 m, 50 m x 720 cm

Transit

Boards available	N/A
Exposure	70%

Cost

1 board/month .... US$ 170

Costs have been increasing at 10% annually.

Sizes

1.2 m x 4 m, 50 m x 75 cm

Restrictions: no cigarette advertising

Source (Outdoor Transit): General Holding, S Map, Top Gen, Bangkok, Thailand: 1989, 1990, 1991, 1992;
(Costs): 12 Promotion, Master Ad, Magic Lamp, Bangkok, Thailand: 1989, 1990, 1991, 1992

Direct Marketing

Direct marketing is still in a relatively undeveloped state. However there are a few rare specialists in the field, in particular, creatives. There is a limited but growing market since more businesses have recognized its applications. There are only a few key players, and still no one is catering full fulfillment services. Quality of names, lists, and postal services' regulations/operations are still poor.

List Broker	*Information Provided*
DM&MT Co., Ltd.	Name, a mailing address with selection services (e.g., age, sex, occupation, residential area etc.)
Allied Marketing DMS	

Telemarketing Companies	*Direct Marketing Association*
DMS (new 1992)	TDMA (Thailand Direct Marketing Association) established in July of 1992

Non-Traditional Media

As rates for television and print are expected to inflate more in the future, there will be more use of outdoor media with the availability of laser, electronic and moving billboards as well as airborne inflatables.

Types Currently Available	Costs in US$
Balloon: - Airship	11,373/1st month, plus 1,569/2nd month on
- Hot Air Balloon Replica	2,549/month
- Sphere	2,549/month
- Blimp	2,549/month
Bus body impact:	20,300.40/20 units/month (1 package (20 units/year) *Not including production cost (55,364.71)
Electric Light Board at T.S.T. Tower:	3,059/month

Sources (Balloon): Media Data Resources, Bangkok, Thailand, 1992; (Bus): Diverse Marketing, Bangkok, Thailand, 1992; (Electric Light Board): Thanayong, Bangkok, Thailand, 1992

Research Sources

Medium Covered	Research Company	Information Provided
TV, Radio, Print, Cinema	Deemar Co., Ltd. 29/5 Soi Saladaeng 1 Saladaeng Road Bangkok	Weekly TV viewing Patterns Telescope (TV reach/frequency analysis) Printscope (Print reach/frequency analysis) Media Index (Annual media survey on TV, radio, print, cinema, population information)
TV, Print, Cinema	Media Focus Co., Ltd. 146/70 Soi Brinakom, Sukhumvit 71 Road, Bangkok	Media spending by brand/category/ etc.
TV, Print, Cinema	Media Data Resources 222 Thansettakis Bldg., 2nd floor Vip Havadee-Rungsit Road, Bangkok	Media spending by brand/category/ etc.

Television Research Currently Available

Research method	Frequency
People Meter	Weekly

Advertising Regulations

By Product

Beverages/Alcohol
Liquor commercials must be aired after 22:00 on TV. No drinking scenes are allowed.
Food/Restaurants
All food advertising needs approval from the FDA. No restrictions for restaurants.
Cigarettes
Cigarette advertising is totally prohibited in all media.
Pharmaceuticals/Drugs
All advertising of pharmaceuticals/drugs needs approval from the FDA.

Advertising To Children

No regulations. All TV commercials are required to be reviewed and approved by the TV and Radio Broadcasting Directing Board before first airing.

By Medium

Television

All ads are required to be reviewed and approved by the TV and Radio Broadcasting Directing Board. Liquor and condom commercials must be aired after 22:00 and no drinking scenes are allowed.

Europe

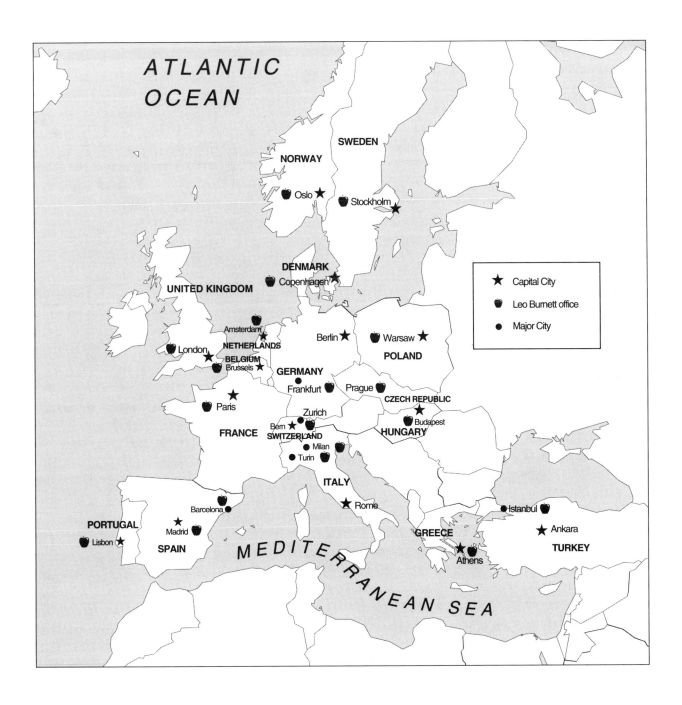

Europe

Regional Summary

There are two significant factors affecting the media markets in Europe. First, the continued deregulation of broadcast media in many European markets. While creating new audiences, deregulation is also leading to an increase in the supply of commercial airtime and to vastly fluctuating costs. Second, new government legislation is restricting activity in a number of the larger markets.

Media Overview

The effects of TV deregulation can be seen in Spain, where the success of the private channels led to huge discounting by state broadcasters. Prices are only now beginning to stabilize from the chaos of deregulation and there are better opportunities for advertisers.

Similarly in Germany, ARD was forced to cut rates for 1993 by 32 percent to ward off competition from the private channels, namely SAT1 and RTL. ZDF looks as if it finished the year undersold. For the first time ever, it would appear Germany is becoming demand-rather than supply-driven.

France has born the brunt of the new legislation. The Loi Sapin effectively bans media broking by prohibiting undisclosed discounting, and the Loi Evin bans tobacco and restricts alcohol advertising. These laws are severely affecting advertising revenues. It will be some time before the print sector really shows signs of recovery.

Italy also is working through the effects of legislation in the aftermath of the Legge Mammi, which controls media ownership. Recent laws on TV sponsorship, introduced to control clutter, will certainly affect the Berlusconi/Publitalia group. Their TV promotions almost certainly will be judged as sponsorship and therefore will be restricted.

The new U.K. ITV franchises finally came into effect in 1993. While revenues from the first half of 1993 were up by 7 percent, it is unlikely they finished on such a positive note (about a 3 percent increase was being forecast). Channel 4 is successfully building share at the expense of ITV3, and BSkyB is now received in 2 million satellite and cable homes, a figure regarded by many as posing a real threat to ITV.

Satellite and cable media continue to develop throughout the rest of Europe, although still not significant enough to achieve critical mass, and very much geared toward small, specialist audiences. National TV continues to take the lion's share of broadcast budgets. The number of homes reached by these pan-European services is increasing. New pan-regional channels are being introduced with Turner's Cartoon Network, stable-mate of CNN, scheduled to be onstream by 1994, and Euronews, a 24-hour news channel, launched early in 1993. Other services owned by U.S. cable programmers are taking their first steps into Europe, Nickelodeon began in the U.K. in September 1993 and plans to expand through much of Europe, joining its sibling MTV in cable homes.

Print owners are also developing new pan-European marketing efforts, with rate cards now being introduced by Axel Springer (for their Auto titles) and Bauer's three-sisters. As yet many local language editions (e.g. *Cosmopolitan, Elle*) are still published under license. Although publishers want to be seen as willing to work across borders, it is not particularly easy, nor does it introduce any significant cost efficiencies.

Throughout Europe, audience measurement is showing signs of convergence. All European countries (bar some Eastern European countries) have people meters. Both the EAAA and ESOMAR are working on ways of coordinating demographics so that research studies can be comparable. Pan-European research continues in the form of the European Businessmen's Readership Survey, Pan-European Survey, and International Airline Travel, measuring upmarket business groups for print, and Pan-European Television Audience Research measuring satellite television.

Liz Workman
Regional Media Manager

Belgium

Area	30,510 km^2
Population (1992)	10,016,623
Population growth rate (1992)	0.3%
GDP	US$ 171.8 billion
GDP/per capita	US$ 17,300
Real growth rate (1991)	1.4%
Capital	Brussels

Population Breakdown

By Sex		*By Age Group*		*By Socio-Economic Status*	
Male	49%	Children	12%	A	12%
Female	51%	Teens	13%	B	28%
		Adults	75%	C	35%
				D	25%

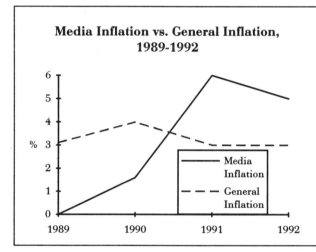

Media Inflation vs. General Inflation, 1989-1992

Number of Households	**4,139,000**

Ownership of household durables

Car	77%
Phone	82%
Washers	82%

(purchasing power equivalent)

GNP distribution by industry

Agriculture	2%
Industry	30%
Services	68%

Exchange rates (US$ to local currency)

1991	0.0303
1992	0.2976

National Holidays

Holiday	*1993 Date*
New Year	January 1
Easter	April 11
Labour Day	May 1
Ascension Day	May 9
Pentecost Monday	May 20
National Holiday	July 21
Assumption Day	August 15
All Saints	November 1
Armistice Day	November 11
Christmas	December 25
French Community	September 27
Flemish Community	July 11

School Holidays

Holiday	*1993 Date*
Autumn Holiday	October 28 - November 1
Christmas Holiday	December 23 - January 3
Easter Holiday	April 12 - April 25 (French region)
	April 5 - April 28 (Flemish region)
Summer Holiday	July 1 - August 31

Major Influences and Trends

Belgian advertisers have been reviewing the method and amount of traditional agency payments because the removal of the surcommission has reduced agencies' margins. These factors have resulted in overstaffing at the agency level.

Concerning the media centers, the situation is now stabilized.

As media ownership becomes more and more concentrated, agency media buyers are forced to deal with increasing difficulties. The tendency among the agencies is to develop other areas of communication in order to increase billings and offer better service to their clients.

Spending Analysis

National advertising spending by medium
based on appropriate year's exchange rate

	1989 US$ MM	1990 US$ MM	1991 US$ MM	1992 US$ MM
TV	213.2	320.7	323.7	347.6
Cinema	11.1	13.8	12.8	13.0
Radio	13.3	21.4	58.5	83.5
Newspaper	225.2	256.7	276.2	305.8
Magazine	210.2	227.0	236.0	231.5
Outdoor	112.4	134.2	138.7	154.4
Total	785.4	973.8	1,045.9	1,135.8

Source: Mediamark

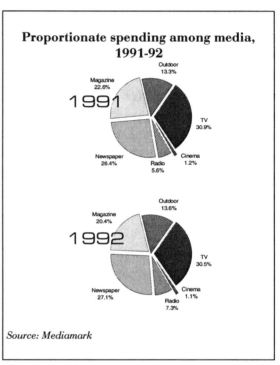

Proportionate spending among media, 1991-92

1991
Outdoor 13.3%
Magazine 22.6%
TV 30.9%
Newspaper 26.4%
Radio 5.6%
Cinema 1.2%

1992
Outdoor 13.6%
Magazine 20.4%
TV 30.5%
Newspaper 27.1%
Radio 7.3%
Cinema 1.1%

Source: Mediamark

Media Buying

At this stage, the situation is fairly stable.

In all likelihood, next year Belgium will begin to experience the effects of the many international changes in media buying (i.e. media buying groups, etc.). In anticipation of these changes, several agencies are considering mergers or changes in structure.

Buying Services with 1992 Billings

Buying Service	Parent Company	US$ MM	Independent/Affiliate
Carat Crystal	Carat	172.6	TBWA, EURO, RSCG, AEGIS
TMP	TMP	163.7	Omnimedia, Square/Media +
Space	Independent	154.8	Leo Burnett, Y&R, DMB&B, Grey, Publicis
Universal Media	Interpublic	119.0	McCann Erickson, Lowe Troost
Initiative Media	Interpublic	92.3	Lintas

Top Advertisers

By Company

Parent Company	Product Categories	US$ MM
Procter & Gamble	Hygiene, Body care	37,801
Unilever	Hygiene, Body care	32,906
Belgian Government	Public service	25,015
BSN Gervais Danone	Food	22,603
GIB Group	Distribution	23,325
Interbrew	Beverages (brewery)	19,205
D'Ieteren	Cars	18,241
L'Oreal	Hygiene, Body care	18,066
Master Foods	Food	16,015
Henkel	Hygiene, Body care	15,069

By Product

Product Category	Advertiser	US$ MM
Car manufacturers	Nissan	10,654
Hygiene & Body care	Dash	4,553
Food	Kelloggs	8,392
Beverages	Coca-Cola	8,422
Distribution	GIB	11,874
Belgian Government	National Lotterie	10,148

Television

Overview

Belgium has both Flemish (North) and French (South) stations. The Flemish public stations BRT1 and BRT2 do not currently broadcast advertising. Advertising in the North is only possible on the commercial channel VTM. All French stations (public RTBF and Tele 21 and private RTL/TV1) broadcast advertising, but use a combined buying module. TVB, with its 2 channels, offers more differentiated programming and therefore obtains a higher coverage than is possible in the North.

Television HH Penetration			Adult Reach
			at 250 GRPs 70%
1992 Penetration	95%	3,932,000	at 500 GRPs 80%
			at 1,000 GRPs 85%

Opportunities

Network	Number of Stations	Ownership	Station Profile	Commercial Minutes/Day	Coverage	Broadcast Hours (Sign-On/Off)
BRT	TV1	State	General	0	31.4%	18:00-23:00 10:00-24:00
	TV2	State	Film, Culture	0	10.0%	19:00-23:00
VTM	VTM	Private	Light Entert.	41	34.6%	15.30-24:00 12:00-24:00
RTBF	RTBF	State	General	14	25.2%	14:00-24:00 11:00-24:00
	TELE21	State	Sports & Music	N/A	4.4%	14:00-24:00 17:00-23:00
RTL	RTL/TVi	Private	Light Entert.	30	22.9%	12:00-24:00 08:00-24:00

Costs

Prime Time TV Costs for :30 in US$				
	1989	1990	1991	1992
TVB (RTL+RTBF)	6,845	7,440	6,696	6,785
VTM	6,889	9,404	11,368	11,904

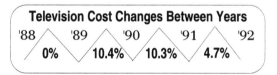

Television Cost Changes Between Years
'88 '89 '90 '91 '92
0%   10.4%   10.3%   4.7%

Audiences/CPM's

Average Cost, Audience, and CPMs by Daypart
(Top 3 stations; :30, national audience, Target=Adults 15+)

Hours	Morning 00:00-12:00	Daytime 12:00-19:00	Prime Time 19:00-22:00	Late Night 22:00-24:00	Weekend 00:00-24:00	Children
Station: VTM						
US$	2,734	2,737	10,185	2,118	5,685	6,253
Avg. Aud. (000)	103	230	679	169	379	37
CPM	26.55	11.90	15.00	12.53	15.00	169.00
Station: RTBF						
US$	N/A	713	6,096	767	2,670	1,002
Avg. Aud. (000)		48	369	65	169	96
CPM		14.85	16.52	11.80	15.80	10.44
Station: RTL/TVi						
US$	1,198	1,518	6,691	928	2,343	2,727
Avg. Aud. (000)	41	138	389	72	148	110
CPM	29.22	11.00	17.20	12.89	15.83	24.79

Audience/Rating by Daypart
Target=North (Public and Commercial channel)

		Household				Adult		
Daypart	Hours	Universe (000)	Hut Levels	Household Rating	Impressions (000)	Universe (000)	Adult Rating	Impressions (000)
Morning	06:00-12:00	2,328.3	N/A	1.0	23	4,684.5	1.0	47
Daytime	06:00-19:00	2,328.3	N/A	5.1	119	4,684.5	4.8	224
Primetime	19:00-22:00	2,328.3	N/A	43.4	1,010	4,684.5	39.6	1,855
Late Night	22:00-24:00	2,328.3	N/A	27.7	645	4,684.5	25.8	1,208
Weekend		2,328.3	N/A	14.4	335	4,684.5	13.8	646
Children's		2,328.3	N/A	N/A	624	4,684.5	9.2	43

Target=South

		Household				Adult		
Daypart	Hours	Universe (000)	Hut Levels	Household Rating	Impressions (000)	Universe (000)	Adult Rating	Impressions (000)
Morning	06:00-12:00	1,810.8	N/A	3.6	65	3,445.1	3.0	103
Daytime	06:00-19:00	1,810.8	N/A	13.0	253	3,445.1	11.0	379
Primetime	19:00-22:00	1,810.8	N/A	49.7	900	3,445.1	43.8	1,509
Late Night	22:00-24:00	1,810.8	N/A	30.8	558	3,445.1	27.9	961
Weekend		1,810.8	N/A	21.7	393	3,445.1	19.5	672
Children's		1,810.8	N/A	N/A	N/A	3,445.1	12.4	427

Scheduling/Regional/Languages

- The most common commercial length is :30 (60%); lengths of :10 to :60 are also available.
- Commercials are aired in blocks throughout the day, both at the beginnings and ends of programs. and during them.
- Additional detail about languages and regional buying is in the Overview to this section.

Children's Programming

Both adult and children's programs accept commercials targeted at children.

CHILDREN'S PROGRAMMING			Universe (000)	Kids' Ratings	Impressions (000)
Station	Hours	Days			
VTM	Whole day	Everyday	623.7	80	498.9
TVB (RTL + RTBF)	Whole day	Everyday	475.7	80	380.6

Radio

Overview

- There are 389 stations in Belgium, 25 of which are in Brussels.
- Ninety-nine percent of all households have radios; the estimated number is 4,142,000. About 35% of automobiles have radios.
- The primary broadcasting languages are French and Flemish.
- Preferences are diverse.
- Commercial lengths available range from :05 to :60.

Ratings

Region	Adult Rating
North	16.0 GRP
South	6.3 GRP

Costs

- Cost changes over time are not comparable because of the arrival of many new stations.

Station	Average Cost	Average CPM	Peak Cost	Peak CPM
BRT1 (North)	392	4.88	1,339	6.84
BRT2 (South)	1,708	4.60	4,419	5.54
Studio Brussel	284	3.15	461	2.97
Radio Donna	246	4.09	417	3.95
RTBF1 (North)	259	7.88	922	7.67
RTBF2 (South)	329	6.44	1,652	7.19
Radio 21	146	2.50	476	3.26

Cable

- Belgium has a very high cable penetration level. Different cable companies cover a specific region with similar programming.
- 85% of households receive cable, many languages are available. Ranked in order of prominence, the top five cable channels are: VTM, BRTN, RTL/TVi, RTBF, and TFI.

Cable Networks	HH Circulation (000)	Programming
TV1 (North and South)	Because of the high density	General entertainment
TV2 (North and South)	of cable distribution in	Cultural, sports
VTM	Belgium most of the	General, soaps, games
RTL/TVi	channels are received by	General, soaps, games
TF1	approximately 85% of the	
FRANCE 2	households. However, there	
FRANCE 3	are regional differences.	

Other cable networks are: NL1, NL2, NL 3, ARD, ZDF, WDR, BBC1, BBC2, ITV, Channel 4, TVE1, Local television (in development).

Satellite

- There is very low satellite dish penetration, largely because of the current popularity of cable. Thus, because of the lack of dishes, satellite channels are distributed via cable.
- The situation is very stable. New satellite channels appear but this is directly linked with cable acceptance.

Satellite Channel	Country of Origin	Language	Programming
TV 5	France	French	
Eurosport	UK	English/Dutch, French, German	Sports
Super Channel	UK/USA	English	Music/old movies
MTV	UK/USA	English	Music
CNN	UK/USA	English	News
RAI	Italy	Italian	Entertainment
TRT	Turkey	Turkish	
RTP	Portugal	Portugese	

Video Cassettes

Roughly 56% of TV households have video cassette recorders (VCRs). Video cassettes in Belgium do not carry commercials, and no change is expected in the near future. Audimeter measures VCR usage.

Cinema

Cinema Cost Changes Between Years

'88	'89	'90	'91	'92
	4%	0%	5%	7%

- Most of the cinemas in Belgium offer commercial time. Lengths available are :20 to :90.
- There are about 588,000 weekly admissions for a universe of over 345 screens.
- The cost of a cinema campaign depends on the period in which you want to be present. During the month of October (which is the best but also the most expensive one), a cinema campaign in the 5 urban centers (Antwerp, Brussels, Gent, Charleroi, Liege) on a total of 166 screens will cost approximately US$ 84,625 for a :30 commercial.

Newspapers

Newspaper Cost Changes Between Years

'88	'89	'90	'91	'92
4%	4%	7%	5%	

Newspaper	Market	Size	Circ. (000)	Avg. Daily Aud. (000)	1 page B&W Cost (US)	Accept Color?
North						
Belang van Limburg	N/A	B	982	316.1	9,899	YES
Gazet van Antwerpen /Gazet van Mechelen	N/A	B	152	508.8	16,907	YES
Het Laatste Nieuws/ Nieuwe Gazet	N/A	B	248	722.1	16,639	YES
De Morgen	N/A	B	256	143.6	5,614	YES
De Standaardgroep/ Nieuwsblad/Gentenaar	N/A	B	323	1,076.9	28,284	YES
Het Volk/Nieuwe Gids	N/A	B	146	521.3	11,535	YES
South						
Le Soir	N/A	B	145	510.1	19,156	YES
La Meuse/Lanterne	N/A	B	103	353.7	14,785	YES
La Nouvelle Gazette, La Province, Le Peuple, Journal & Independence	N/A	B	84	346.5	12,985	YES
La Derniere Heure	N/A	B	70	264.9	10,671	YES
La Libre Belgique/ Gazette de Liege	N/A	B	68	190.4	11,571	YES
Vers L'venir: L'Avenir du Luxembourg, Courier de l'Escaut, Le Jour, Le Rappel	N/A	B	123	430.1	12,760	YES
Nord Eclair: l'Echo du Centre, Le Journal de Mons, Le Journal du Borinage	N/A	B	43	113.3	9,912	YES
L'Echo	N/A	B	21	49.6	7,457	YES
Financieel Ekonomische Tijd	N/A	B	32	103.2	8,871	YES
Grenz Echo	N/A	T	14	12.6	2,325	YES
La Wallonie	N/A	B	48	44.0	7,071	YES
De Lloyd/Le Lloyd	N/A	T	N/A	10.4	5,654	YES

Source: CIM, 1991

Magazines

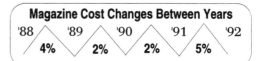

Magazine Cost Changes Between Years

'88	'89	'90	'91	'92
4%	2%	2%	5%	

Magazine	Type	Frequency	Circ. (000)	Audited?	Avg. Issue Aud. (000)	1 page 4/C Cost (US$)
Dag Allemaal/ Zondagsnieuws	N/A	W	380	N/A	1,017	226,600
Kerk en Leven	N/A	N/A	N/A	N/A	988	N/A
Humo	N/A	W	237	N/A	940	260,000
Libelle NL-Rijk der Vrouw	N/A	W	198	N/A	708	270,900
Flair NL	N/A	W	152	N/A	686	233,400
TV Story	N/A	W	172	N/A	672	153,700
Telestar	N/A	W	230	N/A	623	150,000
Knack magazine	N/A	W	127	N/A	611	182,850
De Bond	N/A	N/A	N/A	N/A	564	N/A

Continued on the following page

Magazines, continued

Magazine	Type	Frequency	Circ. (000)	Audited?	Avg. Issue Aud. (000)	1 page 4/C Cost (US$)
Telemoustique	N/A	N/A	N/A	N/A	547	N/A
TV Ekspres	N/A	W	45	N/A	515	86,000
Touring Secours	N/A	N/A	N/A	N/A	492	N/A
Vrouw en Wereld	N/A	N/A	N/A	N/A	454	N/A
Panorama De Post	N/A	W	73	N/A	453	92,200
Touring Wegenhulp	N/A	N/A	N/A	N/A	447	N/A
TEVE - blad	N/A	W	226	N/A	408	81,000
Femmes d'Aujourd'hui-Libelle	N/A	W	116	N/A	382	167,500
Knack WE	N/A	W	127	N/A	527	182,850
Blik	N/A	N/A	N/A	N/A	377	N/A
VIF/EXP.-Pourquoi P.	N/A	N/A	92	N/A	377	182,350
Elga	N/A	M	76	N/A	370	160,000
Joepie	N/A	W	115	N/A	367	110,000
Touring Club Magazine	N/A	N/A	N/A	N/A	355	N/A
Le Soir Illustre	N/A	N/A	N/A	N/A	335	N/A
Telepro	N/A	N/A	N/A	N/A	331	N/A
Paris Match	N/A	N/A	N/A	N/A	307	N/A
Selection	N/A	N/A	N/A	N/A	278	N/A
Het Beste	N/A	N/A	N/A	N/A	272	N/A
Sport '90 Nationale	N/A	N/A	N/A	N/A	264	N/A
Moniteur De L'Auto	N/A	N/A	N/A	N/A	261	N/A
Flair FR	N/A	N/A	N/A	N/A	256	N/A
Feeling	N/A	F	45	N/A	248	99,100
Gael	N/A	M	42	N/A	240	150,000
We L'Express/PP	N/A	N/A	N/A	N/A	233	N/A
Notre Temps/Onze Tijd	N/A	M	100	N/A	223	`125,400
Top Sante	N/A	M	80	N/A	217	95,000
Eigen Aard	N/A	N/A	N/A	N/A	216	N/A
Trends Nationaal	N/A	N/A	N/A	N/A	211	N/A
Cuisine Kreat. Keuken	N/A	N/A	N/A	N/A	205	N/A
Foot/Voetbal Nat.	N/A	N/A	N/A	N/A	202	N/A
Ouders Van Nu/ Kinderen	N/A	N/A	N/A	N/A	195	N/A
KWIK	N/A	N/A	N/A	N/A	187	N/A
BOS	N/A	N/A	N/A	N/A	185	N/A
Art et Decoration	N/A	N/A	N/A	N/A	172	N/A
Park Mail Nat.	N/A	N/A	N/A	N/A	165	N/A
Cosmopolitan NL	N/A	N/A	N/A	N/A	157	N/A
Autogids	N/A	F	25	N/A	143	61,000
New Belg. Business + Industries	N/A	M	27	N/A	135	106,400
L'Instant	N/A	M	110	N/A	122	182,350
Teletip	N/A	N/A	N/A	N/A	120	N/A
Jours de France/ Madame Figaro	N/A	W	19	N/A	109	120,000
Robbedoes/Spirou	N/A	N/A	N/A	N/A	108	N/A
L'Hebdo au Feminin	N/A	W	50	N/A	106	96,400
TV Gids	N/A	N/A	N/A	N/A	102	N/A
7 Extra	N/A	W	30	N/A	101	60,000
Parents	N/A	N/A	N/A	N/A	97	N/A
Avenue	N/A	N/A	N/A	N/A	90	N/A
IK GA Bouwen/Je Vais Construire	N/A	N/A	N/A	N/A	90	N/A
D. Gesondheid	N/A	N/A	N/A	N/A	89	N/A
Modes et Travaux	N/A	N/A	N/A	N/A	88	N/A
Elle FR	N/A	N/A	N/A	N/A	85	N/A
Vie Feminine	N/A	N/A	N/A	N/A	84	N/A
Intermediair National	N/A	N/A	N/A	N/A	79	N/A
Cosmopolitan FR	N/A	M	N/A	N/A	76	67,200
Play Tennis Nat.	N/A	M	30	N/A	74	89,250

Continued on following page

Magazines, continued

Magazine	Type	Frequency	Circ. (000)	Audited?	Avg. Issue Aud. (000)	1 page 4/C Cost (US$)
Premiere	N/A	N/A	N/A	N/A	73	N/A
D. Sante	N/A	N/A	N/A	N/A	69	N/A
Proto's Auto en Sport	N/A	N/A	N/A	N/A	68	N/A
L'Evenement	N/A	N/A	N/A	N/A	65	N/A
Landbouwleven	N/A	N/A	N/A	N/A	62	N/A
Levend Land	N/A	N/A	N/A	N/A	59	N/A
Tu Batis-Je Renove- Bouwen	N/A	N/A	N/A	N/A	57	N/A
Auto Hebdo	N/A	N/A	N/A	N/A	50	N/A

Source: CIM, 1991

Outdoor/Transit

Billboard	**Transit**
Sites available 100,000	**Boards available** 3,129
Lead Time to reserve ....2-10 months	
Exposure 79%	**Exposure** ....N/A
Costs	**Costs**
Average, 1 billboard/month ....US$ 546 From '89-'92, costs have risen by 3%, 10%, 8% and 7% per year, respectively.	**Average, 1 board/month:** ....US$ 121
Sizes	**Sizes**
Not available	0.6 m x 2.75 m, 1.2 m x 1.6 m, 0.68 m x 8m

Direct Marketing

Increasing usage by advertisers; however, direct marketing is not currently tracked in Belgium.

List Broker	*Telemarketing Companies*
M.C.L.S.	CEBECO - Mediaphone
Willy Braillard	Teleperformance
Ketels	*Direct Marketing Association*
Marie Jottrand	Association du Marketing Direct / Vlaamse Direct Marketing Vereniging

Non-Traditional Media

There is increasing interest from advertisers in this category, particularly in the area of interactive media.

Research Sources

Medium covered	Research company	Information provided
All media	CIM - Survey	Audience
	Sobemap	Socio-demographic descriptions
	Place du Champ de Mars 5	Correlation media and product consumption
	1050 Brussels	
TV	Audimeter	Audience/15 min./day
	Sobemap	

Advertising Regulations

By Product

Beverages/Alcohol

Alcohol advertising is generally accepted. However, public channel RTBF and Tele 21 in the south of the country limit advertising for alcoholic beverages which contain more than 10% alcohol. In general, advertising cannot be aimed at children.

Cigarettes

Audio - Visual: forbidden but allowed for sponsoring activities and events
Magazines: 1/1 page
Dailies: 1/2 page
Outdoor: 16 M2
Diversification usually allows for a more impactful and less restricted presence.

Pharmaceuticals/Drugs

Restricted to medical press. It is forbidden to guarantee a healing effect.

Advertising To Children

No product or service which might result in no drugs, no cigarettes, no alcohol.

Czech Republic
(& Slovakia)

Area	127,870 km^2
Population (1992)	15,725,680
Population growth rate (1992)	0.2%
GDP	US$ 108.9 billion
GDP/per capita	US$ 6,900
Real growth rate (1991)	15%
Capital	Prague

Population Breakdown

By Sex		By Age Group	
Male	48.6%	Children, 0-14	21%
Female	51.4%	Teens, 15-29	22%
		Adults, 30-59	39%
		Seniors, 60+	18%

Source: Statistic Yearbook CSFR, 1992

Media Inflation vs. General Inflation, 1989-1992

— Media Inflation   – – – General Inflation

Number of Households	3,700,000

Ownership of household durables
- Car 58%
- Phone 37%
- Washers 66%
  (purchasing power equivalent)

GNP distribution by industry
- Agriculture 8%
- Industry 49%
- Services 43%

Exchange rates (US$ to local currency)
- 1991 .... 0.03389
- 1992 .... 0.03623

Source (Household Durables): Aisa Media, Prague, Czech Republic, 1992

National Holidays

Holiday	1993 Date
New Year's Day	January 1
Easter Monday	April 12
Cyril & Metod	July 5
Jan Hus	July 6
Constitution Day	October 28
Christmas	December 25--26

School Holidays

Holiday	1993 Date
Spring Holdiay	One week in Feb. - March (varies by region)
Summer Holiday	July 1 - August 31
Winter Holiday	Dec. 24 - Jan 2

Major Influences and Trends

Overall

In January, 1993, the former Czechoslovakia split into the Czech and Slovak Republics. Consequently, there have been a number of political and economic implications, all of which have affected the media scene. Overall, in the Czech Republic, we have seen a rapid growth in privatization of industry, growing interest in foreign investment, and an increase in inflation of 18-20%. In Slovakia all changes are much slower.

Tax System

One problematic, recent change is the introduction of the V.A.T. tax system (23% tax in Czech Republic and 25% in Slovakia). In the Czech Republic, the Association of the Advertising Agencies has negotiated the cancellation of this tax for foreign clients.

The effects on the media scene, particularly in the last six months, have been dramatic. The former main federal channel (F1) which had 100% coverage of the CSFR, is now broadcasting under two separate signals (CTI in the Czech Republic and STV 1 in Slovakia). CT 1 continues to attract the largest audiences but still has the most restrictions on advertising, with only 1% of airtime available for commercial sale.

In addition, the first private national TV license was awarded to C.E.T. 21 (the Central European Television For 21st Century) for CT2, the 2nd largest former state channel in the Czech Republic. Full privatization will take effect in January, 1994 with a change in programming format and an increase in available commercial airtime.

The first private regional TV channel 'Premiera' just started broadcasting in Prague and central Czech Republic.

Although IP is still responsible for all national television sales, the Czech and Slovak channels are now purchased separately. Despite the overall reduction in available commercial airtime since the split, prices have increased by 50%. An additional price increase of Czech commercial airtime has already been announced for September 1993 (+15%).

Media 2 Print

There have been no dramatic changes in the print scene. There is no single strong federal publication, so each republic's national dailies just continue to attract similarly sized audiences. International papers and magazines have been launching Czech/Slovak editions. We can already see the improvement in printing/graphic techniques and in the future, we hope to see better distribution, audited circulation, more flexibility for advertisers in terms of creative ad space, and less lead time required for booking and pricing.

Radio

In the past year there has been a significant growth in the number of private radio stations of all formats (about 15 FM stations in Prague at the moment). This has led to a growth in airtime available for sale to advertisers and a number of innovative marketing/promotional opportunities. We expect to see continued growth in the use of radio in the next year.

Outdoor

Outdoor continues to grow at a rapid rate as more western companies enter the scene and/or form joint partnerships with the Czech companies. There has been a proliferation in the types of outdoor advertising available (i.e. transit, bus shelters, billboards, etc.) and despite the steady increases in price (15-20%), the medium continues to grow. We suspect that outdoor will continue to be a viable advertising alternative until television becomes less restrictive.

Advertising Expenditure

Generally, advertising expenditures have been increasing very quickly. KCS 2,421M was spent in 1991, KCS 4,007M in 1992, and KCS 5,108M is predicted for 1993.

The continuous decrease in TV's share of spending (drastic price increases have been prohibitive for all but the biggest ad spenders) is expected to stop in 1994 following the launch of CET 21. This should lead to a plateau in print as well. No major changes are expected in either outdoor or radio.

Source: ARA (Association of the Adv. Agencies), Prague, Czech Republic, 1993

Spending Analysis

National advertising spending by medium
based on appropriate year's exchange rate

	1991 *US$ MM*	*1992* *US$ MM*
TV	36.1	51.8
Radio	13.8	22.2
Print	21.8	44.4
Oudoor	9.3	25.1
Magazine	N/A	N/A
Direct Response	N/A	N/A
Outdoor	N/A	N/A
Other	1.1	1.5
Total	**82.1**	**145.0**

Source: ARA, Prague, Czech Republic, 1993.

Media Buying

- Media buying is mostly done by the advertising agencies.
- Some ad agencies provide other agencies or clients with buying services.
- Media buying agencies exist in Czech Republic.

Buying Services with 1992 Billings

Buying Service	*Market share*	*US$ MM*
Carat	20%	327
Media Drection	11%	115
Omnimedia	10%	166

Top Advertisers (1992 spending)

By Company

Parent Company	*Products*	*Category*	*US$ MM*
P&G	Ariel, Vizir, Blend & Med, Vidal Sassoon, Fairly Ultra	detergents, dentifrice, hair care	5.2
Henkel	Persil, Perwol, Pril, Fa	detergents, house- hold cleaners, toil, soaps, deodorants	2.6
Unilever	Algida	ice creams	1.9
CS Aerolinie	CSA	airlines	1.4
Master Foods	Snickers, Mars, Whiskas, Pedigree Pal	chocolates, animal food	1.1
W.S		direct mail	1.0
Home Shopping		direct mail	1.0
SKODA	Skoda	cars	0.9
Sazka	Sazka	lottery	0.9
Wrigley	Wrigley, Spearmint, Orbit	chewing gum	0.8

By Product

Product Category	*Advertiser*	*US$ MM*
Detergents	P&G	1.1
Dentifrice	P&G	0.9
Cars	Skoda	0.9
Household Cleaners	P&G	0.8

Product Category	*Advertiser*	*US$ MM*
Chewing Gums	Wrigley	0.8
Coffee	Tchio	0.6
Soft Drinks	HBSW	0.5
Butter/Margarine	Unilever	0.5

Source (Top Advertiser Data): Amer Worldwide Research, Czech Republic, 1992.

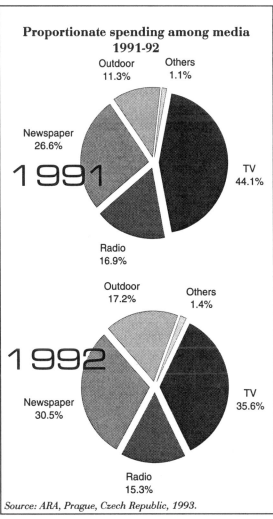

Proportionate spending among media 1991-92

1991
- Outdoor 11.3%
- Others 1.1%
- Newspaper 26.6%
- TV 44.1%
- Radio 16.9%

1992
- Outdoor 17.2%
- Others 1.4%
- Newspaper 30.5%
- TV 35.6%
- Radio 15.3%

Source: ARA, Prague, Czech Republic, 1993.

Television

Overview

After the split of CSFR into the Czech Republic and Slovakia there are:

CT 1   Czech Republic   nationwide

CT 2   Czech Republic   nationwide   (private— will be **CET 21** starting February 4, 1994.)

CT 3   Czech Republic   covers 60% of the country.

Premiera   Regional (Prague) private.

  (Slovakia has two nationwide channels: STV 1, and STV 2)

- In 1992, television household penetration was 98% for the Czech Republic.
- Historically, television household penetration was 95% or higher for the Czech Republic and Slovakia.
  (Sources: Aisa Media 1992, Prague, Czech Republic)
- Commercials (sponsorship) are aired only in specific time blocks at the beginnings and ends of programs.
- Lengths available range from :10 to :60. Sixty percent of all commercials are :30.
- There are no options for local/regional buys.

Opportunities

Network	Number of Stations	Ownership	Station Profile	Commercial Minutes/Day	Coverage	Broadcast Hours (Sign-On/Off)
CT 1	1	State	General	10	CR	06:00-01:00
CT 2	1	State	General	60	CR	08:00-00:30
CT3	1	State	General	14	60% of CR	24 hrs
Premiera	1	Private	Entertainment	80	Prague	10:00-24:00

Costs/ Languages

LANGUAGES	Programming		Commercials
Primary Language	Czech	90%	Czech
Secondary Language	English	8%	none

Television Cost Changes Between Years

'88	'89	'90	'91	'92
N/A%	**N/A%**	**50%**	**150%**	

Audiences/CPM's

Average Cost, Audience, and CPMs by Daypart
(Top 2 stations; :30, national audience, Target=14+)

Hours	Morning 9:00-12:00	Daytime 12:00-16:00	Prime Time 19:15-21:00	Late Night 22:15-23:00	Weekend	Children
Station: CT1						
US$	N/A	N/A	5,166	N/A	Same as week	N/A
Avg. Aud. (000)	N/A	N/A	2,545	N/A		
CPM	N/A	N/A	2.03	N/A		
Station: CT2						
US$	305	365	1,260	900	Same as week	N/A
Avg. Aud. (000)	123	192	830	561		
CPM	2.48	1.90	1.52	1.60		

Source (Avg. Aud.): Aisa Media, Prague, Czech Republic, 1993.

Audiences/Ratings by Daypart (Station = CT1)

	Hours	Household				Adult		
		Universe (000)	Hut Levels	Household Rating	Impressions (000)	Universe (000)	Adult Rating	Impressions (000)
Primetime	19:15-21:00	N/A	N/A	N/A	N/A	2,545	34	865

Source: Aisa Media, Prague, Czech Republic, 1993.

Children's Advertising

There is children's programming on CT2 from 18:00-19:00, but no audience data is available. Both adult and children's programming accept advertising targeted at children.

Radio

Overview

- There are 40 radio stations in the Czech Republic, 39 of them commercial. 15 are in Prague.
- Approximately 98% of all households have radios; the estimated number is 3,626,000. *(Source: Aisa Media, Prague, Czech Republic, 1992.)*
- The primary broadcasting language is Czech. English is also used.
- Prime time is 07:00–09:00 and 16:00-18:00.
- No premiums are required for regional stations. The most popular program types are News and Music.
- Commercial lengths range from :05 to :60.

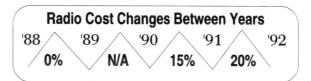

Costs

Daypart Costs/CPMs
(Target=14+)

Daypart	Local Time	Cost :30 US$	Audience (000)	CPM (US$)
Prime Time	07:00-09:00	170	48	3.54
Daytime	12:00-16:00	120	35	3.42
Late Night	22:00-24:00	27	5	5.40

Source: Aisa Media, Prague, Czech Republic, 1993.

Cable

- Cable started in 1992 and still has very limited penetration. A rapid increase is expected, although there is still no research. The system is privately owned
- About 5% of households have cable reception.

Satellite

- There are a growing number of households with satellite dishes. Current research only tracks penetration, which is currently at 14%. *(Source: Aisa Media, Prague, Czech Republic, 1993.)*
- There are currently 20 channels. No restrictions currently exist for satellite imported programs and commercials.

Satellite Channels Available

Satellite Channel	Country of Origin	Language	Programming
CNN	U.S.A.	English	News
Eurosport	U.K.	German, English	Sport
Lifestyle	U.K.	English	Homemakers
MTV	U.K.	English	Music
PRO 7	Germany	German	Movies
I PLUS	Germany	German	Entertainment, News
RTL Plus	Luxembourg	German	Entertainment, News
Sat 1	Germany	German	Entertainment, News
Screensport	U.K.	German, English	Sports
Sky Movies	U.K.	English	Entertainment, Sports
Sky One	U.K	English	Entertainment

Video Cassettes

- About 23.6% of TV-owning households have video cassette recorders (VCRs). However, pre-recorded cassettes do not carry advertising.

Cinema

- There are 2,000 cinemas in the Czech Republic.
- Potential reach over 4 weeks (assuming a schedule of 350 theaters) is 2,700,000.
- Commercials are available in lengths from :30 up.

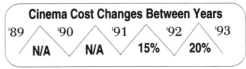

- The average cost of a four-week cinema schedule for a :60 commercial at 26 selected cinemas is US$ 200–$300 per cinema.

Newspapers

There are 5 major national daily papers which accept advertising. Combined circulation is 1.8 million readers. Literacy rate in English is 5-8%.

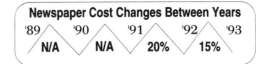

Newspaper	Market	Size	Circ. (000)	Avg. Daily Aud. (000)	1 page B&W (US$)	Accept Color?
Blesk	National	420/297	500	2,338	4,655	Yes
Mladafronta Dnes	National	420/297	400	1,571	4,760	Sat. Issue
Rude'pravo	National	420/297	350	962	3,310	Sat. Issue
Zemedelske	National	420/297	250	703	2,415	No
Hospodarske noviny	National	430/298	140	530	4,480	No

Magazines

The total number of consumer magazines in the Czech Republic is not available. There are 3 major trade and technical magazines and 50 smaller titles.

Magazine	Type	Frequency	Circ. (000)	Audited?	Avg. Issue Aud. (000)	1 page 4/C Cost (US$)
Blesk Mag	Tabloid	Weekly	600	No	2,276	3,415
Vlasta	Women's	Weekly	500	No	2,188	3,375
Tydenik TV	TV Guide	Weekly	450	No	1,759	3,945*
Kvety	G.L.	Weekly	270	No	1,151	5,575
Reflex	G.L.	Weekly	200	No	1,097	3,000
Mlady svet	G.L.	Weekly	180	No	1,299	2,810
Playboy	G.L.	Monthly	50	No	490	3,986

*B&W

Outdoor/Transit

Billboard

Sites available 15,000
Costs, 1 billboard/month............... US$ 200

Billboard Cost Changes Between Years				
'89	'90	'91	'92	'93
N/A	N/A	25%	20%	

Direct Marketing

There are limited direct marketing services in the Czech Republic. List brokers and telemarketing companies do not exist.

Non-Traditional Media

There is currently no use of non-traditional media in the Czech Republic.

Research Sources

Medium Covered	Research Company	Information Provided
TV, Print,Radio	GFK Praha Ujezed 40 Praha 1	Ratings
TV, Print,Radio	AISA Media Prubezna 81 Praha 10	Ratings
TV, Print	Amer World RESEARCH Ltd. Uvalska 25/A Praha 10	Monitoring

Television Research Currently Available

Research Method	Frequency
Interviews - address random	AISA - monthly, quarterly; GFK - twice a year
People Meters	To be developed

Advertising Regulations

By Product

Beverages/Alcohol
No alcohol advertising allowed on TV or radio
Cigarettes
No TV or radio advertising allowed
Pharmaceuticals/Drugs
Only over the counter products, with some restrictions

By Medium

Television
No alcohol or cigarettes; there are restrictions for pharmaceutical products

Denmark

Area	43,070 km²
Population (1992)	5,163,955
Population growth rate (1992)	0.2%
GDP	US$ 91.1 billion
GDP/per capita	US$ 17,700
Real growth rate (1991)	2.0%
Capital	Copenhagen

Population Breakdown

By Sex		*By Age Group*	
Male	49%	Children	11%
Female	51%	Teens	13%
		Adults	76%

Source: Statistisk Arbog, 1993

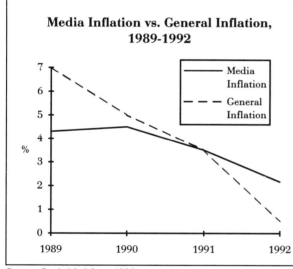

Media Inflation vs. General Inflation, 1989-1992

Source: Statistisk Arbog, 1993

Number of Households	2,330,000

Ownership of household durables

Car	72%
Phone	99%
Washers	78%

(purchasing power equivalent)

GNP distribution by industry

Agriculture	5%
Industry	25%
Services	70%

Exchange rates (US$ to local currency)

1991	0.1600
1992	0.1538

National Holidays

Holiday	*1993 Date*
New Year's	January 1
Easter	March 28, 29
Various National Holidays	April 1, 26; May 9, 20; June 5
Christmas	December 25, 26

School Holidays

Holiday	*1993 Date*
Winter	February (1 week)
Easter	March/April (1 week)
Pentacost	May/June (45 days)
Summer	June/July (7 weeks)
Autumn	October (1 week)
Christmas	December (1/2 week)

Major Influences and Trends

There are primarily fixed rate card prices for all major media categories.

The local TV station - Kanal Denmark Network - and the satellite station TV3 have increased the share of total TV spending, but the TV market is still dominated by the national commercial station, TV2. Both local and satellite channels have increased share by upgrading programming. This has resulted in decreased advertising spending in other major media vehicles, most notably daily newspapers.

Spending Analysis

National advertising spending by medium
based on appropriate year's exchange rate

	1989 US$ MM	1990 US$ MM	1991 US$ MM	1992 US$ MM
TV	128.9	163.6	184.5	243.9
Cinema	--	--	8.8	8.6
Newspaper	660.7	665.4	335.6	338.8
Magazine	225.6	229.0	166.9	133.4
Direct Response	499.5	483.4	--	--
Outdoor	19.0	19.5	16.7	17.3
Other	287.6	295.7	--	
Total	**1,821.4**	**1,856.6**	**712.5**	**742.0**

*The figures from 1989 and 1990 are taken from two different institutes, and 1991 information excludes "Direct Response" and "Other"
Source: AGB Gallup Markedsanalyse, 1993

Media Buying

Media buying is completely dominated by media buying companies like Promedia (Grey), PMI, The Media Partnership and Carat (see table for details).

Buying Services with 1992 Billings

Buying Service	Members	US$ MM
Promedia	Grey Communication	104
The Media Partnership		91
Media Centraler	Ass. of Newspapers	82
Carat Denmark	AEGIS	68
Pool Media Int.	Interpublic	48
Mediapartmenr	Mediacentraler	16

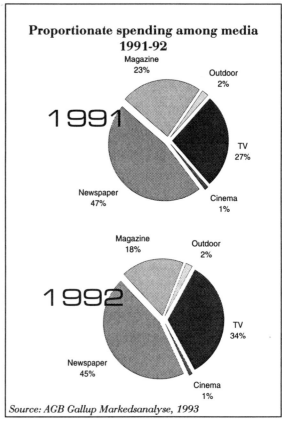

Proportionate spending among media 1991-92

1991
Magazine 23%
Outdoor 2%
TV 27%
Cinema 1%
Newspaper 47%

1992
Magazine 18%
Outdoor 2%
TV 34%
Cinema 1%
Newspaper 45%

Source: AGB Gallup Markedsanalyse, 1993

Daily newspapers - and other media vehicles - struggle due to the loss of market share to television. Therefore, these rate card prices are not expected to increase in 1993-94.

Buying services account for 66% of the market's total expenditures.

Top Advertisers (1992 spending)

By Parent Company

Parent Company	Product Categories	US$ MM
FDB Brugsen	Supermarket (food)	15.2
Dansk Supermarked	Supermarket (food)	13.0
Procter & Gamble	Detergents, Personal Hygiene	12.1
Colgate Palmolive	Personal Hygiene	9.9
Lever	Personal Hygiene	8.5
Magasin	Supermarket (non-food)	6.5
Capilex L'oreal	Haircare	5.3
Kellogg's	Cereal	5.2
CPC Food	Food	4.9
SAS	Airlines	4.4

By Product

Product	Advertisers	US$ MM
Computer and electronics	N/A	72.8
Food	N/A	61.1
Personal Hygiene	N/A	57.7
Transport/cars etc.	N/A	42.3
Houses/Residence	N/A	41.7
Banks, Insurance, etc.	N/A	30.8
Clothing	N/A	30.8
Beverages	N/A	29.9
Travel and Transportation	N/A	29.1
Cleaning articles, etc.	N/A	24.1

Television

Overview

- As mentioned, both local and satellite channels are increasing audience share due to upgraded programming. The national commercial station, TV2, dominates the market.
- Penetration is now estimated at 100%, or 2,330,000 households.

	TV HH Penetration				Adult Reach	
1989	*1990*	*1991*	*1992*	at 250 GRPs	80%
96%	96%	96%	100%	at 500 GRPs	85%
				at 1,000 GRPs	90%

Opportunities

Network	Number of Stations	Ownership	Station Profile	Commercial Minutes/Day	Coverage	Broadcast Hours (Sign-On/Off)
Kanal 2	N/A	N/A	General	60	31%	10
Kanal Danmark	N/A	N/A	General	48	55%	8
TV2	N/A	State-owned	General	72	100%	12
TV3	N/A	TV3/Denmark	General	108	43%	18

Costs/Languages

LANGUAGES	Programming		Commercials
Primary Language	Danish	70%	Danish
Secondary Language	English	25%	English

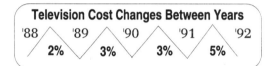

Television Cost Changes Between Years

'88	'89	'90	'91	'92
	2%	3%	3%	5%

Audiences/CPM's

Average Cost, Audience, and CPMs by Daypart
(top 3 stations; :30, urban areas, Target=Adults, April 1993)

Hours	Morning	Daytime	Prime Time	Late Night	Weekend	Children
Station: TV2						
US$	5,061.00*	N/A	983.80	492.60	492.60	N/A
Avg. Aud. (000)	370.0*	N/A	52.7	35.7	35.7	N/A
CPM	13.68*	N/A	18.67	13.79	13.80	N/A
Station: TV3						
US$	704.00	N/A	277.10	576.00	576.00	N/A
Avg. Aud. (000)	32.0	N/A	115.0	77.0	77.0	N/A
CPM	22.00	N/A	2.41	7.48	7.48	N/A
Station: Kanal Denmark						
US$	880.00	N/A	218.50	N/A	N/A	N/A
Avg. Aud. (000)	60.0	N/A	33.0	N/A	N/A	N/A
CPM	14.67	N/A	6.62	N/A	N/A	N/A

Morning/Daytime average

Audiences/Ratings by Daypart (Target=12+)

Daypart	Hours	Household				Adult		
		Universe (000)	Hut Levels	Household Rating	Impressions (000)	Universe (000)	Adult Rating	Impressions (000)
Morning								
Daytime	18:30-19:00	2,237	85	29	649	4,464	19	848
Primetime	19:00-19:30	2,237	85	33	738	4,464	23	1,027
Late Night		2,237	85	12	268	4,464	9	402
Weekend								
Children's								

Scheduling/Regional

- Commercial lengths available include all :05 increments between :10 and :60. The most commonly used length is :30.
- Commercials are aired throughout the day, and in time blocks between programs. Most airing is at beginning and ends of programs. Satellite programs include commercials within programming.
- Almost a quarter (20%) of all TV advertising is bought on a regional basis. Regional costs are approximately 28% that of national costs.

Network	Station	Regions/Hours
TV3	TV3	Larger Cities Monday-Friday (17:45 - 01:25) Saturday-Sunday (08:00 - 10:00, 18:00 - 01:00)
KD (Kanel Dk)	TV Alborg Arhus Kahalen TVO, Fynboen Kanal 2 TV Trekanten	Arhus Alborg Odense Copenhagen Fredericia, Vejle, Kolding
TV Neastved	TV Neastved TV Vestspellanel TV Svenelborg	Neastved Svendborg

Children's Advertising

There is currently no law against placing commercials targeted at children, either between or during children or adult programming. Therefore all programs/blocks are available.

CHILDREN'S PROGRAMMING			Kids'		
Station	Hours	Days	Universe (000)	Ratings	Impressions(000)
TV2	N/A	N/A	833	20	167
TV3	N/A	N/A	391	14	55
KD	N/A	N/A	431	3	13

Source (All Television): AGB Gallup Markedsanalyse

Radio

Overview

- There are 43 local radio stations in Denmark. It is only possible to air national radio spots through this national network of 43 local stations.
- Approximately 98% of all households have radios; the estimated number is 2,283,000. About 56% of automobiles have radios.
- The primary broadcasting language is Danish. English is also used.

- Commercial lengths available range from :10 upwards.
- The most popular program type is Music (Pop/Rock) and News.
- Prime Time is 06:00-18:00.

Costs

Overall Averages

For a :30 radio commercial   Average CPM: US$ 4.80

Ratings

Daypart	Adluit Rating	Adult (000)
06:00-18:00	23	900

Daypart Costs/CPM's

Daypart	Local Time	Cost :30 US$	Audience (000)	CPM (US$)
Prime Time Daytime Late Night	06:00-18:00	4,797	1,100	4.36

Cable

- In Denmark, cable is used mostly for receiving satellite signals. Penetration is 40%.
- There is access mostly to European stations, but some overseas stations are available too, making a total of 32 stations.
- In a few years cable will have digital compression, increasing the number of channels available by a factor of eight. As in the USA, KTAs will introduce a cable-borne signal at the end of 1993.
- English is the primary language on cable; however, German is also used.
- Commercial rates are not available.

Top Cable Channels	Cost	Rating	Commercial Min/Hr
TV3	N/A	45	N/A
Discovery/66	N/A	25	N/A
Kanal Danmark	N/A	N/A	N/A
Kanal 2	N/A	N/A	N/A

Other cable networks

Cable Networks	HH Circulation (000)	Programming
KTAS	275	TV1000, Sverige 1, Lokal
JTAS	165	TV, Sverige 2, Danmark 1
FTS	35	TV2, NRD3, Kanalen, ARD 1, Super Channel Morge 1, ZDF 2, World Net/TV5, BBC, Eurosport, DDR1, DDR2, Filmnet, Scansat/TV3, CNN, MTV, Discovery, Childrens Channel, Nordic, KTAS service, Kanaler, RTL+, Kabel 1 Net, Sat1, Drei Sat, Pro 7, Tele 5

Source (Cable): KTAS

Satellite

- Ninety-three percent of satellite channels are received by cable. There are 7 private dishes in Denmark, including Astra, Intelset and Eotelset.
- Satellite programs and commercials are subject to the rules of the EEC regulations.
- Cururently, penetration is 43%. Within the next five years, 1, 501,900 households are targeted for cable reception.

Channel	Country of Origin	Language	Channel	Country of Origin	Language
CNN	USA	American	Filmnet	Denmark	Danish
TV1000	Scandinavia	Scandinavian	Scansat/TV3	Denmark	Danish
Sverige 1	Sweden	Swedish	CHA	USA	English
Lokal TV's	Denmark	Danish	MTV	U.K.	English
Sverige 2	Sweden	Swedish	Discovery	U.K.	English
Danmark 1	Denmark	Danish	Childrens Channel	U.K.	English
TV2	Denmark	Danish	Nordic	Scandinavia	Scandinavian
NRD3	Germany	German	KTAS	Denmark	Danish
Kanalen ARDI	Germany	German	Servicekanelen	N/A	N/A
Super Channel	U.K.	English	RTL+	Germany	German
Norge 1	Norway	Norwegian	Atel Aet	Denmark	Danish
ZDF 2	Germany	German	Sat 1	Germany	German
Worldnet/TV5	France	French	Drei Sat	Germany	German
BBC	U.K.	English	Pro 7	Germany	German
Eurosport	U.K.	English	Tele 5	Germany	German
DDR 1	Germany	German			
DDR 2	Germany	German			

Source (Satellite): KTAS

Video Cassettes

About 60% of TV households have video cassette recorders. However, tapes rarely carry commercials. The cost is US$ 11,193 per tape. VCR advertising is expected to grow, despite decline in the rental of pre-recorded tapes. DRB - index/Aim and Nielsen/TV-meter -Intomart are the services which measures VCR usage.

Cinema

- There are at least 265 cinemas in Denmark; virtually all offer commercial time.
- Potential reach over 4 weeks is 721,000 viewers.
- Lengths available range from :10 to :60.
- The average cost of a 4-week cinema schedule covering 265 cinemas, is DKK 354,000. Rates have been increasing at no more than 3% annually for two years.

Source (Cinema): Dansk Biograf Reklame

Newspapers

There are 32 national daily papers with a combined circulation of 3,036,381 in Denmark.

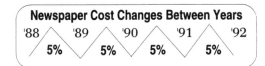

Magazines

There are 48 national consumer magazines published in Denmark.

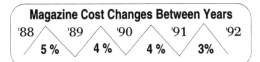

Magazine	Type	Frequency	Circ. (000)	Audited?	Avg. Issue Aud. (000)	1 page 4/C Cost (US$)
Alt for Damene	Women's	Weekly	92	Yes	431	5,808
Bilen	Cars	Monthly	52	Yes	325	3,230
Billed Eladet	Entertain.	Weekly	213	Yes	773	6,595
Bo Bedre	Arrangement of Houses	Monthly	105	Yes	747	6,845
Borsens	Business	2/Monthly	13	Yes	198	4,459
Bac Hyt	Yachting	Monthly	24	Yes	172	3,243
Det Bedste	"Reader's Digest"	Monthly	113	Yes	334	2,555
Fami ie Journalen	Family	Weekly	321	Yes	1,120	8,855
Femina	Women's	Weekly	86	Yes	281	3,833
Herdes Verden	Women's	Weekly	76	Yes	273	3,084
Hjemnet	Family	Weekly	279	Yes	910	6,277
Illustret Videnskab	Science	Monthly	108	Yes	576	4,845
IV	Women's	Monthly	56	Yes	193	3,649
Motor	Cars	22/Year	203	Yes	448	4,974
Samverse	Consumers	10/Year	N/A	Yes	1,210	10,170
Se & Hor	Entertain..	Weekly	311	Yes	1,013	8,034
Sordag	Women's	Weekly	113	Yes	502	3,917
Ude & Hjemme	Family	Weekly	233	Yes	782	5,624

Source : AGB Galup Markedsanalyse, DRB-Index

Outdoor/Transit

Billboard	**Transit**
Sites available .... 16,000 Lead Time to reserve .... 6–12 months Exposure 47%	Boards available.......................... 42,000
Costs	**Costs**

Average, 1 billboard/month
    3.33 m x 2.3 m............................. US$ 48,813
 	
Cost changes
Costs have been rising at about 5% per year.
	Average, 1 board/month:
	    Bus .... US$ 17,380
	    Twin .... US$ 28,112
	Cost changes
	Costs have been rising at about 5% per year.

Sizes	
1.20 m x 1.75 m, 980 m x 2.40 m, 1.00 m x 1.50 m, 0.30 m x 0.48 m, 0.60 m x 0.50 m, 0.36 m x 3.18 m, 0.19 m x 1.58	

Product/Category Restrictions for Outdoor Advertising
Neither pornography nor political advertising is allowed on outdoor or transit media.

Non-Traditional Media

Currently being used are the following:

Go-Cards (Postcards distributed free to restaurants, bars, cafes, etc.)	US$ 0.16 /postcard/2 weeks
Total Bus (buses painted with advertising)	US$ 15,970/1 yr (capital)
Total Trains (trains painted with advertising)	US$ 17,269/1 yr (capital)

Television Research Currently Available

Research Method	*Frequency*
TV Meter	Daily

Advertising Regulations

By Product

Beverages/Alcohol
Regarding alcohol advertising, special attention should be paid to the choice of advertising medium as well as the content and form of the advertisement.

The advertisement should not - directly or indirectly - look or have the appearance of being aggressive or provocative in its style, content, or visuals.

Advertising is not allowed:
1. In schools, in public institutions (i.e. public offices), in hospitals, in institutes of higher education and at places of work, or with appeal to the employees of the place of work (places of sales and public houses are excepted, however).
2. On the pages of the daily papers including Sunday and weekend issues, local or district papers - especially those which deal with sports and youth. Generally the size of the advertisement must not exceed one full page.
3. In publications, including sports magazines, particularly those read by children and young people.

In addition, advertisements for an alcohol product should not:
- Use persons under 30 years as a role model.
- Appeal especially to young age groups.
- Use or picture persons - real or fictional - mentioned by name or recognizable - who are idols for children because of their achievements, occupations, etc.
- Use or show persons such as doctors, dentists, nurses, midwives or people who work within the hospital, sanitary or social sectors.
- Illustrate or mention success as a result of alcohol consumption.

- Use product names of alcoholic beverages on sportswear.
- Use pictures of bottles or any other kind of containers for alcoholic products as advertisements for distinct brand names on sportswear.
- Illustrate or mention that alcohol is wholesome and without risk.
- Invite alcoholic drinking in connection with car driving or at places of work.
- Present or refer to alcohol as a remedy for relieving or solving social and psychological problems.
- Emphasize a high alcohol content..
- Encourage or illustrate alcoholic consumption at work.
- Describe abstinence or temperance related to alcohol negatively.

Cigarettes:
Consumer oriented marketing of cigarettes, fine cut tobacco, cigarette paper and/or cigarette tubes may only take place:
- With the help of display boards, posters, illuminated signs, dummy packs, counter displays, floor displays, change mats, ashtrays, matches, lighters, pocket protectors:
  -In and at tobacco outlets which have no eating or drinking rooms or have these separated from the selling place.
  -On delivery trucks when they are used for normal transport of goods.
- As advertising in:
  -Dailies, including Sunday or weekend issues - however, not in the pages which are particularly meant for children.
  -Periodicals and papers are allowed with the following exceptions:
      Postal packets with no addresses listed.
      Publications targeted at kids, including sport and athletic magazines.
- The advertising size may not exceed 2,000mm column and/or not be larger than one full page.
- Advertising may take place in trade magazines and price-lists to the wholesale and retail trade.
- Marketing may not under any circumstances:
  -Use pictures or drawings of children (i.e. persons who give the impression of being under the age of 30).
  -Use or reproduce persons, real or imaginary, who through their performances or occupations (i.e. entertainment, politics, music, athletics, etc.) appear as idols for children.
  -Use or reproduce persons who are or appear as doctors, dentists, nurses, midwives or who work in hospitals or health services.
  -Use or reproduce persons who appear with names.
  -Appear especially directed to children.
  -Illustrate or refer to any connection between cigarette smoking and success in sports.
  -Illustrate or refer to smoking as being healthy or without risk.
  -In copy or illustration appear aggressive or provoking.

Pharmaceuticals/Drugs
It is prohibited to advertise pharmaceuticals/drugs which may not be peddled or distributed in Denmark in: movies, television, radio, outdoor (posters or traffic), public rooms except pharmacies.

Advertising To Children
Information on children's advertising is found in International Chamber of Commerce and Marketing (ICC) Distribution and Advertising.

By Medium

Television
No beer, alcohol, tobacco, drugs, or political ads are permitted.

Cable
No beer, alcohol, tobacco, drugs, or political ads are permitted.

France

Area	547,030 km²
Population (1992)	57,287,258
Population growth rate (1992)	0.5%
GDP	US$ 1,033.7 billion
GDP/per capita	US$ 18,300
Real growth rate (1991)	1.4%
Capital	Paris

Population Breakdown

By Sex		*By Age Group*		*By Socio-Economic Status*	
Male	51.3%	Children, 0-19	27%	A	10%
Female	48.7%	Teens, 20-39	30%	B	27%
		Adults, 40-59	23%	C	28%
		Seniors, 60-74	13%	D	35%
		Seniors, 75+	7%		

Source: INSEE

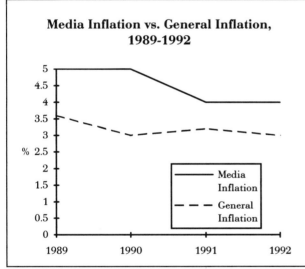

Media Inflation vs. General Inflation, 1989-1992

Media Inflation / General Inflation

Number of Households	21,520,700

Ownership of household durables

Car	75%
Phone	94%
Washers	84%

(purchasing power equivalent)

GNP distribution by industry

Agriculture	2.8%
Industry	38.1%
Services	59.1%

Exchange rates (US$ to local currency)

1991	0.19594
1992	0.18179

Source: (Media Flation) Leo Burnett estimate; (Inflation Rate): INSEE   Source:INSEE

National Holidays

Holiday	*1993 Date*
New Year's	January 1
Easter Monday	April 19
Labor Day	May 1
Memorial Day	May 8
Ascension	May 28
Monday of Whit Sunday	June 8
Bastille Day	July 14
Assumption	August 15
All saints Day	November 1
Armistice WWI	November 11
Christmas	December 25

School Holidays

Holiday	*1993 Date*
All Saints	Oct. 21 - Nov. 2
Christmas	Dec. 21 - Jan. 3
February	Feb. 11 - March 14
Spring	April 9 - May 9
Summer	July 5 - Sept. 6

Major Influences and Trends

The French Media scene has been hit with two powerful blows in 1993: the Sapin Law (which regulates all discounts and which outlaws all rate card deals) and recession. The minor media players are expected to face severe financial problems as advertisers seek to consolidate their investments in a limited number of vehicles in order to secure favorable discounts.

Print is still the major media vehicle, accounting for 45% of total ad spending. Magazines register stable circulations; nonetheless, their revenue has recently dropped, due to the recession and the Evin Law (which bans all tobacco advertising). Furthermore, their position is fragile because of lack of concentration. Dailies are revamping their sales methods and significantly decreasing their rate cards for 4C ads. The distribution system (NMPP) inherited from WWII, should be entirely restructured in order to cut costs. A '2 level system' should be put in place soon, with kiosks distributing all major magazines. (To date, all magazines are available in all 36,000 kiosks).

Conversely, TV ad spending is on the rise, while TV inflation is back (+5%). The state-owned channels (F2 and F3) have been very successfully restructured and their audience share now equals that of TF1 (40%). Radio is maintaining its share of media (12%); a new survey demonstrates its rapid coverage build-up. The major poster contractors, who have suffered severely from recession, are putting forth a new revolutionary survey which provides the audiences of various networks. Furthermore, sale houses are setting up an increasing number of more multimedia deals and sale house packages.

Spending Analysis

National advertising spending by medium
based on appropriate year's exchange rate

	1989 US$ MM	1990 US$ MM	1991 US$ MM	1992 US$ MM
TV	1,969	2,551	2,915	2,955
Cinema	70	90	72	71
Radio	897	1,155	1,265	1,285
Newspaper	3,886	1,603	1,655	1,630
Magazine	3,886	3,385	3,459	3,302
Direct Response	-	-	-	-
Outdoor	983	1,346	1,523	1,432
Total	**11,691**	**10,130**	**10,889**	**11,691**

Source: SECODIP

Media Buying

The French media buying scene has been hit by a new law called the Sapin Law, which took effect on March 31, 1993. This law was designed to establish transparency in buying procedures.

- Ad agencies have become mandatory: advertisers now receive the media invoices directly from the media owners. The agency commission 'principle' no longer exists as no money should come directly from the media owner to the ad agency.
- The rate cards and sales conditions should also be identical for all advertisers (when they buy under the same circumstances).

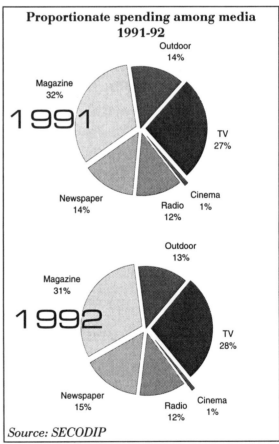

Thus, the law has entailed very complex rate cards which include all kinds of rebates.

Buying Services with 1992 Billings

Buying Service	Parent Company	US$ MM
Carat	Aegis	2,200
Publi Media Service	Publicis/FCB/ Interpublic	1,600
Euro Media	Euro RSCG	1,500
TMP	Grey/DDB/BDDP/O &M/CLM- BBDO/JWT	900
Zenith Club Media	Saatchi/BSB	400

Source: Leo Burnett estimate

The rebates, negotiations and kick-backs related to buyer volumes before the Sapin Law had led to a concentration of media buying in 4 or 5 buying shops. The 'after Sapin' discounts which are 'advertiser-related' give a chance to smaller buyers and advertising agencies as advertisers are beginning to withdraw their media buying from buying consortia to give to affiliates or internal media departments of ad agencies.

Top Advertisers (1992 spending)

By Company

Parent Company	Product Categories	US$ MM
Nestle France SA	Food	220.5
Renault Automobiles	Transportation	216.7
PSA - Peugeot Automobiles	Transportation	139.4
Procter and Gamble	Detergent	133.6
PSA - Citroen	Transportation	118.2
Ford France	Transportation	89.7
Fiat Automobiles	Transportation	81.2
Henkel France	Detergent	72.9
VAG - VW	Transportation	72.7
Lever Bols	Detergent	70.8

Source: SECODIP

By Product

Product Category	Adsvertisers	US$ MM
Transportation	Renault Automobiles	216.7
Detergent	Procter and Gamble	133.6
Leisure	La Francaise des jeux	64.8
Retail	Carrefour Magasins	55.9
Transportation	Renault Automobiles	216.7
Detergent	Procter and Gamble	133.6
Leisure	La Francaise des jeux	64.8
Retail	Carrefour Magasins	55.9
Publishing/ Information	Europe 1 Communication	37.7
Clothing	Kiabi Confection	35.8
Drinks	Evian S.A.E.M.E.	29.6
Food	Nestle France SA	220.5

Source: SECODIP

Television

Overview

Despite recession, TV is still the fastest growing medium (+9% versus year ago in terms of gross adspend). The scene is still dominated by TF1 which accounts for over 40% of the audience and over 54% of total adspending. The state-owned channels, F2 and F3, have been successfully revamped by H. Bourges, who was largely responsible for the successful privatization of TF1. The two stations now work as a team. Their programs are complementary and more upmarket and qualitative than those of TF1. They also combine their efforts to sell their ad space. This synergy between the two channels has resulted in a significant increase in audience share (now equal to that of TF1) and gross ad spending (+27% vs. 1991). Clutter has increased, due to La 5's folding, which has given rise to inflation. Canal +, the private pay TV station, remains by far the most profitable channel (3.7 million subscriptions). M6 has consolidated its position as the youngest audience profile station (13% share of audience). Both channels are strongly investing in cable TV. Arte, the Franco-German cultural station (no advertising), is still very marginal (2% share of audience).

Channel	Funds	Share of Audience*	Share of Adspend**	Programming
TFI	Advertising	41%	54%	Generalist
F2	License + Advertising	24%	17%	Generalist
F3	License + Advertising	15%	8%	Generalist
C+	Subscriptions (90%), Advertising	5%	3%	Movies and Sports
Arte	License	2%		Cultural
M6	Advertising	13%	13%	Series and Movies

*Source: Mediametrie June 93-Adults 15+
**Source: SECODIP 1992

	TV HH Penetration			Adult Reach	
1989	*1990*	*1991*	*1992*	at 250 GRPs	75%
96.6%	96.6%	96.6%	97%	at 500 GRPs	80%
20,2500	20,600	20,600	20,900	at 1,000 GRPs	90%

Sources (TV Household Penetration): CESP/Mediametrie; (Adult Reach): Mediametrie/200 tested planss

Opportunities

Networks	Number of Stations	Ownership	Station Profile	Commercial Minutes/Hr	Coverage	Broadcast Hours (Sign-On/Off)
TF1	1	25% Bouygues 37% Private Shareholdera	General	12	100%	00:00-24:00
France 2	1	State	General	12	100%	00:00-24:00
France 3	1	State	General	12	100%	07:00-01:00
Canal +	1	Havas 25% C. Generale des Eux 214 Private Shareholders 21%	Movies/sports	2 min/break	65%	06:00-04:00
M6	1	C.L.T. (25%) Lyonnaise des Eaux (10%)	Movies U.S. Series	12	75%	00:00-24:00

Costs

Prime Time TV Costs for :30 in US$			
1989	*1990*	*1991*	*1992*
35,411	37,197	32,798	33,782

Source: Leo Burnett estimate

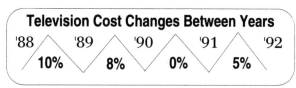

Television Cost Changes Between Years

'88	'89	'90	'91	'92
10%	8%	0%	5%	

Source: Leo Burnett estimate

Audiences/CPM's

Average Cost, Audience, and CPMs by Daypart (Top three stations; Target=Adults 15+)

Hours	Morning 08:00-13:00	Daytime 13:00-20:40	Prime Time 20:40-22:30	Late Night 22:30-03:59	Weekend 12:30-13:40	Children 16:30-17:30
Station: TFI						
US$	15,177	25,317	54,530	18,176	32,722	7,039
Avg. Aud. (000)	3,298	3,385	5,382	1,866	5,295	1,302
CPM	4.60	7.48	10.13	9.74	6.18	5.40
Station: FRANCE 2						
US$	6,180	10,874	29,450	3,272	7,246	1,225
Avg. Aud. (000)	1,432	2,040	3,298	911	1,996	1,042
CPM	4.31	5.33	8.93	3.59	3.63	1.18
Station: FRANCE 3						
US$	1,679	15,232	10,238	N/A	1,818	2,181
Avg. Aud. (000)	1,085	2,561	1,345	N/A	955	868
CPM	1.55	5.95	7.61	N/A	1.90	2.51

Source: Mediametrie, March, 1993

Audience/Ratings by Daypart (National TV, 6 GRPs, Target=Adults 15+, Children 4-14)

	Hours	Household				Adult		
		Universe (000)	Hut Levels	Household Rating	Impressions (000)	Universe (000)	Adult Rating	Impressions (000)
Morning	08:00-13:00	20,900	N/A	4.9	1,024	43,400	4.6	1,996
Daytime	13:01-20:40	20,900	N/A	7.9	1,651	43,400	5.5	2,387
Primetime	08:41-22:30	20,900	N/A	9.5	1,986	43,400	7.6	3,298
Late Night	22:31-03:59	20,900	N/A	4.5	941	43,400	3.9	1,693
Weekend	12:30-13:30	20,900	N/A	7.9	1,651	43,400	6.3	2,734
Children's	16:30-17:30	20,900	N/A	5.6	1,170	43,400	2.8	1,215

Source: Mediametrie, March, 1993

Scheduling/Regional/Languages

- The only language used for programming and commercials is French.
- The most common commercial length is :20. However, lengths from :03 to 2 minutes are available. *(Source: SECODIP)*
- Regional airing is available. Only 1% of all commercials are aired regionally, and the cost is about 130% of a national buy. *(Source: Leo Burnett estimate)*

- Commercials are aired throughout the day for all stations except CANAL + which airs commercials in non-crypted time blocks (12:30–13:30 and 18:30–20:30).
- Commercials are aired only at the beginning and end of programs on public channels, and within programs as well on private channels.

Network	Station	Region	Hours
FRANCE 3	FRANCE 3	12 regions	12:00-13:00; 19:00-20:00
RTL TV	RTL TV	Alsace/Lorraine + cable nationally Provence/Riviera	11:15-12:00; 16:00-12:00; 07:30-12:00

Children's Advertising

CHILDREN'S PROGRAMMING (Target=Kids 4-14)			Universe	Kids' Universe	Impressions
Station	Hours	Days	(000)	Ratings	(000)
TF1	08:00	Mon-Fri	8,050	9.1	732.5
TF1	17:20.	Mon-Fri	8,050	8.5	684.2
TF1	17:40	Sundays	8,050	6.8	547.4
FRANCE 2	18:15	Mon-Fri	8,050	5.5	442.7
FRANCE 3	08:50	Wednesday	8,050	8.2	660.1
M6	09:30	Saturday	8,050	2.5	201.2

Source: Mediametrie March 1993

Radio

Overview

- There are national networks in France, and 55 stations in Paris.
- Approximately 99% of all households have radios; the estimated number is 19,685,000. *(Source: Mediametrie Jan-June 1993)*
- The primary broadcasting language is French; however English broadcasts of the BBC (UK) are also received.
- Commercial lengths range from :05 to 1:30.
- There is no premium for using local FM stations instead of national networks. The most popular program types are music and light entertainment.

Ratings

Daypart	Hours	Adult Rating	Adult (000)
Morning	08:00-08:30	4.7	2,121
Noon	12:30-13:00	3.8	1,704
Early Evening	18:00-18:30	2.5	1,133

Source: Mediametrie Sept. - Dec. 1993/RTL April 1993

Costs

Radio Cost Changes Between Years

'88	'89	'90	'91	'92
8%	4%	5%	6%	

Source: Leo Burnett estimate

For a :30 radio commercial (RTL, April '93) — Average Cost: US$ 2,763 — Average CPM: US$ 2.70

Daypart Costs/CPMs

Daypart	Local Time	Cost :30 US$	Audience (000)	CPM (US$ MM)
Prime Time	07:00 -07:30	8,744	2,334	3.75
Daytime	11:00 - 14:00	3,818	1,835	2.08
Late Night	22:00 - 22:30	100	100	1.00

Source: Mediametrie, Sept.-Dec., 1992; RTL, April 1993

Cable

- After many years of slow growth, cable TV growth has finally taken off. Over 1,100,000 households have subscribed. This is partly due to the support of the government and the private channels (TF1 and M6). *(Source (Number of cable households): AVICA)*
- Penetration has grown from 1% in 1989 to about 5% in 1992. Within the next five years, 2,790,000 households are expected to receive cable broadcasts. *(Source: AVICA/Agence Cable)*
- There are 17 cable channels, all commercial, some privately and some publicly owned.
- French is the primary language used. English broadcasts are also received.
- No Cost, Rating or CPM data is available. The five top cable channels are: EUROSPORT, TV5 EUROPE, Canal J, MTV and RTL TV. *(Source: Sept. 1993 rate cards)*

Cable Networks	HH Circulation (000)	Programming
RTL TV	773	General
TMC	259	General
PARIS PREMIERE	305	General
CANAL J / JIMMY	805 / 610	Children/Series
PLANETE	668	Documentaries
CINE CINEMA	N/A	Movies
CINE CINEFIL	N/A	Movies
MTV EUROPE	798	Music
EUROSPORT	860	Sport
MCM	754	Music
SERIE CLUB	186	Series
CNN	476	News

Source: Cable Marketing April 1993

Satellite

Satellite dishes are still virtually non-existent in France; however, the latest interest of Canal + in satellite dishes is boosting the market. The dishes are getting cheaper and over the last few months 50,000 households have purchased antennas in order to subscribe to 'Canal Satellite' (in order to receive the channels broadcasted via cable). To date, satellite dishes in France total 109,000.

- Pentration is .5%. According to Canal Plus, 800,000 households will receive satellite transmissions within 5 years. *(Source: Leo Burnett estimate)*
- There are 20 channels. No restrictions are currently in effect regarding advertising on satellite broadcasts.

Satellite Channel	Country of Origin	Language	Programming
RTL+	Luxembourg	French	General
TV5 Europe	France	French	General
Eurosport France	France	French	Sports
MCM	France	French	Music
ZDF	Germany	German	General
3 SAT	Germany	German	General
BBC World Service	UK	English	General
Super Channel	UK	English	General
CNN	USA	English	News
Rai Uno	Italy	Italian	General
TVEI	Spain	Spanish	General
RTBF	Belgium	French	General

Continued on following page

Satellite Channel	Country of Origin	Language	Programming
Planete	France	French	Documentaries
Canal J	France	French	Children
Canal Jimmy	France	French	Series
MCM	France	French	Music
Cine/Cinefil	France	French	Movies
Cine Cinema	France	French	Movies

Video Cassettes

Roughly 46% of TV households have video cassette recorders (VCR's). However, video cassettes in France do not carry commercials. There is no service to measure usage, and the situation is not expected to change.

(*Source (Household penetration): CESP*)

Cinema

- There are 4,500 cinemas in France. An average 4 week buy at a cost of US$ 273,000 would show on 1,110 screens and reach 30–35% of the 15-34 year old group.

  Source: Mediametrie/Circuit A

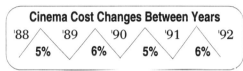

Source: Leo Burnett estimate

Newspapers

There are 11 national daily papers which accept advertising. Combined circulation is 2,100,000

Source (Circulation): OJD

Newspaper	Market	Size	Circ. (000)	Avg. Daily Aud. (000)	1 page B&W Cost (US$)	Accept Color?
France Soir*	National	B	197	880	23,700	Yes
L'Equipe*	National	B	307	1,413	31,100	Yes
L'Humanite*	National	T	63	341	10,700	Yes
La Croix*	National	T	93	256	7,300	Yes
Le Figaro*	National	B	378	1,387	66,400	Yes
Le Monde*	National	T	312	1,575	57,100	Yes
Le Parisien*	N/A	T	394	1,514	33,100	Yes
Liberation*	N/A	T	160	963	15,100	Yes
Le Parisien	National	370 x 260	394	N/A	33,100	Yes
Le Figaro	National	505 x 390	378	N/A	66,400	Yes
Le Monde	National	510 x 375	312	N/A	57,100	Yes
L'Gquipe	National	520 x 375	307	N/A	31,100	Yes
France Soir	National	470 x 340	197	N/A	23,700	Yes
Liberation	National	365 x 285	160	N/A	15,500	Yes
La Croix	National	425 x 295	93	N/A	7,300	Yes
Les Echos	Business	430 x 400	92	N/A	33,700	Yes
L'Humanite	Communist	320 x 258	63	N/A	10,700	Yes
Le Quotidien de Paris	National	390 x 290	46	N/A	10,900	Yes
La Tribune Des Fossrs	Business	400 x 280	42	N/A	13,300	Yes

*Source: CESP 1992; (Average daily readership): CESP 1992; (Circulation): OJD 1992; May 1993 rate cards/Tarif Media

Magazines

There are 320 national consumer magazines, and 210 trade and technical magazines published in France.

Source: Tarif Media

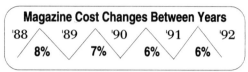

Magazine Cost Changes Between Years

Source: Leo Burnett estimate

Magazine	Type	Frequency	Circ. (000)	Audited?	Avg. Issue Aud. (000)	1 page 4/C (US$)
Ca M'interesse	General	Monthly	308*	N/A	2,799	13,271
Capital	Business	Monthly	225*	N/A	N/A	25,905
Equipe Magazine	Sports	Weekly	373*	N/A	1,964	15,452
Femme Actuelle	Women	Weekly	1,795*	N/A	7,925	41,720
Figaro Magazine	General	Weekly	656*	N/A	2,505	30,901
Ceo	Nature	Monthly	570*	N/A	4,626	32,195
L'FDJ	News	Weekly	216*	N/A	1,394	14,316
L'Expansion	Business	BiMonthly	152*	N/A	762	20,360
L'Express	News	Weekly	580*	N/A	2,535	26,905
Le Chasseur Francais	Nature	Monthly	586*	N/A	2,954	17,670
Madame Figaro	Women	Weekly	607*	N/A	2,236	27,269
Marie Claire	Women	Monthly	574*	N/A	3,589	29,814
Maxi	Women	Weekly	913*	N/A	4,375	16,725
Modes & Travaux	Women	Monthly	870*	N/A	3,871	26,178
Notre Temps	Senior	Monthly	1,056*	N/A	3,899	25,087
Paris Match	General	Monthly	1,072*	N/A	3,564	29,741
Prima	Women	Monthly	1,175*	N/A	4,565	32,813
Selection du Readers'Di	General	Monthly	1,072*	N/A	3,564	19,306
Tele 7 Jours	TV	Weekly	2,980*	N/A	10,711	49,992
Tele Porche	TV	Weekly	1,592*	N/A	6,273	21,778
Tele Star	TV	Weekly	2,002*	N/A	5,999	29,632
Tele Z	TV	Weekly	1,783*	N/A	6,631	21,951
Telelosisirs	TV	Weekly	1,419*	N/A	5,031	24,996
Telerama	TV	Weekly	565*	N/A	2,217	11,271
TV Magazine	TV	Weekly	410*	N/A	1,015	66,499
Voici	Women	Weekly	710*	N/A	3,295	32,813
Art Et Decoration	Home	2M	221	Yes	3,500	14,660
Advantages	Women's	MN	589	Yes	1,848	27,850
Biba	Women's	MN	192	Yes	976	13,452
Ca M'Interesse	General	MN	308	Yes	2,799	13,271
Capital	Business	MN	217	Yes	N/A	25,905
Cosmopolitan	Women's	MN	236	Yes	945	15,852
Dynasteurs Enjeux	General	MN	93	Yes	N/A	14,634
Elle	Women's	W	300	Yes	2,128	22,451
Elle Decoration	Home	2M	129	Yes	1,167	12,325
Enfants Magazine	Home	MN	171	Yes	1,388	13,216
Entreprise	Business	MN	66	Yes	1,052	13,489
Equipe Magazine	Men's	W	371	Yes	1,064	15,452
Expansion	Business	BM	141	N/A	N/A	N/A
Express	General	W	428	Yes	N/A	N/A
Femme Actuelle	Women's	W	1,633	Yes	7,925	41,720
Figaro Magazine	General	W	569	Yes	2,505	30,904
Francais	N/A	N/A	N/A	Yes	N/A	N/A
France Soir	General	D	197	N/A	N/A	N/A
Geo	General	MN	514	Yes	4,626	32,195
Glamour	Women's	MN	95	Yes	430	12,543
L'EDJ	N/A	N/A	N/A	Yes	N/A	N/A
L'Evenement Du	General	W	193	Yes	1,394	14,316
Jeudi	N/A	N/A	N/A	N/A	N/A	N/A
L'Expansion	Business	BM	140	Yes	762	20,380
L'Express	General	W	428	Yes	2,353	26,905
Le Chasseur	General	MN	579	Yes	2,904	17,670
Le Nouvel	Business	W	81	Yes	425	8,897

Continued on following page

Magazines, continued

Magazine	Type	Frequency	Circ. (000)	Audited?	Avg. Issue Aud. (000)	1 page 4/C (US$)
Le Point	General	W	270	Yes	1,394	17,125
Le Revenu Francais	Business	MN	183	Yes	759	16,288
Madame Figaro	Women's	W	568	Yes	2,236	27,269
Maison Marie Claire	Home	MN	165	Yes	1,198	11,742
Marie Claire	Women's	MN	469	Yes	3,589	29,814
Maxi	Women's	W	869	Yes	4,375	16,725
Modes Et Travauex	Women's	MN	815	Yes	3,871	20,178
Notre Temps	General	MN	1,048	Yes	3,899	25,087
Nouvel Observateur	General	W	378	Yes	2,108	20,042
Parents	Women's	MN	302	Yes	3,119	24,269
Paris Match	General	W	648	Yes	3,020	29,741
Premiere	General	MN	211	Yes	1,648	13,907
Prima	Women's	MN	1,128	Yes	4,565	32,813
Readers Digest	General	MN	967	Yes	N/A	N/A
Sante Magazine	Health	MN	473	Yes	4,593	24,724
Selection du	General	MN	967	Yes	3,564	19,308
Studio Magazine	General	MN	84	Yes	735	9,453
Tele 7 Jours	TV Guides	W	2,931	Yes	10,711	49,992
Tele Loisirs	TV Guides	W	1,115	Yes	5,031	24,995
Tele Magazine	TV Guides	W	410	Yes	1,015	6,236
Tele Poche	TV Guides	W	1,499	Yes	6,273	21,778
Tele Star	TV Guides	W	1,790	Yes	5,999	29,632
Tele Z	TV Guides	W	1,780	Yes	6,631	21,951
Telerama	TV Guides	W	561	Yes	2,217	11,271
Top Sante	Health	MN	588	Yes	3,633	22,087
TV Hebdo/Tele K7	TV Guides	W	2,183	No	N/A	42,721
TV Magazine	TV Guides	W	4,178	No	12,013	66,499
Voici	Women's	W	706	Yes	3,295	32,813
VSD	General	W	80	Yes	2,027	8,271

Source (Circulation): OJD France Paid in 1992 /Adult Audience: CESP 1992/ Rates: April 1993 rate cards/Tarif Media

Outdoor/Transit

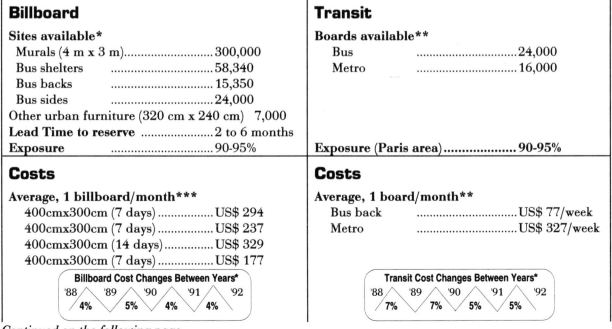

Billboard

Sites available*
- Murals (4 m x 3 m)............................300,000
- Bus shelters 58,340
- Bus backs 15,350
- Bus sides 24,000
- Other urban furniture (320 cm x 240 cm)   7,000
- **Lead Time to reserve** ....2 to 6 months
- **Exposure** 90-95%

Costs

Average, 1 billboard/month***
- 400cmx300cm (7 days)................US$ 294
- 400cmx300cm (7 days)................US$ 237
- 400cmx300cm (14 days)...............US$ 329
- 400cmx300cm (7 days)................US$ 177

Billboard Cost Changes Between Years*

'88	'89	'90	'91	'92
4%	5%	4%	4%	

Transit

Boards available**
- Bus 24,000
- Metro 16,000

Exposure (Paris area)...................90-95%

Costs

Average, 1 board/month**
- Bus back ....US$ 77/week
- Metro   ....US$ 327/week

Transit Cost Changes Between Years*

'88	'89	'90	'91	'92
7%	7%	5%	5%	

Continued on the following page

Outdoor/Transit, continued

Sizes
400 cm x 300 cm., 320 cm x 240 cm ,
120 cm x174 cm, 116 cm x 171 cm,
240 cm x 160 cm, 553 cm x 217 cm

Sizes		
Bus	99 cm x 83 cm	27 cm x 68 cm
Metro	400 cm x 300 cm	120 cm x 176 cm

*Source: Leo Burnett estimate
**Source: Metrobus/Decaux
***Source: Leo Burnett estimate based on April 1993 rate cards

The advertising of tobacco and pharmaceuticals is restricted on outdoor media.

Direct Marketing

The use of direct marketing is increasing in France.

Top Direct Mail List Brokers	*Major Telemarketing Companies*
AX info	Pronytes / Multicontacts
Basse	Teleaction
Cifea DMK	France Telecom
France Telecom / Teleadresses	Matrixx
La Redoute	Teleperformances

Direct Marketing Associations	
A.A.C.C.	Delegation Marketing Direct
SEVPCD	Syndicat des entreprises de ventes par correspondance
ACCE	Association des societes
SMT	Syndicat du Marketing Telephonique
SNCD	Syndicat National de la Communication Directe
UFMD	Union Francaise du Marketing Direct.
UDA	Union des Annonceurs Delegation Marketing Direct

Non-Traditional Media

The use of TV monitors, installed in doctor's waiting rooms and hospital rooms of young mothers, is expanding. TV monitors are expected in supermarkets '93 or '94 (no sound, pictures only). Ads on the back of telephone "credit cards" is growing quickly (high coverage and high OTS levels). Advertising on supermarket caddies is better structured and organized than in previous years.

Research Sources

The CESP is retiring from the survey front. It no longer conducts the surveys, but does monitor their validity (methodology, results, etc.). However, the CESP could still provide the advertising industry with its annual Media Time Survey which provides a breakdown of all activities, and media consumption per target, per daypart, etc. The APPM (Association for the Promotion of Magazines) is presently undertaking its own survey which should be more accurate than in previous years. Concerning TV, Nielsen no longer uses its people meters. Thus, Mediametrie currently has the monopoly in TV audience surveys. Mediametrie is also dynamic on the radio front. It has set up a panel which tracks coverage build-up. Single source survey projects are still under way. However, since Nielsen stopped its TV survey, data no longer comes from a single source (data are merged). SECODIP, an adtracking 'institution,' is also working on the 4th update of its SIMM survey, a database which includes product / brand consumption X media consumption. Survey institutes are concentrating: SECODIP (adspend tracking and single source) has been bought by SOFRES which has set up deals with IRI, which in turn has links with BURKE.

Media Covered	Research Company	Information Provided
All Media	CESP 32, Avenue Georges Mandel 75116 PARIS	Media Time Control of reliability of major media surveys
Print	APPM 7, rue Nicolas Houel 75005 PARIS	Consumer Magazines
	IPSOS 45, rue de Paradis 75010 PARIS	Dailies Upscale Magazines Business Magazines
Radio	Mediametrie 55/63, rue Anatole France 92532 Levallois- Perret Cedex	1/4 H Reach/Duplication
TV	Mediametrie 55/63, rue Anatole France 92532 Levallois-Perret Cedex	Programs/Breaks Audience Reach
	Affimetrie	Network audiences by target on 57 cities
	Avenir 114, rue Gallieni 92100 Boulogn,-Billancourt	
	Dauphin 15, rue de Milan 75009 PARIS	
	Giraudy 92, rue de Courcelles 75008 PARIS	

Television Research Currently Available
People meters, phone bells

Advertising Regulations

By Product

Beverages/Alcohol
Advertising of alcoholic beverages is banned on TV. It is restricted to radio in determined slots, postering and adult print.

Food/Restaurants
No restriction for food. Restaurants are not allowed to advertise if they are considered only retailers.

Cigarettes
Totally banned since January 1993.

Pharmaceuticals/Drug
Advertising for prescription drugs is allowed only in the medical press. There are no restrictions for non-prescriptive drugs.

Advertising To Children
The use of children's advertising is very restricted. It cannot be used to promote adult-related products or recommend product usage.

By Medium

Television

No tobacco; no retail; no edition (magazines, books); no movie releases; no alcohol.

Print

No tobacco advertising is allowed, and no additional alcohol ads can be placed in youth- targeted magazines.

Outdoor

No tobacco.

Cable

Same regulations as TV.

Germany

Area	356,910 km^2
Population (1992)	80,387,283
Population growth rate (1992)	0.5%
Capital	Berlin

Federal Republic of Germany	*Eastern Germany*
GDP.............. US$ 1,331.4 billion	*GDP..............US$ 1,235.8 billion*
GDP/per capita......... US$ 16,700	*GDP/per capita............ US$ 5,870*
Real growth rate (1991)........ 0.7%	*Real Growth Rate (1991)........30%*

Population Breakdown

By Sex	*By Age Group*	*By Socio-Economic Status*
Male 48%	*Children, 0-6............................ 7%*	*A, DM 2,000 .... 17.3%*
Female................................ 52%	*Teens, 7-14................................8%*	*B, DM 2,000-2,999.............24.9%*
	Adults, 15-21 ....8%	*C, DM 3,000-3,999..............21.9%*
	Adults, 22-4 ....30%	*D, DM 4,000+.....................35.9%*
	Adults, 41-60...........................26%	
	Adults, 61+.............................21%	

Source (By Age Group): Statistisches Bundestat: Statistisches Jahrbuch Fuer die Bundesrepublik Deutschland 1993, Bonn, 1992.

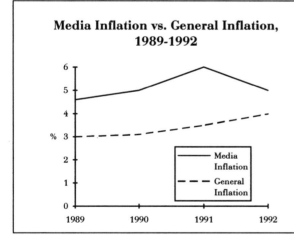

Media Inflation vs. General Inflation, 1989-1992

Number of Households	**34,827,000**

Ownership of household durables

Car................................80%
Phone...........................88%
Washers.......................90%
(purchasing power equivalent)

GNP distribution by industry

Agriculture..................... 2%
Industry 40%
Services 58%

Exchange rates (US$ to local currency)

1991 ....0.6589
1992 ....0.6116

Sources: (No. of Households): GWA, Zahlenund Dalen Fuer die Werbeplanung 1993, Frankfurt, 1992; (Household Durables): Arbeitsgemeinschaft Media Analyse, MA 1993, Frankfurt, 1993; (GNP by Industry): Statisches Jahrbuch fuer die Bundesrepublik Deutschland 1993, Bonn, 1992; (Exchange Rate): ZAW Webung in Deutschland 1993, Bonn, 1992.

National Holidays

Holiday	*1993 Date*
New Year's	January 1
Good Friday	April 1
Easter Monday	April 4
May Day	May 1
Pentecost	May 23
Re-Unification Day	October 3
Day of Receptance and Prayer	November 16
Christmas	December 25, 26

School Holidays

Holiday	*1993 Date*
Christmas	December 23 - January 14
Easter	March 28 - April 15
Pentecost	May 24 - May 25
Summer	July 18 - August 26
Fall	October 17 - October 28

Major Influences and Trends

Looking at 1992 media expenditures, TV shows the most dramatic increase among traditional media, with a revenue increase of 16.8%. The two state channels, ARD and ZDF, saw their share of TV revenue fall from 45% in 1991 to 30% in 1992. Among the private channels, RTL and SAT1 dominate.

The outlook for the next 12 months suggests that TV will continue to be the fastest growing medium in terms of spending.

In January 1993, *Focus*, a weekly news magazine advertised by Leo Burnett Frankfurt, entered the German market as the only competition to *Der Spiegel*. Published by BURDA, it has been very successful, with an average weekly circulation of 600,000 copies.

Spending Analysis

National advertising spending by medium
based on appropriate year's exchange rate

	1989 US$ MM	1990 US$ MM	1991 US$ MM	1992 US$ MM
TV	1,212.9	1,707.4	2,441.0	2,647.1
Cinema	108.9	132.6	148.6	147.3
Radio	419.7	548.8	624.8	600.0
Newspaper	4,463.5	5,198.8	6,391.8	6,415.7
Magazine	2,588.7	3,223.0	3,593.0	3,516.8
Direct Response	1,346.8	1,849.1	2,315.7	2,514.3
Outdoor	337.7	421.0	509.3	515.6
Other	1,660.4	2,061.3	2,516.5	2,639.2
Total	**12,138.6**	**15,142.0**	**18,540.7**	**18,996.0**

Source: ZAW Jahrbuch

Media Buying

Medicom, ranked no. 2, has shown the largest billing increase (23% from 1991 to 1992) New specialists arose (i.e., Media Partnership) and claimed a position among the top buyers. EQUMEDIA (Leo Burnett, Y&R, DMB & B) was recently founded and will soon claim a position among the top five agencies.

Source (Media Buying): Equmedia GmbH, Dominico Madilic, Frankfurt

Buying Services with 1992 Billings

Buying Service	Parent Company	US$ MM
HMS, Wiesbasden		904,800
Mediacom	Grey	797,300
Initiative Media	Lintas	508,000

Proportionate spending among media 1991-92

1991: Outdoor 3%, Other 14%, TV 13%, Radio 3%, Newspaper 35%, Magazine 19%, Direct Response 13%

1992: Outdoor 3%, Other 14%, TV 14%, Radio 3%, Newspaper 34%, Magazine 19%, Direct Response 13%

Source: ZAW Jahrbuch

Buying Service	Parent Company	US$ MM
Universal Com.	McCann/Lowe	487,000
Media Partnership	BBDO/INT/O&M	473,900
Optimedia	Publics/FCB	467,200

Source: Equmedia GmbH, Dominico Madilic, Frankfurt

Top Advertisers (1992 spending)

By Parent Company

Parent Company	Product Categories	US$ MM
Procter & Gamble	Detergents	211
C&A Brenninkmeyer	Retail	194
Springer Verlag	Mass-Media	123
Ferrero	Chocolate/Confectionary	120
Opel	Cars	117
Jacobs Suchard	Chocolate/Coffee	110
Union Dt. Lebensmittelwerke	Food	99
Karstadt	Retail	98
Volkswagen	Cars	97

Source (Top Advertisers-both charts): Schmidt & Pohlmann, Webeaufwendungen

By Product

Product	Advertisers	US$ MM
Cars	Opel	117
Retail	C&A Brenninkmeyer	194
Mass Media	Axel Springer	123
Chocolate/Confectionary	Ferrero	120
OTC Products	Richardson Wick	25
Banks/Savings & Loans	Sparkassen	53
Beer	Krombacher	15
Computer (HW + SW)	IBM	22
Corporation	Bundesministerium Wirtschaft	16
Cans + meat + fish	Langnese	58

Television

Overview

In the last few years, the German TV landscape has experienced a dynamic development. Commercial TV managed to become established, and has been highly successful in important sectors. The trend towards private TV remains positive, as proven by the launching of the newly founded specialized stations on TV, VOX, RTL2, and DSF. Among the private stations, RTL2, which launched in March '93, has the highest growth rate.

Regarding the market share, RTL has maintained its position just behind the public channels ARD and ADF.

Television household penetration is 99%. *(Source: gfK)*

Adult Reach *(Source: gfK)*

	ARD	*ZDF*	*RTL*	*SAT1*
at 250 GRPs	62%	62%	67%	62%
at 500 GRPs	85%	82%	67%	62%
at 1,000 GRPs	85%	82%	67%	62%

Opportunities

Network	Number of Stations	Ownership	Station Profile	Commercial Minutes/Day	Coverage	Broadcast Hours (Sign-On/Off)
ARD	16	Public	41% Juto, Education News 48% Entertainment 5% Sports	20**	100%	16
ZDF	1	Public	40% Juto, Education, News 46% Entertainment 3% Sports	20**	100%	16
RTL	1	Private	40% Juto, Education, News 53% Enterntainment 3% Sports	149	90%	24
SAT1	1	Private	23% Juto, Education, News 55% Enterntainment 2% Sports	142	89%	24
PROF1	1	Private	89% Entertainment 3% Juto, Education	67	80%	24
MTV	N/A	N/A	Only music	N/A	N/A	N/A
Eurosport	N/A	N/A	Only Sports	N/A	N/A	N/A
Super Channel	N/A	N/A	Mixed Programming	N/A	N/A	N/A
TV5	N/A	N/A	Mainly Culture, News	N/A	40%	24

** But not after 8:00pm and on Sundays and Bank Holidays
Source: MC&LB GmbH & Co., Frankfurt

Costs

		1989	*1990*	*1991*	*1992*
Prime Time TV Costs for :30	ARD	94,676	88,893	71,000	73,000
in US$	ZDF	68,967	70,958	70,033	74,535

Source: MC&LB GmbH & Co., Frankfurt

		1993	*1992*	*1991*	*1990*
Television Costs-Change Between	ZDF	10%	64%	2%	0%
Years	ARD	33%	20%	24%	24%
	SAT1	4%	2%	61%	32%
	RTL	10%	52%	1%	16%

Source: MC&LB GmbH & Co., Frankfurt

Audiences/CPM's

Average Cost, Audience, and CPM s by Daypart
(Top three stations, Target=Adults 14+)

Hours	Morning	Daytime	Prime Time	Late Night	Weekend	Children
Station: SAT 1						
US$	1,671	5,013	20,473	3,534	N/A	N/A
Avg. Aud. (000)	288	708	2,652	394	N/A	N/A
CPM	5.80	7.08	7.72	8.97	N/A	N/A
Station: RTL						
US$	2,310	9,038	26,588	2,129	N/A	N/A
Avg. Aud. (000)	414	1,430	2,890	415	N/A	NA
CPM	5.58	6.32	9.20	5.13	N/A	N/A
Station: ZDF						
US$	51,882	N/A	N/A	N/A	N/A	N/A
Avg. Aud. (000)	5057	N/A	N/A	N/A	N/A	N/A
CPM	10.26	N/A	N/A	N/A	N/A	N/A

Audience/Ratings by Daypart
(:30, Target=14+)

Daypart	Hours	Household				Adult		
		Universe (000)	Hut Levels	Household Rating	Impressions (000)	Universe (000)	Adult Rating	Impressions (000)
Morning	6:00-13:00	31,100	54	6	1,866	61,160	2.7	1,651
Primetime	17:00-23:00	31,100	98	53	16,483	61,160	35	21,406
Daytime	13:00-17:00	31,100	72	20	6,220	61,160	11	6,727
Late Night	23:00-6:00	31,100	71	7	2,177	61,160	4	2,446
Weekend	N/A	N/A	N/A	N/A	N/A	61,160	N/A	N/A
Children's	N/A	N/A	N/A	N/A	N/A	N/A	N/A	N/A

Scheduling/Regional/Languages

LANGUAGES	Programming		Commercials
Primary Language	German	100%	German
Secondary Language	English	13%	English

- The most popular length (38%) is :30. Lengths of :25, :40, :45, :60, :60+ are also possible.
- Commercials are aired throughout the day, at the beginnings and ends, and within programs.
- ARD & ZDF use 3-6 blocks of 5-10 mins. between 17:30 and 20:00. Private: Blocks of 1-10 mins are also possible.
- About 19% of all commercials are aired regionally. The cost is from 3% to 29% of the price of national time. (*Source: GWA Zahlen und Daten Fuer die Were planung 1993, Frankfurt, 1992.*)

Source (Scheduling/Regional/Languages): MC&LB GmbH & Co., Frankfurt

Network	Station	Region	Hours
ARD	NDR	ACN I	18:00-20:00
	RB	part/ACN 1	18:00-20:00
	WDR	ACN II	18:00-20:00
	HRI+III	ACN IIIa	18:00-20:00
	SR	part/ACN IIIb	18:00-20:00
	SWF/SDR	ACN IIIb and part of IIIa	18:00-20:00
	BR	ACN IV	18:00-20:00
	SFB	ACN V	18:00-20:00
	NOR	ACN VI	18:00-20:00
	MOR	ACN VII	18:00-20:00

Children's Advertising

Advertising may be directed to children in adult or children's programming. Advertising directed to children or with children should not cause any conflicts with children's interests and should not make use of inexperience.

CHILDREN'S PROGRAMMING			Kids'		
Station	Hours	Days	Universe (000)	Ratings	Impressions (000)
RTL	12h	Sat	6,180	3	185
	6h	Sun	6,180	N/A	N/A
SAT.1	5h	Sat	6,180	2	124
	7h	Sun	6,180	N/A	N/A
Pro 7	3h	Sat	6,180	1	62
	3h	Sun	6,180	N/A	N/A
	3h	Mon-Fri	6,180	N/A	N/A

Source: SPK

Radio

Overview

- There are 188 radio stations in Germany, of which 160 are commercial, and 9 are in Berlin.
- Approximately 98% of all households have radios; the estimated number is 34,103,000. About 75% of automobiles have radios. *(Source: Arbeitsgemeinschaft Media Analyse, MA 1993, Frankfurt, 1993.)*
- The primary broadcasting language is German.
- Commercial lengths available range from :15 up.
- The most popular program types are Pop Music and News.
- No premiums are required. The most popular program types are News and Music.

- Prime Time is 06:00-09:00, with a rating of 29, for 18,150,000 adults.

Costs

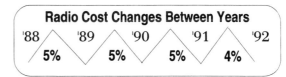

Radio Cost Changes Between Years
'88 — 5% — '89 — 5% — '90 — 5% — '91 — 4% — '92

Daypart Costs/CPMs (Target=Adults 14+)

Daypart	Local Time	Cost :30 US$	Audience (000)	CPM (US$)
Prime Time	06:00-09:00/h	1,766	780	2.26
Daytime	09:00-18:00/h	1,110	580	1.91
Late Night	no national coverage, only few local stations			

Cable

- Currently 14 million households are connected via cable; thus penetration is 46%. 22 million households are targeted to acquire cable in the next five years. *(Source: Telcom/Deutsche Bundespost)*
- The cable system is publicly owned by Telekom. The top five channels are ZDF, ARD, RTL, SAT-1, and Pro7.
- There appears to be a recent trend towards satellite television due to high cable subscription fees.
- German is the primary language on cable; however, English is also used.
- Commercial rates are not available.

Cable Networks	HH Circ. (000)	Programming	Cable Networks	HH Circ. (000)	Programming
SAT1	27,210	Family, Mix*	DSF	18,430	Cultural, Mix*
RTL	27,440	Family, Mix*	3SAT	18,500	Cultural, Mix*
PRO7	20,150	Family, Mix*	Kabelkanal	10,230	Family, Mix*
MTV	17,010	Music	RTL2	11,550	Family, Mix*
Super Channel	10,870	News, Mix*	VOX	16,930	Cultural, Mix*
Eurosport	18,210	Sports	Premiere	15,640	Cinema Films

* Mix: news, entertainment, shows, movies, children's programming
Source: IPA Plus, Frankfurt

Satellite

- The dish market is still booming in Germany. This is due to: a) the relatively high monthly fee of cable networks, and b) fewer opportunities in rural areas to subscribe to cable networks.
- Because of the launch of ASTRA 1c satellite, more and more channels have arisen. At the end of 1993, 18 German language channels will be transmitted via ASTRA Satellite system.
- Because of the technological development of data compression, an increasing number of channels will be launched via satellite.
- Satellite penetration is 32%. No special restrictions apply to satellite-imported programs or commercials.

Source (Satellite): MC & LB GmbH & Co. , Frankfurt/SFK

Satellite Channels Available

Channel	Country of Origin	Language	Programming
SAT1	Germany	German	Entertainment, Culture, News
WDR3	Germany	German	Entertainment, Culture, News
BR3	Germany	German	Entertainment, Culture, News
APN-TV	USA	English	Entertainment, News,
Teleclub	Switzerland	German	Movies
RAI UNO	Italy	Italian	Entertainment, Culture, News
RTL	Luxembourg	German	Entertainment, News
Film Net	Holland	English/Dutch	Movies
3SAT	Germany	German	Entertainment, Culture, News
TV5	France	French	Entertainment, Culture
World Net	USA	English	News
Sky Channel	UK	English	Entertainment, Sports
NRK	Norway	Norwegian	Entertainment, Culture
SVT1	Sweden	Swedish	Entertainment, Culture
SVT2	Sweden	Swedish	Entertainment, Culture
New World Channel	Norway	Various	Religion
Premiere	UK	English	Movies
Children's	UK	English	Children's Programming
Arts	UK	English	Culture
Lifestyle	UK	English	Homemakers
Screen Sport/Sport Channel	UK	German/English/Dutch	Sports
CNN	USA	English	News
MTV Europe	UK	English	Music
BBC 1/2	UK	English	Entertainment, News
MG	France	French	Music, Entertainment, News
LaCinq	France	French	Entertainment, Movies, News
Kanal	France	French	Children's Programming
One World Channel	Scandinavia	English	Information, Culture
Eurosport	UK	German/English/ Dutch	Sports

Source: Kabel und Satellit

Video Cassettes

About 50% of TV households have video cassette recorders (VCRs). However, in Germany, tapes do not carry commercials. G+Y Meter is the service which measures VCR usage.

Source: Arbeitgemeinschaft Media Analyse, MA 1993, Frankfurt, 1993

Cinema

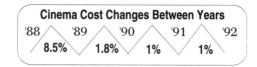

Cinema Cost Changes Between Years				
'88	'89	'90	'91	'92
8.5%	1.8%	1%	1%	

- There are 1,563 cinemas in Germany, 98% of which offer commercial time. *(Source (Percentages): ZAW, Werbungen Deutschland 1993, Bonn, 1992.)*
- Potential reach over 4 weeks is 12%.
- Minimum length is :45.
- The average cost of a 4-week cinema schedule is DM 1,190,900 (US$ 728,356). *(Source: MSA, Richard Reschke, Frankfurt.)*

Newspapers

There are 6 national daily papers which accept advertising. Combined circulation is 5,695,000.

Source: Arbeitgemeinschaft Media Analyse, MA 1993, Frankfurt, 1993.

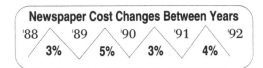

Newspaper Cost Changes Between Years

'88	'89	'90	'91	'92
	3%	5%	3%	4%

Source: ZAW, Werbung in Deutschland, 1993, Bonn, 1992.

Newspaper	Market	Size	Circ. (000)	Avg. Daily Aud. (000)	1 page B&W Cost (US$)	Accept Color?
FAZ	National	Broadsheet	417	970	26,715	Yes
Suddeutsche Zeitung	National	Broadsheet	400	1,090	36,262	Yes
Die Welt	National	Broadsheet	221	620	22,476	Yes
Frankfurter Rundschau	National	Broadsheet	192	620	19,209	Yes
Handelsblatt	National	Broadsheet	145	550	21,959	Yes
Bild	National	Broadsheet	4,320	11,930	241,806	Yes

Source: Arbeitgemeinschaft Media Analyse, MA 1993, Frankfurt, 1993.

Magazines

There are 170 national consumer magazines and 503 trade and technical magazines published in the Netherlands.

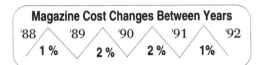

Magazine Cost Changes Between Years

'88	'89	'90	'91	'92
	1%	2%	2%	1%

Source: ZAW, Werbung in Deutschland, 1993, Bonn, 1992

Magazine	Type	Frequency	Circ. (000)	Audited?	Avg. Issue Aud. (000)	1 page 4/C Cost (US$)
Buote	Gen. Interest	Weekly	910	Yes	4,240	37,714
Stern	Gen. Interest	Weekly	1,352	Yes	7,650	59,007
Bild am Sonntag	Gen. Interest	Weekly	2,695	Yes	9,700	64,598
Das Beste	Gen. Interest	Monthly	1,612	Yes	4,390	28,561
Auf einen Blick	TV Guide	Weekly	3,103	Yes	5,530	48,095
Horzu	TV Guide	Weekly	3,009	Yes	9,350	74,154
Super TV	TV Guide	Weekly	568	Yes	1,590	19,336
TV Movie	TV Guide	Bi-weekly	1,814	Yes	N/A	29,345
TV Spielfilm	TV Guide	Bi-weekly	1,311	Yes	3,920	25,687
Brigitte	Women's	Bi-weekly	1,130	Yes	4,100	55,220
Freundin	Women's	Bi-weekly	730	Yes	3,000	34,060
Burda Modcn	Women's	Monthly	548	Yes	1,950	22,690
Cosmopolitan	Women's	Monthly	381	Yes	950	24,835
Madame	Women's	Monthly	107	Yes	420	13,604
Petra	Women's	Monthly	413	Yes	1,350	25,913
Elle	Women's	Monthly	189	Yes	420	19,975
Bild der Frau	Yellow press	Weekly	2,004	Yes	4,050	42,200
Freizeit Revue	Yellow press	Weekly	1,418	Yes	3,210	17,437
Frau im Spiegel	Yellow press	Weekly	767	Yes	2,480	15,442
Tina	Yellow press	Weekly	1,785	Yes	4,310	30,405
Der Spiegel	News Magazine	Weekly	1,174	Yes	6,530	53,405
Focus	News Magazine	Weekly	500	Yes	3,220	20,733
Capital	Economic	Monthly	253	Yes	1,730	28,268
Wirtschaftswocho	Economic	Weekly	149	Yes	870	16,733
ADAC Motorwelt	Motoring	Monthly	11,056	Yes	17,710	109,654
Auto, Motor & Sport	Motoring	Weekly	311	Yes	2,360	33,514
Bravo	Special Interest	Weekly	1,282	Yes	2,530	42,354
Kicker	Special Interest	Weekly	327	Yes	1,940	19,503
Pealhouse	Special Interest	Weekly	230	Yes	410	16,140
Playboy	Special Interest	Weekly	256	Yes	1,270	23,407
Schoner Wohnen	Special Interest	Weekly	342	Yes	2,390	29,643
Geo	Special Interest	Weekly	528	Yes	3,040	38,876

Outdoor/Transit

Billboard		**Transit**	
Sites available		**Boards available**	
Large + Standard 79,170		Trains 7,500	
Extra Large 225,160		Buses 26,000	
Lead Time to reserve .... 90 days			
Exposure 85%		**Exposure** 86%	
Costs		**Costs**	
Average, 1 billboard/month		**Average, 1 board/month** .... N/A	
252 cm x 356 cm .... US$ 244			
59 cm x 84 cm US$ 119			
Cost changes		**Cost changes**	
Prices have been rising at 4% per year.		Prices have been rising at 4% per year.	
Sizes		**Sizes**	
59 cm x 84 cm = 1/1 – Buses: 18 m		Standard Max 18/1 Train: 18 m	

Source: MSA, Richard Reschke, Frankfurt

Tobacco advertising billboards are not allowed within 100 meters of each other. There is also a maximum of 1 site per 300 inhabitants.

Direct Marketing

Overview

Usage of direct marketing is actually increasing faster than traditional advertising vehicles. More packaged goods manufacturers have discovered direct marketing and are building databases to create "private media."

Top Direct Mail Consumer List Brokers	*Information Provided*
AZ Direct Marketing, Gutersloh	Business to business addresses,
Herkur Direktwerbegesellschaft, Einbeck	Private addresses,
Pan Adress, Planegg	Microgeographical segmentation systems,
Schober Direktmarketing, Ditzingen	Business to business, Top-Management lists
MajorTelemarketing Companies	
Profitel, Hamburg	Walter Telemarketing, Karlsruhe
Phone Partner, Dietzenbach	DTM GmbH, Offenbach
	Penny Verkaufsforderung, Heusenstamm
Direct Marketing Association	Deutscher Direktmarketing Verband, Hasengartenstr. 14, D-65189 Wiesbaden

Source: MC & LB GmbH & Co., Frankfurt, 1993.

Non-Traditional Media

No information is available on non-traditional media in Germany.

Research Sources

Medium Covered	Research Company	Information Provided
TV	GfK-Gescllschaft fur Konsumforschung Nordwestring 101 D-90419 Nurnberg	Block ratings via telemeter system
TV/RA/PR/CI	GfK AGMA c.V. (Syndicate) Wolfgangstr. 92 D-60322 Frankfurt/Main	Ratings via panel survey Performance figures via Media Analysis MA

Television research is also available by GfK People Meter weekly and monthly.

Advertising Regulations

By Product

Beverages/Alcohol
Sports heroes cannot appear in ads. Advertising also may not be directed at younger age groups.

Food/Restaurants
There are restrictions concerning diet foods, especially for healthy slogans.

Cigarettes
TV and radio advertising are not allowed. There are restrictions in magazines, cinema, newspaper and outdoor.

Pharmaceuticals/Drugs
Only for over-the-counter products and with several restrictions.

Advertising To Children
Advertising which produces fear or directly asks the consumer to buy the product is not allowed.

Commercial Production
Productions with children are restricted. Showing nude people is restricted, especially in Bavaria. Blasphemy and showing and talking directly about competitive products is forbidden.

By Medium

Television
Minimum 7 seconds, no tobacco advertising.

Print
Tobacco advertising is restricted to a maximum of one full page in magazines and newspapers.

Outdoor
No second tobacco poster within 100 m.

Cable
See Television.

Direct Marketing
Restrictive private laws. No cold solicitations to private persons.

Non-traditional
See Television.

Source (Advertising Regulations): GWA, Werbeplanung 1993, Frankfurt, 1992.

Greece

Area	131,940 km²
Population (1992)	10,264,000
Population growth rate (1992)	0.2%
GDP	US$ 77.6 billion
GDP/per capita	US$ 7,730
Real growth rate (1991)	1.0%
Capital	Athens

Population Breakdown

By Sex
Male 49%
Female................................... 51%

By Age Group
Children, 15-19................... 12.5%
Children, 20-24................... 11.5%
Teens, 25-3......................... 24.0%
Adults, 35-44...................... 18.0%
Adults, 45-54...................... 19.0%
Adults, 55-69...................... 15.0%

By Socio-Economic Status
A, Upper 12.1%
B, Middle............................ 42.8%
C, Lower 45.1%

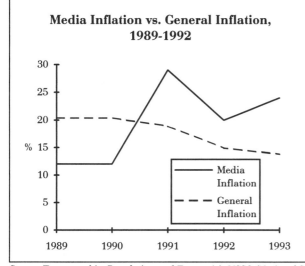

Media Inflation vs. General Inflation, 1989-1992

Legend:
— Media Inflation
-- General Inflation

Number of Households   2,953,000
Ownership of household durables
 Car................................ 31%
 Phone........................... 84%
 Washers........................ N/A
  (purchasing power equivalent)
GNP distribution by industry
 Agriculture............... 16.8%
 Industry 27.3%
 Services 55.9%
Exchange rates (US$ to local currency)
 1991 .... 0.005417
 1992 .... 0.004493

Source (Demographic, Population and Economic): NSSG (National Statistical Services Greece); A.C. Nielsen, Leo Burnett, Athens, Epilogi Magazine

National Holidays

Holiday	1993 Date
New Year's Day	January 1
Epiphany	January 6
Ash Monday	March 14
National Holiday	March 25
Easter Day	May 1
Labor Day	May 1
Whit Monday	June 20
Assumption	August 15
National Holiday	October 28
Christmas Day	December 25

School Holidays

Holiday	1993 Date
Christmas	December 22 - January 6
Three Hierarchs Day	January 30
Easter	April 23 - May 8
Summer	June 15 - September 9
Plus all federal holidays	

Major Influences and Trends

Two events are expected to change the media environment soon, both of which affect television, which absorbs more than 62% of overall advertising spending.

The first change:
Two new TV channels started broadcasting in Autumn of 1993.

The first one is "Star Channel" and is derived from channel "29" after a very strong lifting in names, structure, people, and philosophy. The second one is "Sky TV", owned by Mr. Alafouzos. He also owns the number 1 radio station in Greece ("SKY"). Both stations claim that they will break the duopoly of the two leading channels, Mega and Antenna, which currently dominate TV share in viewing and media budgets.

The second change:
Following some years of hesitation the government decided.in July to give licenses for legal operations to six national and six local private TV channels. These were chosen from the 23 illegal stations which were already broadcasting in the greater Athens area. Surprisly, Sky was denied a license. Rumors say that SKY will buy "Seven X", a private TV station which did receive a license but is faltering.

One of the positive consequences that we expect from this change is the obligation of the legal newcomers to obey the EEC order about maximum advertising time per hour in the commercial channels. Previously, clutter has been a serious problem for the effectiveness of commercials.

Spending Analysis

National advertising spending by medium
based on appropriate year's exchange rate

	1989 US$ MM	1990 US$ MM	1991 US$ MM	1992 US$ MM
TV	123	220.7	300.5	446.6
Cinema	N/A	0.9	0.9	3.3
Radio	22	35.5	31.7	44.4
Newspaper	53.6	94	84.8	89.2
Magazine	80.4	138.6	136	152.5
Direct Response	N/A	N/A	N/A	N/A
Outdoor	20.5	33.9	35.7	29.9
Transporta-tion	N/A	7.8	6.2	3.2
Total	**299.8**	**531.4**	**595.8**	**769.1**

Source: A.C. Nielsen, L.B. Athens

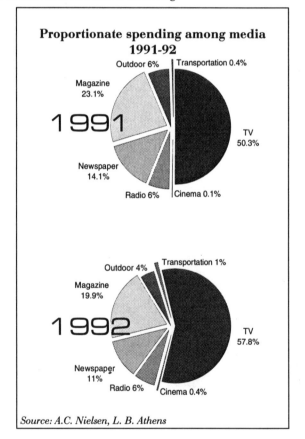

Proportionate spending among media 1991-92

1991
Outdoor 6%
Transportation 0.4%
Magazine 23.1%
Newspaper 14.1%
Radio 6%
Cinema 0.1%
TV 50.3%

1992
Outdoor 4%
Transportation 1%
Magazine 19.9%
Newspaper 11%
Radio 6%
Cinema 0.4%
TV 57.8%

Source: A.C. Nielsen, L. B. Athens

Media Buying

The Greek media buying situation remains stable with six main media shops accounting for half of total advertising spending. The buying services represent approximately 58% of the market's total expenditures.

Buying Services with 1992 Billings

Buying Service	Parent Company	US$ MM
The Media Partnership	BBDO, Bold/O&M, Spot/JWT, Olympic/DDB/ Needham, BBC Grafis, Proad/O&M Conquest Europe, EE/ Alliance	107,832
Greek Media Group	RSCG/Palavidis, BSB, Leo Burnett, GEO/Young & Rubicam, DMB&B, GREY, Alector, Giad	67,395
Initiate Media	Lintas	40,437
Technomedia	Adel/Saatchi & Saatchi, Win, S & S Direct, Magnet	40,437
Universal	McCann Erickson	31,451
Carat	Leoussis, Solid	31,451

Source: LeoBurnett, Athens estimates

Top Advertisers (1992 spending)

By Company

Parent Company	Product /Categories	US$ MM
Lever Hellas	Detergents, Food, Cosmetics, Soap	27.1
Procter & Gamble	Detergents, Soap, Cosmetics	16.9
Greek State	Greek State Services	16.0
Nestle	Food	14.4
Elias	Food, Oil Products	12.1
Colgate-Palmolive	Detergents, Soaps	9.5
Delta	Dairy Products	9.3
3E/Coca Cola	Drinks	8.7
Hasbro Hellas	Toys	8.0
Interamerican	Insurance Company	7.5

Source: Publicity Guide 1992

By Product

Product Category	Advertiser	US$ MM
Liquors	Boutaris	6.6
Detergents	Lever Hellas	27.1
Cars	Hyundai	3.9
Chocolates	Nestle	14.4
Dairy Products	Delta	9.3
Editions	Lambrakis	4.8
Toys	Masbro	8.0
Greek State	Greek State	16.0
Hair Garing Products	Procter & Gamble	16.9
Financial Organization	Interamerican	7.5

Source: Publicity Guide 1992

Television

Overview

- Household penetration is estimated at 99%. *(Sources: AGB Hellas, A. C. Nielsen)*
- Maximum four-week television reach (adults) 89%.

Adult Reach	
at 250 GRPs	65%
at 500 GRPs	73%
at 1,000 GRPs	84%

Opportunities

Network	Number of Stations	Ownership	Station Profile	Commercial Minutes/Hr	Coverage	Broadcast Hours (Sign-On/Off)
ET1	1	State	General	15	98%	07:50 - 02:30
ET2	1	State	General	15	96%	12:30-02:00
ET3	1	State	General	15	75%	16:00 - 00:30
Stations						
MEGA	1	Private	General	15	83%	00:00 - 24:00
Antenna	1	Private	General	15	81%	05:30 - 03:00
New Channel 1	1	Private	General	15	50%	10:00 - 03:00
Star Channel 1	1	Private	General	15	40%	7:00 - 3:00

Source: AGB Hellas, A.C. Nielsen

Costs

Television Cost Changes Between Years

'88   '89   '90   '91   '92
   15%   0%   0%   10%

Audiences/CPM's

Average Cost, Audience, and CPMs by Daypart
(Top three stations, Target=Adults 14+, urban areas, April 1993)

Hours	Morning 08:00-11:59	Daytime 12:00-18:59	Prime Time 19:00-23:00	Late Night 23:25:59	Weekend 15:00-2:300	Children 11:00-00
Station: MEGA						
US$	2,387	2,064	6,128	3,216	3,750	3,44
Avg. Aud. (000)	77	172	383	268	250	48
CPM	31.00	12.00	16.00	12.00	15.00	78.00
Station: ANT1						
US$	1,360	2,142	4,670	3,150	3,200	3,075
Avg. Aud. (000)	85	153	280	210	200	25
CPM	16.00	14.00	16.68	15.00	16.00	123.00
Station: ET1						
US$	351	1,150	4,448	2,052	3,072	2,268
Avg. Aud. (000)	9	50	139	76	96	9
CPM	39.00	23.00	32.00	27.00	32.00	2752.00

Source: AGB Hellas, A.C. Nielsen, Leo Burnett, Athens

Audiences/Ratings by Day part (18% of all commercials;Target=Adults 14+)

Daypart	Hours	HH Universe (000)	Household Rating	HH Impressions (000)
Morning	08:00-12:00	251	5.0	12.6
Daytime	12:00-19:59	682	13.6	92.8
Primetime	20:00-23:00	1,508	30.1	453.9
Late Night	23:00-25:59	1,153	23.0	265.2
Weekend	08:00-25:59	842	16.8	141.5
Children's	08:00-25:59	101	14.1	14.2

(No household or HUT data is available for Greece)
Source: AGB Hellas, Leo Burnett, Athens

Scheduling/ Regional/Languages

LANGUAGES	Programming		Commercials	
Primary Language	Greek	50%	Greek	99.9%
Secondary Language	English	40%	English	0.1%
Tertiary Languages	Portuguese, French, Italian			

- Commercials are aired throughout the day between programs and within programs.
- Commercial lengths range from :10 to :60 with a ceiling grade of :01; 18% of all commercials are :30.

Regional vs. National
Cost for regionally aired :30 commercials average about 32% of national costs.

Only 5% of total TV expenditures are directed to regional stations.

Station	Region	Hours
MEGA	Makedonia	19:00 - 23:00
ANT1	Makedonia	19:00 - 23:00

Source (Scheduling/Regional/Languages): AGB Hellas, Leo Burnett, Athens

Children's Programming

CHILDREN'S PROGRAMMING				Kids'	
Station	Hours	Days	Universe (000)	Ratings	Universe (000)
MEGA	08:00-12:00	Sat.-Sun.	80	11.1	8.9
ANT1	08:00-12:00	Sat.-Sun.	36	5.0	1.8
ET1	08:00-12:00	Sat.-Sun.	14	2.0	.3

Source: AGB Hellas, Leo Burnett, Athens

Radio

Overview

- There are radio stations all over Greece, 96 of them in Athens.
- Approximately 98% of all households have radios; the estimated number is 2,895,000. Approximately 45% of all automobiles have radios.
- The primary broadcasting language is Greek; English is also used.
- No premiums are required. The most popular program types are News and Music.
- Prime Time is 09:00-12:00.

Costs

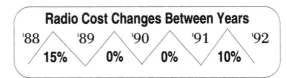

Radio Cost Changes Between Years
'88 / 15% \ '89 / 0% \ '90 / 0% \ '91 / 10% \ '92

Overall Averages for a :30 radio commercial
Average Cost: US$ 190
Average CPM: US$ 0.70

Daypart Costs/CPMs
(Target=Adults; Location=Athens)

Daypart	Local Time	Cost :30 US$	Audience (000)	CPM (US$)
Prime Time	09:00 - 12:00	337	490	0.69
Daytime	12:00 - 17:00	135	296	0.46
Late Night	22:00 - 24:00	108	110	0.98

Source (Radio): A.C. Nielsen, Leo Burnett, Athens

Cable

- The situation regarding cable TV remains stable. There is only one cable station: TVPLUS.
- Commercials are not available; no major changes are expected.

Satellite

- Satellite TV channels are re-broadcast by terrestrial state owned stations in Greece. There are 7 satellite channels, of which 6 are commercial. The number of satellite TV channels will be the same for 1994.
- There are currently no restrictions specifically for satellite imported programs and commercials.
- Satellite penetration is 28.8% of total households, or a total of 850,500 households.

Satellite Channel	Country of Origin	Language	Programming
MTV	United Kingdom	English	Music
CNN	USA	English	News
Eurosport	United Kingdom	English	Sports
RTL	Luxembourg	German	News, Entertainment
Euronews	Europe	English	News
TVE	Spain	Spanish	News, Entertainment
TV5	France	French	News, Entertainment

Video Cassettes

Roughly 43% of TV households have video cassette recorders (VCRs). The use of commercials in pre-recorded tapes is and is expected to remain very small. Negotiations are in progress regarding the regulation of advertising on tapes. AGB is the service which measures VCR usage.

Cinema

- The total number of theaters in Greece is not available. There are 40 cinemas in Athens, where potential reach over 4 weeks is 14% of adults over 16.

- Commercials are available in lengths from :19 to 3 minutes at virtually all cinemas.

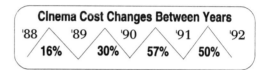

- The average cost of a 4-week cinema schedule for :30 at 26 selected cinemas in Athens and Salonico is US$ 40,437.

Newspapers

There are 16 national daily papers which accept advertising. Combined circulation is 630,943.

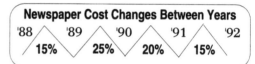

Source (Newspapers): A.C. Nielsen, Leo Burnett, Athens

Newspaper	Market	Size	Circ. (000)	Avg. Daily Aud. (000)	1 Page B&W Cost (US$)	Accept Color?
Morning Issues						
Kathimerini	National	Standard	17	49	3,397	Yes
AVGI	National	Tabloid	2	N/A	1,797	Yes
Makedonia	North Greece	Standard	N/A	56	3,339	Yes
Rizospastis	National	Tabloid	13	43	1,491	Yes
Noon Issues						
Apogevmatini	National	Tabloid	52	136	3,594	Yes
Avriani	National	Standard	22	74	4,044	Yes
Ethnos	National	Tabloid	51	198	4,134	Yes
Eleftherotypia	National	Tabloid	109	297	4,942	Yes
Eleftheros Typos	National	Tabloid	139	415	5,095	Yes
Mesimvrini	National	Standard	12	25	1,262	Yes
Niki	National	Tabloid	17	49	2,359	Yes
TA NEA	National	Tabloid	133	377	6,749	Yes
Thessaloniki	North Greece	Tabloid		74	2,831	Yes
Star	National	Standard	35	56	4,942	Yes
Eleftheros	National	Standard	9	N/A	5,774	Yes
Estia	National	Standard	5	N/A	2,695	No
Eleftheri Ora	National	Standard	2	N/A	5,392	Yes
Sunday and Weekly Issues						
To Vima	National	Standard	187	582	7,764	Yes
Apogevmatini S.	National	Tabloid	86	167	8,696	Yes
Avriani - Logos	National	Tabloid	30	62	2,453	Yes
Sunday Ethnos	National	Tabloid	105	241	3,594	Yes
Sunday Eleftherotypia	National	Tabloid	186	600	6,290	Yes
Sunday Typos	National	Tabloid	120	476	4,718	Yes
Lipon	National	Standard	70	130	3,460	Yes
To Pontiki	National	Tabloid	67	N/A	1,162	Yes
Kathimerini Sun.	National	Standard	68	179	7,189	Yes
To Paron	National	Tabloid	11	12	1,573	Yes
Sports Issues						
Athlitiki Icho	National	Standard	22	80	2,291	Yes
Filathlos	National	Standard	25	62	1,842	Yes
Fos Ton Spor	National	Standard	34	99	3,753	Yes
Ora gia Spor	National	Standard	12	31	2,252	Yes

Source: Media View, A.C. Nielsen, Leo Burnett, Athens

Magazines

There are 27 national consumer magazines which accept advertising. The number of trade and technical magazines is not available.

Magazine Cost Changes Between Years

'88 / '89 / '90 / '91 / '92
15% 28% 30% 20%

Magazine	Type	Frequency	Circ. (000)	Audited?	Avg. Issue Aud. (000)	1 page 4/C Cost (US$)
Athinorama	Athens Guide	Weekly	33	Yes	56	2,224
Auto Week	Supplement	Weekly	77	Yes	56	3,055
Status	Men's	Monthly	14	Yes	68	3,145
4 Wheels	Motoring	Monthly	65	Yes	148	4,942
Tilerama	T/Sradio Guide	Weekly	48	Yes	433	4,268
Ego	Women's	Weekly	26	Yes	136	3,819
Ethnos Spor	Supplement	Weekly	51	Yes	118	2,696
Votre Baute	Women's	Monthly	33	Yes	37	4,044
Einai	Women's	Weekly	28	Yes	173	3,819
Eikones	Gen. Interest	Weekly	24	Yes	167	3,549
Ena	Gen. Interest	Weekly	9	Yes	62	2,696
7 Meres TV	TV & Radio Guide	Weekly	57	Yes	718	4,403
Flash	General Interest	Monthly	12	Yes	37	3,145
Epsilon	General Interest	Weekly	182	Yes	359	4,044
Kai	General Interest	Weekly	15	Yes	161	3,145
Tachidromos	General Interest	Weekly	13	Yes	155	3,505
Oik. Tachi-dromos	Business	Weekly	N/A	Yes	56	2,247
Radiotileorasi	TV & Radio Guide	Weekly	20	Yes	173	1,348
TV Zapping	TV & Radio Guide	Weekly	52	Yes	668	3,189
Tiletheatis	TV & Radio Guide	Weekly	71	Yes	575	4,268
Tilecontrol	TV & Radio Guide	Weekly	41	Yes	272	2,247
Auto Motor and Sportss	Motoring	Monthly	66	Yes	229	4,381
Avantage	Women's	Monthly	17	Yes	49	2,786
Gynaika	Women's	Monthly	30	Yes	198	4,193
Diva	Women's	Monthly	26	Yes	80	3,370
Ekini	Women's	Monthly	99	Yes	87	2,786
Elle	Women's	Monthly	26	Yes	142	4,493
Ichos Hi Fi	Hi'Fi	Monthly	N/A	Yes	31	1,797
Idaniko spiti	House Decoration	Monthly	27	Yes	49	1,887
Idees+Lisis gia Spiti	House Decoration	Monthly	29	Yes	56	1,752
Car & Driver	Motoring	Monthly	26	Yes	62	2,696
Klik	General	Monthly	47	Yes	309	5,392
Cosmopolitan	Women's	Monthly	15	Yes	80	2,370
Makedonia Epiloges	General Interest	Monthly	N/A	Yes	136	2,696
Marie Claire	Women's	Monthly	28	Yes	111	4,493
Max	General	Monthly	34	Yes	111	3,145
Men	Men's	Monthly	19	Yes	49	3,145
Moto	Motoring	Monthly	15	Yes	19	1,348
Prakktiki	Women's	Monthly	36	Yes	56	2,696
Ptisi	Arts/Crafts	Monthly	25	Yes	56	1,797
Pop+Rock	Music	Monthly	N/A	Yes	12	1,483
Pop Corn	Music	Monthly	N/A	Yes	12	1,483
Play Boy	Men's	Monthly	38	Yes	56	3,145
Cinema	Cinema	Monthly	20	Yes	25	1,797
Finai	Women's	Weekly	28	Yes	N/A	5,811
Ti Stin TV	TV & Radio Guide	Weekly	26	Yes	N/A	3,819

Source: Media View, A.C. Nielsen, Leo Burnett, Athens

Outdoor/Transit

Billboard	**Transit**

Sites available (Athens) 5,200
Lead Time to reserve .... 4 weeks
 	
Exposure 94%
	Boards available
	   Subway Wagons 200
	   Yellow Buses 347
	   Green Buses 71
	Exposure (Athens, yellow buses) ... 94%

Costs
Average, 1 billboard/month
   4 m x 8 m .... US$ 521
 	
Billboard Cost Changes Between Years
'88 — '89 — '90 — '91 — '92
54% — 0% — 29% — 20%
	Costs
	Average, 1 board/month:
	   Yellow Bus .... US$ 1,841
	
	Transit Cost Changes Between Years
	'88 — '89 — '90 — '91 — '92
	0% — 33% — 20% — 18%

Sizes 2 m x 4 m, 4 m x 8 m	**Sizes** 2.0 m x 0.6 m, 1.2 m x 0.6 m, 0.6 m x 0.2 m

Direct Marketing

List brokers in Greece rarely provide full list information. Lists are either compiled or bought from "the source." There is no direct marketing association.

Top Direct Mail Consumer List Brokers	*Information Provided*
Bounty	80% of newborns every year
ICAP	Lists of companies
Professional/Unions	Demographics
Telephone Directory	Addresses only

Service 800 is the only telemarketing company. It also acts as a list broker.

Non-Traditional Media

There is currently no use of non-traditional media in Greece.

Research Sources

Medium Covered	*Research Company*	*Information Provided*

All Media	A.C. Nielsen
	   2 Cherokopou
	   7671 Kallithea
		Nielsen monitor service, TV audience ratings, media surveys

	Focus Ltd.
	   54, Vas. Sofias
	   11528 Athens
		Media survey on weekly basis for Athens and Thessaloniki

TV*	AGB Hellas
	   64 L. Riencourt
	   11523 Athens
		TV audience and rating information

	ICAP/Gallup S.A.
	   10 Papadiamandopoulou
	   11528 Athens
		TV audience and rating information

People Meter also reports weekly on television watching.

Advertising Regulations

By Product

Cigarettes
Banned from television, radio and cinema (for films suitable for children under 18).
Pharmaceuticals/Drugs
Banned from all media.
Radio
Advertising of drugs and tobacco is prohibited.

By Medium

Television
Advertising of drugs and tobacco is prohibited.
Print
Advertising of drugs is prohibited.
Outdoor
Advertising of drugs is prohibited.
Cable
Advertising of drugs and tobacco is prohibited.
Direct Marketing
No regulations.

Hungary

Area	93,030 km²
Population (1992)	10,333,327
Population growth rate (1992)	0.1%
GDP	US$ 60.1 billion
GDP/per capita	US$ 5,700
Real growth rate (1991)	7%
Capital	Budapest

Population Breakdown

By Sex
Male 48%
Female................................. 52%

By Age Group
Children, 0-14 .... 20%
Teens, 15-19........................... 7.9%
Adults, 20+ 72.1%

Source: GFK Hungaria Market Research Ltd.

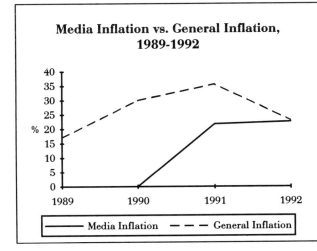

Media Inflation vs. General Inflation, 1989-1992

Number of Households   3,815,000
Ownership of household durables
   Car................................. 46%
   Phone........................... 47%
   Washers........................ N/A
   (purchasing power equivalent)
GNP distribution by industry
   Agriculture.................. 9.5%
   Industry 26.8%
   Services 63.7%
Exchange rates (US$ to local currency)
   1991..................... 0.013398
   1992...........................0.0119

National Holidays

Holiday	1993 Date
New Year's	January 1
National Holiday	March 15
Easter	April 11 - 12
May Day	May 1
Pinkster	May 30 - 31
Constitution Day	August 20
National Holiday	October 23
Christmas	December 25 - 26

School Holidays

Holiday	1993 Date
Winter	December 18 - January 2
Spring	April 1 - 8
Summer	June 11 - September 1

Major Influences and Trends

The media law is still not enacted and the frequency moratorium is only partially absolved, which means that more local and regional radio and TV channels will be granted broadcasting rights.

There is still a ban on national private channels. Tracking sources has proven to be problematic. Data provided for print media, for example, is rarely reliable. But for the sake of international advertising agencies, Hungary's leading publications (e.g. *Nepszabadsag* - Hungary's biggest daily - and *Reader's Digest*) are attempting to bring an official circulation auditing system to Hungary.

The print media market also faces serious distribution problems due to insufficient distribution of the Hungarian post office and other channels. Ownership of print titles is constantly changing and therefore the print quality and the content also change frequently.

Outdoor advertising expenditure has been increasing in recent years. Approximately 65% of total outdoor advertising expenditure is spent on billboards, while the remaining spending is allocated to transport advertising, lamp post sites and small poster structures. It is estimated that approximately 10,400 billboard sites are available in the country, but it seems that there are simply not enough quality billboard sites available to accomodate high season requirements.

Spending Analysis

National advertising spending by medium
based on appropriate year's exchange rate

	1989 US$ MM	1990 US$ MM	1991 US$ MM	1992 US$ MM
TV	10.3	13.8	20.0	51.0
Cinema	4.6	2.8	4.0	3.0
Radio	4.6	5.5	8.0	12.0
Newspaper/Magazine	35.4	52.3	84.0	126.0
Direct Response	1.1	1.4	4.0	15.0
Outdoor	8.0	16.5	20.0	24.0
Other	50.3	45.2	60.0	69.0
Total	**114.3**	**137.5**	**200.0**	**300.0**

Source: Estimations of the Hungarian Advertising Association, Budapest, Hungary, 1993

Media Buying

All television, radio, print and outdoor rates are fixed. However, volume-based discounts are negotiable. Media buying is done through the agencies, except for the big-volume media negotiations, which are often handled by the client. Apart from weak initiatives, no media buying services exist in Hungary.

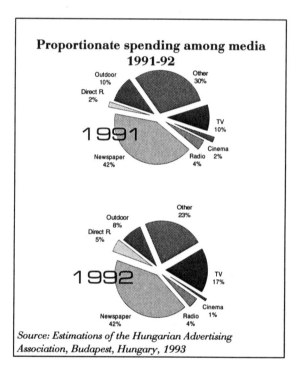

Proportionate spending among media 1991-92

1991: Other 30%, Outdoor 10%, Direct R. 2%, TV 10%, Cinema 2%, Radio 4%, Newspaper 42%

1992: Other 23%, Outdoor 8%, Direct R. 5%, TV 17%, Cinema 1%, Radio 4%, Newspaper 42%

Source: Estimations of the Hungarian Advertising Association, Budapest, Hungary, 1993

Top Advertisers

By Company

Parent Company	Product Categories	US$ MM
Unilever	Laundry Detergent, Ice Creams	4.87
Televital	Direct Mail Companies	4.12
Masterfoods/Mars	Sweets	2.75
Henkel	Detergent, Household Cleaners	2.14
P & G	Shampoo, Sanitary products	1.83
Postabank	Bank Services	1.70
Nestle	Sweets	1.38
MNB/National Bank	Bank Services	1.28
Westel	Radio/Telephone System	1.22
Szerencsejatek Rt.	Game of Hazard	1.21

Source: Amer Ltd., Budapest, Hungary, 1993

By Product

Product Category	Advertiser	US$ MM
Bank Services	Postabank	1.70
Direct Mail Companies	TV Shop	2.81
Newspapers/Magazines	Kepes Europa	.44
Department Stores	Julius Meinl	.65
Cars	Renault	.85
Laundry Detergent	Unilever	4.8
Health Care Products	Esterin	.69
Telecommunication	MATAV Rt.	.81
Coffee	Dowe Egberts	.60
Hair Care	P & G/Wash & Co.	1.83

Source: Amer Ltd., Budapest, Hungary, 1993

Television

Overview

There is still a ban on national private channels. Television channels TV1 and TV2 should experience dramatic changes in sales and programming (e.g. establishing uniform time-slots and pricing structures) in the near future.

Television HH Penetration			Adult Reach	
			at 250 GRPs	65%
1992 Penetration	100%	3,815,000	at 500 GRPs	87%
			at 1000 GRPs	95%

Opportunities

	Number of Stations	Ownership	Station Profile	Commercial Minutes/Day	Coverage	Broadcast Hours (Sign-On/Off)
TV1	1	State	Information, Education, News, Entertainment, Sports	25 - 50	100%	M-F 12:00-14:00 S-S 17:00-19:00
TV2	1	State	Information, Education, News, Entertainment, Sports	21 - 45	99%	M-F 7:00-9:00 S-S 15:00-17:00

Costs

Prime Time TV Costs for :30 in US$	
1991	*1992*
1,875	5,062

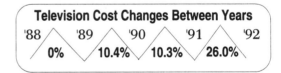

Television Cost Changes Between Years

'88	'89	'90	'91	'92
0%	10.4%	10.3%	26.0%	

Audiences/CPM's

Average Cost, Audience, and CPMs by Daypart
(Top 3 stations, :30 TV, national audience)

Hours	Morning 06:00-12:00	Daytime 14:00-18:55	Prime Time 18:55-20:30	Late Night 22:00-24:00	Weekend	Children
Station: TV1						
US$	473	3,157	5,684	2,526	Depends on	N/A
Avg. Aud. (000)	N/A	953	3,206	900	the time of	
CPM	N/A	3.31	1.77	2.81	the day	
Station: TV2						
US$	473	3,157	4,736	2,526	Depends on	N/A
Avg. Aud. (000)	N/A	879	2,982	900	the time of	
CPM	N/A	3.59	1.59	2.81	the day	

Audiences/Rating by Daypart

		Household				Adult		
	Hours	Universe (000)	Hut Levels	Household Rating	Impressions (000)	Universe (000)	Adult Rating	Impressions (000)
Morning	06:00-12:00	3,815	N/A	6	228.9	8,600	8.5	731
Daytime	19:00-18:55	3,815	N/A	20	763.0	8,600	22.5	1,935
Primetime	18:55-20:30	3,815	N/A	36	1,373.4	8,600	40.2	3,457
Late Night	22:00-24:00	3,815	N/A	15	572.2	8,600	18	1,224
Weekend		N/A	N/A	N/A	N/A	N/A	N/A	N/A
Children's		N/A	N/A	N/A	N/A	N/A	N/A	N/A

Scheduling/Regional

- The most common commercial lengths are :20 and :30 (80%); lengths of :05 and greater are possible.
- Commercials are aired in specific blocks at the beginnings and ends of programs.
- Regional buying is not possible.

Children's Advertising

Currently, there are no restrictions on placement of ads targeted at children. However, no audience data (i.e., kids' ratings) is available.

CHILDREN'S PROGRAMMING			Kids'		
(All Walt Disney shows)			Universe	Universe	Impressions
Station	Hours	Days	(000)	Ratings	(000)
TV1	17:00-19:00	Sunday	856	76	651
TV1	09:00-11:00	Thursday (replay of Sunday program)	856	N/A	N/A
TV1	16:00-18:00	Saturday (every 2nd only)	856	33	282
TV1	19:20-19:30	Monday	856	42	360
TV1	19:20-19:30	Weekday	856	42	360
TV1	19:20-19:30	Friday	856	42	360

Radio

- There are 8 stations in Hungary, 5 of which are commercial and 6 of which are in Budapest.
- Ninety-nine percent of all households have radios; the estimated number is 3,776,000.
- The primary broadcasting language is Hungarian; German and English are also used.
- The most popular progam types are News, Sports, Music and Weather.

- Commercial lengths available range from :05 up.
- An average :30 spot targeted at adults 18+ would cost about US$ 233.
- Regional buying is possible; its cost is less than national buys.
- Cost changes over time before 1992 are not available. Between 1991 and 1992, costs rose almost 72%.
- Prime/Peak time is 06:30-08:30, with an adult rating 12.5 for 1,000,000.

Daypart Costs/CPMs (Target=Adults)

Daypart	Local Time	Avg. Cost :30 US$	Audience (000)	CPM (US$)
Prime Time	06:00 - 08:30	419	1,000	0.42
Daytime	08:30 - 20:00	170	545	0.31
Late Night	20:00 - 24:00	81	100	0.81

Cable

- As the frequency moratorium is partially absolved, more and more local and regional TV channels will be granted broadcasting permission.

- 35% of households currently have cable.
- There are 7 channels.
- The primary language is Hungarian.

Cable Networks	HH Circulation (000)	Cost US$	Rating	Programming
T4	2,500	919	15	Entertainment, Sports, Politics
HTV 30	1,200	625	10	Entertainment
SIO TV	800	375	9	Entertainment

Satellite

- A new satellite channel, Duna TV, was launched in December 1992. It can be received not only in Hungarian homes, but in neighboring countries as well.
- 17% of households have satellite reception.

Satellite Channel	Country of Origin	Language	Programming
Super Channel	UK	English	Entertainment
MTV	UK/USA	English	Music, News
Eurosport	UK	English	Entertainment, Sports
DSF	Germany	German	Sports, Entertainment
CNN	USA	English	News, Entertainment, Sports
RTL Plus	Luxembourg	German	Entertainment, News
RTL 2	Germany	German	Entertainment
SAT 1	Germany	German	Entertainment
PRO 7	Germany	German	Entertainment
3 SAT	Germany	German	Entertainment
Tele5	Germany	German	Entertainment
TV3	France	German	Entertainment, Culture
Screensport	UK	German/English	Sports
Duna TV	Hungary	Hungarian	Entertainment, Culture

Video Cassettes

Roughly 38% of TV households have video cassette recorders (VCRs). Video cassettes in Hungary do not carry commercials, and no service is available to measure VCR usage.

Cinema

- Hungary has 54 cinemas that acccept advertising. Arrangements are made with individual theaters.
- An average :30 spot at one theater costs approximately US$ 132/month.
- Commercial lengths available range from :30 up.
- No information is available on potential reach of cinema advertising in Hungary.

Newspapers

Hungary has 13 national daily papers, with a combined circulation of 1,280,000.

Newspaper Cost Changes Between Years

Costs rose 18% in 1992 over previous years

Newspaper	Market	Size	Circ. (000)	Avg. Daily Aud. (000)	1 page B&W Cost (US$)	Accept Color?
Nepszabadsag	National	Standard	300-360	1000	6,043	No
Nepsvava	National	Standard	150	380	3,376	No
Mai Nap	National	Tabloid	100-120	300	1,633	No
Kurir (Morning)	National	Standard	90	290	2,614	No
Magyar Hirlap	National	Broadsheet	80	230	3,702	Yes
Magyar Nemzet	National	Broadsheet	70	280	2,940	No
Esti Hirlap	National	Tabloid	80	170	1,525	Yes
Napi Vilaggazdasaq	National	Standard	20	80	1,045	No
Vilaggazd.	National	Standard	15	60	1,394	No

Magazines

There are 54 consumer magazines and 32 trade and technical journals published in Hungary.

Magazine Cost Changes Between Years

Costs rose 18% in 1992

over previous years

Magazine	Type	Frequency	Circ. (000)	Audited?	Avg. Issue Aud (000)	1 page 4/C (US$)
Auto-Mag.	Automobiles	Monthly	35	No	120	2,352
Autopiac	Auto	Monthly	40	No	180	2,117
Sport Auto	Auto	Monthly	45	No	N/A	1,949
Motor Revu	Motorbikes	Monthly	30	No	90	1,307
Cash-Flow	Business	Monthly	30	No	30	3,147
Privat Profit	Business	Monthly	40	No	130	2,396
HVG	Business/ Economy	Weekly	130	No	260	3,049
Playboy	Entert./Men	Monthly	36	No	40	2,908
Elite	Women	Monthly	20	No	140	2,287
Voila	Women/ Fashoin	Monthly	35	No	150	1,307
Kismama	Women	Bimonthly	50	No	130	1,742
Pulli	Women	Quarterly	45	No	100	1,525
100xszep	Children	Monthly	75	No	230	1,361
Popcorn	Pop Music	Monthly	65	No	200	2,341
Reader's Digest	Entertainment	Monthly	244	Yes	385	1,960
Reform	Entertainment	Weekly	250	No	1,000	2,504
Tele Mag.	TV Programs	Weekly	525	No	1,575	5,227
Teve Mag.	Entertainment	Weekly	410	No	1,025	5,663

Outdoor/Transit

Billboard	**Transit**
Sites available	**Boards available** ....NA
...............................9,320	
Lead Time to reserve ....5 weeks	
Exposure ....N/A	**Exposure** ....N/A
Costs	**Costs**
Average, 1 billboard/month	**Average, 1 board/month**
4 m x 3 m ....US$ 188	...............................NA
5.1 m x 2.4 m ....US$ 189	
6 m x 3 m ....US$ 216	
Costs have risen 10% between 1991 and 1992.	

Sizes

5.1 m x 2.4 m, 30 cm x 22 cm, 100 cm x 216 cm

Direct Marketing

Overall, direct marketing represents only 5% of total ad spending. It is only used by low quality product advertisers. The quality of mail pieces is very poor.

List Broker	Information Provided
KSH Hungexpo CEG-Info	List of private and company addresses updated quarterly
Top Telemarketing Companies	**Direct Marketing Association**
Teleshop Home Shopping Wunderland Top Trade Margareta	Does not exist.

Non-Traditional Media

More unusual media types are expected to appear, but they will most likely be very expensive. One example is video projections on floating river barges. The cost for a 10 week campaign might be US$ 63,650.

Research Sources

Medium Covered	Research Company	Information Provided
TV/Print/Radio	Amer World Research Budapest, Csatarka (36-1) 188-7858	• Monthly spending data for TV, Print, Radio • Share of spend info. by category • Copies of print ads • Tapes of TV ads
TV/Print/ Outdoor	Mediagnozis 1054 BP. Kalman I.U. 21 1/14 Budapest	• Monthly spend data for TV, Print, Outdoor (no Radio) • Copies of print ads • Tapes of TV ads
TV	AGB/Gallup 1033 Fo ter 1. Zichy Kastely Budapest	• Weekly quarter hour ratings
Magazines/ Newspapers	Mahir Obsereuer 1091 Bp Ulloi eu 51 (36-1) 113-9895	• Observation of ads and articles on basis of selected points of view
Newspapers/ Magazine/TV/ Radio	Szonda Ipos 1081 BP Koztarsasag Ter 3. (36-1) 113-9895	• Audience survey with age, sex breakdown etc., viewing habits, coverage

Television research is available weekly from AGB/Gallup - People Meter, and GFK Diary.

Advertising Regulations

By Product

Beverages/Alcohol
Prohibited. Only point of sale promotions are allowed.

Food/Restaurants
Cannot make "best" claims.

Cigarettes
Prohibited. Only point of sale promotions are allowed.

Pharmaceuticals/Drugs
Restricted to medical press. It is forbidden to guarantee a healing effect.

Advertising To Children
Allowed, but it must not:
- Force them to make contact with strangers.
- Provoke aggressiveness.
- Take unfair advantage of their lack of experience.
- Include anything which causes mental, moral or physical damage to children.
- Suggest a type of behavior not suitable to their age.
- Build a feeling of shame in them when not purchasing advertised product.
- Hurt prestige of parents and teachers.

By Medium

Television
Alcoholic beverages, cigarettes, and drugs are not permitted on public TV and radio. Stations are allowed only 10-12% commercial airtime. No advertising is allowed on national holidays. No private stations can obtain a TV license.

Outdoor
Alcohol, cigarettes, and drugs are not permitted. All sites must be placed a minimum of 20 meters from the side of the road. No sites crossing over road or on road are allowed.

Cable
Airing permission is available to channels airing programs within a range of 40 km.

Italy

Area	301,23 0 km^2
Population (1992)	57,904,628
Population growth rate (1992)	0.2%
GDP	US$ 965.0 billion
GDP/per capita	US$ 16,700
Real growth rate (1991)	1.0%
Capital	Rome

Population Breakdown

By Sex
Male 48%
Female.................................... 52%

By Age Group
Children, 0-4.......................... 4.9%
Teens, 5-14 .... 11.4%
Adults, 15+ 83.7%

By Socio-Economic Status
A, Upper.............................. 10.0%
B, Upper Midde.................. 49.5%
C, Lower Middle................. 33.9%
D, Lower.............................. 6.6%

Source: ISTAT 1992

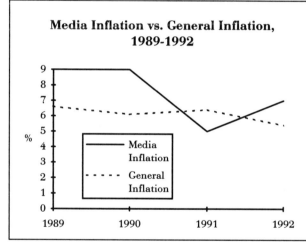

Media Inflation vs. General Inflation, 1989-1992

Legend: Media Inflation; General Inflation

Source: (Inflation rate): Banca D'Italia; (Media Inflation): Leo Burnett estimate

Number of Households	20,263,000

Ownership of household durables
Car.............................. 75.6%
Phone........................ 95.1%
Washers...................... 93.8%
(purchasing power equivalent)

GNP distribution by industry
Agriculture................. 3.6%
Industry 36.9%
Services 59.5%

Exchange rates (US$ to local currency)
1991................... 0.0008711
1992................... 0.0006721

Source: (Statistics): ISTAT 1992

National Holidays

Holiday	1993 Date
New Year	Jan 1
Epiphany	Jan 6
Liberation Day	April 25
Labor Day	May 1
Assumption Day	August 15
All Saints'	Nov 1
Immaculate Conception	Dec 8
Christmas/Boxing Day	Dec 25/26

School Holidays

Holiday	1993 Date
Summer	mid-June - mid-Sept
Christmas	Dec 22 - Jan 6
Easter	Varies, one week around Easter

Major Influences and Trends

In 1992, a series of modifications which were intended to restore order to a number of long term situations actually produced areas of uncertainty. These modifications included:

- Approval of TV broadcasting concessions
- Discussions regarding telepromotion rules
- Agreements and mergers among print concessionaires (Berlusconi/Mondadori, Rizzoli/Rusconi)

Consequently, 1992 was a year of evolution with important changes in terms of space availability and relative costs. These recent changes will most likely be followed by new offers of improved space (quality/profit in TV, costs according to average circulation on specific days for daily print, etc.).

Spending Analysis

National advertising spending by medium
based on appropriate year's exchange rate

	1989 US$ MM	1990 US$ MM	1991 US$ MM	1992 US$ MM
TV	2,501.1	3,214.8	3,709.3	3,191.2
Cinema	17.2	20.6	21.8	17.8
Radio	194.0	244.9	271.2	220.4
Newspaper	1,277.6	1,635.4	1,758.9	1,411.3
Magazine	1,106.8	1,298.3	1,339.5	1,116.8
Outdoor	253.6	299.5	313.6	234.6
Total	**5,350.3**	**6,713.5**	**7,414.3**	**6,192.1**

Source: Media Key, S.R.L.

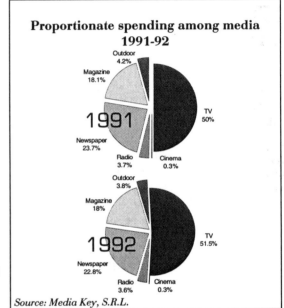

Proportionate spending among media 1991-92

1991
Outdoor 4.2%
Magazine 18.1%
TV 50%
Newspaper 23.7%
Radio 3.7%
Cinema 0.3%

1992
Outdoor 3.8%
Magazine 18%
TV 51.5%
Newspaper 22.8%
Radio 3.6%
Cinema 0.3%

Source: Media Key, S.R.L.

Media Buying

Buying is done for each individual client. Media pricing is usually negotiable and negotiations are made either by clients or agencies/buying services (buying services have had relevant growth in recent years). TV is characterized by the 'duopoly' of RAI and Publitalia. Buying negotiations are most common with Publitalia but are also possible with RAI. Spots are typically purchased without focusing on GRP delivery because audience delivery is not guaranteed by either of the leading Italian stations. With regard to all other media, there is a free market situation, facilitating negotiations.

Top Advertisers

By Company

Parent Company	Product Categories	US$ MM
Ferrero	Confectionery	238.23
Procter & Gamble	Detergents	216.42
Barilla	Pasta	182.93
Fiat Auto	Cars/vehicles	181.26
Sagit	Foods/ready to eat meals	126.18
Saipo	Cosmetics	119.69
Fiat Alfa	Cars/vehicles	117.35
Nestle	Confectionery	115.78
Fiat Lancia	Cars/vehicles	104.68
Renault Italia	Cars/vehicles	97.60

Source: Nielsen, A.C. (N.A.S.A.)

By Product

Product Category	Advertiser	US$ MM
Cars/vehicles	Fiat	166.37
Perfumes	Lancaster	9.24
Watches	SMH	22.09
Food Retail Stores	Coop	27.28
Cosmetics Facial Care	Saipo	27.18
Detergents/HDLS	Procter & Gamble	58.26
Non Food Retail Stores	Standa	30.64
Brioches	Ferrero	88.92
Women's Wear	Max Mara	8.80
Chocolate Bars/Snacks	Ferrero	58.84

Source: Nielsen, A.C. (N.A.S.A.)

Television

Overview

The TV system in Italy is a combination of state and commercial channels. Both accept advertising but in different formats (between programs for state owned, during programs for commercial owned; both broadcast live). There are fixed limits to the amount of advertising permitted on both state and commercial channels. The state channels allow a maximum of 12% advertising per hour and 4% over a week. The commercial stations allow 18% advertising per hour and 15% per week.

	TV HH Penetration				Adult Reach	
1989	*1990*	*1991*	*1992*	at 250 GRPs	68%
99.0%	99.2%	99.1%	99.1%	at 500 GRPs	79%
20,073,000	20,303,000	20,460,000	20,460,000	at 1,000 GRPs	85%

Source (Penetration): Auditel Basic Research; (Adult Reach): Evaluation on Auditel/Marketing TV Service

Costs

Prime Time TV Costs for :30 in US$		
	1991	*1992*
State	30,488	26,010
Commercial	34,989	28,340

Source: Leo Burnett estimate

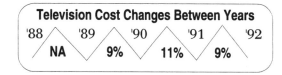

Television Cost Changes Between Years

'88	'89	'90	'91	'92
NA	9%	11%	9%	

Audiences/CPM's

Average Cost, Audience, and CPM's by Daypart (Top 3 stations; :30, national aud. Target=Adults 15+)

Hours	Morning 07:00-12:00	Daytime 12:00-19:30	Prime Time 19:30-22:30	Late Night 22:30-02:00	Weekend VARIOUS	Children VARIOUS
Station: RAI 1						
US$	3,112	13,907	43,810	13,308	22,213	7,410
Avg. Aud. (000)	629	1,873	3,619	948	2,593	290
CPM	4.94	7.43	12.10	14.03	8.56	25.55
Station: CANALE 5						
US$	10,619	17,475	41,065	11,510	8,751	3,172
Avg. Aud. (000)	1,596	2,436	4,246	1,185	1,286	725
CPM	6.65	7.17	9.67	9.71	6.57	4.38
Station: RAI 2						
US$	10,047	13,668	29,194	9,745	!7,658	7,560
Avg. Aud. (000)	1,668	2,223	2,706	1,185	2,012	289
CPM	6.02	6.15	10.78	8.22	8.78	26.16

Source: Spring 1993 rate cards

Audiences/Ratings by Daypart (Target=Adults 15+)

Daypart	Hours	Household				Adults		
		Universe (000)	Hut Levels	Household Rating	Impressions (000)	Universe (000)	Adult Rating	Impressions (000)
Morning	07:00-12:00	20,263	100	1.9	385	48,361	0.8	387
Daytime	12:30-19:30	20,263	100	8.9	1,803	48,361	5.7	2,756
Primetime	19:30-22:30	20,263	100	5.3	1,013	48,361	3.0	1,450
Late Night	22:30-02:00	20,263	100	3.8	770	48,361	2.3	1,112
Weekend	VARIOUS	20,263	100	6.4	1,297	48,361	4.2	2,031
Children's	VARIOUS	20,263	100	2.7	547	48,361	1.2	580

Source: Auditel/Marketing TV Service

Television, continued

Scheduling and Regional

- The most common commercial lengths are :20 and :30 (80%); lengths of :05 and greater are possible.
- Commercials are aired in specific blocks at the beginnings and ends of programs in state TV; they may also be aired within the programs in commercial TV.
- Regional buying is not possible.

Children's Advertising

All programming accepts advertising targeted at children.

Radio

- There are 620 stations in Italy, 5 of which are state-owned; the others are private. 53 of these stations are in Rome, 50 are in Milan. *(Source: AudiRadio, 1991)*
- Ninety-eight percent of all households have radios; the estimated number is 20,234,000. *(Source: ISTAT, 1990)*
- The only broadcasting language is Italian.
- The most popular program types on national stations are News and Sports; on private stations, Music.
- Commercial lengths available range from :07 to :60 and up in private, :15–:40 in state.
- Regional buying is possible; the cost is similar to that of national buys, and there is no premium for buying this way.

Ratings, Adults, 15+ (47,958,000)

Daypart	Adult Rating		Adult (000)	
	State	Commercial	State	Commercial
06:00-09:00	17.0	16.2	8,153	7,787
09:00-12:00	5.1	15.9	2,453	7,619
12:00-15:00	6.9	12.6	3,330	6,055
15:00-18:00	4.7	13.4	2,277	6,438
18:00-21:00	3.7	10.7	1,781	5,124
21:00-24:00	1.8	6.4	848	3,090

(Source: AudiRadio, 1991)

Prime/Peak Time

State	07:00-08:00
Private	09:00-12:00
Young People	14:30-16:30

Cost

Daypart Costs/CPMs (Target=Persons 11+)

Daypart	Local Time	Avg. Cost :30 Unit	Audience (000)	CPM US$
Prime Time				
STATE	07:00-08:30	4,395	1,847	2.38
PRIVATE	09:00-18:00	2,327	3,316	0.70
Daytime				
STATE	09:00-20:00	1,283	369	3.48
PRIVATE	09:00-20:00	2,296	3,095	0.74
Late Night				
STATE	20:00-24:00	163	75	2.17
PRIVATE	20:00-24:00	2,054	1,185	1.73

Source: Spring 1993 rate cards for state and private radio

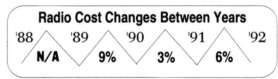

Radio Cost Changes Between Years

'88	'89	'90	'91	'92
N/A	9%	3%	6%	

Source: Leo Burnett estimates

Cable

There is no data available on cable TV in Italy.

Satellite

- Satellite TV is growing but cannot be compared to other countries.
- Programs can only be received via a parabolic aerial system.

Satellite Channel	Country of Origin	Language	Programming
Eurosport	N/A	German, English, Dutch	Sport
Sky Sports	N/A	English	Sport
DSF	Germany	German	Sport
The Movie Channel	UK	English	Movies
Sky Movies Plus	UK	English	Movies
Euronews	N/A	German, English, Spanish, French, Italian	News
CNN	USA	English	News
Sky News	UK	English	News
MTV	USA	English	Music
Sky One	UK	English	Various
UK Gold	UK	English	Various
Children's Channels	UK	English	Children's programs
Super Channel	UK	English	Various
3 Sat	Germany	German	Various
Eins Plus	Germany	German	Various
Sat 1	Germany	German	Various

Source (Satellite): Satellite TV Guide

Video Cassettes

Roughly 38.3% of TV households have video cassette recorders (VCRs). Video cassettes in Italy do carry commercials, but no data is available on units or rates. There is not yet any agency auditing VCR usage in Italy, but AGB/Auditel is expected to produce viewing data soon. *(Source (Percent of households): Auditel Basic Research)*

Cinema

- The total number of cinemas in Italy is unknown, but it is greater than 200,000. All cinemas sell commercial time. *(Source (Number of cinemas): Spring 1993 rate cards)*
- Commercial lengths available include :10, :15, :20, :30, :45, :60 and up.
- Cinema advertising is currently in a period of crisis, and expectations are not good.

Newspapers

Italy has seven national daily newspapers.

Newspaper Cost Changes Between Years

'88	'89	'90	'91	'92
N/A	8%	5%	2%	

Source: Leo Burnett estimates

Newspaper	Market	Size	Circ. (000)	Avg. Daily Aud. (000)	1 Page B&W Cost (US$)	Accept Color?
Il Corriere della Sera	National	400 x 540	677.9	2,806	83,468	Yes
La Repubblica	National	Tabloid	699.9	3,487	76,209	No
La Stampa	Turin	338 x 480	428.0	1,883	61,742	No
Il Messaggero	Rome	370 x 502	269.7	1,419	63,145	Yes
Il Resto del Carlino	Bologna	396 x 513	232.9	1,305	44,274	Yes
La Nazione	Florence	396 x 512	204.9	1,227	44,274	Yes
Il Mattino	Naples	366 x 503	166.5	1,106	38,105	Yes
La Gazzetta del.Mezzogiorno	N/A	N/A	N/A	557	N/A	N/A
Il Giornale	National	356 x 520	156.4	711	28,948	No
SPORTS DAILIES						
Gazzetta dello Sport	National	400 x 545	427.6	3,344	38,104	No
Corriere Sport-Stadio	National	395 x 530	270.3	1,869	35,201	No
FINANCIAL						
Il Sole 24 Ore	National	395 x 535	303.9	1,454	50,806	Yes

Sources: (Circulation): Ads 1992; (Audience): Audipress 93/I; (Cost B/W): Spring 1993 rate cards

Magazines

There are 114 consumer magazines, and 1,686 trade and technical publications in Italy.

Source: Audipress/ISTAT

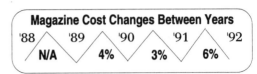

Source Leo Burnett estimates

Magazine	Type	Frequency	Circ. (000)	Audited?	Avg. Adult Aud (000)	1 page 4/C Cost (US$)
TV Sorrisi e Canzoni	Entertainment TV	Weekly	2,248.9	Yes	10,705	59,140
Famiglia Cristiana	Family	Weekly	1,078.3	Yes	5,416	38,710
Gioia	Women	Weekly	440.1	Yes	2,425	43,615
Donna Moderna	Women	Weekly	634.4	Yes	3,715	36,828
Panorama	News	Weekly	529.6	Yes	4,714	4,489.2
Espresso	News	Weekly	362.5	Yes	3,175	33,570
Gente	Family/News	Weekly	814.6	Yes	4,976	40,725
Quattroruote	Cars/Sport	Monthly	713.7	Yes	7,677	29,267
Tuttomusica-Spettacolo	Music/Leisure	Monthly	477.5	Yes	2,279	13,306
Topolino	Kids/Cartoons	Weekly	498.7	Yes	3,249	14,785
Casaviva	Interior Decorating	Monthly	299.8	Yes	2,218	21,370
Airone	Nature	Monthly	138.4	Yes	1,618	20,161
Color Supplements						
Venerdi (weekly supplement to La Republica)		Weekly	877.2	Yes	4,786	40,215
7 (Saturday supplement to Corriere Dalla Sera)		Weekly	689.3	Yes	3,002	44,354

Sources: (Circulation) Ads; (Audience): Audipress 93/I; (Cost 4/C): Spring 1993 rate cards

Outdoor/Transit

Billboard	**Transit**
Sites available (Public)................N/A (Private)...............31,300** Lead Time to reserve ....2-10 months Exposure 79%	Boards available ....3,129 Exposure ....N/A
Costs Average, 1 billboard/15 days*** 6 m x 3 m ....US$ 470 6 m x 3 m ....US$ 329-$437 **Billboard Cost Changes Between Years*** '88 / '89 / '90 / '91 / '92 N/A / 13% / 8% / 10%	**Costs** Average, 1 board/month: **Available upon request** **Transit Cost Changes Between Years*** '88 / '89 / '90 / '91 / '92 N/A / 13% / 8% / 10%
Sizes 6 m x 3 m, 1 m x 1.4 m, 1.4 m. x 2 m	**Sizes** 3 m x 0.7 m, 1.2 m x 0.7 m, 1.2 m x 0.45 m

*Sources: * Leo Burnett estimate; **INDE Affissioni; *** Spring 1993 rate cards*

Direct Marketing

Direct Marketing is still a growing market in Italy.

List Broker	Information Provided
Cemit	General list suppliers
Olinet	General list suppliers
Addressvit	General list suppliers
CEDAP	General list suppliers
Dun & Bradstreet Kosmos	List of companies supplied
Telemarketing Companies	**Direct Marketing Associations**
Tellemme	Aidim, Corso Venezia 16, Milan
Teleperformance	Assodirect, Via Larga 19, Milan
Telemarketing Italia	
Telesurvey	
Cemit	

Non-Traditional Media

This area is in continual growth. Direct response, promotions, PR, and sponsorship are evident.

Research Sources

Medium Covered	Research Company	Information Provided
TV	Auditel	Audience for HHs and ind. 4+ years-breakdown by: territory, city size, socio/economic level, homemakers, 12 age groups, sex, presence of children, educational level
Periodicals	Audipress Via Larga 19 Milan	Number of readers, reading frequency, origin of copy read, socio/demographic groups, psychographic profile, 6 monthly/120 periodicals audited
Dailies	Audipress Via Larga 19, Milan	Number of readers, reading frequency, socio/demographic groups, 6 monthly/53 dailies audited
Cinema		Research not continuous, last available information is dated 1986 and provides data on cinema-goers by age and socio/demographic groups
Radio	Audiradio Via Larga 19, Milan	Audience rating per min, socio/demographic groups. Stations audited: state radios, private networks and local stations in each province
Ads	Ads Via Larga 19, Milan	Circulation and research for dailies and periodicals

Television Research is available by people meter daily on-line, or printed weekly and monthly.

Advertising Regulations

By Product

Beverages/Alcohol

In TV spots, presenting the consumption of alcoholic beverages as an integral part of sports activities, study, work or driving is prohibited. Casting people under 25 years old is also prohibited. Cartoons or drawings which may be of interest to children cannot be used. Alcoholic beverage ads can only be aired after 20:30 state TV and after 15:30 on commercial channels. *(Source: State TV regulation)*

Cigarettes

Banned by law on all media.

Pharmaceuticals/Drugs

Approval must be obtained from the Ministry of Health for any advertising of pharmaceuticals or drugs. An authorized number must be written on every ad. TV storyboards must be approved by SACIS (Code of Advertising Self Discipline) and authorization must then be obtained from the Ministry of Health. The directions "read the instructions carefully" must be clear in audio and video. People younger than 18 can only play passive roles (cannot present products) in ads.

Advertising To Children

All channels (radio and TV) insist that advertising messages addressed to children are clear and do not encourage dangerous behavior either physically or mentally.

Commercial Production

None. In general comparative advertising is prohibited.

By Medium

Television

Mammi Law enforces limitations regarding: advertising clutter, advertising within cartoons and artistic/educational programs, broadcasting concessions

Outdoor

New highway code restrictions on billboards and illuminated advertising (must not obstruct visibility for motorists or be confused with road signs).

Netherlands

Area	37,330 km^2
Population (1992)	15,112,064
Population growth rate (1992)	0.6%
GDP	US$ 249.6 billion
GDP/per capita	US$ 16,600
Real growth rate (1991)	2.2%
Capital	Amsterdam

Population Breakdown

By Sex
Male 49%
Female................................... 51%

By Age Group
Children, 0-19 ....24.6%
Teens, 20-39.........................32.9%
Adults, 40-64........................29.4%
Seniors, 65+ 13%

By Socio-Economic Status
A 17.2%
B1 ....21.5%
B2 ....18.8%
C 35.5%
D...7.0%

Source: Central Bureau for Statistics, 1993

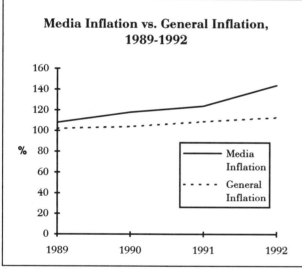

Media Inflation vs. General Inflation, 1989-1992

Legend:
— Media Inflation
- - - General Inflation

Source (Media Inflation): VEA MIB, 1993

Number of Households   6,241,000
Ownership of household durables
   Car................................. 65%
   Phone............................ 48%
   Washers........................ 80%
   (purchasing power equivalent)
GNP distribution by industry
   Agriculture.................... 4%
   Industry 31%
   Services 65%
Exchange rates (US$ to local currency)
   1991 ....0.5530
   1992 ....0.5453

Source: Central Bureau for Statistics, 1993

National Holidays

Holiday	1993 Date
New Years Day	January 1
Christmas	December 25 - 26
Good Friday	April 1
Ascension Day	May 12
Whitsunside	May 22 - 23
Easter	April 3 - 4

School Holidays

Holiday	1993 Date
Autumn (Middle & North regions)	October 17-October 15
Autumn (South region)	October 24-November 1
Christmas (all)	December 19-January 3
Winter (Middle & South regions)	February 20-Febraury 28
Winter (North region)	February 27-March 7
Spring (all)	April 30-May 9

Major Influences and Trends

The TV market is still developing. This year we have seen the launch of airtime sales on Filmnet Plus, the subscription movie and events channel. On the first of October, the Netherlands saw the launch of RTL5, the second private commercial TV channel. Print is suffering as a result from these TV developments and the effects of the recession. Newspapers suffer most with severe losses in spending for cars, daily goods and personal recruitment.

Radio is still developing with new channels and formats becoming more available. Outdoor and cinema remain stable amidst the turmoil.

The market is becoming more short term in both buying and objectives. Plans are rarely commited to for the whole calendar year. Advertisers seek the short term comforts of heavy promotional support for their brands. This is specifically true for cars, audio/video and other durables

Spending Analysis

National advertising spending by medium
(based on appropriate year's exchange rate)

	1989 US$ MM	1990 US$ MM	1991 US$ MM	1992 US$ MM
TV	272	340	391	464
Cinema	8	8	10	12
Radio	52	59	100	116
Newspaper	1,275	1,337	1,398	1,351
Magazine	946	1020	802	825
Direct Response	1,239	1,269	1,441	1,558
Outdoor	138	126	248	302
Other	132	160	597	705
Total	**4,062**	**4,319**	**4,987**	**5,333**

Source: VEA 1993

Media Buying

The market is more or less settling, since all key players are now active. There is a trend to place media strategy within the advertising agency and media buying, optimization and administration with the media agency. Buying services represent 70% of the market's total expenditures. All the buying services below are agency affiliated except Carat Nederland, which is independent.

Buying Services with 1992 Billings

Buying Service	Marketshare	1992 Billings (US $ MM)
The Media partnership	35%	327
Carat Nederland	12%	115
Initiative Media	18%	166
EQUMEDIA	12%	109
Media Exposure	12%	109
Universal Media	12%	109

Source: Adformatie

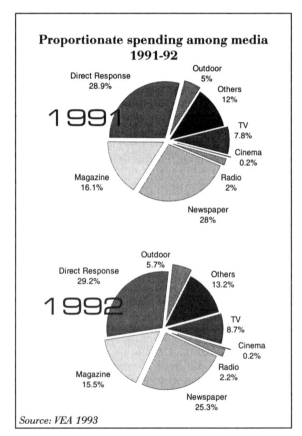

Proportionate spending among media 1991-92

1991
Direct Response 28.9%
Outdoor 5%
Others 12%
TV 7.8%
Cinema 0.2%
Radio 2%
Newspaper 28%
Magazine 16.1%

1992
Direct Response 29.2%
Outdoor 5.7%
Others 13.2%
TV 8.7%
Cinema 0.2%
Radio 2.2%
Newspaper 25.3%
Magazine 15.5%

Source: VEA 1993

Top Advertisers(1992 spending)

By Company

Parent Company	Product Categories	US$ MM
Procter & Gamble		27.1
Albert Heijn	Supermarket	16.9
Capital lever		16.0
RVD (Rijks Voorlichtings Dienst)	Government	14.4
		12.1
Van den Bergh foods	Food company of Unilever	9.5
Heineken		9.3
PTT Post		8.7
PTT Telecom		8.0
Nestle		7.5
Bols		

Source: Adformatie, Feb. 02, 1993.

Television

Overview

	Adult Reach	
	at 250 GRPs	62.5%
	at 500 GRPs	125%
	at 1,000 GRPs	150%

- Two new channels emerged in 1993.
- TV advertising share increasing at the cost of print.
- There are more and more scattered TV audiences.
  Penetration is now estimated at 98%, or 6,116,000 households.
- Prices are more or less stable.

Opportunities

Network	Number of Stations	Ownership	Station Profile	Commercial Minutes/Day	Coverage	Broadcast Hours (Sign-On/Off)
NL1		State	ABC	39	98%	14:00-24:00
NL2		State	ABC	35	98%	14:00-24:00
NL3		State	ABC	30	98%	14:00-24:00
RTL4		Public	CD	90	97%	07:00-03:00
Kindernet		Public	Kids	20	70%	07:00-10:00
From October 1, 1993						
RTL5		Public	Highly educated/ men/youth	60	±70%	17:00-02:00

Costs

Prime Time TV Costs for :30 in US$			
1989	1990	1991	1992
N/A	7,089	7,634	8,180

Television Cost Changes Between Years

'88 — 15% — '89 — 40% — '90 — 21% — '91 — 27% — '92

Audiences/CPM's

Average Cost, Audience, and CPMs by Daypart
(Top 3 stations, :30 national TV Target=Adults, urban areas, April 1993)

Hours	Morning 7:00-9:00	Daytime 14:00-18:00	Prime Time 18:00-22:30	Late Night 22:30-24:00	Weekend	Children
Station: NL1					same as	
US$	N/A	2,181	5,453	3,817	week	N/A
Avg. Aud. (000)	N/A	245	552	276		N/A
CPM	N/A	8.90	9.88	13.83		N/A
Station: NL2						
US$	N/A	3,272	6,544	4,908		N/A
Avg. Aud. (000)	N/A	240	588	504		N/A
CPM	N/A	13.63	11.12	9.74		N/A
Station: RTL4						
US$	1,091	2,727	8,725	5,453		N/A
Avg. Aud. (000)	N/A	360	972	588		N/A
CPM	N/A	7.58	8.98	9.27		N/A

Audiences/Ratings by Daypart (National broadcast, :30, Target=13+)

| Daypart | Hours | Household | | | | Adults | | |
		Universe (000)	Hut Levels	Household Rating	Impressions (000)	Universe (000)	Adult Rating	Impressions (000)
Morning	7:00-9:00	4,361	N/A	0.8	35	12,210	1	122
Daytime	14:00-18:00	4,361	N/A	2.6	113	12,210	3	366
Primetime	18:00-22:30	4,361	N/A	8.0	349	12,210	9	1,099
Late Night	22:30-24:00	4,361	N/A	4.5	196	12,210	5	611
Weekend								
Children's								

Scheduling/Regional/Local/Languages

LANGUAGES	Programming		Commercials
Primary Language	Dutch	60%	Dutch 90%
Secondary Language	English&		English
	German	40%	

- Commercials are aired in specific time blocks. Public notices are aired at the beginning and ends of programs; commercials are aired at the beginning, end and within programs.

- Commercial lengths available include all :05 increments between :10 and :60, although lengths greater than :60 are also available. The most commonly used length (31%) is :30.
- Regional buys are available; however, only 2% of all commercials are bought regionally. Rates vary.

Children's Advertising

Advertising may be directed to children in adult or children's programming. The children's universe is estimated at 1,850,000 children; impressions at 160.9, and ratings for the children's universe are 8.7.
Source: All television information from Informart

Radio

Overview

- There are 5 state-owned radio stations in the Netherlands, of which only Radio 5 is non-commercial. Concert Radio, Eurojazz, Sky Radio, Holland FM, RTL Radio, Love Radio, Radio 538, Radio Noordzee are privately owned.
- Approximately 98% of all households have radios; the estimated number is 6 million. No data is available on radios in automobiles.

Radio Cost Changes Between Years

'88 — '89 — '90 — '91 — '92
8% — 17% — 52% — 163%

- The primary broadcasting language is Dutch. English is also used.
- Commercial lengths available range from :10 to :60 in :05 increments; commercials longer than :60 are also possible.
- No premiums are required. The most popular program types are news and music.
- Prime Time is 09:00-12:00.

Costs

Overall Averages

For a :30 radio commercial	Average Cost: US$ 873
	Average CPM: US$ 2.00

Daypart Costs/CPMs (Target=Adults)

Daypart	Local Time	Cost :30 Unit	Audience (000)	CPM (US$)
Prime Time	7:00-9:00	1,830	617	2.97
Daytime	7:00-19:00	1,260	495	2.55
Late Night	23:-24:00	608	30	20.27

Source: All radio information from Informart

Cable

- Holland has very high cable penetration: 87%, or about 5,400,000 cable households. The average household gets 15 commercial channels via cable. There is only one non-commercial channel. *Source: Informart*
- Cable is fully- or semi–government-owned. It is also subsidized, and there are city-wide monopolies.
- No new dramatic growth is anticipated.
- Dutch is the primary language on cable; however, English, French and German are also used. The top cable channels are RTL4, NL3, NL2, NL1 and BRT1.

Satellite

- Satellite channels are distributed by cable. Most stations are part of the European/Worldwide networks.
- Satellite programs and commercials are subject to the rules of the EEC Media Directives.
- The recent growth is expected to stop. Perhaps another 3.5% of the total households will acquire satellite access in the next five years. *Source: Informart*

Satellite Channels Available

Channel	Country of Origin	Language	Programming
CNN	USA	American	Cable/D.B.S. dish reception
Super Channel	USA	English, Dutch, German	Cable, D.B.S. dish reception
Eurosport	France, USA	English, Dutch, German, French	Cable/D.B.S. dish reception
MTV	UK	English, American	"
TV5*	Belgium, France, Switzerland, Canada	French	"
Kindernet	Holland	Dutch (subtitled)	"
Filmnet Plus	France, Holland	Dutch (subtitled)	"
Filmnet Movies*	France, Holland	Dutch (subtitled)	"
RTL+	Germany	German	"
Discovery Channel	USA/UK	English	"

* Non Commercial   Source: Intomart/N&W-LB

Video Cassettes

About 53% of TV households have video cassette recorders (VCRs). However, tapes rarely carry commercials, and this is not considered a significant medium for advertising in the Netherlands. Intomart is the service which measures VCR usage.

Cinema

- There are at least 180 cinemas in the Netherlands, and virtually all offer commercial time.
- Potential reach over 4 weeks is 15%.
- Lengths available are as follows:
    - 30-45 sec.
    - 46-60 sec.
    - 66-110 sec.
    - 111-150 sec.
- The average cost of a two-week cinema schedule providing total coverage of Amsterdam, Rotterdam, the Hague and Utrecht (59 theaters) is US$ 15,201.

Source (Cinema Information): Bioscoop Reclame Handboek 1993

Newspapers

There are 6 national daily and 43 regional/local papers which accept advertising.

Source: VEA M/B 1993

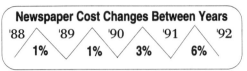

Newspaper Cost Changes Between Years

'88	'89	'90	'91	'92
	1%	1%	3%	6%

Source: VEA M/B 1993

Newspaper	Market	Size	Circ. (000)	Avg. Daily Aud. (000)	1 page B&W Cost (US$)	Accept Color?
Algemeen Dagblad	National	5,500 mm	397	1,285	23,779	Y
Financieele Dagblad	National	5,500 mm	38	215	14,936	Y
NRC Handelsblad	National	5,500 mm	248	525	30,372	Y
Telegraaf	National	5,500 mm	709	2,014	38,539	Y
Trouw	National	5,500 mm	120	293	12,117	Y
Vokskrant	National	5,500 mm	343	849	23,723	Y

Sources (Circulation): Handboek V/D, Ned. PERS 1993; (Audience): SUMMO; (Cost B/W): CEBUCO 1993

Magazines

There are 170 national consumer magazines and 503 trade and technical magazines published in the Netherlands.

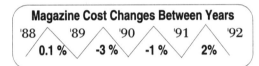

Magazine Cost Changes Between Years

'88	'89	'90	'91	'92
	0.1%	-3%	-1%	2%

Source: VEA M/B 1993

Magazine	Type	Frequency	Circ. (000)	Audited?	Avg. Issue Aud. (000)	1 page 4/C Cost (US$)
Autoweek	S.I.	weekly	139,754	Y	592	6,456
Autovisie	S.I.	bi-weekly	57,023	Y	372	4,174
Autokompioen	S.I.	bi-weekly	78,052	Y	743	4,509
Doe-het-zelf	Home	monthly	141,042	Y	865	6,778
Eigen Huis & Interieur	Home	monthly	64,909	Y	759	7,461
Grasduinen	S.I.	monthly	68,766	Y	668	8,779
Kampioen	S.I.	monthly	1,637,119	Y	4,195	11,102
Kinderen	S.I.	monthly		Y	637	7,640
Ouders van nu	S.I.	monthly	157,593	Y	786	7,689
Reizen	S.I.	monthly	37,992	Y	N/A	2,984
Tip	S.I.	monthly	137,713	Y	577	7,498
VT Wonen	Home	monthly	180,860	Y	1,077	10,508
Waterkampioen	S.I.	bi-weekly	55,292	Y	334	3,785
Pauze	Youth	monthly	565,000	N	N/A	17,668
Avrobode	RTV guide	weekly	902,589	Y	1,938	17,706
EO Visie	RTV guide	weekly	120,332	Y	274	2,299
Mikro Gids	RTV guide	weekly	417,862	Y	822	4,144 (B&W!)
NCRV Gids	RTV guide	weekly	466,391	Y	1,027	10,197
Studio	RTV guide	weekly	261,625	Y	558	5,857
Televizier	RTV guide	weekly	280,763	Y	701	15,399
Troskompas	RTV guide	weekly	635,205	Y	1,453	8,103
VARA TV-mag.	RTV guide	weekly	556,141	Y	1,214	12,629
Veronica	RTV guide	weekly	1,119,749	Y	3,000	17,530
VPRO Gids	RTV guide	weekly	202,367	Y	263	5,727
Intermediair	Business	weekly	210,476	Y	649	15,541
Management Team	Business	bi-weekly	121,518	Y	513	7,882
Quote	Business	monthly	35,000	N	N/A	7,127
Aktueel	Entertain	weekly	101,511	Y	1,334	5,153
Playboy	Men's	monthly	129,165	Y	524	9,434
Penthouse	Men's	monthly	92,078	Y	268	7,226
Het Beste	Family	monthly	387,639	Y	1,013	12,078

Continued on the following page

Magazines, continued

Magazine	Type	Frequency	Circ. (000)	Audited?	Avg. Issue Aud. (000)	1 page 4/C Cost (US$)
Nieuwe Revu	Entertain	weekly	160,001	Y	1,629	9,456
Panorama	Entertain	weekly	196,362	Y	2,039	10,655
Prive	Gossip	weekly	493,038	Y	2,364	15,837
Story	Gossip	weekly	417,546	Y	2,353	11,506
Weekend	Gossip	weekly	371,346	Y	1,644	6,489
Man	Men's	monthly	27,236	Y	104	3,888
Esquire	Men's	bi-monthly	30,000	Y	N/A	3,708
Elsevier	Opinion	weekly	123,087	Y	566	9,308
Vrij Nederland	Opinion	weekly	92,925	Y	374	7,097
HP/De Tijd	Opinion	weekly	85,000	Y	214	5,794
Finance	Opinion	monthly	42,500	Y	N/A	4,362
Ski Magazine	Sports	bi-monthly	99,000	N	180	5,019
Sport Int'l.	Sports	monthly	44,589	Y	317	3,500
Voetbal Int'l.	Sports	monthly	188,598	Y	1,047	6,180
Ariade	Womens/SI	monthly	635,205	Y	501	13,142
Avantgarde	Womens	monthly	46,563	Y	387	6,489
Avenue	Womens	monthly	48,284	Y	356	7,730
Cosmopolitan	Womens	monthly	132,372	Y	496	10,808
Elegance	Womens	monthly	60,957	Y	380	7,730
Knip	Womens/Si	monthly	160,085	Y	703	7,383
Libelle	Womens	monthly	778,724	Y	3,184	27,560
Margriet	Womens	monthly	539,103	Y	2,508	21,828
Nouveau	Womens	monthly	154,822	Y	465	10,481
Opzij	Womens	monthly	60,359	Y	205	4,305
Viva	Womens	weekly	136,789	Y	601	79,667
Top 10	Pop music	3-weekly	120,000	N	NA	4,090
Yes	Youth/Women	weekly	174,033	Y	726	8,474
Elle	Womens	monthly	85,000	N	184	8,343
Marie Claire	Womens	monthly	84,368	Y	165	7,716

Sources (Circulation and costs B/W): Handboek V.D. NED PERS 1993; (Reach and Audit): SUMMO

Outdoor/Transit

Billboard	**Transit**
Sites available ....5,500 **Lead Time to reserve** ....3 months	**Boards available** City Trams ....110 National Buses ....400 City Buses ....133 Trainwagon sides 600
Exposure 45%	Costs rose in 1990 but not since.
Costs **Average, 1 billboard/month** 116 cm x 118 cm ....US$ 464 **Cost changes** Prices have risen, but package periods have also.	**Costs** **Average, 1 board/month** ....varies by size **Cost changes** No cost changes since 10% in 1990.
Sizes 332 cm x 236 cm	**Sizes** Transit buses.................................. 845 cm x 709 cm Tram boarding side .... 1280 cm x 50 cm Tram non boarding side............ 1780 cm x 50 cm Train...47 cm x 62 cm

Direct Marketing

Relatively advanced infrastructure and postal system. One of Europe's top DM users (per capita). First signs of environment/privacy 'backlash' have appeared in mailbox stickers saying 'No unaddressed direct mail'. Addressed mail concentrated in traditional sectors (finance, insurance, funds solicitations, subscriptions, retail). Growing use in non-traditional sectors (FMCG etc.).

Top Direct Mail (Consumer) List Brokers	Information Provided
Goe Markeprofiel	broad spectrum (no buying history)
Hulsink Direct Marketing	address, buying history
Direct List Services	address, interest area
Schober Direct Marketing	address, interest area
Omnidata	broad spectrum (no buying history)
Telemarketing Companies	Direct Marketing Association
Bell Sell	D.M.I.N.
Services Network telefoondiensten	(Direct Marketing Institute Netherlands)
Telecom Direct Almere	Weerdestein 96
Vierhand	1083 GG Amsterdam
Marke-Tel	Tel. 31-20-6429595

Non-Traditional Media

Non-traditional media is not noticeable in The Netherlands.

Research Sources

Media Covered	Research Company	Information Provided
TV/Radio	Intomart P.O. Box 10004 1201 DA Hilversum	Radio/TV audience data
TV/cinema/ press/outdoor	SUMMO Vliegtuigstraat 26 losg CL Amsterdam	Audience data, product usage, buying frequency, socio-economic and demographic information

Television research is available by people meter within 24 hours.

Advertising Regulations

By Product

Beverages/Alcohol

For all alcoholic beverages (containing 1.5% or more alcohol by volume) restrictions are the same. Main restrictions for all media types: advertising messages may not be specially aimed at minors/children or persons who appear to be minors. Audiovisual commericials must contain an educational slogan ('Enjoy a drink, but only moderate' and/or 'Keep it pleasant, drink moderate.') and air for a minimum of 3 seconds.

Source: Code for Alcoholic Beverage

Food/Restaurants:

Since November 1, 1991 advertising of sweets can also be broadcast before 20:00. Advertising of sweets must display the symbol of a toothbrush.

Cigarettes

No tobacco advertising on TV, radio, some magazines (youth/sports) and public transport (buses, trams, trains). Ad restrictions are expected for cinema placement starting in 1996.

Advertising may not be aimed at minors (<18yrs). In all tobacco advertising a warning-line must be carried. Note: No restrictions for pipe tobacco and cigars!

Source: Code for Cigarettes and Shag.

Pharmaceuticals/Drugs

Medical drugs, weight reducers etc., are subject to screening by experts (KOAGG/KAMA).

Norway

Area	324,220 km^2
Population (1992)	4,294,876
Population growth rate (1992)	0.5%
GDP	US$ 72.9 billion
GDP/per capita	US$ 17,100
Real growth rate (1991)	4.1%
Capital	Oslo

Population Breakdown

By Sex		*By Age Group*	
Male	49%%	Children, 1-14	18%
Female	51%%	Teens, 15-19	8%
		Adults, 19+	74%

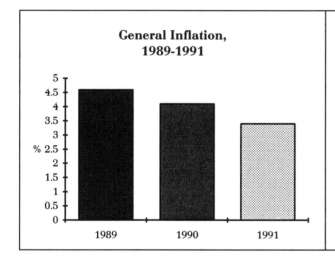

General Inflation, 1989-1991

Number of Households	1,800,000

Ownership of household durables

Car	74%
Phone	93%
Washers	96%

(purchasing power equivalent)

GNP distribution by industry

Agriculture	N/A
Industry	N/A
Services	N/A

Exchange rates (US$ to local currency)

1991	N/A
1992	0.17857

National Holidays

Holiday	*1993 Date*
New Year's Day	January 1
Maundy Thursday	April 16
Good Friday	April 17
Easter Monday	April 20
Labor Day	May 1
Constitution Day	May 17
Ascension Day	May 28
Whit Sunday	May 7
Whit Monday	May 8
Christmas Day	December 25
Boxing Day	December 26

School Holidays

Holiday	*1993 Date*
Summer Vacation	June 20-August 20
Easter Holiday	April 12-13
Christmas	December 17-January 4
Autumn Holiday	September 17-24
Winter Holiday	February 5-15

Major Influences and Trends

Media independents currently dominate the media market in Norway. Advertising agencies have been re-structured to accommodate for the prominence of these buying clubs, with most ad agencies choosing to absolve internal media departments and leave the media buying to the independents.

Spending Analysis

National advertising spending by medium
based on appropriate year's exchange rate

	1989 US$ MM	1990 US$ MM	1991 US$ MM	1992 US$ MM
TV	17	67	142	290
Cinema	46	53	50	47
Radio	8	19	27	24
Newspaper	1,332	1,420	1,381	1,294
Magazine	247	295	250	232
Outdoor	32	48	71	80
Other	33	43	36	N/A
Total	**1,715**	**1,945**	**1,957**	**1,977**

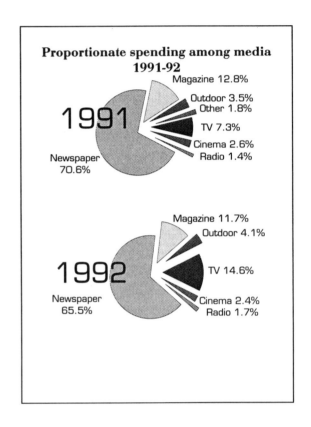

Proportionate spending among media 1991-92

1991
Newspaper 70.6%
Magazine 12.8%
Outdoor 3.5%
Other 1.8%
TV 7.3%
Cinema 2.6%
Radio 1.4%

1992
Newspaper 65.5%
Magazine 11.7%
Outdoor 4.1%
TV 14.6%
Cinema 2.4%
Radio 1.7%

Media Buying

There are three huge media independents who account for 80-90% of the media market. Very few agencies currently have their own media departments, the majority are letting the independents do all media buying

Buying Services
Carat Intermedia
Media Marketing
Reklame Formidling
Carat Mediakanalen
Media Plus

Television

There are two national channels, which cover 50% of the country. Only one of these accepts advertising. The national commercial station is currently expanding and campaigns must be booked several weeks early. This is a change for Norway and has led to increased ad rates.

Other facts about Norwegian TV
- Prime time costs were US$ 11,900 for :30 in 1990. Costs rose 150% in 1991. No recent data has been compiled.
- Norwegian is the only language used.
- The most common commercial length is :30. Other lengths, starting with :10 and increasing in :10 increments to :60, are also available.
- Commercials are aired throughout the day. TV2 and TVN air in blocks, TV3 in breaks.
- Advertising directed to children is not allowed.
- There are no regional advertising opportunities.

TV HH Penetration		Adult Reach	
Station	*% of total HH*		
TV2	90%	at 250 GRPs	68%
TV3	45%	at 500 GRPs	79%
TVN	50%	at 1000 GRPs	85%

Radio

- In Norway, there are 1 national, 3 state-owned, and about 400 local radio stations. About 25 of these are located in Oslo, but only 5 are large enough to be appealing to most advertisers.
- Ninety-eight percent of all households have radios; the estimated number is 1,764,00.

- The only broadcasting language is Norwegian.
- The most popular program type is light entertainment.
- Commercial lengths available vary; a maximum of 15% of air time is available overall.
- No average rates are available for an average :30 spot.

Cable

- Cable is becoming increasingly important in the market as penetration slowly builds. Penetration is increasing by 2-3% every year. It is currently at about 49% of all households, or 882, households.
- There are 2 commercial cable channels.. Norwegian is the only language used.

Norway's Cable Channels

	Cost US$ Per Point	Rating	Commercial Min/Hour
TV Norge	2.50	8	20% (12)
TV3	2.30	3	20% (12)

Satellite

- Satellite is in the beginning stages in Norway. It is expected to slowly increase in penetration. At this time there is no data on it.

Satellite Channel	Country of Origin	Languuage
Swedish TV1	Sweden	Swedish
Swedish TV2	Sweden	Swedish
TV3	Sweden	Scandinavian
TVNorge	Norway	Norwegian
TV 4	Norway	Norwegian
TV2	Norway	Norwegian
Eurosport	Great Britain	English
Super Channel	Great Britain/Italy	English
MTV	Great Britain	English

Video Cassettes

Roughly 50% of TV households in Norway have video cassette recorders (VCRs). Video cassettes in Norway do carry commercials. Both rates and number of advertisers per tape vary. The situation is stable. People meters are used to measure VCR usage.

Cinema

- About half of the cinemas in Norway offer commercial time. Lengths vary from :10 to :60.
- Over 4 weeks, an ad run at 400 theaters would reach about 17% of the total population.
- The cost of a cinema campaign varies.

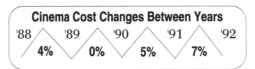

Cinema Cost Changes Between Years				
'88	'89	'90	'91	'92
4%	0%	5%	7%	

Newspapers

- Norway has 2 national daily newspapers, with a combined circulation of 900,000.
- Literacy rate in English is 95%.

Newspaper	Market	Size	Circ. (000)	Avg. Daily Aud. (000)	1 Page B&W Cost (US$)	Accept Color?
Aetenposter	N/A	Broadsheet	275	756	17	Yes
Dughladet	N/A	Tabloid	225	921	8	Yes
VG	N/A	Tabloid	315	1,322	11	Yes
Bergens Fidenale	N/A	Broadsheet	96	260	7	Yes
Adresslavisen	N/A	Broadsheet	90	241	7	Yes
Stavanger Altenblak	N/A	Broadsheet	71	179	5	Yes

Magazines

Norway has 40 consumer magazines and about 500 trade and technical publications. Rates and circulation information are not available.

Magazine	Type	Frequency	Audited?	Avg. Issue Aud. (000)	1 page 4/C Cost (US$)
Hjmet	Family/Women	Monthly	N/A	N/A	N/A
Motor	Motor	Monthly	N/A	N/A	N/A
Se & Hor	Entertainment	Weekly	N/A	N/A	N/A
Norsk ukeblad	Family/Women	Monthly	N/A	N/A	N/A
Allers	Family/Women	Weekly	N/A	N/A	N/A
Illustrert Viten.	Political Science	Monthly	N/A	N/A	N/A
Familien	Family/Women	Bi-monthly	N/A	N/A	N/A
Vi Menn	Men	Weekly	N/A	N/A	N/A
Det Beste	Reader's Digest	Monthly	N/A	N/A	N/A
Bonytt/Hjem & F.	Home Leisure	Monthly	N/A	N/A	N/A
KK	Women	Weekly	N/A	N/A	N/A
Oknomisk Rapport	Economic/Business	Monthly	N/A	N/A	N/A
Na	Entertainment	Weekly	N/A	N/A	N/A
Det Nye	Youth/Women	Monthly	N/A	N/A	N/A
Jakt & Fiske	Hunting/Fishing	Monthly	N/A	N/A	N/A
Programbladet	TV Magazine	Weekly	N/A	N/A	N/A
Foreldre & Barn	Parents	Monthly	N/A	N/A	N/A
Villmarksliv	Hunting/Fishing	Monthly	N/A	N/A	N/A
Bil	Car Magazine	Monthly	N/A	N/A	N/A
Kapital	Economic/Business	Monthly	N/A	N/A	N/A
Football	Football	8 edits/yr.	N/A	N/A	N/A
Batnytt/Seilas Batliv	Sailing/Boat	8 edits/yr.	N/A	N/A	N/A
Topp	Youth	Monthly	N/A	N/A	N/A
Hytteliv	Cottage/Leisure	Monthly	N/A	N/A	N/A

Direct Marketing

Direct marketing is currently an important media vehicle in Norway and is becoming increasingly significant.

Non-Traditional Media

Non-traditional media is becoming increasingly important in Norway. Ads on toilets in restaurants, on balloons (blimps), on shopping carts, etc.

Research Sources

Medium Covered	Research Company
Newspaper	Gallup
Magazine, TV	MMI
Radio	

TV research is available by TV meters, weekly and monthly.

Outdoor/Transit

Billboard		**Transit**	
Sites available 5,000		Boards available ....all buses	
Lead time to reserve ....min: 3 months			
Costs		**Costs**	
Average, 1 billboard/month ....varies		Average, 1 board/month: ....varies	
Sizes	2 m x 3 m	**Sizes**	25 cm x 35 cm

Advertising Regulations

By Product

Beverages/Alcohol
Since March 1, 1977, advertising for beverages containing alcohol has been prohibited. Furthermore, all advertising for products and raw materials for home production of wine is prohibited.

Cigarettes
A ban on advertising for tobacco (cigarettes, cigars, tobacco, pipes, cigarette paper, and other smoking articles - lighters excepted) has been in effect since July 1, 1975. In principle, the restriction includes all types of advertising aimed at the public, and point of sale activities are also strongly restricted.

Pharmaceuticals/Drugs
Advertising of medical products must be approved in advance by the Ministry of Health.

Advertising To Children
'Be careful'

Sources Consulted

Reklamebyra Foreningen, Norway
SSB Norway, *Statistical Yearbook*

Poland

Area	312,680 km^2
Population (1992)	38,385,617
Population growth rate (1992)	0.4%
GDP	US$ 162.7 billion
GDP/per capita	US$ 4,300
Real growth rate (1991)	5%
Capital	Warsaw

Population Breakdown

By Sex		*By Age Group*		*By Socio-Economic Status*	
Male	48%	Children, 0-14	25%	A	26%
Female	52%	Teens, 15-29	21%	B	38%
		Adults, 30-59	39%	C	17%
		Adults, 60+	15%	D	19%

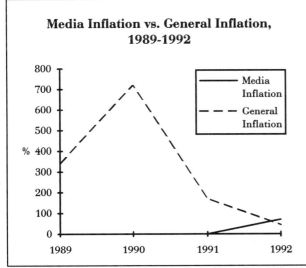

Media Inflation vs. General Inflation, 1989-1992

Number of Households	11,967,000

Ownership of household durables
- Car.............................34.1%
- Phone.......................25.0%
- Washers.....................64.1%
  (purchasing power equivalent)

GNP distribution by industry
- Agriculture..................8.9%
- Industry 44.9%
- Services 46.2%

Exchange rates (US$ to local currency)
- 1991 ....0.000086956
- 1992 ....0.000060894

Source: Statistical Yearbook 1992, Chief Central Statistical Office, Warsaw, Poland, April-Dec. 1992

National Holidays

Holiday	*1993 Date*
New Year	January 1
Easter	April 19 - 20
Labor Day	May 1
3rd of May Constitution	May 3
Corpus CHristi	June 18
Ascension Day	August 15
All Saints Day	November 1
Independence Day	November 11
Christmas	December 25 - 26

School Holidays

Holiday	*1993 Date*
Winter Holidays	January 27 - February 9
Summer Holidays	July 1 - August 31

Major Influences and Trends

- Agencies buy and negotiate media directly with media owners. Big companies such as Procter & Gamble or Master Foods make use of the Agency of Record system.

- There are networks of regional TV, radio and press. Contact with one such TV or radio station can facilitate booking all regions through one central point.

Spending Analysis

National advertising spending by medium
1992 data for period April-December 1992

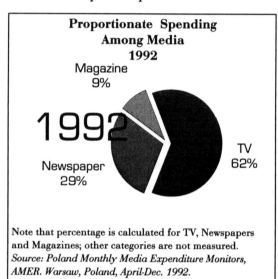

Proportionate Spending Among Media 1992

Magazine 9%

1992

Newspaper 29%

TV 62%

Note that percentage is calculated for TV, Newspapers and Magazines; other categories are not measured.
Source: Poland Monthly Media Expenditure Monitors, AMER. Warsaw, Poland, April-Dec. 1992.

Media Buying

- Media buying is typically done by advertising agencies.
- Buying services are emerging.

Top Advertisers

By Company

Parent Company	Product Categories	US$ MM
Procter & Gamble	Household Articles, Personal Care	14.9
Lever Polska	Household Articles, Personal Care	14.8
Henkel	Household Articles, Personal Care	6.4
Benckiser	Health & Beauty Care	5.7
Masterfoods	Foodstuffs	5.2
L'Oreal	Health & Beauty Care	3.9
Johnson & Johnson	Health & Beauty Care	3.2
Colgate	Health & Beauty Care	2.2
P.Z.U.	Insurance Company	1.7
Home Shopping	Various items	1.5

By Product

Product Category	Advertiser	US$ MM
Laundry Detergents	Ariel	2.3
Automoblies	Renault	.15
Shampoos	Poly Kur	.787
Candies/Confectionary	Mentos	.32

Television

Overview

- National government Polish TV consists of two channels with local programming 30 minutes per day. There are also several private stations that are not yet legal, as well as a legal satellite channel.
- Available commercial lengths include: :06, :15, :20, :35, :40, :45, :60, :65. Of these, :30 is the most popular, accounting for 50% of all commercials. *(Source (:30 data): PTV rate cards, Biuro Rzklamy TVP, Warsaw, Poland, April-Dec. 1992.)*
- Commercials can be aired only in time blocks; it is posible to open a new time block before or after some TV programs. No commercials are allowed within programs on government channels.

Audiences/CPM's

Average Cost, Audience, and CPMs by Daypart
(Top Two Stations, :30, national audience, Target=Adults 16+)

Hours	Morning 07:00 - 09:00	Daytime 09:00 - 19:00	Prime Time 19:00 - 21:30	Late Night 21:30 - 02:00	Weekend	Children
Station: I						
US$	560	2,450	4,450	2,560	3,300	2,600
Avg. Aud. (000)	1,300	2,800	11,830	2,680	5,420	2,350
CPM	0.43	0.88	0.38	0.96	0.61	1.12
Station: II						
US$	1,390	1,760	2,360	1,760	1,690	1,050
Avg. Aud. (000)	1,450	1,680	5,390	1,940	2,160	1,120
CPM	0.96	1.05	0.44	0.91	0.78	0.94

Sources: PTV rate cards, Biuro Rzklamy TVP, Warsaw, Poland, Jan.-Dec. 1992; Weekly TV Audience Monitor, OBOP. Warsaw, Poland, April-Dec. 1992.

Audience/Ratings by Daypart (Target=Adults, 16+)

| Daypart | Hours | Household | | | | Adult | | |
		Universe (000)	Hut Levels	Household Rating	Impressions (000)	Universe (000)	Adult Rating	Impressions (000)
Morning	07:00-09:00	11,967	239	N/A	N/A	28,898	4	1,156
Daytime	09:00-19:00	11,967	1,795	N/A	N/A	28,898	2	578
Primetime	19:00-21:30	11,967	4,787	N/A	N/A	28,898	22	6,358
Late Night	21:30-02:00	11,967	2,393	N/A	N/A	28,898	6	1,734
Weekend		11,967	2,992	N/A	N/A	28,898	10	2,890
Children's		11,967	N/A	N/A	N/A	28,898	5	1,445

Source:: Wykorzystanie Mediow w Polsce, V-VI 1992; Radio i Telewizja; GfK Polonia Institute, Warsaw, Poland, Oct.-Dec. 1992.

Regional/Languages

LANGUAGES	Programming	Commercials
Primary Language	Polish	Polish
Secondary Language	English (1%)	None

40% of all advertising is bought regionally.

Network	Station	Region	Hours
Regional	TV Warsaw, Lodz, Lublin, Gdansk, Poznan, Katowice, Szczecin, Krakow, Wroclaw	100% coverage	18:00 - 18:30 / 18:00 - 21:00 Friday
Polonia 1	Network of 12 regional stations	35% coverage	08:00 - 23:00

Children's Advertising

The children's universe of TV targets has not been estimated. TVP1 and 2 will take ads to children in adult programming but children are not monitored by rating service.

Station	Hours	Days
TVP 1	09:30-10:00	Everyday
TVP 1	19:00-19:30	Everyday
TVP 2	08:30-09:00	Everyday
TVP 2	08:00-09:00	Saturday

Radio

- There are 24 radio stations in Poland, 7 of which are in Warsaw.
- Seventy percent of all households have radios; the estimated number is 11,331,000.
- The primary broadcasting language is Polish; English is also used.
- The most popular program types are news, local information and music.

- Commercial lengths available include: :05, :10, :15, :20, :30, :40, :45, :60.
- Alternatives to national airing include using satellite capabilities to air commercials regionally using a network link, or purchasing local air time on an individual basis.

Radio, continued

- An average :30 spot would cost about US$ 200, or CPM US$ 0.50.
- Regional buying is possible; there is no premium for buying regionally

Daypart Costs/CPMs

Daypart	Local Time	Avg.Cost :30 US$	Audience (000)	CPM
Prime Time	06:00 - 09:00	375	840	0.44
Daytime	09:00 - 19:00	189	560	0.34
Late Night	after 19:00	125	280	0.44

Ratings

Daypart	Adult Rating	Adult (000)
06:00 - 09:00	2	56

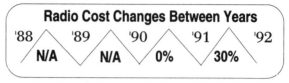

Sources (Radio): Wykorzystanie Mediow w Polsce, V-VI, 1992; (Radio): Telewizja GfK Polonia Institute, Warsaw, Poland, Oct.-Dec. 1992; (Different radio stations' rate cards), Poland, Jan.-Dec. 1992.

Satellite

- There are two Polish satellite program sources:
- TV Polonia is government-owned.
- PolSAT is privately owned, broadcast from the Netherlands.

Currently, there are 2,273 satellite receivers, which represent 19% of the households in Poland. Within the next 5 years, the total is expected to grow to 2,992, or 25% of the total households.

Foreign channels received in Poland

Satellite Channel	Origin	Language
RTL	Germany	German
SAT 1	Germany	German
Tele 5	Germany	German
Pro 7	Germany	German
3 Sat	Germany	German
Eurosport	British	English
Sky Channel	British	English
MTV	British	English

Sources (Satellite): Wykorzystanie Mediow w Polsce, V-VI, 1992; (Radio): Telewizja GfK Polonia Institute, Warsaw, Poland, Oct.-Dec. 1992.

Cable

There are currently limited facilities for cable in Poland.

Video Cassettes

- Currently, about 41% of TV households in Poland have video cassette recorders.
- There is no service that measures VCR usage in Poland.
- VCR tapes do not currently carry commercials. Commercialization is not expected.

Cinema

- There is little interest in Cinema, since quality control is poor and attendance is low.
- Commercial lengths available are :30 and :60.

Newspapers

- 95% of the national daily papers accept advertising.
- Total national newspaper circulation is available through GfK Pentor.
- Agency estimates 20% English literacy.

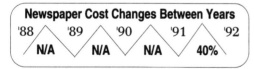

Newspaper	Avg. Daily Aud.(000)
Gazeta Wyborcza	3,300
Rzeczpospolita	800
Express Wieczorny	800
Sztandar Mlodych	700

Source: Press 1992 (Spring, Autumn), Instytut Badania Opinii i Rynku "Pentor". Warsaw, Poland, June 1992, Dec. 1992.

Magazines

Poland has 40 consumer magazines, and an unknown number of trade and technical publications.

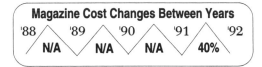

Magazine	Audited?
Wprost	No
Twoj Styl	No
Sukces	No
Antena	No
Kobieta i Zycie	No
Przyjaciolka	No
Polityka	No
Dziewczyna	No
Poradnik Domowy	No
Kobieta i Styl	No

Outdoor/Transit

Billboard		Transit	
Sites available 5,000		**Boards available**	
Lead Time to reserve ....4-6 weeks		2,000	
Exposure ....N/A		Exposure 60-80%	
Costs		**Costs**	
Average, 1 billboard/month		Average, 1 board/month:	
..............................US$ 300		1 bus ....US$ 278	
In 1992, outdoor and transit costs rose approxixmately 20%			
Sizes			
Size varies greatly.			

Direct Marketing

Limited direct marketing in Poland.

Research Sources

Non-Traditional Media

The opportunities represented by non-traditional media have not yet been explored in Poland.

Medium Covered	Research Company	Information Provided
TV, Newspapers, Magazines	AMER	Advertising spending
Newspapers, TV, Magazines, Radio	GfK, Pentor, Estymator	Readership, Ratings, Demographics
TV	OBOP	Ratings
	GfK	Ratings, Demographics

Advertising Regulations

By Product

Beverages/Alcohol
No alchohol advertising permitted.

Food/Restaurants
No restrictions.

Cigarettes
Not allowed on TV or radio.

Pharmaceuticals/Drugs
OTC advertising became legal in December 1993.

Advertising to children
No information.

Commercial Production
Background may be in foreign language but text must be in Polish.

By Medium

Television
No alcohol or cigarette advertising is allowed on TV.

Print
Advertising cannot attempt to aggressively influence people to smoke cigarettes or drink alcohol, but it may inform about such products existing on the market.

Outdoor
Generally similar to print, but local authorities may allow some cigarette and alcohol advertising.

Portugal

Area	92,080 km²
Population (1992)	10,448,509
Population growth rate (1992)	0.4%
GDP	US$ 87.3 billion
GDP/per capita	US$ 8,400
Real growth rate (1991)	2.7%
Capital	Lisbon

Population Breakdown

By Sex		By Age Group		By Socio-Economic Status	
Male	47.6%	Children	25%	A	4.5%
Female	52.3%	Teens	17%	B	10.7%
		Adults	58%	C	52.9%
				D	81.9%

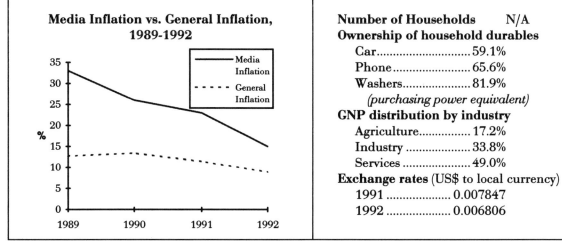

Media Inflation vs. General Inflation, 1989-1992

Number of Households	N/A

Ownership of household durables
- Car 59.1%
- Phone 65.6%
- Washers 81.9%

(purchasing power equivalent)

GNP distribution by industry
- Agriculture 17.2%
- Industry 33.8%
- Services 49.0%

Exchange rates (US$ to local currency)
- 1991 .... 0.007847
- 1992 .... 0.006806

Source (Demographics, Population and Economics): Marktest, "1993-General and Marketing Facts" and "Consumidor 92", Lisbon, Portugal.

National Holidays

Holiday	1993 Date
New Year's Day	January 1
Carnival	March 2
Easter Friday	April 9
Easter Sunday	April 11
Freedom Day	April 25
Labor Day	May 1
Portugal Day	June 10
Corpus Christi	August 15
Assumption	August 15
Republic Day	October 5
All Saint's Day	November 1
Independence Day	December 1
Imaculate Conception	December 8
Christmas	December 25

School Holidays

Holiday	1993 Date
Easter	April 5-16
Summer	June 30-September 14
Christmas	December 18-January 4

Major Influences and Trends

The most important development in the Portuguese media market has been the recent arrival of private TV. The 2 new stations are: SIC (October '92) and TVI (February '93).

Total ad spending tends to be relatively stable, with multi-nationals growing due to enhanced distribution, but with many smaller local companies cutting back because of short-term economic problems. As a result, price increases have slowed down.

Although TV has experienced significant structural shifts because of the arrival of private channels, the other media have not gone through any major changes recently. However, as private TV becomes more influential, national radio stations, newspapers and magazines may all face reduced revenues.

Spending Analysis

National advertising spending by medium
based on appropriate year's exchange rate

	1989 US$ MM	1990 US$ MM	1991 US$ MM	1992 US$ MM
TV	136.1	181.3	258.2	295.0
Radio	25.1	32.6	45.3	56.6
Newspaper	56.9	71.2	104.7	106.5
Magazine	48.9	83.3	120.5	127.1
Outdoor	19.0	46.3	66.6	68.7
Total	286.0	414.7	595.3	653.9

Source: Sabatina, "Publivar-V4 '91" and "Publivar-V4 '92", Lisbon, Portugal.

Media Buying

In Portugal, the media market is driven by volume. Available bonuses are awarded due to the amount of volume placed on the market. However, tariff costs are fixed. As a result, all ad agencies are grouping or buying through buying service groups.

Buying Services with 1992 Billings

Buying Service	Parent Company	US$ MM
JET	Joao M./Extensao/Team P	135.6
MEGAMEIOS	Universal/Iniciativas//Others	128.6
TMP	JWT/Ogilvy/DDB&G/ BBDO	109.6
OPTIMEDIA	FCB Group/	82.2
PMP	Publimeios/Media Planning	50.4
CARAT	Carat	27.1
OUTRAS/DIR		120.0

Source: Sabatina "Publicidade no exterior", Lisbon, Portugal, 1992.

Top Advertisers (1992 Spending)

By Company

Parent Company	Product Categories	US$ MM
Industrias Lever Portuguesa	Hygiene and Beauty	23.8
Renault Portuguesa	Cars	13.3
Fiat Auto Portuguesa	Cars	11.2
Nestle Portugal	Food	10.7
Procter & Gamble	Hygiene and Beauty	8.9
FIMA Industria Alimentar	Margarine	7.7
SIVA-S.Imp Veiculos Auto	Cars	7.5
Automoveis Citroen	Cars	7.1
IGLO-Industries Cclados	Frozen Food	7.1
Grupo Refrigor	Drinks	6.9

By Product

Product Category	Advertiser	US$ MM
Hygiene and Beauty	Industrias Lever Portuguesa	23.8
Transports	Renault Portuguesa	13.3
Food Products/Services	Nestle Portugal	10.7
General Interests/Objects/ Domestics	Sony Portugal	4.4
Equipment/Services	Telecom Portugal	3.1
Clothes/Comfort	Sapataria Charles	2.8
Culture/Information	Filmes Lusomundo	1.8

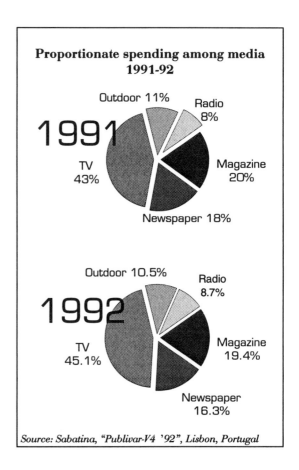

Proportionate spending among media 1991-92

1991
Outdoor 11%
Radio 8%
TV 43%
Magazine 20%
Newspaper 18%

1992
Outdoor 10.5%
Radio 8.7%
TV 45.1%
Magazine 19.4%
Newspaper 16.3%

Source: Sabatina, "Publivar-V4 '92", Lisbon, Portugal

Television

LANGUAGES	Programming	Commercials		Adult Reach
				at 250 GRPs 60%
Primary Language	Portuguese	Portuguese		at 500 GRPs 80%
Secondary Language	English	None		at 1000 GRPs 90%

Source: C/LB based on AGB data Lisbon, Portugal, 1992.

Audiences/CPM's/Costs

Average Cost, Audience, and CPMs by Daypart
(Top 3 Stations, :30, national audience,
Target=Housewives)

Television Cost Changes Between Years

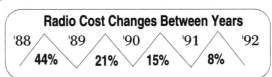

'88 30% '89 27% '90 25% '91 20% '92

	Hours	Morning 08:00-12:00	Daytime 12:00-20:00	Prime Time 20:00-22:00	Late Night 22:00-01:00	Weekend	Children
Station: RTP1							
US$		973	3,614	15,410	5,516	8,994	N/A
Avg. Aud. (000)		85.6	347.1	1,095.5	546.1	624.3	N/A
CPM		11.37	10.41	14.07	10.10	14.40	N/A
Station: RTP2							
US$		973	1,246	2,124	2,178	2,573	N/A
Avg. Aud. (000)		22.3	105.8	127.4	194.6	101.6	N/A
CPM		43.63	11.78	16.67	11.19	25.32	N/A
Station: SIC							
US$		N/A	1,317	1,964	1,414	1,409	N/A
Avg. Aud. (000)		N/A	91.1	183.1	193.4	102.4	N/A
CPM		N/A	14.45	10.73	7.31	13.76	N/A

Source (All television): C/LB based on AGB data Lisbon, Portugal, 1992.

Scheduling/Regional

- All commercials are aired nationally.
- The most common commercial length is :20; other available lengths are :08, :10, :15, :25, :30, :45, and :60.
- Commercials are aired in blocks throughout the day, at the beginning and within programs.

Children's Advertising

Children's advertising is accepted in all adult programming on all stations. Kids' audiences vary.

Radio

- There are 16 radio stations, all in Lisbon. There are also regional networks and local radio stations.
- The primary broadcast language is Portuguese.

Radio Cost Changes Between Years

'88 44% '89 21% '90 15% '91 8% '92

- Commercial lengths available are :08, :15, :20, :30 and :60.
- Primetime for radio is 07:00-10:00.

Daypart Costs/CPM's

Daypart	Local Time	Avg. Cost :30 US$	Audience (000)	CPM (US$)
Prime Time	07:00-10:00	483.00	219	2.21
Daytime	10:00-20:00	178.50	85	2.10
Late Night	20:00-01:00	94.50	47	2.01

Source (Radio): Marktest, "Bareme", Lisbon, Portugal, 1992

Ratings

Daypart	Adult Rating	Adult (000)
07:00-10:00	2.8	200
10:00-20:00	1.1	79
20:00-01:00	0.6	43

Cable

There is no cable in Portugal. During the next three years, cable should become available.

Satellite

There are no facilities for satellite reception in Portugal.

Cinema

Cinemas in Portugal carry advertising in lengths of :20 to :60 or longer.

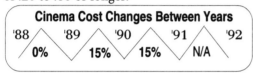

Cinema Cost Changes Between Years

'88	'89	'90	'91	'92
0%	15%	15%	N/A	

Source: C/LB

Newspapers

Literacy rate in English is 30%.
Cost and circulation data is not available.

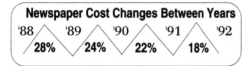

Newspaper Cost Changes Between Years

'88	'89	'90	'91	'92
28%	24%	22%	18%	

Source: C/B based on AGB data

Daily Newspaper
Correio da Mauha
Jornal de Noticias
O Publico
Diario de Noticias
A Capital

Video Cassettes

Approximately 48% of Portuguese TV households have video cassette recorders (VCRs), but pre-recorded tapes do not carry advertising. VCR usage is measured by the AGB/Marktest (Meters).

Magazines

Cost and circulation data is not available.

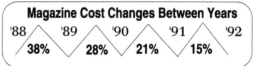

Magazine Cost Changes Between Years

'88	'89	'90	'91	'92
38%	28%	21%	15%	

Source: C/LB

Magazine	Audited?
Maria	Yes
Maxima	Yes
Marie Claire	No
Activa	No
Elle	Yes
Guia	Yes
Mulher Moderna	Yes
Selec. Reader's Digest	Yes
Nova Gente	Yes
Sabado	Yes
TV Guia	Yes
TV 7 Dias	Yes
Grunde	Yes
Reportagem	N/A
Auto Motor	Yes
Turbo	No
Bola Magazine	No
Exame	Yes
Forum Estudante	Yes
Visao	N/A

Outdoor/Transit

Billboard

| Sites available | ....3,000 |
| Lead Time to reserve | ....1 week firm |

Costs

Average, 1 billboard/month

| 4m x 3m | US$ 588 |
| 8m x 3m | US$ 1,020 |

Billboard Cost Changes Between Years

'88	'89	'90	'91	'92
30%	26%	13%	15%	

Transit

Boards available

.................................4,000

Costs

Average, 1 board/month:

.............................US$ 70.60

Transit Board Cost Changes Between Years

'88	'89	'90	'91	'92
20%	18%	12%	10%	

Continued on the following page

Sizes	Sizes
Outdoor Billboards: 4 m x 3 m, 8 m x 3 m	1.20 m x 1.76 m

No tobacco advertisements are allowed outdoors.

Source (Cost changes): C/LB

Direct Marketing

N/A

Non-Traditional Media

There is little or no activity with non-traditional media in Portugal.

Research Sources

Medium Covered	Research Company	Information Provided
TV, Radio, Press, Outdoor	Sabatina Av.Ant.Aug.Aguiar No. 30-1 Dt. 1100 Lisboa	Investments control Copies of Advertising
TV and Press	Markfest Rua S. Jose No. 183-2 1000 Lisboa	Investments control Ratings of sports on TV Based on AGB data survey
TV, Radio, Press, Cinema	Markfest (see above)	Audience survey through personal interviews, with breakdown by sex, age, etc. Viewing habits, categories of products, consumption, etc.
TV, Radio, Press, Cinema	Eurotests Av. Eng.Arantos Oliveira, 5-Slj 1900 Lisboa	Audience survey through personal interviews, with breakdown by sex, age, etc. Viewing habits, categories of products, consumption, etc.
TV	ECOTEL Av. Eng.Arantos Oliveira, 5-Slj 1900 Lisboa	People meter control
TV	AGB Portugal Rua Luciano Cordeiro, 23 C 1100 Lisboa	
Press	APCT R. Rodrigo da Fonseca, 204-4 Dt. 1000 Lisboa	Print run and circulation

Advertising Regulations

By Product

Beverages/Alcohol
Not allowed if minors are targeted or if linked to physical exercises, driving, therapeutics, stimulant or sedative effects. Ads cannot infer a connection between alcohol and social success or other advantages. TV and radio ads arc only allowed from 21:30 until 07:00.

Food/Restaurants
No restrictions.

Cigarettes
Totally prohibited, except:

> the sponsoring of car races for the world or European championships
> with government permission to support during the first 6 month period
> the launch of a new product or brand in the market

Pharmaceuticals/Drugs
Allowed only for non-prescription drugs (i.e. aspirin).

Advertising To Children
Cannot exploit the trust of fathers or teachers or contain elements that can damage children's moral and physical integrity. Minors can be the main actors in advertising when there is a direct relationship between them and the product or service announced.

Commercial Production
No restrictions. Foreign made TV commercials cannot participate in the National Advertising Film Festival.

By Medium

No advertising regulations are available by medium.

Spain

Area	504,750 km^2
Population (1992)	39,118,399
Population growth rate (1992)	0.2%
GDP	US$ 487.5 billion
GDP/per capita	US$ 12,400
Real growth rate (1991)	2.5%
Capital	Madrid

Population Breakdown

By Sex		*By Age Group*		*By Socio-Economic Status*	
Male	48.6%	Children	12%	A, Upper	5%
Female	51.4%	Teens	14%	B, M+U.	54%
		Adults	74%	C, L-M	26%
				D, Lower	15%

Sources: INE (Institutuo Nacional de Estadistica) and EGM (Estudio General de Medios, AIMC)

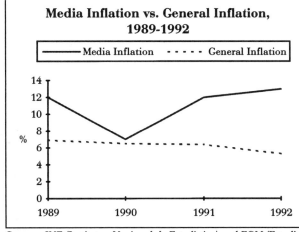

Media Inflation vs. General Inflation, 1989-1992

Number of Households   11,350,000
Ownership of household durables
Car 59%
Phone 77%
Washers 92%
    (purchasing power equivalent)
GNP distribution by industry
Agriculture 6%
Industry 38%
Services 56%
Exchange rates (US$ to local currency)
1991 .... 0.010424
1992 .... 0.008023

Sources: INE (Institutuo Nacional de Estadistica) and EGM (Estudio General de Medios, AIMC); (Media Inflation): VLD

National Holidays

Holiday	*1993 Date*
New Year	January 1
Epiphany	January 6
Easter	2nd week of April
Summer	1 month (July/August usually)
National Day	October 12
Constitutional	December 6
Christmas	December 25

School Holidays

Holiday	*1993 Date*
Easter	2nd week of April
Summer	June 23 - September 14
Christmas	December 20 - January 7

Major Influences and Trends

- The Spanish media market has seen enormous developments since the deregulation of TV in 1990. Until then, the only TV available was state TV. In 1990, the Antena 3 and Tele 5 private networks were started in Madrid and Barcelona. Gradually their penetration grew to cover more cities. Currently private TV has a penetration around 85%.
- Because TV has become so easily accessible to smaller advertisers, other media has suffered. This situation is also exacerbated by the economic crisis experienced throughout most of Europe.
- Carat and Pubintegral have clearly dominated the buying scene since their merger.

Spending Analysis

National advertising spending by medium
based on appropriate year's exchange rate

	1989 US$ MM	1990 US$ MM	1991 US$ MM	1992 US$ MM
TV	1,660	2,385	3,098	4,077
Cinema	12	15	19	15
Radio	214	274	296	243
Newspaper	633	906	967	860
Magazine	492	645	689	620
Outdoor	63	57	93	198
Other	N/A	N/A	N/A	N/A
Total	3,074	4,282	5,162	6,013

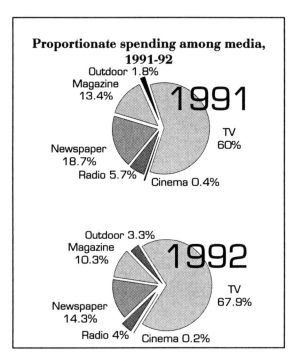

Proportionate spending among media, 1991-92

1991: Outdoor 1.8%, Magazine 13.4%, Newspaper 18.7%, Radio 5.7%, Cinema 0.4%, TV 60%

1992: Outdoor 3.3%, Magazine 10.3%, Newspaper 14.3%, Radio 4%, Cinema 0.2%, TV 67.9%

Media Buying

- Agencies and buying shops negotiate with media.
- Media are not controlled monopolistically, but the trend is to belong to big media groups.

Buying Services with 1992 Billings

Buying Service	Parent Company	US$ MM
Carat Spain	Carat	802.3
Media Planning	--	601.7
TMP	JWT/Bosm/Tiempo BBDO/Tandem DB	296.9
Central Media	BSB Group	280.8
C.I.C.M.	NW Ayer	240.7
Universal Media	McCann	208.6

Buying Service	Parent Company	US$ MM
Equamedia	LB/Y.R./Grey/DMBB	200.6
Multicompra	CID/PCA	200.6
Inciativa de Medios	Lintas	184.5
Optimedia	FCB	128.4
Mass Media	BBDP	120.3
Medai Services	Contrapunto/ Publicidad 96	120.3
Others	(Mediating/DA/ Central de compras)	120.3

Source (Media Buying): Annuncios (magazine)

Top Advertisers (1992 Spending)

By Company

Parent Company	Product Categories	US$ MM
Grupo Unilever	Food/Cleaning/Health & Beauty	87.2
Fasa Renault	Automobile	86.7
Citroen Hispania S.A.	Automobile	83.2
El Corte Ingles S.A.	Department Store	71.5
Procter & Gamble Espana S.A.	Cleaning/Food/Health & Beauty	62.9
Grupo Nestle	Food	53.5
S.E.A.T.	Automobile	53.4
Peugeot-Talbot Espana S.A.	Automobile	52.9
Ford Espana S.A.	Automobile	52.6
Leche Pascual S.A	Food	50.8

By Product

Product Category	Advertiser	US$ MM
Automobile	Renault	86.7
Automobile	Citroen	83.2
Department Store	El Corte Ingles	71.5
Health & Beauty	Procter & Gamble	62.9
Automobile	S.E.A.T.	53.4
Automobile	Peugeot	52.9
Automobile	Ford	52.6
Food	Pascual	50.8
Food	Nestle	46.8
Automobile	Fiat	45.8

Television

Overview

In 1992 the TV market has grown 6%. Penetration is now 99%.

	TV HH Penetration			Adult Reach	
1989	*1990*	*1991*	*1992*	at 250 GRPs	70%
98.5%	98.5%	98.9%	99%	at 500 GRPs	85%
10,540,000	11,037,000	11,225,000	11,682,000	at 1,000 GRPs	91%

Opportunities

National

Networks	Number of Stations	Ownership	Station Profile	Commercial Minutes/Day	Coverage	Broadcast Hours (Sign-On/Off)
TVE	2	Government	General	49	95	07:00-04:00
Tele 5	1	Private	General	135	82	07:00-03:15
ANI3	1	Private	General	80	82	06:45-02:45
Canal +	1	Private	Decoded (Movie)	10	69	24 Hours

Regional

Networks	Number of Stations	Ownership	Station Profile	Commercial Minutes/Day	Coverage	Broadcast Hours (Sign-On/Off)
TV3	2	Government–Catalan	General	30	16	07:30-02:00
TM3	1	Government–Madrid	General	42	13	08:00-03:15
C9	1	Government–Valencia	General	42	9	08:00-02:30
ETB	2	Government–Pafs Vasco	General	17	5	09:00-01:00
C. Sur	1	Government–Andalucia	General	32	20	08:00-02:00
TVG	1	Government–Galicia	General	27	8	09:00-01:30

Costs

Prime Time TV Costs for :30 in US$			
1989	*1990*	*1991*	*1992*
60,100	75,400	80,400	56,200

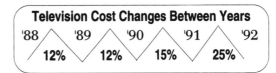

Television Cost Changes Between Years

'88   '89   '90   '91   '92
12%   12%   15%   25%

Audiences/CPM's

Average cost, Audience, and CPMs by Daypart

(Top 3 three stations; :30, national audience; Target=Adults 16+)

Hours	Morning 09:30-12:30	Daytime 14:30-16:30	Prime Time 21:30-23:00	Late Night 24:00-01:00	Weekend ALL	Children 17:00-19:30
Station: TVE						
US$	1,303	37,708	59,721	49,341	19,442	13,539
Avg. Aud. (000)	373	3,569	4,438	1,788	1,320	1,500
CPM	3.49	10.57	13.46	27.60	14.73	9.03
Station: Tele 5						
US$	4,513	24,269	53,653	22,865	27,538	17,650
Avg. Aud. (000)	259	1,508	2,955	1,614	1,031	1,110
CPM	17.42	16.09	18.16	14.17	26.71	15.90
Station: Antena 3						
US$	6,318	22,063	54,396	11,003	25,954	18,453
Avg. Aud. (000)	340	1,482	2,071	1,407	746	999
CPM	18.58	14.89	26.27	7.82	34.79	18.47

Audience Ratings by Daypart (Target=Adults 15+)

Daypart	Hours	Household Universe (000)	Hut Levels	Household Rating	Impressions (000)	Adult Universe (000)	Adult Rating	Impressions (000)
Morning	08:00-13:30	10,690	N/A	6.1	652	29,717	4.5	1,337
Daytime	13:45-17:00	10,690	N/A	32.4	3,463	29,717	27	8,024
Primetime	21:00-23:00	10,690	N/A	50.7	5,420	29,717	42.3	12,570
Late Night	13:15-04:00	10,690	N/A	15.3	1,635	29,717	13.1	3,893
Weekend	All	10,690	N/A	17.2	1,839	29,717	15.3	4,546
Children's	17:00-19:30	10,690	N/A	22.3	2,384	29,717	18.6	5,527

Source: Sofres A.M.E.G.M.

Scheduling/Regional/Languages

LANGUAGES

	Programming	Commercials
Primary	Spanish (Castillian)	Spanish (Castillian)
Secondary	Catalan (6%), Valenciano (4%)	Catalan (6%)
	Gallego (2%), Vasco (2%)	

Network	Station	Region	Hours
TVE	TVE1-TVE2	National	All
TVE5	TVE 5	National	All
Antena 3	Antena 3	National	All
Canal +	Canal +	National	All

- Commercials are aired throughout the day, within programs and at their beginnings and ends.
- Sixty percent of all commercials are :20. Other lengths may be available.

- 20%of all commercial time is purchased on a regional basis. Costs are proportional to the audience in each case.

Children's Advertising

Advertising may be directed to children in connection with any programming.

Radio

- There are 1200 radio stations in Spain, all of which are commercial and 22 of which are in Madrid.
- Ninety-six percent of all households have radios; the estimated number is 11,331,000.
- The primary broadcasting language is Castillian Spanish; Catalan is also used.
- The most popular program types for adults are Sports, News, and Magazines; and music for teens.
- Commercial lengths available range from :15 up.
- An average :30 spot targeted at adults 18+ would cost about 519,500.

- Regional buying is possible; there is no premium for buying regionally.
- Prime/peak time for radio is 10:00–11:00, with an adult rating of 18.9, based on a universe of 6,057,000.

Radio Cost Changes Between Years

'88	'89	'90	'91	'92
6%	8%	8%	12%	

Daypart Costs/CPMs (Target=Persons 14+)

Daypart	Local Time	Avg.Cost :30 US$	Audience (000)	CPM (US$)
Prime Time	11:00-12:00	1,203	1,600	0.75
Daytime	14:00-15:00	1,444	640	2.27
Late Night	24:00-01:00	4,167	320	13.02

Cable

Cable TV is beginning during 1993 in local areas like Sevilla and Cantabria.

Satellite

17 satellite channels are accessible in Spain, only 35 % of the households can receive satellite broadcasts.

Satellite Channel	Country of Origin	Language
Galavision	Mexico	Spanish
Eurosport	France	French/English
Sky Channel	Great Britan	English
TV 5	France	French
CNN	USA	English
RAI 1-2	Italy	Italian

Satellite Channel	Country of Origin	Language
MTV	–	English
SAT 1	Germany	German
RTL	Luxemburg	German
Screensport	–	English
BBC	Great Britan	English

Video Cassettes

Roughly 48% of TV households have video cassette recorders (VCRs). Video cassettes in Spain do not carry commercials, and no change is expected in the near future. E.G.M. measures VCR usage via personal interviews.

Cinema

| Cinema Cost Changes Between Years |
| '88 /\ '89 /\ '90 /\ '91 /\ '92 |
| N/A \/ 17% \/ 40% \/ N/A |

- Of the 2,000 cinemas in Spain, 90% offer commercial time, in lengths from :15 to :120.
- Over 4 weeks, the potential reach of a commercial is 38.15% of the people 14 and older.
- Cinema is a creative media, useful for local support.

Newspapers

Spain has 5 national daily newspapers with a combined circulation of approximately 2,500,000.

Newspaper Cost Changes Between Years
'88 /\ '89 /\ '90 /\ '91 /\ '92
N/A \/ 10% \/ 7% \/ 15%

Newspaper	Market	Size	Circulation (000)	Avg. Daily Aud. (000)	1 Page/B&W Cost (US$)	Accept Color?
El Pais	Madrid	Tabloid	407	1,423	12,144	No
ABC	Madrid/Seviile	Tabloid	327	N/A	11,128	Yes
Marca	N/A	Tabloid	315	1,395	6,875	N/A
El Periodico	Cataluna	Tabloid	180	720	5,279	No
AS	Madrid	Tabloid	151	629	5,833	Yes
El Mundo	Madrid	Tabloid	186	623	8,940	No
La Vanguardia	Cataluna	Tabloid	206	614	7,750	Yes
Diario 16	Madrid	Tabloid	125	414	10,417	No
La Voz de Galicia	Galicia	Tabloid	106	397	5,083	No
Diario Vasco	N/A	Tabloid	93	330	2,950	N/A
Sport	N/A	N/A	78	309	3,150	N/A
Levante	N/A	N/A	43	240	2,920	N/A
La Verdad	N/A	N/A	9	227	1,800	N/A
El Mundo Deportive	N/A	N/A	61	210	3,250	N/A
Sur	N/A	N/A	40	201	3,160	N/A
El Heraldo de Vigo	N/A	N/A	N/A	199	1,830	N/A
Co Espanol	Pais Vasco	Tabloid	136	560	3,370	No
Do Vasco	Pais Vasco	Tabloid	92	330	2,848	No
Antena TV	N/A	Broadsheet	288	N/A	N/A	N/A
Blanco Y Negro	N/A	Broadsheet	554	N/A	N/A	N/A
Correo Espanol	N/A	Tabloid	134	N/A	N/A	N/A
El Dominical	N/A	Broadsheet	364	N/A	N/A	N/A
El Mundo Siglo XXI	N/A	Tabloid	112	N/A	N/A	N/A
Gente D 16	N/A	Broadsheet	182	N/A	N/A	N/A
Magazine La Vang.	N/A	Broadsheet	400	N/A	N/A	N/A
Magazines El Mundo	N/A	Broadsheet	191	N/A	N/A	N/A
S.D. El Pais	N/A	Broadsheet	1047	N/A	N/A	N/A
Suplemento Semanal	N/A	Broadsheet	766	N/A	N/A	N/A

Sources: (Circulation) O.J.D. (Oficina para Justificación de Difusion); (Audience) E.G.M.

Magazines

Spain has 250 consumer magazines, and about 750 trade and technical publications.

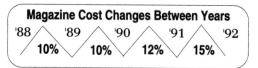

Magazine	Type	Frequency	Circ. (000)	Audited?	Avg. Issue Aud. (000)	1 page 4/C Cost (US$)
Tele Indiscreta	TV Guides	Weekly	1,122	Yes	3,419	11,472
Tele Programa	TV Guides	Weekly	1,190	Yes	3,178	12,435
Pronto	Women's	Weekly	818	Yes	3,022	12,796
Hola	Heart Mag.	Weekly	624	Yes	2,544	15,845
Muy Interesante	General	Monthly	297	Yes	2,130	11,633
Semana	Women's	Weekly	361	Yes	1,738	9,025
Supertele	TV Guides	Weekly	700	Yes	1,731	10,429
Lecturas	Women's	Weekly	345	Yes	1,679	10,028
Diez Minutos	Women's	Weekly	400	Yes	1,598	9,025
Interviu	General	Weekly	212	Yes	1,140	12,034
Burda	Women's	Monthly	85	Yes	1,129	7,942
Mia	Women's	Weekly	263	Yes	1,119	8,825
TV Plus	TV Guides	Weekly	330	Yes	962	5,535
Super Pop	Youth	Fortnightly	340	Yes	898	5,616
Jueves, el	General/Humor	Weekly	140	Yes	884	2,286
Tiempo	General	Weekly	145	Yes	752	10,429
Clan TV	N/A	N/A	N/A	N/A	744	N/A
Cosmopolitan	Women's	Monthly	180	Yes	711	11,031
Ragazza	Youth	Monthly	140	Yes	594	7,020
Fotogramas	Cinema & Video	Monthly	134	Yes	579	5,616
Autopista	Motoring	Weekly	44	N/A	N/A	5,120
Cambio 16	General	Weekly	68	Yes	109	9,790
Casa 16	Interior Des.	Monthly	52	N/A	N/A	7,290
Conocer	General	Monthly	83	N/A	N/A	4,370
Crecer Feliz	Children's	Monthly	68	Yes	134	7,410
El Mueble	Interior Des.	Monthly	96	Yes	226	8,120
Elle	Women's	Monthly	133	Yes	170	14,300
Epoca	General	Weekly	78	N/A	N/A	7,700
Fantastic	Cinema & Video	Monthly	45	N/A	N/A	3,540
Geo	General	Monthly	42	N/A	N/A	7,500
Hola, S.A	Romance	Weekly	656	Yes	1,288	17,500
Man	Men's	Monthly	53	N/A	N/A	6,870
Marie Claire	Women's	Monthly	87	Yes	126	11,040
Mia	Women's	Weekly	276	Yes	452	9,580
Motociclismo	Motoring	Weekly	56	N/A	N/A	3,700
Motor 16	Motoring	Weekly	36	N/A	N/A	5,250
Natura	General	Monthly	67	Yes	105	4,830
Nueva Estilo	Interior Des.	Monthly	120	Yes	311	9,160
PC Magazine	Information	Monthly	36	N/A	N/A	4,540
PC World	Information	Monthly	46	N/A	N/A	5,310
Penthouse	Men's	Monthly	67	N/A	N/A	6,250
Ser Padres Hoy	Children	Monthly	101	Yes	151	7,700
Solo Moto 30	Motoring	Monthly	31	N/A	N/A	3,310
Telva	Women's	Weekly	108	Yes	N/A	11,040
Tribuna	General	Weekly	92	N/A	N/A	7,450
Vogue	Women's	Monthly	50	Yes	130	12,080
Woman	Women's	Monthly	125	Yes	101	13,330

Source (Circulation): O.J.D. (Oficina para Justification de Difusion); (Audience): E.G.M.

Sunday Supplements

	Circulation(000)
El Pais	1,151
El Mundo	814
Blanco y Negro	731

	Circulation(000)
Antena Semanal	N/A
La Vanguardia	364
Suplemento Semanal	1,027

Outdoor/Transit

Billboard	**Transit**
Sites available	Boards available
40,000	2,500
Lead Time to reserve 3-4 months, with a guarantee of one month, possible pre-emption	
Exposure 79%	**Exposure** ....N/A
Costs	**Costs**
Average, 1 billboard/month	Average, 1 board/month:
8 m x 3 m ....US$ 562	1 bus ....US$ 278
4 m x 3 m ....US$ 280	

Billboard Cost Changes Between Years

'88	'89	'90	'91	'92
	7%	5%	5%	5%

Transit Cost Changes Between Years

'88	'89	'90	'91	'92
	10%	12%	5%	6%

Sizes	**Sizes**
8 m x 3 m, 4 m x 3 m, 6 m x 4 m	Different

Direct Marketing

List Brokers	*Information*
B.D. Mail	Official Register of Population
Euromailing	Government Traffic Department
Sevdio	Private files, etc.
Coditel	
Camerdata	

Telemarketing Companies
Teleaction
Marketing Telefonico
Iberphone
Markel

Direct Marketing Associations
Asociacion Espanola de Marketing Directo
Asociacion Espanola de Agenciac de Publicidad

Non-Traditional Media

There is a large diversity of non-traditional media in Spain, and the field is expanding rapidly.

Research Sources

Medium Covered	*Research Company*	*Information Provided*
TV, Magazine, Press, Cinema, Radio, VCR	AIMC/FGM Capitan Haya, 61 24th Floor, Office 3 28008 Madrid	Audience information through personal interview
TV*	SOFRES Pza. Csrlos Trias Beltran, 7 Edif. Sollube 4° Pl. 28020 - Madrid	
TV*	Audimeter Sobemap	Audience/15 min./day

TV Research is available from Recall every 3 months, and from People Meter daily.

Advertising Regulations

By Product

Beverages/Alcohol
Advertising alcoholic beverages containing a higher alcoholic content than 20% is prohibited on TV.

Cigarettes
Tobacco advertising is not allowed on TV.

Pharmaceuticals/Drugs
Must be authorized by Health Ministry.

Advertising To Children
Various qualitative restrictions.

By Medium

Television
Included in 'Ley General de la Publicidad' (Advertising Law).

Sweden

Area	449,964 km^2
Population (1992)	8,602,157
Population growth rate (1992)	0.4%
GDP (1992)	US$ 197.8 billion
GDP/per capita	US$ 23,000
Real growth rate (1991)	–1.1%
Capital	Stockholm

Population Breakdown

By Sex		*By Age Group*	
Male	49.4%	Children	12.0%
Female	50.6%	Teens	12.5%
		Adults	75.5%

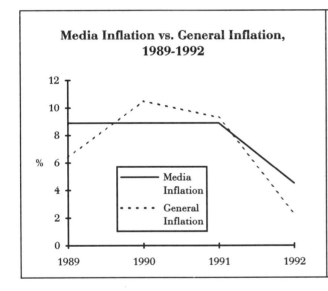

Media Inflation vs. General Inflation, 1989-1992

Number of Households   3,830,170

Ownership of household durables

Car	58%
Phone	96%
Washers	75%

(purchasing power equivalent)

GNP distribution by industry

Agriculture	4%
Industry	28%
Services	68%

Exchange rates (US$ to local currency)

1991	0.1823
1992	0.1374

National Holidays

Holiday	1993 Date
New Year's	January 1
Easter	April 9, 11 12
Various National Holidays	May 1, 20, 30, 31, June 26, November 6
Christmas	December 25, 26

School Holidays

Holiday	1993 Date
Winter	March 1 - 7
Easter	April 5 - 12
Summer	June 10 - August 18
Christmas	December 22 - January 6

Major Influences and Trends

Market Structure

The media market is almost 100% controlled by media buying companies. This structure has been in place for the last 10-15 years and is expected to continue.

Media

Major changes have recently occured in the television market. TV4, the terrestrial national commercial TV channel—which started in March '92—now has a penetration of 90% and the satellite channels TV3 and TV5 now have penetrations of 48% and 39%. Due to the start of TV4, the TV5 share of total spending is expected to increase over the next few years, and TV3 and TV5 are expected to fight for their share of market by improving their programming.

Spending Analysis

National advertising spending by medium
based on appropriate year's exchange rate

	1989 US$ MM	1990 US$ MM	1991 US$ MM	1992* US$ MM
TV	0	59	181	238
Cinema	14	15	16	14
Radio	0	0	0	0
Newspaper	1,127	1,150	1,084	869
Magazine	165	162	296	210
Outdoor	69	88	82	70
Total	**1,375**	**1,474**	**1,659**	**1,401**

* '91 exchange rates have been used.

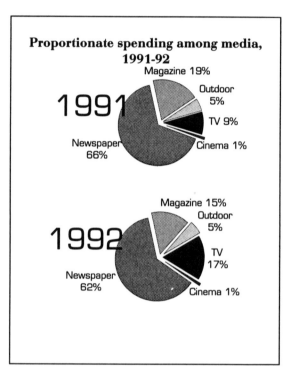

Proportionate spending among media, 1991-92

1991
Magazine 19%
Outdoor 5%
TV 9%
Cinema 1%
Newspaper 66%

1992
Magazine 15%
Outdoor 5%
TV 17%
Cinema 1%
Newspaper 62%

Media Buying

- It is possible to negotiate with all the different media. Negotiations can only be done on a client by client basis because buying clubs are not allowed.

- Buying services do exist and account for 52% of the market's total expenditures.

Top Advertisers (1992 Billings)

By Company

Parent Company	Product Categories	US$ MM
KF	Retail/HyperStore	67
ICA AB	Retail/HyperStore	64
Procter & Gamble	Fast moving consumer goods	27
Televerket	Telefon company	25
Volvo	Automobiles	18
Colgate-Palmolive	Fast moving consumer goods	17
Vivo-Favor	Retail/Supermarket	16
Hennes & Mauritz	Clothing, cosmetics, etc.	14
Lever AB	Fast moving consumer goods	14
Kapp Ahl	Clothing	13

Buying Services with 1992 Billings

Buying Service	Parent Company	US$ MM
Carat	Carat	220
Media Marketing Gruppen	Grey Parily	219
Media Broker	N/A	68
Inserator	KF	42
Gester & Co.	N/A	34
Lintas	N/A	34

Source: Affars Varlden - May '93

Television

Overview

For stations and penetration, see Major Influences and Trends, preceding.
Actual costs have generally increased due to increased TV penetration.

Prime Time TV Costs for :30 in US$				Adult Reach	
1989	*1990*	*1991*	*1992*	at 250 GRPs	69%
N/A	1,400	10,000	41,500	at 500 GRPs	79%
				at 1,000 GRPs	86%

Audiences/CPM's

Average Cost, Audience, and CPMs by Daypart
(Top three stations, national audience, Target=Adults 16+)

Hours	Morning	Daytime 06:00-19:00	Prime Time 19:00-23:00	Late Night 23:00 -	Weekend	Children
Station: TV3						
US$	N/A	2,233	6,166	618	618	N/A
Avg. Aud. (000)		24	147	24	24	
CPM		93.04	41.95	25.75	25.75	
Station: TV4						
US$	3,715	2,107	18,585	3,449	N/A	N/A
Avg. Aud. (000)	120	89	341	166		
CPM	30.96	23.67	54.50	20.78		
Station: TV5						
US$	N/A	N/A	1,237	N/A	N/A	N/A
Avg. Aud. (000)			86			
CPM			14.38			

Audiences/Ratings by Daypart (Target=Adults15-74)

Daypart	Hours	Household				Adult		
		Universe (000)	Hut Levels	Household Rating	Impressions (000)	Universe (000)	Adult Rating	Impressions (000)
Morning	06:00-09:00	3,548	N/A	N/A	N/A	5,732	2.1	120
Daytime	09:00-18:00	3,548	N/A	N/A	N/A	5,732	1.6	92
Primetime	19:00-23:00	3,548	N/A	N/A	N/A	5,732	5.9	338
Late Night	23:00-24:00	3,548	N/A	N/A	N/A	5,732	2.9	166
Weekend		3,548	N/A	N/A	N/A	5,732	N/A	N/A
Children's		3,548	N/A	N/A	N/A	5,732	N/A	N/A

Scheduling/Regional/Languages

- Primary language for both programming and commercials is Swedish. English is also used.
- The most common commercial length is :30; :10 is the minimum amount of time.
- Commercials are aired in blocks throughout the day on TV3 and TV5; but TV4 allots specific time blocks between programs.
- Only 30% of all TV advertising is bought on a regional basis. Regional costs are approximately 26% that of national costs.

Regional Schedules

Station	Region	Hours
TV Stockholm	Greater Stockholm	weekdays 17:00-17:55
TV Skane	Malmo	weekdays 17:00-17:55
Kanal Goteborg	Goteborg	weekdays 17:00-17:55

Children's Advertising

Children's programming is accepted on TV3 and TV5 with no limitations. TV4 does not allow advertising targeted at children under age 12.

TV3 is by far the most popular channel among children.

CHILDREN'S PROGRAMMING			Kids		
Station	Hours	Days	Universe (000)	Ratings	Impressions (000)
TV3	08:00-09:25	Sat.-Sun.	582	11.2	65.2

TV5 does not broadcast any children's programs. TV4 is subject to restrictions. (See advertising regulations.)
Source (Television): TV3, TV4 and TV5

Radio

- There are 3 national non-commercial radio stations and 60 local commercial stations in Sweden, ten of them are located in the main city.
- Approximately 96% of all households have radios; the estimated number is 2,600,000. About 50% of cars have radios.
- The primary broadcasting language is Swedish; however some programming is in English.
- Primetime is 07:00-09:00 and 16:00-18:00.
- The most popular program types are Rock/Pop and News.
- Commercial lengths range from :10-:60; no overall costs are available.

Cable

- Cable is most used for receiving satellite signals. There is access to most European stations, as well as some overseas stations. The cable system is publicly (government) owned.
- There are currently 35 cable channels; 31 are commercial, 4 are not.
- 1,723,600 households currently have cable, representing 45% of Swedish households.
- Cable penetration is not expected to increase much over the next 5 years.

- The primary broadcasting language is Swedish; the secondary language is English.

Top 5 Cable Channels (no costs or ratings available)
TV3 - exclusively for Sweden
TV5 - Nordic countries
MTV
Eurosport
Z-TV - exclusively for Sweden

Satellite

- 10% private dishes; 90% via cable.
- Satellite penetration is at 54%; reaching approximately 2,191,000 households.
- 220,000 households have a private dish – Astra, Intel and Euteldal.
- More are expected to receive satellite within the next five years.

- There are currently 90 channels received, 85 are commercial and EEC regulations apply to imported programs and commercials.
- Sales are expected to increase due to lower prices.

Video Cassettes

- About 70% of TV households have video cassette recorders (VCRs). Rented tapes (major titles only) carry an average of 7-10 sponsors per tape with an average cost of US$ 6,870 for a :30 spot.
- There is very little interest among advertisers in VCR advertising.

Cinema

- After a few years of decline, cinema usage has recently started to increase.
- The number of cinemas is not available but 100% of Swedish cinemas offer commercial time in :10 spots.
- The average cost of a four week cinema schedule (based on 550 theaters) is US$ 55,000.

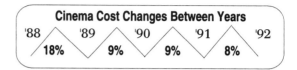

Cinema Cost Changes Between Years
'88 — '89 — '90 — '91 — '92
18% — 9% — 9% — 8%

Newspapers

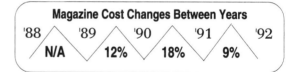

Newspaper Cost Changes Between Years
'88 — '89 — '90 — '91 — '92
N/A — 8% — 11% — 8%

- Only regional daily papers in Sweden accept advertising, national dailies do not.
- The literacy rate in English is 72%.

Daily Newspaper	Market	Size	Circulation (000)	Avg. Daily Aud. (000)	1 page/B&W Cost (US$)	Accept Color?
Expressen	N/A	N/A	N/A	1,431	9,350	Yes
Aftonbladet	N/A	N/A	N/A	1,084	8,380	Yes
Dagens Nyheter	N/A	N/A	N/A	905	20,400	Yes
Goteborg-Posten	N/A	N/A	N/A	599	14,040	Yes
J Dag	N/A	N/A	N/A	526	8,560	Yes
Svenska Dagbladet	N/A	N/A	N/A	489	18,160	Yes

Source (Newspapers): Each individual newspaper

Magazines

There are 150 consumer magazines and 250 trade/technical magazines published in Sweden.

Magazine Cost Changes Between Years
'88 — '89 — '90 — '91 — '92
N/A — 12% — 18% — 9%

Magazine	Type	Frequency	Circulation (000)	Audited?	Avg Issue Aud. (000)	1 page/4/C Cost (US$)
ICA-kurieren	General	Weekly	509	Yes	1,828	11,300
Var bostad	Housing	Weekly	982	Yes	1,074	9,600
Land	General	Weekly	382	Yes	875	9,700
Hemmets Journal	General	Weekly	288	Yes	724	6,300
Allers	General	Weekly	283	Yes	650	5,800
Hemmet Veckotidning	General	Weekly	N/A	Yes	623	5,200
Allas Veckotidning	General	Weekly	198	Yes	540	3,400
Hant i Veckan	General	Weekly	164	Yes	537	6,100
Alt om Mat	Food	Weekly	145	Yes	529	5,500
Alt i Hemmet	Housing	Weekly	114	Yes	450	N/A

Outdoor/Transit

Billboard	**Transit**
Sites available .... 12,000 Lead Time to reserve .... 6-12 months Exposure 84%	Boards available .... 16,000 Exposure (metro) 89%
Costs	**Costs**

Average, 1 billboard/month
    18 pages (420 x 300) .... US$ 473
    8 pages (280x 200)........................ US$ 210
 	
 Billboard Cost Changes Between Years
 '88   '89   '90   '91   '92
 18%   14%   12%   21%
	Average, 1 board/month
	    Buses .... US$ 150
	    Trains(11) .... US$ 760
	
	 Transit Board Cost Changes Between Years
	 '88 '89 '90 '91 '92
	 12% 13% 11% 15%

Sizes	**Sizes**
Large Billboards: 420 cm x 320 cm; Billboards: 280 cm x 200 cm; Posters (3 sided): 140 cm x 300 cm, Posters: 100 cm x 150 cm	Buses: 400 cm x 70 cm, 140 cm x 50 cm

Restrictions for Outdoor Advertisements:
Advertising for alcoholic beverages (except Class 1 beer) and tobacco is prohibited. Ads with political or religious content and ads for charity organizations are also not permitted.

Direct Marketing

- Direct Mail in Sweden accounts for approximately 18% of the total advertising expenditure and is thus a significant medium. Direct Mail is particularly effective, and specific target groups can be reached via the public database.
- All organizations engaged with distribution and data processing are members of Swedish Direct Marketing Association (SWEDMA).

List Broker	**Direct Marketing Association**

UniMedia AB
   Box 1143
   436 23 ASKIM
 Adressgruppen
   Kungsg 58
   11 22 STOCKHOLM
 Adresskompaniet
   S.Malarstrand 45
   118 25 STOCKHOLM
 DM-Bolaget
   101 50 STOCKHOLM
 and
   405 10 GOTEBORG
 Direct Key
   Upplandsg 81-83
   113 44 STOCKHOLM
	Swedma (Swedish Direct Marketing Assoc.)
	   Box 14038
	   104 40 STOCKHOLM

Non-Traditional Media

Currently being used are the following non-traditional media.

Type	Currently Available	Costs
In-Store Media		
posters on carts in supermarkets	11,000 sites	US$ 24,420 for 1 month
Arme Vision		
Large screen (video/cinema-like) broadcast at army barracks every weekday	39 stations	US$ 4,120 - 4 x/hour (:30) for 1 month
Station SJ Television		
Commercials on monitors at train stations around Sweden Reach 100,000	40 sites in 33 cities	Costs: US$ 4,780 for 1 month, :30 spots

Research Sources

Medium Covered	Research Company	Information Provided
TV	Nielsen/MMS Box 1032 164 21 Kista	People Meter Data
Cinema	Burke Marketing Information AB Box 14093 400 20 Goteborg	Day After Recall
Outdoor	W & D Marknadsinformation AB Box 1260 111 82 Stockholm	Recall, reach, frequency, etc.
	Ake Wissing & Co Odeng 62 113 22 Stockholm	Recall, reach, frequency, etc.
Newspaper/ Magazine	IMU-Testologen AB Sollentunay. 84 191 93 Sollentuna	Reach, frequency, etc.
	TEMO Testhuset AB Box 1359 171 26 Solna	Reach, frequency, etc.

Television research currently available is Nielsen People Meter, weekly.

Advertising Regulations

By Product

Beverages/Alcohol
Advertising for spirits, wine and strong beer are banned. Advertising for light beer is limited by certain restrictions.

Food/Restaurants
Nutritional claims are allowed. There are restrictions on references to the medical professions and to people portrayed as doctors. Advertisements for baby food are submitted to the 'Voluntary Code of Ethics for Marketing Infant Foods' guidelines, applied by industry and controlled by the Food Administration.

Cigarettes
Advertising for tobacco must be moderate—meaning that it must not be aggressive and not encourage the use of tobacco. No advertisements are allowed in magazines or other publications directed towards

younger people. Similarly, sport magazines can not be used. All advertising must be kept within a maximum size and must contain a health warning. TV, direct mail, outdoor, and cinema can not be used.

Pharmaceuticals/Drugs

Advertising for medical products must not give misleading information. Statements from doctors can only be used if the source can be documented.

Advertising To Children

Advertising directed to children and young people should not be presented in such a way as to exploit their natural credulity and loyalty. Neither should it be presented in such a way that children and young people could be harmed physically, psychologically or morally.

Advertising directed to children may not invite orders by mail/phone, and may not indicate the approximate price of toys. It is not permitted to offer premiums, gifts, participation in competitions, compare brands, use celebrities, use children as endorsers, or to use children as presenters, when they are not knowledgeable about the product. Advertising for war toys is banned.

No TV advertising should be targeted at children under the age of 12 and is not allowed immediately before and after programs addressed to children. Furthermore, persons or characters playing a prominent part in children's programs are not allowed to appear in commercials.

Commercial Production

The main rule is that 'all advertising should be legal, decent, honest and truthful.' All advertising should be in accordance with proper marketing practices and should not mislead consumers or trades people.

By Medium

Television

No tobacco, alcoholic beverages (except light beer) or prescription medicine are allowed.

Print

No alcoholic beverages (except light beer) or prescription medicine are allowed. Tobacco advertising is limited to 3/4 DIN A4-page.

Outdoor

No alcoholic beverages (except light beer), or prescription drugs are allowed. Ads with political or religious content and advertising for charity are not permitted.

Cable

EEC-regulations.

Direct Marketing

No alcoholic beverages (except light beer) or prescription medicine are allowed. Must not be targeted to people under age 16.

Switzerland

Area	41,290 km²
Population (1992)	6,828,023
Population growth rate (1992)	0.6%
GDP	US$ 147.4 billion
GDP/per capita	US$ 21,700
Real growth rate (1991)	0.2%
Capital	Bern

Population Breakdown

By Sex		*By Age Group*		*By Socio-Economic Status*	
Male	48%	Children, 0-9	10%	A	5%
Female	52%	Teens, 10-19	14%	B	45%
		Adults, 20+	76%	C	44%
				D	6%

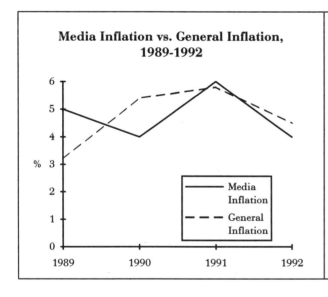

Media Inflation vs. General Inflation, 1989-1992

Number of Houdseholds	2,871,000

Ownership of household durables

Car	78%
Phone	87%
Washers	55%

(purchasing power equivalent)

GNP distribution by industry

Agriculture	5%
Industry	35%
Services	60%

Exchange rates (US$ to local currency)

1991	1,50 SFr.
1992	1,50 SFr.

National Holidays

Holiday	1993 Date
New Year's	January 1
Good Friday	September 4
Easter	November 4

School Holidays

Holiday	1993 Date
Spring	April 24 - May 8
Summer	July 17 - August 21
Autumn	November 9 - 23

Source (All information this page): Annual Statistic Yearbook 1993

Major Influences and Trends

Although on December 6, 1992 Switzerland declined the opportunity to join the European Community, the Swiss media market has many typical European features. Expenditures on advertising are stagnating/stagflating, the commercial TV market is being liberalized, and media-buying is becoming more and more concentrated.

This situation suggests the following future developments in the Swiss media market:
1. Due to the generally insecure economic situation in Switzerland, the growth of the media market throughout the last few years will not continue (i.e. there will be a stagnation or even a stagflation).
2. The tough competition linked with high media inflation will lead to an even stronger shifting from traditional media (especially print) to activities below the line.
3. Newspaper: continuing concentration of media buying.
4. Magazines: Due to heavy losses in advertising and circulation, several magazines have recently been discontinued.
5. Television: Positive development due to the liberalization of commercial sector and growing inventory of commercial TV stations.
6. Outdoor/Cinema/Radio: Limited development within their roles as complementary media vehicles.

There will be a continuing concentration in media buying due to international pressure as well as set-ups of new media agencies and joint ventures of advertising agencies.

In the near future, although Switzerland will not become a member of the European Community, the media market will have to go through the same problems and developments as the European media market.

Spending Analysis

National advertising spending by medium,
based on appropriate year's exchange rate

	1989 US$ MM	1990 US$ MM	1991 US$ MM	1992 US$ MM
TV	123	144	141	146
Cinema	10	13	13	13
Radio	15	20	23	26
Newspaper	604	693	689	697
Magazine	294	370	384	378
Outdoor	101	103	119	112
Other	--	2	5	
Total	**1,147**	**1,345**	**1,374**	**1,372**

Source: Media Focus/Nielsen CH-Hergiswil

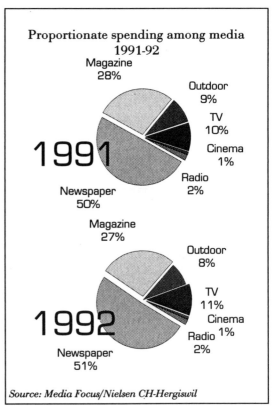

Proportionate spending among media 1991-92

1991
Magazine 28%
Outdoor 9%
TV 10%
Cinema 1%
Radio 2%
Newspaper 50%

1992
Magazine 27%
Outdoor 8%
TV 11%
Cinema 1%
Radio 2%
Newspaper 51%

Source: Media Focus/Nielsen CH-Hergiswil

Media Buying

- Generally fixed media rate (not negotiable).
- Media-buying services have been expanding since 1990.
- In 1991 buying services represented 10% of the market's total expenditures (US$ 130 MM).

Buying Services with 1992 Billings

Buying Service	Parent Company	US $ MM	Independent/ Affiliate
Qualimedia	Lintas, McCann	46	Publi Media Intern.
TMP Media	BBDO, O+M, DDB JW	46	TMP
Optimedia	Publicis, FCR	20	Media Team Europe
Zenith	Saatchi & Saatchi, ZKG	12	Zenith
Eurospace	TBWA, Carat	7	Eurospace

Top Advertisers (1991 Spending)

By Company

Parent Company	Product Categories	US$ MM
Migros	Retail	55.6
Coop	Retail	44.3
Toyota	Automotive	19.4
General Motors	Automotive	17.1
Denner	Retail	15.2

* 1992 Spending information N/A
Source: Media Focus/Nielsen CH-Hergiswil

By Product

Product Category	Advertiser	US$ MM
Automotive	Toyota	209.8
Trade/Wholesale	Migros	166.9
Medical	Clinic	88.1
Banking	SBC	88.1
Furniture	Mobel Plister	74.1

Source: Media Focus/Nielsen CH-Hergiswil

Television

Television Cost Changes Between Years

'88	'89	'90	'91	'92
5%	4%	2%	3%	

Adult Reach	
at 250 GRPs	40%
at 500 GRPs	60%
at 1,000 GRPs	80%

Source: AG Fuer das Werbefemsehen, CH-Bern

Audiences/CPM's

Average Cost, Audience, and CPMs by Daypart
(Top Three Stations, :30, national audience, Target=Persons 6-74)

Hours	Morning 12:00-14:00	Daytime 14:00-17:00	Prime Time 18:00-23:00	Late Night 23:00-08:00	Weekend 18:00-23:00	Children N/A
Station: German						
US$	2,300	2,500	23,300	2,300	12,000	
Avg. Aud. (000)	125	200	1,020	160	812	N/A
CPM	18.40	12.50	22.84	14.38	14.78	
Station: French						
US$	1,200	750	7,400	1,700	7,400	
Avg. Aud. (000)	91	35	325	130	325	N/A
CPM	13.19	21.43	22.77	13.08	22.77	
Station: Italian						
US$	230	200	1,200	230	1,300	
Avg. Aud. (000)	11	15	50	13	53	N/A
CPM	20.91	13.33	24.00	17.69	24.53	

Audiences/Ratings by Daypart

Daypart	Hours	Household				Adult		
		Universe (000)	Hut Levels	Household Rating	Impressions (000)	Universe (000)	Adult Rating	Impressions (000)
Morning	12:00-19:00	N/A	N/A	N/A	N/A	N/A	27	N/A
Daytime	14:00-17:00	N/A	N/A	N/A	N/A	N/A	4	N/A
Primetime	18:00-23:00	N/A	N/A	N/A	N/A	N/A	3	N/A
Late Night	13:00-01:00	N/A	N/A	N/A	N/A	N/A	31	N/A
Weekend	Sunday	N/A	N/A	N/A	N/A	N/A	N/A	N/A
Children's	N/A							

Scheduling/Languages

LANGUAGES	Programming		Commercials
Primary Language	German	70%	German
Secondary Language	French	25%	French

- 32% of commercial spots sold are :30 in length and time is available in increments of :01 from :05 to :90.

- Commercials are aired throughout the day in specific time blocks at the beginning and end of programs as well as within programs.
- All commercials are aired nationally.

Children's Advertising

ADULT PROGRAMMING			Kids		
Station	Hours	Days	Universe (000)	Ratings	Impressions (000)
SRG	All	All	451	6	27

CHILDREN'S PROGRAMMING			Kids		
Station	Hours	Days	Universe (000)	Ratings	Impressions (000)
German	14:00-17:00		451	6	27

Source: AG Fuer das Webefemsehen, CH-Bern

Radio

- In the main city there are 3 national radio stations.
- Over 30 local stations exist carrying no premiums for regional or local commercials.
- The primary broadcast language is German and the secondary language is French.
- The most popular program types are News and 'Middle of the Road.'
- Commercial lengths are available from :10-:60.
- Primetime for radio is 12:00-13:00 and no ratings are available.
- No average audience or CPM information is available.

Radio Cost Changes Between Years
'88 — '89 — '90 — '91 — '92
3%   5%   2%   3%

Daypart/Prime Time

Daypart	Local Time
Prime Time	06:00 - 08:00
Daytime	10:00 - 14:00
Late Night	18:00 - 22:00

Source: Leo Burnett Media CH-Zurich

Cable

Teleclub is the only cable channel in Switzerland.

Regional cable is used as a complementary vehicle during national campaigns and they carry no advertising.

The primary broadcast language is German, the secondary language is French.

(Source: AG Fuer das Werbefemsehen, CH-Bern)

Satellite

There are 10 satellite channels that carry no advertising in Switzerland

Satellite is an ongoing market and 2-3% of TV households are expected to receive satellite within the next five years. *(Source: AG Fuer das Werbefemsehen, CH-Bern)*

Most European satellite channels are aired via cable.

Video Cassettes

About 40% of the TV households in Switzerland have video cassette recorders (VCRs); however pre-recorded tapes do not carry commercial advertising. *(Source: AG Fuer das Werbefemsehen, CH-Bern)*

Cinema

Cinemas in Switzerland do carry advertising with commercial lengths from :20-:90. No cost or four week reach information is available.

Source (Cinema information): Central Film AG, CH-Zurich

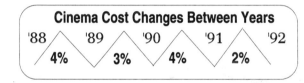

Cinema Cost Changes Between Years

'88	'89	'90	'91	'92
4%	3%	4%	2%	

Newspapers

Literacy rate in English is 30%.

Newspaper Cost Changes Between Years

'88	'89	'90	'91	'92
5%	4%	6%	4%	

Source: Leo Burnett Media, CH-Zurich

Daily Newspaper	Market	Size	Circulation (000)	Avg. Daily Aud. (000)	1 page B&W Cost (US$)	Accept Color?
Blick	N/A	N/A	N/A	760	N/A	N/A
NZZ	N/A	N/A	N/A	388	N/A	N/A
Tages Anzeiger	N/A	N/A	N/A	738	N/A	N/A
La Suisse	N/A	N/A	N/A	207	N/A	N/A

Magazines

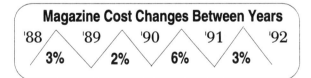

Magazine Cost Changes Between Years

'88	'89	'90	'91	'92
3%	2%	6%	3%	

Magazine	Type	Frequency	Circ. (000)	Audited?	Avg. Issue Aud. (000)	1 page 4/C Cost (US$)
Schwetz Illustrierte	N/A	N/A	N/A	Yes	N/A	N/A
Sonutags-Blick	N/A	N/A	N/A	Yes	N/A	N/A
Illustre	N/A	N/A	N/A	Yes	N/A	N/A

Outdoor

Billboard

Sites available	 150,000
Lead Time to reserve	.... One year adv.
Exposure	.... 60-80%

Costs

Average, 1 billboard/month

B4	$20
B12	$70
12 m^2 x 2,000	

Billboard Cost Changes Between Years

'88 ⟋⟍ '89 ⟋⟍ '90 ⟋⟍ '91 ⟋⟍ '92
  4%   3%   3%   5%

No size information is available

Direct Marketing

Direct Marketing is the most important current advertising medium (41%) and still growing.

Top Direct Mail Consumer List Brokers

List Broker	Information Provided
AWZ, Bern	Catalogs
Direct Mail Company	Catalogs
Jaeggi & Weibel, Zurich	Catalogs

Direct Marketing Association

Schori Veriband for Direct Marketing

Source (Direct Marketing): Leo Burnett Media, CH-Zurich.

Research Sources

Medium Covered	Research Company	Information Provided
Print, Cinema	WEMF Bachmattstr. 53 8048 Zurich	MACH 92 (Basic) MACH 92 (Consumers)
Television	AGW Gincomcttistrasse 15 3000 Bern 15	Telecontrol
Radio	SRG Giacomettistrasse 15 3000 Bern 15	SRG Mediastudie

Advertising Regulations

By Product

Beverages/Alcohol
Not allowed on TV and Radio. Restricted in Outdoor and Cinema.

Cigarettes
See Beverages/Alcohol.

Pharmaceuticals/Drngs
Restricted on TV and Radio.

Advertising to Children
Certain moral codes.

By Medium

Television
Limited advertising time (30 minutes) and restrictions on ad placement.

Outdoor
Restrictions for cigarettes and alcohol.

Turkey

Area	780,580 km²
Population (1992)	59,640,143
Population growth rate (1992)	2.1%
GDP	US$ 198 billion
GDP/per capita	US$ 3,400
Real growth rate (1991)	1.5%
Capital	Ankara

Population Breakdown

By Sex		*By Age Group*		*By Socio-Economic Status*	
Male	51.3%	Children, 0-14	37.5%	A	5%
Female	48.7%	Teens, 15-19	10.7%	B	7%
		Adults, 20+	51.8%	C	32%
				D	43%

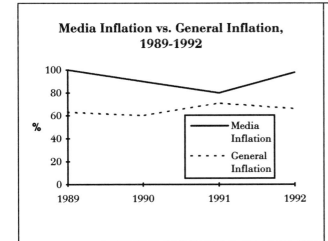

Media Inflation vs. General Inflation, 1989-1992

Number of Households	11,300,000

Ownership of household durables

Car	14%
Phone	45%
Washers	90%
(purchasing power equivalent)	

GNP distribution by industry

Agriculture	14%
Industry	35%
Services	51%

Exchange rates (US$ to local currency)

1991	0.00228832
1992	0.00014432

National Holidays

Holiday	*1993 Date*
New Years Day Holiday	January 1
Ramadan Holiday	April 4 - 6
Nat. Sovereignty Day	April 23
Youth and Sports Day	May 19
Kurban Holiday	June 11 - 14
Victory Day	August 30
Republic Day	October 29

School Holidays

Holiday	*1993 Date*
Semester Holiday	January 25 - February 9
Summer Holiday	June 6 - September 13

Major Influences and Trends

The Turkish media enviroment has continued its rapid growth and has become a scene of ever increasing competition.

The TV market has been transformed by the launch of several channels in the last year, and the radio airwaves have been saturated with FM radio stations. Above all, the proliferation of new broadcast media is accelerating the development of media planning and buying, although available media research is limited.

Television has become a more complex medium than ever. The number of channels recently increased to 13, including 6 on public TV TRT. As the number of channels has increased and commercial airing time has augmented, commercial breaks have become more cluttered and share of viewership per channel has decreased. Until the 1990 launch of InterSTAR, a Turkish language satellite service based in Germany, Turkish Radio and Television (TRT) was a monopoly. Agencies booked a year's air time in advance for their clients. This contract system has now died out and TRT is being forced to be more flexible.

TRT1's dominance in the market has been eroded by three leading private stations. Once the government introduces private TV officially, many expect TRT to surrender some of its frequencies to these private channels.

Show TV and Kanal 6 are now competing to become the leading Turkish channel, followed by InterSTAR, TRT1, Teleon (sister company of InterSTAR) and HBB. Almost all channels are servicing the same telecast schedule consisting of films, game shows, entertainment and soccer. TGRT (new channel of the newspaper Turkiye) started officially broadcasting in May, 1993, and another newspaper's channel Sabah TV Satel is now broadcasting test airings. Satel is expected to start officially broadcasting by the beginning of July, 1993 and will rename itself ATV at this time. With the introduction of new private channels, TRT is losing its portion of the already reduced share of media budgets typically spent on TV.

The radio market was also very active in the last year with the establishment of new private FM radio stations. The year ended with over 50 private stations broadcasting locally . However, in April 1993, the government suspended the broadcasting of private FM stations. Ex-private radio owners are hoping to start broadcasting again in June, 1993, with the permission of the newly formed government and prime minister.

Newspapers have engaged in fierce competition among themselves and against TV channels. The three biggest publishers have resorted to continuous promotions to reinforce their position in the market. Sabah, Hurriyet and Milliyet are now locked in a campaign to win readers with promotions offering free encyclopedias. All spend heavily on advertising. The "Encyclopedia War" among these three publishers will finish by the end of October, 1993, and it has not yet been determined whether the readers will stay with newspapers once they have all the encyclopedia volumes. However, it is certain that once the encyclopedia promotion is over, the daily cumulative newspaper circulation (which is currently about 4 million) will suffer due to less reader duplication. Most households now buy more than one newspaper in order to acquire more encyclopedia sets.

Although magazines have limited circulation in Turkey, the quality and quantity of magazines have been increasing. Most of the developments have been seen within the special interest magazines.

These recent developments in the Turkey media market have resulted in the improvement of media planning and buying services.

In order to respond to the volume and complexity of the media environment, independent media buying companies have begun to carrry out the media buying function for many clients.

Currently, there are four media buying companies operating in Turkey:

Equmedia, formed in December 1992 with the initiation of Leo Burnett, offers media buying services to partner agencies' clients.

Media Gold, a joint company of Cenajans/Grey and Guzel Sanatlar/Saatchi and Saatchi, plans and buys media. However, Media Gold's levy of a ten percent commission from media owners has not pleased everybody.

Other media buying companies are Media Plus which serves Alic/BBDO clients in Turkey, and Universal Media the in-house media company of McCann-Ericson.

It is very difficult to make definite projections in an unstable media environment. However, here are some estimations for the short-term:

The law proposal to break the state's monopoly in TV and radio broadcasting will be approved by Turkish National Assembly.

The TV and radio market will reach a saturation point and local and special interest broadcasting will gain importance.

Media giants, owning multi-media channels, will increase their power which will lead to private media monopolies.

The importance of media planning and buying will keep increasing, forcing the establishment of adequate media research tools in Turkey.

Spending Analysis

National advertising spending by medium
based on appropriate year's exchange rate

	1989 US$ MM	1990 US$ MM	1991 US$ MM	1992 US$ MM
TV	191.3	128.6	312.3	549.2
Cinema	N/A	N/A	4.1	3.3
Radio	3.0	2.2	1.2	1.9
Newspaper	213.1	117.0	266.3	459.2
Magazine	39.6	18.8	53.6	82.2
Total	447.0	266.6	637.5	1,095.8

Media Buying

Developments in Turkey's media market are accelerating changes in the media buying scene. There are currently four buying companies. There are also rumors that Carat is looking for opportunities in the Turkish market. Buying companies are not very active at the moment, however many people expect they will bring a variety and dynamism to the market in the very near future.

Agencies which form media buying companies represent 27.7% of total market.

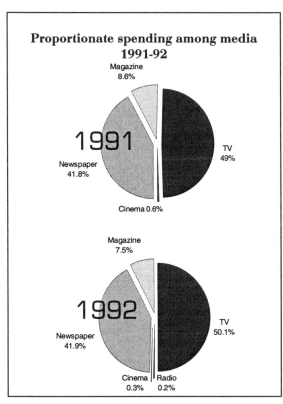

Proportionate spending among media 1991-92

Buying Services

Buying Service	Parent Company
Equmedia	Markom/Leo Burnett Raklamevi/Y & R Adam/Birlesik Reklancilik/Yorum/Euro RSCG
Media Gold	Canajans/Young, and Guzel Sanatlar/S and 9
Media +	Alice & BBDO
Universal Media	McCann-Ericson

Top Advertisers

By Company

Parent Company	Categories	US$ MM
Imar Bankasi	Finance	29.77
Alo Bilgi	Telemarketing	23.05
Seat/Super Oto	Automobile	15.37
Sabah	Press	15.37
Hurriyet	Press	14.36
Alo Ultra Deterjan	Household Cleaners	13.81
Milliyet	Food	12.23
Ariel Ultramatik Det.	Household Cleaners	9.67
Pepsi-Cola	Beverages	9.55
Blendax	Cosmetics	9.54

By Product

Product Category	Advertiser	US$ MM
Finance	Imar Bankasi	29.77
Telemarketing	Al Bilgi	23.05
Automotive	Seat/Super Oto	15.80
Press	Sabah	15.37
Household Cleaners	Alo Ultra Deterjan	13.81
Cosmetics	Blendax	9.54
Entertainment	Super FM	6.87
Companies	Milpa	8.74
Food	Algida	3.97
Household Durables	Arcelik TV	3.77

Television

Overview

See **Major Trends** for details.
Television penetration level has been at 99.4%
since 1990; reaching about 11,230,000
households.

Adult Reach	
at 250 GRPs	70%
at 500 GRPs	90%
at 1,000 GRPs	100%

Opportunities

Network	Number of Stations	Ownership	Station Profile	Commercial Minutes/Day	Coverage	BroadcastHours (Sign-On/Off)
TRT	TV1	State	General	8	99.4	07:00-02:00
TRT	TV2	State	Slightly Sophisticated	11	92.5	18:00-24:00
TRT	TV3	State	Sophisticated	1	79.1	20:00-24:00
TRT	TV4	State	Education	-	42.8	17:00-23:00
TRT	INT/AVR.	State	General	-	N.A.	15:00-02:00
TRT	GAPTV	State	Education	10	N.A.	12:00-18:00
Prime Media	STAR	Private	General	31	72.3	07:00-02:00
ARS	Show TV	Private	General	53	71.4	07:00-02:00
ART1	Kanal 6	Private	General	38	44.7	07:00-01:00
SATEL	ATV	Private	General	17	N.A.	07:00-01:00
Hos Group	HBB	Private	General	11	29.1	07:00-01:00
Ihlas Holding	TGR7	Private	General	26	N.A.	07:00-01:00

Costs

Prime Time TV Costs for a :30 in US$			
1989	1990	1991	1992
N/A	8,000	8,500	12,000

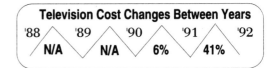

Television Cost Changes Between Years

'88	'89	'90	'91	'92
	N/A	N/A	6%	41%

Audience/CPM's

Average Cost, Audience, and CPMs by Daypart
(Top 3 Stations:, :30, national audience)

Hours	Morning 07:00-12:00	Daytime 12:00-18:30	Prime Time 18:30-24:00	Late Night 24:00-07:00	Weekend	Children 16:20-18:30
Station: SHOW TV						
US$	2,750	3,200	12,500	1,300	N/A	3,200
Avg. Aud. (000)	1,470	1,053	4,228	95	N/A	1,366
CPM	1.87	3.04	2.95	13.68	N/A	2.34
Station: KANAL 6						
US$	2,200	4,200	13,500	900	N/A	4,200
Avg. Aud. (000)	1,221	1,770	4,710	207	N/A	1,898
CPM	1.80	2.37	2.87	4.35	N/A	2.21
Station: InterSTAR						
US$	2,400	5,250	14,250	900	N/A	5,250
Avg. Aud. (000)	577	896	3,870	151	N/A	1,232
CPM	4.16	5.86	3.68	5.96	N/A	4.26

Audiences/Ratings by Daypart (Target=People 18+)

Daypart	Hours	Household				Adult		
		HH Universe (000)	Hut Levels	Household Rating	Impressions (000)	Universe (000)	Adult Rating	Impressions (000)
Morning	07:00-12:00	11,300	N/A	N/A	N/A	36,000	10.46	3,765
Daytime	12:00-18:30	11,300	N/A	N/A	N/A	36,000	11.95	4,302
Primetime	18:30-24:00	11,300	N/A	N/A	N/A	36,000	35.23	12,683
Late Night	24:00-07:00	11,300	N/A	N/A	N/A	36,000	2.22	799
Weekend	N/A	11,300	N/A	N/A	N/A	N/A	N/A	N/A
Children's	16:30-18:30	N/A	N/A	N/A	N/A	N/A	14.2	5,112

Scheduling/Regional/Languages

- The most common commercial lengths are :20 and :30; other lengths vary.
- All programming is in Turkish.
- State TV airs commercials in specific time blocks; private TV airs commercials throughout the day.
- 99%of all commercial advertising is on a national basis; 1% are regional/locally broadcast. Costs for regionally aired commercials are 10% of those for national buys.
- Alternatives to airing commercials nationally are available on the TRT network on station GAP TV in the east region between 12:00 and 18:00 hours at approximately 10% of the cost.

Children's Advertising

All programming accepts advertising targeted at children.

Radio

- There are approximately 100 radio stations in Turkey; 20 of which are in Istanbul.
- 90% of all households have radios; the estimated number is 10,170,000.
- The primary broadcasting language is Turkish; the News is also broadcast in English, German and French.
- The most popular program type is musical.

- Regional/local commercial buying is possible, and carries a US$5,000 premium per :30 commercial spot.
- Commercial lengths vary; no CPM's are available.
- The Prime/Peak Time for radio is 08:00-10:00 and 16:00-02:00; no ratings are available.

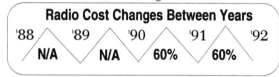

Radio Cost Changes Between Years

'88	'89	'90	'91	'92
N/A	N/A	60%	60%	

Cable

- Cable is at the introduction stage, and has been installed in about 90,000 homes representing only 0.7% of the total households in Turkey.
- The cable system is publicly owned.
- Turkish is the primary broadcast language; English is the secondary language.
- A state-owned communication company and Ericssonare Partners are installing cable in the majority of cable TV homes. One million more households are expected to receive cable within the next five years.
- 20 cable channels currently exist of which 18 are commercial.
- Legal legislation will most likely place restrictions on cable prices.

Satellite

- There are 12 satellite channels accessible in Turkey; less than 1% of Turkish households are expected to receive satellites within the next five years.

- 11 satellite stations are commerecial and there are no regualtions or restrictions that apply to imported programs and commercials.

- Special antennas and municipality dishes are available. The most widely received stations are RTL Plus, SAT1, S. Channel, Tele5, and CNN.

- An increase in the number of satellite channels is expected, but cable should expand more quickly than satellite.

Satellite Channel	Country of Origin	Language	Programming
RTL Plus	Luxembourg	German	General
SAT1	Germany	German	General
Sky Channel	UK	English	General
SAT3	Germany	German	General
Super Channel	UK	English	Music/General
BBC TV	UK	English	News/General
Raiuno	Italy	Italian	General
Eurosport	Germany	English	Sports
CNN	USA	English	News
TVS	France	French	General
Raidue	Italy	Italian	General
TVE	Spain	Spanish	General

Video Cassettes

- About 17% of TV households (or 15% of all households) have video cassette recorders (VCRs).
- Video cassettes in Turkey do carry advertising and the number of sponsors per tape varies; costs are determined through negotiations depending on the movie category.
- AGR is the service that measures VCR usage.
- As the number of TV channels increases, the usage decreases.

Cinema

- The quality of movies and the number of moviegoers is expected to increase.
- Of 316 cinemas surveyed, 47% offer commercial time in various lengths; costs and potential reach are not available.

Cinema Cost Changes Between Years

'88	'89	'90	'91	'92
300%	200%	200%	200%	

Newspapers

There are 20 national daily Turkish newspapers which accept advertising; their combined circulation is 4,000,000.
The literacy rate in English is 10%.

Newspaper Cost Changes Between Years

'88	'89	'90	'91	'92
N/A	95%	70%	90%	

Newspaper	Market	Size	Circulation (000)	Avg. Daily Aud. (000)	1 page B&W Cost (US$)	Accept Color?
Sabah	National	Broadsheet	774	7,740	27,600	Yes
Hurriyet	National	Broadsheet	665	6,384	22,400	Yes
Milliyet	National	Broadsheet	397	1,786	23,400	Yes
Turkiye	National	Broadsheet	299	957	19,500	Yes
Bugun	National	Broadsheet	189	246	20,600	Yes
Meydan	National	Broadsheet	162	162	20,600	Yes
Fotomac	National	Broadsheet	128	141	42,600	Yes
Fotospor	National	Broadsheet	116	162	43,600	Yes
Zaman	National	Broadsheet	105	115	14,000	Yes
Cumburiyet	National	Broadsheet	57	160	12,800	Yes

Magazines

Turkey has 10 consumer magazines and 134 trade/technical magazines.

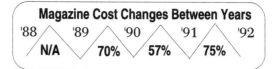

Magazine Cost Changes Between Years

'88	'89	'90	'91	'92
N/A	70%	57%	75%	

Magazine	Type	Frequency	Circulation (000)	Audited?	Avg. Issue Aud. (000)	1 page4/C Cost (US$)
AktGel	Entertainment/ News	Weekly	23	No	23	7,100
Tampo	Entertainment/ News	Weekly	20	No	18	7,500
Penthouse	Men's	Monthly	120	No	105	5,500
Playmen	Men's	Monthly	50	No	45	5,250
Cosmopolitan	Women's	Monthly	25	No	23	5,500
Burda	Women's	Monthly	40	No	36	4,500
Bluejean	Entertainment	Monthly	60	No	6	5,700
Free	Entertainment	Monthly	35	No	4	3,500
Autoshow	Automotive	Weekly	30	No	27	4,500
October	Automotive	Weekly	25	No	23	3,500
Ekonomist	Business	Weekly	20	No	18	6,750

Outdoor/Transit

Billboard

Sites available	5,000 approx.
Lead Time to reserve	2 weeks
Exposure	N/A

Costs

Average, 1 billboard/month

70 m x 100 cm	US$ 475
90 m x 125 cm	US$ 125

Transit

Sizes vary and are not standard.
Transit Board advertising exists, costs are negotiable; no other information is available.

Regional restrictions exist for tobacco, alcohol and pharmaceuticals and apply to all outdoor advertising.

Billboard Cost Changes Between Years

'88	'89	'90	'91	'92
40%	70%	50%	50%	

Direct Marketing

Direct Marketing is gaining importance as a media vehicle which can reach a very qualified target audience. There is no Direct Marketing Association.

List Broker	Information Provided
DAP Research Co.	Product Usage/Demographics
Piar-Gallup	Demographics
PEVA-GFK	Product Usage
Datajans	Product Usage/Demographics

Telemarketing Companies	
Kanual Market	All product categories
Art Pazarlama	More durable goods
EVPA	More consumer goods
ALO BILGI	Special interest goods

Non-Traditional Media

Increased usage of non-traditional media is expected. Types currently available include: in-store, direct mailing, and computerized media; costs vary.

Research Sources

Medium covered	Research company	Information Provided
TV	AGB	TV viewership, national spendings
	Anadolu & Bilegim	
	Indo Cd. No:20	
	Celiktepe/Instanbul	
	Narajans	
Print	Strateji Aragtarma	TV register readership
	Yeniyoi Sk. 5/6	
	Gayrettepe/Instanbul	
Radio	Strateji Arastirma	General radio listening
Cinema	Fida film	Viewership and profiles
Direct Marketing	DAP	Full
General	Advertising Association	All above

Television Research Currently Available

Research Method	Frequency
People Meter	People Meter, weekly with monthly summaries

Advertising Regulations

By Product

Beverages/Alcohol
Not allowed on TV and Radio.
Food/Restaurants
No restrictions.
Cigarettes
Not allowed on TV and radio.
Pharmaceuticals/Drugs
Not allowed on TV, radio, outdoor, and only allowed on print for product launches.
Advertising To Children
Monitoring of TV commercials.
Commercial Production
No restriction.

By Medium

Television
New television regulations will be ready by the end of 1993.
Print
Pharmaceutical advertisements are not allowed.
Outdoor
Varies according to municipality regulations of each city.
Cable
Depends on new television regulations.
Direct Marketing
Available upon request.
Non-traditional
Available upon request.

Sources Consulted

AGB-Anadolu Research Corp., Monthly Reports
AGB-Anadster Research Corp., Monthly Reports, 1993.
Anadolu University, Jan., 1993
Bilegim Research Co., 1993
Consumption Patterns by Piar-Gallup, 1991
Fida Film, 1993
Media Owners
PTT
Srategi Research, 1993
Stale Institute of Statistics Yearbook of 1992
Zel-Nielsen Research Company, 1993

United Kingdom

Area	244,820 km^2
Population (1992)	57,797,514
Population growth rate (1992)	0.3%
GDP	US$ 915.5 billion
GDP/per capita	US$ 15,900
Real growth rate (1991)	1.9%
Capital	London

Population Breakdown

By Sex		*By Age Group*		*By Socio-Economic Status*	
Male	48.3%	Children, 0-9	14%	A	3%
Female	51.7%	Teens, 10-19	13%	B	16%
		Adults, 20+	73%	C	51%
				D	16%
				E	14%

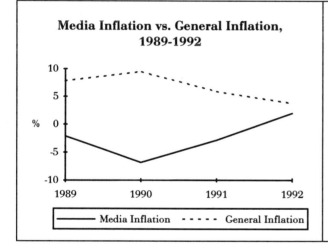

Media Inflation vs. General Inflation, 1989-1992

— Media Inflation   - - - - - General Inflation

Number of Households	11,900,000

Ownership of household durables
Car................................72%
Phone...........................93%
Washers.......................88%
   (purchasing power equivalent)
GNP distribution by industry
Agriculture.................. 1.8%
Industry 27.7%
Services 70.5%
Exchange rates (US$ to local currency)
1991 ....1.906
1992 ....1.515

National Holidays

Holiday	1993 Date
New Year's	January 1
Good Friday	April 9
Easter Monday	April 12
May Day Holiday	May 3
Spring Holiday	May 31
Late Summer Holiday	August 30
Christmas Day	December 25
Boxing Day	December 26

School Holidays*

	Holiday	1993 Date
England and Whales	Christmas	December 18 - January 6
	Half Term	February 15 - February 19
	Easter	April 5 - 16
	May Half Term	May 22 - June 1
	Summer Holidays	July 17 - September 7
	Autumn Half Term	October 25 - 29
Scotland	Christmas	December 18 - January 6
	Easter	April 3 - 21
	May Half Term	May 1 - 8
	Summer Holidays	June 26 - August 24
	Autumn Half Term	October 18 - 22

Each Regional Education Authority decides its own holiday dates so the figures above are the average of the dates used.

Major Influences and Trends

The UK media scene is undergoing profound and radical change. In terms of television, the separate selling of Channel 4 and the growth of satellite have resulted in a competitive market for television airtime. Facing their loss of monopoly conditions, the Channel 3 companies are frantically reorganizing themselves in terms of ownership and sales to be as competitive as possible. The number of available regions are expected to shrink from 13 to 4-5 over the next 12 months.

The whole issue of new technology is also raising its head; cable is at least beginning to make substantial inroads and the ITC is moving towards policy statements on digital television.

Print has been badly hit by the recession and continues to be highly competitive.

Radio is expanding quickly: two national stations have been launched and regional stations are in the pipeline as the existing local franchises are all being readvertised. Thus, we can expect a totally different radio market in the future. However, revenue growth still lags behind.

Cinema and outdoor are both presenting and marketing themselves in a far more professional way in the face of increased competition from other media.

Spending Analysis

National advertising spending by medium
based on appropriate year's exchange rate

	1989 US$ MM	1990 US$ MM	1991 US$ MM	1992 US$ MM
TV	N/A	N/A	4,408	3,754
Cinema	N/A	N/A	80	68
Radio	N/A	N/A	284	233
Newspaper	N/A	N/A	5,240	4,234
Magazine	N/A	N/A	3,940	3,134
Direct Response	N/A	N/A	1,706	1,432
Outdoor	N/A	N/A	509	430
Total	**N/A**	**N/A**	**16,167**	**13,285**

Source: Advertising Association Year Book 1992

Media Buying

The media buying scene continues to fragment in the UK. In addition to the growth of media independents, there is an increasing trend towards media affiliates (agencies floating off their media departments and then letting them pitch for media business only).

Little has happened on the buying club front. Most agencies which are currently involved in clubs use them more for research purposes than media buying clout.

Buying Services with 1992 Billings

Buying Service	Parent Company	1992 US$ MM	Independant/ Affiliate
Zenith	Saatchi	468.5	Affiliate
Initiative Media	Lintas	202.2	Affiliate
TMD Carat	Carat	163.5	Independent
Media Centre	DMB&B	149.7	Affiliate
O&M Media	O&M	126.2	Affiliate

Source: Register Meal 1992 UK

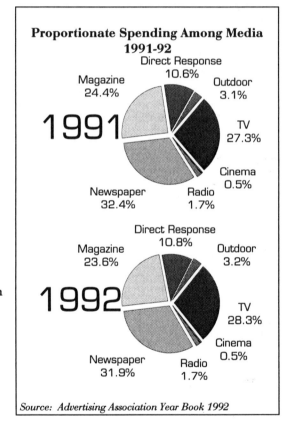

Proportionate Spending Among Media 1991-92

1991
Direct Response 10.6%
Magazine 24.4%
Outdoor 3.1%
TV 27.3%
Cinema 0.5%
Radio 1.7%
Newspaper 32.4%

1992
Direct Response 10.8%
Magazine 23.6%
Outdoor 3.2%
TV 28.3%
Cinema 0.5%
Radio 1.7%
Newspaper 31.9%

Source: Advertising Association Year Book 1992

Top Advertisers

By Company

Parent Company	Product Categories	US$ MM
Procter & Gamble	Household Products	143.3
Lever Brothers	Household Products	118.8
Kellogg	Breakfast Cereals	92.9
Ford	Motor	76.5
British Telecom	Public Utilities	73.2
Vauxhall Motors	Motor	62.8
Procter & Gamble	Health & Beauty	56.6
Elida Gibbs	Health & Beauty	53.1
Bass Brewers	Brewing	51.6
Mars Confectionery	Confectionery	51.6

Source: *Register Meal 1992 UK*

By Product

Product Category	Advertiser	US$ MM
Retail	Tesco	78.9
Fast Food	McDonald's	25.4
Public Utilities	British Telecom	18.3
Household Products	Persil Micro Liquid	18.3
Motors	Renault Clio	18.1
Holiday & Travel	Lunn Poly	17.7
Financial	Abbey National	16.4
Media	Sky	15.5
Beers	Carling Black Label	14.7
Tobacco	Benson & Hedges Silk Cut	13.6
Food/Drink	NDC Milk	13.6
Toys/Games	Sega	5.9

Source: *Register Meal 1992 UK*

Television

Overview

See Major Influences

Television HH Penetration				Adult Reach	
1989	*1990*	*1991*	*1992*	250 GRPs	75%
97%	97%	97%	98%	500 GRPs	85%
21,139	21,885	22,054	22,077	1,000 GRPs	91%

Opportunities

Network	Number of Stations	Ownership	Station Profile	Commercial Minutes/Day	Coverage	Broadcast Hours (Sign-On/Off)
ITV	N/A	N/A	General	147	N/A	N/A
Angelia	N/A	N/A	N/A	147	N/A	N/A
Border	N/A	N/A	N/A	128	N/A	London M-F
Carlton	N/A	N/A	N/A	147	N/A	N/A
Central TV	N/A	N/A	N/A	147	N/A	N/A
Grampian	N/A	N/A	N/A	147	N/A	N/A
Granada	N/A	N/A	N/A	147	N/A	N/A
HTV	N/A	N/A	N/A	193	N/A	London Sa-Su
LNT	N/A	N/A	N/A	147	N/A	N/A
Meridian	N/A	N/A	N/A	147	N/A	N/A
STV	N/A	N/A	N/A	147	N/A	N/A
ULSTER	N/A	N/A	N/A	147	N/A	N/A
West Country	N/A	N/A	N/A	147	N/A	N/A

Costs

Prime Time TV Costs for :30 Adult CPM's in US$			
1989	*1990*	*1991*	*1992*
10.15	10.15	10.66	11.10

Audience/CPM's

Average Cost, Audience, and CPMs by Daypart
(Top 3 Stations, :30. national audience, Target=Adults)

Hours	Morning 06:00-09:29	Daytime 09:30-17:25	Prime Time 17:25-22:59	Late Night 23:00-05:59	Weekend	Children
Station: GMTV						
US$	6,650	N/A	N/A	N/A	N/A	N/A
Avg. Aud. (000)	809	N/A	N/A	N/A	N/A	N/A
CPM	8.22	N/A	N/A	N/A	N/A	N/A
Station: ITV						
US$	N/A	17,802	71,529	8,646	N/A	N/A
Avg. Aud. (000)		1,921	7,123	1,072	N/A	N/A
CPM		9.27	10.04	8.06	N/A	N/A
Station: CH4						
US$	583	32,664	12,065	1,167	N/A	N/A
Avg. Aud. (000)	131	901	1,289	648	N/A	N/A
CPM	4.45	36.25	9.36	1.80	N/A	N/A

Audience/Ratings by Daypart

Daypart	Hours	Household Universe (000)	Hut Levels	Household Rating	Impressions (000)	Adult Universe (000)	Adult Rating	Impressions (000)
Morning	06:00-09:29	22,168	N/A	5.5	1,219	N/A	N/A	N/A
Daytime	09:30-17:24	22,168	N/A	6.4	1,418	N/A	N/A	N/A
Primetime	17:25-22:59	22,168	N/A	21.1	4,677	N/A	N/A	N/A
Late Night	23:00-05:59	22,168	N/A	4.2	931	N/A	N/A	N/A
Weekend	09:30-05:59	22,168	N/A	N/A	NA	N/A	N/A	N/A
Children's	16:00-17:00	22,168	N/A	6.0	1,330	N/A	N/A	N/A

Scheduling/Regional/Languages

LANGUAGES	Programming		Commercials
Primary Language	English	99%	English
Secondary Language	Welsh	1%	1
	One of ITV's regional stations has 25% of programs transmitted in Welsh		

- 45% of all commercials are :30; others are available in multiples of :10.
- Commercials are aired throughout the day in center breaks and end breaks.
- On the movie channel on Sky there are no center breaks available in the films.

- 85% of commercials are aired nationally; of the 15% aired on a regional/local level no cost comparisons are available.
- The national stations are GMTV, all satellite channels and Channel 4 (although Channel 4 can be sold regionally). All ITV stations are regional.
- Channel 4 can be bought as 6 separate macro regions: London, Midlands, North, Scotland, South and Ulster. ITV stations are: Carlton, (London Weekly), LWT (London Weekend), Central, Granada, North, Anglia, STV, HTV, Grampian, Border, Westcountry and Ulster.

Children's Advertising

All adult programming will accept advertising targeted at children, but most advertisers take advantage of specific children's programming during weekday afternoons and weekend mornings.

Source (All television data): BARB 1992 UK

Radio

- The United Kingdom has 130 radio stations. The 12 stations in London are Jazz FM, Kiss FM, Captial FM, Capital Gold, Newstalk, Talkback, Melody, WNK, LGR, Choice FM, RTM and Spectrum.
- Household penetration percentages are not available. Automobile penetration is 18%.

- The primary broadcast language is English.
- On AM stations the most popular program type is Golden Oldies; while a Top 40 format is most popular on FM radio.
- Commercial spots are available in :20, :30, :40, :50, :60 and :60+. Costs are not available.
- Regional programming is achieved by individual stations splitting frequencies across regions. There is no additional cost for buying regionally. *(Source: JICRAR 1992, RAB 1992)*
- Prime/Peak time is 06:00-09:00. Adult rating is 7 for an audience of 3,176,000.

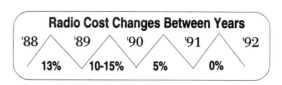

Daypart Costs/CPM's

Daypart	Local Time	Avg. Cost :30 US$	Audience (000)	CPM (US$)
Prime Time	06:00 - 09:00	12,753	7,084	1.80
Daytime	09:00 - 18:00	12,849	8,566	1.50
Late Night	18:00 - 24:00	4,630	3,307	1.40

Cable

- There are 3 cable channels: Bravo, Discovery, and Superchannel.
- Cable growth is predicted to increase at a faster rate than dish sales. The reason is a large amount of investment from US companies who see the huge potential for development in the increasingly competitive field of telecommunications.
- In 1992 cable reached 473,415 households in the UK. By 1994, 1,250,000 households are expected to have cable access.
- The primary broadcast language is English.

Source (Cable data): CTA 1992

*Cable Networks (owners)	HH Circulation (000)
Telewest	75,888
Comcast	72,905
Videtron	67,297
Southwestern Bell	53,672
Nynex	40,047
CVC	39,065
Devanha Group	25,805
General Cable	24,895

*All cable networks provide the same basic programming.

Satellite

- Satellite has shown rapid growth since the launch of Sky TV on the Astra satellite in February 1989 and BSkyB and Marco Polo satellites in April 1990.
- Current penetration is approximately 14% of UK homes. Among certain groups (children, young adults, housewives with children) this figure is over 20%. Penetration is expected to reach 50% by the year 2000.
- All BSkyB services will be encrypted by 1994 with different price ties enabling access to premium programming (i.e. movie channel, sports).

Satellite Channels	
Sky One	Nickelodeon
Sky News	MTV
Movie Channel	Bravo
UK Gold	QVC
Sky Sports	Family Channel
Movies Gold	Discovery
TNT	CNN
Eurosport	

Satellite Penetration (MM)				
	Dish	Cable	Total	Penetration
July 1993	2.53	.836	3.36	15.2%
Jan. 1994	2.86	.940	3.80	17.2%
July 1994	3.15	1.000	4.15	18.8%

Source (Satellite data): BARB 1992

Video Cassettes

- About 69% of UK homes have video cassette recorders (VCRs).
- BARB measures VCR usage.

- Pre-recorded tapes do carry advertising, but VCR advertising is still viewed as a specialist segment. Usage is increasing.

- Cost depends on film (ranges from £2,000-£70,000).

Cinema

Cinema Cost Changes Between Years
'88   '89   '90   '91   '92
26.7%   7.3%   4.9%   2.2%

Cinemas in the United Kingdom do carry advertising in any multiple of 10 seconds. Continued growth is expected.

Newspapers

Newspaper Cost Changes Between Years
'88   '89   '90   '91   '92
3.5%   4.4%   5.9%   4.5%

The literacy rate in English is 99%.

Daily Newspaper	Market	Size	Circulation (000)	Avg. Daily Aud. (000)	1 page/B&W Cost (US$)	Accept Color?
Daily Mail	N/A	T	1,737	4,777	19,516	YES
Daily Express	N/A	T	1,512	3,938	20,825	YES
Today	N/A	T	545	1,690	5,712	YES
Daily Star	N/A	T	798	2,407	10,780	YES
Daily Mirror	N/A	T	2,762	7,841	25,900	YES
Sun	N/A	T	3,544	9,841	30,500	YES
Financial Times	N/A	B	286	729	28,224	YES
Daily Telegraph	N/A	B	1,036	2,767	34,500	YES
Independent	N/A	B	368	1,102	14,000	YES
Guardian	N/A	B	413	1,466	15,500	YES
Times	N/A	B	379	1,181	7,250	YES

Source: NRS Oct-Mar 1993

Source (Newspaper data): NRS 1992

Magazines

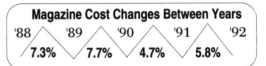

Magazine Cost Changes Between Years
'88   '89   '90   '91   '92
7.3%   7.7%   4.7%   5.8%

Magazine	Type	Frequency	Circ. (000)	Audited?	Avg. Issue Aud (000)	1 page 4/C Cost (US$)
TV Times	N/A	Weekly	1,114	Yes	9,600	N/A
Radio Times	N/A	Weekly	1,593	Yes	12,700	N/A
TV Quick	N/A	Weekly	709	Yes	7,000	N/A
What's on TV	N/A	Weekly	1,431	Yes	9,500	N/A
Woman	N/A	Weekly	717	Yes	12,500	N/A
Woman's Own	N/A	Weekly	700	Yes	15,500	N/A
Woman's Realm	N/A	Weekly	390	Yes	N/A	N/A
Woman's Weekly	N/A	Weekly	827	Yes	8,700	N/A
Chat	N/A	Weekly	450	Yes	5,700	N/A
Me	N/A	Weekly	431	Yes	N/A	N/A
Best	N/A	Weekly	572	Yes	9,450	N/A
Bella	N/A	Weekly	1,122	Yes	14,850	N/A
Take a Break	N/A	Weekly	1,345	Yes	13,500	N/A
My Weekly	N/A	Weekly	448	Yes	N/A	N/A
People's Friend	N/A	Weekly	484	Yes	N/A	N/A
Hello!	N/A	Weekly	488	Yes	6,050	N/A
Family Circle	N/A	Monthly	405	Yes	6,050	N/A
Good Housekeeping	N/A	Monthly	446	Yes	7,990	N/A
Essentials	N/A	Monthly	421	Yes	N/A	N/A
Prima	N/A	Monthly	682	Yes	9,135	N/A
Woman & Home	N/A	Monthly	410	Yes	4,680	N/A
Cosmopolitan	N/A	Monthly	473	Yes	8,420	N/A
Reader's Digest	N/A	Monthly	1,521	Yes	N/A	N/A

Continued on following page

Magazines, continued

Magazine	Type	Frequency	Circ. (000)	Audited?	Avg. Issue Aud. (000)	1 page 4/C Cost (US$)
BBC Good Food	N/A	Monthly	549	Yes	11,064	N/A
Sunday Magazine	N/A	Weekly	4,969	N/A	31,500	N/A
You Magazine (MOS)	N/A	Weekly	2,016	N/A	17,875	N/A
Sunday Mirror Mag.	N/A	Weekly	2,016	N/A	N/A	N/A
Sunday Express Mag.	N/A	Weekly	1,761	N/A	22,400	N/A
Sunday Times Mag.	N/A	Weekly	1,176	N/A	47,000	N/A
Just Seventeen	N/A	Monthly	205,044	YES	4,350	N/A
Homes & Gardens	N/A	Monthly	189,911	YES	3,943	N/A
Vogue	N/A	Monthly	138,167	YES	4,450	N/A
Observer Magazine	N/A	Weekly	536,000	N/A	7,000	N/A

Source (Magazine data): ARC 1992

Outdoor/Transit

Billboard

Sites available 126,000
Lead Time to reserve .... 8-12 weeks adv.

Exposure 50-90%

Costs

Average, 1 billboard/month
1.52 x 1.02 (vertical)...................... US$ 77
1.8 x 1.2 (vertical) .... US$ 230
3.05 x 6.1 (horizontal) .... US$ 540
3.05 x 12.19 (horizontal) .... US$ 2,015

Billboard Cost Changes Between Years
'88   '89   '90   '91   '92
   10%   5-15%   5%   4%

Sizes

45 (60' x 40'), 125 (60' x 120')., 165 (120' x 180')
485 (120' x 120'), 965 (480' x 120')

Transit

Boards available
150,000 (Underground)
90,000 Buses (Sides/Rears)
Also escalator panels, taxi interior and exterior panels.
Exposure (Buses) 80%

Costs

Average, 1 board/month:
Varies
Bus sides   .... US$ 125-215

Transit Board Cost Changes Between Years
'88   '89   '90   '91   '92
   1%   10%   1%   1%

Sizes

Varies according to region.

Restrictions are dependent on local authority/landlord and for certain sizes, the following may be prohibited: Tobacco, Religion, Alcohol, Contraceptives, Political.

Direct Marketing

Direct Mail volumes have continued to rise despite the recession (5.7% increase in 1992 versus 1991 and a 7.5% increase in the 1st quarter of 1993 versus 1992).

List Broker	Information Provided
CCN Systems	Demographics using census and electoral role and credit rating data (MOSIAC).
CACI	Demographics using census and electoral role data (ACORN).

Top Telemarketing Companies	Direct Marketing Association
Merit Direct	Data Protection Association
Programs	
Decisions	
Telecom Potential	

Non-Traditional Media

Non traditional media are becoming both more available and accessible.
Types currently available include: Interactive Television, Computer Games, and Virtual Realty.
Costs are negotiable

Research Sources

Medium Covered	Research Company	Telephone Number
TV	BARB	081-761-9119
Press	NRS	071-379-0366
Cinema	Caviar	071-439-9531
Radio	Ratar	071-729-2646
Outdoor	Oscar	071-637-7763

Advertising Regulations

Advertising restrictions for alcohol, cigarettes and pharmaceutical/drugs are tight. Outlined below are the main regulations.

Beverages/Alcohol
Advertising may not be addressed, particularly to the young. Anyone shown drinking should clearly be over 25. Children may not be seen or heard.
No advertising may feature any personality whose example young people are likely to follow.
Advertising should not be based on a dare or imply failure to those who do not accept the challenge of a particular drink.
Ads cannot imply that drinking is essential to social success or that any drink can contribute towards sexual success or make the drinker more attractive to the opposite sex.
Advertisements should not place undue emphasis on the alcoholic strength of drinks.
Advertising may not be linked with driving or with the use of potentially dangerous machinery.
Advertisements should not encourage or appear to condone over-indulgence. Repeated buying of alcohol should not be implied.

Food/Restaurants
Available on request.

Cigarettes
No cigarette advertising is allowed on TV/Cinema/Radio.
Advertisements must carry a government health warning.

Ads should not encourage people to start smoking, or encourage smokers to smoke in excess. A cigarette left in the mouth cannot be shown.
Ads cannot claim directly or indirectly that smoking is a sign of manliness, courage or daring, or that smoking enhances the female charm. Also, advertisements cannot claim that there is a link between smoking and sexual success.
No ads can appear to be wholly or mainly directed toward young people.
New EEC Directives on tobacco advertising are currently under discussion.

Pharmaceuticals/Drugs
Advertisements must be literal, no superiority claims are allowed unless they can be proven.
Advertisements must not encourage excessive use of a product.
Ads may not imply a cure for the ailment, illness or disease, as distinct from the relief of symptoms.
No contraceptive or pregnancy testing ads are allowed on TV.

Advertising To Children
No ad can be shown which may result in harm to a child mentally, physically or morally.
Ads for toys, games and similar products must include an indication of price.
Others available on request.

Middle East

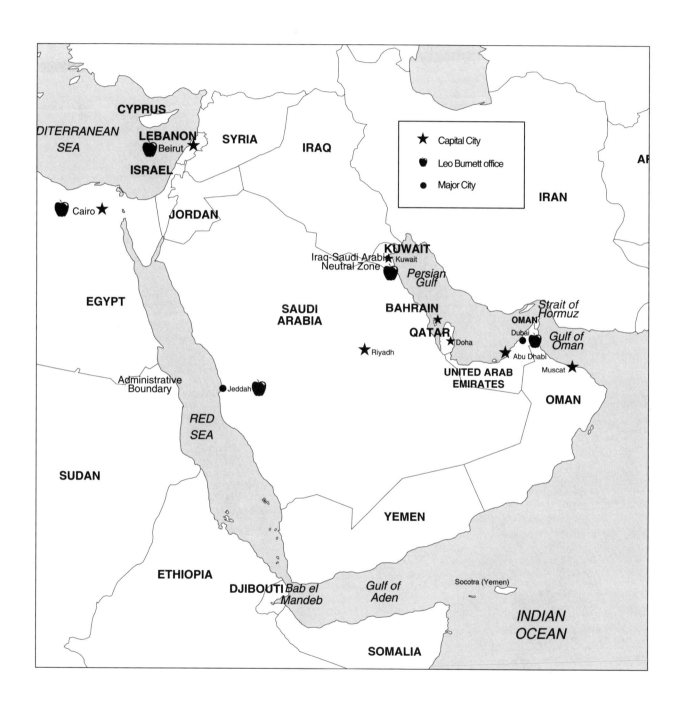

Middle East

Regional Summary

The Middle East's media economy has grown over the past ten years with different countries demonstrating different rates of growth. The negative impact of the 1990/91 'Gulf Crisis' on the media economy reversed almost instantaneously after the war ended.

Media Dynamics–New Technologies

Satellite

In 1991, during the Gulf Crisis, the Arab Gulf Cooperation Council (AGCC) witnessed the start of the Satellite Boom. At the time, satellites were used by network news stations to provide up-to-the minute coverage of the Gulf War. Today, satellite dishes are becoming a necessity in residential compounds in some AGCC countries. A precise count of homes receiving satellite transmissions is not available at this stage. ARABSAT transmits CNN International, Star TV and Dubai Satellite TV to the Middle East, North East Africa, parts of the Near East and Eastern Europe.

Kuwait and Bahrain have designated local national transmission TV channels to re-broadcast satellite programs.

Cable

Two cable stations began operations in Dubai, United Arab Emirates (UAE) and Qatar in May 1993. Currently neither network is commercial. Both networks are subscription-based and charge US$ 50 monthly for 10 channels.

The Current Media Scene

Print remains the medium where most advertising dollars are spent in the Middle East. Pan-regional and national publications exist. The 40 pan-regional vehicles, better known as pan-Arab publications, have five classifications: socio-political, social, feminine, general interest and sports. There is one pan-Arab newspaper.

There are also pan-Gulf publications which include a few daily newspapers and magazines (which fall into the five basic categories mentioned above) and serve the countries of Saudi Arabia, Kuwait, U.A.E., Bahrain, Qatar and Oman.

On the TV front, viewing options have expanded in the Middle East Region at varying levels in different countries. In Lebanon for example, TV has grown to be the most important medium. Satellite and Cable TV are producing fragmentation in viewership habits. An estimated 90 regional TV stations are serving approximately 10 million households.

A few television stations cross borders between the Arab Gulf Cooperative Council (AGCC) countries during certain periods of the year. Currently, the spillover is measured in a few countries like Saudi Arabia and Bahrain.

Raja Sowan
Regional Media Director

Bahrain

Area	620 km^2
Population (1992)	551,513
Population growth rate (1992)	3.1%
GDP	US$ 4.0 billion
GDP/per capita	US$ 7,500 (1990)
Real growth rate (1988)	6.7%
Capital	Manama

Exchange rate (US$ to local currency)	1991	2.6522
	1992	2.6522

Population Breakdown

Nationals

By Sex		By Age Group	
Male	50%	Children, 0-9	28.1%
Female	50%	Teens, 10-14	11.4%
		Adults, 15+	60.5%

Non-Nationals

By Sex		By Age Group	
Male	67.8%	Children, 0-9	9.0%
Female	32.2%	Teens 10-14	3.7%
		Adults, 15+	87.3%

Source: Birks Sinclair & Associates Ltd., GCC Market Report 1992

National Holidays

Holiday	1993 Date
New Year	January 1
Eid Al Fitr*	April 11
Eid Al Adha*	April 20
Islamic New Year*	July 23
Prophet's Birthday*	August 1
Ashoura*	August 1,2
National Day	December 16

School Holidays

Holiday	1993 Date
Summer Break	Mid-June to Mid-September

* *Muslim holidays cannot be pre-determined as they are based on the sightings of the moon as per the Muslim lunar calendar.*

Major Influences and Trends

- Media buying and media consortia are not prevalent.
- Basic media (eg. TV) are Government controlled/owned.
- Viewing habits have become more significant after the Gulf War.
- Governments, broadcasters and advertisers are paying more attention to television. This has lead to technological developments and a growing demand for quality programs which has resulted in a change in the government television industry.
- Another important audio-visual phenomena is the ever growing popularity of Satellite Television in the Arabian Peninsula.

- Dubai Satellite Television is the most recent audio-visual entrant which broadcasts 24 hours and offers a wider variety of programming than the local stations. This will probably lead to audience fragmentation and the survival of the fittest, i.e., better fragmentation and the acceptance of country-by country split run advertising. (Star TV was the first to accept split run advertising in Bahrain via the BBC.)

Spending Analysis

National advertising spending by medium,
based on appropriate year's exchange rate

	1989 US$ MM	1990 US$ MM	1991 US$ MM	1992 US$ MM
TV	4.8	5.1	6.3	15.8
Newspaper	5.3	5.2	5.6	8.1
Magazine	0.8	0.7	0.6	0.7
Total	**10.9**	**11.0**	**12.5**	**24.6**

Source: Pan Arab Research Center Advertising Monitoring Reports 1989, 1990, 1991, 1992

Media Buying

- Media pricing is generally non-negotiable.
- Basically advertising agencies deal with media; some small advertisers approach the media directly.
- Structured media buying services are not available.
- Ownership is diversified. Government normally owns TV in addition to one or two print media vehicles. Others are enterprise driven.

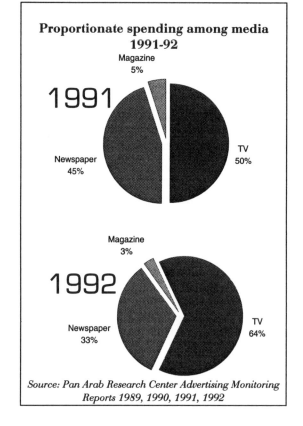

Proportionate spending among media 1991-92

1991 — Magazine 5%, Newspaper 45%, TV 50%

1992 — Magazine 3%, Newspaper 33%, TV 64%

Source: Pan Arab Research Center Advertising Monitoring Reports 1989, 1990, 1991, 1992

Top Advertisers (1992 Spending)

By Company

Parent Company	Product Categories	US$ MM
Marlboro	Cigarettes	0.182
Rothmans	Cigarettes	0.139
Saudia	Sterilized Milk	0.137
Singapore Airlines	Airlines	0.120
Gulf Air	Airlines	0.109
Kuwair and Bahrain	Banks	0.109
Clorox	Bleach	0.107
National Bank of Bahrain	Special services	0.106
Mitsubishi	Passenger cars	0.105
AC Delco	Auto parts	0.094

By Product

Product Category	US$ MM
Financial services	3.60
Retail stores	2.30
Restaurants/Hotels/Clubs•	1.31
Road Vehicles	1.15
Communications and public services	1.07
Professional services	1.02
Travels/Hotels/Resorts	0.96
Publishing media	0.77
Jewelery and accessories	0.76
Equipment	0.74

Television

	TV HH Penetration				Adult Reach	
1989	1990	1991	1992		at 250 GRPs	78%
98%	98%	98%	98%		at 500 GRPs	80%
					at 1,000 GRPs	87%

Opportunities

Network	Number of Stations	Ownership	Station Profile	Commercial Minutes/Day	Coverage	Broadcast Hours (Sign-On/Off)
1	2	Government	General	44	National	
Channel 4	Arabic		General / Commercial	44	National	Weekday / Weekend 16:00 - 24:00
Channel 55	English		General / Commercial	44	National	Weekday / Weekend 17:00 - 23:00
Channel 44	Arabic		General / Commercial	44	National	Weekday / Weekend 11:00 - 20:00
Channel 57 (Star TV - Asia BBC Transmission)	English		General / Commercial	44	National	Weekday / Weekend 01:00 - 24:00

Costs

- The average cost for a Prime Time :30 commercial is US$ 490.

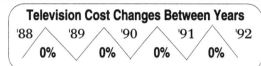

Television Cost Changes Between Years

'88 — 0% — '89 — 0% — '90 — 0% — '91 — 0% — '92

Audiences/CPM's

Average Cost, Audience, and CPMs by Daypart
(Top 2 Stations, :30, national audience, Target=Adults 6+)

Hours	B Time	Peak Time	A Time
Station: Channel 4 (Arabic)			
US$	225	490	371
Avg. Aud. (000)	16	132	45
CPM	14	3.71	8.24
Station: Channel 55 (English)			
US$	225	490	371
Avg. Aud. (000)	3	81	56
CPM	75	6.05	6.63

Audiences/Rating by Daypart (Target: Adults 16+)

| Daypart | Hours | Household | | | | Adult | | |
		Universe (000)	Hut Levels	Household Rating	Impressions (000)	Universe (000)	Adult Rating	Impressions (000)
Primetime	19:00-21:00	Channel I	N/A	N/A	N/A	325	41	132
Primetime	19:00-21:00	Channel II	N/A	N/A	N/A	325	25	81
Late Night	21:00-off	Channel I	N/A	N/A	N/A	325	14	45
Early Time	21:00-off	Channel II	N/A	N/A	N/A	325	17	56
Early Time	Before 18:00	Channel I	N/A	N/A	N/A	325	5	16
		Channel II	N/A	N/A	N/A	325	1	3

Scheduling/Regional/Languages

- In Bahrain 75% of all commercials are :30; other available lengths are :20, :45, and :60.
- Commercials are aired in specific time blocks at the beginning and end of programs.
- All commercial time is aired on a national level.

- The average household audience of a :30 TV commercial broadcast on national TV:
  - Males: 31.2%
  - Females: 56.7%

LANGUAGES	Programming		Commercials	
Primary Language (Channel 4)	Arabic	100%	Arabic	100%
Secondary Language (Channel 55)	English	90%	English	

Children's Advertising

All adult programming accepts advertising directed to children.

CHILDREN'S PROGRAMMING			Kids		
Station	Hours	Days	Universe (000)	Ratings	Impressions (000)
All	16:00-18:00	All	N/A	N/A	N/A

Radio

- In Bahrain 93% of all households (237,000) have radios.
- There are 2 radio stations, both are commercial.
- The primary broadcast language on the AM station is Arabic; on the FM station, it is English.
- The most popular programs are news bulletins.
- Commercial lengths available are :15, :30, :45, and :60.

Daypart Costs/CPMs

Daypart	Local Time	Avg. Cost :30 US$	Audience (000)	CPM (US$)
Prime Time	12:00-18:00	66	N/A	N/A
Daytime	07:00-09:00	66	N/A	N/A
Late Night	After 21:00	53	N/A	N/A

Prime/Peak Time for Radio

Arabic AM	13:00-15:00 and 07:00-09:00
English FM	14:00-16:00 and 07:00-09:00

Cable

Cable TV is not available in Bahrain.

Satellite

- Four satellite stations—MBC, ESC, Star TV, and a new entrant called Dubai Satellite Television—are making forays into the Arabian peninsula. MBC and ESC are the dominant satellite players in the region.
- Excellent production value coupled with better programming and coverage are the distinct features of satellite service.
- A major milestone in satellite television occured when Star TV partnered with Bahrain TV to accept 'Split Run' advertising in Bahrain only.
- All four of the satillite stations are commercial and restrictions are confined to the laws of each country.

Satellite Channel	Country of Origin	Language	Programming
M.B.C.	London	Predominant Arabic/English	A mix of sports, music, comedy drama, current affairs, news based programmes, science fiction etc.
Star TV	Hong Kong	English	Same as above
ESC	Cairo	Arabic	Same as above
Dubai Satellite TV	Dubai-U.A.E.	Arabic/English	Same as above

Video Cassettes

- About 71% of TV households have video cassette recorders (VCRs). Video cassettes in Bahrain do carry commercials; the average is 5–7 sponsors per tape. The Pan Arab Research Center (PARC) measures VCR usage. The average cost of a :30 commercial is US$ 250.
- A downward trend is expected in VCR viewership trends due to the development of satellite TV.

Cinema

- There are 11 theaters in Bahrain which offer commercial lengths of :30 and :60.
- Roughly 7% of adults are regular cinemagoers (mostly Asians).
- Cinema is a dying medium due to the influx of video, MBC and Star TV.
- All cinemas offer commercial time.

Newspapers

The 3 national daily newspapers have a combined circulation of 56,000; all accept advertising and there is a 20-25% literacy rate in English.

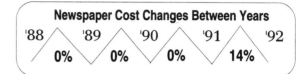

Newspaper Cost Changes Between Years
'88 — 0% — '89 — 0% — '90 — 0% — '91 — 14% — '92

Daily Newspaper	Market	Size	Claimed Circ. (000)	Avg. Daily Aud. (000)	1 page/B&W Cost (US$)	Accept Color?
Akhbar Al Khaleej	National	Broadsheet	25	105	2,095	Yes
Al Ayam	National	Broadsheet	21	25	2,128	Yes
Gulf Daily News	National	Tabloid	10	41	1,756	Yes

Magazines

Bahrain has 2 consumer magazines and no trade or technical magazines.

Magazine	Type	Frequency	Circ. (000)	Audited?	Avg. Issue Aud. (000)	1 page 4/C Cost (US$)
Gulf Panorama	Leisure & General Interest	Monthly	15	No	17	1,700
This is Bahrain (English)	Leisure & Local Information update	Quarterly	15	No	4	1,369

Outdoor/Transit

- There are 13 unipole sites available in Bahrain that are seen by 100,000 to 225,000 people per month.
- They are 6.9 m x 3.18 m and cost US$ 930 for one month; 2-4 weeks in advance is the time needed to reserve this advertising space. Tobacco and alcoholic beverage advertising is prohibited.

Direct Marketing

Al Hilal is the only list broker which provides mailing lists with demographic information.

List Broker	Information Provided
Al Hilal	Mailing lists with demographic information

Non-Traditional Media

There is currently no use of non-traditional media in Bahrain.

Research Sources

Medium Covered	Research Company	Information Provided
TV, Cinema, Video, Radio, Magazines, Newspaper	Pan Arab Research Center P.O. Box 24744, 13108 Safat, Kuwait. Tel: 2450783/2450786 Telex: 23770 Pareho Kt	Media Surveys Ad spending monitoring Copy monitoring

Advertising Regulations

Overall

- Any media vehicle or medium will adhere to the laws of the country.
- Any form/content which does not conform with cultural and religious sensitivities is disallowed.
- Public representation of Gulf women should conform to strict tradition.
- Exaggeration is seen as the most unacceptable trend in advertising and indeed is interpreted as a form of lying with the intention of misleading the consumer.
- Wild dancing, revealing dress, violent scenes, intimate scenes , etc. are not allowed.

By Product

Beverages/Alcohol
No restrictions/regulations for non-alcoholic beverages.
Alcohol advertising is banned.
Cigarettes
Tobacco advertising is prohibited on TV.
Pharmaceuticals/Drugs
Prior approval from Ministry of Health is required.

By Medium

Television
Any commercial aired is subject to approval by the local Censorship Committee.
Alcohol and tobacco are banned.
Print
Alcohol and related products are banned.
Outdoor
Alcohol and related products are banned.
Direct Marketing
The following categories are banned:
   Inflammable goods
   Pornographic material
   Alcohol and alcoholic beverages

Sources Consulted

Bahrain Seas, 4, 1988
Media Research Data: Pan Arab Research Center (PARC), *Bahrain Media Index, 1989*

Egypt

Area	1,001,450 km²
Population (1992)	56,368,950
Population growth rate (1992)	2.3%
GDP	US$ 39.2 billion
GDP/per capita	US$ 720
Real growth rate (1991)	2%
Capital	Cairo

Population Breakdown

By Sex		*By Age Group*		*By Socio-Economic Status*	
Male	51%	Children	40%	A&B	6%
Female	49%	Teens	19%	C	36%
		Adults	41%	D	58%

Source (Demographics): Central Agency for Public Mobilization & Statistics, Egypt, Feb., 1993

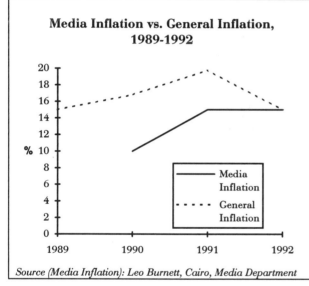

Media Inflation vs. General Inflation, 1989-1992

Source (Media Inflation): Leo Burnett, Cairo, Media Department

Number of Households	11,780,000

Ownership of household durables
- Car.................................. N/A
- Phone............................. N/A
- Washers.......................... N/A

(purchasing power equivalent)

GNP distribution by industry
- Agriculture.................... 20%
- Industry 23%
- Services 57%

Exchange rates (US$ to local currency)
- 1991 .....................L.E. 3.30
- 1992 .....................L.E. 3.34

Source (GDP by industry, inflation rate): The Economist
Intelligence Unit Estimates, UK, 4th Quarter, 1992

National Holidays

Holiday	*1993 Date*
Easter Monday	April 18 *
Sinai Liberation Day	April 25
Labor Day	May 1
Ramadan Bairam	March 11, 12, 13 *
Revolution Day	July 23
Courban Bairam	May 19, 20, 21 *
Islamic New Year	June 9 *
Armed Forces Day	October 6
Prophets Birthday	August 18 *

School Holidays

Holiday	*1993 Date*
Evacuation day	June 18
Suez City day	October 24

Some holidays' dates cannot be predetermined exactly because they are based on sightings of the moon.

Major Influences and Trends

Both print and broadcast media vehicles are owned and operated by the government (public sector), and thus no main influences and media trends are available to report.

Spending Analysis

National advertising spending by medium,
based on appropriate year's exchange rate

	1989 US$ MM	1990 US$ MM	1991 US$ MM	1992 US$ MM
TV	30	33	23.6	35.5
Cinema	2.0	2.0	3.0	2.0
Radio	4.0	5.0	3.0	0.2
Newspaper	45.0	48.0	39.5	61.7
Magazine	8.0	11.0	8.6	17.2
Outdoor	8.0	7.0	10.0	7.0
Total	**97.0**	**106.0**	**87.7**	**123.6**

*Source: Leo Burnett, Cairo, Media Department, estimates; (1991 data):
Pan Arab Research Center (PARC), Dubai*

Media Buying

Television is government owned and maintains fixed and non-negotiable prices.

Newspaper and magazine rates continue to be negotiable off the rate card directly between publishers and local clients, making it extremely difficult for ad agencies to beat prices obtained by large local companies. Some big local government advertising institutions play the role of buying services for other small-to-medium agencies who prefer not to deal with complicated government (TV) administration and comply with their rules and regulations, (namely bank guarantee and short notice payment).

Buying services account for approximately 50% of the market's total expenditures.

(Source: Leo Burnett, Cairo, Media Department Monitoring)

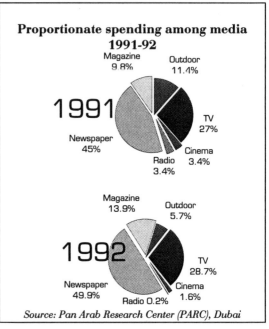

Proportionate spending among media 1991-92

1991: Magazine 9.8%, Outdoor 11.4%, TV 27%, Cinema 3.4%, Radio 3.4%, Newspaper 45%

1992: Magazine 13.9%, Outdoor 5.7%, TV 28.7%, Cinema 1.6%, Radio 0.2%, Newspaper 49.9%

Source: Pan Arab Research Center (PARC), Dubai

Buying Services with 1992 Billings

Buying Service	US$ (000)
Al Ahram	9,244
Al Akhbar	2,636
S.E.P.	2,214

Source: Leo Burnett, Cairo, Media Department Monitoring

Top Advertisers (1992 Spending)

By Company

Parent Company	Product Categories	US$ MM
Procter & Gamble	Soap/Toothpaste/Shampoo/ Detergent/Sanitary Pads	1.6
Unilever	Soap/Toothpaste/Shampoo/ Detergent/Deodorant	1.3
Nestle	Yogurt/Ice Cream/Baby Foods	0.8
Pepsi Int'l	Soft drinks	0.7
Shamaadan	Biscuits/Tea	0.6
Fine Foods	Soup/Tomato Sauce/Creme Chantill	0.4
Gawhara	Tea/Sanitary Ware	0.3
Flora	Tissues	0.3
Henkil	Detergent	0.3
Chipsy	Snacks	0.3

Source: Leo Burnett, Cairo, Media Department Monitoring

By Product

Product Category	Advertiser	US$ MM
Shamaadan (biscuit)	Akhbar	0.540
Omo (detergent)	Ahram	0.499
Ariel (detergent)	Saatchi & Saatchi	0.496
Pepsi (soft drink)	Impact	0.352
Al Gawhara (tea)	S.E.P.	0.322
Flora (tissue)	Senior	0.293
Camay (soap)	AMA LB	0.274
Persil (detergent)	Impact	0.274
Fine Foods (soup)	Look	0.273
Chispy	Ahram	0.252

Source: Leo Burnett, Cairo, Media Department Monitoring

Television

Adult Reach	
at 250 GRPs	65%
at 500 GRPs	75%
at 1,000 GRPs	85%

Overview

In Egypt, TV is the most easily accessible medium for the general
population. 90% of the population has had television access for 4 years. The total number of TV
households is 9,400,000. *(Source: Leo Burnett, Cairo, Media Department estimates)*
Programming and commercials are mainly in Arabic with a limited number of programs (news, serials,
films) in English and French.

Opportunities

Network	Names of Stations	Ownership	Station Profile	Commercial Minutes/Day	Coverage	Broadcast Hours (Sign-On/Off)
1	1st ch.	Government	General	90	95%	10:00-24:00
	2nd ch.	Government	General (Education)	30	65%	10:00-24:00
	3rd ch.	Government	General (Greater Cairo)	20	20%	14:00-24:00
	4th ch.	Government	Local (Canal Zone)	10	10%	13:00-24:00
	5th ch.	Government	Local (Alexandria)	10	10%	16:30-24:00

Costs

Prime Time TV Costs for :30 in US$			
1989	*1990*	*1991*	*1992*
1,500	1,850	1,850	1,850

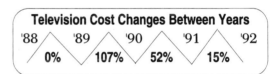

Television Cost Changes Between Years
'88 — '89 — '90 — '91 — '92
0% 107% 52% 15%

Audiences/CPM's

Average Cost, Audience, and CPMs by Daypart
(Top 3 Stations, :30, national audience)

Hours:	Morning 6:00-12:00	Daytime 12:00-18:00	Prime Time 18:00-22:00	Late Night 22:00-23:00	Weekend 18:00-22:00	Children 16:00-18:00
Station 1						
US$ (000)	1,000	1,850	1,000	1,850	N/A	1,850
Avg. Aud. (000)	939	5,760	617	4008	N/A	939
CPM	1.06	0.32	1.62	0.46	N/A	1.97
Station 2						
US$ (000)	N/A	1,850	1,000	1,850	N/A	1,850
Avg. Aud. (000)	N/A	548	681	1,560	N/A	548
CPM	N/A	3.38	1.47	1.19	N/A	3.38
Station 3						
US$ (000)	N/A	1,000	N/A	N/A	N/A	N/A
Avg. Aud. (000)	N/A	210	N/A	N/A	N/A	N/A
CPM	N/A	4.76	N/A	N/A	N/A	N/A

Audiences/Rating by Daypart

Daypart	Hours	Household				Adult		
		Universe (000)	Hut Levels	Household Rating	Impressions (000)	Universe* (000)	Adult Rating	Impressions (000)
Morning	10:00-13:00	N/A	N/A	N/A	N/A	26	7.6	2
Daytime	15:01-15:30	N/A	N/A	N/A	N/A	26	15.8	4
Primetime	19:15-19:30	N/A	N/A	N/A	N/A	26	50.2	13
Late Night	22:15-22:30	N/A	N/A	N/A	N/A	26	50.4	13
Weekend	22:15-22:30	N/A	N/A	N/A	N/A	26	49	13
Children's	---	N/A	N/A	N/A	N/A	--	--	-

*Calculation of total adult population based on PARC Research.

Scheduling/Regional/Languages

LANGUAGES	Programming		Commercials
Primary Language	Arabic	90%	Arabic
Secondary Language	English	10%	English

Source: Leo Burnett, Cairo, Media Department estimates

- Commercials are available in :10, :20, :30, :45 and :60 lengths; 80% of all commercials are :30 long.
- Egyptian TV has 3 to 4 advertising breaks daily in specific time blocks mainly at the beginning of programs; with limited commercials at the end or within programs.
- About 4% of all commercials are aired on a regional/local level; the cost is 50% that of national air time. *(Source: Leo Burnett, Cairo, Media Department estimate)*

Regional Channels and Schedules

Network	Station	Region	Hours
1	3rd Ch.	Greater Cairo	17:00-23:00
	4th Ch.	Canal Zone	18:00-22:00
	5th Ch.	Alexandria	17:00-22:00

Children's Advertising

All adult programming accepts advertising targeted at children.

CHILDREN'S PROGRAMMING			Kids'		
Station	Hours	Days	Universe (000)	Ratings	Impressions (000)
1st ch.	Morning	Friday	14,530	N/A	N/A
2nd ch.	Morning	Friday	14,530	N/A	N/A

Radio

- The penetration level of radio is 95%; broadcasting reaches about 9,940,000 households. *(Source: Leo Burnett, Cairo, Media Department estimate)*
- In Egypt there are 16 radio stations; all are located in Cairo and 7 are commercial.
- The primary broadcasting language is Arabic; English is secondary. The most popular program types are request programs: Noon Request and Evening–Request.
- Commercials are available in :10, :20, :30, :45 and :60 lengths. There are no alternatives to national air time.

Ratings

Daypart	Adult (000)
Prime Time	16,779
Daytime	665
Late Night	998

Daypart Costs/CPMs

Local Time	Avg. Cost :30 US$	Audience (000)	CPM (US$)
08:00-10:00	180	1502	0.12
14:00-19:00	180	648	0.28
10:00-14:00	270	83	3.25
19:00-24:00	180	48	3.75

- There was a 15% cost change in 1990; no others are available.

Cable

Cable is not available in Egypt.

Satellite

- The Egyptian Satellite Station (ESC) is the only station transmitted via satellite; it is a commercial station, but it is not received in Egypt. It is aimed at Arab Gulf Countries, namely Saudi Arabia, Kuwait and U.A.E.
- The ESC broadcasts in Arabic, programming includes Arabic serials, news and films.
- Other satellite channels are available only in households that own a satellite dish; these are few.

Video Cassettes

About 9% of all Egyptian households have video cassette recorders (VCRs); representing 10% of all TV households. *(Source: Leo Burnett, Cairo, Media Department estimate)* VCR usage is measured by the Pan Arab Research Center. Pre-recorded tapes carry between 9 and 15 sponsors per tape at an average cost of US$ 700 per tape.

Cinema

Based on a survey of 250 theaters the potential reach over a 4 week period is 9% of the population. About 85% of all theaters offer commercial time in :10, :30, :60, :120 and :180 lengths. *(Source: Leo Burnett, Cairo, Media Department estimate)* The average cost of a 4 week cinema schedule is US$ 540 for Deluxe and US$ 150 for First Class.

Newspapers

Egypt has 12 national daily newspapers that accept advertising with a combined circulation of 7,000,000. *(Source: As claimed by newspapers)* The literacy rate in English is about 4%.

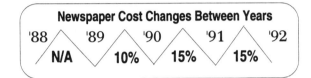

Daily Newspaper	Market	Size	Circulation (000)	Avg. Daily Aud. (000)	1 page/B&W Cost (US$)	Accept Color?
Al Akhbar	National	53x38	1,891	12,279	23,500	Yes
Al Ahram	National	53x38	2,600	10,837	23,500	Yes
Al Gumhuria	National	58x42	1,500	5,096	23,500	Yes
Al Wafd	National	58x42	700	3,228	---	Yes
Al Messa	National	58x42	600	1,966	8,640	Yes
Egyptian Gazette	National	58x42	40	900	15,120	Yes
Le Progres	National	58x42	30	950	15,120	Yes
Journal D'Egypt	National	58x42	30	800	15,120	Yes
Al Ahram A Missai	National	53x38	120	500	5,088	Yes

Magazines

There are 27 consumer and trade magazines published in Egypt. Two technical publications, *Bus. Monthly* and *Al Ahram Al-Iktissadi* also exist.

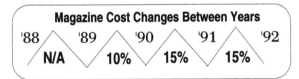

Magazine	Type	Frequency	Circ. (000)	Audited?	Avg. Issue Aud. (000)	1 page 4/C Cost (US$)
Hawaa	Women	Weekly	220	Yes	1,316	2,000
Akher Saa	Sports	Weekly	400	Yes	1,452	3,200
Radio & TV	Complete Weekly Guide	Weekly	100	No	1,115	2,200
Al Mussawar	Political	Weekly	220	Yes	816	4,600
October	Social	Weekly	300	Yes	1,590	3,300
Kawakeb	Entertainment	Weekly	120	Yes	825	2,500
Sabah El Kheir	General Interest	Weekly	60	No	618	4,400
Rose El Youssef	General News	Weekly	60	No	578	5,300
Al Ahram Al Iktissadi	Business	Weekly	170	Yes	104	20,700
Nisf El Donia	Women	Weekly	400	Yes	1,504	2,200
Kolenas	General News	Weekly	120	Yes	252	13,300
Al Ahram El Riyadhi	Sports	Weekly	320	Yes	579	4,800
Horriyati	General News	Weekly	120	No	751	4,400
Akhbar El Riyadha	Sports	Weekly	150	Yes	450	2,200
Akhbar El Hawades	Hawades	Weekly	70	Yes	200	2,200

Outdoor/Transit

Billboard	Transit
Sites available ....9,000+ (flexible)* Lead Time to reserve ....6 weeks adv. Exposure (prime, metro sites) 55-75%*	Boards available ....4,500* Exposure (metro) 90%
Costs Average, 1 billboard/month 3 x 8M .... US$ 60 **Billboard Cost Changes Between Years** '88 — '89 — '90 — '91 — '92 12% 20% 17% 30%	**Costs** Average, 1 board/month: ....US$ 50 **Transit Cost Changes Between Years** '88 — '89 — '90 — '91 — '92 7% 15% 15% 20%
Sizes 2 m x 3 m 6 m x 6 m 3 m x 4 m 6 m x 8 m 3 m x 6 m 6 m x 12 m 3 m x 8 m 6 m x 16 m 4 m x 8 m 8 m x 16 m	**Sizes** 1 m x 1.5 m 2 m x 6 m 3 m x 3 m 3 m x 4 m

Source: Leo Burnett, Cairo, Media Department estimate

Product/Category Restrictions for Outdoor Advertisements
- Liquor and alcohol are banned.
- Cigarette ads are allowed but with health warning.

Direct Marketing

Direct marketing is not a very advanced media vehicle, however it is extensively used by hotels, travel agencies, courier companies, financial institutions and fashion houses, mostly for the A and B Income Group Community.

Non-Traditional Media

Supermarket in-store video/TV is available in approximately 50 of the major stores in Cairo. Costs are as follows:

>   :30 = US$ 600 for one week
>   :45 = US$ 700 for one week
>   :60 = US$ 760 for one week.

Closed advertising circuits in underground stations available in approximately 5 stations.

>   :10 = US$ 220 for one month
>   :20 = US$ 320 for one month
>   :30 = US$ 420 for one month
>   :45 = US$ 580 for one month
>   :60 = US$ 740 for one month

Research Sources

Medium Covered	Research Company	Information
All media	PARC (Pan Arab Research Center, W.L.L) Member of Gallup Int'l	Ratings by media of adult population based on socio-economic factors.

Television Research Currently Available

Research Method	Frequency
Random	Yearly
Door to door	
Surveys	

Advertising Regulations

By Product

Beverages/Alcohol
Advertising of alcohol/beverages is banned in Egypt for religious reasons.
Food/Restaurants
No regulations.
Cigarettes
Cigarette advertising is banned from all broadcast media, it is allowed in all print and outdoor media with a health warning.
Pharmaceuticals/Drugs
Advertising for medicine is not allowed in all media. Beauty/health products with medical composition like anti-dandruff, shampoo, toothpaste...need ministry of health clearance prior to airing. Very limited - special permission needed from Ministry of Health.
Advertising To Children
Should not exploit children's innocence and affect their personality. Advertising should not cause any mental and physical harm and should not exploit their superficial reaction.

By Medium

Television
No cigarette advertising.
No alcohol advertising.
No sexy appearance (dress).
No medicine advertising.
Print
No alcohol advertising.
No medicine advertising.
Outdoor
No alcohol advertising.
No medicine advertising.
In-store video and Underground closed circuits video
No alcohol advertising.
No cigarettes advertising.
No medicine advertising.

Source (Regulations): Egyptian Central Advertising Department Rules & Regulations, 1993

Kuwait

Area	17,820 km^2
Population (1992)	1,378,613
Population growth rate (1992)	N/A
GDP	US$ .75 billion
GDP/per capita	US$ 6,200
Real growth rate (1991)	50%
Capital	Kuwait

Exchange rate (US$ to local currency)	1991	3.3278
	1992	3.3278

Population Breakdown

Nationals

By Sex		By Age Group	
Male	56%	Children, 0-9	21.1%
Female	44%	Teens, 10-14	11.4%
		Adults, 15+	67.5%

Non-Nationals

By Sex		By Age Group	
Male	78.9%	Children, 0-9	6.2%
Female	21.1%	Teens, 10-14	2.0%
		Adults, 15+	91.8%

Source: Birks Sinclair & Associates LTd., GCC Market Report 1992

National Holidays

Holiday	1993 Date
Lailat Al-Miraj*	January 11
Lailat Al-Bara'a*	February 17
Ramadhan begins*	February 18
Lailat Al-Qadar*	April 1
Eid Al Fitr*	April 4
Pilgrimage begins*	June 2
Eid Al Adha*	June 11
Islamic New Year*	July 1
Ashoora*	July 1
The Holy Prophet*	September 9
Mohammed's birthday*	September 29

*Muslim holidays cannot be pre-determined as they are based on the sightings of the moon as per the Muslim lunar calendar.

School Holidays

Holiday	1993 Date
Arabic schools	3 weeks in February-March (mid term break)
	Mid June-Mid September (summer holidays)
English schools	2 weeks for Christmas and New Year's
	2 weeks for Easter
	Mid June-Mid September (summer holidays)
Indian schools	As per the English schools. Plus a couple of days for major Indian festivals
European schools	As per the English schools
Japanese schools	A week for New year's and a couple of days for major Japanese festivals

Major Influences and Trends

- Media buying/media consortia are not prevalent.
- Basic media (e.g. TV) are government controlled/owned.
- Viewing habits have become more significant after the Gulf War.
- Governments, broadcasters and advertisers are paying growing attention to television. This has led to technological developments and a growing demand for quality programs which has created/resulted in a change in the government television industry.
- Another important audio-visual phenomena is the ever growing popularity of satellite based television stations like MBC, ESC, Star TV and the most recent Dubai satellite launched in May '93.
- The satellite television stations are offering many more channels and longer broadcasting hours, which will probably lead to audience fragmentation and the survival of the fittest (i.e., better programming).
- Kuwait TV has dedicated three local channels that terrestrially re-broadcast satellite TV channels, namely MBC, ESC, and CNN.

Spending Analysis

National advertising spending by medium
based on appropriate year's exchange rate

	1989 US$ MM	1990 US$ MM	1991 US$ MM	1992 US$ MM
TV	21.7	13.4	2.2	13.0
Newspaper	59.3	40.2	19.6	50.0
Magazine	17.9	13.4	2.4	14.0
Total	**99.0**	**67.0**	**24.2**	**77.0**

Source: Pan Arab Research Center (PARC), Advertising Monitoring Reports, 1989, 1990, 1991 and 1992

Proportionate spending among media 1991-92

1991
- Magazine 10%
- TV 9%
- Newspaper 81%

1992
- Magazine 18%
- TV 17%
- Newspaper 65%

Source: Pan Arab Research Center (PARC), Advertising Monitoring Reports, 1989, 1990, 1991 and 1992

Media Buying

- Media pricing is generally non-negotiable.
- Basically advertising agencies deal with media. Some small advertisers approach the media directly.
- Structured media buying services are not available.
- Ownership is diversified. Government normally owns TV in addition to one or two print media vehicles. Others are enterprise driven.
- Buying services do not exist.

Top Advertisers (1992 Spending)

By Company

Parent Company	Categories	US$ MM
Chevrolet	Passenger Cars	1.80
Marlboro	Cigarettes	1.56
Rothmans	Cigarettes	1.41
Al Ghanim	Used car dealers	1.40
Nissan	Passenger cars	1.07
N.B.K.	Banks	0.99
Toyota	Passenger cars	0.86
Honda	Passenger cars	0.68
Gulf Bank	Banks	0.60

By Product

Product Category	US$ MM
Road vehicles	13.8
Retail stores	6.4
Tobacco products	5.4
Financial services	4.3
Publishing media	4.2
Cosmetics and beauty aids	3.5
Electronics entertainment equipment	3.2
Jewelry and accessories	2.8
Professional services	2.7
Restaurants/Hotels/Clubs	2.3

Television

	TV HH Penetration				Adult Reach	
					at 250 GRPs	36.5%
1989	*1990*	*1991*	*1992*		at 500 GRPs	47.5%
98%	98%	99%	99%		at 1,000 GRPs	49.0%

Opportunities

Networks	Number of Stations	Ownership	Station Profile	Commercial Minutes/Day	Coverage	Broadcast Hours (Sign-On/Off)
1	2	Government	General		National	
	I Arabic Channel	Government	General	12	78.0%	All Week
	II English Channel	Government	General	6	60.0%	All Week

Costs

Prime Time TV Costs for :30 in US$				
	1989	*1990*	*1991*	*1992*
Channel I	966	1,449	1,449	1,449
Channel II	745	1,449	1,449	1,449

TV Cost Changes Between Years

In 1989, Channel I costs increased 50% and Channel II costs increased 94%. Neither channel has had cost increases since.

Audiences/CPM's

Average Cost, Audience, and CPMs by Daypart
(Top 2 Stations, :30, national audience, Target=All adults)

Hours	Morning 6:00-12:00	Daytime 12:00-18:00	Prime Time 18:00-22:00	Late Night 22:00-23:00	Weekend 18:00-22:00	Children 16:00-18:00
Station: Channel I (Arabic)						
US$	932	1,190	1,449			
Avg. Aud. (000)	52	40	140			
CPM	17.92	29.75	10.35			
Station: Channel II (English)						
US$	932	1,190	1,449			
Avg. Aud. (000)	7	28	30			
CPM	133.14	42.50	48.30			

Audiences/Rating by Daypart

Daypart	Hours	Household Universe (000)	Hut Levels	Household Rating	Impressions (000)	Adult Universe (000)	Adult Rating	Impressions (000)
Ch. 1								
Morning	Early	N/A	N/A	N/A	N/A	912	4.4	40
Daytime	Selected	N/A	N/A	N/A	N/A	912	15.4	140
Primetime	Excellent	N/A	N/A	N/A	N/A	912	5.7	52
Ch. II								
Children	Early	N/A	N/A	N/A	N/A	912	0.8	7
Daytime	Excellent	N/A	N/A	N/A	N/A	912	3.1	28
Primetime	Selected	N/A	N/A	N/A	N/A	912	3.3	30

Scheduling/Regional/Languages

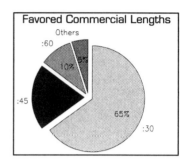

Favored Commercial Lengths

LANGUAGES	Programming		Commercials
Primary	Arabic	95%	Arabic
Secondary	English	80%	English

Commercial lengths available include :10, :15, :20, :30, :45, :60, :75, :90, and :120.

Children's Advertising

All programming accepts advertising directed to children.

Radio

- There are 22,700 households with radios in Kuwait, about 99% of all households; 98% of the automobiles also have radios.
- Kuwait has 3 radio stations , all non-commercial, broadcasting primarily in Arabic; English is the secondary language.
- Maximum listening is estimated to be during early morning (07:00-09:00) and around early afternoon (13:00-15:00) at the time of the hourly news bulletins.

Cable

Cable is not available in Kuwait.

Satellite

- A very recent development on Kuwait TV is the introduction of the satellite station called 'Kuwait Space Channel' K.S.C. K.S.C. is directly controlled by the Ministry of Information. It is non-commercial and it's main purpose is to support the National cause.
- New satellite entrants like MBC and Star TV are making forays into the peninsula of Arabia. Excellent production values and styles coupled with livelier programming and slicker new coverage are the distinctive features of these services.
- A buoyant audio-visual medium, satellite may become a dominant audio visual buy in a TV mix strategy.
- MBC reaches 200,000 TV homes, about 550,000 adults. This number is expected to double within the next 5 years.
- There are 3 satellite channels; 2 of them are commercial.

Satellite Channel	Origin	Language	Programming
M.B.C.	London	Predominantly Arabic/ English	Each channel offers a mix of sports, music, comedy, current
Star TV	Hong Kong	English	affairs, news based programs,
ESC	Cairo	Arabic	science fiction, etc.
Dubai Satellite TV	Dubai - U.A.E.	Predominantly Arabic/ English	

Video Cassettes

The Pan Arab Research Center measures video cassette recorder (VCR) usage and estimates that 90% of all households have video cassette recorders. Pre-recorded tapes carry sponsors. The average costs are US$ 590 for Egyptian films and US$ 358 for Arabian serials.

Cinema

- Kuwait has 13 theaters and potentially reaches 3% of all adults (16+) over a 4 week period. All cinemas offer commercial time with spots of :15, :30, :45 and :60 available. The average cost of a 4 week schedule is US$ 1,719.
- Cinema is considered a dying medium.

Newspapers

There are 9 national daily newspapers that accept advertising with a combined circulation of 588,000.

The literacy rate in English is about 70%.

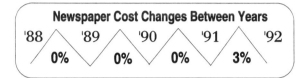

Newspaper Cost Changes Between Years

'88   '89   '90   '91   '92
   0%   0%   0%   3%

Daily Newspaper	Market	Size	Circulation (000)	Avg. Daily Aud. (000)	1 page/B&W Cost (US$)	Accept Color?
Al Qabas	National	Broadsheet	115	361	6,210	Yes
Al Watan	National	Broadsheet	61	249	6,210	Yes
Al Anba	National	Broadsheet	114	301	6,210	Yes
Al Seyassah	National	Broadsheet	155	71	6,013	Yes
Al Rai Al Aam	National	Broadsheet	84	41	6,013	Yes
Arab Times (English)	National	Broadsheet	16	72	5,011	Yes
Kuwait Times (English)	National	Broadsheet	43	38	5,011	Yes

Magazines

Seven consumer magazines are published in Kuwait. There have been no rate changes in the last 4 years.

Magazine	Type	Frequency	Circ. (000)	Audited?	Avg. Issue Aud. (000)	1 page 4/C Cost (US$)
Al Nahda	Social/Political	Weekly	40	No	50	4,658
Al Yaqza	Social/Political	Weekly	70	No	109	6,400
Al Riyadhi Al Arabi	Social/Political	Weekly	30	No	33	4,700
Al Majales	Social/political	Weekly	50	No	67	4,400
Hayatuna	General Interest	Weekly	10	No	48	2,070
Al Arabia	Social/Political	Monthly	25	No	68	1,000
Kuwait TV and Radio Guide	Guide	Weekly	80	No	16	1,466

Outdoor/Transit

- Outdoor sites are available on buses, at the airport and nodal highway points, and as private sites on building tops.
- The cost of a neon sign includes manufacture of sign, 2 years maintenance contract, municipality fees, annual rental fees which could vary from site to site and rental charged by the owner.
- A 14 m x 5 m neon sign might be expected to cost US$ 98,994 for 5 years.

Sizes

Types of Sign	Outdoor Sizes	Transit Sizes
Neon	14 m x 5 m	2.4 m x 0.6 m
Height of Arabic letters	1.29 m	
Height of English letters	0.76 m	

Product/Category Restrictions for Outdoor Advertisements

Cigarettes, feminine hygiene products, airlines, alcohol and lighters may not be advertised on outdoor signs.

Direct Marketing

Direct marketing is not an active medium in Kuwait.

Non-Traditional Media

There is no evidence of the use of non-traditional media in Kuwait.

Research Sources

Medium Covered	Research Company	Information Provided
TV, Radio, Cinema Newspaper, Magazines	Pan Arab Research Center P.O. Box 24744 13108 Safat Kuwait	Adults 16+ penetration; segmented by sex, age, nationality, origin and geographical area of Kuwait.
Video		Psychographics and lifestyles of those surveyed.

Television Research Currently Available

Research Method	Frequency	Research Method	Frequency
Random house to house surveys Face to face interviews	Annually	Diary method Phone survey (CATI system)	Annually Quarterly

Advertising Regulations

Overall

Any media vehicle or medium will adhere to the laws of the land.

Any form/content which is culturally revealing is disallowed.

Public representation of Gulf women should conform to strict tradition.

Exaggeration is seen as the most unacceptable trend in advertising and indeed is interpreted as a form of lying with the intent of misleading the consumer.

Wild dancing, revealing dress, violent scenes, intimate scenes etc. are not allowed.

By Product

Beverages/Alcohol

No restrictions/regulations for non-alcoholic beverages. Alcohol advertising is banned.

Food/Restaurants

Subject to Ministry of Health approval.

Cigarettes

Not accepted on television or outdoor. Cinema advertising is restricted.

All advertisements must carry health warning. Size of health warning must be 10% of the advertisement.

Advertisement must be aimed at adults only.

Pharmaceuticals/Drugs

Advertising pharmaceuticals/drugs is banned.

By Medium

Television

Any commercial aired is subject to the discretion of local TV authorities.

Sources Consulted

Media Research Data: Pan Arab Research Center, (PARC) *Kuwait Media Phone Survey*, 1992

Lebanon

Area	10,400 km^2
Population (1992)	3,439,115
Population growth rate (1992)	1.6%
GDP	US$ 4.8 billion
GDP/per capita	US$ 1,400
Real growth rate (1991)	N/A
Capital	Beirut

Population Breakdown

By Sex		*By Age Group*		*By Socio-Economic Status*	
Male	48%	Children	37%	A	8%
Female	52%	Teens	12%	B	30%
		Adults	51%	C	36%
				D	25%

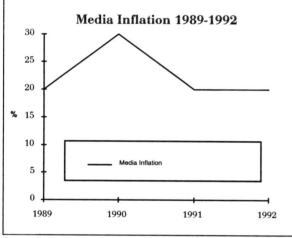

Media Inflation 1989-1992

Number of Households   580,000
Ownership of household durables
  Car .... N/A
  Phone .... N/A
  Washers .... N/A
  (purchasing power equivalent)
GNP distribution by industry
  Agriculture 15%
  Industry 27%
  Services 58%
Exchange rates (US$ to local currency)
  1991 .... 0.00125
  1992 .... 0.00057

Source (Population and demographics estimates): UNRWA (UN) 1986

National Holidays

Holiday	1993 Date
New Year	January 1
St. Maron	February 9
Labor Day	May 1
Assumption Day	August 115
Independence Day	November 22
Christmas Day	December 25
Good Fridays & Mondays	Not Fixed
Eid El Fitr	Not Fixed
Eid El Adha	Not Fixed
Muslims New Year	Not Fixed
Prophet's Eid	Not Fixed

School Holidays

There is no data available on school holidays in Lebanon.

Major Influences and Trends

Media space is negotiated and bought by advertising agencies on behalf of their clients, with the exception of 2 to 3 important local clients who do their own negotiations, since their accounts are handled by more than 1 agency.

Media ownership is enterprise driven, except for 1 TV station, Tele Liban, which is state owned.

The government's 'laissez-faire' policy has led to the proliferation of audio-visual media; in the area of 10,452 km^2 with 3 million inhabitants, there are more than 48 TV stations (national and regional).

However, TV audiences view the major networks.

Spending Analysis

National advertising spending by medium
based on appropriate year's exchange rate

	1989 US$ MM	1990 US$ MM	1991 US$ MM	1992 US$ MM
TV	15	13	19	27
Cinema	N/A	N/A	0.4	0.6
Radio	4	2	3	4
Newspaper	2.7	1	1.8	2
Magazine	1.5	0.4	0.6	0.8
Outdoor	N/A	2	3	3.5
Total	**23.2**	**18.4**	**27.8**	**37.9**

Source: Estimation of STAT figures

Media Buying

- Media buying is done exclusively by advertising agencies.
- Negotiations for media costs are also undertaken by agencies' media staff.
- There are no monopolies; however one large media group controls the largest medium, TV.
- There are no buying clubs or services.

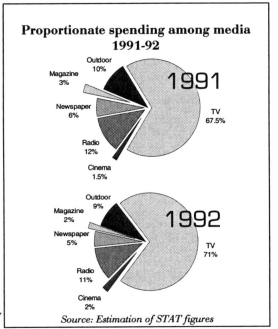

Proportionate spending among media 1991-92

Source: Estimation of STAT figures

Top Advertisers (1992 Spending)

By Product

Product Category	US$ MM
Cigarettes	3.280
Whisky	2.890
Snacks	2.430
Boutiques	1.570
Soft Drinks	1.450
Autos	11.65

Source: Estimation of STAT figures

Television

	Television HH Penetration			
	1989	*1990*	*1991*	*1992*
	96%	96%	98%	98%

Source: Audiences as per Mass Institute Surveys

Opportunities

Networks	Number of Stations	Ownership	Station Profile	Commercial Minutes/Day	Coverage	Broadcast Hours (Sign-On/Off)
LBC	1	Private	General	N/A	National	07:00-24:00
Teleliban	2	State	General	N/A	National	12:00-24:00
C33	1	Private	General	N/A	Urban	16:00-24:00
MTV	1	Private	General	N/A	National	07:00-24:00
Mashrek	1	Private	General	N/A	Semi-National	17:00-24:00
NTV	1	Private	General	N/A	Urban	16:00-24:00
Future	1	Private	General	N/A	Semi-National	16:00-24:00
CVN	1	Private	General	N/A	Urban	18:00-24:00

Costs

Prime Time TV Costs for :30 in US$			
1989	*1990*	*1991*	*1992*
600	750	1,200	1,250

Source: Audiences as per Mass Institute Surveys

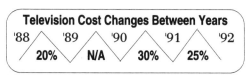

Television Cost Changes Between Years

'88   '89   '90   '91   '92
   20%   N/A   30%   25%

Source : Audiences as per Mass Institute Surveys

Audiences/CPM's

Average Cost, Audience, and CPMs by Daypart
(Top 3 Stations, :30, national audience, Target=All adults)

Hours	Morning 6:00-12:00	Daytime 12:00-18:00	Prime Time 18:00-22:00	Late Night 22:00-23:00	Weekend 18:00-22:00	Children 16:00-18:00
Station: LBC						
US$	200	300	2,000	1,000	300	300
Avg. Aud. (000)	105	105	693	567	168	N/A
CPM	1.90	2.86	2.09	1.76	1.79	N/A
Station: Teleliban		12.00	19.30	21.30	17.00	17.30
US$	N/A	N/A	1,200	600	200	200
Avg. Aud. (000)	N/A	N/A	231	126	42	42
CPM	N/A	N/A	5.19	4.76	4.76	4.76
Station: MTV	09:00	13:00	20:30	22:00		
US$	N/A	N/A	500	400	N/A	N/A
Avg. Aud. (000)	N/A	N/A	126	126	N/A	N/A
CPM	N/A	N/A	3.97	3.17	N/A	N/A

Source: Audiences as per Mass Institute Surveys

Audiences/Rating by Daypart (Target=Adults 15+)

Daypart	Hours	Household				Adult		
		Universe (000)	Hut Levels	Household Rating	Impressions (000)	Universe (000)	Adult Rating	Impressions (000)
Morning	N/A	N/A	N/A	N/A	N/A	N/A	N/A	N/A
Daytime	N/A	N/A	N/A	N/A	N/A	N/A	N/A	N/A
Primetime	20:00	N/A	N/A	N/A	N/A	2,100	45	945
Late Night	N/A	N/A	N/A	N/A	N/A	N/A	N/A	N/A
Weekend	N/A	N/A	N/A	N/A	N/A	N/A	N/A	N/A
Children's	N/A	N/A	N/A	N/A	N/A	N/A	N/A	N/A

Scheduling/Regional/Languages

LANGUAGES	Programming		Commercials
Primary	Arabic	60%	Arabic
Secondary	English	35%	English
	French	15%	French

- The most common commercial lengths are :30 and :60; air time is available at any length.
- Commercials are aired throughout the day at the beginning and end of programs and within them.

- Alternatives to national airtime is available on regional/local stations. 5% of all commercials are aired at the regional/local level and the costs is 5% of national air time.

Network	Region	Hours
Fayha TV	North	Anytime during
Bekaa TV	Bekaa	the evening
BTC	Zahle	

Children's Advertising

ADULT PROGRAMMING				Kids'	
Station	Hours	Days	Universe (000)	Ratings	Impressions (000)
LBC	19:00	All Week	N/A	N/A	N/A
TL	18:30	All Week	N/A	N/A	N/A
MTV	18:00	All Week	N/A	N/A	N/A

CHILDREN'S PROGRAMMING				Kids'	
Station	Hours	Days	Universe (000)	Ratings	Impressions (000)
LBC	18:00	All Week	N/A	N/A	N/A
TL	17:30	All Week	N/A	N/A	N/A
MTV	18:30	All Week	N/A	N/A	N/A

Radio

- In Lebanon there are 530,000 households with radios; both household and automobile penetration is at 98%.
- There are 68 radio stations, 64 are commercial and 40 are located in Beirut.
- The primary broadcasting language is Arabic; English is secondary.
- The most popular program types are news and variety.
- Alternatives to national air time exist on regional stations; commercial time is available at any length with a :30 spot costing an average of US$ 30.

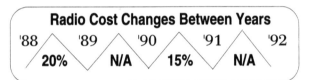

Radio Cost Changes Between Years

'88	'89	'90	'91	'92
20%	N/A	15%	N/A	

Daypart Costs/CPMs (Target=All Adults)

Daypart	Local Time	Avg. Cost :30 US$	Audience (000)	CPM US$
Prime Time	07:15	35	N/A	N/A
Daytime	14:15	35	N/A	N/A
Late Night	21:00	15	N/A	N/A

Prime/Peak Time for Radio

Daypart	Adult Rating	Adult (000)
07:15-14:00	30	630

Cable

There is no information available on cable in Lebanon.

Satellite

A limited number of affluent households are equipped with satellite access.

Video Cassettes

No information is available about video cassette recorder (VCR) usage in Lebanon.

Cinema

- Lebanon has 30 theaters all of which offer commercial time.
- Based on a survey of 15 cinemas, the potential reach over a 4 week period is 20%.

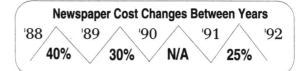

Cinema Cost Changes Between Years

'88		'89		'90		'91		'92
	20%		N/A		30%		30%	

- Commercial time is available in any length with the average cost of a 4 week cinema schedule US$ 600 per theater.

Newspapers

- All of the national daily newspapers in Lebanon accept advertising and have a combined circulation of 130,000. The literacy rate in English is estimated at 40%.

Newspaper Cost Changes Between Years

'88		'89		'90		'91		'92
	40%		30%		N/A		25%	

Daily Newspaper	Market	Size	Circulation (000)	Avg. Daily Aud. (000)	1 page/B&W Cost (US$)	Accept Color?
Al Nahar	National	52 x 8	30,000	150,000	5,400	Yes
Al Safir	National	52 x 8	20,000	120,000	4,160	Yes
Al Diyar	National	52 x 8	30,000	150,000	4,400	No
Al Anwar	National	52 x 8	40,000	40,000	2,500	Yes
Al Hayat	National	52 x 8	6,000	18,000	3,000	Yes
Al Liwa'	National	52 x 8	3,500	40,500	2,000	Yes
L'orient Le Jour	National	52 x 8	15,000	67,500	5,400	Yes

Magazines

Magazine Cost Changes Between Years

'88		'89		'90		'91		'92
	30%		N/A		15%		15%	

20 consumer magazines and 10 trade/technical magazines are published in Lebanon.

Magazine	Type	Frequency	Circ. (000)	Audited?	Avg. Issue Aud. (000)	1 page 4/C Cost (US$)
Magazine	General	Weekly	15	No	75	850
Massira	General	Weekly	10	No	55	750
Revue du Liban	General	Weekly	8	No	40	900
Commerce du Levant	Business	Bi-weekly	5	No	10	750

Outdoor/Transit

Billboard

Sites available	5,000
Lead Time to reserve	8 weeks adv.
Exposure	................................30-75%

Costs

Average, 1 billboard/month

3 m x 2 m ....US$ 80

Billboard Cost Changes Between Years

'88 ⟋⟍ '89 ⟋⟍ '90 ⟋⟍ '91 ⟋⟍ '92
20%　　15%　　10%　　20%

Sizes

4 m x 2 m, 3 m x 2 m

Direct Marketing

There is no information available on direct marketing in Lebanon.

Non-Traditional Media

The use of non-traditional media in Lebanon is expanding. There is in-store advertising, and computer-animated billboards.

Research Sources

Medium Covered	Research Company	Information
All Media	PARC	Media coverage and viewership habits
All Media	Mass Reach	Since Feb. '93, TV research by questionnaire, quarterly

Advertising Regulations

By Product

Cigarettes
10% of advertising space allocated to health warning.

By Medium

Television
All TV commercials should be cleared by government censorship services.

Oman

Area	212,460 km^2
Population (1992)	1,587,581
Population growth rate (1992)	3.5%
GDP	US$ 10.6 billion
GDP/per capita (1990)	US$ 6,925
Real growth rate (1989)	0.5%
Capital	Muscat

Exchange rate (US$ to local currency)	1991	2.6076
	1992	2.6076

Population Breakdown

Nationals

By Sex		By Age Group	
Male	50.6%	Children, 0-9	33.3%
Female	49.4%	Teens, 10-14	12.8%
		Adults, 15+	53.9%

Non-Nationals

By Sex		By Age Group	
Male	81.7%	Children, 0-9	4.1%
Female	18.3%	Teens, 10-14	1.8%
		Adults, 15+	94.1%

Source: Birks Sinclair & Associates Ltd. GCC Market Report 1992.

National Holidays

Holiday	1993 Date
Prophet's Accession to Heaven*	February 2
Eid Al Fitr*	April 5
Eid Al Adha*	June 14
Islamic New Year*	July 6
Prophet's birthday*	August 14
National Day	November 7,8

School Holidays

Holiday	1993 Date
Summer break	Mid June to mid September

Muslim holidays cannot be pre-determined as they are based on the sightings of the moon as per the Muslim lunar calendar.

Major Influences and Trends

- Media buying groups and media consortia are not prevalent.
- Basic media (e.g. TV) are government controlled/owned.
- Viewing habits have become more significant since the Gulf War.
- Governments, broadcasters and advertisers are paying more attention to television. This has led to technological developments and a growing demand for quality programs which has created/resulted in a change in the Government's television industry.
- Cable television has started in Dubai and Qatar, however the initial reaction/response is not up to the industry's expectations.
- Another important audio-visual phenomena is the ever growing popularity of the satellite based television stations like MBC, ESC, Star TV and the most recent Dubai Satellite launched in May '93.
- The satellite television stations are offering many more channels and longer broadcasting hours.
- This probably will lead to audience fragmentation and the survival of the fittest (i.e., better programming).

Spending Analysis

National advertising spending by medium
based on appropriate year's exchange rate

	1989 US$ MM	1990 US$ MM	1991 US$ MM	1992 US$ MM
TV	3.7	4.4	4.6	9.5
Newspaper	6.0	6.7	7.0	8.0
Magazine	0.6	1.2	1.2	0.7
Total	**10.3**	**12.3**	**12.8**	**18.2**

Source: Pan Arab Research Center (PARC) Advertising Monitoring Reports, 1989, 1990, 1991, 1992.

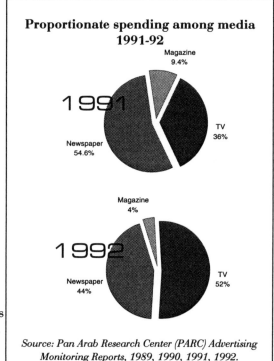

Proportionate spending among media 1991-92

1991
Magazine 9.4%
TV 36%
Newspaper 54.6%

1992
Magazine 4%
TV 52%
Newspaper 44%

Source: Pan Arab Research Center (PARC) Advertising Monitoring Reports, 1989, 1990, 1991, 1992.

Media Buying

Media pricing is generally non-negotiable.
Basically, advertising agencies deal with media. Some small advertisers approach the media directly.
Structured media buying services are not available.
Ownership is diversified. The government normally owns TV/Radio in addition to one or two print media vehicles.
Others are enterprise-driven.
Buying services do not exist.

Top Advertisers (1992 Spending)

By Company

Parent Company	Product Categories	US$ MM
Al Jamil	Baby diapers	0.32
Sohar	Corn oil	0.29
Pampers	Baby diapers	0.28
Minara	Sunflower oil	0.27
Ford	Passenger cars	0.24
Daewoo	Passenger cars	0.24
Bahar	Laundry detergents	0.23
Honda	Passenger cars	0.20
Pantene	Shampoo	0.19
Toyota	Passenger cars	0.17

By Product

Product Category	US$ MM
Road vehicles	3.50
Laundry detergents	1.10
Personal hygiene and health	0.92
Cosmetics and beauty aid	0.88
Dairy products	0.85
Retail stores	0.81
Baby care/baby hygiene	0.77
Tobacco products	0.71
Financial services	0.66

Television

	Television HH Penetration		
1989	*1990*	*1991*	*1992*
NA	90%	90%	90%

Opportunities

Net-works	Number of Stations	Ownership	Station Profile	Commercial Minutes/Day	Coverage	Broadcast Hours (Sign-On/Off)
1	1	Government	General	18.17	National	Weekday 15:00 - 00:30 Weekend 10:00 -02:30

Costs

TV costs have not changed in the last four years. There is no average cost, but a schedule as shown below.

Ordinary Time:	US$ 1,104
Peak Time:	US$ 1,519
Fixed:	US$ 1,795

Audiences/CPM's

Average viewership is 87.5% male and 92.8% female. Rating data is not available.

Scheduling/Regional/Languages

LANGUAGES	Programming		Commercials
Primary	Arabic	80%	Arabic
Secondary	English	20%	English

- Commercial lengths available are :15, :30, :45, :75, :90, :105 and :120; 75% of all commercials are :30 in length.

- Air time for commercials is scheduled throughout the day at the beginning and end of programs. 100% of commercial air time is sold on a national level.

Children's Advertising

All programming accepts advertising directed to children

Radio

- In Oman there are 346,500 households with radios; the household penetration level is 99% and the automobile penetration level is 98%.
- There are 2 radio stations, 1 is commercial and both are located in Muscat.
- The primary broadcasting language is Arabic; English is secondary.
- Commercial time is available in :15, :30, :45 and :60 spots.
- There have been no cost changes in the last four years.

Daypart Costs/CPM's

Daypart	Local Time	Avg. Cost :30 US$
Prime Time	Ordinary Time	104
Daytime	Peak Time	117
Late Night	Fixed Time	130

Ordinary Time: Spots transmitted at any time period allocated by the station.
Peak Time: Spots transmitted adjacent to programs specified by the advertiser.
Fixed Time: Spots transmitted adjacent to main news bulletins.

Cable

There is no cable information available for Oman.

Satellite

Satellite is a buoyant audio-visual medium that is becoming an important buy in a TV mix strategy. 3 satellite stations (i.e., MBC, ESC, Star TV and a new entrant called Dubai Satellite Television) are making forays in the peninsula of Arabia wherein MBC and ESC have established themselves as dominant satellite players in this region. Excellent production values and styles coupled with better programming and slicker new coverage are the distinctive features of satellite services.

There are currently 4 commercial satellite stations in Oman; restrictions that apply to imported programs and commercials are confined to the laws of the country.

Satellite Channel	Country of Origin	Language	Programming
M.B.C.	London	Predominantly Arabic/English	Each channel offers a mix of sports, music, comedy, current affairs, news-based programs, science fiction, etc.
Star TV	Hong Kong	English	
ESC	Cairo	Arabic	*Same as above*
Dubai Satellite TV	Dubai - U.A.E.	Predominantly Arabic/English	*Same as above*

Video Cassettes

About 78% of all households in Oman have video cassette recorders (VCRs); which is 84% of the TV households. VCR usage is measured by PARC/Gallop and Seas Analysis. Current rates for VCR commercials are shown at the right.

Cost of VCR advertising in US$

	:30	:45	:60
Arabic	900	1,150	1,350
Hindi	2,000	2,700	3,200

Cinema

- Cinema is a fading medium due to the advent of video, cable, and satellite television. However, the wide screen will attract select audiences.
- Based on a survey of 29 theaters, available commercial lengths include :15, :30, :45, :60 and :120.
- There have been no cost changes in the last four years.

Newspapers

Oman has 4 national daily newspapers that accept advertising and have a combined circulation of 76,500.

Newspaper Cost Changes Between Years

'88	'89	'90	'91	'92
0%	0%	0%	7.5%	

Daily Newspaper	Market	Size	Circulation (000)	Avg. Daily Aud. (000)	1 page/B&W Cost (US$)	Accept Color?
Oman Daily	National	Broadsheet	21.0	NA	4,108	Yes
Al Wattan	National	Broadsheet	23.5	NA	4,134	Yes
Oman Daily Observer	National	Broadsheet	17.0	NA	4,134	Yes
Times of Oman	National	Broadsheet	15.0	NA	3,858	Yes

Magazines

There are 6 consumer magazines published in Oman.

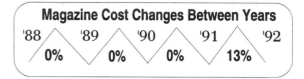

Magazine	Type	Frequency	Circ. (000)	Audited?	Avg. Issues Aud. (000)	1 page 4/C Cost (US$)
Al Adnan	News	Weekly	10.0	No	NA	386
Al Akidah	News	Weekly	10.0	No	NA	520
Al Nahda	News	Weekly	10.0	No	NA	520
Al Omaneya	News	Weekly	21.5	No	NA	520
Oman	News	Weekly	10.5	No	NA	910
Al Usra	Family	Weekly	12.6	No	NA	522

Outdoor/Transit

Billboard

Sites available
- Panel advertising in sports stadiums
- Bus panels on Oman National Transport
- Neon signs on building

Lead Time to reserve .... 4 to 6 weeks

Transit

Boards available

Bus Panels 245

Costs

Average, 1 billboard/month

1 page (12.9 m x 3.6 m) .... N/A

Costs

Average, 1 bus board/month

Large .... US$ 287

Medium .... US$ 274

Small .... US$ 91

Sizes (Buses)

	Large	Medium	Small
Near Side Panel	6.0 m x 0.45 m	4.5 m x 0.45 m	2.8 m x 0.4 m
Off side Panel	6.2 m x 0.5 m	5.1 m x 0.5 m	2.7 m x 0.45 m
Near Side Panel	1.2 m x 0.4 m	1.2 m x 0.4 m	

Product/Category Restrictions for Outdoor Advertisements

Cigarette/Tobacco products need prior approval from the Municipality.

Direct Marketing

Direct marketing is not available in Oman. Jacobsons Direct Mailing is a company that provides database directories.

The following product categories are, by 'convention,' banned: Inflammable goods, pornographic material, alcohol and alcoholic beverages.

Non-Traditional Media

Information on the use of non-traditional media in Oman is not available.

Research Sources

Medium covered	Research company	Information
TV, Press, Outdoor Radio, Cinema	Al Omaneya P.O. Box 6303 Ruwi, Muscat Sultanate of Oman	Market statistics, commercial media

No television research is currently available. Birks & Sinclair provide population and demographic estimates.

Advertising Regulations

Overall

- Any media vehicle or medium must adhere to the laws of the country.
- Any form/content which is culturally revealing is disallowed.
- Public representation of Gulf women should conform to strict tradition.
- Exaggeration is seen as the most unacceptable trend in advertising and indeed is interpreted as a form of lying with the intent of misleading the consumer.
- Wild dancing, revealing dress, violent scenes, intimate scenes, etc. are not allowed.

By Product

Beverages/Alcohol
No restrictions/regulations for non-alcoholic beverages.
Alcohol advertising is banned.

Cigarettes
Restricted to print media and some outdoor advertisements.
Statutory to incorporate a Government warning.

Pharmaceuticals/Drugs
Prior approval from Ministry of Health is required.

Financial Advertising
Prior approval from the Central Bank of Oman is required for all media.

By Medium

Television
Cigarettes/Tobacco products are not allowed.

Print
Cigarettes/Tobacco related advertising is permitted in press.

Outdoor
Cigarette/Tobacco related advertising is permitted and is subject to prior approval from the Municipality.

Qatar

Area	11,000 km²
Population (1992)	484,387
Population growth rate (1992)	3.2%
GDP	US$ 7.4 billion
GDP/per capita	US$ 15,000
Real growth rate (1990)	N/A
Capital	Doha

Exchange rate (US$ to local currency)	1991	0.28346
	1992	0.28346

Population Breakdown

Nationals

By Sex		By Age Group	
Male	50.3%	Children, 0-9	35.7%
Female	49.7%	Teens, 10-14	13.0%
		Adults, 15+	51.3%

Non-Nationals

By Sex		By Age Group	
Male	76.0%	Children, 0-9	11.2%
Female	24.0%	Teens, 10-14	3.8%
		Adults, 15+	85.0%

Source: Birks Sinclair & Associates, Ltd. GCC Market Report 1992.

National Holidays

Holiday	1993 Date
New Year's	January 1
Accession Day*	February 11
Ramadhan*	February 22
Eid Al Fitr*	April 4
Eid Al Adha*	June 3
Ashora*	July 13
Independence day	July 23
Prophet's birthday*	October 1

School Holidays

Holiday	1993 Date
Summer break	Mid June to mid September

Muslim holidays cannot be predetermined as they are based on the sightings of the moon as per the Muslim lunar calendar.

Major Influences and Trends

- Media buying/media consortia are not prevalent.
- Basic media (e.g. TV) are Government controlled/owned.
- Viewing habits have become more significant since the Gulf War.
- Governments, broadcasters and advertisers are paying more attention to television. This has led to technological developments and a growing demand for quality programs which has created/resulted in a change in the Government's television industry.

- Cable television has started in Dubai and Qatar, however the initial reaction/response is not up to the industry's expectations.
- Another important audio-visual phenomena is the ever growing popularity of the satellite based television stations like MBC, ESC, Star TV and the most recent Dubai Satellite launched in May '93.
- The satellite television stations are offering many more channels and longer broadcasting hours.
- This apparently will lead to audience fragmentation and a survival of the fittest (i.e., better programming).

Spending Analysis

National advertising spending by medium,
based on appropriate year's exchange rate

	1989 US$ MM	1990 US$ MM	1991 US$ MM	1992 US$ MM
TV	2.7	3.8	3.6	5.0
Newspaper	7.4	6.3	5.4	9.4
Magazine	0.8	0.7	0.9	1.2
Total	**10.9**	**10.8**	**9.9**	**15.6**

Source: Pan Arab Research Center Advertising Monitoring Reports 1989, 1990, 1991 and 1992

Media Buying

- Media pricing is generally non-negotiable.
- Basically advertising agencies deal with media. Some small advertisers approach the media directly.
- Structured media buying services are not available.
- Ownership is diversified. Government normally owns TV/Radio in addition to one or two print media vehicles. Others are enterprise driven.
- There are no buying services in Qatar.

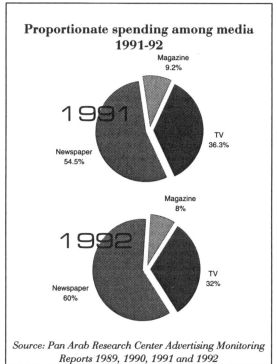

Proportionate spending among media 1991-92

1991
Magazine 9.2%
TV 36.3%
Newspaper 54.5%

1992
Magazine 8%
TV 32%
Newspaper 60%

Source: Pan Arab Research Center Advertising Monitoring Reports 1989, 1990, 1991 and 1992

Top Advertisers (1992 Spending)

By Company

Parent Company	Product Categories	US$ MM
Marlboro	Cigarettes	0.19
Jeep	4 wheel drive	0.18
Dunhill lights	Cigarettes	0.17
Chevrolet	Passenger cars	0.15
Shabab El-Yom	Magazines/Newspapers	0.14
Buick	Passenger cars	0.13
BMW	Passenger cars	0.12
Gulf Air	Airlines	0.11
Mazda	Passenger cars	0.10
Tide with Bleach	Laundry detergents	0.10

By Product

Product Category	Advertiser	US$ MM
Retail stores	2.20	134.51
Road vehicles	2.10	79.94
Jewelry and accessories	0.90	43.81
Cosmetics and beauty aids	0.77	41.64
Tobacco products	0.75	27.23
Professional services	0.69	11.65
Publishing media	0.64	
Diary products	0.69	
Laundry detergents	0.55	
Electronic entertainment equipment	0.48	

Television

	TV HH Penetration				Adult Reach	
1989	*1990*	*1991*	*1992*	at 250 GRPs	73%
95%	95%	95%	95%	at 500 GRPs	82%
				at 1,000 GRPs	89%

Overview

- The TV penetration level is at 95% reaching a total of 17,000 households.
- No ratings are available.

Opportunities

Network	Number of Stations	Ownership	Station Profile	Commercial Minutes/Day	Coverage	Broadcast Hours (Sign-On/Off)
1	2	Government	General	5.2	National	Weekday 16:00 - 23:59
						Weekend 16:00 - 23:59

Costs

Prime Time TV Costs for :30 in: US$				
	1989	*1990*	*1991*	*1992*
Special Time	434	434	551	551
A. Time	310	310	413	413

Television Cost Changes Between Years

'88	'89	'90	'91	'92
	0%	30%	0%	0%

Audiences/CPM's

Average Cost, Audience, and CPMs by Daypart (:30)

Hours	Morning 6:00-12:00	Daytime 12:00-18:00	Prime Time 18:00-22:00	Late Night 22:00-23:00	Weekend 18:00-22:00	Children 16:00-18:00
Station: Qatar Arabic	Special Time					
US$	N/A	N/A	551	N/A	N/A	N/A
Avg. Aud. (000)	N/A	N/A	113	N/A	N/A	N/A
CPM	N/A	N/A	4.88	N/A	N/A	N/A

Scheduling/Regional/Languages

LANGUAGES	Programming		Commercials
Primary	Arabic	100%	Arabic
Secondary	English	90%	English

- Commercial lengths available are :10, :15, :30, :45, and :60; the most common length is :30

- Air time for commercials is scheduled throughout the day in specific time blocks at the beginning and end of programs. 100% of commercial air time is sold on a national level.

Children's Advertising

- All adult programming accepts advertising targeted at children.
- No ad breaks fall within children's programming. However, all children's programming accepts children's advertising.

Radio

- In Qatar, there are 175,000 households with radios; the household penetration level is 99% and the automobile penetration level is 98%.
- There are 2 radio stations, both are located in Dubai and neither one is commercial.
- The primary broadcasting language is Arabic; English is secondary.

Cable

Qatar Cable Vision kicked off in May 1993. The cable system is privately owned by the Qtel company. At the inception stage the number of subscribers was below industry expectations. Qatar Cable Vision has a 'basic service' wherein a subscriber is entitled to 12 channels with an option of choosing premium channels (5 total) at an additional cost. The primary broadcasting language is Arabic; English and French are the secondary languages.

Cable HH Penetration			
1989	*1990*	*1991*	*1992*
2.6%	6%	7%	7%
80,000	679,900	763,500	1,200,00

Cable Networks	Programming
CNN International	24 hours
Egyptian Space Channel	11:00-02:00
MBC	13:00-00:30
CFI (French)	08:30-01:30
BBC - Star Asia	00:00-23:25
Prime sports - Star Asia	01:00-21:00
Star Plus - Star Asia	02:00-21:30

Cable Networks	Programming
Dubai Space Channel	00:00-12:00
MTV - Star Asia	24 hours
Zee TV + Pakistan TV	00:00-22:00
Educational	10:00-20:30
Programs	20:30-23:00
One of the GCC TV programs	15:00-19:00

Satellite

- Satellete is a buoyant audio-visual medium becoming an important audio-visual buy in a TV mix strategy.
- 3 satellite stations (i.e., MBC, ESC, Star TV) and a new entrant called Dubai Satellite Television are making forays in the peninsula of Arabia where MBC and ESC have established themselves as dominant satellite players in this region.
- Excellent production values and styles coupled with better programming and slicker new coverage are the distinctive features of satellite services.
- There are currently 4 commercial satellite stations in Oman; restrictions that apply to imported programs and commercials are confined to the laws of the country.

Satellite Channel	Country of Origin	Language	Programming
M.B.C.	London	Predominantly Arabic/English	Each channel offers a mix of sports, music, comedy, current affairs, news based programs, science fiction, etc.
Star TV	Hong Kong	English	*Same as above*
ESC	Cairo	Arabic	*Same as above*
Dubai Satellite	Dubai	Predominantly Arabic/English	*Same as above*

Video Cassettes

About 70% of all households in Oman have video cassette recorders (VCRs); totalling 74% of the TV households. VCR usage is measured by PARC/Gallop and Seas Analysis. Pre-recorded tapes carry an average of 5 to 7 sponsors per tape; the cost is US$ 294 per :45 spot. Due to the influx of MBC and Star TV, video viewership patterns might get affected.

Cinema

- Based on a survey of 8 theaters in Qatar all offer commercial time in :30, :45 and :60 spots. The average costs are US$ 138 or :30, US$ 165 for :45 and US$ 193 for :60.
- Cinema is a fading medium due to the advent of video, MBC, Star TV and Cable TV.

Newspapers

In Qatar, there are 4 national daily newspapers that accept advertising and have a combined circulation of 105,000. The literacy rate in English is estimated at 25%.

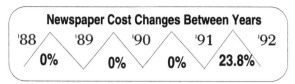

Daily Newspaper	Market	Size	Claimed Circulation (000)	Avg. Daily Audience (000)	1 page/B&W Cost (US$)	Accept Color?
Arrayah	National	Broadsheet	30	119	2,755	Yes
Al Arab	National	Broadsheet	45	52	2,479	Yes
Al Sharaq	National	Broadsheet	20	49	1,377	Yes
Gulf Times Daily	National	Broadsheet	10	107	1,515	Yes

Magazines

There are 9 consumer magazines published in Qatar.
Magazine costs have not changed in the last four years in Qatar.

Magazine	Type	Frequency	Circ. (000)	Audited?	Avg. Issue Aud. (000)	1 page 4/C Cost (US$)
Akhbar Al Ousbou (Arabic)	Pan Arab News	Weekly	21.0	No	5	716
Al Adh	General News		15.0	No	11	567
Al Jawhara (Arabic)	Womens	Monthly	23.0	No	10	567
Al Saquer Al Riyadhi	Sports		5.0	No	NA	Non-Commercial
Al Qummah (Arabic)	General Interest Consumer related	Monthly	80.0	No	NA	386
Al Mourshed (Arabic/English)	Maps, Guides	Bi-Monthly	5.0	No	NA	794
Diaruna Wal Alam (Arabic/English)	Energy, Oil, Gas	Monthly	5.0	No	NA	Non-Commercial
This is Qatar	Local Business Maps, Guides	Bi-Monthly	10.0	No	NA	1,790

Outdoor/Transit

Qatar has a relatively limited circuit of street posters. There are 13 sites (Unipoles) available plus signs in the airport terminal. A 6 to 8 week advance reservation is necessary; the average cost of one transit board for one month is US$ 2,750.

Direct Marketing

There is no information available on direct marketing in Qatar.

Non-Traditional Media

There is no information available on non-traditional media in Qatar.

Research Sources

Medium Covered	Research Company	Information Provided

TV, Newspapers, Magazines, Video	Pan Arab Research Center (PARC)
	    P.O. Box 24744
	    Safat-Kuwait
	    Tel: 2450783/0
	    Tlx: 23770 Pancho Kt.
		Adults 16+ penetration segmented by sex, age, nationality, origin and geographical area of Qatar residence.
		Psychographics of those surveyed.

Advertising Regulations

Overall

Any media vehicle or medium will adhere to the laws of the country.
- Any form/content which is culturally revealing is disallowed.
- Public representation of Gulf women should conform to strict tradition.
- Exaggeration is seen as the most unacceptable trend in advertising and indeed is interpreted as a form of lying with the intention of misleading the consumer.
- Wild dancing, revealing dress, violent scenes, intimate scenes, etc. are not allowed.

By Product

Beverages/Alcohol
No restrictions/regulations for non-alcoholic beverages.
Alcohol advertising is banned.
Cigarettes
Tobacco advertising is permitted only in the print media and on video.
Pharmaceuticals/Drugs
Banned.

By Medium

Television
Any commercial aired is subject to the approval by the local censorship committee.
Alcohol and tobacco are banned.
Print
Alcohol and related products are banned.
Outdoor
Alcohol and related products are banned.

Sources Consulted

Media Research Data: Pan Arab Research Center (PARC), *Qatar Media Index*, 1989

Saudi Arabia

Area	1,945,000 km²
Population (1992)	17,050,934
Population growth rate (1992)	3.3%
GDP	US$ 104 billion
GDP/per capita	US$ 5,800
Real growth rate (1991)	1.5%
Capital	Riyadh

Population Breakdown

By Sex		*By Age Group*	
Male	59.5%	Under 15	59.5%
Female	40.5%	Adults, 15-75	40.5%

Number of Households 1,300,000

Ownership of household durables

Car	N/A
Phone	N/A
Washers	N/A

(purchasing power equivalent)

GNP distribution by industry

Agriculture	6%
Industry	50%
Services	44%

Exchange rates (US$ to local currency)

1991	0.26738
1992	0.26702

National Holidays

Holiday	*1993 Date*
Ramadan	3rd week of March
Hajj	4th week of April
Summer	1st week of July to 2nd week of September

School Holidays

Holiday	*1993 Date*
Ramadan	3rd week of March
Hajj	4th week of April

Source (Population and demographics estimates): Media Information Analysis Database (M.A.I.D.)and Pan Arab Research Center (P.A.R.C.)

Major Influences and Trends

- Only a few media are available: TV, Print, Outdoor.
- Satellite stations have seen a significant increase in penetration in Saudi as cost of dishes has gone down drastically and are now affordable.
- Saudi TV has seen a minor drop in ratings, reflecting the audiences that were picked up by the satellite channels.

Spending Analysis

National advertising spending by medium
based on appropriate year's exchange rate

	1989 US$ MM	1990 US$ MM	1991 US$ MM	1992 US$ MM
TV	48.5	46.1	45.5	59.9
Newspaper	105.5	116.0	129.8	114.9
Outdoor	17.4	12	13.0	15.0
Total	**171.4**	**174.1**	**188.3**	**189.8**

Media Buying

- Saudi TV has no deals and no cost negotiations.
- There are no buying services in Saudi Arabia.
- Print costs are flexible to an extent and deals can be made. Basically, print media is handled by two major media houses.

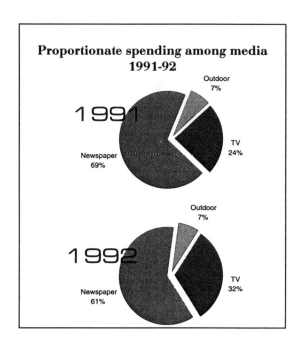

Proportionate spending among media 1991-92

1991
Outdoor 7%
Newspaper 69%
TV 24%

1992
Outdoor 7%
Newspaper 61%
TV 32%

Top Advertisers (1992 Spending)

By Company

Parent Company	Product Categories	US$ MM
Toyota	Automobile	7,533
Procter & Gamble	Paper Products/Health & Beauty Care/Dishwashing Liquid	7,230
Unilever	Health & Beauty Care/Dishwashing Liquid	2,673
Nissan	Automobile	2,365
Nestle	Dairy Products	1,592
Kraft General Foods	Cheese/Concentrate Juice	1,352
Fromogerie Bell	Cheese	1,026
Clorox	Detergent	953
Al Alali	Dairy	603
Braun	Shaving Razor	600

By Product

Product Category	Advertiser	US$ MM
Automobile	Toyota	7,533
Diapers	Pampers	1,003
Detergent	Clorox	953
Cheese	Kraft	762
Carbonated Cola	Pepsi	735
Shampoo	Head & Shoulders	716
Facial Lotion	Oil of Olay	670
Milk	Al Alali	603
Shaving Razor	Braun	600
Coffee	Nescafe	575

Television

Overview

	TV HH Penetration		
1989	1990	1991	1992
96%	96%	97%	98%

- Saudi TV: The local station is the dominant station followed by the satellite channels. The eastern Saudi province benefits from Bahrain TV and the western province has spillover from Egypt TV during summer time.
- The TV penetration level in Saudi Arabia is at 98%. There have been no cost changes in the last four years.
- The maximum four-week adult reach at 1000 GRPs is 62% on Channel 1.

Opportunities

Networks	Number of Stations	Ownership	Station Profile	Commercial Minutes/Day	Coverage	Broadcast Hours (Sign-On/Off)
Ch. 1 (Arabic)	1	Government	Religious/Educational	35	National	10:00-13:00 16:00-24:00
Ch. 2 (English)	1	Government	Entertainment/Sports	2	National	17:00-01:40

Costs

Prime Time TV Costs for :30 in US$		
1989	*1990*	*1991*
3,204	3,204	3,204

Audiences/CPM's

Average Cost, Audience, and CPMs by Daypart
(:30, national audience)

Hours	Morning 10:00-13:00	Daytime 12:00-21:00	Prime Time 21:00-24:00
Station: Channel 1			
US$	1,068	2,136	3,204
Avg. Aud. (000)	971	345	2,670
CPM	1.10	6.20	1.20
Hours		*17:00 22:00*	*22:00-24:00*
Station: Channel 2			
US$	N/A	1,335	2,003
Avg. Aud. (000)	N/A	516	1,821
CPM	N/A	2.59	1.10

Audiences/Rating by Daypart

Daypart	Hours	Household				Adult		
		Universe (000)	Hut Levels	Household Rating	Impressions (000)	Universe (000)	Adult Rating	Impressions (000)
Morning	10:00-13:00	4200	34	1428	5100	14	714	184
Daytime	12:00-21:00	4200	17	714	5100	12	612	429
Primetime	21:00-24:00	4200	55	2310	5100	43	2193	918
Late Night	N/A	N/A	N/A	N/A	N/A	N/A	N/A	490
Weekend	N/A	N/A	N/A	N/A	N/A	N/A	N/A	367
Children's	N/A	N/A	N/A	N/A	N/A	N/A	N/A	612

Scheduling/Regional/Languages

- The most common commercial length is :30, accounting for 80% of all commercials sold. Other lengths available are :15, :45, :60 and :120.
- Commercial air time is sold in specific time blocks at the beginning and end of programs only.

- All commercial advertising is sold on the national level.

LANGUAGES	Programming		Commercials
Primary (Channel 1)	Arabic	100%	Arabic
Secondary (Channel 2)	French	4%	Arabic/
	Others	1%	English

Radio

Radio advertising information is not available.

Cable

Cable is not available in Saudi Arabia.

Satellite

- The estimated satellite penetration level in Saudi Arabia is 25%.
- An increase to approximately 40% is expected within the next 5 years.
- There are twelve satellite channels broadcast on Arab SAT; all are commercial.

Satellite Channels	Satellite Channels
Middle East Broadcasting Center	Kuwait TV
	Jordan
Egypt Satelite Channel	Abu Dhabi
SATV 1	Morocco
SATV 2	Oman
Dubai TV	CFI
CNN	

Video Cassettes

Video cassette recorder (VCR) data is not available for Saudi Arabia.

Cinema

Cinema advertising information for Saudi Arabia is not available.

Newspapers

Saudi Arabia has 13 national daily newspapers that accept advertising. The combined circulation is 928,000 and the literacy rate in English is estimated at 60%.

Daily Newspaper	Market	Size	Circulation (000)	Avg. Daily Aud.(000)	1 page/B&W Cost (US$)	Accept Color?
Asharq Al Awsat*	National	53x35.5	220	N/A	10,933	No
Arab News**	National	53x35.5	59	N/A	7,200	No
Al Riyadiyah*	National	53x35.5	87	N/A	6,667	No
Al Nadwa*	Western	53x35.5	40	N/A	3,456	No
Al Madina*	Western	53x35	57	N/A	5,760	Yes
Al Bilad*	Western	53x37	60	N/A	5,760	No
Okaz*	Western	53x35.5	198	N/A	7,915	Yes
Saudi Gazette**	Western	53x35.5	30	N/A	5,066	Yes
Al Yaum*	Eastern	53x35.5	65	N/A	5,760	Yes
Al Riyadh*	Central	52x35.5	50	N/A	6,556	Yes
Jazerrah*	Central	52x35.5	93	N/A	5,760	Yes
Riyadh Daily**	Central	52x35.5	8	N/A	3,816	No
Al Muslimoon*	National	53x35.5	114	N/A	5,300	No

*Arabic
**English

Magazines

There are 8 consumer magazines published in Saudi Arabia.

Magazine Cost Changes Between Years				
'88	'89	'90	'91	'92
0%	0%	0%	15%	

Magazine	Type	Frequency	Circ. (000)	Audited?	Avg. Adult Aud. (000)	1 page 4/C Cost (US$)
Majalla	Socio/Political	Weekly	142	Yes	900	6,000
Asharq Al Awsat	General	Weekly	157	Yes	1,269	5,200
Sayidati	Women's	Weekly	157	Yes	1,629	5,733
Kolenas	Women's	Weekly	87	No	747	3,810
Iqraa	Socio/Political	Weekly	47	No	243	2,000
Al Yamamah	Socio/Political	Weekly	40	No	393	1,600
Ahlan (In-flight)	Leisure & Holiday	Monthly	150	No	1,161	8,931
Basim	Children's	Weekly	44	Yes	144	2,133

Outdoor/Transit

Billboard	Transit
Sites available .... 10,000 Lead Time to reserve .... 4 weeks	Boards available On Buses only

Costs
 	
Average, 1 billboard/month
    1 (4.27 m x 14.64 m)..................... N/A
	Costs
	
	Average, 1 board/month
	    .... US$ 360

Sizes 4.2 m x 14.6 m 0.60 m x 4.00 m 3.04 m x 2.03 m 0.60 m x 2.00 m 1.17 m x 1.73 m 0.40 m x 2.00 m 3.00 m x 12.00 m	**Sizes** 0.60 m x 1.10, 0.64 m x 1.45

Direct Marketing

Direct Marketing information is not available.

Non-Traditional Media

No information about non-traditionl media in Saudi Arabia is available.

Research Sources

Medium covered	Research company	Information Provided

TV/Video/PR	Media Analysis Info Database
	    Abalkhail Building
	    2nd Flr. Room 204
	    POB 20688
	    Jeddah Saudi Arabia
	    Tel/Fax 6530853
		Monthly advertising

	Pan Arab Research Center
	    (PARC) W.L.L.L.L.
	    POB 50114, Dubai
	    Tel: 376696 Fax: 344456
		Yearly media penetration studies (TV & press readership)

Television Research Currently Available

Research Method	Frequency
Sample (representing adults) answering a questionnaire media habits	Yearly

Advertising Regulations

By Product

Beverages/Alcohol
Prohibited.
Food/Restaurants
Not prohibited.

Cigarettes

Strictly prohibited in TV and local press but indirect advertising is always possible.

Pharmaceuticals/Drugs

Not allowed as long as it is registerd at the Ministry of Health.

Advertising To Children

Dangerous scenes that kids may imitate are prohibited.

By Medium

Television

No cigarettes, no alcoholic beverages, no females (if hair is unveiled).

Print

No cigarettes, no alcoholic beverages allowed.

Outdoor

Faces are not allowed to show. No cigarettes and no alcoholic beverages allowed.

Sources Consulted

Media Information Analysis Database (M.A.I.D.)
Pan Arab Research Center (P.A.R.C.)

U.A.E.

Area	83,600 km^2
Population (1992)	2,522,315
Population growth rate (1992)	5.4%
GDP	US$ 33.7 billion
GDP per capita	US$ 14,100
Real growth rate (1991 est.)	11%
Capital	Abu Dhabi

Exchange rate (US$ to local currency)	1991	0.2725
	1992	0.2725

Population Breakdown

Nationals

By Sex		*By Age Group*	
Male	50.2%	Children, 0-9	36.2%
Female	49.8%	Teens, 10-14	13.9%
		Adults, 15+	49.9%

Non-Nationals

By Sex		*By Age Group*	
Male	66.9%	Children, 0-9	14.3%
Female	33.1%	Teens, 10-14	5.0%
		Adults, 15+	80.7%

Source (Population and demographic estimates): Birks Sinclair & Associates, Ltd. GCC Market Report 1992.

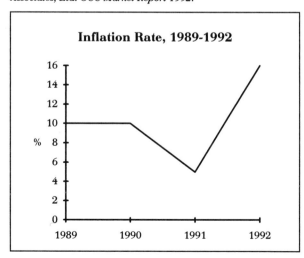

Inflation Rate, 1989-1992

National Holidays

Holiday	1993 Date
Isra & Miraj* (The Prophet's Night Journey to Heaven)	February 9
Eid Al Fitr*(End of Ramadan)	April 1
Eid Al Adha*(The Feast of Sacrifice)	April 20
Muslim New Year/Ashura*	July 22/August 1
Mawlid Al-Nabi* (Prophet Mohammed's birthday)	October 1
Prophet Mohammed's birthday	

School Holidays

Summer	June-Mid September
Christmas	December 22-January 5

*Muslim holidays cannot be pre-determined as they are based on the sightings of the moon as per the Muslim lunar calendar.

Major Influences and Trends

- Media buying/media consortia are not prevalent.
- Basic media (e.g. TV) are Government controlled/owned.
- Viewing habits have become more significant since the Gulf War.

Governments, broadcasters and advertisers are paying more attention to television. This has led to technological developments and a growing demand for quality programs which has created/resulted in a change in the government's television industry.

Cable television has started in Dubai and Qatar; however, the initial reaction/response is not up to the industry's expectations.

Another important audio-visual phenomena is the ever growing popularity of the satellite based television stations like MBC, ESC, Star TV and the most recent Dubai Satellite launched in May '93.

The satellite television stations are offering many more channels and longer broadcasting hours.

This probably will lead to audience fragmentation and the survival of the fittest (i.e. better programming).

Spending Analysis

National advertising spending by medium
based on appropriate year's exchange rate

	1989 US$ MM	1990 US$ MM	1991 US$ MM	1992 US$ MM
TV	21.2	21.7	21.7	32.9
Newspaper	43.0	41.9	58.6	57.0
Magazine	6.4	6.3	5.6	9.9
Total	**70.6**	**69.9**	**85.9**	**99.8**

Source: Pan Arab Research Center (PARC) Advertising Monitoring Reports 1989, 1990, 1991, 1992

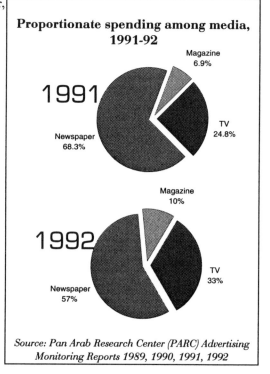

Proportionate spending among media, 1991-92

1991
Magazine 6.9%
TV 24.8%
Newspaper 68.3%

1992
Magazine 10%
TV 33%
Newspaper 57%

Source: Pan Arab Research Center (PARC) Advertising Monitoring Reports 1989, 1990, 1991, 1992

Media Buying

- Media pricing is generally non-negotiable.
- Basically advertising agencies deal with media. Some small advertisers approach the media directly.

- Structured media buying services are not available.
- Ownership is diversified. Government normally owns TV/Radio in addition to one or two print media vehicles. Others are enterprise driven.

Top Advertisers (1992 spending)

By Company

Parent Company	Product Categories	US$ MM
Al Shuruq	Magazines/Newspapers	1.35
Toyota	Passenger cars	1.06
Emirates Airlines	Airlines	0.72
Chevrolet	Passenger cars	0.47
Honda	Passenger cars	0.45
Tide with bleach	Laundry detergents	0.44
Riyadhal Al Shabab	Magazines/Newspapers	0.41
Ariel Ultra	Laundry detergents	0.40
OMO	Laundry detergents	0.40
Nido	Powdered milk	0.39

By Product

Product Category	US$ MM
Retail stores	11.15
Road vehicles	8.5
Cosmetics and beauty aids	7.1
Jewelry and accessories	6.8
Electronics entertainment equipment	4.5
Publishing media	4.3
Financial services	4.2
Entertainment	4.0
Travels/Hotels/Resorts	3.5
Dairy products	3.1

Television

- Household penetration is estimated at 93%.
- There are 3 cities where broadcasts originate, and offer multiple channels for different languages.
- Commercial lengths include :05, :20, :30, :35, :45, :50, :60. Eighty percent of all commercials are :30.

Adult Reach	
at 250 GRPs	54.6%
at 500 GRPs	67.1%
at 1,000 GRPs	71.4%

Opportunities

Networks	Number of Stations	Ownership	Station Profile	Commercial Minutes/Day	Coverage	Broadcast Hours (Sign-On/Off)
Dubai	2	Government	General	14.6	National	WD 16:00 - 00.00
						WE 14.00 - 02.00
Abu Dhabi	2	Government	General	14.6	National	WD 12.00 - 00.00
						WE 16.00 - 02.00
Sharjah	1	Government	General	14.6	National	WD 16:00 - 00.00
						WE 14.00 - 02.00

WD=Weekday, WE = Weekend

Costs

Prime time TV costs for :30 in US$				
	1989	1990	1991	1992
Abu Dabhi	658	658	681	681
Dubai	604	631	817	817
Sharjah	N/A	441	518	518

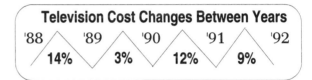

Television Cost Changes Between Years

'88   '89   '90   '91   '92

14%   3%   12%   9%

Audiences/CPM's

Average Cost, Audience, and CPMs by Daypart

(Top 3 stations, :30, national audience, Target=Adults 15+)

Station Abu Dhabi	Peak Time	Station: Dubai	Peak Time	Station: Sharjah	Peak Time
US$	954	US$	1,076	US$	518
Avg. Aud. (000)	292	Avg. Aud. (000)	249	Avg. Aud. (000)	47
CPM	3.27	CPM	4.32	CPM	11.02

Audience/Rating by Daypart (Target=Adults 25-44)

Daypart	Hours	Households Universe (000)	Households Hut Levels	Households Household Rating	Households Impressions (000)	Adult Universe (000)	Adult Adult Rating	Adult Impressions (000)
Primetime	Abu Dhabi	N/A	N/A	N/A	N/A	1,260	23	292
Primetime	Dubai	N/A	N/A	N/A	N/A	1,260	20	249
Primetime	Sharjah	N/A	N/A	N/A	N/A	1,260	4	47

Scheduling/Regional/Languages

	Arabic Channels of Dubai & Abu Dhabi	English Channels of Dubai & Abu Dhabi	Sharjah
Primary	95% Arabic	96% English	80% Arabic
Secondary	5% English	2% Hindi/Urdu, 2% French	18% English, 2% Urdu

Commercials are aired throughout the day, at the beginnings and ends of programs. There are no regional buys.

Children

There is programming directed towards children, but no analytical data is available about the audience.

CHILDREN'S PROGRAMMING			Kids		
Station	Hours	Days	Universe(000)	Ratings	Impressions(000)
Dubai (Arabic)	14:20-15:30	All	NA	NA	NA
Dubai (English)	14:15-18:30	All	NA	NA	NA
Abu Dhabi (Arabic)	12:30-13:00	All	NA	NA	NA
Abu Dhabi (English)	17:00-18:30	All	NA	NA	NA
Sharjah	16:45-17:30	All	NA	NA	NA

Radio

Overview

- There are five radio stations in the U.A.E., of which three are commercial. Two are in the main city. All radio broadcasting is local.
- Two stations broadcast in Arabic, two in English and one broadcasts in a mixture of Arabic and various Asian languages.

Ratings

Time	Adult Rating	Adult (000)
07:30	6.1	77
09:30	2.5	32
14:30	1.6	20
17:30	1.3	16
20:30	1.0	12

- Household penetration is 92%, or 1,216,000 households. However, 98% of automobiles have radios. The most popular programs on AM are music and listeners' complaints. Most popular on FM are music and news programs.
- Commercial time is sold in units of :15, :30, :45 and :60.
- Radio costs rose 23% between 1991 and 1992. Prior to that they were stable.
- Main news bulletins are broadcast every hour, primarily during the morning. Prime/Peak time for radio is 07:00-09:00 and early afternoon (13:00-15:00).

Costs

Averages by Daypart (Dubai FM)

Daypart	Local Time	Avg. Cost :30 US$	Audience (000)	CPM (US$)
Prime Time	07:00-10:00	74	38	1.95
Daytime	10:00-13:00	82	31	2.65
Late Night and	14:00-19:00	67	5	13.40
Early Evening	19:00-Close			

Cable

Overview

- Dubai Cable TV (CABLE VISION) kicked off in May 1993. At its inception, the number of subscribers was below expectations (currently estimated at 1,500 subscriptions).
- Dubai Cable TV has a basic service in which a subscriber receives 6 channels plus an option of choosing 4 movie stations at an additional cost.
- A wait and watch policy needs to be adopted as Dubai cable TV is presently only available in the emirates of Dubai and not a national cable option.

Cable Channels/Cost

There are 6 'basic' and 4 movie channels, none of which are commercial (all are government-owned). All broadcast primarily in Arabic, secondarily in English, French, and Urdu. In the charts below, the first 6 channels are 'basic' channels that broadcast 24 hours a day.

Top Cable Channels

BASIC CHANNELS	Monthly Cost US$	MOVIE/CHILDREN'S CHANNELS	Monthly Cost US$
Prime Sports - Asia		Arabic Movie Channel	11
ESC		English Movie Channel	19
CNN	47	Hindi Movie Channel	11
CFI		Documentaries/Children's Channel	10
Dubai Satellite			
BBC - Asia			

Satellite

- 3 satellite stations, MBC, ESC, Star TV, and a new entrant called Dubai Satellite Television are making forays in the peninsula of Arabia where MBC and ESC have established themselves as the dominant satellite players in this region.
- Excellent production values and styles coupled with better programming and slicker news coverage are the distinctive features of satellite services.
- A buoyant audio-visual medium, is becoming an important audio-visual buy in a TV mix strategy.

Satellite Channel	Country of Origin	Language	Programming
M.B.C.	London	Predominantly Arabic/ English	A mix of sports, music, comedy, current affairs, news based programs, science fiction, etc.
Star TV	Hong Kong	English	*Same as above*
ESC	Cairo	Arabic	*Same as above*
Dubai Satellite	Dubai-U.A.E.	Predominantly Arabic/English	*Same as above*

Video Cassettes

Overview

- Of TV-owning households, 84% also have a video cassette recorder (VCR).
- Prerecorded tapes may carry commercials from as many as 6-10 sponsors.
- PARC/Gallup measures usage.
- Usage may be affected by the growth of cable TV.

Costs

	US$		
	:30	:45	:60
Arabic	900	1,150	1,350
Hindi	2,000	2,700	3,200

Cinema

- U.A.E. has 22 cinemas. They are regularly visited by 14% of the population, mostly young males and Asians.
- All cinemas offer commercial time. Commercial lengths available include :15, :30, :45, :60 and :120.
- Average cost of a 4-week cinema schedule (:30 at one cinema) is US$ 1,634.
- No historial data is available on cinema.

Newspapers

- There are 9 national and 43 regionally circulated daily newspapers in the U.A.E. The combined circulation of the national papers is 1,019,000.
- No data is available on English literacy.
- Costs rose 12.5% in 1992 versus the previous year.

Newspaper	Market	Size	Circ. (000)	Avg. Daily Aud. (000)	1 Pg./B&W Cost (US$)	Accept Color?
Al Ittihad	National	Broadsheet	76	298	4,159	Yes
Al Khaleej	National	Broadsheet	67	310	4,159	Yes
Al Bayan	National	Broadsheet	60	182	4,159	Yes
Khaleej Times	National	Broadsheet	56	363	4,621	Yes
Gulf News	National	Broadsheet	54	319	5,275	Yes
Emirates News	National	Broadsheet	21	10	2,354	Yes
Al Fajr	National	Broadsheet	25	5	4,033	Yes
Al Wahda	National	Broadsheet	20	13	3,800	Yes

Magazines

There are 7 consumer magazines in the U.A.E. and 3 trade/technical publications. Magazine costs rose 33% in 1992 over 1991. Rates and circulation information are as follows.

Magazine	Type	Frequency	Circ. (000)	Audited?	Avg. Issue Aud (000)	1 pg/4/C Cost (US$)
Arriyadah Walshabab	Sports/Social	Weekly	100	ABC	217	1,962
Zahrat Al Khaleej	Socio Feminine	Weekly	69	ABC	242	2,044
Hyatt Annas	Feminine	Monthly	47	No	NA	2,398
Al Sharuq	Political	Weekly	NA	No	NA	1,962
What's On	General Interest	Monthly	22	No	85	1,907
Emirates Woman	Women's	Quarterly	10	No	61	1,771
Gulf Weekly	General Interest	Weekly	55	No	243	2,044
Weekend	General Interest	Weekly	56	No	250	2,125
Gulf	Business	Monthly	5	No	NA	625
Commercial Trade & Industry	Business	Weekly	5	No	34	1,090
UAE Digest	Business	Monthly	10	No	NA	750

Outdoor/Transit

Outdoor advertising opportunities in the U.A.E. are tremendous, however it is regulated by the municipality.
- Billboards are available with a 6-8 week advance reservation.
- The average cost of one transit board is US$ 2,750 per month.

Direct Marketing

- There is no direct marketing association, and there are no telemarking companies in the U.A.E.
- The following products are banned from direct marketing: inflammable goods, pornographic material, alcohol and alcoholic beverages.

List Broker	Information Provided
Xerox	Data base directories
Dubai World Trade Center	Same
Jacobsons Direct Mailing	Same

Non-Traditional Media

Trends/Expectations

There is a trend toward the emergence of more targeted advertising/media.

Types Currently Available

- High-definition electronic screens in Outdoor.
- 3,000 showings of :10 spots/month cost US$ 5,102.

Research Sources

Medium Covered	Research Company	Information Provided
All Media	Pan Arab Research Center (P.A.R.C.) P.O. Box 5803 Dubai - U.A.E.	Adults 15+ penetration: Segmented by demographics, sex, age, nationality, origin and geographic area of U.A.E. residence. Psychographics of those surveyed.
TV	PARC	New installed TV meters in U.A.E.

Television Research Currently Available

Research Method	Frequency
Multi-stage probability sampling	Annually

Advertising Regulations

Overall

- Any media vehicle or medium will adhere to the laws of the country.
- Any form/content which is culturally revealing is disallowed.
- Public representation of Gulf women should conform to strict tradition.
- Exaggeration is seen as the most unacceptable trend in advertising and indeed is interpreted as a form of lying with the intention of misleading the consumer.
- Wild dancing, revealing dress, violent scenes, intimate scenes, etc. are not allowed.

By Product

Beverages/Alcohol
No restrictions/regulations for non-alcoholic beverages.
Alcohol advertising is banned.
Cigarettes
Restricted to print media, video and some outdoor advertisements.
Statutory to incorporate a government health warning.
Pharmaceuticals/Drugs
Prior approval from Ministry of Health is required.

By Medium

Television
Any commercials aired are subject to the approval by the local Censorship Committee.
Alcohol and tobacco are banned.
Print
Alcohol and related products are banned.
Outdoor
Alcohol and related products are banned.

Sources Consulted

Pan Arab Research Center, *JICME U.A.E. Media Index*, 1992

Media Research Data: Readership based on *U.A.E. Seas*, June 6, 1992

Latin America

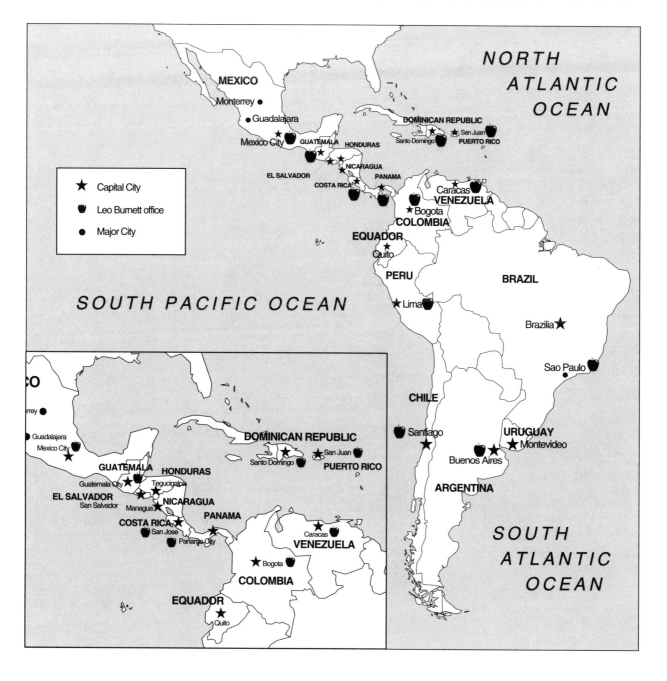

Latin America

Regional Summary

Political/economic overview

The economy of the Latin American Region appears to be moving ahead slowly despite a variable—and in some cases rather high—inflation index. The economic growth is accompanied by stable political situations in most Latin American countries. These two factors—slow economic growth and reduced political risk-combined with open markets and regional trade agreements are helping to make Latin America a more lucrative market. The economies of Mexico, Chile and Argentina are leading the way for economic development. Colombia, Brazil and Venezuela are following a similar pattern.

Media overview

Television is the main medium throughout the region. Programming is also similar throughout the region, soap operas, sports and U.S. produced series are the most popular programs. Cigarette and alcohol advertising are allowed (with some limitations) in all countries except Venezuela. Cable penetration is growing slowly, as is its commercialization—more networks are beginning to accept advertisements. The satellite arena is also growing slowly.

Regional media buying has emerged throughout Latin America. Regional TV buys can be done on Univision (Televisa), Telemundo, CNN and ESPN on cable/satellite. Unfortunately, no audience information is available for cable, satellite, VCR usage, etc.

In many countries, TV measurement services have made the transition towards people meters. These are primarily offered by the IBOPE company.

As for print media, newspapers seem to be experiencing a small growth in the share-of-investments due to strong retail and finance categories. Recently, an agreement between the leading newspapers in the region, one in each country, is allowing advertisers to buy space in any of the participating papers, through the local 'partner.' Some discounts can be achieved this way.

The importance of magazines varies from country to country. Strong publishing groups are present (e.g., Abril, Editorial America). Some titles are becoming more regionally important: *Time, Vision, America Economia, Cambio 16 America, Newsweek,* etc.

Radio is still a developing medium throughout the region—although Colombia is an exception. Finally, the areas of direct marketing and promotional activities are growing dramatically.

Javier Salas
Vice President, Business Development
and Communications Director

Argentina

Area	2,766,890 km²
Population (1992)	32,901,234
Population growth rate (1992)	1.1%
GDP	US$ 101.2 billion
GDP/per capita	US$ 3,100
Real growth rate (1991)	5.5%
Capital	Buenos Aires

Population Breakdown

By Sex	*By Age Group*	*By Socio-Economic Status*
Male 49%	Children, 0-12 .... 31%	A, B, & C1 .... 15%
Female.................................. 51%	Teens, 13-19............................ 9%	C2 .... 36%
	Adults, 20+ 60%	D&E 49%

Media Inflation vs. General Inflation, 1989-1992

The general inflation rate in Argentina has decreased from almost 5,000% in 1989 to about 18% in 1992.

Media inflation has decreased from about 46.5% in 1989 to only 1.4% in 1992.

Number of Households	10,096,875

Ownership of household durables
- Car................................ N/A
- Phone........................... N/A
- Washers........................ N/A

(purchasing power equivalent)

GNP distribution by industry
- Agriculture................... N/A
- Industry .... N/A
- Services .... N/A

Exchange rates (US$ to local currency)
- 1991 .... 0.0000101
- 1992 .... 1.01

National Holidays

Holiday	*1993 Date*
New Year's Day	January 1
Holy Friday	April 7
Labor Day	May 1
1st National Government	May 25
Malvinas Isles Sovereignity Declaration	June 10
Flag Day	June 20
National Independence Day	July 9
Gen. San Martin Commemoration Death	August 17
Race Day	October 12
Christmas	December 25

School Holidays

Holiday	*1993 Date*
Winter Holidays	July 18 - July 31
Teacher's Day	September 11
Student's Day	September 21
Summer Holidays	December 14 - March 7

Major Influences and Trends

There has been consolidation of media ownership in the market:

- Clarin newspaper bought Mitre radio and Station 13.
- La Nacion newspaper bought Del Plata radio.
- Station 13, an open channel, created a special news channel called 'Todo Noticias' that airs via satellite to the cable channels throughout the entire country.
- Station 9 bought Libertad radio.
- TELEFE (Station 11) bought Continental radio and is the owner of Atlantida publishing (magazines).
- Cablevision is the owner of America radio, El Cronista newspaper and Channel 2 on open TV.
- Each medium sells advertising independently, cross-media discounts are not available.

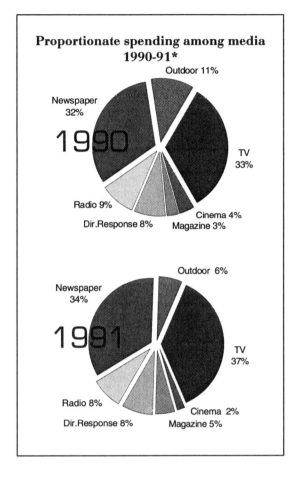

Proportionate spending among media 1990-91*

Spending Analysis

National advertising spending by medium
based on appropriate year's exchange rate

	1988 US$ MM	1989 US$ MM	1990 US$ MM	1991* US$ MM
TV	277.4	131.6	251.1	391.0
Cinema	38.1	14.9	27.7	19.7
Radio	101.4	37.0	72.4	81.6
Newspaper	360.5	169.6	238.0	366.3
Magazine	40.3	19.3	24.6	56.1
Direct Response	137.3	45.5	58.4	89.0
Outdoor	139.2	47.4	79.7	67.7
Other	97.7	91.6	107.4	
Total	**1,191.1**	**556.8**	**859.3**	**1,071.4**

* The 1992 data is not available, (has not been published by the Argentine Chamber of Advertisers)

Media Buying

Media buying is handled by ad agencies on behalf of clients. For TV buying only, the agencies combine clients' budgets to achieve buying volume and discounts.

Buying Services with 1992 Billings

Buying Service	Parent Company	US$ MM
Espacios	Ogilvy and Mather, David Ratto BBDO, McCann Erickson, Nexo, Pragma FCB, Colonese - Lintas, Lautrec and Voz e Imagen	110,460,037
Raul Naya Prod.	Raul Naya	98,870,829
Multimix	Casares Grey & Asociados, Leo Burnett and Gowland	53,577,346
Olam	FSD Young and Rubicam and Yuste Publicidad	19,933,391
Fax S.A.	Fiat	18,213,172
Aude	Aurora	18,101,563
Kenia S.A.	Kenia	14,496,484
Nobleza Piccardo	Nobleza Piccardo	13,608,986
Excel S.A.	Philip Morris	12,452,039
Radvic	Radvic	10,356,286

Top Advertisers (1992 Total Spending)

By Company

Parent Company	Product Categories	US$ MM
Lever Y Asoc.	Cleaning and beauty products	47.6
Pepsi Cola	Carbonated beverages	27.7
Molinos	Food	27.6
Coca-Cola	Carbonated beverages	27.0
Philip Morris	Tobacco	23.8
Nobleza Piccardo	Tobacco	22.8
Refinerias de Maiz	Food	22.6
Nestle	Food	19.9
Mastellone	Food	18.5
Aurora Grundig	Household appliance	15.8

By Product

Product Category	Advertiser	US$ MM
Carbonated beverages	Pepsi Cola	25.9
Tobacco	Marlboro/Philip Morris	14.5
Milk Products	LaSerenisima/Mastellone	14.1
Soups	Knoor/Ref. de Maiz	14.0
Deodorant	Rexina/Lever y Asoc.	8.2
Food	Maggi/Nestle	8.0
Cars	Peugeot/Sevel	7.2
Soap	Drive/Lever y Asoc.	5.9

Television

	TV HH Penetration			Adult (ABC, 20-49) Reach	
1989	*1990*	*1991*	*1992*	at 250 GRPs	77%
94.2%	95%	95%	95%	at 500 GRPs	79%
7,382	9,413	9,592	9,592	at 1,000 GRPs	89%

Opportunities

Network	Number of Stations	Ownership	Station Profile	Commercial Minutes/Day	Coverage	Broadcast Hours (Sign-On/Off)
America	2	Private	General Public Interest	240	CAP. & GBA	10:00-24:00
ATC S.	7	Government	General Public Interest	288	National	24 Hour
S. 9	1	Private	General Public Interest	180	National	10:00-24:00
S. 11 Tel	1	Private	General Public Interest	156	National	12:00--01:00
S. 13	1	Private	General Public Interest	180	CAP. & GBA	12:00-01:00

Costs

Prime Time TV Costs for :30 in US$			
1989	*1990*	*1991*	*1992*
820.0	1,563.9	3,952.8	7,113.1

Television Cost Changes Between Years
'88 '89 '90 '91 '92
7,254% 1,861% 203% 80%

Audiences/CPM's

Average Cost, Audience, and CPMs by Daypart
(Top 3 Stations, :30, national audience, Target=Adults 20-40, Children 6-12, ABCD)

Hours	Morning Sign On-14:00	Daytime Sign On/Off	Prime Time 19:00-24:00	Late Night 24:00-Sign-Off	Weekend Sign On-Off	Children Sign On-Off
Station: 9						
US$	2,771.0	3,858.0	5,750.0	3,480.0	3,341.0	2,271.0
Avg. Aud. (000)	82.0	58.9	92.2	20.5	43.5	17.7
CPM	33.79	65.50	62.36	169.75	76.80	128.30
Station: 11						
US$	2,536.0	4,775.0	7,039.0	2,020.0	2,699.0	2,559.0
Avg. Aud. (000)	35.9	83.3	137.1	87.1	74.3	67.8
CPM	70.64	57.32	51.34	23.19	36.32	37.74
Station: 13						
US$	1,782	4,460	8,339.0	N/A	2,286.0	1,658.0
Avg. Aud. (000)	60.2	78.1	87.1	N/A	76.9	54.7
CPM	29.60	57.10	95.74	N/A	29.72	30.31

Audiences/Rating by Daypart (Target=Adults, ABC 20-49)

Daypart	Hours	Household				Adult		
		Universe (000)	Hut Levels	Household Rating	Impressions (000)	Universe (000)	Adult Rating	Impressions (000)
Morning	Sign On-14:00	3,238	42.6	8.5	275.2	1,281	3.0	38.4
Daytime	Sign On-Sign Off	3,238	39.3	7.9	255.8	1,281	3.8	48.6
Primetime	19:00-24:00	3,238	56.2	9.4	304.3	1,281	6.5	83.2
Late Night	24:00- Sign Off	3,238	13.3	2.7	87.4	1,281	1.8	23.0
Weekend	Sign On-Sign Off	3,238	59.2	5.9	191.0	1,281	3.4	43.5
Children's	Sign On-12:00 16:00-19:00	3,238	24.5	9.8	317.3	1,281	3.0	38.4

Scheduling/Languages

- Commercials are aired throughout the day within programs, in their corresponding breaks (e.g., in a one hour program the average number of breaks is 4). In the commercial break, the spot can be aired at the beginning or at the end of the break. Commercials can also be aired as program sponsors.
- There is no standard length. The most commonly bought commercial length is :30, and the official, but variable, minimum is :10.
- The only language used for programming and commercials is Spanish.

Regional

There are no national TV open networks in Argentina. Therefore, to have national reach it is necessary to air the commercial locally in Capital Federal Suburbs and in each province.

ATC Station 7 has a system of booster stations with national reach and a cable service that broadcasts ATC transmissions.

It is estimated that a total of 1,411,000 homes in the rest of the country (outside of Capital and GBA) are associated with a cable system. Spots placed on cable do achieve national reach.

Also, Station 11 (TELEFE - Capital Federal) is broadcast to the whole country via satellite. That transmission reaches Uruguay, Bolivia, Paraguay, Chile and the south of Peru and Brazil as well.

Children's Advertising

Programming which accepts advertising to children

ADULT PROGRAMMING				Kids'	
Station	Hours	Days	Universe (000)	Ratings	Impressions (000)
11	21:00-22:00	Wednesday	570	34.0	193.8
11	21:00-22:00	Tuesday	570	28.2	160.7
13	20:00-21:00	Thursday	570	27.9	159.0
11	20:00-21:00	Mon-Fri	570	20.1	114.6
11	21:00-22:00	Monday	570	19.2	109.4

CHILDREN'S PROGRAMMING (Target= 6-12 years old)				Kids'	
Station	Hours	Days	Universe (000)	Ratings	Impressions (000)
11	16:00-17:00	Mon-Fri	570	17.1	97.4
13	12:00-13:00	Mon-Fri	570	17.0	96.9
13	17:00-18:00	Mon-Fri	570	14.2	80.9
11	18:00-19:00	Mon-Fri	570	6.8	38.8
2	11:00-12:00	Mon-Fri	570	5.4	30.8
13	17:00-18:00	Mon-Fri	570	8.2	46.7

Radio

- There are 247 AM and FM radio stations in Argentina, all of which are commercial. 15 AM and 11 FM stations are located in Capital Federal and GBA.
- The household penetration is estimated at 98% (9,895,000 households).
- The primary broadcast language is Spanish; English is secondary.

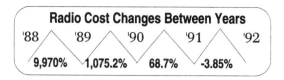

Radio Cost Changes Between Years				
'88	'89	'90	'91	'92
9,970%	1,075.2%	68.7%	-3.85%	

- The most popular program types are
  -News/General Interest
  -Magdalena Tempranisimo on Mitre Radio
  -Tiempos Modernos on Continental Radio

Ratings

Daypart	Adult Rating	Adult (000)
09:00-12:00	6.5	105.2

National/Regional

The following radio stations transmit by satellite to the entire country. The rest of the radio stations depend on the reach of the broadcasting waves.

LS5 Radio Rivadavia: Broadcasts to the whole country by:
- *Contract with Video Cable Color.* The associates to this closed circuit can also obtain 100% of Rivadavia's programming and commercials.
- *Air radios.* Retrieve satellite signal by parabolic antenna.

LR9 Radio America: The same as Rivadavia, broadcasts to the whole country by satellite.

LR6 Radio Mitre: Since August 1991, this radio broadcasts to the whole country in both AM and FM.

Daypart Costs/CPMs (Target=Adult 20-40, ABC)
Buying units for commercials are in seconds, not by :30 units; no restrictions are placed on length.

Daypart	Local Time	Avg. Cost /:30 US$	Avg. Aludience (000)	CPM (US$)
Prime Time (Mon-Fri)	06:00-12:00	441	66.4	6.65
Daytime (Mon-Fri)	06:00-24:00	281	35.6	7.89
Late Night (Mon-Fri)	00:00-06:00	84	1.6	52.50

Cable

- There are 37 commercial cable channels in Argentina.
- Cable household penetration is growing steadily in the Capital Federal and GBA.
- This is an important medium for specific targets, but the total number of people who subscribe to cable is not measured.

- The primary broadcast language is Spanish; other languages used are English, Italian, Portuguese, and German.

Cable Household Penetration		
1989	1990	1991
4.9%	5.0%	9.4%
132,000	185,000	329,000

Top Cable Channels (Local Operators)	Rating	Commercial Min/Hr
Channel 3 - Cablesport (VCC)	9.6	2-4
Channel 5 - Women's Station (VCC)	9.6	2-4
Channel 3 - Nowadays (CV)	13.5	2-4
Channel 5 - Films (CV)	14.6	2-4
Channel 17 - Sports (CV)	9.5	2-4

Cable Networks	Programming	Cable Networks	Programming
Cartoon Network	Children's Programming	Television de Chile	Programming from Chile
ESPN	Sports	TVC-Television Francesca	Programming from France
ECO	News, General Interest	CNN	News
TVE-Television Espanola	Programming from Spain	World Net	U.S., General Information
TNT	Family Programming	Television Alemana	Programming from Germany
Music Television	Music Videos	Manchette	Brazilian Network
HBO	Movies (no pay-cable)	La Rai	Programming from Italy

Satellite

Satellite Channel	Country of Origin	Satellite Channel	Country of Origin
Ch. 27	TVC-Television Francesca	Ch. 33	Local
Ch. 28	Local	Ch. 34	Local
Ch. 29	CNN	Ch. 35	Local
Ch. 30	World Net - U.S. General Information	Ch. 36	Manchete-Brazilian TV
Ch. 31	Local	Ch. 37	La Rai-Italian TV
Ch. 32	German Television		

Video Cassettes

- Approximately 26.9% of all households in the Capital Federal have video cassette recorders; representing 26.1% of TV households.
- VCR usage is measured by IBOPE.
- Pre-recorded tapes do carry advertising.
- The number of sponsors per tape depends on the commercial length. Some clients want to be exclusive advertisers.
- Average cost per commercial is US$ 5 per number of movie copies released. Also, costs vary by film.
- So far, very low advertising presence has been evident in this medium.

Cinema

- There are 125 cinemas in Buenas Aires (CAP FED and GBA own 60 of them) and 65 more in the rest of the country.
- All cinemas offer commercial time with spots ranging from:15 to :60.

- The average cost of a four week cinema schedule is US$ 95,500 for :30 (based on 45-120 theaters).

Newspapers

There are 384 national daily papers which accept advertising.

Daily Newspaper	Market	Size	Circulation (000)	Avg. Daily Aud. (000)	1 page B&W Cost (US$)	Accept Color?
NATIONAL						
Clarin	CAP. & GBA	Tabloid	715.1	444.9	16,368	Yes
La Nacion	CAP. & GBA	Broadsheet	209.7	264.2	27,490	Yes
Ambito Financiero	CAP. & GBA	Tabloid	125.0*	120.0	17,604	Yes
El Cronista	CAP. & GBA	Tabloid	60.0*	57.0 Est.	10,019	Yes
Bs. As. Herald	CAP. & GBA	Tabloid	20.0*	14.2 Est.	8,221	Yes
La Prensa	CAP. & GBA	Broadsheet	42.5*	1.9	16,374	Yes
Pagina 12	CAP. & GBA	Tabloid	130.0	147.4	11,514	Yes
PROVINCIAL						
El Litoral	Santa Fe	Broadsheet	32.5	31.2 Est.	8,322	Yes
La Capital	Rosario	Broadsheet	53.1	55.2 Est.	19,998	Yes
La Nueva	Bahia	Broadsheet	33.1	31.2	5,454	No
Provincia	Blanca Cordoba	Broadsheet	82.0	81.3 Est.	14,889	Yes
La Voz del Interior	Mendoza	Broadsheet	60.3	57.8 Est.	6,464	Yes
Los Andes	Tucuman	Broadsheet	70.3	67.4 Est.	9,686	No
La Gaceta		Broadsheet				

* Target=Adults 20-40, ABC

Magazines

There are more than 12 consumer magazines which accept advertising in Argentina, and 542+ trade and technical magazines.

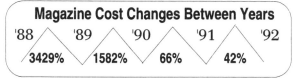

Magazine	Type	Frequency	Circ. (000)	Audited?	Avg. Issue Aud. (000)	1 page 4/C Cost (US$)
Billiken	Children	Weekly	162.8	Yes	13.0	3,393
Emanuelle	Women's	Monthly	60.0	No	50.6	4,000
Para Ti	Women's	Monthly	66.9	Yes	62.7	7,423
Mia	Women's	Weekly	150.9	Yes	38.0	5,151
El Grafico	Sports	Weekly	84.7	Yes	77.6	5,201
Conozca Mas	General	Monthly	121.3	Yes	50.7	5,252
Somos	Public Interest	Weekly	15.4	Yes	15.0	4,100
Gente	Economical	Weekly	197.1	Yes	166.5	8,837
Mercado	Political, Current Affairs	Monthly	15.6	Yes	14.4	5,400
Apertura	Economical/Political	Monthly	N/A	Yes	13.3	5,000
Muy Interesante	General Public Interest	Monthly	N/A	Yes	142.3	6,565
Noticias	Current Affairs/ Political	Weekly	N/A	No	122.3	11,488

Outdoor/Transit

Billboard	**Transit**
Sites available Capital Federal: 33,000 Greater Buenos Aires: 15,000 Rest of Country: 10,000 **Lead Time to reserve** .... 4 weeks adv.	**Boards available**.......................... N/A

Costs	**Costs**
Average, 1 billboard/month Poster panels (30 units) .... US$ 87,365 CPM Posters .... US$ 8,333 **Billboard Cost Changes Between Years** '88 '89 '90 '91 '92 5026% 1100% 63% 30%	**Average, 1 board/month** Subway boards.............................. US$ 161 Taxis(Publitax, illuminated x 100 units) .... US$ 23,473 Comparisons between previous years cannot be made because there is no mesurement service available.

Sizes	**Sizes**
CPM 1.48 m x 1.10 m Poster Panels 7.30 m x 3.50 m	Illuminated indicators inside subways: 0.74 m x 1.10 m Publitax: 1.08 m x 0.36 m

There are no restrictions on outdoor advertising.

Direct Marketing

The only available direct marketing source is Asociacion Argentina de Marketing Directo.

List Brokers	*Telemarketing Companies:*	*Direct Marketing Association*
VR Tovec y Asociados (Lease/sale/ purchase of lists. Maintains data base.) Multiletter S.A. Martin Meyer S.A. Di Paola & Peydro Celano y Asociados	VR Tovec y Asociados Di Paola y Peydro Ines Rusquellas Full Sale Direcciones Lar S.A.	AMDA (Asociacion de Marketing Directo de Argentina)

Research Sources

Medium Covered	*Research Company*	*Information Provided*
Magazines	Asociacion Arg. de Editores de Revistas Esmeralda 672	Titles, distribution, and readers, and circulation.
Radio	Asociaciones Radioifusoras Privadas Argentinas Paseo Colon 797	Broadcasters per zone
TV/Radio/Print	Mercados & Tendencias Talcahuano 750 9no IPSA Cerrito 1054 Piso 8 y 13	Audience and readership per zone

Continued on following page

Research Sources, continued

Research Company	Information Provided

IBOPE
  Carlos Pellegrini 445 Piso 8
IVAT
  B. de Yrigoyen 678)	

Instituto Verificador de Circulaciones Av de Mayo 1370 ler piso)	Circulation & Distribution of each medium per zone
Agencia los Diarios Sarmiento 1236)	Publication Control

Television Research Currently Available

Research Method	Frequency
Mercados & Tendencias - Household Meters/Diaries	Rating/Share/GRP/Reach/Frequency/GRPs simulation. Weekly: TV Capital and GBA, Daily: per schedules Monthly: rest of the country
IPSA - Daily Booklet	Same as above
IBOPE	Same as above
IVAT	Daily information per schedules

Advertising Regulations

By Product

Beverages/Alcohol

Can not encourage improper alcohol consumption or minimize the consequences of abuse.

Can not represent young people, sportsmen, scientists or teachers, consuming these beverages.

Can not show alcohol as a way of overcoming anxiety, distress, tiredness or of improving the bodily fitness in general.

Can not transmit situations, atmosphere, content, music or other elements, directed to people younger than 21 years old.

Commercials about alcohol/beverages cannot include sex or violence.

Commercials about products produced in Argentina must present the 'Industria Argentina' inscription horizontally and very visibly.

Cigarettes

Cigarette consumption should not be associated with sports, but advertising participation in sports events is acceptable.

Commercials about new tobacco treatment procedures or cigarette production process, referring to low tar and nicotine contents, should be restricted to real, probable effects.

Pharmaceuticals/Drugs

There must be an authorization from the national department of public health. Each commercial must contain the phrase 'IN CASE OF DOUBT, CONSULT YOUR DOCTORS.'

Advertising To Children

Commercials directed to children can not show either dangerous elements (drugs, disinfectants, insecticides, etc.) near a child or display a child using household appliances (ovens, stoves, etc.).

Kids can not appear driving any kind of adult vehicle.

Commercial Production

Radio Broadcast Law Number 22285 Art. Number 23 says   ' ...all Commercials Must Be Of National Production.'

By Medium

Television

Can not schedule cigarette commercials on TV programs only directed to people younger than 21 years old.

Radio

Can not schedule cigarette commercials on radio programs only directed to people younger than 21 years old.

Cinema

Can not schedule cigarette commercials during films intended for kids.

Promotions

Can not promote or distribute cigarettes to people younger than 21 years old at schools or universities.

Sources Consulted

Censo Nacional de Poblacion y Vivienda 1991

Multimedios y Marketing

Brazil

Area	8,511,965 km²
Population (1992)	158,202,019
Population growth rate (1992)	1.8%
GDP	US$ 358 billion
GDP/per capita	US$ 2,300
Real growth rate (1991)	1.2%
Capital	Brazilia

Population Breakdown

By Sex		*By Age Group*		*By Socio-Economic Status*	
Male	49.4%	Children, 0-14	34.4%	A	8.0%
Female	50.6%	Teens, 15-19	20.3%	B	21.0%
		Adults, 20+	45.4%	C	38.0%
				D&E	33.0%

Source: Anuario Estadistico Brasil (IBGE) 1992

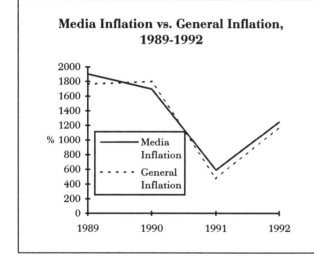

Media Inflation vs. General Inflation, 1989-1992

Number of Households	36,905,000

Ownership of household durables

Car	22.7%
Phone	18.2%
Washers	68.1%

(purchasing power equivalent)

GNP distribution by industry

Agriculture	9.1%
Industry	34.3%
Services	56.6%

Exchange rates (US$ to local currency)

1991	0.0000300
1992	0.0000229

Source: Anuario Estatico Brasil (IBGE) 1992

National Holidays

Holiday	1993 Date
New Year's Day	January 1
Carnival	February 15
Saint's Day	April 9
Tiradentes	April 21
Labor Day	May 1
Corpus Christi	June 2
Independence Day	September 7
St. Aparecida	October 12
All Saints Day	November 12
Christmas	December 25

School Holidays

Holiday	1993 Date
Summer	December 1-February 15
Winter	July 1-July 30

Major Influences and Trends

Brazil is experiencing a trend towards segmentation in television, with subscription TV broadcast stations becoming more numerous everyday.

This concept is still in its infancy stage and primarily located in the main Brazilian cities.

Spending Analysis

National advertising spending by medium,
based on appropriate year's exchange rate

	1989 US$ MM	1990 US$ MM	1991 US$ MM	1992 US$ MM
TV	1,086	1,342	1,070	1,137
Radio	151	219	220	93
Newspaper	484	654	525	468
Magazine	275	245	176	161
Outdoor	30	48	34	8
Other	24	41	10	52
Total	**2,051**	**2,549**	**1,913**	**1,919**

Source: Meio and Mensagem 1993

Media Buying

Media negotiations in Brazil are done within the agency and sometimes the client is present. The negotiations vary according to client, product category and the ranking of the media vehicle.

There are no real buying service bureaus in Brazil. There is a company named 'Bureau,' but they only sell traditional media services. This is because the media vehicles refuse to work with a real bureau/buying service. When a client has more than one brand advertising agency, the agencies work together as a 'Media Central' to negotiate the total client budget (for all the products).

Proportionate spending among media 1991-92

1991: TV 56%, Newspaper 28%, Magazine 9%, Outdoor 2%, Radio 5%

1992: TV 59%, Newspaper 24%, Magazine 9%, Outdoor 3%, Radio 5%

Source: Meio and Mensagem 1993

Top Advertisers (1992 Spending)

By Company
By Product

Parent Company	Product Categories	US$ MM
Ind. Gesy Lever Ltda.	Consumer Products	62.9
Nestle Indl. Coml Ltda.	Food	38.5
Globex Utilidades S/A	Commerce	32.1
Bco. Estado S.Paulo	Finance	31.5
Commerce Des.Mercantil S/A	Finance	29.8
Arisco Prods.Alimenticios Ltda.	Food	27.5
Mappin Casa AnloBrasil S/A	Commerce	27.0
Cia. Cigarros Souza Cruz	Tobacco	26.8
Golden Cross Assist. Inter. Saude	Health	26.7
General Motors Brasil S/A	Autos	26.0

Source: Meio and Mensagem 1993

Product Category	US$ MM
Commerce	817.1
Service	606.6
Education	365.4
Toys	312.1
Foods	295.3
Finance	267.1
Perfumary	194.9
Construction	180.7
Photo/Optical	160.4
Drinks	128.1

Source: Meio and Mensagem 1993

Television

Overview

- TV in Brazil has 96% penetration in the major cities. The leading network, Rede Globo TV, achieves 55% share of viewers in primetime.
- Subscription broadcast stations do not yet have significant enough participation to compete with the VHF broadcast stations, but they do capture the upper-income audiences. Subscriptions already exceed 100,000.

TV Household Penetration				Adult Reach	
1989	*1990*	*1991*	*1992*	at 250 GRPs	63%
64.5%	64.5%	72.7%	73.5%	at 500 GRPs	71%
22,470	23,122	26,573	27,509	at 1,000 GRPs	80%

Source: IBOPE, Sao Paulo

Opportunities

Networks	Number of Stations	Ownership	Station Profile	Commercial Minutes/Hour	Coverage	Broadcast Hours (Sign-On/Off)
Globo	83	Private	General	Avg. 15	99.9%	07:00-02:30; WD 7:00-19:00
SBT	57	Private	General	Avg. 15	76.8%	07:00-02:30; WD 7:00-19:00
Bondeirantes	33	Private	General	Avg. 15	65.4%	07:00-02:30; WD 7:00-19:00
Manchete	40	Private	General	Avg. 15	59.1%	07:00-02:30; WD 7:00-19:00
Record	13	Private	General	Avg. 15	N/A	07:00-02:30; WD 7:00-19:00
Other	9	Private	General	Avg. 15	N/A	07:00-02:30; WD 7:00-19:00
Education	21	Goverrnment	Educational	Avg. 15	N/A	07:00-02:30; WD 7:00-19:00

Costs

Prime Time TV Costs for :30 in US$			
1989	*1990*	*1991*	*1992*
15,000	21,500	23,387	33,779

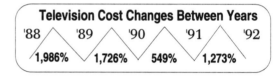

Television Cost Changes Between Years
'88 / '89 / '90 / '91 / '92
1,986% / 1,726% / 549% / 1,273%

Audiences/CPM's

Average Cost, Audience, and CPMs by Daypart
(Top 3 Stations, :30, national audience, Target=Adults 15+)

Hours	Morning 08:00-12:00	Daytime 12:00-20:00	Prime Time 20:00-22:00	Late Night 22:00-01:00	Weekend	Children
Station: Globo						
US$	5,008	10,665	33,779	8,288	13,644	5,282
Avg. Aud. (000)	3,358	7,835	22,386	5,597	10,074	4,477
CPM	1.49	1.36	1.51	1.48	1.35	1.18
Station: SBT						
US$	2,988	5,750	11,756	8,272	9,006	2,907
Avg. Aud. (000)	1,119	3,358	5,597	2,238	N/A	N/A
CPM	2.67	1.71	2.10	3.70	N/A	N/A
Station: Bandeirantes						
US$	1,058	2,228	4,691	1,058	4,311	N/A
Avg. Aud. (000)	358	1,119	1,119	1,009	1,489	N/A
CPM	2.96	1.99	4.19	1.05	2.91	N/A

Source: Midia Dados 1992 and Grupo de Midia

Audiences/Rating by Daypart (Target=Adults 15+)

Daypart	Hours	Household				Adult		
		Universe (000)	Hut Levels	Household Rating	Impressions (000)	Universe (000)	Adult Rating	Impressions (000)
Morning	07:00-12:30	27,199	18	10	2,720	81,688	5	4,084
Daytime	12:30-18:00	27,199	40	22	10,880	81,688	14	11,436
Primetime	18:00-22:00	27,199	71	50	13,599	81,688	30	24,506
Late Night	23:30-02:00	27,199	23	12	3,264	81,688	8	6,535
Weekend	08:00-02:00	27,199	43	24	11,696	81,688	17	13,887
Children's	08:00-12:30	27,199	20	11	2,992	81,688	7	5,718

Source: IBOPE 1993

Scheduling/Regional/Languages

- The only language used in TV broadcasting is Portuguese.
- 70% of all commercials are bought locally; prices vary with markets.
- The most common commercial length (70%) is :30; other available lengths are :05, :10, :15, and :60.

- Commercials are aired throughout the day, at the beginning and end of programs, and within programs.

Children's Advertising

All adult programming accepts advertising targeted at children.

CHILDREN'S PROGRAMMING (Target = Kids 2-14)			Kids'		
Station	Hours	Days	Universe (000)	Ratings	Impressions (000)
Globo	08:00-12:40	M-Sat	35,818	8	2,865
Globo	11:00-12:00	Sun	35,818	7	2,507
Globo	10:00-10:30	Sun	35,818	4	1,433
SBT	08:30-11:00	Sun	35,818	4	1,433
SBT	10:15-12:15	M-Sat	35,818	5	1,791
SBT	15:00-17:30	M-F	35,818	5	1,791
Manchete	17:00-18:30	M-F	35,818	2	716
Manchete	08:00-10:00	M-F	35,818	1	358

Radio

- Brazil has 1,519 AM and 1,127 FM stations, most of which are commercial.
- In Sao Paulo there are 26 AM and 27 FM stations, of which 1 AM and 2 FM stations do not accept advertising. *(Source: Midia Dados 1993)*

Daypart Costs/CPMs
(:30 Radio Commercial, Target=Adults +15, Sao Paulo Metro Area, 1 station)

Daypart	Local Time	Avg. Cost :30 US$	Audience (000)	CPM (US$)
AM				
Prime Time	08:00-10:00	402	448	0.90
Daytime	06:00-19:00	161	305	0.53
Late Night	22:00-24:00	60	42	1.44
FM				
Prime Time	10:00-12:00	267	418	0.64
Daytime	06:00-19:00	216	234	0.92
Late Night	22:00-24:00	139	85	1.64

Source: IBOPE 1993

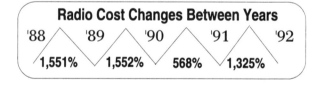

Radio Cost Changes Between Years

'88	'89	'90	'91	'92
1,551%	1,552%	568%	1,325%	

- The only broadcast language in radio is Portuguese.
- The most popular program on FM is Hit Parade of Music, which is segmented by target. On AM, programs directed to housewives and news are popular.
- Commercial lengths available are :15, :30, :45, and :60.

Ratings

	Daypart	Adult Rating	Adult (000)
AM	08:00-10:00	5.5%	763
FM	10:00-12:00	10.4%	1,458

Source: Market - Sao Paulo

Cable

Cable and UHF channels are slowly beginning to emerge. There is no research available.

Satellite

Brazil only has a satellite relay broadcast via 'BrasilSat' which belongs to the National Communication Company.

Satellite Channel	Country Of Origin	Programming
TVA		
ESPN	U.S.A.	Sports
CNN	U.S.A.	News
Cartoon Network	U.S.A.	Children's Programming
GloboSat		
TNT	U.S.A.	Movies, family programming
Deutsche Welle	Germany	German TV
FOX	U.S.A.	General
Worldnet	U.S.A.	–
TVE	Spain	Spanish TV
ECO	Mexico	News, general
TV Cinq	France	French TV

Source: GloboSat/TVA

Video Cassettes

Of TV households in Brazil, 19% have video cassette recorders (VCRs). There is no service to measure VCR usage, and tapes that carry advertising are rare.

Cinema

- 408 cinemas in Brazil accept advertising.
- Net reach over 4 weeks for a target of Adults 15+ is 21%. GRPs are 38, and average frequency is 1.9. *(Source: Morplan)*
- 60% of all commercials in cinemas are :30.

Cinema Cost Changes Between Years

'88	'89	'90	'91	'92
1,562%	1,458%	613%	1,209%	

- Average cost of a 4-week schedule at up to 20 theaters is US$ 2,683.
- As creative prices drop, this medium will continue growing.

Newspapers

In Brazil, newspaper is a regional/local medium. There are no national newspapers.

Newspaper Cost Changes Between Years

'88	'89	'90	'91	'92
1,542%	1,506%	629%	1,271%	

Daily Newspaper	Market	Size	Circulation (000)	Avg. Daily Aud. (000)	1 page/B&W Cost (US$)	Accept Color?
Folha de S.Paulo	Sao Paulo	Standard	Sunday 604	Sunday 707	Sunday 79,684	Yes
			Weekday 399	Weekday 786	Weekday 54,290	Yes
O Estado de Sao Paulo	Sao Paulo	Standard	Sunday 451	Sunday 995	Sunday 65,628	Yes
			Weekday 399	Weekday 774	Weekday 54,290	Yes
Gazeta Mercantil	Sao Paulo	Standard	Weekday 53	Weekday 59	Weekday 34,438	Yes
O Globo	Rio de Janeiro	Standard	Sunday 544	Sunday 2067	Sunday 37,090	Yes
			Weekday 265	Weekday 742	Weekday 22,478	Yes
Jornal do Brasil	Rio de Janeiro	Standard	Sunday 187	Sunday 452	Sunday 31,800	Yes
			Weekday 129	Weekday 245	Weekday 20,468	Yes
Zero Hora	Porto Alegre	Tabloid	Sunday 232	Sunday 440	Sunday 5,160	Yes
			Weekday 106	Weekday 159	Weekday 4,578	Yes

Source: Edictor/IVC

Magazines

There are 283 consumer magazines and about 587 technical and trade magazines in Brazil. *(Source: Midia Dados 1993)*

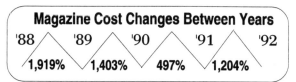

Magazine	Type	Frequency	Circ. (000)	Audited?	Avg. Issue Aud. (000)	1 page 4/C Cost (US$)
Veja	General	Weekly	820	Yes	4,162	31,625
Veja Sao Paulo	General	Weekly	240	Yes	1,368	15,815
Playboy	Men's	Monthly	303	Yes	2,335	16,798
Exame	Business	Monthly	127	Yes	372	18,952
Claudia	Women's	Monthly	289	Yes	1,434	18,217
Quatro Rodas	Sports & Auto	Monthly	190	Yes	1,426	15,333

Source: Edictor/IVC

Outdoor/Transit

Billboard	**Transit**

Sites available 25,780
Lead Time to reserve ....4 weeks
Exposure 60-80%
 	
Costs
 	
Average, 1 billboard/month
   3.0 m x 9.0 m, pref. location........US$ 946
 	
Billboard Cost Changes Between Years
'88   '89   '90   '91   '92
2,268%   1,544%   690%   1,203%
	Transit boards are still an emerging advertising option. There is difficulty appraising them within the Brazilian market.
	
	Costs
	
	Average, 1 unit/month
	   Varies by vehicle (trains, taxis, subway)

Sizes 3.0 m x 9.0 m, 3.6 m x 6.0 m, 2.3 m x 6.0 m	**Sizes** Trains: 1.0 m x 0.36 m, Taxis: 1.0 m x 0.10 m, Subway: 0.68 m x 0.67 m

Direct Marketing

The direct marketing companies in Brazil offer different mailing lists by target groups. For example, doctors, women or industries.

List Broker	Information	Direct Marketing Association
Abril	Magazine Readers/Subscriber Lists	Associacao Brasileira De Marketing Direto
Direta	Different Mailings by Target	
Alvo	Different Mailings by Target	
JE	Different Mailings by Target	
Lettersshop	Different Mailings by Target	

Non-Traditional Media

There is currently no use of non-traditional media in Brazil.

Research Sources

Medium covered	Research company	Information Provided
Newspapers and Magazines	I.V.C R. Joao Adolfo, 118-6 andar Conj.601 Sao Paulo-SP	Circulation Verification Institute Circulation Analysis
TV, Radio, Newspapers, Outdoor, Magazine	Nielsen Av. Bernardino de Campos - 98 14 andar Sao Paulo-SP	Competitive Data (Spending/GRP) Media Spending By Year
TV, Radio	IBOPE R Sete de Abril, 230 Sao Paulo-SP	Audience Rating by Market and Household/Target
TV, Radio, Newspaper, Magazine, Cinema	Marplan Av. Nove de Julho, 40 - 8 andar Sao Paulo-SP	Penetration by Target and Market

Television Research Currently Available

Research Method	Frequency
I.V.C - Checking (if spots actually ran)	Monthly
Nielsen- Checking (if spots actually ran)	Monthly
Ibope - People Meter/Recall	Weekly/Monthly
Marplan - Recall	Yearly

Advertising Regulations

By Product

Beverages/Alcohol
Alcohol advertisements only allowed on TV after 21:00 (to 05:00).
Cigarettes
Cigarette advertisements only allowed on TV and radio after 21:00 (to 05:00) with the warning 'Smoking detrimental to health.'
Pharmaceuticals/Drugs
Restrictions pertain basically to selling (prescriptions), endorsements (doctors), etc.
Advertising To Children
Must portray real people.

By Medium

There are no particular regulations by medium.

Chile

Area	756,950 km^2
Population (July 1992)	13,528,945
Population growth rate (1992)	1.6%
GDP	US$ 30.5 billion
GDP per capita	US$ 2,300
Real growth rate (1991 est.)	5.5%
Capital	Santiago

Population Breakdown

By Sex
Male 49.4%
Female 50.6%

By Age Group
Children, 0-14 .... 30.5%
Teens, 15-25 .... 18.3%
Adults, 25+ 51.2%

By Socio-economic Status
A & B 2.0%
C 53.0%
D 35.0%
E 10.0%

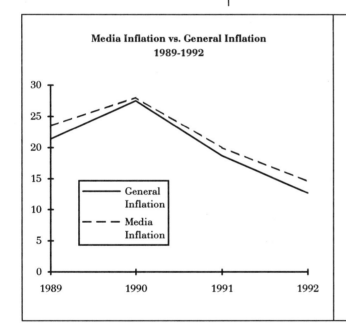

Media Inflation vs. General Inflation
1989-1992

Legend: General Inflation; Media Inflation

Number of households 2,974,623
Ownership of household durables
Car 30.0%
Phone 58.8%
Washers .... N/A
(purchasing power equivalent)
GNP distribution by industry
Agriculture: 7.8%
Industry: 34.5%
Services: 57.7%
Exchange rate (US$ to local currency)
1991 .... 0.002871
1992 .... 0.002551

National Holidays

Holiday	1993 Date
New Year's Day	January 1
Easter	April 9-10
Labor Day	May 1
National	May 21
Corpus Christi	June 10
St. Peter, St. Paul	June 29
Assumption	August 15
National	September 11
Independence	September 18-19
All Saints Day	November 1
Immaculate Conception	December 8
Christmas	December 25

School Holidays

Holiday	1993 Date
Summer	December 17— March 7
Winter	2 weeks in July
Independence	September 13 — 19

Major Influences and Trends

The emergence of the people meter, the TV measuring system, redistributed spendings to each TV channel. Although new ratings were 40% lower, it didn't decrease the total investment in television.

New formats in traditional media have developed, especially in Outdoor.

Media	Media Growth	Negotiation Frequency	Principal Purchase Place	Ownership
Press	Stable	Every Semester	Santiago	Private
TV	Growing	Annual	Santiago	Private-University
Radio	Stable	Every Semester	National	Private
Cinema	Stable	Every Month	Santiago	Private
Outdoor	Growing	Every Semester	National	Private
Magazines	Low	Every Semester	Santiago	Private
Cable	Growing	Every Semester	Santiago	Private

Spending Analysis

National Advertising spending by medium
based on appropriate year's exchange rate

	1989 US$ MM	1990 US$ MM	1991 US$ MM	1992 US$ MM
TV	68.1	82.4	108.4	156.9
Cinema	0.4	0.4	0.5	0.8
Radio	17.2	20.4	26.0	37
Newspaper	56.1	64.4	84.2	121.2
Magazine	11.7	13.5	14.8	15.8
Outdoor	4.1	5.4	8.4	12.8
Total	**157.7**	**186.5**	**242.3**	**344.4**

Media Buying

- All media pricing is negotiable. Agencies and/or clients deal with media; acting as middlemen between client and media. Both media and the clients pay 15% commission to the agency.
- There are no buying services in Chile

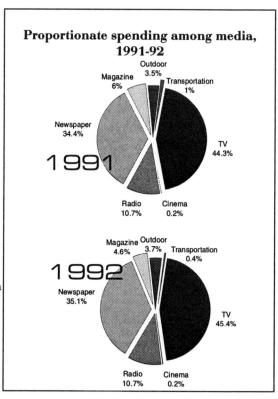

Proportionate spending among media, 1991-92

1991
- Outdoor 3.5%
- Magazine 6%
- Transportation 1%
- Newspaper 34.4%
- TV 44.3%
- Radio 10.7%
- Cinema 0.2%

1992
- Magazine 4.6%
- Outdoor 3.7%
- Transportation 0.4%
- Newspaper 35.1%
- TV 45.4%
- Radio 10.7%
- Cinema 0.2%

Top Advertisers (1992 spending)

By Company

Parent Company	Product Categories	US$ MM
Lever Chile	Detergent/Drive	19.6
Nestle Chile S.A.	Coffee/Nescafe	13.9
CCU S.A.	Beer/Cristal	11.8
CMPC	Napkins/Abolengo	6.6
Falabella S.A.	Department Store/Falabella	6.1
Sociedad Productora de Leche	Milk/Super Shake	5.9
Almacenes Paris	Department Store/Almarcenes Paris	5.5
P&G Chile	Toothpaste/Odontine	5.3
Centenario S.A.	Cookies/Galletas McKay	4.8
Embotelladora Andina	Soft drinks/Coca Cola	4.6

By Product

Product Category	US$MM
Department Stores	30.0
Cars	15.0
Banks	13.0
Soft drinks	12.6
Telephone and Services	11.6
Shampoo	10.1
Official Announcements	9.8
Beer	9.7
Casino and Games of Chance	6.9

Television

Overview

	TV HH Penetration						
	1989	*1990*	*1991*	*1992*			
Capital	93%	95%	95%	96%	**Adult Reach**		
	1,010	1,160	1,276	2,855	at 250 GRPs	69.0%	
Regions	85%	87%	87%	89%	at 500 GRPs	80.4%	
	1,444	1,528	1,681	2,648	at 1,000 GRPs	88.0%	

- Household penetration is estimated at 96% in the capital city; 89% in outlying regions.
- There are 11 channels. The top three have national coverage. Spanish is the only language used.
- Commercial lengths range from :10 to :60 in increments of :05; 31% of all commercials are :30.

Opportunities

Networks	Number of Stations	Ownership	Station Profile	Commercial Minutes/Day	Coverage	Broadcast Hours (Sign-On/Off)
TVN	120	Government	General	105	98.0%	06:30-02:30
TV 13	44	Catholic Univ.	General	159	92.0%	09:00-02:30
TV 9	23	Megavision (Private)	General	115	78.7%	09:00-00:30
TV 4	1	Private	General	125	40.1%	11:30-02:30
TV 11	5	Univ. of Chile	General	103	68.2%	06:30-01:30
TV 5 Valpo.	1	Catholic Univ.	General	90	50.7%	09:00-00:00
Telenorte	11	Univ. of Norte	General	N/A	10.8%	07:30-02:00
TV9 Concepcion	1	Catholic Univ	Genral	NA	12.6%	14:30-00:00
TV 10 Valdivia	1	Univ. of Chile	General	N/A	5.9%	07:00-22:30
TV 8 LaSerena	1	Catholic Univ.	General	N/A	3.7%	07:00-24:30
TV 7 Pto. Montt	1	Catholic Univ.	General	N/A	0.6%	14:30-23:30

Audiences/CPM's

Average Cost, Audience, and CPMs by Daypart
(Top three stations, national audience, Target=Adults 25-44)

Hours	Morning 06:30-14:30	Daytime 14:31-20:00	Prime Time 20:01-23:30	Late Night 23:31-02:30	Weekend 15:00-21:00	Children 11:00-13:30
Station: TV-13						
US$	470	663	3,440	663	1,678	356
Avg. Aud. (000)	3.9	20.8	73.8	39.3	36.2	12.4
CPM	120.50	31.90	46.60	16.90	46.30	28.70
Station: TV-7						
US$	816	1,658	3,163	1,446	893	255
Avg. Aud. (000)	12.3	13.9	49.3	23.8	17.7	13.1
CPM	66.4	119.30	64.20	60.70	50.50	19.50
Station: TV-9						
US$	539	619	2,326	1,378	619	445
Avg Aud. (000)	3.6	14.9	29.3	16.9	19.1	10.8
CPM	149.70	41.50	79.40	81.50	32.40	41.20

Audiences/Rating by Daypart (National broadcasts; Target=Adults 25-44)

Daypart	Hours	Households				Adult		
		Universe (000)	Hut Levels	Household Rating	Impressions (000)	Universe (000)	Adult Rating	Impressions (000)
Morning	06:30-14:30	986	16.0	5.8	57.1	771	1.6	12.3
Daytime	14:31-20:00	986	40.7	7.8	76.9	771	1.8	13.9
Primetime	20:01-23:30	986	58.8	13.6	134.1	771	6.4	49.3
Late Night	23:31-02:30	986	25.4	7.4	73.0	771	3.1	23.8
Weekend	15:00-21:00	986	42.7	6.7	66.1	771	2.3	17.7
Children's	11:00-13:30	986	22.9	5.0	49.3	771	1.7	13.1

Costs

Prime time TV costs for :30 in US$			
1989	1990	1991	1992
1,633	1,945	2,735	3,245

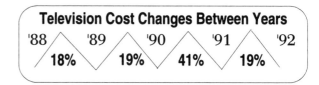

Television Cost Changes Between Years

'88 — '89 — '90 — '91 — '92

18%   19%   41%   19%

Scheduling/Regional

Commercials are aired throughout the day, at the beginnings and ends of programs. Local buys are available at about 7.9% of the cost of equal time on national stations (for :30). For example, a :30 commercial on a national station might cost the advertiser US$ 3,571.40; while the same time on a regional station would cost US$ 281.40.

Station	Region*	Hours
TV 13: Channel 5 and 9	VIII and XI	10:00-01:30
TV 7: Channels 7, 10 & 9	VIII, IX, XII Regions and Central Zone	06:30-02:00

Chile is divided into 13 regions, according to present legislation.

Children's Advertising

There are no restrictions regarding advertising targeted at children in adult or children's programming. Family, kids and pre-school programming runs all day on Saturdays and Sundays.

CHILDREN'S PROGRAMMING				Kids'	
Station	Hours	Days	Universe (000)	Ratings	Impressions (000)
Channel 13	10:15-12:15	Mon-Fri	428	3.4	162
	16:30-19:00	Mon-Fri	428	5.7	323
Channel 7	11:00-12:15	Mon-Fri	428	1.3	255
	18:15-20:00	Mon-Fri	428	3.8	510
Channel 9	11:00-11:30	Mon-Fri	428	4.1	384
	16:00-18:00	Mon-Fri	428	7.2	695

Radio

Overview

- There are 404 radio stations in Chile. All of them are commercial. Of these, 46 are located in Santiago.
- Spanish is the only language used for broadcasting.
- Household penetration is 97%, or 2,885,400 households. The most popular programs are News and Sports.
- Any commercial length is available upon request. Most commonly used are :20 and :30.

- Commercials can be aired only through a network system of linked stations carried on specific programs e.g., News. (Similiar to syndication.) Prime Time is 09:00 to 13:00.

Costs

National spots are 35% more expensive than regional ones.

Daypart Costs/CPMs

Daypart	Local Time	Avg. Cost :30 US$	Audience (000)	CPM (US$)
Prime Time	09:00-13:00	1,175	14.5	81
Daytime	13:01-23:00	870	8.9	97
Late Night	23:01-03:00	825	4.5	183

Cable

Overview

- Cable is available in 78,000 households in Santiago. 7,000 homes are reached via broadcast microwaves and 71,000 homes via cable. Penetration is as high as 20% in high socio-economic groups, and constitutes 7.9% of the total households overall.
- A continuous increase of subscribers and channels is expected. One hundred thousand households in Santiago are expected to have cable by the end of 1998.
- There are 51 cable channels, 14 are commercial.

- The primary languages for cable are Spanish and English. Portuguese, Italian and French are also used.

Cable Channels/Cost

Top Cable Channels	Cost US$	Commercial Min/Hr
Space	21.00	2
TNT	28.00	1
CNN	23.00	1
ESPN	23.00	1

Local Cable Operators	HH Circulation (000)	Programming
Intercom (Cable	28	CNN-ESPN-HBO-TNT
Metropolis (Cable)	43	Space-NC-Spectro-RAI
TV Max (Microwaves)	7	ECO-TVE-DW-Manchete-Oglobo-MTV-TVS-Worldnet

Video Cassettes

- Of TV households, 21% have video cassette recorders (VCRs).
- Due to international restrictions, advertising in video cassette films is not allowed. There is no commercial advertising on VCR tapes, nor is there any measuring service for their use.

Cinema

- Chile has 91 cinemas. The capacity of a single cinema over a month is 77,200 people.
- All cinemas offer commercial time. Commercial lengths available include :15, :20, :25, :30, :35, :40, :45, :50, :55, and :60.
- Average cost of a 4-week cinema schedule (:30 at one cinema) is US$ 1,276.
- No historial data is savailable on cinema. This is a slow-growing medium. There are no reliable audience or spending measurements.

Newspapers

- There are 9 national and 43 regionally circulated daily newspapers in Chile. The combined circulation of the national papers is 1,019,000.
- No data is available on English literacy.
- Costs rose 12.5% in 1992 versus the previous year.

Newspaper	Market	Size	Circ. (000)	Avg. Daily Aud. (000)*	1 Page B&W Cost (US$)	Accept Color?
El Mercurio	National	Standard	190	744	13,175	Yes
La Tercera	National	Tabloid	200	642	6,530	Yes
La Cuarta	National	Tabloid	130	387	1,475	Yes
Las Ultimas Noticias	National	Tabloid	163	433	3,426	Yes
La Epoca	National	Tabloid	21	52	3,790	Yes
La Nacion	National	Tabloid	35	63	1,374	Yes
El Diario	National	Tabloid	20	67	1,256	Yes
La Estrategia	National	Tabloid	45	66	7,411	Yes

*Santiago

Magazines

There are 55 Chilean consumer magazines, and 50 trade/technical publications. Rates and circulation information are as follows.

Magazine	Type	Frequency	Circ. (000)	Audited?	Avg. Issue Aud. (000)	1 page 4/C Cost (US$)
Cosas	Misc	Bi-weekly	32	No	192	2,761
Caras	Misc	Bi-weekly	15	No	82	2,850
Vanidades	Women's	Bi-weekly	25	No	75	2,769
Paula	Women's	Bi-weekly	25	No	100	2,959
Que Pasa	Informative	Weekly	26	No	78	2,156
Hoy	Informative	Weekly	22	No	35	1,836
Master Club	Misc	Monthly	230	No	448	3,814
Visa Magazine	Misc	Monthly	130	No	219	3,444
Mundo Diners	Misc	Monthly	46	No	132	2,832

Outdoor/Transit

Billboard

Non-transit-owned billboard advertising is available, but there are no reservations in advance, and no data is available on the number of boards.

Sizes

Outdoor	Size	1 Month(US$)
Road Billboard	4 m x 12 m	602.1
Superlight	4 m x 12 m	5,986.5
Backlight	4 m x 12 m	13,382.4

Transit

Transit advertising includes boards categorized as 'underway' and outdoor billboards. (See below)

Sizes

Underway	Size	1 Month(US$)
Transparency	130 x 330 cm	1,873.2
Big Billboards	180 x 330 cm	992.4
Inside wagons	29 x 74 cm	36.2
Outdoor		
Traffic Billboard	155 x 100 cm	1,117.4
Bus Stop Billboard	155 x 100 cm	606.9
City Billboard	180 x 330 cm	165

There are no restrictions for advertising in Outdoor media.

Direct Marketing

Direct Marketing is a new media option; however, because it is scarcely used, its effectiveness has not yet been proven.

Major Telemarketing Companies	Information
Agencia de Marketing Directo Ditborn & Urzeta Santa Maria St. 2812 Providencia Phone: 2342444	Demographics, socioeconomic level, lifestyle, buying power, product preference and usage attitudes and values, historical/purchasing cycles
Young & Rubicam: Direct Marketing Orquideas St. 979 Providencia Phone: 2319239	*Same as above*

Continued on following page

Direct Marketing, continued

Major Telemarketing Companies	Information
Carlos Muller & Asociados Condell St. 888 Providencia Phone: 6352265	Demographics, socioeconomic level, lifestyle, buying power, product preference and usage attitudes and values, historical/purchasing cycles
North y Asociados S.A. Orrego Luco St. 160 Providencia Phone: 2326610	*Same as above*
Sales S.A. Diagonal Paraguay St. 490 Providencia Phone: 6381994	*Same as above*
Direct Marketing Association	
Asociacion de Marketing Directo de Chile, A.G.	

Non-Traditional Media

Trends/Expectations

There is a trend toward the emergence of more targeted advertising/media.

Types Currently Available

High-definition electronic screens in Outdoor.
3,000 showings of :10 spots/month
Costs: US$ 5,102/month

Research Sources

Medium covered	Research company	Information provided
TV	Time Media Eliodoro Yanez St 2864, Santiago, Chile	Household ratings Target ratings
Radio	SEARCH Bilbao St. 2841 Santiago, Chile	Household ratings Target ratings
Newspaper	SEARCH *(See above for address)*	Household ratings Target ratings
Magazines	SEARCH *(See above for address)*	Household ratings Target ratings

Television Research Currently Available

Research Method	Frequency
People meters (Monday - Sunday, 24 hrs)	Weekly

Advertising Regulations

By Product

Beverages/Alcohol
Spots cannot air before 22:00 on TV.
Cigarettes
Advertising must have the warning in all media: 'Tobacco may cause cancer.' National
TV spots cannot be aired before 22:00 on TV.
Pharmaceuticals/Drugs
Only advertising for non-prescription products can be aired.

By Medium

Television
Cigarettes and alcoholic beverages
Can only advertise after 22:00. Competitive products cannot be advertised continuously.
Print
Competitive products cannot be printed on the same page.
Outdoor
Advertising must not distract drivers.

Sources Consulted

"Informe sobre Chile 1993", Editorial Gestion Ltda., Santiago, Chile, 1993. (Report includes information from the Instituto Nacional de Estadisticas (INE), Centro Latinoamericano Demografico (CELADE), Organismo de Planificacion (ODEPLAN) and the Central Bank of Chile.)

"Estudio de los Grupos Socioeconomicos de Chile", Instituto Consultor en Comercializacion y Mercado Limitada (ICCOM), Santiago, Chile, 1993.

MEGATEC S.A. (Advertising Data Bank), Santiago, Chile, 1993.

"Study of audience measuring with people meter system," Time Media S.A., Santiago, Chile, 1993.

"Audience level measuring study of radio and reading level of newspapers and magazines", Search Marketing S.A., Santiago, Chile, 1993.

Asociacion de Radiodifusores de Chile (ARCHI).

Colombia

Area	1,138,910 km^2
Population (1992)	34,296,941
Population growth rate (1992)	1.9%
GDP	US$ 45 billion
GDP/per capita	US$ 1,300
Real growth rate (1991)	3.7%
Capital	Bogota

Population Breakdown

By Sex
Male 50%
Female................................. 50%

By Age Group
Children...............................29%
Teens 13%
Adults...................................58%

By Socio-Economic Status
A..2%
B...6%
C..55%
D..37%

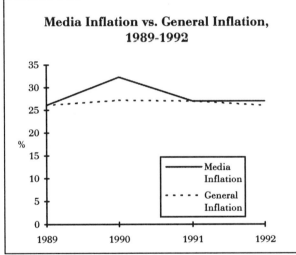

Media Inflation vs. General Inflation, 1989-1992

Legend:
— Media Inflation
···· General Inflation

Number of Households	5,185,807

Ownership of household durables
Car................................ 40%
Phone........................... N/A
Washers........................ 33%
(purchasing power equivalent)

GNP distribution by industry
Agriculture................... 25%
Industry 35%
Services 40%

Exchange rates (US$ to local currency)
1991 .... 0.0001665
1992 .... 0.0001459

Source: DANE-Republica Bank and Leo Burnett Research

National Holidays

Holiday	1993 Date
New Year's	January 1
Epiphany	January 11
St. Joseph's Day	March 22
Holy Week	April 8-9 (Thur-Fri)
Labor Day	May 1
Ascension Day	May 24
Corpus Christi	June 14
Sacred Heart	June 21
St. Peter and St. Paul's Day	July 5
National Independence Day	July 20
Boyaca's Battle	August 7
Virgin Mary's	August 16

Holiday	1993 Date
Christopher Columbus Day	October 18
All Saint's Day	November 1
Cartagena's Independence	November 15
Immaculate Conception	December 8
Christmas Day	December 25

School Holidays

Holiday	1993 Date
Calendar "A"	November - February
Calendar "B"	May - August
Calendar "C"	December-January/June-July

Major Influences and Trends

Political and economic factors did not have a marked affect on Colombia's media scene in 1992. All TV stations are still government owned and operated. Tough production laws limit foreign influence. A majority of the commercial production must be done by Colombians or in Colombia specifically. There has been an overall increase in advertising spending due to an economic upturn. New magazines have emerged in the market although their circulations are low.

Spending Analysis

National advertising spending by medium
based on appropriate year's exchange rate

	1989 US$ MM	1990 US$ MM	1991 US$ MM	1992 US$ MM
TV	128.0	290.6	297.8	445.8
Radio	33.6	93.6	130.0	187.6
Newspaper	35.7	78.8	86.7	106.2
Magazine	12.5	29.6	27.0	35.7
Total	**209.8**	**492.6**	**541.5**	**775.3**

Source: Infoanalisis Colombia, Dec. 1992

Proportionate spending among media 1991-92

1991: Radio 24%, Magazine 5%, Newspaper 16%, TV 55%

1992: Radio 21%, Magazine 5%, Newspaper 14%, TV 60%

Source: Infoanalisis Colombia, Dec. 1992

Media Buying

- Agencies as well as clients negotiate with the media.
- TV costs are negotiable.
- Programmers are responsible for selling commercial time on the networks.
- Newspapers and magazines publish standard rates and only traditional agency discounts are applied.
- Radio offers great possibilities for negotiation, although 70% of radio inventory is controlled by two large monopolies.
- Buying services do not exist.
- Direct advertiser negotiations represent 40% of the market total.

Top Advertisers (1992 Spending)

By Company

Parent Company	Product Categories	US$ MM
Colgate	Fab/Powder Detergent	19.4
Inextra	Inextra/Powder Detergent	14.4
Postobon	Pepsi/Soft Drink	13.0
Cogra Lever	Sunsilk/Shampoo	11.4
Nestle	La Lechera/Milk	7.7
Bavaria	Bararia/Beer	7.0
Coca-Cola	Coca-Cola/Soft Drink	6.7
Cia Nal de Chocolates	Sello Rojo/Instant Coffee	4.9
Varela	Juno/Soap	4.1
Cicolac	Klim/Powder Milk	4.1

Source: Infoanalisis

By Product

Product Category	Advertiser	US$ MM
Fab/Powder Detergent	Colgate	7.3
Coca-Cola/Soft Drink	Coca-Cola	6.4
Lot Instantanea/Lottery	Wintech	3.1
Aguila Roja/Coffee	Aguila Roja	2.5
Klim/Powder Milk	Cicolac	2.4
Pert Plus/Shampoo	Inextra	2.3
Colgate/Tooth Paste	Colgate	1.8
Camay/Soap	Inextra	1.6
Pony Malta/Soft Drink	Bavaria	1.5
Aguila/Beer	Bavaria	1.4

Source: Infoanalisis

Television

TV HH Penetration				Adult Reach (ABC, 20-49)	
1989	*1990*	*1991*	*1992*	at 250 GRPs	40%
70%	70%	70%	70%	at 500 GRPs	65%
3,412	3,486	3,629	4,303	at 1000 GRPs	88%

Sources: (HH) Leo Burnett estimate; (Reach) A. C. Nielsen

Opportunities

Networks	Number of Stations	Ownership	Station Profile	Commercial Minutes/Hour	Coverage	Broadcast Hours (Sign-On/Off)
Channel 1	1	Government	General	10	90%	10:00-14:30; 16:00-00:10, WK08:00-00:00
Channel A	1	Government	General	10	90%	10:00-14:00, 16:00-00:00, WK08:00-00:00
Channel 3	1	Government	Cultural		30%	17:00-00:00, WK14:30-23:00
Regional Channels						
Telecaribe	1	Government	General	10	30%	12:00-00:00, WK12:00-24:00
Telepacifico	1	Government	General	10	30%	12:00-00:00, WK12:00-24:00
Teleantioquia	1	Government	General	10	30%	12:00-00:00, WK12:00-24:00
Telecafe	1	Government	General	10	30%	12:00-00:00, WK12:00-24:00

Source: Leo Burnett

Costs

Prime Time TV Costs for :30 in US$			
1989	*1990*	*1991*	*1992*
1,400	2,600	2,250	2,807

Television Cost Changes Between Years
'88 — '89 — '90 — '91 — '92
30% 35% 20% 14%

Source (:30 costs and cost changes): Leo Burnett

Audiences/CPM's

Average Cost, Audience, and CPM's by Daypart
(Top 3 Stations, :30, national audience, Target=Persons 18+)

Hours	Morning 08:00-12:00	Daytime 12:00-19:00	Prime Time 19:00-22:30	Late Night 22:30-00:30	Weekend 08:00-00:30	Children 08:00-00:30
Station: Channel 1						
US$	913	1,000	2,813	750	1,906	913
Avg. Aud. (000)	1,550	1,880	5,820	580	1,940	1,747
CPM	0.9	0.9	0.8	1.3	1.3	0.9
Station: Channel A						
US$	1,750	3,125	2,800	763	2,625	1,750
Avg. Aud. (000)	1,550	1,880	5,820	580	1,940	1,747
CPM	2.5	2.5	0.8	1.3	1.3	1.0

Audiences/Rating by Daypart

Daypart	Hours	Household				Adult		
		Universe (000)	Hut Levels	Household Rating	Impressions (000)	Universe (000)	Adult Rating	Impressions (000)
Morning	08:00-12:00	5,185	40	18	933	19,790	10	1,979
Daytime	12:00-19:00	5,185	55	30	1,556	19,790	9	1,780
Primetime	19:00-22:30	5,185	63	32	1,659	19,790	20	3,958
Late Night	22:30-00:30	5,185	8	3	156	19,790	8	1,583
Weekend	08:00-00:30	5,185	40	20	1,037	19,790	17	3,364
Children's	08:00-00:30	5,185	30	16	830	9,980	14	1,397

Scheduling/Regional/Languages

- Spanish is the only language used in all programming and commercials.
- The most common commercial lengths are :10, :15, :20, :40, :45, :50, and :60.
- Commercials are aired throughout the day for 10 minutes/hour; 4 minutes at the beginning and 3 minutes at the end of programs.
- Both national and regional ad placement is available. About 17% of all commercials are aired regionally, where the cost is 35% that of national time. *(Source: Leo Burnett)*

Network	Hours
Telecaribe	All regional networks air programming during the following hours: M-F 10:00-14:30, 16:00-00:10, and 08:00-00:00.
Telepacifico	
Tele Antioquia	
Telecafe	N/A

Children's Advertising

All adult programming accepts advertising targeted at children.

ADULT PROGRAMMING				Kids'	
Station	Hours	Days	Universe (000)	Ratings	Impressions (000)
Ch. 1 & A	16:00-19:00	M-F	9,980	16	1,597
Ch. 1 & A	08:00-12:00	Sat-Sun	9,980	14	1,397

Radio

- In Colombia there are 660 radio stations; 545 of them are commercial and 55 are located in the main city.
- About 36% of the automobiles have radios.
- The broadcast language is Spanish.
- Regional placement is available and no premiums are paid for local broadcasting.

Radio Cost Changes Between Years

'88 — 26% — '89 — 30% — '90 — 35% — '91 — 20% — '92

- The most popular program types are News and Sports. Prime/Peak times are 06:00-09:00 and 18:00-19:00.
- Available commercial lengths are :05, :10, :15, :20, :30, :40, 45, and :60.

Ratings

Daypart	Adult Rating	Adult (000)
06:00-09:00	4.3	559
12:00-14:00	4.0	520
18:00-19:00	3.0	390

Source (All radio data): Ministerio Comunicaciones

Daypart Costs/CPMs

Daypart	Local Time	Avg. Cost :30 US$	Audience (000)	CPM (US$)
Prime Time	06:00-10:00	625	221.5	2.81
Daytime	10:00-18:00	326	119.9	2.71
Late Night	18:00-24:00	305	91.8	3.31

Cable

- Cable is available only in the main cities (Bogota, Medellin, Cali and Barranquilla)
- The penetration level is estimated at 4%, representing about 207,400 households.

Cable HH Penetration		
1989	1990	1991
1.7%	1.8%	1.9%

- There are 10 cable channels (all are currently non-commercial) and the cable system is privately owned.
- Cable in Colombia does not accept advertising. Cable reach is limited to upper income level households in a few cities.
- Spanish is the primary broadcast language, English is secondary.

Cities with Cable Access	HH Circulation (000)
Bogota	118.2
Medellin	33.2
Cali	30.0
Barranquilla	26.9

Cable Networks

Ch. 44 Sports	Ch. 52 TNT Classic Movies	Ch. 60 HBO Movies
Ch. 48 International	Ch. 56 News	Ch. 62 Family Programming

Source (All cable data): DANE

Satellite

- Satellite is still in the developmental stages. Most homes with satellite currently receive U.S. satellite networks with U.S. advertising. It is not yet possible to purchase air time locally.
- The satellite penetration level is 16% which represents 829,600 households.
- There are 15 channels (all non-commercial).

Source: DANE

Satellite Channel	Country of Origin	Language	Programming
Galaxy	USA	English and Spanish	Movies, Sports, News, Soap operas and News-movies
Disney-E	USA	English	Family programming
Showtime-E	USA	English	Movies
ESPN	USA	English	Sports
TMC-E	USA	English	Movies
Cinemax	USA	English	Movies
Galavision		English	General
HBO-E	USA	English	Movies
Discovery	USA	English	Educational
CNN	USA	English	News

Source: TV-Orbita Magazine

Video Cassettes

There are 357,700 Colombian households currently using video cassette recorders (VCRs)—which represents 8% of TV households. *(Source:DANE)*

Cinema

- There are 380 cinemas in Colombia, all offering commercial time.

- Commercial lengths available include :15, :20, :30, :40, :60, :90 with the average cost of a :60 spot at one theater/one time being US$ 360.

Source (All cinema data): Leo Burnett

Cinema Cost Changes Between Years

'88   '89   '90   '91   '92

20%   20%   20%   20%

- Over 4 weeks the average reach is 98,000 people for all cinemas.

Newspapers

- Colombia has 2 national daily newspapers with a combined circulation of 510,200
- The literacy rate in English is less than 2%.

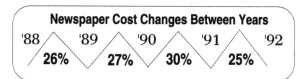

Daily Newspaper	Market	Size	Circulation (000)	Avg. Daily Aud. (000)	1 page/B&W Cost (US$)	Accept Color?
El Tiempo	National	Broadsheet	256.4	7,949	8,450	Yes
El Espectador	National	Broadsheet	206.8	641	8,275	Yes
La Prensa	National	Tabloid	27.5	85	1,407	Yes
Nuevo Siglo	National	Broadsheet	28.0	87	5,590	Yes
La Republica	National	Broadsheet	12.1	38	5,962	Yes
El Colombiano	Antioquia	Broadsheet	93.8	291	5,051	Yes
El Pais	Valle	Broadsheet	84.0	261	4,550	Yes
El Heraldo	Atlantico	Broadsheet	72.0	224	4,840	Yes

Source (All newspaper data): Leo Burnett and newspapers themselves

Magazines

There are 32 consumer magazines and 96 trade and technical magazines published in Colombia.

Magazine	Type	Frequency	Circ. (000)	Audited?	Avg. Issue Aud. (000)	1 page 4/C Cost (US$)
Cromos	Entertainment	Weekly	50	No	250	1,923
Selecciomes	Entertainment	Weekly	85	No	595	1,947
Semana	Business	Weekly	120	Yes	720	2,876
Vanidades	Women's	Bi-weekly	54	No	162	2,813
Buenhogar	Women's	Bi-weekly	48	No	144	2,382

Source (All magazine data): Leo Burnett and magazines themselves

Outdoor/Transit

Billboard

Sites available .... 1,900 to 3,100
Lead Time to reserve .... 6 weeks

Costs

Average, 1 billboard/month (in 4 main cities only)
12 x 4 m	....	US$ 633
16 x 4 m	....	US$ 785
18 x 5 m	....	US$ 1,011

Billboard Cost Changes Between Years

'88 — 25% — '89 — 23% — '90 — 27% — '91 — 28% — '92

Transit

Boards available
.... 4,000+

Costs

Average, 1 board/month:
.... US$ 96

Transit Cost Changes Between Years

'88 — 20% — '89 — 20% — '90 — 20% — '91 — 20% — '92

Sizes

8 m x 3 m, 12 m x 4 m

Sizes

2.50 m x 0.50 m, 1.00 m x 0.70 m

Source (All outdoor/transit data): Leo Burnett

Direct Marketing

The direct marketing scene has not even begun to develop in Colombia. Carvaja is the only company beginning to provide lists and there are no direct marketing associations.

Non-Traditional Media

There are video monitors that air movies, music videos, etc. on cross-country buses and public transit buses.

Research Sources

Medium Covered	Research Company	Information Provided
TV, Radio	A.C. Nielsen Calle 80 No. 5-81 Bogota Colombia	TV monthly audience by age, social class (in 6 regions and 15 cities) Reach and frequency TV, Radio checking (spot verification) Monthly competition report TV monthly audience (regional)
Radio	C.N.C. Diagonal 34 No. 5-89 Bogota PUBLIDATOS Calle 59 No. 5-02 Bogota	Radio audience Radio audience
TV, Radio Newspaper, Magazine	INFOANALISIS Cra. 13 A #78-58 Bogota	Monthly competitions

Television research currently available includes monthly diaries.

Advertising Regulations

By Product

Beverages/Alcohol
Advertising for beverages with an alcohol content of over 12% is allowed after 22:30, but it must include a health warning in both audio and video. Beer and wine advertising must be aired after 19:00, but there are no other restrictions.

Food/Restaurants
No promotions

Cigarettes
Cigarette advertising is allowed on TV only after 23:00 with a health warning in both audio and video.

Pharmaceuticals/Drugs
There are some pharmaceutical advertising restrictions on TV imposed by Instituto Nacional de Television (National TV Institute) and the Department of Public Health. Print advertising is allowed only in medical magazines.
Advertising for popular (over-the-counter) medicine is allowed on TV, but is under the control of the Department of Public Health.

Advertising Regulations, continued

Advertising To Children
No restrictions

Commercial Production
A 'mixed commercial' is understood to be the one made by Colombian producers with national and/or foreign models in which foreign production is limited to the post production services made by computer, laboratory, tricks or stock shots, as long as the latter does not exceed the third part of the total length of the commercial. Commercials produced simultaneously with stock shots and computers may not be authorized.

The mixing of sound with national as well as 'mixed commercials' must be done in the country and with Colombian personnel.

Regarding commercials filmed or recorded by Colombians abroad; all commercials must be submitted to Inravision in order to verify that they were made by Colombian personnel.

By Medium

Television
Cigarette advertising is allowed on TV only after 23:00 with a health warning in both audio and video. Advertising for beverages with an alcohol content of over 12% is allowed after 22:30, but it must include a health warning in both audio and video. Beer and wine advertising must be aired after 19:00, although there are no other restrictions.

Costa Rica

Area	51,100 km^2
Population (1992)	3,187,085
Population growth rate (1992)	2.4%
GDP	US$ 5.9 billion
GDP/per capita	US$ 1,900
Real growth rate (1991)	2.5%
Capital	San Jose

Population Breakdown

By Sex		*By Age Group*	
Male	*51%*	*Children*	*32%*
Female	*49%*	*Teens*	*15%*
		Adults	*53%*

Source:Oficina Nacional de Censos y Estad isticas, San Jose, Costa Rica, July 1993.

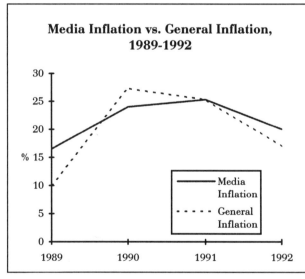

Media Inflation vs. General Inflation, 1989-1992

Number of Households	673,882

Ownership of household durables
- Car .... N/A
- Phone .... N/A
- Washers .... N/A

(purchasing power equivalent)

GNP distribution by industry
- Agriculture 16%
- Industry 44%
- Services 40%

Exchange rates (US$ to local currency)
- 1991 .... 0.007313
- 1992 .... 0.007267

National Holidays

Holiday	1993 Date
New Year's Day	January 1
Labor Day	May 1
Independence Day	September 15
Thursday-Friday Holy Week	March-April
Christmas	December 25

School Holidays

Holiday	1993 Date
New Year's Day	January 1
San Jose Day	March 19
Thursday-Friday Holy Week	March-April
Juan Santamaria	April 11
Labor Day	May 1
Guanacaste Join to C.R.	July 25
Los Angeles Virgin	August 2
Mother's Day	August 15
Independence Day	September 15
Columbus Day	October 12
Christmas	December 25

Major Influences and Trends

Improved technology is now reaching Costa Rica, allowing local TV networks to receive live programming like the World Cup and the OTIS Music Awards from other countries' off satellite feeds, instead of programming received with three-month delays.

Magazines are becoming very influential as an advertising medium, although still in the infancy stage. Newspaper advertising is still the primary print vehicle in Costa Rica.

Spending Analysis

National advertising spending by medium
based on appropriate year's exchange rate

	1989 US$ MM	1990 US$ MM	1991 US$ MM	1992 US$ MM
TV	34.4	32.8	32.8	53.8
Radio	5.2	9.1	9.1	12.1
Newspaper	22.9	23.4	21.0	27.4
Magazine	2.0	2.7	2.5	3.7
Total	**64.5**	**68.0**	**65.4**	**97.0**

Source: Gerente General, J. Francisco Correa, Servicios Publicitarios, Guadalupe, Costa Rica, July, 1993.

Media Buying

The broadcasters are very open for negotiations. Television and magazines are more rigorous and there are few newspaper facilities.
Negotiations can be done directly by the client, by agency, or both.

In Costa Rica, buying services do not exist.

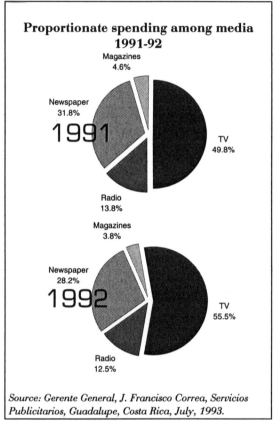

Proportionate spending among media 1991-92

1991
Magazines 4.6%
Newspaper 31.8%
TV 49.8%
Radio 13.8%

1992
Magazines 3.8%
Newspaper 28.2%
TV 55.5%
Radio 12.5%

Source: Gerente General, J. Francisco Correa, Servicios Publicitarios, Guadalupe, Costa Rica, July, 1993.

Top Advertisers/1992 Total Spending

By Company

Parent Company	Product Categories	US$ MM
Republic Tobacco	Cigarettes	1.79
Colgate	Home Products	1.76
Demasa	Snacks, Corn Products	1.65
Dos Pinos	Milk Derivates	1.47
Cerveceria C.R.	Beer	1.25
Tabacalera C.R.	Cigarettes	1.18
Lasca	Airlines	1.02
Cikora	Local Stores	0.96
Perifericos	Supermarket	0.94
La Nacion	Newspapers	0.94

Source: Gerente General, J. Francisco Correa, Servicios Publicitarios, Guadalupe, Costa Rica, July, 1993.

By Product

Product Category	Advertiser	US$ MM
Supermarket	Perifericos	0.540
Airlines	Lacsa	0.477
Department Stores	El Globo	0.438
Paint	Kativo (Protecto)	0.402
Beer	Cerveceria C.R. (Imperial)	0.395
Paint	Pintica (Glidden)	0.381
Newspaper	La Republica	0.356
Department Stores	La Gloria	0.351
Detergent	Irex	0.351
Corn Meal	Demasa (Masarica)	0.335

Source: Gerente General, J. Francisco Correa, Servicios Publicitarios, Guadalupe, Costa Rica, July, 1993.

Television

- Costa Rica has 12 television networks, 2 of which are government-run.
- The UHF channels are beginning to become better known; 6 UHF channels currently exist.

TV HH Penetration			Adult Reach	
1990	*1991*	*1992*	at 250 GRPs	60%
86%	86%	88%	at 500 GRPs	80%
550.1	550.1	599.8	at 1000 GRPs	90%

Opportunities

Network	Number of Stations	Ownership	Station Profile	Commercial Minutes/Hour	Coverage	Broadcast Hours (Sign-On/Off)
Canal 2	1	Brenes & Coll (Private)	General	11	88%	06:00-24:00
Canal 4	1	A. Vargas (Private)	General	11	90%	09:00-24:00
Canal 6	1	M. Sotela (Private)	General	11	90%	09:00-24:00
Canal 7	1	O. Picado (Private)	General	11	95%	06:00-24:00
Canal 9	1	A. Vargas (Private)	General	11	90%	17:00-24:00
Canal 11	1	O. Picado (Private)	General	11	60%	15:00-24:00
Canal 13	1	Government	General	11	95%	13:00-24:00
Canal 15	1	University of Costa Rica (Government)	Educational	N/A	40%	N/A
Canal 19	1	Private	General	11	60%	12:00-24:00

Costs

Prime Time TV Costs for :30 in US$			
1989	*1990*	*1991*	*1992*
147	171	208	257

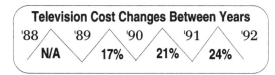

Television Cost Changes Between Years
'88 / N/A / '89 / 17% / '90 / 21% / '91 / 24% / '92

Audiences/CPM's

Average Cost, Audience, and CPMs by Daypart
(Top 3 Stations, :30, national audience, Target=Households)

Hours	Morning 06:00-12:00	Daytime 12:00-18:00	Prime Time 18:00-21:00	Late Night 21:00-Sign Off	Weekend All Day	Children 14:00-18:00
Station: 7						
US$	83	83	383	307	257	83
Avg. Aud. (000)	65.2	109.3	150.9	54.8	101.7	27.2
CPM	1.27	0.76	2.54	5.6	2.52	3.05
Station: 6						
US$	80	80	366	264	237	80
Avg. Aud. (000)	40.4	72.8	109.6	47.3	81.2	33.0
CPM	1.98	1.10	3.34	5.58	2.91	2.42
Station: 2						
US$	72	94	307	94	158	72
Avg. Aud. (000)	30.1	18.8	27.3	29.4	28.3	1.9
CPM	2.32	5	11.24	3.20	5.58	37.9

Audiences/Rating by Daypart (Target=Households)

Daypart	Hours	Household				Adult		
		Universe (000)	Hut Levels	Household Rating	Impressions (000)	Universe (000)	Adult Rating	Impressions (000)
Morning	06:00-12:00	212	N/A	N/A	N/A	615	2.2	13.53
Daytime	12:00-18:00	212	N/A	N/A	N/A	615	3.0	18.45
Primetime	18:00-21:00	212	N/A	N/A	N/A	615	5.5	33.83
Late Night	21:00-Sign-Off	212	N/A	N/A	N/A	615	3.4	20.91
Weekend	N/A	212	N/A	N/A	N/A	615	3.7	22.76
Children's	14:00-20:00	212	N/A	N/A	N/A	615	3.8	23.37

Scheduling/Regional/Languages

Language	Programming		Commercials
Primary Language	Spanish	95%	Spanish
Secondary Language	English	5%	English

- The most common commercial length (75%) is :30; other available lengths are :15, :20, :40, :45, and :60.
- Commercials are aired throughout the day, at the beginning and within programs.

- There are no regional buying options, but some channels' coverage (i.e., Ch 11 and Ch 19) is primarily limited to the metropolitan area. Only 3% of all advertising is not planned nationally.

Network	Region	Hours
Channel 11	Metropolitan	15:00-23:00
Channel 19	Metropolitan	12:00-24:00

Children's Advertising

ADULT PROGRAMMING				Kids'	
Station	*Hours*	*Days*	*Universe (000)*	*Ratings*	*Impressions (000)*
Canal 2	18:00-20:00	M-Sun	182	2.8	5.1
Canal 4	18:00-20:00	M-Sun	182	0.6	1.1
Canal 6	18:00-20:00	M-Sun	182	14.9	27.2
Canal 7	18:00-20:00	M-Sun	182	18.3	33.4

CHILDREN'S PROGRAMMING				Kids'	
Station	*Hours*	*Days*	*Universe (000)*	*Ratings*	*Impressions (000)*
Canal 6	14:00-18:00	M-Sun	182	12.9	23.5
Canal 7	14:00-18:00	M-Sun	182	15.1	27.6

Source (All television data): Gerente General, J. Francisco Correa, Servicios Publicitarios, Guadalupe, Costa Rica, July, 1993.

Radio

- There are 71 radio stations, 59 of which are commercial, 47 commercial and 4 non-commercial stations are in San Jose.
- 95%, or 640,000 households have radios.
- Local advertising is possible; there is no premium.
- Spanish is the primary language used in radio broadcasting. English is also used.
- The most popular program types are La Patada (comedy) and Deportes (sports).
- Standard commercial lengths are :15, :30 and :60.

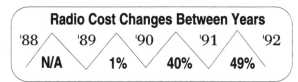

Radio Cost Changes Between Years

'88	'89	'90	'91	'92
N/A	1%	40%	49%	

- Primetime for radio is 06:00-11:00.

Daypart Costs/CPMs (in Local Currency)

Daypart	Local Time	Avg. Cost :30 US$	Avg. Rating	CPM (US$)
Prime Time	06:00-10:00	607	7.9	76.84
Daytime	10:00-18:00	607	4.9	123.88
Late Night	18:00-20:00	607	2.7	224.81

Source (All radio data): Gerente General, J. Francisco Correa, Servicios Publicitarios, Guadalupe, Costa Rica, July, 1993.

Cable

Overview

- Costa Rica has two cable systems: Cabletica, which is currently without open channels for commercials, and Cable Color, which has six channels that accept advertising.
- There are a total of 49 privately owned cable channels; of which only 4 are commercial.
- The primary broadcasting language is Spanish; English is secondary.

Trends/Outlook

- Cable television's audience is more upscale than TV's upper middle class audience. Therefore, it does not represent important competition for TV.
- Cable television is growing among the upper and middle classes. Within the next five years, 42,500 households are expected to receive cable.
- Cable networks are sold locally in package deals.

Cable HH Penetration			
1989	*1990*	*1991*	*1992*
1.9%	2.1%	3.9%	3.9%
13,000	14,000	26,000	26,500

Top Cable Channels	*Cost US$*	*Commercial Min/Hr*
CNN	33	13
ESPN	33	13
TNT	33	2
Cable TV Guide	33	11

Cable Networks	*HH Circulation (000)*	*Programming*
Cable Color	13,500	Sports, News, Movies
Super Canal	5,000	Sports, News
Cable Tica	8,000	Sports, News, Movies

Cable Networks	*Programming*	*Cable Networks*	*Programming*
Univision	U.S. Spanish-language programs	WOR-New York	General U.S. programming
Cable TV Guide	Informative Guide	World Net - Channel 41	News, politics
Multivisoin	Family programming	CNBC	Financial News
CNN Headline News	News	WPIX-New York	General U.S. programming
Telecentro	Family programming, movies	Television Espanola	Programs from Spain
Teletica	Family programming, movies	USA Network	General U.S. programming
CNN Telemundo	News	KTLA-Los Angeles	General U.S. programming
WGN Chicago	General U.S. programming	NBC Network	General U.S. programming
SUR	Programming from Peru	TVA Music Channel	Music videos
Canal II	Sports	A&E-Arts & Entertainment	Cultural, general U.S.
ESPN International	Sports (English)	ABC Network	General U.S. programming
SINART	Educational, cultural	CBS Network	General U. S. programming
HBO-Ole TV	Movies 24 hours	Deutsche Welle TV	Programming from Germany
TNT English	Movies 24 hours (English)	Rai Italiano	Programming from Italy
Cine Canal	Movies 24 hours	Channel 29	Movies, sitcom, sports, music
TNT Spanish	Movies 24 hours (Spanish)	Channel 38 Stereo	Movies, music
TV5 Frances	French programming	Channel 19	Movies
Cartoon Channel	Children's programming	TBN-Trinity Broadcasting	Religious, family programming
CNN News	News	Channel 8 - NBC News	International News

Source (All cable data): Cable Color, Pavas, Costa Rica, July, 1993.

Satellite

See Major Trends and Cable sections for information about satellite reception in Costa Rica.

Cinema

- There are 71 cinemas in Costa Rica, all of which offer commercial time.
- Based on 13 theaters, a commercial will reach about 975,000 people per month.

Source (All cinema data): Publitesis, San Jose, Costa Rica, July, 1993.

Newspapers

There are 4 national daily newspapers which accept advertising with a combined circulation of 318,333.

Video Cassettes

No data is available about video cassette recorder usage in Costa Rica.

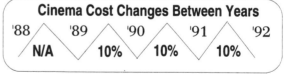

Cinema Cost Changes Between Years

'88	'89	'90	'91	'92
N/A	10%	10%	10%	

- An average cost for a 4-week schedule at 13 theaters is about US$ 4,355.
- Available commercial lengths include :30 and :60.

Newspaper Cost Changes Between Years

'88	'89	'90	'91	'92
N/A	23-27%	20%	22%	

Daily Newspaper	Market	Size	Circulation (000)	Avg. Daily Aud. (000)	1 page/B&W Cost (US$)	Accept Color?
La Nacion	National	Tabloid	103	492	857	Yes
La Republica	National	Tabloid	65	281	607	Yes
La Prensa Libre	National	Tabloid	60	247	500	Yes
El Extra	National	Tabloid	90	N/A	569	Yes

Source (All newspaper data): Gerente General, J. Francisco Correa, Servicios Publicitarios, Guadalupe, Costa Rica, July, 1993.

Magazines

There are 29 consumer magazines and 11 trade and technical magazines in Costa Rica.

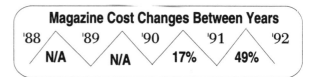

Magazine	Type	Frequency	Circ. (000)	Audited?	Avg. Issue Aud. (000)	1 page 4/C Cost (US$)
Perfil	Women's	15 Days	21	No	105	769
Rumbo	News	8 Days	6	No	30	505
Tambor	Children's	15 Days	14	No	86	442
Cable Guia	TV Guide	Monthly	N/A	N/A	N/A	N/A
La Industria	Economy	Trimestral	N/A	N/A	N/A	N/A
Actualidad Economica	Economy	Monthly	8	Yes	32	442
Panorama	News	8 Days	7	Yes	42	560
Comercio Exterior	Economy	Bimonthly	N/A	N/A	N/A	N/A

Source (All magazine data): Gerente General, J. Francisco Correa, Servicios Publicitarios, Guadalupe, Costa Rica, July, 1993.

Outdoor/Transit

Billboard

Sites available......................25-30 per month
Lead Time to reserve ....N/A
Exposure 50-60%

Costs

Average, 1 billboard/month
9 m x 3 m   ....US$ 161

Billboard Cost Changes Between Years

'88	'89	'90	'91	'92
20%	25%	20%	20%	

Sizes

Billboards   9 m x 3 m

Transit

Boards available............................... 45
  (32 side panels and 13 back panels)
Exposure (metro)...............................65%

Costs

Average, 1 board/month
Buses   ....US$ 597

Transit Board Cost Changes Between Years

'88	'89	'90	'91	'92
15%	30%	15%	N/A	

Sizes

Buses: Side panels   70 m x 4.5 m
         Back panels   60 m x 1.5 m

Outdoor boards must be located 200 meters away from the central line of the road, and 100 meters away from the main roads and railroad intersections.

Source (All Outdoor/transit data): Publicidad Original Limitada Tibas, Costa Rica, July, 1993.

Direct Marketing

The trend is for advertisers to use direct marketing services directly, instead of through their advertising agency.

List Broker	Information Provided
Credomatic	Names, income, address, age, etc. (all information provided on credit card applications)

Top Telemarketing Company
Garnier Directo

Non-Traditional Media

There is no information available on the use of non-traditional media in Costa Rica.

Research Sources

Medium Covered	Research Company	Information Provided
TV	Consejo Nacional de la Publicidad	TV ratings
Radio	Camara Nacional de Radio	Radio rating

TV Research is available monthly from TV Recall/Coincidental Radio, and quarterly from the latter.

Advertising Regulations

By Product

Beverages/Alcohol
TV advertising is only permitted after 19:00. Alcohol advertising is not permitted on Sundays or holidays, and it is not allowed in sports events, or in teen, children, sporting and cultural programming.
Cigarettes
It is the same as beverages and alcohol. However, cigarette advertising can't be aired before 20:00.
Pharmaceuticals/Drugs
Efficacy claims in advertising are regulated. Wording cannot be misleading or imply false remedies. Advertising is limited to non-prescription medicine.
Commercial Production
Only Central American talent is permitted for the audio/voice-overs in commercials on air.

By Medium

Television
Commercials may not go on air without their respective documents for radio control permission.
Print
Newspapers cannot accept ads that are 5 or 7 columns wide.
Outdoor
Transit boards have to be located 200 meters away from the central line of the road, and 100 meters away from the main roads and railroad intersections.

Dominican Republic

Area	48,730 km^2
Population (1992)	7,515,892
Population growth rate (1992)	1.9%
GDP	US$ 7 billion
GDP/per capita	US$ 950
Real growth rate (1991)	2%
Capital	Santo Domingo

Population Breakdown

By Sex		*By Age Group*		*By Socio-Economic Status*	
Male	50.8%	Children, 0-14	38.0%	A	3.3%
Female	49.2%	Teens, 15-19	11.0%	B	5.0%
		Adults, 20-40+	51.0%	C	28.9%
				D	62.8%

Source: Oficina Nacional de Estadistica

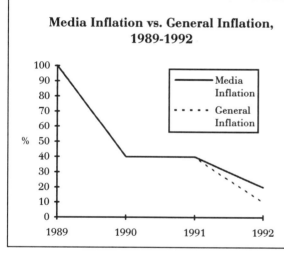

Media Inflation vs. General Inflation, 1989-1992

Number of Households	1,330,927

Ownership of household durables

Car	N/A
Phone	N/A
Washers	N/A

(purchasing power equivalent)

GNP distribution by industry

Agriculture	15.0%
Industry	25.0%
Services	60.5%

Exchange rates (US$ to local currency)

1991	0.10411188
1992	0.07787462

National Holidays

Holiday	1993 Date
New Year's	January 1
Reyes Magos Day (Three Kings Day)	January 6
Virgen Altagracia Day	January 21
Duarte Day	January 26
Independence Day	February 27
Saint's Friday (Good Friday)	April 17
Labor Day	May 1
Corpus Christi	June 10
Restoration	August 16
Virgen Mercedes Day	September 24
Race Day/V Centenary	October 12
Christmas	December 25

School Holidays

Holiday	1993 Date
Summer Vacation	June 5 - September 1
Christmas Vacation	December 22 - January 9

Major Influences and Trends

Television is the primary medium in Santo Domingo. However, radio has been quite important over the last several years.

Spending Analysis

National advertising spending by medium
based on appropriate year's exchange rate

	1989 US$ MM	1990 US$ MM	1991 US$ MM	1992 US$ MM
TV	2,291.0	1,780.0	1,815.2	1,289.9
Radio	1,458.0	1,424.0	2,042.1	1,382.0
Newspaper	N/A	356.0	680.7	368.8
Outdoor	N/A	N/A	N/A	30.5
Total	**3,749.0**	**3,560.0**	**4,538.0**	**3,071.2**

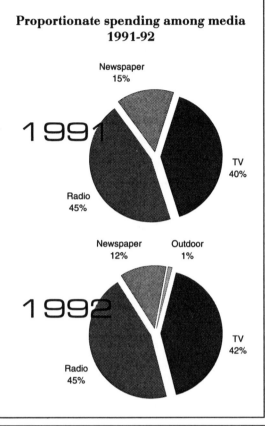

Proportionate spending among media 1991-92

1991: Newspaper 15%, TV 40%, Radio 45%

1992: Newspaper 12%, Outdoor 1%, TV 42%, Radio 45%

Media Buying

- All media pricing is negotiable.
- The agencies handle negotiations directly with the media.
- Upfront negotiations are conducted with all media on an annual basis.
- Buying services do not exist.

Top Advertisers (1992 Spending)

By Company

Parent Company	Product Categories	US$ MM
Bargelo	Rum	60.0
Cerveceria Nacional Dominicana	Beer	45.9
Leon Jimenes (Philip Morris)	Cigarettes	42.6
Brugal	Rum	35.8
Sociedad Industrial Dominicana	Cleaning and food products	35.2
Bermudez	Rum	33.7
Distribuidora Corripio (P&G)	Packaged goods	33.5
Colgate-Palmolive	Packaged goods	32.1
IGLO-Industries Cclados	Frozen Food	7.1
Grupo Refrigor	Drinks	6.9

Source: Centro de Informacion Computarizada

Television

Overview

Although television has remained quite stable over the last several years, stations are lobbying the government to authorize networks to expand into the interior provinces via local stations. If this is achieved, advertisers will be able to buy by zones. The broadcasting language is Spanish.

TV HH Penetration (in Santo Domingo)				Adult Reach	
1989	1990	1991	1992	at 250 GRPs	78%
36%	84.7%	84.7%	89.9%	at 500 GRPs	95%
280,000	362,700	362,700	364,500	at 1,000 GRPs	99%

Opportunities

Network	Channels	Ownership	Station Profile	Commercial Minutes/Hour	Coverage	Broadcast Hours (Sign-On/Off)
Teleantillas	2, 13	Private	General	22	90%	06:00-24:00
RTVD	4, 5, 12	State Owned	General	22	96%	08:00-24:00
Circuito Independencia	6	Private	General	22	96%	06:00-05:00
Rahintel	7, 11	Private	General	22	80%	06:00:24:00
7 Cibao	7	Private	General	Approx 22	(Santiago)	10:00-24:00
Color Vision	9, 11	Private	General	22	92%	06:00-01:00
Telesistema	11, 9	Private	General	22	90%	11:00-24:00
TV-13	13	Private	General	22	(Capital)	10:00-24:00

Source: Stations themselves

Costs

Prime Time TV Costs for :30 in US$			
1989	1990	1991	1992
N/A	248	296	340

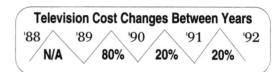

Television Cost Changes Between Years

'88	'89	'90	'91	'92
N/A	80%	20%	20%	

Audiences/CPM's

Average Cost, Audience, and CPM's by Daypart
(Top 3 Stations, :30, national audience, Target=Adults 20-40)

Hours	Morning 06:00-12:00	Daytime 12:00-18:00	Prime Time 19:00-23:00	Late Night 23:00-01:00	Weekend 12:00-20:00	Children 14:00-17:00
Station: Ch. 2 (Teleantillas)						
US$	140	200	340	200	280	104
Avg. Aud. (000)	22.5	77.5	167.5	40.0	30.0	10.0
CPM	6.22	2.58	2.02	5.00	9.33	10.4
Station: Ch. 9 (Color Vision)						
US$	128	264	320	344	320	240
Avg. Aud. (000)	17.5	132.5	90.0	75.0	217.5	187.5
CPM	7.31	1.99	3.55	4.58	1.47	1.28
Station: Ch. 11 (Telesistema)						
US$	N/A	208	352	280	224	104
Avg. Aud. (000)	N/A	185.0	165.0	25.0	27.5	85.0
CPM	N/A	1.12	2.13	11.2	8.14	1.22

Audiences/Rating by Daypart

Daypart	Hours	Household				Adult		
		Universe (000)	Hut Levels	Household Rating	Impressions (000)	Universe (000)	Adult Rating	Impressions (000)
Morning	06:00-12:00	664	106	2.7	17.9	466	4.8	22.5
Daytime	12:00-18:00	664	370	19.1	126.8	466	27.9	130.0
Primetime	19:00-23:00	664	339	17.5	119.3	466	25.2	117.5
Late Night	23:00-01:00	664	361	7.4	49.1	466	13.4	62.5
Weekend	12:00-20:00	664	408	12.4	82.3	466	21.5	100.0
Children's	14:00-17:00	664	71	18.3	121.5	198	37.9	75.9

Source: Market Probe

Scheduling/Regional/Languages

- The only language used in programming and commercials is Spanish.
- Commercials are aired throughout the day both at the beginning and end and within programs.
- Of all commercials sold, 80% are :30 and 20% are :20 and :15.

- Other lengths available are :10, :15, :40, :45 and :60.
- Opportunities for regional/local commercial buys exist only on Channel 7 in Santiago between 10:00 and 24:00; the cost is 30% that of a national buy for a :30 spot. Such buys account for 2% of commercial spending.

Children's Advertising

All adult programming accepts advertising targeted at children.

| CHILDREN'S PROGRAMMING | | | | Kids' | |
Station	Hours	Days	Universe (000)	Ratings	Impressions (000)
Ch. 2	16:00-16:30	M-F	1,025	1.2	12.3
Ch. 6	08:00-12:00	Sat	1,025	1.3	13.3
Ch. 7	14:00-15:00	M-F	1,025	1.7	17.4
Ch. 7	08:00-12:00	Sat	1,025	3.9	40.0
Ch. 7	08:00-12:00	Sun	1,025	5.3	54.3
Ch. 9	14:00-16:00	M-F	1,025	18.3	187.5
Ch. 9	08:00-12:00	Sat	1,025	6.3	64.6
Ch. 11	14:30-17:00	M-F	1,025	9.3	95.3

Source: Market Probe

Radio

- There are 255 commercial radio stations in the Dominican Republic, of which 65 are located in Santo Domingo.
- The primary broadcast language is Spanish; English is also used.
- Penetration levels are at 97% in households and 80% in automobiles.
- Commercial time is available in lengths of :10, :15, :20, :30, :45, and :60.

Ratings

Daypart	Adult Rating	Adult (000)
Prime Time	21.8	329.7
Daytime	9.9	203.6
Late Night	1.1	14.3

Source: Market Probe

Radio Cost Changes Between Years

'88	'89	'90	'91	'92
N/A	N/A	22%	32%	

Averages by Daypart (Target=Adults 20-40)

Daypart	Local Time	Avg. Cost :30 US$	Audience (000)	CPM (US$)
Prime Time	06:00-14:00	24	395.7	0.06
Daytime	14:00-19:00	24	227.4	0.10
Late Night	19:00-24:00	16	14.3	1.12

Cable

Cable HH Penetration		
1990	1991	1992
12%	12%	5%

- Overall cable penetration has decreased (from 12% to 5%) since international cable laws went into effect. Pirating of restricted channels, like the movie channels, has been nearly eliminated.
- Roughly 25,000 households have cable.
- There are 22 privately owned cable channels; 5 of them are commercial.

Top Cable Channels	Cost US$	Commercial Min/Hr
CNN	30	15
ESPN	30	15
MTV	30	15
USA Network	22	15
TCN-10 (Local)	18	20

- If the local cable operator, CODETEL, acquires the rights to restricted channels, subscription numbers may rise again.
- English is the primary broadcast language for cable. Spanish is the secondary language.

Satellite

There is no information regarding satellite reception in the Dominican Republic available.

Video Cassettes

Video cassettes are not an advertising medium in the Dominican Republic.

Cinema

- There are 95 cinemas in the Dominican Republic of which 95% offer commercial time.
- Commercial lengths available are :30, :60, and :90 and the average cost of a 4 week schedule is US$ 640.

- There will probably be a drop in both number of theaters and audiences due to increasing ticket prices.

Newspapers

There are 10 national daily newspapers in the Dominican Republic; all accept advertising. The combined circulation is 344,000.

Daily Newspaper	Market	Size	Circulation (000)	Avg. Daily Aud. (000)	1 page B&W Cost (US$)	Accept Color?
Listin Diario	National	Standard	63	194.3	1,840	Full Color
Hoy	National	Standard	48	102.3	1,480	Full Color
El Siglo	National	Standard	37	104.1	1,200	Full Color
El Caribe	National	Standard	28	21.5	920	Three Color
Nuevo Diario	National	Tabloid	15	60.0	500	Three Color
La Informacion	National	Standard	15	15.6	432	Full Color
El Sol	National	Tabloid	20	14.6	456	Three Color
El Nacional	National	Tabloid	58	154.0	800	Full Color
Ultima Hora	National	Tabloid	35	114.8	616	Full Color
La Noticia	National	Tabloid	20	38.4	456	Full Color

Source (All newspaper data): Publications themselves

Magazines

The number of consumer magazines in the Dominican Republic is not certain. There are 5 trade and technical magazines.

Magazine	Type	Frequency	Circ. (000)	Audited?	1 page 4/C Cost (US$)
Bohio	Tourist	Quarterly	20	No	960
La Cotica	Tourist - in 5 languages	Yearly	30	No	1,600
Tobogan	Children	Monthly	30	No	200
Ysabela	Variety	Monthly	20	No	450
Al Detalle	Business	Monthly	10	No	360
Dominican Business	Business/Economic	Monthly	15	No	640
Mundo de Las Negocias	Business	Monthly	20	No	480
Bannca	Banking	Monthly	20	No	420
Rio	Real Estate	Bi-monthly	15	No	360

Source: Publications themselves

Outdoor/Transit

Billboard	**Transit**
Sites available ....4,000 Exposure 20-60%	Exposure 60%

Costs
 	
Average, 1 billboard/month
   12 ft x 24 ft ....US$ 160
	Costs
	
	Average, 1 board/month
	   Buses ....N/A

Billboard Cost Changes Between Years

'88	'89	'90	'91	'92
	N/A	100%	60%	40%

Transit Board Cost Changes Between Years

'88	'89	'90	'91	'92
	N/A	100%	60%	40%

Sizes	**Sizes**
Billboards 12 ft x 24 ft	Transit Boards 3 ft x 9 ft

Direct Marketing

Direct Marketing is not a significant medium in the Dominican Republic.

Non-Traditional Media

Non-Traditional media are not yet used in the Dominican Republic.

Research Sources

There are no research companies, list brokers, telemarketing companies, or direct marketing associations in the Dominican Republic.

Advertising Regulations

By Product

Beverages/Alcohol
Alcohol advertising is not permitted during children's programs.
Cigarettes
See Beverages/Alcohol.

By Medium

Television
The maximum number of commercials per hour allowed is 15.
Outdoor
Outdoor sites must be located 40 meters away from highways.

Ecuador

Area	283,560 km²
Population (1992)	10,933,143
Population growth rate (1992)	2.2%
GDP	US$ 11.5 billion
GDP/per capita	US$ 1,070
Real growth rate (1991)	2.5%
Capital	Quito

Population Breakdown

By Sex		*By Age Group*		*By Socio-Economic Status*	
Male	*49.7%*	*Children*	*26.7%*	*A&B*	*25.0%*
Female	*50.3%*	*Teens*	*24.0%*	*C*	*15.2%*
		Adults	*49.3%*	*D*	*36.6%*
				E	*45.7%*

Source: Indice Estadistico/Ecuador, 1990, 1991

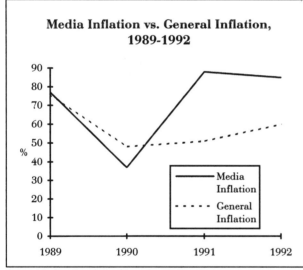

Media Inflation vs. General Inflation, 1989-1992

Number of Households	2,226,000

Ownership of household durables
- Car.............................37.8%
- Phone........................20.7%
- Washers.....................10.3%
  (purchasing power equivalent)

GNP distribution by industry
- Agriculture...................N/A
- Industry ....N/A
- Services ....N/A

Exchange rates (US$ to local currency)
- 1991 ....0.1100
- 1992 ....0.1850

Source: Indice Estadistica/Ecuador, 1990, 1991

National Holidays

Holiday	*1993 Date*
New Year's	January 1
Carnaval	March 2
Holy Friday	April 17
Labor Day	May 1
Independence Day	May 24/August 10
Simon Bolivar Birthday	July 24
Guayaquil Foundation Day	July 25
Guayaquil Independence Day	October 9
Columbus Day	October 12
All Souls Day	November 2
Cuenca Independence Day	November 3
Quito Foundation Day	December 6
Christmas	December 25

School Holidays

Holiday	*1993 Date*
Highland:	
Easter	April 13-17
Summer Vacations	July 15-October 15
Christmas	December 22-January 6
Coastal Area:	
End of School Year	December 15-March 15

Major Influences and Trends

- Total media spending in Ecuador breaks out as follows: TV (54.6%), Radio (8.7%), Newspapers/Magazines (29.7%), and Outdoor (6.8%).
- Clients and agencies are moving towards a more diverse media mix to achieve better cost efficiencies.

Spending Analysis

National advertising spending by medium
based on appropriate year's exchange rate

	1989 US$ MM	1990 US$ MM	1991 US$ MM	1992 US$ MM
TV	N/A	N/A	31,818	32,051
Cinema	N/A	N/A	144	102
Radio	N/A	N/A	4,548	5,128
Newspaper	N/A	N/A	15,454	15,384
Magazine	N/A	N/A	2,272	2,051
Outdoor	N/A	N/A	4,400	4,002
Total	N/A	N/A	**58,636**	**58,718**

Source: Teleamozonas (Local TV station, private)

Media Buying

Ad agencies handle media buying and negotiate directly with TV stations. A few clients handle their media buying, but this is very unusual.
Buying services do not exist.

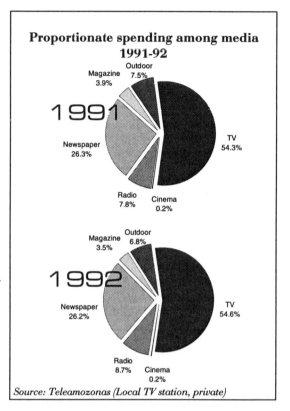

Proportionate spending among media 1991-92

1991: Magazine 3.9%, Outdoor 7.5%, TV 54.3%, Newspaper 26.3%, Radio 7.8%, Cinema 0.2%

1992: Magazine 3.5%, Outdoor 6.8%, TV 54.6%, Newspaper 26.2%, Radio 8.7%, Cinema 0.2%

Source: Teleamozonas (Local TV station, private)

Top Advertisers/1992 Spending

By Product

Product Category	US$ MM
Banking	4.1
Government	2.6
Soft Drinks	2.3
Lottery	1.6
Toothpaste	1.5

Product Category	US$ MM
Rum	1.4
Municipality	1.2
Beer	0.6
Oil (Cooking)	0.5

Source: Teleamozonas

Television

TV HH Penetration			
1989	*1990*	*1991*	*1992*
90.2%	91.2%	92.4%	93.4%

Source: Indice Estadistico, Ecuador, 1990, 1991

Overview

The market is controlled by five national TV stations that are both national and regional. They are Ecuavisa, Teleamazonas, Mabonas, Gamavision, Telecentro and Telesistemas.

Opportunities

	Number of Stations	Ownership	Station Profile	Commercial Minutes/Day	Coverage	Broadcast Hours (Sign-On/Off)
Ecuavisa	2	Private	Comm./Entertain./News	170	National	07:00-24:00
Teleamazonas	1	Private	Comm./Entertain./News	170	National	07:00-24:00
Gamavision	1	Private	Comm./Entertain./News	170	National	07:00-24:00
Telecentro	1	Private	Comm./Entertain./News	170	National	07:00-24:00
Telesistema	1	Private	Comm./Entertain./News	170	National	07:00-24:00
Teletrece	1	Private	Comm./Entertain./News	170	Regional	07:00-24:00
Teleandina (UHF)	1	Private	Comm./Entertain./News	170	Regional	07:00-24:00
C.E.R.	1	Private	Comm./Entertain./News	170	Regional	07:00-24:00
Manavision	1	Private	Comm./Entertain./News	170	Regional	07:00-24:00

Source: Indice Estadistico Ecuador, 1990, 1991

Costs

Prime Time TV Costs for :30 in US$				
	1989	1990	1991	1992
TVB	6,845	7,440	6,696	6,785
VTM	6,889	9,404	11,368	11,904

Source: Agency Information

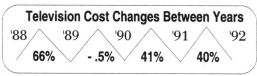

Television Cost Changes Between Years

'88	'89	'90	'91	'92
66%	-.5%	41%	40%	

Source: Agency Information

Audiences/CPM's

Average Cost, Audience, and CPM's by Daypart
(Top 3 Stations, :30, Target=national audience)

Hours:	Morning 11:00-17:00	Daytime 17:00-20:30	Prime Time 20:30-24:00	Late Night 24:00-2:00	Weekend	Children
Station: Ecuavisa						
US$	102.5	400	795	256.4	Same as Weekdays	N/A
Avg. Aud. (000)	257.8	783.5	363.3	45.8		N/A
CPM	0.4	0.5	2.19	5.6		N/A
Station: Telecentro						
US$	174.3	620.5	912.8	158.9	Same as Weekdays	N/A
Avg. Aud. (000)	78.2	241.5	245.4	70.4		N/A
CPM	2.2	2.56	3.7	2.25		N/A
Station: Teleamazonas						
US$	112.8	256.4	920.5	276.9		N/A
Avg. Aud. (000)	318.5	229.8	518.6	30.9		N/A
CPM	0.35	1.10	1.80	8.96		N/A

Source: Agency Information

Audiences/Rating by Daypart

Daypart	Hours	Household				Adult		
		Universe (000)	Hut Levels	Household Rating	Impressions (000)	Universe (000)	Adult Rating	Impressions (000)
Morning	11:00-17:00	2,079	10.2	3.2	66.5	5,032	2.4	120.7
Daytime	17:00-20:30	2,079	55.0	24.0	499	5,032	16.3	820.2
Primetime	20:30-24:00	2,079	50.5	22.0	457.4	5,032	12.0	603.8
Late Night	24:00-2:00	2,079	3.0	1.5	31	5,032	0.4	20.1

Source: Agency Information

Scheduling/Regional/Languages

- Spanish is the only language used in Ecuadorian TV broadcasting.
- About 70% of all commercials are :30; other lengths available are :20; :40 and :60.
- Commercials are aired throughout the day both at the beginning, end and within programs.

- Advertising may be targeted separately at the costal or highland regions at all hours.
- About 20% of all commercials are aired on a regional/local basis. The cost of local advertising is 30% and regional is 60% that of nationally aired time.

(Source: Agency Information)

Children's Advertising

For adult programming, the children's universe of 2,755,000 provides an average of 2,369 impressions, and an average rating of 8.6.

| CHILDREN'S PROGRAMMING | | | | Kids' | |
Station	Hours	Days	Universe (000)	Ratings	Impressions (000)
All	15:00-17:00	Mon.-Sat.	2,755	28.4	782.4

Source (Children's Advertising): Agency Information

Radio

- There are 312 radio stations in Ecuador, all but 10 of which are commercial. 80 stations are in Quito.
- Ninety-eight percent (of 2,181,000) households have radios. Automobile pentration is roughly 17.1%.
- Spanish is the only language used for radio broadcasting.
- The most popular program types are modern music and news.
- Commercial lengths available are :20, :30, :40 and :60.

Source (Radio): Indice Estadistico Ecuador, 1990, 1991.

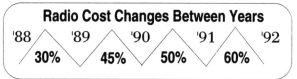

Radio Cost Changes Between Years

'88 '89 '90 '91 '92
30% 45% 50% 60%

- Radio advertising may be bought on a regional basis, without premium.

Rating

Daypart	Adult Rating	Adult (000)
14:00-15:00	1.3	13.2

Daypart Costs/CPMs (Target=Young Adults)

Daypart	Local Time	Avg. Cost :30 US$	Audience (000)	CPM
Prime Time	14:00-15:00	6.00	17	0.35

Cable

- Cable penetration is currently 0.7% of total households (approximately 16,000) and is limited to upper income households. However, in the next five years 25% of total households are expected to subscribe.
- Of the 33 privately owned cable channels that currently broadcast in Ecuador, only 3 are commercial and these are local cable channels.
- Most of the channels received via cable are U.S. channels. Only three cable channels provide local programming, which includes news, sports, and movies.

Source (Cable): Agency Information

- The primary broadcast language is English; Spanish, French and Portuguese are also used.
 The Cinemania movie channel has a circulation of 16,000 and offers 20 commercial spots.

Cable Networks	Programming
Cinemania	Movies
Cable Deportes	Sports
Cable Noticias	News
NBC	U.S. Programming
CBS	U.S. Programming
ABC	U.S. Programming
TNT	Movies
TLC	Educational

Satellite

Satellite is still in the developmental stages in Ecuador. *(Source: Agency Information)*

Video Cassettes

About 33.5% of TV households in Ecuador have video cassette recorders (VCRs). Pre-recorded tapes do not carry advertising. *(Source: Agency Information)*

Cinema

- Based on the 22 theaters registered in Quito, the potential reach over a four week period is 680,000.
- All cinemas offer commercial time in lengths of :30, :40 and :60.
- Very few TV spots are appropriate for cinema. There is a decrease in cinema usage as an advertising medium.

Source: Agency Information

Newspapers

Ecuador has 2 national daily papers that accept advertising. Their combined circulation is 200,000.

Daily Newspaper	Market	Circulation (000)	Avg. Daily Aud. (000)	1 page B&W Cost (US$)	Accept Color?
El Comercio	National	160	800	2,800	Yes
Universo	National	200	1,000	2,900	Yes
Telegrafo	National	55	275	764	Yes
Hoy	National	60	300	1,813	Yes
Manabita	Manabi	6	30	226	Yes
Mercurio	Cuenca	13	65	698	Yes

Source (Newspapers): Agency Information

Magazines

Magazine	Type	Frequency	Circ. (000)	Audited?	Avg. Issue Aud. (000)	1 page 4/C Cost (US$)
Vistazo	News/Social	2x/month	72	No	216	1,498
Estadio	Sports	Weekly	36	No	108	487
Hogar	Women's	Monthly	47	No	141	1,079
La Otra	News/Social	2x/month	50	No	150	887
Diners	News	Monthly	35	No	105	233
Elite	Social	Monthly	35	No	105	641
15 Dias	Politics	2x/month	25	No	75	902

Source: Agency Information

Outdoor/Transit

Billboard	Transit
Sites available ... .N/A Lead Time to reserve ....negotiated individually. Exposure 50-80%	Boards available ....N/A Exposure (metro) ....80% (in Quito)
Costs Average, 1 billboard/month 8 m x 4 m ....US$ 137	**Costs** Average, 1 board/month: (per sq. meter) ....US$ 4.00

Direct Marketing

Direct marketing is in a very early stage of development.

Non-Traditional Media

Non-traditional media is not used in Ecuador.

Research Sources

Medium Covered	Research Company	Information
TV, Radio	Cidem	TV and radio ratings
TV, Radio	IPSA	TV and radio ratings

Television research is currently available in two forms: monthly by diary, and daily by audio meters. The latter technique is in an early stage of development.

Advertising Regulations

By Product

Beverages/Alcohol
Alcohol advertising cannot be aired before 20:30.
Children or outstanding sports figures should not be used as models.
Outdoor ads cannot be placed near schools or stadiums.
Food/Restaurants
No restrictions.
Cigarettes
Same as alcohol.
Pharmaceuticals/Drugs
Advertising material needs to be approved by the Health Ministry.
Advertising To Children
No restrictions.
Commercial Production
No restrictions.

By Medium

Television is a self-regulated medium with a few restrictions on advertising against alcohol, cigarettes and pharmaceutical drugs.
There are no restrictions on Print, Outdoor, Cable, Direct Marketing or Non-traditional media.

El Salvador

Area	21,040 km^2
Population (1992)	5,574,279
Population growth rate (1992)	2.2%
GDP	US$ 5.5 billion
GDP/per capita	US$ 1,010
Real growth rate (1991)	3%
Capital	San Salvador

Population Breakdown

By Sex
Male 50%
Female 50%

By Age Group
Children, 0-10 .... 32%
Teens, 11-19 .... 22%
Adults, 20+ 46%

By Socio-Economic Status
A 5%
B 0%
C 35%
D 60%

Media Inflation vs. General Inflation, 1989-1992

Number of Households   N/A
Ownership of household durables
Car 23.6%
Phone 22.3%
Washers .... N/A
(purchasing power equivalent)
GNP distribution by industry
Agriculture .... N/A
Industry .... N/A
Services .... N/A
Exchange rates (US$ to local currency)
1991 .... N/A
1992 .... 0.1142857

National Holidays

Holiday	1993 Date
New Year's Day	January 1
Holy Week	April 8-10
Labor Day	May 1
August Holiday	August 4-6
Independence Day	September 15
All Saint's Day	November 2
Christmas	December 25

School Holidays

Holiday	1993 Date
Holy Week	April 5-20
Labor Day	May 1
Mother's Day	May 10
Father's Day	June 17
Teacher's Day	June 22
August Holiday	August 2-6
Independence Day	September 15
Columbus Day	October 12
All Saint's Day	November 2
First Independence Announcement	November 5

Major Influences and Trends

Television

In El Salvador, Telecorporacion Salvadorena media group, owned by Mr. Boris Ezerschy, has 88% of the audience share of TV. This media group controls all TV negotiations requiring advertisers to commit advertising dollars up front with their station. Commercials less than :30 are not allowed.

Radio

There has been a considerable increase in rates this last year due to the new technology of CD lasers used in the transmission of radio programs.

Print

Even though El Salvador is the smallest country in the area, the daily circulation of newspapers is one of the highest in Central America.

Spending Analysis

National advertising spending by medium

based on appropriate year's exchange rate

	1989 US$ MM	1990 US$ MM	1991 US$ MM	1992 US$ MM
TV	N/A	N/A	9.3	15.2
Radio	N/A	N/A	3.0	4.6
Newspaper	N/A	N/A	7.5	11.4
Other	N/A	N/A	0.2	0.6
Total	**N/A**	**N/A**	**20.0**	**31.8**

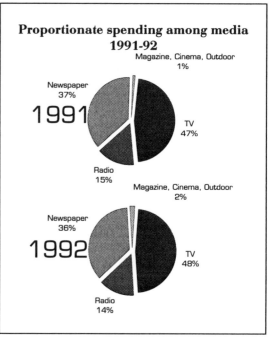

Proportionate spending among media 1991-92

1991
- Newspaper 37%
- Magazine, Cinema, Outdoor 1%
- TV 47%
- Radio 15%

1992
- Newspaper 36%
- Magazine, Cinema, Outdoor 2%
- TV 48%
- Radio 14%

Media Buying

As previously explained, TV negotiations require annual upfront commitments from advertisers. A second contract, finalized later in the year, allows for a maximum of a 20% increase on this initial sum. Thus, the channels maintain control, and are able to predict each client's yearly investment.

Top Advertisers

By Product

Product Category	Advertiser
Tropicana/Soft drinks	Val.Agroindustra
Margarine/Detergents/Toothpaste	Unisola
Perfumes Carrel	Dist. Zablah
Lottery	Loteria NAC
Aspirin/Antacid/Cold Medicine	Bayer Miles
Cereals/Maizena	Comersal Colgate
Pollo Campero/Pollo Indio	Los Cedros
Electricity	Cel
Food/Perfume/Milk/P&G	Dist Zablah

Television

Overview.

- TV penetration in San Salvador as of 1992 is 94.3%.
- The 4 channels of 'Telecorporacion Salvadorena' (2, 4, 6, and 21 in the capital) are leaders in the market and handle the majority of the investments.
- Stations sign-on at noon and air their own programming until 05:45; commercial time is available after 05:45 until 24:00.

Opportunities

Network	Ownership	Station Profile	Commercial Minutes/Day	Coverage	Broadcast Hours (Sign-On/Off)
Ch. 2	Private	Family	221	80%	05:45-24:00*
Ch. 4	Private	Sports	209	70%	05:45-24:00*
Ch. 6	Private	Cinema	227	70%	05:45-24:00*
Ch. 12	Private	General	160	80%	05:45-24:00
Ch. 21	Private	General	50	Capital	05:45-24:00**

**Commercials begin at 12:00 noon.
*From noontime, each channel has its own programs.

Costs

Prime Time TV Costs for :30 in US$			
1989	*1990*	*1991*	*1992*
N/A	140	167	201

Television Cost Changes Between Years				
'88	'89	'90	'91	'92
	N/A	19%	20%	18%

Audiences/CPM's

Average Cost, Audience, and CPMs by Daypart
(Top 3 Stations, :30, national audience, Target=Adults)

Hours	Morning	Daytime	Prime Time	Late Night	Weekend	Children
Station: Ch.2						
US$	156	52	320	86	320	52
Avg. Aud. (000)	8.3	11.9	9.6	9.7	11.6	13.3
CPM	18.77	4.36	33.33	8.84	27.59	3.91
Station: Ch.4						
US$	156	57	229	130	190	57
Avg. Aud. (000)	5.5	5.2	6.9	5.9	7.5	5.4
CPM	28.33	10.99	33.13	22.0	25.40	10.58
Station: Ch.6						
US$	156	113	299	139	448	N/A
Avg. Aud. (000)	1.3	3.8	14.5	11.3	12.6	N/A
CPM	120.00	29.73	20.62	12.30	35.52	N/A

Audiences/Rating by Daypart (Target=Adults)

Daypart	Hours	Household				Adult		
		Universe (000)	Hut Levels	Household Rating	Impressions (000)	Universe (000)	Adult Rating	Impressions (000)
Morning						107.9	2.0	2.2
Daytime		Household audience not measured in El Salvador.				107.9	2.6	2.8
Primetime						107.9	10.5	11.3
Late Night						107.9	1.6	1.7
Weekend						107.9	6.8	7.3
Children's						107.9	5.6	6.0

Scheduling/Regional/Languages

- Spanish is the only language used in TV broadcasting in El Salvador.
- The most common (70%) commercial length is :30. Other available lengths are :20, :40, and :60.

- Commercials are aired throughout the day both at the beginning, end and within programs.
- Regional air time is available on Channel 21 in the capital between the hours of 05:45 and 24:00.

Children's Advertising

All programming accepts advertising targeted at children.

Radio

- Approximately 95% of the households in El Salvador have radios.
- There are 82 radio stations in El Salvador, all of which are commercial, and 40 of which are in San Salvador.
- All stations offer air time in lengths of :05-:60 for advertising. Alternatives do exist for regional and local commercial time and no premiums are charged.
- The primary broadcasting language is Spanish; English is also used.

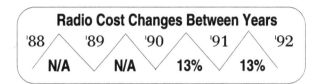

Daypart Costs/CPMs (Target=Adults 20+)

Daypart	Local Time	Cost :30 US$	Audience (000)	CPM (US$)
Prime Time	06:00-12:00	11.25	42.2	0.27
Daytime	12:00-18:00	11.25	31.0	0.36

- Prime/Peak time for radio is 06:00-12:00.
- The most popular program type is Music.

Cable

- Although the cable industry has emerged in El Salvador, local TV stations have proven to be tough competitors for cable networks.
- Cable penetration level is only 2%.
- There are 14 privately owned cable stations, none of which accept advertising. Cable ratings are not measured.
- The primary broadcasting language is English; Spanish is secondary.

Cable Networks	Programming	Cable Networks	Programming
TNT	Movies	NBC	U.S. programming
Cartoon Network	Children's programming	SUR	Programming from Peru
Canal de las Estrellas	Entertainment	Family Channel	Family programming
CNN	News 24-hours	Discovery Channel	Family, educational
Univision	Spanish-language programming	ABC	U.S. programming
HBO Ole	Movies	WGN-Chicago	U.S. programming
CBS	U.S. programming	ESPN	Sports

Satellite

El Salvador has minimal satellite penetration and it is exclusively upscale.

Video Cassettes

An estimated 53.5% of all households have video cassette recorders (VCRs), however pre-recorded tapes do not carry advertising.

Cinema

In El Salvador there are 66 theaters. Commercial time is available in :30 spots at an average cost of US$ 206 for a 4 week advertising schedule in one theater.

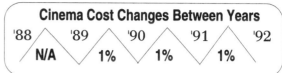

Cinema Cost Changes Between Years

'88	'89	'90	'91	'92
N/A	1%	1%	1%	

Newspapers

There are 5 national daily newspapers all of which accept advertising and have a combined circulation of 322,000.

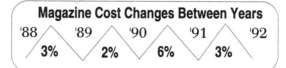

Newspaper Cost Changes Between Years

'88	'89	'90	'91	'92
20%	29%	13%	14%	

Daily Newspaper	Market	Size	Circulation (000)	Avg. Daily Aud. (000)	1 page B&W Cost (US$)	Accept Color?
La Prensa Grafica	National	Tabloid	108	N/A	765	Yes
El Diario de Hoy	National	Tabloid	96	N/A	707	Yes
La Noticia	National	Tabloid	35	N/A	363	Yes
Diario El Mundo	National	Tabloid	53	N/A	383	Yes
Diario Latino	National	Tabloid	30	N/A	363	Yes

Magazines

El Salvador has 27 consumer magazines.

Magazine Cost Changes Between Years

'88	'89	'90	'91	'92
3%	2%	6%	3%	

Magazine	Type	Frequency	Circ. (000)	Audited?	Avg. Issue Aud. (000)	1 page 4/C Cost (US$)
TV Guia	Television	Bi-weekly	20	No	N/A	9
Mercadeo	Marketing	Quarterly	1	No	N/A	20
Aces	-	2x/year	8	No	N/A	20
Banca	Finance	Quarterly	2	No	N/A	23
Udes	Business	Quarterly	2	No	N/A	23
Semana	Politics	Bi-weekly	10	No	N/A	30
Sus Hijos	Education	Quarterly	15	No	N/A	20
Aventura	Children's	Bi-weekly	10	No	N/A	20
Eventos	Sports	Monthly	1	No	N/A	19
El Exportador	Export	Quarterly	2.5	No	N/A	20
Mujer	Women's	Bi-weekly	20	No	N/A	13
Integral	-	3x/year	15	No	N/A	N/A
Colorea	Children's	1x/14 mon.	12	No	N/A	13
Gente	General	Monthly	N/A	No	N/A	22

Outdoor/Transit

Billboards 30 m x 10 m are available at an average cost of US$ 217 for one month. Reservations need to be made 4 weeks in advance. There has been a 20% cost increase each year for the last three years.

Direct Marketing

The only list broker in El Salvador is Wealth Builders. They provide information by zone and by socio-economic levels. There are neither telemarketing companies nor direct marketing associations.

Non-Traditional Media

There is no use of non-traditional media in El Salvador.

Research Sources

Medium Covered	Research Company	Information
TV	Multivex	Ratings by program day and hour Published semi-annually

Advertising Regulations

By Product

Beverages/Alcohol
All models advertising beverages/alchohol must be 18 years or older. Alcohol advertising is allowed after 19:00.

Cigarettes
All models advertising cigarettes must be 18 years or older. Cigarette advertising is allowed after 19:00.

Pharmaceuticals/Drugs
Health Department authorization.

By Medium

Television
Commercials under :30 are not accepted in programs.

Print
Full color inserts in newspapers have to be 21 inches in length; magazine insertions must be full page.

Cable
Cable does not accept advertising.

Sources Consulted

Asociacion Salvadrena de Agencias de Publicidad (ASAP)
Estadisticas Y Censas, 1991-1992
Multivex
Multivex Salvador

Guatemala

Area	108,890 km²
Population (1992)	9,784,275
Population growth rate (1992)	2.4%
GDP	US$ 11.7 billion
GDP/per capita	US$ 1,260
Real growth rate (1991)	3%
Capital	Guatemala City

Population Breakdown

By Sex		*By Age Group*		*By Socio-Economic Status*	
Male	50.0%	Children	29.4%	A	4.5%
Female	50.0%	Teens	23.0%	B	11.0%
		Adults	47.6%	C	84.5%

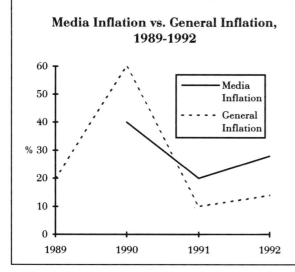

Media Inflation vs. General Inflation, 1989-1992

Media Inflation
General Inflation

Number of Households   1,804,560
Ownership of household durables
  Car 36.3%
  Phone 36.1%
  Washers .... N/A%
  (purchasing power equivalent)
GNP distribution by industry
  Agriculture .... N/A
  Industry .... N/A
  Services .... N/A
Exchange rates (US$ to local currency)
  1991 .... 0.2271665
  1992 .... 0.190476

National Holidays

Holiday	*1993 Date*
New Years' Day	January 1
Holy Week	March 27-April 7
Labor Day	May 1
Army Day	June 30
Assumption Day	August 13
Independence Day	September 15
Anniversary of the 1944 Revolution	October 20
All Saints Day	November 1
Christmas	December 25

School Holidays

Holiday	*1993 Date*
New Year's Day	January 1
Holy Week	March 27-April 7
Labor Day	May 1
Mother's Day	May 10
Fathers Day	June 17
Teacher's Day	June 25
Assumption Day	August 15
Independence Day	September 15
Anniversary of the 1944 Revolution	October 20
All Saints Day	November 1
Christmas	December 25
Also, 2 weeks in June, July and most of November and December	

Major Influences and Trends

Television

Of the four local (VHF) channels the two leading stations in audience share (3 & 7) belong to the same owner, Angel Gonzalez. Advertisers are often required to commit 100% share of dollars to the leading stations like 3 & 7. The advertiser benefits with additional bonus spots at no additional charge.

Radio

Apparently, the most important radio networks in the country are getting together to ensure that the rates are similar between one radio network and the other. This will also lead to similar negotiations, and depending on the total budget, it may be possible to better negotiate with every radio network. Radio is a vehicle that is becoming more united and strong. We are also looking at the possibility of unification of city and country radio networks that will reach more people (by selling programs as packages).

Print

A print war has recently begun. There have been 2 major events that could have a major effect on this medium.

1. A presidential candidate (and owner of a newspaper owner) was murdered in July '93. It is not known exactly what will happen, but it is believed that the structure of the newspaper will change while circulation will increase.

2. A new newspaper just came out in July '93. Its name is *La Republica* and it will compete against the major newspaper in the country. Major product launchings have occured via newspapers recently, and there is a war among the titles for more subscribers. The deals and negotiations are getting more aggressive each day.

Spending Analysis

National advertising spending by medium
based on appropriate year's exchange rate

	1989 US$ MM	1990 US$ MM	1991 US$ MM	1992 US$ MM
TV	30.7	48.7	42.4	38.5
Cinema	0.1	0.1	0.1	0.2
Radio	15.0	10.0	26.8	27.7
Newspaper	13.0	16.7	29.2	32.0
Magazine	1.0	1.2	3.9	3.9
Outdoor	0.6	7.9	9.5	
Total	**60.4**	**84.6**	**111.9**	**108.6**

Media Buying

Top Advertisers

By Product

Product Category	Advertiser
Product Category	Advertiser
Beer	Cerveza Gallo
Soft Drinks	Pepsi
Tobacco	Rubios
Analgesics	Asprina
Detergents	Dona Blanca
Cereals	Corn Flakes
Fast Food	McDonald's
Tooth Paste	Colgate
Banks	G&T

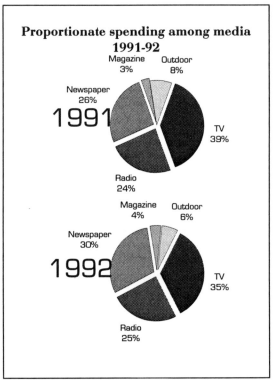

Proportionate spending among media 1991-92

1991
- Magazine 3%
- Outdoor 8%
- Newspaper 26%
- TV 39%
- Radio 24%

1992
- Magazine 4%
- Outdoor 6%
- Newspaper 30%
- TV 35%
- Radio 25%

Buying services do not exist.

Television

Channels 3 & 7 are the leaders in audience numbers. The TV penetration level has risen dramatically (to approximately 1,492,000 households) due to the decline in cable penetration.

	TV HH Penetration			Adult Reach	
1989	*190*	*1991*	*1992*	at 250 GRPs	60%
56%	65%	71%	71%	at 500 GRPs	80%
				at 1000 GRPs	90%

Opportunities

Networks	Number of Stations	Ownership	Station Profile	Commercial Minutes/Day	Coverage	Broadcast Hours (Sign-On/Off)
3	26	Private*	General	155	90%	24 hours
5	3	Army	Education/General	--	60%	09:30-23:30
7	26	Private*	Soap Operas/Sports/News	115	90%	06:00-24:00
11	12	Private	Soap Operas/News	75	70%	05:30-22:30
13	6	Private	Family	30	50%	15:00-22:30
UHF 21	1	Private	Religion/Education	--	100% (Cap)	12:00-24:00
UHF 25	1	Private	Musical	--	100% (Cap)	10:00-23:00

Channels 3 and 7 are owned by Angel Gonzalez

Costs

Prime Time TV Costs for :30 in US$			
1989	*1990*	*1991*	*1992*
142.90	180.92	342.86	400.00

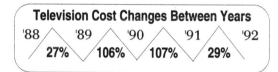

Television Cost Changes Between Years

'88   '89   '90   '91   '92
27%   106%   107%   29%

Audiences/CPM's

Average Cost, Audience, and CPMs by Daypart
(Top 3 Stations, :30, national audience, Target=Adults 15+)

Hour	Morning 6:00-12:00	Daytime 12:00-18:00	Prime Time 18:00-22:00	Late Night 22:00-23:00	Weekend 18:00-22:00	Children 16:00-18:00
Station: Ch. 3						
US$	245	245	482	482	482	245
Avg. Aud. (000)	35.8	73.1	388.9	50.7	293.9	69.3
CPM	6.83	3.35	1.42	9.51	1.64	3.53
Station: Ch. 7						
US$	156	161	375	375	375	161
Avg. Aud. (000)	13.4	100.00	338.9	237.2	429.7	37.9
CPM	11.66	1.61	1.11	1.58	0.87	4.24
Station: Ch. 11						N/A
US$	147	147	482	482	482	N/A
Avg. Aud. (000)	3.0	4.5	9.0	20.9	13.6	N/A
CPM	49.11	32.74	53.57	23.07	35.45	N/A

Audiences/Rating by Daypart (Target=Adults 15+)

Daypart	Hours	Household				Adult		
		Universe (000)	Hut Levels	Household Rating	Impressions (000)	Universe (000)	Rating	Impressions (000)
Morning	06:00-12:00					1,190	4.0	47.6
Daytime	12:00-18:00	Household information is not measured in Guatemala.				1,190	12.3	146.4
Primetime	18:00-22:00					1,190	26.2	311.8
Late Night	22:00-24:00					1,190	11.1	132.1
Weekend	18:00-24:00					1,190	25.2	299.9
Children's	16:00-18:00					1,190	4.5	53.6

Scheduling/Regional/Languages

Regional Airing

Station	Region	Hours
Ch. 21	Capital	12:00-24:00
Ch. 25	Capital	12:00-23:00

- Spanish is the only language used in TV broadcasting

- About 80% of all commercials are :30; also available are :15, :20, :40, :45, :60 and :90.
- Commercials are aired throughout the day at the beginning, end and within programs.
- Regional airing of commercials is available but only accounts for about 1% of the total spending.

Children's Advertising

Programming which accepts advertising directed to children

ADULT PROGRAMMING				Kids'	
Station	Hours	Days	Universe (000)	Ratings	Impressions (000)
3	18:00-22:00	Mon-Sun	301.1	29.3	88.2
7	18:00-22:00	Mon-Sun	301.1	22.5	67.8
11	18:00-22:00	Mon-Sun	301.1	0.2	0.6
13	18:00-22:00	Mon-Sun	301.1	0.1	0.3

CHILDREN'S PROGRAMMING				Kids'	
Station	Hours	Days	Universe (000)	Ratings	Impressions (000)
3	16:00-18:00	Mon-Fri	301.1	23.0	69.3
7	14:00-15:00	Mon-Fri	301.1	21.0	63.2

Radio

- There are 140 commercial radio stations; 45 are located in Guatemala City.
- About 91% of all Guatemalans have radios in their homes, totalling 1,912,600 households.
- The primary broadcasting language is Spanish; English is secondary and the most popular program type is musical.
- Commercials are available in ;10, :15, :20, :30, :40, :45, and :60 spots; no premiums are paid for local purchases.
- Prime/Peak time is between 08:00 and 10:00.

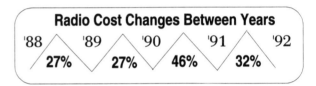

Radio Cost Changes Between Years

'88 — 27% — '89 — 27% — '90 — 46% — '91 — 32% — '92

Daypart Costs/CPMs
(Target=Persons 8+, Capital)

Daypart	Local Time	Avg.Cost :30 US$	Audience (000)	CPM (US$)
Prime Time	8:00-10:00	13.40	73.3	0.36
Daytime	14:00-16:00	13.40	22.4	0.60
Late Night	18:00-20:00	13.40	4.5	2.98

Cable

A Cable regulation law has been in effect since September 1992. Since then subscriptions have decreased because subscription fees were increased while the premium channels were canceled from the basic cable options.

- The cable penetration level in Guatemala City is 45% (about 812,100 households) down from 50% in 1991. A continued decline is expected within the next five years.
- There are currently 36 privately owned cable stations; only 10 of which are commercial.
- English is the primary broadcasting language; Spanish is secondary.

Cable Networks	HH Circulation (000)	Programming
Mayacable	23	
MTV		Music Videos
Home Cinema		Movies
Cartoon Network		Children's
Lifetime		Family Programming
ESPN International		Sports
CNN		News
Kaminal TV		Movies
Intercable	60	
Teledrama		Soap Operas
Triple A		Movies
CNN		News
Cartoon Network		Children's
TNT		Movies, Family
SUR		Peruvian TV

Satellite

No satellite channels are broadcast in Guatemala at this time.

Video Cassettes

An estimated 30% of the TV households in Guatemala City have video cassette recorders (VCRs); however, there is no service that measures usage and pre-recorded tapes do not carry advertising.

Cinema

- There are 60 cinemas in Guatemala and 60% of them offer commercial time. The potential reach over a 4 week period is 25,200 people per theater.
- Commercial lengths are between :30 and :60; the average cost of a 4 week schedule is US$ 227 for one theater.

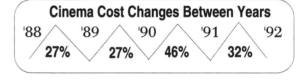

Cinema Cost Changes Between Years

'88	'89	'90	'91	'92
27%	27%	46%	32%	

Newspapers

- There are 5 national daily newspapers that accept advertising; the combined circulation is 251,000.
- The minimum size for a B/W print ad is 20 meters and 28 meters for a color ad.

Newspaper Cost Changes Between Years

'88	'89	'90	'91	'92
20%	30%	29%	20%	

Daily Newspaper	Market	Size	Circulation (000)	Avg. Daily Aud. (000)	1 page B&W Cost (US$)	Accept Color?
Presa Libre	National		110	450	840	Yes
El Grafico	National		45	88	700	Yes
Siglozi	National		55	203	600	Yes

Magazines

There are 29 consumer magazines and 10 trade
and technical magazines published in Guatemala.

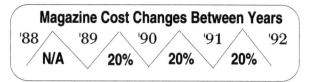

Magazine	Type	Frequency	Circ. (000)	Audited?	Avg. Issue Aud. (000)	1 page 4/C Cost (US$)
Cronica	Politics/Economy	Weekly	10.0	No	N/A	980
Critica	Politics/Economy	Bi-weekly	12.0	No	N/A	780
Polemica	General	Monthly	5.0	No	NA/	533
Empresa	Marketing	Monthly	5.0	No	NA/	750
A Donde	Tourist	Monthly	3.0	No	N/A	600
Gerencia	Management	Monthly	2.0	No	N/A	680
Vanidades*	Women's	Bi-weekly	5.4	No	N;A	1,450***
Buen Hogar	Home	Bi-weekly	5.0**	No	N/A	1,300***
Ideas	Home	Monthly	3.3**	No	N/A	1,100***
Cosmopolitan	Women's	Monthly	3.2**	No	N/A	1,250***

Central American Edition
**Guatemala Circulation*
***Regional Cost*

Outdoor/Transit

Billboard	**Transit**
Sites available 6,000	Boards available 600
Exposure (max.) 22%	Exposure .... 25% (city)
Lead Time to reserve .... 5 weeks	
Costs	**Costs**
Average, 1 billboard/month	Average, 1 board/month:
64 m x 3 m .... US$ 100	.... US$ 144.29

Billboard Cost Changes Between Years

'88	'89	'90	'91	'92
	10%	20%	15%	15%

Transit Board Cost Changes Between Years

'88	'89	'90	'91	'92
	20%	20%	15%	N/A

Sizes	**Sizes**
Billboards No limitations	Transit Boards 3.66 m x 0.76 m
	81 cm x 61 cm

Direct Marketing

Cemaco, Diners Bi-Credit, Master Card and Siglo
XXI are the top five list brokers; all of them
provide information by S.E.L. Zone. There is no
direct marketing association.

List Broker	Information Provided
Cemaco	By S.E.L. Zone*
Diners	By S.E.L. Zone
Bi-Credit	By S.E.L. Zone
Master Card	By S.E.L. Zone
Siglo XXI	By S.E.L. Zone

Socio economic levels (S.E.L.) are used to divide areas into zones.

Non-Traditional Media

There is no use of non-traditional media in Guatemala.

Research Sources

Medium covered	Research company	Information Provided
TV, Radio, Newspapers, Magazines	Empresa De Investigacion De Mercadeo Multivex 3 Calle 2-50, Zona 9	Rating by programs, day and hour

TV research is available bi-monthly from Multivex Recall.

Advertising Regulations

By Product

Beverages/Alcohol
Need a broadcast permit from the Food & Beverage division of the Health Department.
Food/Restaurants
Need a broadcast permit from the Food & Beverage division of the Health Department.
Cigarettes
The model must be over 18 years old. Need a permit. No cigarette commercials can air before 20:00.
Pharmaceuticals/Drugs
Broadcasting permit/health permit required.
Advertising To Children
Broadcasting permit required.
Commercial Production
Commercials can be transmitted outside city limits, but a counterbalance is required. The announcer must be local.

By Medium

Television
Commercial spots of less than :15 are not accepted within programs. Every commercial has to have a broadcasting permit.
Print
The minimum length of a B/W newspaper page is 20 inches; for a color page, the minimum length is 28 inches.
Cable
Local cable operators cannot transmit premium channels (HBO, Cinema, Request, Galavision, Univision) on basic cable.

Sources Consulted

Asistercia Ejecutura
Multivex

Honduras

Area	112,090 km²
Population (1992)	5,092,776
Population growth rate (1992)	2.8%
GDP	US$ 5.2 billion
GDP/per capita	US$ 1,050
Real growth rate (1991)	-0.3%
Capital	Tegucigalpa

Population Breakdown

By Sex
Male 50%
Female 50%

By Age Group
Children, 0-19 .... 57.8%
Adults, 20+ 42.2%

By Socio-Economic Status
A 2%
B 8%
C 20%
D 70%

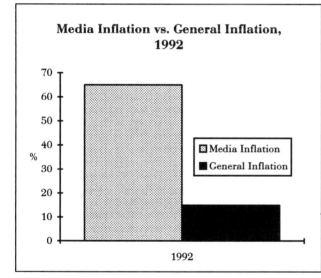

Media Inflation vs. General Inflation, 1992

- ⊠ Media Inflation
- ■ General Inflation

Number of Households 1,046,100
Ownership of household durables
  Car 3.5
  Phone .... N/A
  Washers .... N/A
      (purchasing power equivalent)
GNP distribution by industry
  Agriculture .... N/A
  Industry .... N/A
  Services .... N/A
Exchange rates (US$ to local currency)
  1991 .... 0.1754386

National Holidays

Holiday	1993 Date
New Year's	January 1
Labor Day	May 1
San Francisco Morazan	October 3
Americas's Discovery	October 12
Army Day	October 21
Christmas	December 25

School Holidays

Holiday	1993 Date
America's Day	April 14
Tree Day	May 30
Student's Day	June 11
Flag Day	June 14
Lempira's Day	July 20
Independence Day	September 20
Independence Pliegos	September 28
San Francisco Morazan	October 3
America's Discovery	October 12
Army Day	October 21

Major Influences and Trends

Unlike other Central American countries where a majority of the population lives in the capital city or in its direct vicinity, in Honduras the population is divided among the cities of Tegucigalpa and San Pedro Sula. As a result, media tends to be more decentralized than in other countries.

For example, each of the two major cities publish their own local newspaper although each paper circulates to the other as well. Radio stations tend to be scattered throughout the country.

Cable penetration is higher outside the two metro areas due to low coverage of the main TV channels there.

Spending Analysis

National advertising spending by medium
based on appropriate year's exchange rate

	1989 US$ MM	1990 US$ MM	1991 US$ MM	1992 US$ MM
TV	N/A	5.3	5.9	6.7
Cinema	N/A	.1	.1	0.1
Radio	N/A	4.6	4.9	5.9
Newspaper	N/A	3.5	3.8	4.4
Magazine	N/A	0.2	0.2	0.2
Outdoor	N/A	0.1	0.1	1.1
Total	**N/A**	**13.8**	**15.0**	**18.4**

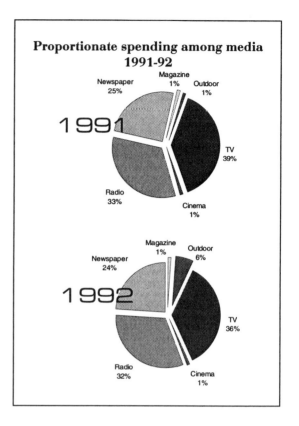

Proportionate spending among media 1991-92

1991: Newspaper 25%, Magazine 1%, Outdoor 1%, TV 39%, Cinema 1%, Radio 33%

1992: Newspaper 24%, Magazine 1%, Outdoor 6%, TV 36%, Cinema 1%, Radio 32%

Media Buying

TV and radio negotiations are primarily controlled by the monopoly that owns the leading stations. Advertisers are required to commit 100% share to earn bonus air time from the station.

Top Advertisers

By Company

Prarent companyy	Product Categories
Cerveceria Hondurena, S.A.	Coca Cola, Imperial, National, Soft Drinks, Beer
Fabrica de Manteca y Jabon Atlantida	La Blanquita, Lempira, Detergent Soap, Margarine
Taca	Airlines
Numar de Honduras	Margarine/Clover Brand, Corona/Oil
Sterling Products	
Miles	
Tabacalera Hondurena	Cigarettes
Colgate	Detergent/Toothpaste
Grupo Galeria	
Banco Atlantida	Bank

By Product

Product Category	Advertiser
Margarine/Oil	Clover Brand Products
Automobiles	Toyota
Fast Food	Burger King
Soft Drinks	Pepsi
Milk (Liquid)	Leyde
Hardware	Larach & Company
Milk (Powder)	Anchor
Electric Devices	Comun
Beer	Nacional
Banks	Banco Atlantide

Television

TV HH Penetration			
1989	1990	1991	1992
43%	40%	N/A	45%

Television penetration is low (45%), totaling 470,700 households. Measurement studies for TV are made every four years, thus negotiations must be based on a planner's judgment. As in Guatemala and El Salvador, the leading TV channels are controlled by a media monopoly, Telesistema Hondureno. This group's stations typically attract up to 80% of the TV viewers.

Opportunities

Channels	Number of Stations	Ownership	Station Profile	Commercial Minutes/Day	Coverage	Broadcast Hours (Sign-On/Off)
5-9-13	3	Private	Soap Operas /Sports	306	85%	07:30-23:30
3-7	2	Private	Action/Movies/ Children/News	240	80%	11:30-23:00
7 & 4	2	Private	Children/Movie/ Soap Opera	144	30%	15:00-23:30
9 & 2	3	Private	Cultural/Soap Operas	288	70%	06:00-24:00
21	1	Private	Movies	324	60%	00:00-24:00
6	1	Private	Action/Cultural	324	40%	06:00-23:00

Costs

Prime Time TV Costs for :30 in US$			
1989	1990	1991	1992
N/A	80.0	97.00	116.00

Television Cost Changes Between Years

'88	'89	'90	'91	'92
	N/A	21%	20%	9%

Audiences/CPM's

Average Cost, Audience, and CPMs by Daypart
(Top 3 Stations, :30, national audience)

Hours	Morning 7:00-12:00	Daytime 12:00-18:00	Prime Time 18:00-22:00	Late Night 22:00-24:00	Weekend 18:00-22:00	Children
Station: 5						
US$	89.90	176.25	222.81	93.75	235.00	N/A
Avg. Aud. (000)	77.9	270.1	210.0	59.3	N/A	N/A
CPM	1.15	.65	1.06	1.58	N/A	N/A
Station: 3 & 7						
US$	46.88	68.75	116.72	96.88	96.88	46.88
Avg. Aud. (000)	13.8	24.1	65.1	12.8	N/A	20.7
CPM	3.40	2.85	1.79	7.57	N/A	2.26
Station: 7 & 4						
US$	N/A	36.62	106.25	80.31	96.41	38.62
Avg. Aud. (000)	N/A	17.3	62.6	59.2	N/A	20.1
CPM	N/A	2.23	1.70	1.36	N/A	1.92

Audiences/Rating by Daypart

Daypart	Hours	Household Universe (000)	Hut Levels	Household Rating	Impressions (000)	Adult Universe (000)	Adult Rating	Impressions (000)
Morning	07:00-12:00					1,199	3.9	46.8
Daytime	18:00-22:00					1,199	9.3	111.5
Primetime	12:00-18:00		Household information is not available			1,199	5.9	70.7
Late Night	22:00-24:00					1,199	4.4	52.8
Weekend	18:00-22:00					1,199	N/A	N/A
Children's						1,199	1.6	19.2

Scheduling/Regional/Languages

- Spanish is the only language used in TV broadcasting.
- Negotiations are based on volume of share. There are no specifically regional buys.
- Commercials are aired throughout the day at the beginning and end of programs and within them.
- Lengths available are :20, :30, :40, :45 and :60; and 90% of all commercials are :30.

Children's Advertising

Programming which accepts advertising directed to children

| ADULT PROGRAMMING | | | | Kids' | |
Station	Hours	Days	Universe (000)	Ratings	Impressions (000)
Ch. 5	18:30-19:00	Mon-Sun	98.5	N/A	N/A
Ch. 7&4	19:00-21:00	Mon-Fri	98.5	N/A	N/A

| CHILDREN'S PROGRAMMING | | | | Kids' | |
Station	Hours	Days	Universe (000)	Ratings	Impressions (000)
Ch. 5	14:00-16:00	Mon-Fri	98.5	N/A	N/A
Ch. 7&4	15:00-17:30	Mon-Fri	98.5	N/A	N/A
Ch. 3&7	11:30-12:30	Mon-Sun	98.5	N/A	N/A

Radio

- Virtually all of the 1,046,100 households in Honduras have radios.
- There are 166 commercial radio stations, 34 are located in Tegucigalpa.
- The primary broadcasting language is Spanish; English is secondary.
- Music is the most popular program type.
- Peak/Prime times for radio are 06:00-12:00 for music and 05:00-07:00 for news.

Radio Cost Changes Between Years

'88	'89	'90	'91	'92
	N/A	N/A	28%	20%

- Available commercial lengths are :15, :20, :30 and :45.

Prime/Peak Time

Daypart	Programming
06:00-12:00	Music
05:00-07:00	News

Cable

- New cable laws are expected to go into effect soon. At that point, cable costs are expected to increase by 300%.
- There are 25 privately owned cable channels available, but none accept advertising.
- The current penetration level is 11% in the capital city and 20% in all other cities.
- English is the primary broadcast language; Spanish is secondary.

Cable Networks	Programming	Cable Networks	Programming
Galavision	Spanish-language programming	Cartoon Channel	Children's programming
CNN	News	WGN-Chicago	U.S. programming
MTV	Music videos	Canal de las Estrellas	Entertainment
Cinemax	Movies	ESPN	Sports
SUR	Programming from Peru	Discovery Channel	Family, educational
HBO	Movies	TNT	Movies
Movie Channel	Movies	Request	-
ABC	U.S. programming	Nickelodeon	Children's programming
CBS	U.S. programming		

Satellite

No information about satellite reception in Honduras is available.

Video Cassettes

An estimated 7% of the TV households in Honduras have video cassette recorders. There is currently no service that measures usage and pre-recorded tapes do not carry advertising.

Cinema

- Honduras has 45 cinemas; 30% of which offer :60 commercial spots.
- The average cost for a 4 week cinema schedule is about US$ 87.71.

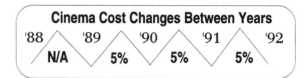

Cinema Cost Changes Between Years

'88	'89	'90	'91	'92
N/A	5%	5%	5%	

Newspapers

There are 4 national daily newspapers that accept advertising and have a combined circulation of 158,000.

Newspaper Cost Changes Between Years

'88	'89	'90	'91	'92
N/A	75%	25%	20%	

Daily Newspaper	Market	Circulation (000)	Avg. Daily Aud. (000)	1 page B&W Cost (US$)	Accept Color?
La Prensa	San Pedro	42	N/A	304.69	Yes
La Tribuna	Tegucigalpa	42	N/A	304.69	Yes
Tiempo	San Pedro	36	N/A	304.69	Yes
El Heraldo	Tegucigalpa	38	N/A	304.69	Yes

Magazines

Honduras has 15 consumer magazines.

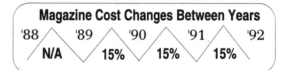

Magazine Cost Changes Between Years

'88	'89	'90	'91	'92
N/A	15%	15%	15%	

Magazine	Type	Frequency	Circ. (000)	Audited?	Avg. Adult Aud. (000)	1 page 4/C Cost (US$)
Cambio Empresarial	General	Monthly	5	No	N/A	278
Ventas Y Mercadeo	Business	Monthly	1	No	N/A	278
Panorama	General	Weekly	9	No	N/A	500
Hablemos Claro	General	Monthly	6	No	N/A	314
Revista As	Sports	Monthly	6	No	N/A	278

Outdoor/Transit

- The average one month cost for a billboard (9 ft x 27 ft) is US$ 70.
- Reservations need to be made 3 weeks in advance.
- Costs have changed by 12% per year for the last three years.

Direct Marketing

There is no direct marketing activity in Honduras.

Non-Traditional Media

There is no use of non-traditional media in Honduras.

Research Sources

Medium Covered	Research Company	Information Provided
TV, Radio, Press	Price Waterhouse	Rating by program day and hour (measured every four years)
TV, Radio	C.I.M.	Rating by program day and hour (per agency request. High premium. Agency exclusivity).

Television Research Currently Available

Research Method	Frequency
Recall	Every four years

Advertising Regulations

By Product

Beverages/Alcohol
Television advertising is permitted after 19:00 only.
Cigarettes
Television advertising is permitted after 19:00 only.

By Medium

Outdoor
There are restrictions regarding the location of the transit boards that surround boulevards and some specific areas. Transit boards must be located 25 meters from the center of the road.

Mexico

Area	1,972,550 km^2
Population (1992)	92,380,721
Population growth rate (1992)	2.3%
GDP	US$ 289 billion
GDP/per capita	US$ 3,200
Real growth rate (1991)	4%
Capital	Mexico City

Population Breakdown

By Sex
Male 49%
Female 51%

By Age Group
Children, 0-12 .... 33%
Teens, 13-18 .... 15%
Adults, 19-29 .... 20%
Adults, 30-44 .... 17%
Adults, 45+ 15%

By Socio-Economic Status
A&B, US$ 2,880+* 4%
C, US$ 960 to US$ 2,879* 33%
D, US$ 80 to US$ 959* 63%
*Monthly income

Source: Gamma Mexico

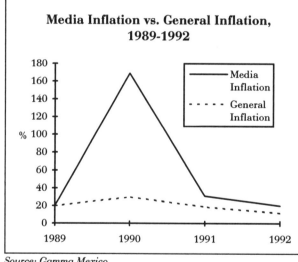

Media Inflation vs. General Inflation, 1989-1992

— Media Inflation
---- General Inflation

Source: Gamma Mexico

Number of Households	17,112,672

Ownership of household durables
Car 47%
Phone .... N/A
Washers .... N/A
(purchasing power equivalent)

GNP distribution by industry
Agriculture 9%
Industry 41%
Services 50%

Exchange rates (US$ to local currency)
1991 .... 0.0003203
1992 .... 0.0003200

National Holidays

Holiday	1993 Date
New Year's Day	January 1
Constitution Day	February 5
Benito Juarez Anniversary	March 21
Good Friday/Passover/Easter	April 8/9
Labor Day	May 1
Independence Day	September 16
Revolution Day	November 20
Christmas	December 25

School Holidays

Holiday	1993 Date
Battle de Puebla Day	May 5
Mother's Day	May 10
Columbus Day	October 12
All Saints Day	November 1
Day of the Dead	November 2
Day of Virgin of Guadalupe	December 12
Vacations	Last two weeks in December

Major Influences and Trends

Televisa still controls the majority of general media buying in Mexico; in TV it owns 85% of the television stations nationwide and one of the two major cable systems, Cablevision. Televisa is also the main supplier of outdoor boards and it owns the strongest magazine group, Editorial America.

The government channels, Ch. 7 & 13, were sold in July 1993. 'Grupo Radio Televisora del Centro' are the new owners. This may bring about a better and more competitive TV industry. This same group also bought 127 cinema theaters named 'COTSA,' and a production company named 'Estudios America.'

In the magazine industry, specialized titles are becoming more numerous each year because the trend is towards target segmentation. Circulation audits are starting to become more important, as well.

Radio groups are becoming stronger by offering better quality programming and more attractive packages to advertisers. Cable TV is also growing.

Spending Analysis

National advertising spending by medium
based on appropriate year's exchange rate

	1989 US$ MM	1990 US$ MM	1991 US$ MM	1992 US$ MM
TV	607.5	1,121.9	1,469.4	2,111.2
Cinema	5.5	7.3	18.7	20.4
Radio	92.1	134.6	212.4	321.5
Newspaper	100.5	141.3	183.1	217.3
Magazine	63.1	69.9	96.9	124.3
Outdoor	38.9	54.3	67.4	101.4
Total	**907.6**	**1,529.2**	**2,047.9**	**2,896.1**

Source: Anuazio de Inversion Publicitaria/A.C. Nielsen, Mexico, 1992

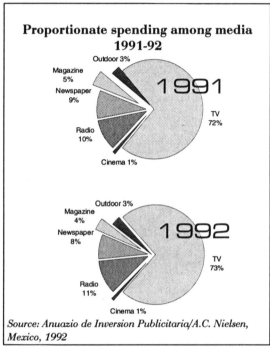

Source: Anuazio de Inversion Publicitaria/A.C. Nielsen, Mexico, 1992

Media Buying

Television. TV is bought through annual advance payments, with fixed rates and time bonuses of up to 300%. Bonuses granted by Televisa during negotiations may cross to other Televisa owned media. Clients typically handle the negotiations directly.

Radio. There are all kinds of negotiations in radio. There are several groups which represent radio stations, sharing the business in a competitive environment.

Magazines. There are all kinds of contracts, including payment in advance with a 30%-100% bonus.

Newspapers. There are newspaper groups that arrange the buying. In Mexico, local newspapers are stronger than national newspapers.

Outdoor. Vendors are open to any kind of negotiations. The many options in outdoor can be contracted by different time periods.

Buying services. Do exist; however there are no important companies.

Top Advertisers (1992 Spending)

By Company

Parent Company	Product Categories	US$ MM
PepsiCo.	Soft drink	134.51
Colgate Palmolive	Cleaners, Detergents, Soap	79.94
Procter & Gamble	Detergents, Hygiene articles	77.16
Bimbo	Food	43.81
Bacardi & Co.	Liquor	41.64
Kimberly Clark	Health, Hygiene, Beauty	38.32
Domecq	Liquor	37.51
Unilever	Detergent, Hygiene articles	37.36
Coca Cola	Soft drink	37.35
La Moderna	Cigarettes	34.87

Source: A.C. Nielsen Co., Mexico/Anvario, 1992

By Product

Product Category	Advertiser	US$ MM
Non-alcoholic beverages	PepsiCo.	134.51
Health and Beauty products, Cleaning products	Colgate	79.94
Food	Bimbo	43.81
Liquor	Bacardi & Co.	41.64
Banks	Bancomer	27.23
Autos	Nissan	11.65

Source: A.C. Nielsen Co., Mexico/Anvario, 1992

Television

Overview

Televisa owns the largest television network, comprised of channels 2 and 5, thereby controlling the television market in Mexico.

Television HH Penetration			
1989	*1990*	*1991*	*1992*
72.8%	72.8%	85%	85%
11,355	10,740	12,540	14,621

Source: AMAP/Media Data, 1992

Television is negotiated and paid for one year in advance, with advertisers negotiating directly with the media, primarily Televisa.

Opportunities

Net-works	Number of Stations	Ownership	Station Profile	Commercial Minutes/Day	Coverage	Broadcast Hours (Sign-On/Off)
CH 2	148	Televisa (Private)	Local productions, soap operas, contest programs.	384	96%	00:00-24:00
CH 13*	83	TV Azteca	Productions of other countries, soap operas, contest programs and family programming.	288	81%	06:00-02:30
Semi-network						
CH 5	33	Televisa (Private	Entertainment, cartoons, police series, family programming.	384	68%	07:00-02:00
CH 7*	77	TV Azteca	Will have teen programming.	288	75%	06:00-02:30
CH 11	43 (By Cable systems)	IPN - Cultural (Public)	Cultural	192	29%	07:00-24:00
CH 6	114 (By cable systems)	Teleprogramas De Mexico (Private)	Productions of other countries, soap operas, contest programs and family programming.	N/A	11%	00:00-24:00

During 1992 both channels transmitted exactly the same programming.
Source: AMAP/Media Data, 1992

Costs

Prime Time TV Costs for :30 in US$			
1989	*1990*	*1991*	*1992*
16,462	34,153	51,889	59,520

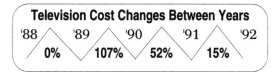

Television Cost Changes Between Years

'88 — '89 — '90 — '91 — '92
0% 107% 52% 15%

Audiences/CPM's

Average Cost, Audience, and CPMs by Daypart
(Top 3 Stations, :30, national audience, Target=Adults 15+)

Hours	Morning 7:00-14:00	Daytime 14:00-19:00	Prime Time 19:00-23:00	Late Night 23:00-07:00	Weekend 07:00-23:00	Children 14:00-21:00
Station: Ch 2						
US$	29,760	59,520	59,520	59,520	44,640	44,640
Avg. Aud. (000)	177.5	453.0	899.9	483.6	349.0	376.9
CPM	167	131	66	123	128	118
Station: Ch 5						
US$	14,110	20,832	28,080	14,110	21,000	21,000
Avg. Aud. (000)	30.6	104.1	238.8	220.4	226.5	380.5
CPM	461	200	118	64	92.7	55
Station: Ch 13						
US$	4,410	8,830	17,660	4,410	10,300	10,300
Avg. Aud. (000)	36.7	42.9	146.9	32.4	55.1	54.4
CPM	120	206	120	136	187	189

Source: IBOPE Mexico Avg., Jan.-Dec. 1992

Audiences/Rating by Daypart (Target=Adults 19-44)

Daypart	Hours	Household				Adult		
		Universe (000)	Hut Levels	Household Rating	Impressions (000)	Universe (000)	Adult Rating	Impressions (000)
Morning	07:00-14:00	3,166	18	6	190	6,122	3	184
Daytime	14:00-19:00	3,166	46	9	285	6,122	7	429
Primetime	19:00-23:00	3,166	63	23	728	6,122	15	918
Late Night	23:00-07:00	3,166	10	15	475	6,122	8	490
Weekend	07:00-23:00	3,166	43	13	412	6,122	6	367
Children's	14:00-21:00	3,166	53	12	380	6,122	10	612

Source: IBOPE Avg., Jan.-Dec. 1992

Scheduling/Regional/Languages

- All Mexican programming is in Spanish.
- Commercials are available in :20, :30, :40 and :60 lengths; 60% of all commercials are :20 and another 30% are :30.
- Commercials are aired throughout the day, both at the beginning and end of programs and during them.
- As an alternative to national buying, local air time is available on all stations in all markets by individual buys. Local buying totals 57% of advertising spending and costs approximately 10% that of national air time (the cost varies by market).

Children's Advertising

Programming which accepts advertising directed to children

ADULT PROGRAMMING				Kids'	
Station	Hours	Days	Universe (000)	Ratings	Impressions (000)
Ch. 2	17:00-20:00	M-F	3,624	14	507
	21:00-23:00	M-F	3,624	8	290
	18:00-23:00	Sat-Sun	3,624	9	326
Ch. 5	21:00-23:00	M-Sat	3,624	4	145
	10:00-24:00	Sun	3,624	4	145
Ch. 13	21:00-23:00	M-F	3,624	1	36

CHILDREN'S PROGRAMMING				Kids'	
Station	Hours	Days	Universe (000)	Ratings	Impressions (000)
Ch. 2	07:00-10:00	Sun	3,624	11	399
	20:00-21:00	M-F	3,624	18	652
Ch. 5	14:00-21:00	M-Sat	3,624	10	362
Ch. 13	19:00-21:00	M-F	3,624	4	145

Source: IBOPE, Mexico 1993

Radio

- Radio penetration is at 98%; a total of 16,770,400 households. About 83% of the automobiles in Mexico have radios.
- Of the 923 radio stations, 920 are commercial and 58 are in Mexico City.
- Spanish is the primary broadcasting language; English is secondary. News is the most popular program type.
- Commercials are available in :05, :10, :20, :30, :40 and :60 lengths and no premiums are paid for regional or local airing.

Radio Cost Changes Between Years

'88	'89	'90	'91	'92
	25%	60%	35%	53%

- There are two alternatives to national commercial air time: using satellite capabilities to air commercials regionally via a network link, or purchasing local air time on an individual basis.
- Peak/Prime time for radio is 07:00-13:00 for Households. Prime time for automobiles is 07:00-09:00, 13:00-15:00 and 15:00-19:00.

Ratings

Daypart	Mexico City Adult Rating	Adult (000)
06:00-11:00	.3	48.1
11:00-16:00	.4	64.1
16:00-21:00	.3	48.1

Source (Radio): Radiometer I.N.R.A., 1993

Daypart Costs/CPMs (Target=Adults 19-44)

Daypart	Local Time	Avg. Cost :30 US$	Audience (000)	CPM (US$)
Prime Time	08:00-12:00	240	4,557.3	53.90
Daytime	13:00-19:00	75	4,050.9	18.58
Late Night	20:00-24:00	75	1,519.1	49.56

Cable

There are two major privately owned subscription cable systems. Cablevision and Multivision (scrambled) reach 174 cities in 29 states. Cable penetration is about 7%; totalling 1,200,000 households. It is a growing medium, and because cable distributors are still increasing their coverage and number of channels, a growth in subscriber numbers (3,000,000 households are expected to subscribe within the next 5 years) and improved quality of programming are anticipated. At the present time however, open TV is still stronger.

In Mexico City there are 41 cable channels; 21 of which are commercial. Spanish is the primary broadcasting language; English is secondary.

Cable HH Penetration			
1989	*1990*	*1991*	*1992*
2.6%	6%	7%	7%
80,000	679,900	763,500	1,200,00

Top Cable Channels	Cost US$	Commercial Min/Hr
Multideporte	10,391	6
ABC, CBS, NBC	6,432	6
Movie Cable	6,432	6
TNT	10,391	6
TVC	8,320	6

Cable Networks	HH Circulation (000) National/Mexico City	Programming
Movie Cable	800/170	Movies
Super Canal	800/170	Music videos and movies
Nuestro Cable	800/170	Family programming
TNT	800/175	Movies
Multideporte	800/175	Sports
ZAZ	800/175	Cartoons/Movies
Tele UNO	314/175	U.S. TV Series
AS	297/175	U.S. TV Series
CNN	314/175	News
TVC	800/-	Family programming
Canal 6	800/-	Family programming

Satellite

- In Mexico, it is expensive for consumers to have the option of receiving a satellite signal. Consumers have to buy the parabolic dish and a decoder. Last year, the decoder was unavailable in Mexico. As a result, the satellite signal is being received by less people. Cable TV's penetration is replacing satellite territory. Satellite penetration is not expected to increase significantly.
- Satellite reaches about 17,100 households; only 1% of the total Mexican households. About 25,000 households are expected to subscribe in the next 5 years.
- There are currently 50 satellite channels; however satellite is not a commercial advertising medium.
  Source: Directorio Canitec, 1992

All of the channels listed below are broadcast in English from the USA.

Satellite Channel	Programming	Satellite Channel	Programming
KUSA ABC	News	Cinemax	Movies
KRMA PBS	General	HBO	Entertainment
Sports Channel	Sports	Family Channel	Entertainment
KMGH CBS	News	Life Time	Entertainment
Prime Ticket	Movies	Prime Network	General
Home Sports	Sports	Weather Channel	News
Channel America	Sports	New England Channel	Sports
Channel Chicago	News	MTV	Music videos
KCNK NBC	Sports	The Movie Channel	Movies
Channel Ohio	Sports	Nickelodeon	General
Prime Network	Entertainment	Playboy Channel	Entertainment
International	Movies	CNN	News
Viewer's Choice	Sports	Superstation TBS	Entertainment
Prime Sports	Sports	WGN	General
KWGN	News	ESPN	Sports
Sunshine Network	News	Discovery Channel	Entertainment
Comedy Central	Comedy	TNT	Movies
Pay Per View	Movies, events	The Nashville Network	General
Encore	General	U.S.A.	General
Disney Channel	Family	Arts & Entertainment	Entertainment
FLIX	General	Cable Video Store	Movies
Country Music TV	Music videos	Sports South Headline	News
Showtime	Movies	Home Team Sports	Sports

Video Cassettes

Video cassette recorders (VCRs) are used by 52% of the TV households in Mexico; totalling 38% of all households. Pre-recorded tapes do not carry advertising and commercialization is not expected although VCR penetration should increase. IBOPE MEXICO measures every signal that is received on TV via Channel 3. This includes VCR, satellite signals and video games.

Cinema

- There are 1,998 urban, 618 suburban and 1,763 rural theaters in Mexico; 98% offer commercial time.
- Based on 130 cinemas in Mexico City, the potential 4 week reach is 4.5%.

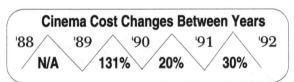

Cinema Cost Changes Between Years				
'88	'89	'90	'91	'92
N/A	131%	20%	30%	

- Commercial lengths available are :10, :20, :30, :40 and :60 and the average cost of a 4 week schedule in 130 theaters is US$ 460.

Urban theaters in the city are segmented into categories based on the quality/type of service.

There are no audience measurements and none are expected to develop.

Now that Grupo Radio TV del Centro has purchased the 'COTSA' group of theaters, many improvements in quality and service are anticipated. The new name for the theater group is ECOCINES.

Newspapers

There are 6 national daily newspapers that accept advertising. The combined circulation is about 1,374,000 with the main circulation concentrated in Mexico City. There is an estimated 10% English literacy rate.

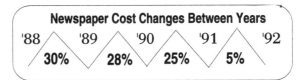

Daily Newspaper	Market	Size	Circulation (000)	Avg. Daily Readership (000)	1 page B&W Cost (US$)	Accept Color?
Diario de Mexico	Mexico City	Standard	21	42	3,353	Yes
Esto	Mexico City	Tabloid	150	300	1,366	Only supplements
Excelsior	National	Standard	140	280	5,270	Yes
El Economísta	Mexico City	Tabloid	30	60	1,856	1 additional color
El Financiero	National	Tabloid	90	135	2,028	Yes
El Heraldo de Mexico	National	Standard	40	280	4,840	Yes
El Nacional	Mexico City	Standard	20	40	2,880	Yes
El Sol de Mexico	Mexico City	Standard	25	68	4,384	Yes
El Universal	National	Standard	160	304	5,271	Yes
La Aficion	Mexico City	Tabloid	18	36	1,504	Yes
La Jornada	Mexico City	Tabloid	45	113	2,363	Yes
La Prensa	National	Tabloid	200	460	2,035	Yes
Novedades	National	Standard	50	315	5,270	Yes
Ovaciones	Mexico City	Both	120	240	4,416	Additional colors
Summa	Mexico City	Tabloid	15	30	1,549	Yes
The News	Mexico City	Tabloid	25	58	2,416	Yes
Uno mas Uno	Mexico City	Tabloid	40	60	2,848	No
El Informador	Guadalajara	Standard	50	130	1,455	Yes
El Occidental	Guadalajara	Standard	35	91	1,322	Yes
El Norte	Monterrey	Standard	125	250	2,850	Yes
El Porvenir	Monterrey	Standard	25	75	1,825	Yes

Magazines

332 consumer magazines and 451 trade and technical magazines are published in Mexico.

Magazine	Type	Frequency	Circ. (000)	Audited?	Avg. Issue Aud. (000)	1 page 4/C Cost (US$)
America Economia	Business	Monthly	17.6	No	35	4,480
Activa	Women's	Bi-monthly	45.9	Yes	92	6,880
Automundo Deportivo	Sports	Monthly	150	No	300	609
Buenhogar	Women	Bi-monthly	61.6	Yes	123	6,880
Business Mexico	Business	Monthly	4	No	8	4,412
Caminos del Aire	In-flight	Monthly	125	No	875	13,280
Casas y Gente	Decoration	Monthly	20	No	40	5,760
Claudia	Women's	Monthly	181	No	362	4,646
Computer World	Computers	Bi-monthly	10	No	20	5,365
Contenido	General	Monthly	180	Yes	358	6,432
Cosmopolitan	Women's	Monthly	161.7	Yes	324	9,600
Decision	Business	Monthly	30	No	90	548
Deporte Ilustrado	Sports	Monthly	40	No	80	4,416
Ejecutivos de Finanzas	Finance	Monthly	15	Yes	30	4,672
Escala	In-flight	Monthly	110	No	1,029	12,432
Eres	Teens	Bi-monthly	730	No	1,460	13,248
Expansion	Business	Bi-monthly	26.3	Yes	53	5,629

Continued on following page

Magazine	Type	Frequency	Circ. (000)	Audited?	Avg. Issue Aud. (000)	1 page 4/C Cost (US$)
Geomundo	General	Monthly	57	Yes	114	2,720
Golf Pro-Am	Sports	Monthly	16	No	32	3,200
Golden Penthouse	Men's	Monthly	38	No	76	4,416
Harper's Bazzar	Women's	Bi-monthly	20	No	40	4,960
Hombre	Men's	Monthly	32	No	64	2,720
Ideas para su hogar	Women's	Monthly	42	Yes	84	2,880
Impacto	Politics	Monthly	150	No	300	1,545
Kena	Women's	Monthly	100	No	200	7,365
Maria Orsini	Gourmet	Bi-monthly	21	No	41	4,800
Mecanica Popular	Men's	Monthly	110	Yes	210	9,126
Mexico Desconocido	Geography	Monthly	72	Yes	35	6,502
Muy Interesante	Science	Monthly	234	Yes	466	5,120
Newsweek	General	Weekly	20	No	40	4,552
Orbit	TV Program	Monthly	28	No	56	5,952
Orbita	TV Program	Monthly	100	No	299	7,888
Personal Computing	Computers	Monthly	N/A	No	N/A	3,774
PC Magazine	Computers	Monthly	27	Yes	54	4,960
Playboy	Men's	Monthly	148	No	295	7,040
Progreso	Business	Monthly	9	No	31	3,194
Selecciones	General	Monthly	880	Yes	3,000	4,816
Shape	Sports	Monthly	75	No	150	4,429
Siempre	Politics	Weekly	100	No	200	2,240
Teleguia	TV Program	Weekly	709	Yes	1,418	10,240
Tiempo Libre	Showbusiness	Weekly	95	No	190	1,024
Tu	Teens	Monthly	125	Yes	249	4,800
TV Novelas	Women's	Bi-Weekly	938	Yes	1,876	14,400
Vanidades	Women's	Bi-Weekly	229	Yes	657	10,560
Vogue	Women's	Monthly	50	No	200	6,544

Outdoor/Transit

Billboard

Sites available 15,418
Lead Time to reserve .... 4 to 8 weeks

Exposure 1-30%

Transit

Boards available
   Subway Panel 450
   Inside Subway 20,000
   Taxis 70,000
Exposure (metro) 15%
      (in Mexico City)

Costs

Average, 1 billboard/month
   1 page (12.9 m x 3.6 m) .... US$ 1,093

Billboard Cost Changes Between Years

'88	'89	'90	'91	'92
	20%	30%	18%	15%

Costs

Average, 1 board/month
   Subway Panels .... US$ 530
   Inside Subways .... US$ 19.50
   Taxis .... US$ 207

Transit Cost Changes Between Years

'88	'89	'90	'91	'92
	19%	30%	18%	15%

Continued on following page

Outdoor/Transit, Continued

Sizes	Sizes
Standard Billboards–2.9 m x 3.6 m	Subway Panels–3.49 m x 1.74 m
Double Billboards–12.9 m x 7.2 m	Lateral–0.46 m x 0.24
Back Light–....... 12.0 m x 4.0 m	Buses–1.00 m x 6.00 m
.... 12.0 m x 8.0 m	Taxis–0.80 m x 0.30 m
.... 15.0 m x 4.0 m	
Unipost–15.0 m x 4.0 m	
Bus Stop (Top, Left/Right)–6 m x 3.6 m	
Tridinamic–12.9 m x 3.6 m	
Ultra 'Q'–7.2 m x 7.2 m	

Product/Category Restrictions for Outdoor Advertisements
- There are some avenues where the government allows only a certain number of billboards.
- Billboards must be placed at least 100 meters away from each another.
- Eliminate billboards from visually cluttered avenues. (Self-regulated)
- Cigarette and alcoholic beverage advertising must have a health warning phrase.
- No nudity allowed.

Direct Marketing

Direct marketing is becoming more important among advertisers. The number of suppliers and advertisers has increased since 1990. Options include direct response, telemarketing, direct mail, and data bases.

List Broker	Information

Direcciones S.A.
  Lago Winnipeg 163 Tacuba
  11410, Mexico City
	Business lists, consumer lists, laser printing, computer services, letter shop.

Respuesta Directa S.A. de C.V.
  Peten 12 Narvarte
  03020 Mexico City
	Business lists, consumer lists, laser printing, computer services, letter shop, door-to-door services.

Imagen	Consumer lists.

Telemarketing Companies		Direct Marketing Association
Telemantra		Asociacion Mexicana de
Entelsa		Mercadotecnia Directa
Ticket Master (In Mexico since 1990)	Becoming successful in the telemarketing area.	

Non-Traditional Media

The trend is for media forms to be segmented by geographic areas and targets. Costs vary by medium.
Types of non-traditional media that are currently available:
On the streets: Mailboxes, public timeclocks, bus stops.
In supermarkets: Bags, directories, cars, monitors, audio, etc.
Others: In airports, schools, restaurants, stadiums, social events, yellow pages, etc.

Research Sources

Medium Covered	Research Company	Information Provided
TV	IBOPE Mexico Bruno Traven 60 Mexico, City	Ratings and reach and frequency in Mexico City.
	A.C. Nielsen Blvd. A. Camacho 191, Mexico, City	Competitive weekly activity, monthly competitive report and annual spending in major markets.
	INRA Av. Coyoacan 1870 Mexico, City	Monthly ratings in major markets.
Radio	A.C. Nielsen	Annual spending
	INRA	Monthly ratings in major markets.
Magazines/Press	A.C. Nielsen	Annual spending
	Moctezuma y Asociados	Reach, habits and profiles.

Television Research Currently Available

Research Method	Frequency	Research Method	Frequency
IBOPE Ratings, Reach & Frequency People meters, Set meters and diaries.	Weekly	INRA Ratings coincidentally	Monthly

Advertising Regulations

By Product

Beverages/Alcohol
Advertising copy for alcoholic beverages must be self-regulated. Consumer promotions must be cleared by the Secretary of Commerce. The Secretary of Public Education supervises the correct use of language. Alcoholic beverage advertising must have a health warning phrase in the copy.

Food/Restaurants
Consumer promotions must be cleared by the Secretary of Commerce. The Secretary of Public Education supervises the correct use of language. In the case of food, a health phrase must be included.

Cigarettes
Advertising copy for cigarettes must be approved by the Secretary of Health. Consumer promotions must be cleared by the Secretary of Commerce. The Secretary of Public Education supervises the correct use of language. Cigarette advertising must have a health warning phrase in the copy.

Pharmaceuticals/Drugs
Consumer promotions must be cleared by the Secretary of Commerce. The Secretary of Public Education supervises the correct use of language.

Advertising To Children
Consumer promotions must be cleared by the Secretary of Commerce. The Secretary of Public Education supervises the correct use of language.

Commercial Production
Several regulations by the same ministries mentioned above, depending on the category.

By Medium

Television
Cigarette and alcohol advertising must be aired after 21:00 and 22:00, respectively, and must have a health warning phrase.

Print
Cigarette and alcoholic beverage advertising must have a health warning phrase.

Outdoor
There are some avenues where the government allows only a certain number of billboards. Billboards must be placed at least 100 meters away from each another. Eliminate billboards from visually cluttered avenues (self regulated).
Cigarette and alcoholic beverage advertising must have a health warning phrase.
No nudity allowed.

Cable
Cigarette and alcohol advertising can only air after 21:00 and 22:00, respectively, and must have a health warning phrase.

Nicaragua

Area	129,494 km²
Population (1992)	3,878,150
Population growth rate (1992)	2.8%
GDP	US$ 1.6 billion
GDP/per capita	US$ 425
Real growth rate (1991)	1.0%
Capital	Managua

Population Breakdown

By Sex
Male 48%
Female................................... 52%

By Age Group
Children, 0-10...................... 33.5%
Teens, 11-19........................ 24.5%
Adults, 20+.......................... 42.0%

By Socio-Economic Status
A 28%
B... 0%
C... 0%
D.. 72%

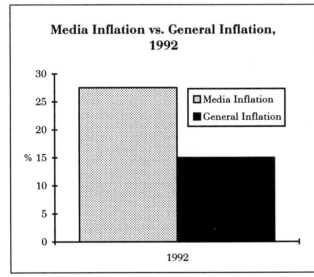

Media Inflation vs. General Inflation, 1992

☒ Media Inflation
■ General Inflation

Number of Households	**N/A**

Ownership of household durables
Car.................................. 3.5
Phone........................... N/A
Washers........................ N/A
(purchasing power equivalent)

GNP distribution by industry
Agriculture.................... N/A
Industry .... N/A
Services .... N/A

Exchange rates (US$ to local currency)
1991 .... N/A
1992 ....0.2000

National Holidays

Holiday	1993 Date
New Year's Day	January 1
Holy Week	April
Labor Day	May 1
Independence Day	September 14, 15
Christmas	December 25

School Holidays

Holiday	1993 Date
New Year's Day	January 1
Holy Week	April
Labor Day	May 1
Independence Day	September 14, 15
Christmas	December 25

Major Influences and Trends

Under the Sandinist Government, advertising was barely active, but during the last two years the advertising industry has started growing again. The two channels that existed during the Sandinist Government have begun to improve their programs. Two new channels have emerged and hopefully during the next few years more commercial TV channels will emerge. Advertising is still minimal.

Television
TV coverage is directed to the Pacific area, where the capital city and major cities are located (these are the major markets). In Managua, TV household penetration reached 93% in 1992. International companies are beginning to invest again and hopefully there will be an improvement in TV coverage.

Radio
Radio is strong in Nicaragua, and the most popular programs are news and sports, primarily baseball.

Spending Analysis

National advertising spending by medium
based on appropriate year's exchange rate

	1992 *US$ MM*
TV	7.8
Cinema	N/A
Radio	8.9
Newspaper	6.7
Magazine	N/A
Outdoor	N/A
Total	**23.8**

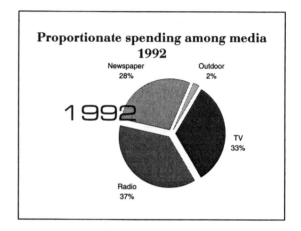

Proportionate spending among media 1992

Newspaper 28%
Outdoor 2%
TV 33%
Radio 37%

Media Buying

TV stations negotiate based on volume of investment and offer bonus space for specific spending levels. There is no saturation in the media market since the number of clients advertising is still low. Buying services do not exist.

Television

The growth of TV stations in this country and improvement in programming of channel 2 (leader) will increase TV's usage by advertisers in a short period of time. Penetration levels are only measured in Managua and currently stand at 93%.

Opportunities

Channels	Number of Stations	Ownership	Station Profile	Commercial Minutes/Day	Coverage	Broadcast Hours (Sign-On/Off)
2	1	Private	Soap Operas	65	Pacific Coast	8:00-23:00
4	1	Private	Movies/News	17	Pacific Coast	8:00-23:00
6	1	Government	Soap Operas/ Movies/Series	45	National/Except East	8:00-23:00
8	1	Private	Movies	24	Capital	12:00-23:00

Costs

Costs rose by 5% in 1992.

Audiences/CPM's

Average Cost, Audience, and CPMs by Daypart
(Top 3 Stations, :30, national audience)

Hours:	Morning 8:00-12:00	Daytime 12:00-18:00	Prime Time 18:00-22:00	Late Night 22:00-23:00	Weekend	Children
Station: 2						
US$	40.83	66.50	210.83	210.83	N/A	N/A
Avg. Aud.* (000)	63.4	110.9	237.7	63.4		
CPM	0.64	0.60	0.88	3.32		
Station: 6						
US$	40.83	66.50	210.83	210.83	N/A	N/A
Avg. Aud.* (000)	55.5	55.6	39.6	15.9		
CPM	0.73	11.90	5.32	13.25		
Station: 8						
US$	N/A	31.33	87.83	87.83	N/A	N/A
Avg. Aud.* (000)	N/A	23.8	55.5	55.5		
CPM	N/A	1.31	1.58	1.58		

Household ratings are not measured in Nicaragua. These are people ratings.

Scheduling/Regional/Languages

- The only broadcasting language is Spanish.
- Commercials are aired throughout the day in :20, :30 and :40 time spots. 88% of all commercials are :30.
- All networks have regional coverage. Channel 8 is the only channel that has sole coverage of the capital.

Children's Advertising

All programming accepts advertising directed to children.

Radio

- Ninety-three percent of the households in Managua have radios.
- There are 66 radio stations, all in Managua.
- The most popular program types are sports and news.
- Spanish is the primary broadcast language, although English is also used.
- Commercial time is available in :10, :20, :30, :40 and :60 spots and no premiums are paid for regional or local advertising.

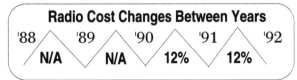

Radio Cost Changes Between Years

| '88 | '89 | '90 | '91 | '92 |
| N/A | N/A | 12% | 12% | |

Prime/Peak Time for Radio

Local Time	Avg. Rating	Avg.Cost :30 US$
08:00-12:00	5.0	10

- The average cost of a :30 radio commercial for a target audience of people 8+ ABCD is US$ 10.94, while the average CPM is US$ 1.01.

Cable

- This medium was established in 1990 and several of the programs are in Spanish from Mexican channels.
- No cable regulations exist and the cable industry suffers from severe pirating.
- There are 22 privately owned cable channels, none are commercialized or measured; they reach about 7.5% of all households in Nicaragua.

- Most broadcasting is in Spanish; English is the secondary language.

Cable Networks	Programming
Ch. 5 - Mexico	Programming from Mexico
HBO	Movies
Univision	Spanish-language programming
Ch. 6 - Mexico	Programming from Mexico
CNN	News 24-hours

Satellite

No satellite channels are broadcast in Nicaragua at this time.

Video Cassettes

An estimated 20% of the TV households in Managua have video cassette recorders (VCRs) ; however pre-recorded tapes do not carry advertising.

Cinema

There are only 5 cinemas in Nicaragua and only one offers commercial time.

Newspapers

Nicaragua has 4 national daily newspapers that accept advertising. They have a combined circulation of 135,000. Newspaper costs rose 13.6% in 1992.

Daily Newspaper	Size	Circulation (000)	Avg. Daily Aud. (000)	1 page B&W Cost (US$)	Accept Color?
La Prensa	6 col x 20 in	40	1,975	No	Yes
Barricada	6 col x 20 in	40	1,104	Yes	
El Nuevo/Diario	8 col x 20 in	45	1,975	No	
La Tribuna	Tabloid	15	500	No	

Magazines

There are 25 consumer magazines published in Nicaragua.

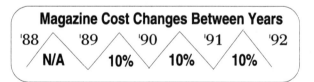

Magazine Cost Changes Between Years

'88	'89	'90	'91	'92
N/A	10%	10%	10%	

Magazine	Type	Frequency	Circ. (000)	Audited?	Avg. Issue Aud. (000)	1 page4/C Cost (US$)
El Pais	Economy	Monthly	10	No	1,225	980
El Publicista	Publicity	Monthly	2	No	1,270	780
Pensamiento	Economy	Monthly	N/A	No	720	N/A
La Ternera	Cattle	Monthly	3	No	440	533
Observador	Economy	Monthly	70	No	935	750

Outdoor/Transit

- A billboard 9 ft x 48 ft costs US$ 105.00 for one month.
- Reservations need to be made three weeks in advance.
- Rates rose by 15% in 1992.

Direct Marketing

Direct marketing does not exist in Nicaragua.

Non-Traditional Media

There is no use of non-traditional media in Nicaragua.

Research Sources

Medium covered	Research company	Information Provided
TV, Radio, Press	Multivex 3 Calle 2-50, Zona 9	Rating by program/by day/by hour TV measured annually by Recall
TV	M&R	Rating by program/by day/by hour TV measured semi-annually by Recall

Advertising Regulations

Advertising regulations have not been established in Nicaragua.

Sources Consulted

Instituto Nicaraguense Estadistico y Censo (INEC)

Panama

Area	78,200 km^2
Population (1992)	2,529,902
Population growth rate (1992)	2.0%
GDP	US$ 5.0 billion
GDP/per capita	US$ 2,040
Real growth rate (1991)	9.3%
Capital	Panama City

Population Breakdown

By Sex
Male 50.6%
Female............................... 49.4%

By Age Group
Children, 0-10 .... 23.8%
Teens, 11-19 .... 21.8%
Adults, 20+ 54.4%

By Socio-Economic Status
A 7.0%
B 0.0%
C 33.0%
D 60.0%

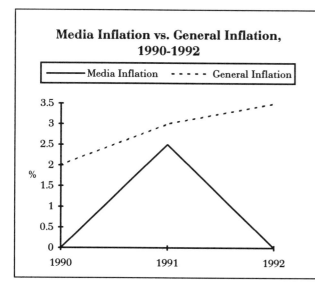

Media Inflation vs. General Inflation, 1990-1992

—— Media Inflation   - - - - General Inflation

Number of Households   600,000
Ownership of household durables
   Car 35.0%
   Phone .... N/A
   Washers .... N/A
   (purchasing power equivalent)
GNP distribution by industry
   Agriculture 11.3%
   Industry 9.4%
   Services 8.8%
Exchange rates (US$ to local currency)
   1991 .... 1.00
   1992 .... 1.00

National Holidays

Holiday	1993 Date
New Year's Day	January 1
Memorial Day	January 9
Carnivals	February 20
Easter	April 1
Labor Day	May 7
Panama Foundation	August 15
Columbus Day	October 12
Independence Day	November 3
Independence (Villa de Los Santos)	November 10
Independence (Spain)	November 28
Mother's Day	December 8
Christmas	December 25

School Holidays

Holiday	1993 Date
Children's Day	November 1
Mid-Year Vacations	July 23 - August 9
Student's Day	September 26
Summer Vacations	December - April

Major Influences and Trends

Television

Television is the most important medium and it is very effective in providing excellent penetration and total coverage. Panamanian media is saturated because there are only three channels for 2,466,000 million people, which means much lower CPM's for advertisers.

The three channels have national coverage and the Department of Justice & Government controls and assigns the broadcast frequencies.

Radio

Radio audiences are divided between many different broadcasting stations, and although there is no radio research, experience shows that radio can be used as a complementary medium to extend reach to audiences in urban and rural areas (D/E). Radio is also used to reach younger audiences in the socio-economic ABC segment by buying broadcasts (mostly on FM stations) which target this segment.

Newspapers

Newspaper is effective for advertisers who need to be more extensive and explanatory in their message. This is especially true in Panama since there are no local magazines. However, there are no circulation audits which would provide the relative cost of print vehicles.

Spending Analysis

National advertising spending by medium
based on appropriate year's exchange rate

	1989 US$ MM	1990 US$ MM	1991 US$ MM	1992 US$ MM
TV	N/A	N/A	46.8	57.3
Radio	N/A	N/A	4.2	4.6
Newspaper	N/A	N/A	17.9	22.3
Total	N/A	N/A	68.9	84.2

Media Buying

Agencies buy TV, radio, newspapers, billboards, magazines, and cinema, for an 18% commission. Every TV channel gives the client a discount or bonus time depending on the amount the client will commit. Buying services do not exist.

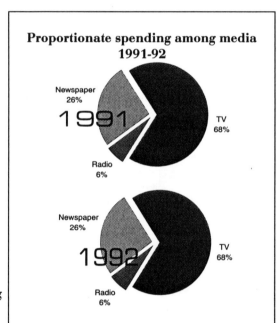

Proportionate spending among media 1991-92

1991
Newspaper 26%
TV 68%
Radio 6%

1992
Newspaper 26%
TV 68%
Radio 6%

Top Advertisers (1992 Spending)

By Company

Parent Company	Product Categories	US$ MM
Almacen El Lider	Male/Female Clothes	3.02
Almacen Piccolo	Male Clothes	1.31
Dorval	Shoes	1.04
Cerveceria Nacional	Various Beers	1.01
Panasonic	Electric Appliances	.95
Nissan	Cars	.92
Colgate-Palmolive	Soap, Toothpaste	.89
Tabacalera Istmena,S.A.	Cigarettes	.70
Farmacias Arrocha	Drugstore	.69
Audiofoto Internacional	Electric, Audio & Photographic Appliances	.66

Television

In Panama, there are three private channels: 4, 13, and 2. The two other channels, 11 and 5, are educational channels. In 1992, TV household penetration reached 65.1% (390,600).

Adult Reach	
at 250 GRPs	3,323,731
at 500 GRPs	6,647,462
at 1,000 GRPs	3,294,924

Opportunities

	Number of Stations	Ownership	Station Profile	Commercial Minutes/Hour	Coverage	Broadcast Hours (Sign-On/Off)
Channel 4	1	Fernando Eleta A.	General Programs	12	National	06:00-12:00
Channel 13	1	Nicolas Gonzalez Revilla	General Programs	12	National	06:00-12:00
Channel 2	1	Grupo Motta	Sports/General Programs	12	National	06:00-12:00
Channel 11	1	Government	Educational	None	Metropolitan	N/A
Channel 5	1	Government	Educational	None	Metropolitan	N/A

Costs

Prime Time TV Costs for :30 in US$			
1989	1990	1991	1992
N/A	400	460	423

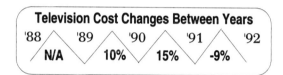

Television Cost Changes Between Years

'88 — '89 — '90 — '91 — '92
N/A — 10% — 15% — -9%

Audiences/CPM's

Average Cost, Audience, and CPMs by Daypart
(Top 3 Stations, :30, national audience, Target=Persons 20+)

Hours	Morning 06:00-12:00	Daytime 12:30-18:00	Prime Time 18:30-20:30	Late Night 20:30-24:00	Weekend 06:00-12:00	Children 08:00-11:00/ 15:00-17:00
Station: Channel 4						
US$	125.00	225.00	495.00	165.00	270.00	60.00
Avg. Aud. (000)	N/A	N/A	N/A	N/A	N/A	N/A
CPM	N/A	N/A	N/A	N/A	N/A	N/A
Station: Channel 13						
US$	75.00	210.00	450.00	145.00	300.00	60.00
Avg. Aud. (000)	N/A	N/A	N/A	N/A	N/A	N/A
CPM	N/A	N/A	N/A	N/A	N/A	N/A
Station: Channel 2						
US$	68.00	80.00	325.00	165.00	100.00	50.00
Avg. Aud. (000)	N/A	N/A	N/A	N/A	N/A	N/A
CPM	N/A	N/A	N/A	N/A	N/A	N/A

Audiences/Rating by Daypart (Target=Persons 20+)

Daypart	Hours	Household				Adult		
		Universe (000)	Hut Levels	Household Rating	Impressions (000)	Universe (000)	Adult Rating	Impressions (000)
Morning	06:00-12:00	406	N/A	33.2	134.8	316	13.6	42.9
Daytime	12:30-18:30	406	N/A	52.7	214.0	316	22.2	70.1
Primetime	18:30-20:30	406	N/A	84.2	341.9	316	44.3	139.8
Late Night	20:30-24:00	406	N/A	64.5	261.9	316	41.1	129.7
Weekend	06:00-12:00	406	N/A	66.4	269.6	316	40.7	128.4
Children's	08:00-11:00 15:00-17:00	406	N/A	51.3	208.3	316	65.2	205.8

Scheduling/Regional/Languages

- All programming in Panama is in Spanish.
- Commercial time is available in :10, :15, :20, :30, :40, :45 and :60 spots; 80% of all commercials are :30.
- Commercials are aired in specific blocks before, within and after programs.

- A maximum of 25 spots per 10 minutes is allowed.
- Only national channels accept advertising, metropolitan channels are government owned and do not accept commercials.

Children's Advertising

Programming which accepts advertising directed to children

| ADULT PROGRAMMING | | | | Kids' | |
Station	Hours	Days	Universe (000)	Ratings	Impressions (000)
Channel 4	09:30-11:30	Sat.-Sun.	15,137	12.6	1,907
	15:00-17:00				
	13:00-15:00	Mon.-Fri.	15,137	9.5	1,438
	07:00-09:00				
Channel 13	06:00-24:00.	Sunday	15,137	18.6	2,815
	13:00-15:00	Mon.-Fri.	15,137	9.7	1,468
	19:00-21:00				
Channel 2	19:00-20:00	Mon.-Sat.	15,137	6.5	1,378

| CHILDREN'S PROGRAMMING | | | | Kids' | |
Station	Hours	Days	Universe (000)	Ratings	Impressions (000)
Channel 4	09:30-11:30	Mon.-Fri.	15,137	30	4,541
	15:00-17:00				
	09:00-11:30	Fri.-Sat.	15,137	30.1	4,556
	11:30-12:30	Saturday	15,137	11.8	1,786
	14:00-17:00	Sat.-Sun.	15,137	14.2	2,240
	13:30-17:00				
Channel 13	17:30-18:00	Mon.-Fri.	15,137	41.8	6,327
	15:00-18:00	Sunday	15,137	24.8	3,754
	09:30-11:30	Mon.-Fri.	15,137	23.3	3,527
	15:30-17:30				
	10:30-11:30	Sunday	15,137	13.9	2,104
	14:00-16:30	Sat.-Sun.	15,137	8.3	1,256
	13:00-15:00				
Channel 2	08:00-09:00	Mon.-Fri.	15,137	11.9	1,801
	14:30-16:00				
	08:00-10:00	Saturday	15,137	17.2	2,604
	08:00-10:00	Sunday	15,137	17.9	2,710

Source (Television): Panamenca Communications Int., S.A.

Radio

- Radio penetration in Panama is 88%; about 433,546 households.
- There are 78 national stations, all are commercial and 42 are located in Panama City.
- The primary language used for broadcasting is Spanish; English is secondary.
- The most popular program types are News and Music.
- Commercials are available in :10, :15, :20, :30, :40 and :60 spots.

- Radio costs rose 10% from 1990 to 1991 and 15% from 1991 to 1992.
- Prime times in Panama are from 06:00 - 09:00 and 17:00 - 18:30. These are primarily news broadcasts.

Daypart Costs/CPMs
(Target=Persons 8+ in capital)

Daypart	Local Time	Avg. Cost :30 US$
Prime Time	06:00-09:00	25.00
Daytime	12:00-17:00	8.00
Late Night	19:00-22:00	8.00

Cable

The one local cable operator in Panama, Cable Onda 90, is private. They broadcast via 28 channels and have made arrangements with the local TV stations to air programming on UHF channels because they are not able to sell advertising on cable. This is expected to cause a decrease in share for the local channels. The primary broadcasting language is English; Spanish is also used.

The top cable channels are HBO OLE, CNN, ESPN, TBS and Cartoon Network.

Satellite

Satellite dishes in Panama have access to all U.S. cable networks (see U.S. section for a list of networks). In addition, there is access to the following foreign-language channels via satellite:

Satellite Channel	Language
Antenna Greece	Greek
Arab Network of America	Arabic
CBC French-East	French
CBC Parliamentary Network	French
Canal de Noticias	Spanish
CNI Newswire	Spanish
CTFM	French
Deutsche Welle	German
Galtavision	Spanish
Gems TV	Spanish
International Channel	N/A
NHK	Japanese
RAI/USA Network	Italian
RTP	Portuguese
SCOLA	N/A

Satellite Channel	Language
Super Canal	Spanish
SUR	Spanish
Telemundo	Spanish
TV Asia	Hindi
TV Japan(NHK)	Japanese
TV5	French
Univision	Spanish
XEIPN-Mexico City	Spanish
XEW-Mexico City	Spanish
XEWH-Hermosillo	Spanish
XHDF-Mexico City	Spanish
XHFM-Veracruz	Spanish
XHGC	Spanish
XHIMT-Mexico City	Spanish
XHTV-Mexico City	Spanish

Video Cassettes

An estimated 70% of the TV households in Panama have video cassette recorders (VCRs). Pre-recorded tapes do not carry advertising.

Cinema

Of the 30 theaters in Panama, only 3% offer commercial time (:30 and :60 spots). For a 4 week schedule, each :30 spot costs US$ 400.00 and each :60 spot costs US$ 600.00.

Newspapers

There are 5 national daily newspapers that accept advertising; they have a combined circulation of 155,000.

Daily Newspaper	Market	Size	Circulation (000)	Avg. Daily Aud. (000)	1 page B&W Cost (US$)	Accept Color?
La Prensa	National	Standard	35-40	160-192	970.00	Yes
Panama America	National	Standard	19-21	91-101	630.00	Yes
La Estrella de Panama	National	Standard	17-21	82-101	630.00	Yes
El Siglo	National	Tabloid	25-35	120-158	375.00	No
La Critica	National	Tabloid	25-38	120-182	375.00	No

Magazines

Magazines received in Panama are U.S. or Central America editions of the titles. No magazines are published locally.

Magazine	Type	Frequency	Circ. (000)	Audited?	Avg. Issue Aud. (000)	1 page 4/C Cost (US$)
Vanidades	Women's	N/A	5.2	No	N/A	N/A
Buenhogar	Women's	N/A	5.1	No	N/A	N/A
Cosmopolitan in Spanish	Women's	N/A	5.2	No	N/A	N/A
Coqueta	Teen's	N/A	3.5	No	N/A	N/A
TV	Teen's	N/A	3.7	No	N/A	N/A
Ideas	Women's	N/A	2.5-3.0	No	N/A	N/A
Harper's Bazaar	Women's	N/A	.5	No	N/A	N/A
Cosmopolitan in English	Women's	N/A	.5	No	N/A	N/A
Good Housekeeping	Women's	N/A	1.0	No	N/A	N/A
Popular Mechanic	Men's	N/A	.5	No	N/A	N/A
Redbook	Women's	N/A	.4	No	N/A	N/A
Architectural Digest	Architecture	N/A	.5	No	N/A	N/A

Outdoor/Transit

Billboard	**Transit**
Sites available .... no limitations Lead Time to reserve .... 1 month Exposure .... N/A	Boards available .... no limitation Exposure (metro) 78%
Costs Average, 1 billboard/month .... US$ 400 (10% cost change from previous year)	**Costs** Average, 1 board/month: .... US$ 300
Sizes 10 ft x 32 in, 20 ft x 50 in, 12 ft x 24 in.	**Sizes** 120 in x 33 in, 72 in x 24 in, 24 in x 24 in.

Direct Marketing

There is no direct marketing activity in Panama.

Non-Traditional Media

There is no use of non-traditional media in Panama.

Research Sources

Medium covered	Research company	Information provided
TV Newspaper	Panamerica Communications, Int. S.A.	Recall method used every 6 months

Advertising Regulations

By Product

Beverages/Alcohol

"If you drink, don't drive" warning must be included in TV spots after 18:00. Warning must also be included in print, except for outdoor and P.O.P. material. There should not be any scenes with people drinking alcoholic beverages.

Food/Restaurants

Spots have to be approved by the Joint Health Minister.

Cigarettes

The same as alcohol warning but with a non-smoking message.

Both TV commercials and print ads cannot include scenes of people smoking. The models chosen for the advertisements must be older than 18.

Pharmaceuticals/Drugs

Depending on what kind of medicine you want to advertise, it has to be approved by the Joint Health Minister.

By Medium

Television

New commercials on air must be approved by the Joint Health Ministry.

Source Consulted

Media Research Data: Leo Burnett, Panama

Peru

Area	1,285,220 km^2
Population (1992)	22,767,543
Population growth rate (1992)	2.0%
GDP	US$ 20.6 billion
GDP/per capita	US$ 920
Real growth rate (1991)	2.4%
Capital	Lima

Population Breakdown

By Sex		*By Age Group*		*By Socio-Economic Status*	
Male	*50.3%*	*Children*	*36.9%*	*A*	*4.0%*
Female	*49.7%*	*Teens*	*20.6%*	*B*	*22.0%*
		Adults	*42.5%*	*C*	*45.0%*
				D	*29.0%*

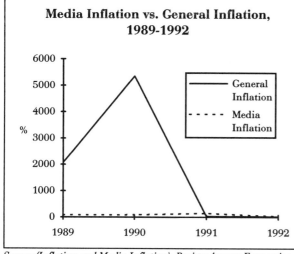

Media Inflation vs. General Inflation, 1989-1992

— General Inflation
- - - - Media Inflation

Number of Households	**1,299,700**

Ownership of household durables

Car	N/A
Phone	N/A
Washers	N/A

GNP distribution by industry

Agriculture	6.0%
Industry	31.0%
Services	63.0%

Exchange rates (US$ to local currency)

1991	0.8786
1992	0.5180

Source (Inflation and Media Inflation): Revista Avance Economica and Revista Mensual Enero, 1993.

Source (GNP by Industry): Perven numeros, Cuanto S. A., Lima, Peru, 1992.

National Holidays

Holiday	*1993 Date*
New Year's	December 31 - January 1
Holy Thursday	April 8
Holy Friday	April 9
Labor Day	May 1
Saint Peter and Saint Paul Day	July 5
National Holiday	July 28 - 29
Santa Rosa de Lima Day	September 6
Angamos Combat	November 1
All Saint's Day	November 1
Christmas Holiday	December 24 - 25

School Holidays

Holiday	*1993 Date*
Vacations	May 18 - 24
	July 20 - August 10
	October 19 - 25
	December 14 - March 8

Source: Elaboracion LB/Causa

Major Influences and Trends

- The main medium in Peru is television.
- America Television (TV-4) was sold in early 1993 to Televisa of Mexico.
- In the main interior cities, Arequipa, Cusco, Cajamarca and Huanuco, new private local TV channels have emerged.
- There has been an emergence of comparitive advertisement where the competitive brand is shown and its disadvantages are touted.
- Although the overall circulation numbers in print vehicles have decreased as a result of lower readership levels, new magazines and newspapers have entered the market.
- The importance of alternative media is growing. These include signage on bus stops, taxis and buses.

Source: Elaboracion LB/Causa

Spending Analysis

National advertising spending by medium
based on appropriate year's exchange rate

	1989 US$ MM	1990 US$ MM	1991 US$ MM	1992 US$ MM
TV	226.0	177.7	161.0	198.1
Cinema	15.1	11.9	8.2	4.8
Radio	0.6	0.6	7.3	14.3
Newspaper	5.8	3.9	10.6	13.9
Magazine	2.1	4.4	1.9	3.6
Outdoor	1.4	1.1	1.0	2.4
Other	0.6	0.5	--	--
Total	**251.6**	**200.1**	**190.0**	**237.1**

Source: Supervision Nacional de comerciales Resumenes Anuales de Inversion, Elaboracion LB/Causa, 1989, 1990, 1991, 1992.

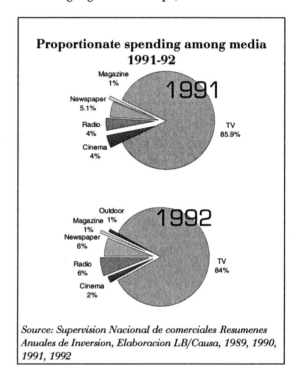

Proportionate spending among media 1991-92

Source: Supervision Nacional de comerciales Resumenes Anuales de Inversion, Elaboracion LB/Causa, 1989, 1990, 1991, 1992

Media Buying

Companies with large advertising budgets can negotiate with the media directly. Others negotiate using agencies. In many cases, intermediaries are used to buy radio and newspapers in the interior of the country.
Source: Elaboracion LB/Causa

Newspapers and magazines are negotiable. There are no media monopolies in Peru.
Buying services do not exist

Television

Overview

Television in Peru is divided into dayparts. Different types of programming air in each daypart. The breakout is as shown in the table on the right.

Programming by Daypart

Morning	News
Daytime	Soap operas
Children's	Cartoons
Prime Time	Imported programming dubbed to Spanish
Late Night	Adult programming

Television HH Penetration					Adult Reach	
1989	1990	1991	1992		at 250 GRPs	59%
86.3%	85.0%	88.7%	88.9%		at 500 GRPs	69%
					at 1,000 GRPs	95%

Opportunities

Network	Number of Stations	Ownership	Station Profile	Commercial Minutes/Hr	Coverage	Broadcast Hours (Sign-On/Off)
Latinoamericana de Radiodifusora TV2	1	Private (Baruch Ivcher)	General	12	National	24 hr
America Television TV 4	1	Private (America N. Gonzales Televisa)	General	12	National	24 hr
Panamerica Television TV5	12	Private (M. Delgado Parker)	General	12	National	12:30-14:30 Wkd. 08:00-14:30
Andina de Television ATV - Ch. 9	3	Private (Julio Vera Gutierrez)	General	12	Lima/North / South	12:00-14:30
R.T.P. TV7	11	Government (C. Lecca Arrieta)	Education/ General	12	National	24 hr
Empresa Radiodifusora S.A.	1	Private (Vittorio de Ferrari)	General	12	National	12:00-24:00
Global TV 13	1	Private	General	12	National	

Costs

Prime Time TV Costs for :30 in US$			
1989	1990	1991	1992
3,395	3,214	1,839	1,500

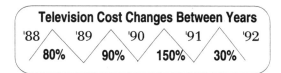

Television Cost Changes Between Years

'88 — 80% — '89 — 90% — '90 — 150% — '91 — 30% — '92

Audiences/CPM's

Average Cost, Audience, and CPMs by Daypart
(Top 3 Stations, :30, national audience, Target=Adults 15+)

Hours	Morning 06:00-12:00	Daytime 12:00-16:00	Prime Time 19:00-23:00	Late Night 23:00-00:00	Weekend 12:00-00:00	Children 16:00-19:00
Station: TV 2						
US$	650	650	1,200	1,300	800	650
Avg. Aud. (000)	278	90	260	197	200	122
CPM	2.34	7.22	4.62	6.60	4.00	5.33
Station: TV 5						
US$	566	1,600	2,500	1,700	2,000	850
Avg. Aud. (000)	127	385	314	197	219	168
CPM	4.50	4.20	8.00	8.63	9.13	5.10
Station: TV 9						
US$	N/A	540	900	630	630	450
Avg. Aud. (000)	N/A	95	339	209	203	146
CPM	N/A	5.70	2.70	3.01	3.10	3.10

Audiences/Rating by Daypart (Target: Adults 18+)

Daypart	Hours	Household				Adult		
		Universe (000)	Hut Levels	Household Rating	Impressions (000)	Universe (000)	Adult Rating	Impressions (000)
Morning	06:00-12:00	1,041	42.2	7.0	72.9	3,676	2.6	95.6
Daytime	12:00-16:00	1,041	53.5	7.6	79.1	3,676	3.4	125.0
Primetime	19:00-23:00	1,041	72.9	10.4	108.3	3,676	5.4	198.5
Late Night	23:00-24:00	1,041	48.3	6.9	71.8	3,676	3.6	132.3
Weekend	12:00-24:00	1,041	56.7	8.1	84.3	3,676	3.7	136.0
Children's	16:00-19:00	1,041	49.1	7.0	72.9	3,676	2.9	106.6

Scheduling/Regional/Languages

- All programming in Peru is in Spanish.
- Currently 80% of all commercials are :30; other lengths available are :10, :15, :20, :40, :50 and :60.
- Commercial time is sold by rotations or by daypart and are aired both at the beginning and end of programs and within them. Alternatives for airing commercials exist on the ATV Network, (Station TV-9 in the Lima/North/South regions) between 12:00 and 02:00. About 10% of all commercials are aired on a regional/local level at 20% the cost of national air time for a :30 spot.

Children's Advertising

Programming which accepts advertising directed to children

ADULT PROGRAMMING				Kids'	
Station	Hours	Days	Universe (000)	Ratings	Impressions (000)
TV-2	20:00-21:00	Sun	779	15.3	119.2
TV-5	20:00-21:00	Sat	779	25.1	195.5
TV-9	21:00-22:00	Sat	779	12.6	98.2

CHILDREN'S PROGRAMMING				Kids'	
Station	Hours	Days	Universe (000)	Ratings	Impressions (000)
TV-2	19:00-19:30	Sun	779	12.2	95
TV-5	08:00-12:00	Sat-Sun	779	18.0	140.2
TV-9	14:00-16:00	Sat-Sun	779	8.9	69.3

Sources (Television): C. P.I. Sintonia Auditorios Televisivos; Resumenes Mensuales, Lima, Peru; Revista 17.65 Mensual, Lima, Peru; Programacion Proporcionada para los canales; Supervision Nacional de comerciales. Tarifas Impresa de los canales.

Radio

- The Peruvian radio penetration level is 97.2%; about 1,132,200 households.
- Lima has 50 commercial stations. Spanish is the only broadcast language.
- News and Sports are the most popular program types.
- Commercials are available in multiples of :10 up to :60. The average costs of a :30 spot is US$ 90 on the National Network and US$ 60 on the Lima Network. Spots are sold in rotations, not by daypart.

Radio Cost Changes Between Years

'88		'89		'90		'91		'92
	80%		90%		150%		30%	

- Regional and local air time costs an average of 70% that of national time and are available on Panamericana.
- Prime/Peak time is from 06:00 to 12:30.

Ratings

Daypart	Adult Rating	Adult (000)
06:00-24:00	1.9	107.4

Sources (Radio): C. P.I. Sintonia Radial AM/FM, 1992; Supervision Nacional de comerciales. Tarifas Impresa de las Emisoras.

Cable

Telecable, which is a privately owned cable TV company, offers subscriptions and delivers 22 TV channels from different countries. *(Source: Elaboracion LB/Causa)*

Satellite

Direct-to-home satellite channels do not exist in Peru. *(Source: Elaboracion LB/Causa)*

Video Cassettes

7.9% of all Peruvian households have video cassette recorders (VCRs), which represents 12.1% of the TV households. Pre-recorded tapes do not carry advertising. *(Source: C.P.I. Estudio de Tenencia TV, 1992)*

Cinema

- There are 81 cinemas in Peru; based on a survey of 64 theaters, the potential reach over a four week period is 70%.
- All theaters offer :60 commercial spots at an average cost of US$ 12,722 for a 4 week schedule at 37 cinemas in Lima.

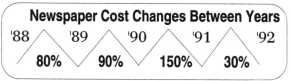

Cinema Cost Changes Between Years

'88	'89	'90	'91	'92
	80%	90%	150%	30%

Source (Cinema): Publicin S.A., Lima, Peru; Tarifas Impresas, 1992.

Newspapers

All national daily newspapers in Peru accept advertising; the literacy rate in the national language is 100% for adults 15+ in Lima. Newspaper circulation is not audited in Peru.

Newspaper Cost Changes Between Years

'88	'89	'90	'91	'92
	80%	90%	150%	30%

Source (Newspapers): Estudio de Lectoria y Perfilde Lectores de Diaros y Revistas; C.P.I. Reportes, 1992; Tarifas Impresas de Diarios y Revistas.

Newspaper	Market	Size	Circulation (000)	Avg. Daily Aud. (000)	1 page/B&W Cost (US$)	Accept Color?
Comercio	National	Broadsheet	108.0	660.0	4,719	Yes
OJO	National	Tabloid	81.0	326.0	1,787	Yes
Republica	National	Tabloid	58.5	248.4	2,383	Yes
Onda	National	Tabloid	54.0	85.1	1,657	Yes
Expreso	National	Tabloid	54.0	204.3	1,937	Yes
Extra	National	Tabloid	22.5	109.3	1,450	Yes
Popular	National	Tabloid	22.5	64.6	2,331	No
El Peruano	National	Broadsheet	31.5	50.3	1,658	Yes
Tercera	National	Tabloid	13.5	N/A	N/A	Yes
Gestion	Naitonal	Tabloid	16.2	28.4	1,399	No
El Mananero	National	Tabloid	81.0	150.9	663	Yes
Super Idolo	National	Tabloid	54.0	92.3	1,533	Yes
El Pueblo	Arequipa	Broadsheet	13.5	N/A	646	Yes
Correo	Arequipa	Tabloid	5.4	N/A	317	No
Arequipa Al Dia	Arequipa	Tabloid	4.5	N/A	300	Yes
El Sol	Cusco	Tabloid	3.6	N/A	227	Yes
La Industria	Chiclayo	Broadsheet	16.2	N/A	1,371	Yes
El Diario	Chimbote	Tabloid	4.5	N/A	499	Yes
El Faro	Chimbote	Tabloid	3.6	N/A	197	Yes
Correo	Huancayo	Tabloid	2.3	N/A	317	Yes
La Voz	Huancayo	Tabloid	2.7	N/A	194	Yes
El Matutino	Iquitos	Tabloid	2.7	N/A	518	Yes
El Tiempo	Piura	Tabloid	10.8	N/A	296	No
Correo	Piura	Tabloid	10.8	N/A	317	No
La Industria	Trujillo	Broadsheet	16.2	N/A	1,371	Yes
Satelite	Trujillo	Tabloid	5.4	N/A	444	Yes
Correo	Tacna	Tabloid	7.2	N/A	317	No

Source: Elaboracion LB/Causa; C.P.I. Estudio de Lectoria, 1992.

Magazines

32 consumer magazines are published in Peru.
Magazine circulation is not audited.

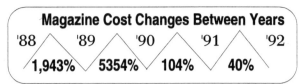

Magazine	Type	Frequency	Circ. (000)	Audited?	Avg. Issue Aud. (000)	1 page 4/C Cost (US$)
Actualidad Economica	Economy	Monthly	3,080	No	N/A	1,200
America Economia	Economy	Monthly	880	No	N/A	8,600
Avance Economica	Economy	Monthly	2,640	No	N/A	1,200
Caretas	Politics/Current Affairs	Weekly	22,000	No	N/A	2,800
Cosas	Current Affairs	Bimonthly	8,800	No	N/A	2,200
Cuanto	Statistical	Monthly	4,400	No	N/A	2,700
Debate	Economy	Bimonthly	6,160	No	N/A	2,490
Efficacia	Economy	Monthly	2,640	No	N/A	1,750
Empresas & Empresarios	Management	Monthly	1,320	No	N/A	900
Gente	Politics/Current Affairs	Weekly	22,000	No	N/A	3,300
Gerencia	Management	Monthly	2,640	No	N/A	1,600
Globo	Horoscope	Monthly	4,400	No	N/A	2,700
Industria Peruana	Industry	Monthly	1,760	No	N/A	1,350
La Tortuga	Current Affairs	Bimonthly	1,760	No	N/A	3,200
Marketing Estrategias	Marketing	Monthly	1,760	No	N/A	1,350
Mercadeo Latino	Marketing	Monthly	1,760	No	N/A	1,350
Mineria	Mining	Monthly	2,200	No	N/A	1,200
Morena	Female	Monthly	13,200	No	N/A	2,750
Oiga	Politics/Current Affairs	Weekly	13,200	No	N/A	2,800
Proceso Economico	Economy	Monthly	1,320	No	N/A	2,400
Proyeccion	Managemnt	Monthly	2,200	No	N/A	1,500
Quehacer	Politics	Bimonthly	6,600	No	N/A	2,000
Semana Economica	Economy	Weekly	6,160	No	N/A	1,790
SI	Politics/Current Affairs	Weekly	16,160	No	N/A	2,900
Teleguia	TV Magazine	Bimonthly	13,200	No	N/A	700
Telecolor	TV Magazine	Bimonthly	8,800	No	N/A	1,600
The Peru Report	Management	Bimonthly	2,640	No	N/A	2,700
1/2 De Cambio	Economy	Monthly	4,400	No	N/A	1,700
1/2 De Marketing	Marketing	Monthly	4,400	No	N/A	1,700
Vanidades	Female	Bimonthly	14,960	No	N/A	1,600
Buen Hogar	Female	Bimonthly	14,960	No	N/A	1,600
Vea	Female	Monthly	13,200	No	N/A	2,750

Source: Elaboracion LB/Causa; C.P.I. Estudio de Lectoria, 1992

Outdoor/Transit

The average cost for a 3.60 m x 7.20 m billboard in Peru is US$ 140; reservations are needed one month in advance.   *(Source: Elaboracion LB/Causa)*

Direct Marketing

- There are no specialized direct mail companies. Banks, federal organizations, markets, travel agencies and magazines serve as the top mail consumer list brokers in Peru.
- There is no activity in telemarketing, nor any direct marketing association.

Non-Traditional Media

There is no use of non-traditional media in Peru.

Research Sources

Medium Covered	Research Company	Information Provided
TV, Radio	*Compania Peruana de Investigacion Rio de Janerio #150-Miraflores	Diary Method
Newspaper, Magazines, TV, Radio	Teledatum	Survey

*TV research is available daily, weekly and monthly from Teletron People Meter.

Advertising Regulations

By Product

Beverages/Alcohol

Advertising of alcoholic drinks containing a high percentage of alcohol will only be permitted after 21:00 and children cannot be used as models.

Cigarettes

Cigarette advertising will only be permitted after 21:00. It is also forbidden to have cigarette advertising without labeling it with a danger of consumption warning.

Pharmaceuticals/Drugs

Pharmaceutical drugs which require a doctor's prescription for purchase require labeling, although non-prescription drugs do not.

Commercial Production

Restrictions were dropped beginning in 1992. Foreign produced commercials are now allowed to air in Peru.

Puerto Rico

Area	9,104 km²
Population (1992)	3,776,654
Population growth rate (1992)	1.0%
GDP	US$ 7.4 billion
GDP/per capita	US$ 15,000
Real growth rate (1990)	N/A
Capital	San Juan

Population Breakdown

By Sex		*By Age Group*		*By Socio-Economic Status*	
Male	48%	Children, 2-11	19%	A	10%
Female	52%	Teens, 12-17	12%	B	37%
		Adults, 18+	69%	C	30%
				D	23%

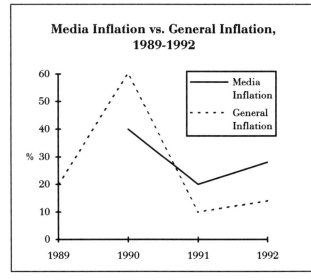

Media Inflation vs. General Inflation, 1989-1992

Number of Households   1,051,810

Ownership of household durables

Car	68%
Phone	68%
Washers	93%

(purchasing power equivalent)

GNP distribution by industry

Agriculture	28%
Industry	24%
Services	48%

Currency = US$

National Holidays

Holiday	1993 Date
New Year's Day	January 1
Epiphany	January 6
Martin Luther King	January 20
George Washington Birthday	February 17
Memorial Day	May 25
Good Friday	April 17
Independence Day	July 4
Labory Day	September 7
Thanksgiving	November 26
Christmas	December 26

Local Holidays

Holiday	1993 Date
Hostos	January 11
Jose de Diego	April 16
Munoz Rivera	July 17
Constitution Day	July 25
Jose Celso Barbosa	July 27
La Raza	October 12
Veterano	November 11
Descubrimiento de PR	November 19

School Holidays

Holiday	1993 Date
Same as Federal and Local	
Dia del Arbol	November 20

Spending Analysis

National advertising spending by medium
based on appropriate year's exchange rate

	1989 US$ MM	1990 US$ MM	1991 US$ MM	1992 US$ MM
TV	120.0	88.4	110.0	114.1
Cinema	3.0	2.2	2.3	3.3
Radio	46.4	35.1	37.0	52.0
Newspaper	150.0	99.4	143.0	158.0
Magazine	8.0	9.4	10.3	10.7
Outdoor	N/A	6.8	7.0	7.5
Other	2.6	N/A	N/A	N/A
Total	**330.0**	**241.3**	**309.6**	**345.6**

Proportionate spending among media 1991-92

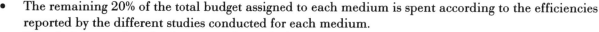

Media Buying

- The primary media are negotiated at the begin-ning of each year. On average, approximately 80% of the total budget assigned to each medium is committed upfront, obtaining rate card discounts, protection on negotiated rates and benefits on specific properties.
- TV buying (generally 80% of budget) is deter-mined by the efficiency of each program, as per monthly viewership studies.
- The remaining 20% of the total budget assigned to each medium is spent according to the efficiencies reported by the different studies conducted for each medium.
- Negotiations are done by the agency for each client separately.
- Annual contracts are signed by the agency and the client.
- Buying services do not exist.

Top Advertisers (1992 Spending)

By Company

Parent Company	US$ MM TV Rate Card
Procter & Gamble	22.3
Colgate Palmolive	8.7
Unilver	9.0
Anheuser Busch, Inc.	6.3
Kellogg Products	4.7
Sterling Products	5.4
Farmacias Walgreens	3.6
Cosmair Caribe	3.0
Grande Supermarket	2.9
Puerto Rico Telephone Co.	2.9

By Product

Product Category	US$ MM TV Rate Card
Theater, Entertainment	23.2
Fast Foods & Restaurants	17.0
USA Local Governments	14.1
Beers & Malts	13.0
Detergent	9.1
Communications Systems	8.2
Professional Service	8.1
Pharmaceutical, Drug Products	8.0
Household Cleaners	7.8
Network Island Stations	7.7

Television

Overview

- The television penetration level is 98%, reaching 1,029,400 households.
- Soap operas, movies, news, talk shows, comedy and sitcoms are the most common types of programming. Channels 2, 4, 11 and 7 have a combined 90% share of total TV households.

Adult Reach		*Morning*	*Daytime*	*Primetime*	*L.Night*	*Weekend*
	at 250 GRPs	31%	41%	63%	47%	75%
	at 500 GRPs	32%	44%	84%	50%	84%
	at 1,000 GRPs	33%	45%	88%	51%	88%

Opportunities

Network	Number of Stations	Ownership	Station Profile	Commercial Minutes/Hr	Coverage	Broadcast Hours (Sign-On/Off)
WKAQ-TV Ch. 2	2	Telemundo Inc. (Private)	General	12	97%	06:00-01:00
WAPA-TV Ch. 4	2	Pegasus (Private)	General	12	95%	06:00-02:00
WLII-TV Ch. 11	1	Mallrite Co. (Private)	General	12	95%	06:00-02:00
WSTE-TV Ch. 7	1	Siete Grandes Television, Inc. (Private)	General	12	90%	07:00-24:00
WIPR-TV Ch. 6	1	Government of P.R. (Government)	General	None	90%	07:30-00:30
WMTJ-TV Ch. 40	1	Ana G. Mendez Foundation (Public)	Educational	Sponsorship	–	07:30-00:30
WSJU-TV Ch. 18	2	International Broadcasting Corp. (Private)	U.S. Programming	12	75%	06:00-23:30
WPRV-TV Ch. 13	2	Private	U.S. Programming	12	–	07:00-23:30

Costs

Prime Time TV Costs for :30 in US$			
1989	*1990*	*1991*	*1992*
1,826	2,008	2,210	2,340

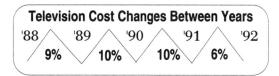

Television Cost Changes Between Years

'88		'89		'90		'91		'92
	9%		10%		10%		6%	

Audiences/CPM's

Average Cost, Audience, and CPMs by Daypart
(Top 3 Stations, :30, Target=Adults 18+)

Hours	Morning Sign-On-12:00	Daytime 12:00-18:00	Prime Time 18:00-22:00	Late Night 22:00-24:00	Weekend 18:00-22:00	Children M-F 15:00-17:00
Station: CH. 2						
US$	512	1,525	2,636	700	1,865	50.8
Avg. Aud. (000)	9.1	154.3	307.5	171.5	348.9	114.6
CPM	8.66	9.88	8.57	4.08	5.35	4.43
Station: CH. 4						
US$	433	988	2,540	444	1,280	402
Avg. Aud. (000)	34.7	108.9	208.5	143.0	134.1	35.5
CPM	12.47	9.16	12.18	3.10	9.51	11.32
Station: CH. 11						
US$	279	572	1,843	189	83	347
Avg. Aud. (000)	50.0	61.4	219.8	84.3	147.3	27.7
CPM	5.58	9.31	8.38	2.24	6.82	12.52

Audiences/Rating by Daypart (Target=Adults 18+)

Daypart	Hours	Household				Adult		
		Universe (000)	Hut Levels	Household Rating	Impressions (000)	Universe (000)	Adult Rating	Impressions (000)
Morning	Sign-On-12N	1,029	19.1	5.4	55.6	2,280	2.1	47.9
Daytime	12:00-18:00	1,029	34.6	9.6	98.8	2,280	4.7	107.2
Primetime	1800-22:00	1,029	59.1	17.8	183.2	2,280	10.8	246.3
Late Night	22:00-00:00	1,029	34.6	10.2	104.9	2,280	5.8	132.3
Weekend	18:00-22:00	1,029	51.7	15.1	155.4	2,280	9.2	209.8
Children's	15:00-17:00	1,029	35.0	9.9	101.9	2,280	2.6	59.3

Scheduling/Regional/Languages

LANGUAGES	Programming		Commercials
Primary Language	Spanish	93%	Spanish
Secondary Language	English	7%	English

Regional Airing

Network	Station	Region	Hours
Channel 2	WORA Ch. 5	West	Same as network
Channel 4	WOLE Ch. 12	West	Same as network

- About 70% of all commercials are :30; other lengths available are :15, :45 and :60.
- Commercials are aired throughout the day, at the beginning, end and within programs.
- Regional and local buying accounts for 5% of the total; the cost is 25% that of national air time.

Children's Advertising

Programming which accepts advertising directed to children

ADULT PROGRAMMING			Kids'		
Station	Hours	Days	Universe (000)	Ratings	Impressions (000)
Ch. 2	18:00-22:00	M-Sun	617	9.9	61.2
Ch. 4	18:00-22:00	M-Sun	617	8.7	53.5
Ch. 11	18:00-22:00	M-Sun	617	9.2	57.0

CHILDREN'S PROGRAMMING			Kids'		
Station	Hours	Days	Universe (000)	Ratings	Impressions (000)
Ch. 2	15:00-17:00	M-F	617	18.6	114.6
Ch. 4	15:00-17:00	M-F	617	5.8	35.5
Ch. 11	15:00-17:00	M-F	617	4.5	27.7
Ch. 2	Sign-on-11:00	Sat	617	11.1	68.3
Ch. 4	Sign-on-11:00	Sat	617	5.2	32.4
Ch. 11	Sign-on-11:00	Sat	617	8.9	54.9
Ch. 2	Sign-on-11:00	Sun	617	8.4	51.9
Ch. 4	Sign-on-11:00	Sun	617	4.4	27.1
Ch. 11	Sign-on-11:00	Sun	617	11.0	67.8

Radio

- There is a 98% radio penetration level in Puerto Rico; representing 834,700 households.
- San Juan has 28 of the 109 radio stations in Puerto Rico; 108 stations are commercial.
- The primary broadcasting language is Spanish. English is secondary. Music and talk shows are the most popular.

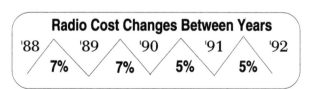

Radio Cost Changes Between Years

| '88 | '89 | '90 | '91 | '92 |
| | 7% | 7% | 5% | 5% |

- National air time costs 30% more than regional and local air time. Commercial lengths available are :15, :30, :45 and :60.

Daypart Costs/CPM's (Target=Persons 18+)

Daypart	Local Time	Avg. Cost :30 Unit US$		Audience(000)		CPM (US$)	
		National	Regional	National	Regional	National	Regional
Prime Time	18:00-22:00	98	24.00	80.6	12.0	1.22	2.00
Daytime	12:00-18:00	75	22.00	30.0	10.2	2.50	2.15
Late Night	22:00-24:00	46	20.00	15.9	2.5	2.89	8.00

Cable

- There are 24 cable channels of which 6 are commercial.
- The primary broadcasting language is English; Spanish is secondary.
- Few cable operators in Puerto Rico sell commercial time for local advertisers.
- Some cable homes subscribe to the basic service for the purpose of improving local TV reception.
- Currently, there is no cable TV measurement, but it will be available starting January '94 as part of Mediafax monthly reports.
- Total cable universe is approximately 267,644. Approximately 42% of total subscribers have an annual income of US$ 15,000+. Within the next five years 30% of all TV households (308,820) are expected to subscribe to cable.

Cable HH Penetration			
1989	1990	1991	1992
20%	22%	24%	26%
203,880	226,533	246,232	267,644

Top Cable Channel	Primtime (US$)	Prime R.O.S.* (US$)	Comm Min /Hr
MTV	55	42	2
ESPN	105	83	2
USA	55	42	1
CNN	55	42	2
NBC	110	45	2

R.O.S. = Run of Schedule–Media buy that guarantees that spots will run in a variety of dayparts.

Cable Operators	Cable Franchise Areas (as reported by cable operators)
Cable TV of Greater San Juan	San Juan, Bayamon (Partial), Carolina, Rio Piedras, Trujillo Alto, Guaynabo, Isla Verde, Santurce, Hayo Rey, PTA de Tierra (Partial)
Community Cablevision	Levittown, Toa Baja, Toa Alta, Catano
Telecable of P.R.	San Juan, Bayamon, Carolina, Guaynabo, Toa Baja, Trujillo Alto, Catano, Loiza, Canovanas, Juncos, Las Piedras, Caguas, Cayey, Naranjito, Comerio, Vega Alta, Toa Alta, Dorado
Cablevision International	Vega Baja, Vega Alta, Manati, Dorado, Arecibo, Camuy, Hatillo, Barceloneta, Canovanas, Loiza, Rio Grande, Luquillo, Fajardo, Ceiba, Naguabo
Buenavision	Caguas, Juncos, San Lorenzo, Gurabo, Humacao, Las Piedras, Yabucoa, Aguas, Buenas, Cidra, Cayey
Teleponce Cable TV	Ponce, Juana Diaz, Yauco, Guayanilla, Penuela
Cablevision de Mayaguez	Mayaguez
Cable TV Del Noroeste	Aguadilla, Isebela, Quebradillas, Aguada, Moca
Dom's Cable TV	San German, Lajas, Cabo Rojo, Hormigueros, Sabana Grande, Maricao, Guanica
Cable TV Atlantic	Lares, San Sebastian, Utuado, Morovis, Ciales, Corozal, Florida, Orocovis

Cable Networks	Programming	Cable Networks	Programming
C-Span	Congress USA	Lifetime	Movies, Better Living
C-Span II	Congress USA	Comedy Central	Comedy
QVC	Shopping Channel	The Family Channel	Programs Oriented to Family
QVC II	Shopping Channel	The Weather Channel	24-Hours Weather Information
WSN	Shopping Channel	E! TV	Entertainment, News
EWTN	Religious	The Learning Channel	Educational
WABC	ABC Network-NY.	TBN	Trinity Network
WBBM-TV	CBS Network-Chicago	USA Network	Family Oriented Programs
WXIA-TV	NBC Network-Atlanta	MTV	Music Videos
ESPN	Sports Programming	VH-1	Music Videos
American Movie Classics	Movie Classics	Nickelodeon	Children's Programming
The Discovery Channel	Science, History, Travel, Nature	Arts & Entertainment	Arts, Movies, Specials
TNT	Movies, Specials, Sports	Bravo	Movies, Concerts
TBS-TV	Movies, Specials, Sports	Cinemax	Movies, Specials, Comedy
WWOR-TV	Movies, Specials, Sports	The Disney Channel	Family Oriented Programs
WGN-TV	Movies, Specials, Sports	HBO (Home Box Office)	Movies, Specials, Sports
WFIX	Movies, Specials, Sports	Showtime	Movies, Specials, Sports
WSBK	Movies, Specials, Sports	The Movie Channel	Movies
CNN	24-Hour News		

Satellite

- An increasing number of satellite dishes are currently being distributed. There is no current measurement of households using dishes but given the lower costs and increased accessibility, there will probably be a greater number of users.
- There are 8 non-commercial satellite channels with 12,000 subscribers reaching only 1% of all households.

Satellite Channel	Country of Origin	Language	Programming
WGN	USA	English	Movies, Specials, Sports
WTBS	USA	English	Movies, Specials, Sports
WOR	USA	English	Movies, Specials, Sports
WXIA	USA	English	Movies, Specials, Sports
WABC	USA	English	Movies, Specials, Sports
WBBM	USA	English	Movies, Specials, Sports
EWTN	USA	English	Religious programming

Video Cassettes

- Puerto Rico has 564,829 households with video cassette recorders (VCRs). This represents 54% of all households and 55% of TV households. Mediafax is the service that measures VCR usage. Pre-recorded tapes do not carry advertising.
- During the past five years, there has been a proliferation of video chain stores such as Blockbuster Videos. The proliferation of title rentals has increased competition against local and cable TV stations.

Cinema

- Based on 101 theaters the weekly attendance rate is 126,514.
- 90% of the cinemas offer commercial time in :30 and :60 lengths.
- The cinema industry is in continuous growth.

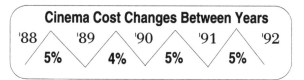

Cinema Cost Changes Between Years

'88 5% '89 4% '90 5% '91 5% '92

- The average cost per theater is US$ 173.25 for :30 and US$ 288.75 for :60.

Newspapers

Puerto Rico has 3 island-wide daily newspapers that accept advertising; the literacy rate is 91% in Spanish and 43% in English.

Newspaper Cost Changes Between Years
'88 / 8% \ '89 / 8% \ '90 / 9% \ '91 / 10% \ '92

Newspaper	Market	Size	Circulation (000)	Avg. Daily Aud. (000)	1 page/B&W Cost (US$)	Accept Color?
El Nuevo Dia	National	13" x 6 cols.	216.1	750.6	4,524	Yes/add cost 4/C
El Vocero	National	13" x 6 cols.	240.5	761.0	3,900	Yes/add cost 4/C
San Juan Star	National	13.5" x 6 cols	34.3	59.8	3,645	Yes/add cost 4/C

Combined circulation island-wide daily papers
Monday-Friday=499,513 (3 newspapers)
Saturday=442,350 (3 newspapers)
Sunday=256,111 (2 newspapers)

Readership Profile	El Nuevo Dia	El Vocero	San Juan Star
Sex			
Male	46.1%	50.1%	72.5%
Female	53.9%	49.9%	27.5%
Socio-Economic			
High/Middle High	15.1%	6.0%	57.5%
Middle	42.4%	40.6%	37.5%
Middle Low/Low	41.3%	71.6%	2.5%
Age			
12-17	14.2%	14.0%	12.5%
18-34	42.4%	40.6%	37.5%
35-69	43.4%	45.4%	50.0%

Magazines

There are 17 consumer magazines and 6 trade/technical magazines published in Puerto Rico.

Magazine Cost Changes Between Years
'88 / 3% \ '89 / 3% \ '90 / 5% \ '91 / 4% \ '92

Magazine	Type	Frequency	Circ. (000)	Audited?	Avg. Issue Aud. (000)	1 page 4/C Cost (US$)
TV Guides						
Teve-Guia	TV-Guide	Weekly	44	N/A	N/A	840
Vea	TV-Guide	Weekly	57	N/A	N/A	930
Artistas	Show Business	Bi-Weekly	16	N/A	N/A	550
TV-Novelas	Show Business	Monthly	27	N/A	N/A	1,095
Women's						
Buenhogar	Housekeeping	Bi-weekly	16	N/A	N/A	1,975
Vanidades	International	Bi-weekly	19	N/A	N/A	2,600
Bazaar	Women's	Monthly	12	N/A	N/A	2,970
Cosmopolitan	Women's	Monthly	18	N/A	N/A	2,920
Ideas	Home Ideas	Monthly	15	N/A	N/A	1,330
Imagen	Women's	Monthly	71	N/A	N/A	3,800
Caras	Women's	Monthly	31	N/A	N/A	3,500
Selecciones	Reader's Digest	Monthly	59	N/A	N/A	2,100
Youth						
Euforia	Teens	Monthly	30	N/A	N/A	2,530
Tu	Teens	Monthly	15	N/A	N/A	1,585
Men's						
Geomundo	Men's	Monthly	18	N/A	N/A	1,265
Hombre de Mundo	Men's	Monthly	6	N/A	N/A	1,900
Automundo	Men's/Cars	Monthly	N/A	N/A	N/A	2,748
Business						
Comercio y Produccion	Industry	Monthly	5	N/A	N/A	1,056
Business Puerto Rico	Business	Monthly	15	N/A	N/A	2,900

Continued on following page

Magazines, continued

Magazine	Type	Frequency	Circ. (000)	Audited?	Avg. Issue Aud. (000)	1 page 4/C Cost (US$)
General						
San Juan City Mag.	Business/Industry	Monthly	60	N/A	N/A	3,000
Bellas Artes	Theater Programs	Monthly	50	N/A	N/A	1,600
Buena Salud	Nutrition /Health	Monthly	57	N/A	N/A	3,500
Guest Informant	Tourism	Annually	50	N/A	N/A	11,700

Outdoor/Transit

Billboard

Sites available .... N/A
Lead Time to reserve .... 1 month adv.

Costs

Average, 1 billboard/month
   6 m x 12 m .... US$ 525

Billboard Cost Changes Between Years

'88	'89	'90	'91	'92
8%	8%	5%	5%	

Sizes

12 m x 24 m, 11 m x 23 m, 6 m x 12 m,
and 3 m x 6 m

Transit

Boards available
   Bus Shelters .... US$ 350
   Bus(inside) .... US$ 600
   Taxi Top .... US$ 330

Costs

Average, 1 board/month
   Bus Shelters .... US$ 426
   Bus (inside) .... US$ 11.50
   Taxi Top .... US$ 60.50

Transit Board Cost Changes Between Years

'88	'89	'90	'91	'92
6%	6%	5%	5%	

Sizes

Bus Shelters	69 cm x 49 cm
Buses (Inside)	21 cm x 22 cm
Taxi Top	14 cm x 38 cm

There are no restriction on products or categories.
Billboards are restricted as to location of site, location of signage on site (i.e., roof tops) and size.

Direct Marketing

Growing participation by major clients.

List Broker	Information Provided	Telemarketing Companies
Informatch	Household addresses, professional	Direct Response (Division of Casiano Communications)
Compu Mailing	Household addresses, professional	Target Marketing Services, Inc.
Direct Marketing & Media Group	Business addresses, officers	Voice of Information Processing, Inc.
Casiano Communications	Subscriber names, addresses/telephone numbers for magazines like Caribbean Business, Imagen, Buena Salud	Informatch

Direct Marketing Association
Local Chapter of Direct Marketing Association President: Carlos Cusnier (809) 721-5050

Research Sources

Medium Covered	Research Company	Information Provided
TV	Mediafax Ponce de Leon 1606 Piso 9, Santurce P.R. 00906	TV HH share by channel, by broad dayparts Broad daypart audience detail Household & target ratings
Radio	Asesores Asociados Call Box 8313 San Juan, P.R. 00906	Average ratings, shares Audience by specific station
Newspaper & Magazine	Asesores Asociados (see above)	Readership study Readership profiles Readership by newspaper or magazines

TV research is available monthly by meter, and quarterly by meter and diary.

Advertising Regulations

Beverages/Alcohol
Alcohol advertisements can only air on television after 21:00.

Cigarettes
Cigarette advertising is not allowed on television or radio (FCC Regulation).

Outdoor
Billboards are restricted as to location of site, location of signage on site (i.e., roof tops) and size.

Sources Consulted

ABC Circulation Audit Newspaper, Rate Cards
Cable Senior Management/Mediafax/Rate Card
Guastello Film, Rate Card
Individual Suppliers
Mediafax R/F, Telmar Inf.
Medium Senior Management
Official Government Correspondence
Publish Record Service
Puerto Rico 1990 Census
Radio Measurement: Asesores Asociados Rate Cards
Senior Management/Magazine Rate Cards
Sono Film, Rate Card
TV Measurement: Mediafax Rate Cards
TV Measurement: Mediafax TV Management

Uruguay

Area	176,220 km²
Population (1992)	3,141,533
Population growth rate (1992)	0.6%
GDP	US$ 9.1 billion
GDP/per capita	US$ 2,935
Real growth rate (1992 est.)	2.3%
Capital	Montevideo

Population Breakdown

By Sex		*By Age Group*		*By Socio-Economic Status*	
Male	47%	Children	23%	A	11%
Female	53%	Teens	11%	B	31%
		Adults	66%	C	45%
				D	13%

Source: Busqueda (weekly economic publication), Promedios

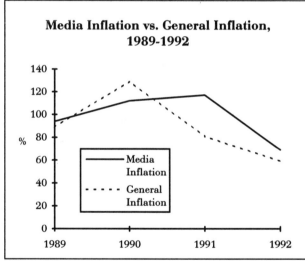

Media Inflation vs. General Inflation, 1989-1992

Legend: Media Inflation; General Inflation

Number of Households	**900,000**

Ownership of household durables
Car	37%
Phone	55%
Washers	N/A

(purchasing power equivalent)

GNP distribution by industry
Agriculture	10%
Industry	29%
Services	61%

Exchange rates (US$ to local currency)
1991	0.4955401
1992	0.3304692

Sources: Busqueda (weekly economic publication), Promedios

National Holidays

Holiday	*1993 Date*
New Year's	January 1
Labor Day	May 1
Constitution Day	July 18
National Independence Day	August 25
Christmas Day	December 25

School Holidays

Holiday	*1993 Date*
Easter Holidays	April 12-18
Winter Holidays	July 5-19
Summer Holidays	December 7-March 8

Major Influences and Trends

- The media with the strongest influence in the country are those that originate from the capital, Montevideo. These are referred to as Capital TV, Capital Press and Capital Radio.
- An increase in outdoor advertising, sales promotions, event sponsorships and merchandising is evident.
- The three private capital TV stations, (4, 10 & 12) cooperatively own a network (RUTSA) covering the provinces and competing with the state national TV system.
- Agencies have access to two different measurement and competitive sources which provide an accurate evaluation of the media and of target audiences, thus minimizing margins of error which may exist in these systems.
- These systems enable agencies to evaluate and optimize media planning and appraise different target audiences according to their buying potential, against a multimedia mix.

Spending Analysis

National advertising spending by medium
based on appropriate year's exchange rate

	1989 US$ MM	1990 US$ MM	1991 US$ MM	1992 US$ MM
TV	26.2	27.6	30.5	35.1
Cinema	.5	.3	.2	.2
Radio	12.2	12.2	11.9	13.8
Newspaper	16.7	16.5	16.2	18.5
Outdoor	2.0	2.1	2.4	2.7
Other	3.9	4.2	4.7	5.6
Total	**61.4**	**62.9**	**65.9**	**75.9**

Source: AUDAP (Uruguaian Advertising Agencies Association)

Media Buying

Media buying is done directly by agencies. It is possible to negotiate annual discounts with all media.

Buying services do not exist.

Television

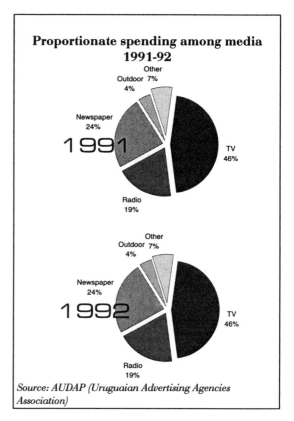

Proportionate spending among media 1991-92

1991: TV 46%, Radio 19%, Newspaper 24%, Outdoor 4%, Other 7%

1992: TV 46%, Radio 19%, Newspaper 24%, Outdoor 4%, Other 7%

Source: AUDAP (Uruguaian Advertising Agencies Association)

Overview

44% of Uruguay's population is located in the capital city of Montevideo. In the capital, there are three private TV stations (the leading stations in audience share) and a state TV station (with cultural programming). In the provinces, there are two networks (one private and one state) plus local TV stations. The TV household penetration level has been at 95% (about 855,000 households) for the last 4 years.

TV HH Penetration				Adult Reach
				at 250 GRPs 80%
1989	1990	1991	1992	at 500 GRPs 87%
95%	95%	95%	95%	at 1,000 GRPs 89%

Opportunities

Network	Number of Stations	Ownership	Station Profile	Commercial Minutes/Day	Coverage	Broadcast Hours (Sign-On/Off)
RUTSA	17	Private	General	80	National	17:00-01:00
S.N.T.	13	State	Cultural	122	National	07:00-02:00
Canal 4	1	Private	General	149	Capital	11:00-02:00
Canal 7	1	Private	General	90	Southern Region	11:00-02:00
Canal 10	1	Private	General	175	Capital	11:00-02:00
Canal 11	1	Private	General	100	Eastern Region	11:00-02:00
Canal 12	1	Private	General	160	Capital	11:00-02:00
Canal 2	1	Private	General	130	Eastern Region	07:00-02:00

Costs

Prime Time TV Costs for :30 in US$			
1989	1990	1991	1992
311.9	321.3	428.6	500.0

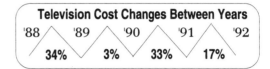

Television Cost Changes Between Years

'88 ⟋ '89 ⟋ '90 ⟋ '91 ⟋ '92
34%   3%   33%   17%

Audiences/CPM's

Average Cost, Audience, and CPMs by Daypart
(Top 3 Stations, :30, national audience)

Hours	Morning 11:00-17:30	Daytime 17:30-19:30	Prime Time 19:30-22:00	Late Night 22:00-Sign off	Weekend	Children
Station: 4						
US$	266.25	330.00	626.25	446.25	N/A	N/A
Avg. Aud. (000)	77.22	91.52	243.10	128.70	N/A	N/A
CPM	3.45	3.61	2.58	3.46	N/A	N/A
Station: 10						
US$	266.25	330.00	626.25	446.25	N/A	N/A
Avg. Aud. (000)	54.34	138.71	228.8	107.25	N/A	N/A
CPM	4.90	2.38	2.74	4.16	N/A	N/A
Station: 12						
US$	266.25	330.00	626.25	446.25	N/A	N/A
Avg. Aud. (000)	65.78	134.42	251.68	118.69	N/A	N/A
CPM	4.05	2.45	2.49	3.76	N/A	N/A

Source: Promedios

Audiences/Rating by Daypart (Target=Adults 20+)

Daypart	Hours	Household				Adult		
		Universe (000)	Hut Levels	Household Rating	Impressions (000)	Universe (000)	Adult Rating	Impressions (000)
Morning	11:00-17:30	397	15.5	5.1	20.6	859	4.2	36
Daytime	17:30-22:00	397	28.2	10.2	40.4	859	9.4	81
Primetime	19:30-22:00	397	50.1	16.8	66.6	859	15.5	133
Late Night	22:00-02:00	397	14.3	4.7	18.9	859	4.4	38
Weekend	N/A	N/A	N/A	N/A	N/A	N/A	N/A	N/A
Children's	N/A	N/A	N/A	N/A	N/A	N/A	N/A	N/A

Household data is estimated. Household information is not measured in Uruguay as a whole, only in the capital (Montevideo). Accordingly, such measurements should only be used directionally for the rest of the country.

Scheduling/Regional/Languages

- The only language used for broadcasting is Spanish. *(Source: Promedios)*
- Commercial lengths available are :20, :25, :30, :35, :45 and :60; 70% of all commercials are :35.
- Commercials are aired throughout the day both at the beginning and end of programs and within them.
- Alternatives to nationally aired commercials do exist (see table); regional/local buying accounts for 95% of the total advertising spending.

Network	Station	Region	Hours
Canal 11	1	Treinta Y Tres	17:00-01:00
Canal 8	1	Salto	17:00-01:00
Canal 3	1	Paysandu	17:00-01:00
Canal 12	1	Fray Bentos	17:00-01:00
Canal 3 & 8	2	Colonia	17:00-01:00
Canal 7	1	Tacuarembo	17:00-01:00
Canal 12	1	Melo	17:00-01:00
Canal 11	1	Maldonado	11:00-01:30
Canal 9	1	Rocha	17:00-01:00
Canal 10	1	Bella Union	17:00-01:00
Canal 10	1	Rivera	17:00-01:00
Canal 3	1	Artiga s	17:00-01:00
Canal 3	1	Rio Branco	17:00-01:00
Canal 4	1	Chuy	17:00-01:00
Canal 9	1	Paso de Los Toros	17:00-01:00
Canal 7	1	Pan de Azucar	08:30-02:30
Canal 2	1	Maldonado	07:00-02:00
Canal 4	1	Montevideo	11:00-02:00
Canal 10	1	Montevideo	11:00-02:00
Canal 12	1	Montevideo	11:00-02:00

Costs compared to national commercials

Area	:30 Cost	
National	US$ 187.5	(SNT) (State channel, low rating)
Local (Average)	US$ 20.87	
Regional	US$ 626.25	(Montevideo)
Regional	US$ 435.75	(Rutsa)

Children's Advertising

Programming which accepts advertising directed to children

ADULT PROGRAMMING				Kids'	
Station	Hours	Days	Universe (000)	Ratings	Impressions (000)
10	20:30	Wed	304.9	39	120.1
4	20:30	Mon	304.9	39	118.9
12	19:30	Mon	304.9	12	36.6
12	19:30	Fri	304.9	11	33.5
4	19:30	Sat	304.9	33	100.6

Average rating for highest rated hour of measurement during the top five adult programs that quarter.

CHILDREN'S PROGRAMMING				Kids'	
Station	Hours	Days	Universe (000)	Ratings	Impressions (000)
4	20:30	Sun	304.9	46	140.25
4	20:30	Thur	304.9	42	128.05
12	12:00	Mon-Fri	304.9	30	91.47
12	12:00	Sun	304.9	33	100.61
4	09:30	Sat	304.9	27	82.32

Average rating for highest rated hour of measurement during the top five kids programs that quarter.

Radio

- Radio penetration is 100% in homes (900,000 households); and about 80% (266,400) in automobiles.
- There are 160 radio stations, 156 of them are commercial; and of the 36 stations located in Montevideo, 32 are commercial.
- All programming is in Spanish and the most popular program types are musical, sports and news/talk.
- There are 4 radio stations with national coverage in Uruguay and 3 news broadcasts by network. The rest are local radio stations.
- All radio stations charge different rates, varying according to region, audience, and segmentation of the audience.
- Commercial lengths available are :10, :15, :20, :30, :35 and :40.

Daypart Costs/CPM's (Target=Adults 20+; Avg. of Main Montevideo Radio Stations)

Daypart	Avg. Cost :30 US$	Avg. Audience (000)	CPM (US$)
Located	50	7.7	6.4
Rotation	25	7.7	3.2

Ratings
Prime/Peak Time for Radio

Daypart	Adult Rating	Adult (000)
07:00-12:00	40	771

Cable

There is no cable TV yet in Uruguay. Permits were granted in late 1993 for the provinces.

Satellite

There are no direct-to-home satellite operations originating in Uruguay. Installed satellite dishes receive TV stations from other countries.

Video Cassettes

Video cassette recorder (VCR) usage is measured by Promedios; about 35% of all TV households have VCRs. Fifty percent of the companies allow advertising on pre-recorded tapes. The average is 2 sponsors per tape; the cost is US$ 0.83 per cassette.

Cinema

- Uruguay has 42 theaters; based on the 33 in Montevideo, the potential reach over a 4 week period is 7% of the population in the capital. Commercial time is available in 80% of the theaters.
- Commercial lengths available are :30, :40 and :60 for an average cost of US$ 17.00 per second (per theater).
- In Montevideo, advertising through this medium is very low, but in Punta Del Este (Uruguay's international resort) it is important, and currently being monopolized by Argentinian advertisers.

Newspapers

There are 5 national daily newspapers that accept advertising; the combined circulation is 251,000.

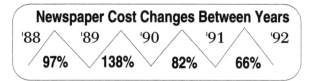

Newspaper Cost Changes Between Years
'88 / '89 / '90 / '91 / '92
97% \ 138% \ 82% \ 66%

Daily Newspaper	Market	Size	Circulation (000)	Avg. Daily Aud. (000)	1 page B&W Cost (US$)	Accept Color?
El Dia	National	Tabloid	7.7	25.4	3,600	Yes
El Pais	National	Standard	50.9	167.9	7,000	Yes
La Manana	National	Tabloid	3.0	9.8	2,800	Yes
El Observador	National	Tabloid	3.0	9.8	2,900	Yes
Ultimas Noticias	National	Tabloid	7.1	23.5	3,000	Yes
El Diario	National	Tabloid	7.1	23.5	2,800	No
La Republica	National	Tabloid	18.3	60.5	3,400	No

Estimated data. No circulation data available in Uruguay.

NOTE: Negotiated rates can be 20-40% less than listed prices.

Magazines

Although there are 500,000 magazine readers in Uruguay, there are no significant magazines published in the country. These Uruguayan readers consume foreign magazines, most of them published in Argentina.

Outdoor/Transit

Billboard	**Transit**
Sites available 2,600	Boards available 1,500
Lead Time to reserve* ....8 weeks	
Exposure ....300,000 per mo.	
Costs	**Costs**
Average, 1 billboard/month	Average, 1 board/month
10 m x 4 m ....US$ 160	...............................US$ 133
4 m x 3 m ....US$ 185	
7 m x 3 m ....US$ 235	
During the 1988-1992 period, the annual average increase in local currency has been 95%.	
Sizes	**Sizes**
4.00 m x 3.00 m	Bus 2.60 m x 0.65 m
7.00 m x 3.00 m	1.00 m x 0.40 m
	0.72 m x 0.30 m

Source: Publibus
*Source: Publicartel

Direct Marketing

Direct marketing is not very developed in Uruguay, but it is growing.

Non-Traditional Media

There has been an increase in the usage of non-traditional media, sales promotions; event sponsorships and merchandising in 1992.

Research Sources

Medium Covered	Research Company	Information Provided
TV/Radio/Newspaper	Promedios Bvar. Artigas 1098 Montevideo	Rating/reach/frequency GRP simulation multi-media
TV/Radio/Newspaper	Marketing Investigadores Assoc. Guayabo 1522 Montevideo	*Same as above*
TV	Mediciones y Mercado 25 de Mayo 463 P2 Montevideo	Broadcasting controls
TV	Telecontrol Ltda. Gabota 1390, Apt. 002	Broadcasting controls

TV research is available on weekly and monthly basis. Diary method is used.

Advertising Regulations

By Product

Cigarettes
All tobacco advertising must be labelled with 'Smoking is hazardous for your health.'

Pharmaceuticals/Drugs
Medicines requiring a physician's prescription cannot be advertised. All medicine advertisements must be labelled with 'Consult your physician.'

By Medium

Outdoor
Tobacco advertising is forbidden on Montevideo buses.

Venezuela

Area	912,050 km^2
Population (1992)	20,675,970
Population growth rate (1992)	2.4%
GDP	US$ 52.3 billion
GDP/per capita	US$ 2,590
Real growth rate (1991)	9.2%
Capital	Caracas

Population Breakdown

By Sex		By Age Group		By Socio-Economic Status	
Male	50%	Children, 0-5	13%	A,B	2%
Female	50%	Teens, 5-14	24%	C	21%
		Adults, 15-29	28%	D	37%
		Adults, 30-44	19%	E	40%
		Adults, 45-59	10%		
		Adults, 60+	6%		

Source: Fuente: DATOS, C.A. 1993

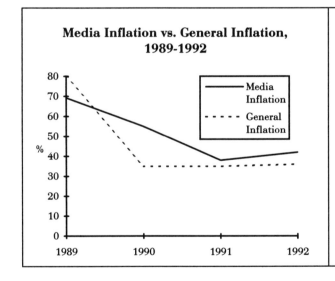

Media Inflation vs. General Inflation, 1989-1992

Number of Households   657,400
Ownership of household durables
Car 40%
Phone 41%
Washers 60%
(purchasing power equivalent)
GNP distribution by industry
Agriculture 45%
Industry 38%
Services 17%
Exchange rates (US$ to local currency)
1991 .... 0.01534
1992 .... 0.01147

National Holidays

Holiday	1993 Date
Columbus Day	October 12
Independence Day	April 19
Labor Day	May 1
Carabobo Battle	June 24
Signature Independence	July 5
Simon Bolívar	July 24

School Holidays

Holiday	1993 Date
Carnival	March 12
Easter	March 15
Teacher's Day	January 15
Youth Day	February 12
Christmas	December 25
Summer Vacation	July 15 to September 30

Major Influences and Trends

- Television holds the largest share of advertising expenditure (60+%).
- Local TV stations are growing, both in number and coverage.
- State-owned TV channels have returned to commercial status.
- Regional cut-in available on one national TV station.
- Cable/satellite dish penetration is increasing.
- There is a growing number of trade magazines.
- Only one media buying consortium exists for each group of agencies.
- All media are negotiable.
- There have been attempts to further regulate advertising activity for some categories, including cigarettes, and alcoholic beverages.
- There is growing activity in direct marketing.
- Cable television is becoming commercial.

Spending Analysis

National advertising spending by medium
based on appropriate year's exchange rate

	1989 US$ MM	1990 US$ MM	1991 US$ MM	1992 US$ MM
TV	181.4	462.7	287.5	384.4
Cinema	3.2	4.2	4.6	5.7
Radio	6.5	8.3	13.9	11.5
Newspaper	116.6	120.9	134.8	143.4
Magazine	9.7	12.5	13.9	17.2
Outdoor	6.5	8.3	9.3	11.5
Total	**324.0**	**417.0**	**463.7**	**573.7**

Source: Fuente. (1) IVP (Instituto Venezolano Publicitario), 1989, 1990, 1991, 1992.

Media Buying

Clepsidra is the only media buying company in existence. For the time being, it negotiates and buys for a group of companies: ARS (Local), Target/DDB Needham, ETC/DMB&B (Local Affiliate), and GHERSY/BSB (Local Affiliate). 1992 billings amounted to US$ 9,321,000 which is 8.6% of the market's total expenditures.

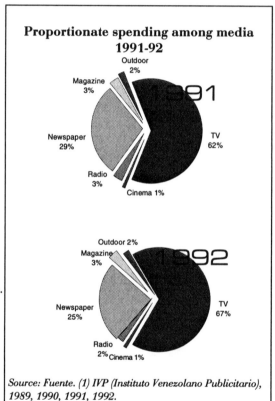

Proportionate spending among media 1991-92

Source: Fuente. (1) IVP (Instituto Venezolano Publicitario), 1989, 1990, 1991, 1992.

Top Advertisers (1992 Spending)

By Company

Parent Company	Product Categories	US$ MM
ODC	Media/Supermarkets/Dept.stores	24.6
Procter&Gamble	Detergents/Toiletries	21.6
Cruz Verde Group	Cleaning Products	19.7
Empresas IBC	Media/Books/Records/Airlines	9.9
Mercantil Group	Financial services	9.0
Latinoamericana Group	Financial services/Insurance	7.7
Banco Latino Group	Financial services	7.0
Colgate Palmolive	Detergents/Toiletries	6.9
Heinz Foods	Foods	6.0
Polar Groups	Beer/Malt/Food	5.4

Source: Fuente. IVP (Instituto Venezolano Publicitario), 1992.

By Product

Advertiser	Product Category	US$ MM
Sonorodven	Records	7.5
Sonografica	Records	2.8
Bank Services	Banco Mercantil	5.6
Bank Services	Banco Progreso	5.5
Bank Services	Banco Latino	5.0
Dept. Store	Maxy´s	4.3
Malt	Maltin Polar	3.7
Ketchup	Ketchup Heinz	2.7
Soft Drink	Pepsi-Cola	2.1
Liquid Cleanser	Lavansan	3.7

Source: Fuente. IVP (Instituto Venezolano Publicitario), 1992.

Television

	TV Household Penetration				Adult Reach
1989	**1990**	**1991**	**1992**		at 250 GRPs 70%
89%	89%	89%	89%		at 500 GRPs 92%
					at 1,000 GRPs 99%

Source:(Penetration): Fuente Datos, C.A., 1993

Opportunities

Networks	Number of Stations	Ownership	Station Profile	Commercial Minutes/Day	Coverage	Broadcast Hours (Sign-On/Off)
R.C.T.V	1	Private	General	266	Nat'l(95%)	06:00-01:00
Venevision	1	Private	General	266	Nat'l(95%)	06:00-01:00
Televen	1	Private	General	266	Nat'l (90%)	24 hours
VTV-5	1	Government	Cultural	0 (non-comm.)	Nat'l (95%)	17:00-24:00
VTV-8	1	Government	General	266	Nat'l (95%)	07:00-24:00
Local NCTV	1	Private	General	256	Local (28%)	06:00-24:00
TAM	1	Private	General	256	Local (47%)	06:00-24:00
Telecaribe	1	Private	General	256	Local (7%)	06:00-24:00
TRT	1	Private	General	256	Local (5%)	14:00-24:00
Televicentro	1	Private	General	256	Local (6%)	16:00-24:00
Telesol	1	Private	General	256	Local (4%)	12:00-24:00

Costs

Prime Time TV Costs for :30 is US$			
1989	**1990**	**1991**	**1992**
1,900	2,008	2,585	2,585

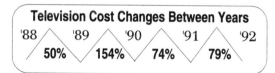

Television Cost Changes Between Years

'88	'89	'90	'91	'92
	50%	154%	74%	79%

Audiences/CPM's

Average Cost, Audience, and CPMs by Daypart
(Top 3 Stations, :30, national audience, Target=Adults ABCD/16-54)

Hours	Morning 06:00-11:30	Daytime 12:00-18:00	Prime Time 18:00-22:00	Late Night 22:00-24:00	Weekend 08:30-24:00	Children 16:00-19:00
Station: R.C.T.V						
US$	306	1,376	3,823	1,529	1,950	688
Avg. Aud. (000)	209.0	919.8	1,365.7	689.8	425.0	418.1
CPM	1.46	1.50	2.80	2.22	4.59	1.65
Station: Venevision						
US$	298	1,032	3,498	1,813	2,581	602
Avg. Aud. (000)	174.2	557.4	745.6	557.4	439.0	411.1
CPM	1.71	1.85	4.69	3.25	5.88	1.46
Station: Televen						
US$	105	397	1,740	890	672	223
Avg. Aud. (000)	41.8	69.7	97.5	41.8	153.3	279
CPM	2.52	5.70	17.84	21.28	4.38	8.00

Source: CVI/IVOPE, 1993

Audiences/Rating by Daypart (Target=Adults ABCD /16-54 years and Children / 5-14 years, ABCD)
Current TV research does not measure homes, only people. Hut refers to total (%), adults watching TV.

Daypart	Hours	Household			Adult			
		Universe (000)	Household Rating	Impressions (000)	Universe (000)	PUT Levels	Adult Rating	Impressions (000)
Morning	06:00-11:30	3,854	N/A	N/A	6,968	6.3	1.6	111.5
Daytime	12:00-18:00	3,854	N/A	N/A	6,968	22.4	5.6	390.2
Primetime	18:00-22:00	3,854	N/A	N/A	6,968	32.3	8.1	564.4
Late Night	22:00-24:00	3,854	N/A	N/A	6,968	19.2	4.8	334.5
Weekend	08:30- 24:00	3,854	N/A	N/A	6,968	15.2	3.8	264.8
Children's *	16:00-19:00	3,854	N/A	N/A	2,654	27.3	6.8	180.5

*Households are not measured in Venezuela
Source (PUT and Adult Universe): CVI, IBOPE, 1993

Scheduling/Regional/Languages

- The only broadcasting language in Venezuela is Spanish.
- Lengths available for commercials are negotiable; 55% of all commercials are :30, 35% are :20, 8% are :40 and 2% are :60.
- Commercials are aired throughout the day both at the beginning and end of programs and within them.

- Alternatives to airing commercials nationally exist on the R.C.T.V. network in 4 regions all day. Only 4% of all advertising is on the regional/local level and the cost is 60% that of national air time.

Children's Advertising

All adult programming accepts advertising directed to children.

CHILDREN'S PROGRAMMING				Kids'	
Station	Hours	Days	Universe (000)	Ratings	Impressions (000)
RCTV	19:30-20:00	Mon	6,820	18.4	1,254.9
RCTV	20:00-20:30	Thur	6,820	17.9	1,220.9
RCTV	09:00-11:00	Sat	6,820	11.2	763.9
Venevision	17:30-18:00	M-F	6,820	10.9	743.4
Venevision	16:00-16:30	M-F	6,820	15.3	1,043.5
Venevision	18:00-18:30	M-F	6,820	10.5	716.2

Source (Universe): CVI, IBOPE, 1993

Radio

- Venezuela has 221 AM stations and 94 FM stations; 312 of them are commercial. 27 AM stations and 21 FM stations are located in Caracas; 45 of which are commercial. *(Source: Fuente: Publicacion Profesional Publicitaria 1993)*
- The primary broadcasting language is Spanish; other programming is in Italian, Arabic, and Portuguese. Music, news and sports are the most popular program types.
- Spot radio bought on individual stations is not subject to premiums. Radio is usually bought on a local/regional basis.
- Common commercial lengths are :20, :30, :40, :50 and :60; other lengths are negotiable. The average cost of :30 on a 1 x 30 rotation L/S (Caracas) is US$ 21.67; with an approximate CPM of US$ 13.

Penetration

	% of Total HH	Radio HH (000)
Radio	90	3,898.8**
Automobiles	40% (Est.)**	2,412.2*

*50% of households have 2+ cars
**Source: Fuente: JDC Orientacion, C.A., 1992, 1993

Audience/Costs
Target: Adults 10+/ABCDE/Caracas/Homes

Daypart	Local Time	Avg. Cost :30 US$	Audience (000)	CPM (US$)
Prime Time	06:00-12:00	24	161.5	0.15
Daytime	12:00-19:00	20	111.6	0.18

Source: CVI, IBOPE, 1993

Prime/Peak Time for Radio

Daypart	Adult Rating	Adult (000)
06:00-09:00	9.9	161.5

Source: CVI, IBOPE, 1993

Cable

- Two systems, Cablevision and Omnivision, are very active. They offer signals from satellite. Both face some technical difficulties but they are expanding their coverage.
- These systems are not truly 'cable.' Programming is sent via a codified signal.
- There have been continuous yearly increases in subscriber numbers. Cable will continue growing, and is expected to reach up to 500,000 households within the next 5 years.
- There are 22 privately owned cable channels of which 19 are commercial.
- Spanish is the primary broadcasting language; English is secondary.

Cable HH Penetration			
1989	*1990*	*1991*	*1992*
0.8%	2.3%	3.7%	4.0%
30,000	85,000	140,000	152,000

Source: Datos, C.A., 1989, 1990, 1991, 1993

Top Cable Channels	Cost (US$)	Commercial Min/Hour
CNN	2,210	4
Omnivision Multicanal	2,210	4
The Best TV	335	4
Eco Galavision	335	4
ESPN	2,210	4

Cable Operators	HH Circulation (000)	Programming
Cablevision	23.0	Variety
Omnivision Multicanal	129.0	Variety

Cable/Channel	Country of Origin	Language	Programming
CableVision			
PSN	USA	English	Sports
The Best TV	USA	English	News (CBS/NBC)
USA Network	USA	English	Variety
TVE	Spain	Spanish	Variety
Eco/Galavision	Mexico	Spanish	News/Variety
Nickelodeon	USA	English	Cartoons
Cartoon Network	USA	English	Cartoons
A&E	USA	English	Variety
CineCanal	Mexico	Spanish	Movies
NBC	USA	Spanish	News
OmniVision/Multicanal			
Channel 12	Venezuela	Spanish	Variety
HBO-OLE	Venezuela	Spanish	Movies
CNN	USA	English	News
ESPN	USA	English	Sports
TNT	USA	English	Movies
USA Network	USA	English	Variety
A&E	USA	English	Variety
Cablecito	Venezuela	Spanish	Cartoons
RAI	Italy	Italian	Variety
TVE	Spain	Spanish	Variety
TVM	USA	English	Video/Music
Fox	USA	Spanish	Variety

Satellite

- There is strong penetration (2.6% of total HH) despite codified signals. *(Source: Datos,C.A., 1993)*
- People have to buy the parabolic dish and a decoder. There is a magazine that contains all the information and monthly programming.
- Increasing penetration is expected (300,000 by 1998). Almost every new building is equipped with a dish.
- All of the channels listed below broadcast in English, and their programming originates in the U.SA.

Satellite Channels				
Galaxy 5	**Galaxy 5**	**Galaxy 5**	**Galaxy 5**	**Telstar**
Disney -E	ESPN	MAX-W	HN	Channel 12
TBN	FAM	TNT	A&E	Channel 20
CNN	TDC	TNN	SHO-E	
WTB-S	CNBNC/FNN	USA-E	VCPPV-1	
WGN	TMC-W	BET	Life-E	
SCI-FI	HBO-E	MEU		

Video Cassettes

16% of all Venezuelan households have video cassette recorders (VCRs), which is 17.9% of the TV households. *(Source: Datos, C.A., 1993)* Pre-recorded tapes carry an average of one sponsor per tape. The cost of advertising is highly negotiable.

Cinema

- There are 340 theaters that reach an estimated 1,700,000 people each 4 weeks. *(Source: P.P.P. Ano, 1993)*
- All cinemas offer commercial time; common lengths for advertising are :20, :30, :40 and :60 with other lengths negotiable.

Cinema Cost Changes Between Years

'88	'89	'90	'91	'92
514%	25%	25%	59%	

- The average cost of a 4 week cinema schedule is US$ 200.73.
- A decrease in number of theaters and audiences is expected due to increasing ticket prices.

Newspapers

There are 13 national daily newspapers that accept advertising; the combined circulation is 1,633,000.

Newspaper Cost Changes Between Years

'88	'89	'90	'91	'92
140%	22%	41%	49%	

Daily Newspaper	Market	Size	Circulation (000)	Avg. Daily Aud. (000)	1 page B&W Cost (US$)	Accept Color?
El Nacional	National	Standard	175.0	437.2	2,527	Yes
El Universal	National	Standard	170.0	N/A	2,527	Yes
Diario de Caracas	National	Tabloid	95.0	237.5	1,950	Yes
The Daily Journal	National	Tabloid	10.5	26.2	1,156	Yes
Meridiano	National	Tabloid	213.5	533.7	1,147	Yes
Mundo	National	Standard	189.0	472.5	1,950	Yes
Ultimas Noticias	National	Tabloid	230.0	575.0	1,204	Yes
Impulso	Lara State	Standard	60.0	476.0	2,255	Yes
Carabobeno	Carabobo State	Standard	60.0	150.0	2,125	Yes
El Siglo	Aragua State	Standard	60.0	150.0	1,835	Yes
La Nacion	Tachira	Standard	45.0	112.5	1,060	Yes
El Tiempo	Anzoategui	Tabloid	50.0	125.0	573	Yes
Correo del Caroni	Bolivar State	Standard	59.0	147.5	2,527	Yes

Source (Newspaper): Fuente de Datos P.P.P. de cado ano solicitado, 1989, 1990, 1991, 1992.

Magazines

65 consumer magazines and 130 trade/technical magazines are published in Venezuela.

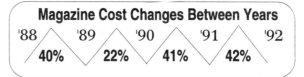

Magazine	Type	Frequency	Circ. (000)	Audited?	Avg. Issue Aud. (000)	1 page 4/C Cost (US$)
Hombre de Mundo	Male	Monthly	81.2	No	N/A	1,453
Numero	Management	Monthly	25.0	No	120	2,523
Buenhogar	Women's	Bi-Weekly	79.2	No	94	2,018
Cosmopolitan	Women's	Monthly	72.2	No	94	2,018
Vanidades	Women's	Bi-Weekly	105.6	No	N/A	2,217
Gaceta Hipica	Horse Racing	Weekly	175.0	No	N/A	942
Computer News	Computers	Bi-Weekly	15.0	No	30	895
Dinero	Finance	Monthly	23.0	No	36	2,810
Producto	Mktg./Advg.	Monthly	31.0	No	60	3,584
Elite	General Interest	Weekly	75.0	No	187	687
Publicidad y Mercadeo	Mktg./Advg.	Bi-Weekly	10.2	No	25	2,606
Ellas	Female	Monthly	23.2	No	58	687
Ideas	Female	Monthly	50.0	No	125	1,503
Variedades	Female	Monthly	58.6	No	146	850
Exceso	Present Time	Monthly	30.0	No	75	2,810
Gerente Venezuela	Management	Monthly	25.0	No	62	3,268
Geomundo	Geography	Monthly	60.8	No	152	1,452
Zeta	General Interest	Weekly	48.0	No	120	516
Paginas	Female	Bi-weekly	71.8	No	143	687
Bohemia	General Interest	Weekly	69.4	No	173	857
Coqueta	Female	Bi-weekly	105.6	No	264	1,510
Kena	Female	Bi-weekly	73.5	No	183	687
Harper's Bazaar	Female	Monthly	50.0	No	125	2,097
Inversiones Venezuela	Management	Monthly	25.0	No	62	2,901
Mecanica Popular	Male	Monthly	62.0	No	155	1,452
Etiqueta	Female	Monthly	10.0	No	25	1,789
Ronda	Female	Weekly	104.0	No	260	659
Venezuela Grafica	Show Business	Weekly	79.0	No	197	494
Venezuela Farandula	Show Business	Weekly	80.0	No	200	659
Tu	Female	Monthly	70.0	No	175	1,510

Source (Magazine): Fuente de Datos P.P.P. de cado ano solicitado, 1989, 1990, 1991, 1992.

Outdoor/Transit

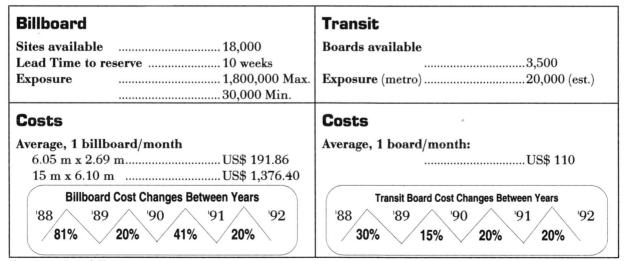

Billboard		**Transit**	
Sites available 18,000		**Boards available**	
Lead Time to reserve .... 10 weeks		3,500	
Exposure .... 1,800,000 Max.		**Exposure** (metro) ....20,000 (est.)	
..............................30,000 Min.			

Costs

Average, 1 billboard/month
6.05 m x 2.69 m.............................. US$ 191.86
15 m x 6.10 m .... US$ 1,376.40

Costs

Average, 1 board/month:
.... US$ 110

Continued on following page

Outdoor/Transit, continued

Sizes		Sizes	
66.66 m x 3.05 m	3.35 m x 1.50 m	Bus Shelters	1.2 m x 1.76 m
15 m x 6.10 m	2.70 m	Bus Panels	0.8 m x 1.50 m
Others	6.05 m x 2.69 m	Metro Displays	0.65 m x 0.51 m
		Metro Dioramas	1.76 m x 1.22 m

Direct Marketing

This discipline is just getting shape in Venezuela.

List Broker	*Information Provided*	*Top Telemarketing Company*	*Direct Marketing Association*
Credimatico TDC (Visa Mastercard)	Credit Card holders	Guia Util	Asociacion Venezolana de Mercadeo Directo
Diners Club	Credit Card holders		
Dun & Bradstreet	As required		

Non-Traditional Media

Non-traditional media currently available are printed walls, street signage, shopping cars, hot screen TV, scent strips, and computer disks. Costs vary and new alternatives become available every day.

Research Sources

Medium covered	*Research company*	*Information*
Television	Datos, C.A.	R&F Study - national (7 cities)
	Apartado 5957	Weekly breakdown by age, sex, economic level, etc.
	Caracas 1010-A, Venezuela	
	MD/Mr. Andrew Templeton	
Television	C.V.I	R&F Study - national (5 cities)
	C/Veracruz, Las Mercedes	
	Edifc. Aba, Mezz.	Weekly breakdown by age, sex, economic level, etc.
	Caracas 1060, Venezuela	
	MD/Mr. Rodolfo Barreda	
Radio	J.D.C	Radio audiences by station (4 main cities)
	CD/El Carmen	
	Centro Empresarial	Sex, age, socio-economic class, in both homes and
	Dos Caminos, Piso,	vehicles
	Of. IZ-F, Caracas, Venezuela	
	MD/Mr. Carlos Diaz	
Radio	DATOS C.A.	Annual analysis by rating area
		Reach by socio-economic class and dayparts

TV research is available monthly with weekly breakdowns by panel, diary, reach frequency studies.

Advertising Regulations

By Product

Beverages/Alcohol
Banned on both TV and Radio

Food/Restaurants
None

Cigarettes
Banned on both TV and radio

Pharmaceuticals/Drugs
There must be an authorization from the national department of Public Health. Each commercial must contain, the phrase 'In case of doubt, consult your doctor.'

Advertising To Children
None

Commercial Production
A mixed commercial is understood to be the one made by Venezuelan producers, with national and/or foreign models in which foreign production is limited to the post-production services made by the computer, laboratory, tricks or stock shots, as long as the latter does not exceed the third part of the total length of the commercial. The announcer must be local.

Source: P.P.P. (Publicacion Profesional Publictana), 1993.

By Medium

Television
Maximum 15 min/per hour, maximum 4/breaks per hour.

Outdoor
Location 50 m away from highways.

Cable
Maximum 4 min/per hour, maximum 2 min/breaks per hour.

North America

North America

Regional Summary

The media economies of the United States and Canada generally remain soft, waiting for the end of the recession. In both Canada and the United States media prices are becoming increasingly negotiable; even print media, which long resisted this trend, is showing signs of moving from fixed rates to negotiated prices.

Key Dynamics–New Technologies

Canadian Cable

About three quarters of Canadian homes have cable, allowing the cable system to serve as a means of television regulation. Recently the Canadian Radio, Television and Telecommunications Commission (CRTC) announced decisions bringing Canadian television to a 300 channel standard. Such policies are in response to the expansion of non-Canadian satellite program availability which threatens CRTC's ability to regulate viewing of non-Canadian program sources.

CRTC regulations aim to protect Canadian television ownership, limiting non-Canadian programming. Hoping to counter the rise of satellite program options, the CRTC recently began accepting applications for additional specialty channels to expand Canadian viewing alternatives. As many as 12 new channels are expected by the beginning of 1995.

The CRTC is seeking legislative means to regulate non-Canadian direct broadcast satellite (DBS) transmissions into the country. Also, recent changes in the percentage of foreign specialty programming allowed on Canadian cable services may further limit access to U.S. cable networks such as CNN and Arts & Entertainment (A&E).

U.S.A. Viewing Options

Television viewing options continue to expand in the United States. The U.S. television industry expects important developments in areas such as digitalization, compression and multiplexing, which will allow even more channels.

It is not clear when this increased channel capacity will occur. Much depends on the ability of stations and program originators to invest in the physical requirements of the new technology. Current coaxial cable carries roughly 90 channels. Multiplexing is expected to bring 120-150 channels. With digitalization, compression and fiber optics, some predict as many as 500 channels.

One key test of fiber optic technology is the Orlando, Florida launch of Time-Warner's Full Service Network in 1994. This test involves 4,000 homes receiving fully interactive television through a fiber optic 'cable' network. People in these homes will be able to select personalized programming line-ups and purchase products through their televisions. Several other interactive services are in testing, though of much more limited scope. The outcome of such tests will influence the future of this form of media.

Pan-Regional Availabilities

The majority of North American media are available only in the originating country. Relatively few vehicles cross borders between countries; among those that do, pricing is usually kept separate by country.

As mentioned earlier, some U.S. produced cable programs are available to Canadian viewers. According to the Nielsen Canada Cable Meter Index Report, A&E, CNN and The Nashville Network have the three largest Canadian audiences of U.S. cable in Canada. These cable feeds are priced and purchased separately from U.S. buys.

In print, many of the large U.S. magazines include some Canadian readership. Further, several magazines offer Canadian editions including: *Reader's Digest, National Geographic*, and *Time Canada*. Each of these titles offers discounts in conjunction with U.S. buys.

Canadian households along the border can receive signals from local U.S. stations. Some key border markets are: Bangor, Maine; Buffalo, New York; Burlington, Vermont; Plattsburgh, New York; Detroit, Michigan; Rochester, New York; Seattle-Tacoma, Washington; Spokane, Washington; and Waterstown, New York.

Beyond Canada and the United States, some media vehicles cross the southern U.S. border into Latin America. Two U.S.-based television companies in Miami, Florida, Telemundo and Univision, are expanding their services. Both companies use satellites to feed Spanish language programming to U.S. Hispanic homes and to Latin America, and expect to include Spain in the coming year. Television buys from these services can be negotiated to cover Spanish-speaking homes across regions.

Major U.S. magazines with Latin American editions are *Business Week International, Reader's Digest, National Geographic, Newsweek International* and *Time Latin America*. These titles list regional group discount options, some in conjunction with U.S. buys.

For cable television, some U.S. cable networks provide programming available in Latin America (e.g., CNN, ESPN). Usually Latin American feeds are sold separately from U.S. feeds.

Finally, like Canada, some local market broadcast television in the United States can be received by homes across the border in Mexico. Currently the U.S. and Mexican television sources do not measure such spill. Likely markets include: El Paso, Texas; McAllen-Brownsville, Texas; San Diego, California; and Tuscon, Arizona.

Dick Hobbs
Senior Vice President and
WorldWide Media Director

Canada

Area	9,976,140 km²
Population (1992)	27,351,501
Population growth rate (1992)	1.3%
GDP	US$ 521.5 billion
GDP/per capita	US$ 19,400
Real growth rate (1991)	1.1%
Capital	Ottawa

Population Breakdown

By Sex		*By Age Group*		*By Socio-Economic Status*	
Male	49%	Children, under 12	14%	A,US$ 75+M	11%
Female	51%	Teens, 12-17	9%	B,US$ 50-75M	19%
		Adults, 18+	77%	C,US$ 25-50M	38%
				D,US$ 25M or under	32%

Source: Statscan, Survey of Markets, 1992

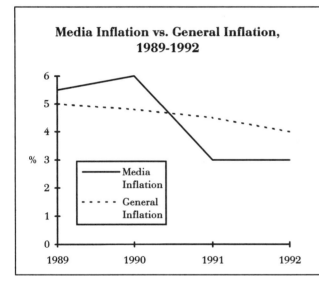

Media Inflation vs. General Inflation, 1989-1992

Number of Households   10,350,000

Ownership of household durables

Car	81%
Phone	99%
Washers	68%

(purchasing power equivalent)

GNP distribution by industry

Agriculture	2%
Industry	26%
Services	72%

Exchange rates (US$ to local currency)

1991	0.857251
1992	0.780800

Source: Statscan, Survey of Markets, 1992

National Holidays

Holiday	*1993 Date*
New Year's	January 1
Good Friday	April 9
Victoria Day	May 24
St. Jean-Baptiste (P.Q.)	June 24
Canada Day	July 1
Civic Day	August 2
Labor Day	September 6
Thanksgiving	October 11
Christmas	December 27
Boxing Day	December 28

School Holidays

Holiday	*1993 Date*
Grade 1 - 12/13:	Varies by year and by school board
Mid-term Break	March 16 - 20
Summer	June 26 - September 7
Christmas Holiday	Dec. 18, 1993 - Jan. 2, 1994
Grade 1 - 8 only:	
Remembrance Day	November 11
P.A. or P.H. Days	5 - 8 days throughout the year

Major Influences and Trends

The reality of 100 channel television is apparent. The neutral approach to media planning has been adopted. Media plans are developed, combining traditional media with secondary/ non traditional media, delivering a more personalized, relevant and actionable media program.

Spending Analysis

National advertising spending by medium,
based on appropriate year's exchange rate

	1989 US$ MM	1990 US$ MM	1991 US$ MM	1992 US$ MM
TV	1,230.1	1,317.2	1,366.0	1,263.3
Cinema	N/A	N/A	N/A	-
Radio	634.2	674.7	620.2	578.9
Newspaper	2,551.1	2,676.8	1,674.6	1,563.2
Magazine	1,094.0	1,213.9	895.6	754.7
Direct Response	1,716.1	1,809.7	1,405.4	1,360.2
Outdoor	606.4	655.3	692.7	621.5
Other	-	-	778.1*	751.9*
Total	**7,831.9**	**8,347.6**	**7,432.6**	**6,893.7**

* includes yellow pages.

Media Buying

All media pricing is negotiable. Broadcast costs are driven by supply and demand. The press publish rate cards but adherence is not universal.

Agencies/buying services purchase on behalf of advertisers. No large advertisers operate an in-house media buying group. Buying services are numerous (25+). There are two large respected companies. Growth of traditional buying services is flat. All Canadian media are Canadian owned and operated. Three large groups control 75% of English language television. Two large groups represent the majority of consumer magazines and dailies.

Buying services account for approximately 20% of the market's total expenditures. *(Source:Marketing Magazine/Leo Burnett estimate)*

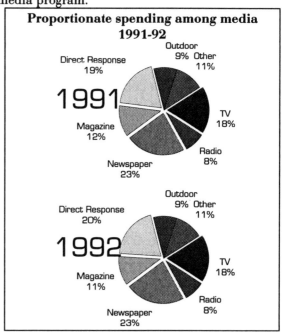

Proportionate spending among media 1991-92

1991
- Direct Response 19%
- Magazine 12%
- Newspaper 23%
- Radio 8%
- TV 18%
- Outdoor 9%
- Other 11%

1992
- Direct Response 20%
- Magazine 11%
- Newspaper 23%
- Radio 8%
- TV 18%
- Outdoor 9%
- Other 11%

Buying services with 1990 billings

Buying Service*	Parent Company	US$ MM
Harrison, Young, Pesonan & Newell		180
McKim Media Group	N. W. Ayer	170
Media Initiatives Canada	McLaren Lintas	150
Media Buying Services		129
Genesis Media	Vickers & Benson/ Media Canada	120

* *MajorBuying Services only*
** *Extremely difficult to obtain accurate figures*
(Source:Marketing Magazine/Leo Burnett estimate)

Top Advertisers (1992 Spending)

By Company

Parent Company	Product Categories	US$MM
Government of Canada	Various	145.1
General Motors of Canada	Automotive	139.6
Proctor & Gamble	Various	127.5
The Thompson Group	Various	104.6
Sears Canada	Department Store	75.6
The Molson Companies	Alcohol (Beer)	73.5
Eaton's of Canada	Department Store	59.3
BCE	Telecommunications	57.3
John Labatt Ltd.	Alcohol (Beer)	52.4
Imasco	Financial	49.8

Source: Marketing Magazine and MMS Annual Spending Summary

By Product

Product Category	Advertiser	US$MM
Automotive	General Motors	139.6
Toiletries and Cosmetics	Procter & Gamble	127.5
Retail	Sears Canada	75.6
Breweries	The Molson Companies	73.5
Financial	Imasco	49.8
Food	Kraft General Foods Group	48.5
Entertainment	Paramount Communications	44.7
Restaurants	McDonald's	43.1
Soft Drinks	Pepsico	33.8

Source: Marketing Magazine and MMS Annual Spending Summary

Television

TV HH Penetration				Reach against adults	
1989	*190*	*1991*	*1992*	at 250 GRPs	62%
99%	99%	99%	99%	at 500 GRPs	78%
N/A	9,678,000	9,826,000	10,246,500	at 1000 GRPs	85%

Overview

- Demand flat across Canada
- Ontario still a sellers market
- People meter surveyed on a national level
- Market meter still in development
- Additional specialty channels will increase audience fragmentation

Opportunities

Net-works	Number of Stations	Ownership	Station Profile	Coverage	Broadcast Hours (Sign-On/Off)
Atlantic TV System (Regional)	1 (28 Transmitters)	Privately Owned	Entertainment, News, Sports	97%	06:00-02:00
Atlantic Satellite Network (Satellite-to-Cable/Regional)			Offered in Conjunction with Above		06:00-02:00
Maritimes Indep. TV (Regional)	1 (+7 Transmitters)		Local, City Oriented	N/A	06:00-02:00
Sask. TV Network (Regional)	4 (+1 Affiliate)	Privately Owned	Entertainment, News, Sports	9%	
CBC Eng.	38 (Including 25 Affiliates)	Crown Corp.	News, Information, Public Affairs, Entertainment	98%	07:00-03:00
CBC Fr.	20 (Including 8 Pre-broadcasting stations)	Crown Corp.	Lifestyle, News, Information, Public Affairs, Entertainment	99%	07:30-02:00
CTV-Eng.	18 (Plus 6 Affiliates)	Privately Owned by Stations	Entertainment, News, Sports	97%	06:30-04:00
TVA-Fr.	10	Privately Owned by Member Stations	News, Public Affairs, Sports, Variety	99%	06:25-02:00
Global-Eng.	1 (+9 Transmitters)	Privately Owned	Entertainment, News, Sports	98%	06:00-04:00
Radio Quebec (Regional)	17	Publicly Owned	Entertainment, News, Information, Education	98%	08:00-10:00
Quatre Saisons - Fr. (Regional)	9	Privately Owned	Entertainment, News, Sports	94%	10:00-02:30

* All networks allow 12 minutes/hour except CBC (10 minutes/hours) and specialty channels (8 minutes/hour)

Costs

Prime Time TV Costs for :30 (in US$)				
	1989	*1990*	*1991*	*1992*
CBC English (US prime)	10.0	11.0	11.0	11.0
CBC French	8.2	11.0	11.0	11.5
CTV English	14.6	15.5	16.0	15.0
TVA French	9.9	10.5	11.0	10.0
Global	4.7	4.5	5.5	6.5
Quatre Saisons	3.7	3.2	3.5	3.0
Radio Quebec	N/A	N/A	N/A	N/A

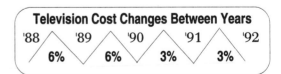

Television Cost Changes Between Years
'88 '89 '90 '91 '92
6% 6% 3% 3%

Audiences/CPM's

Average Cost, Audience, and CPMs by Daypart
(Top 2 Stations, :30, national audience, Target=Adults 18-49)

Hours	Morning	Daytime	Prime Time	Weekend	Children
Station: English					
US$	857	1,633	9,430	1,084	44,640
Avg. Aud. (000)	105	265	980	165	376.9
CPM	8.16	6.16	9.62	6.56	118
Station: French					
US$	1,092	857	6,900	N/A	21,000
Avg. Aud. (000)	235	206	750	N/A	380.5
CPM	4.64	4.16	9.20	N/A	55

Audiences/Rating by Daypart

Daypart	Hours	Household Universe (000)	Hut Levels	Household Rating	Impressions (000)	Adult Universe (000)	Adult Rating	Impressions (000)
Morning	08:00-12:00	9,826.2	13	7.1	697.0	20,062.0	4.3	862.7
Daytime	12:00-18:00	9,826.2	22	6.6	648.5	20,062.0	4.0	802.5
Primetime	18:00-23:00	9,826.2	54	13.2	1,297.1	20,062.0	7.9	1,584.9
Late Night	23:00-02:00	9,826.2	17	1.8	176.9	20,062.0	1.1	220.7
Weekend	12:00-18:00	9,826.2	27	3.9	383.2	20,062.0	2.3	461.4
Children's	08:00-12:00	9,826.2	13	1.8	176.9	20,062.0	1.1	220.7

Scheduling/Regional/Languages

LANGUAGES	Programming	Commercials
Primary Language		
English stations	English	English
French statoins	French	French
Secondary Language		
Multi-lingual pay TV services	Cathay - Cantonese, Mandarin & East Indian	Indian & Cantonese
	Telelatino - Italian & Portuguese	Italian
	Chinavision - Cantonese & Mandarin	Cantonese & Mandarin

- According to the 1991/92 CMDC *Media Digest*, 80% of all commercial time sold is in :30 spots; some other available commercial lengths are :15, :45, :60, :90 and :120.
- Commercial time is aired throughout the day in 2 or 3 minute clusters both at the beginning and end of programs and within them.
- All stations in all markets sell time in all dayparts on a selective basis. 80% of all commercials are aired on a regional/local basis; costs are 20-100% that of national air time depending on the region.
  (Sources (Regional Costs): TVB/Marketing Magazine)

Children's Advertising

Adult Programming
All English adult programming accepts advertising to children. Individual advertisers or station managers may exercise discretion and choose to avoid certain commercials in certain programming. Also, advertising to children must remain within the Advertising Standards Councils' guidelines and get Telecaster Committee approval.

Children's Programming
The CTV Network, YTV on basic cable nationally, and English language independents accept children's advertising assuming it meets the above state approvals.
CBC English does not accept advertising to children in children's programming.
The province of Quebec prohibits all advertising to children.

Radio

- The penetration level of radio in Canada is 98.7%; reaching about 9,550,700 households.
- There are 703 radio stations of which 575 are commercial. 20 stations are located in Toronto.
- English is the primary language used for broadcasting; secondary languages are French, Italian and Cantonese. The most popular program types are M.O.R./Easy Listening and Country music.
- CBC and CBC FM are the only radio Networks in Canada and are non-commercial. There are limited syndicated programs used on network basis.

- Some Regional Networks exist but radio is planned and purchased primarily on a market-by-market basis.
- Commercial time is available in :15, :30 and :60 spots. The costs vary significantly by market and stations.
- Peak/Primetime hours are at breakfast time between 07:00 and 09:00.

Ratings

Daypart	Adult Rating	Adult (000)
06:00-10:00	28	5,570
10:00-15:00	23	4,582
15:00-19:00	19	3,873
19:00-24:00	8	1,687

Cable

- Cable household penetration has stabilized at 72% in 1992 reaching 7,375,700 households. 3 to 5% more households are expected to receive cable within the next 5 years.
- Cable is divided into Basic and Pay. Within Pay, many option exist for English, French and multi-lingual stations. Packages also include non-commercial movie channels, U.S. stations (e.g., WTBS, WGN) as well as A&E, CNN.
- The cable system is privately owned. There are 9 English channels (4 are commercial), 6 French channels (2 are commercial) and 3 Multilingual (all commercial).
- The primary languages used to broadcast are English and French (predominantly English); Italian and Cantonese are the secdondary languages.

Cable Networks	HH Circulation (000)	Programming
TSN (English)	6,000	Sports - live and taped professional and amateur, sports, news
RDS (French	1,800	As above, in French language
Much Music	5,400	Music videos, news, interviews, concerts
Musique Plus (French)	1,800 (Quebec)	As above, with French language hosts
Telelatino (Multi-lingual)	706	Italian/Spanish sports, movies, documentaries, news general.
Chinavision (Multi-lingual)	111	Chinese news, movies, dramas, soaps, general.
Cathay International	16	Chines/Vietnamese (B.C.)
Vision (English)	6,300	Multi-faith religions programming, arts, education and general.
Weather Network (English)	6,700	Weather
Metromedia (French)	1,200	Weather
Youth TV (YTV) English	6,300	Kids, Teens and All Family
TV 5 (French)	4,800	International French programming (France).
CBC Newsworld (English)	6,600	24 hr. News and information.

Continued on following page

Cable, continued

Cable Networks	HH Circulation (000)	Programming
Family Channel (Eng.)	380	Family entertainment - Pay
The Movie Network/Superchannel	N/A	Movies - Pay
Canal Famille (Fr.)	N/A	Family
Super Eran (Fr.)	N/A	Movie - Pay

Satellite

- There are three satellite stations that originate in Canada. The Ankik E1 and Satellite and E2 act as rebroadcasters of signals to remote Canadian communities. The CANCOM group of stations (11 stations) extend their normal off-air broadcast reach primarily to non-cable communities. Pay cable and U.S. services, some syndicated events, and regional networks also use satellite to extend their reach.
- Although homes with satellite dishes have the ability to pick-up international channels, television viewing by satellite represents only .6% of total viewing. BBM estimates that only 2-3% of homes have dishes.
- The satellite subscriber market in Canada is currently in decline due to changing broadcasting/programming arrangements. Stations that were received off-air previously, have now been scrambled and viewers must now pay high costs to receive a similar number of stations. However, more stations are coming out on satellite offering viewers more variety. Canadian consumers are waiting for stability in the broadcast/programming area. The broadcasters/programmers are awaiting U.S. market developments from upcoming Direct Broadcast Satellite Groups (launching in U.S. as early as Fall '93).
- There are 20 satellite channels of which 16 are commercial. A wide variety of U.S. channels can also be received; the most popular are U.S. Movie and Sports channels. (See U.S. Satellite channel listings)

Video Cassettes

- About 69% of all households in Canada have video cassette recorders; which is 72% of all TV households.
- VCR usage (TV recorded material) is measured by both BBM and Nielsen . BBM grouped all the above under VCR usage, while Nielsen, with people meter, is attempting to credit recorded TV programs to the program or station. In-depth reports on VCR viewing have not been updated since 1985.
- Very few pre-recorded tapes carry commercials; those that do have an average of 1 to 3 sponsors per tape. The costs of this type of advertising varies.
- VCR usage will continue to lag ownership growth. Current records indicate VCR usage accounting for less than 4% of total viewing share. Zipping/zapping information not available in Canadian market.

Cinema

- Canada has more than 1,000 theaters.
- There are 543 markets with 801 (78%) indoor theaters and drive-in theaters that offer cinema advertising (1989 Film Canada Yearbook).

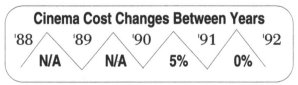

Cinema Cost Changes Between Years

'88	'89	'90	'91	'92
	N/A	N/A	5%	0%

- Commercial time is available in lengths of :30, :60 and :90. The average cost of a 4 week cinema schedule with National Cineplex is US $175,000.

Newspapers

27% of Canadians are functionally literate in either of the two official languages (English or French).

There are 2 (Financial Post (T), Globe & Mail (B)) national daily newspapers that accept advertising.

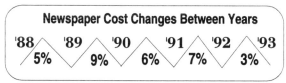

Newspaper Cost Changes Between Years					
'88	'89	'90	'91	'92	'93
5%	9%	6%	7%	3%	

The combined circulation is 384.2M (2/3 of circ. in Ontario as they are essentially Toronto papers).

Daily Newspaper	Market	Size	Circulation (000)	Avg. Daily Aud. (000)	1 page/B&W Cost (US$)	Accept Color?
English						
The Vancouver Sun	Vancouver	Broadsheet	193.7	456	12,929	Yes
The Province	Vancouver	Tabloid	172.4	440	4,132	Yes
Times-Colonist	Victoria	Broadsheet	78.4	162	4,444	Yes
Calgary Herald	Calgary	Broadsheet	121.3	303	8,583	Yes
Calgary Sun	Calgary	Tabloid	70.0	203	2,400	Yes
Edmonton Journal	Edmonton	Broadsheet	159.2	342	10,660	Yes
Edmonton Sun	Edmonton	Tabloid	84.1	206	2,698	Yes
Leader Post	Regina	Broadsheet	67.1	84	3,303	Yes
Star Phoenix	Saskatoon	Broadsheet	60.3	100	3,258	Yes
Free-Press	Winnipeg	Broadsheet	151.9	265	7,632	Yes
Winnipeg Sun	Winnipeg	Tabloid	44.3	111	1,869	Yes
Hamilton Spectator	Hamilton	Broadsheet	113.7	236	7,895	Yes
Kitchener-Waterloo Record	Kitchener	Broadsheet	75.1	155	4,793	Yes
London Free Press	London	Broadsheet	112.0	181	7,099	Yes
Ottawa Citizen	Ottawa	Broadsheet	173.1	281	10,456	Yes
Ottawa Sun	Ottawa	Tabloid	52.7	122	2,127	Yes
Sudbury Star	Sudbury	Broadsheet	27.3	N/A	2,345	Yes
Toronto Star	Toronto	Broadsheet	494.7	1,345	23,621	Yes
Toronto Sun	Toronto	Tabloid	252.9	925	5,425	Yes
Gazette	Montreal	Broadsheet	158.5	341	9,266	Yes
Record	Sherbrooke	Broadsheet	5.5	N/A	731	Yes
Times-Transcript	Moncton	Broadsheet	43.5	46	2,263	Yes
The T.G./E.T.G.	Saint John	Broadsheet	56.8	90	2,900	Yes
Cronc-Hrld/Mail Star	Halifax	Broadsheet	138.9	181	5,439	Yes
Cape Breton Post	Sydney	Broadsheet	31.8	N/A	2,445	Yes
Telegram	St. John's	Broadsheet	40.2	N/A	2,586	Yes
Financial Post	National	Tabloid	78.5	257	6,613	Yes
Globe & Mail	National	Broadsheet	311.2	908	29,378	Yes
French						
Le Droit	Ottawa	Tabloid	33.8	82	1,569	Yes
Le Quotidien	Chicoutimi	Tabloid	28.3	67	1,382	Yes
Le Devoir	Montreal	Broadsheet	24.0	N/A	4,989	Yes
Le Journal de Montreal	Montreal	Tabloid	281.6	709	6,996	Yes
La Presse	Montreal	Broadsheet	186.6	498	11,313	Yes
Le Journal de Quebec	Quebec City	Tabloid	98.8	207	3,225	Yes
Le Soleil	Quebec City	Broadsheet	96.8	182	7,266	Yes
La Tribune	Sherbrooke	Broadsheet	33.8	52	1,687	Yes
Le Nouvelliste	Trois Rivieres	Broadsheet	50.9	94	3,556	Yes

Magazines

There are 497 consumer magazines and 626 trade and technical magazines published in Canada.

Magazine Cost Changes Between Years					
'88	'89	'90	'91	'92	'93
5%	4%	6%	2%	2%	

Magazine	Type	Frequency	Circ. (000)	Audited?	Avg. Issue Aud. (000))	1 page 4/C Cost (US$)
English						
Canadian	Inflight	Monthly	92.3	CCAB	255	9,291
Canadian Geographic	General Interest	6/yr.	249.8	ABC	772	7,168
Canadian House & Home	Homes	8/yr.	104.8	ABC	556	7,133
Canadian Living	Women's	13/yr.	592.6	ABC	1,965	17,096
Chatelaine	Women's	Monthly	911.5	ABC	2,219	23,369
City & Country Home	Homes	6/yr.	60.7	ABC	N/A	7,023
Enroute	Inflight	Monthly	111.5	CCAB	235	10,470
Equinox	General Interest	6/yr.	173.0	ABC	601	7,812
Flare	Women's	Monthly	190.4	ABC	585	9,573
Harrowsmith	General Interest	6/yr.	155.3	ABC	413	6,000
Homemaker's	Women's	8/yr.	1,291.6	CCAB	1,265	18,443
Images	Women's	4/yr.	400.0	CCAB	N/A	11,595
Maclean's	News	Weekly	579.0	ABC	2,020	18,068
Modern Woman	Women's	Monthly	774.0	N/A	N/A	16,537
Reader's Digest	General Interest	Monthly	1,266.5	ABC	2,726	21,054
Saturday Night	General Interest	7/yr.	76.7	ABC	N/A	9,830
Select Homes & Food	Homes	8/yr.	167.5	ABC	535	7,414
Time	News	Weekly	354.5	ABC	1,585	14,289
TV Guide	TV & Radio	Weekly	810.2	ABC	1,613	14,074
You	Women's	4/yr.	207.2	CCAB	185	6,243
French						
L'Actualite	News	20/yr.	221.7	ABC	560	9,362
Chatelaine	Women's	Monthly	193.1	ABC	583	7,636
Clin D'Oeil	Women's	Monthly	73.6	ABC	276	4,661
Coup de Pouce	Women's	13/yr.	153.2	ABC	458	5,918
Elle Quebec	Women's	Monthly	66.3	ABC	N/A	4,650
L'Essentiel	Women's	Monthly	91.1	ABC	225	4,255
Femme Plus	Women's	Monthly	75.2	ABC	211	3,529
Le Lundi	General Interest	Weekly	68.2	ABC	680	4,115
Madame au Foyer	Women's	8/yr.	310.3	CCAB	283	4,607
Selection du R. Digest	General Interest	Monthly	327.9	ABC	654	7,281
Sept Jours	News	Weekly	159.0	ABC	809	5,852
TV Hebdo	TV & Radio	Weekly	240.9	ABC	606	5,095

Outdoor/Transit

Billboard	**Transit**
Sites available ....28,000+	Boards available
Lead Time to reserve .... 1 to 6 months	.............................400,000+
(Dependent upon medium, market and time of year)	
Exposure .... Max: 81%	Exposure (metro) 87%
(A18+ @ 75 Daily GRP's)	(A18+ @ 75 Daily GRP's)

Continued on following page

Outdoor/Transit, continued

Costs	**Costs**

Average, 1 billboard/month
10ft. x 20ft.   ....US$ 875
	Average, 1 board/month:
	    Exterior King: ....US$ 250
	    Interior Single:.............................US$ 12.50
	    (Production additional)

Billboard Cost Changes Between Years
'88 6% '89 6% '90 5% '91 4% '92

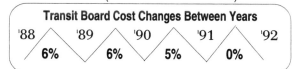

Transit Board Cost Changes Between Years
'88 6% '89 6% '90 5% '91 0% '92

Sizes	**Sizes**

Backlights: 10 ft x 30 ft and 10 ft x 20 ft
Urbanites: 10 ft x 23 ft
Super Posters/Posters: 10 ft x 20 ft
Omni Posters: 16 ft x 12 ft (vertical)
Series 10: 10 ft x 45 ft
Big Boards/ Series 14: 14 ft x 48 ft
Spectaculars (various): 20 ft x 40 ft to 20 ft x 52 ft
Big Boards: 16 ft x 52 ft
Airport -Exterior: 10 ft x 30 ft
Airport - Interior: 10 ft x 30 ft
Airport - Interior Airboards: 50 ft x 40 ft
Airport - Interior Spectaculars: 8 ft x 12 ft
                                       to 8 ft x 16 ft
Transit Shelter/Shelterlites: 48 ft x 66 ft
Pillar-Ads: 46 3/4 in x 68 1/4 in
Pillarbox: 26 3/4 in x 68 1/4 in
Mall Posters: 43 in x 60 in
	Interior Transit 11 ft x 35 ft and 11 ft x 70 ft
	Exterior Transit 30 ft x 139 ft (King)
	21 ft x 70 ft (Seventy)
	Subway 28 ft x 20 ft (Door Card)
	6 ft x 4 ft (Station Lite)
	48 ft x 62 ft (Station Poster)
	66 ft x 144 ft (Super Poster)
	21 ft x 50 ft (Backlit 50's)
	38 ft x 98 ft (Backlit 100's)
	10 ft x 33 ft (Metro-Space)
	  Metron digital Space
	  Super Buses (Painted)

Product/Category Restrictions

All Outdoor
- Alcohol prohibited, except in Ontario (cannot be posted within 600 ft. of schools and churches.
- All outdoor in Quebec must be in French.
- All outdoor on D.O.T. (Department of Transportation) property (e.g., airports) in Quebec, French must be positioned first.

Mall Posters
- Alcohol prohibited except Ontario, Quebec and Manitoba
- All Quebec locations must be in French.

Transit
- Alcohol limitations on quantities of Interior Cards:
- Only 1 brand per company per vehicle
- Only 2 cards for every 15 cards in each vehicle
- Only 5 platform posters per level per station in subways
- Alcohol prohibited on exterior transit except some drinking moderation allowed in some regions.

Political
- Some restrictions on municipal.
- None allow slogans or position statements.

Religious
- Some communities refuse religious.

Direct Marketing

Direct marketing is growing in Canada. The importance of it is more relevant in view of the shrinking economy, and need for fast results. Some agencies have set up Direct Marketing groups under the company or as separate units. Names of direct mail consumer list brokers are not available.

Direct Marketing Association
Canadian Direct Marketing Association
1 Concorde Gate Suite 607
Don Mills, Ontario M3C 3N6
391-2362

Advertising Restrictions on Direct Marketing
There is no specific legislation regarding direct marketing activities. This branch of the advertising business has its own 'code of ethics and standards of practice', published by the Canadian Direct Marketing Association.

Non-Traditional Media

There is a trend toward increased usage of non-traditional media to provide integrated marketing efforts. Some types that are currently available are in-store, couponing, packaging and sponsorship event marketing. Suppliers are open to ideas; costs are not available.

Research Sources

Research company	Information Provided
TV & Radio	
A.C. Nielsen Co. of Canada Ltd. 160 McNabb Street Markham, Ontario L3R 4B8 BBM (Bureau of Broadcast Measurement) 1500 Don Mills Road Suite 305 Don Mills, Ontario M3B 3L7	BBM and Nielsen are the syndicated rating services in Canada. Each produces surveys of network TV plus market-by-market and station-by-station television audience estimates and program ratings. Nielsen provides metered TV network measurement. BBM also surveys radio and produces estimates of Canadian audiences to all its member radio stations. It participates with Radio Bureau and Radio Stations to produce the Radio Product Measurement (RPM) Study.
Magazine	
PMB (Print Measurement Bureau) 77 Bloor Street West Suite 1502 Toronto, Ontario M5B 1M2	Measures primary and total audience for print, i.e., consumer and business magazines, their quantitative and qualitative reading habits. Also measures product usage to audience demographic and psychographic data, nationally and by region, or major markets. PMB also collects data for other media i.e., time spent on TV, Radio, Outdoor, Newspaper and Mall visits, and Transit.
Business Publications	
Survey of Business & Professional Managerial Canadians c/o Financial Post 777 Bay Street Toronto, Ontario M5W 1A7	Syndicated research on reading habits sponsored by some of the major business magazines. Available research includes; audience demographics -their purchase influence, position in the business, exclusive readership and interest levels.

Continued on following page

Research Sources, continued

Newspaper	

Newspaper Marketing Bureau, Inc.
  10 Bay Street
   Water Park Place Suite 201
   Toronto, Ontario M5J 2R8
(Also offices in Montreal and
Vancouver)
	Oversees NADBANK, which is the source for daily newspaper readership habits, sectional readership, product purchase behavior, service usage, and other media habits (radio & TV) are available on a market-by-market, regional or national basis (33 markets in total).

Magazine/ Newspapers	

ABC - Audit Bureau of Circulations
  151 Bloor Street West
  Suite 850
  Toronto, Ontario M5S 1S4
 	
CCAB- Canadian Circulations Audit
Board
  188 Eglinton Avenue East
  Suite 304
  Toronto, Ontario M4P 2X7
	Publishers Statements and Audit Reports of Circulation in a standardized format detailing circulation by region and trade distribution. ABC requires 70% paid circulation and business publications 50% paid or non-paid direct request. It publishes FAS-FAX 5-Year Trend Reports and Canadian Circulation of U.S. Magazines. CCAB audits publications whose circulation is any combination of Paid or controlled.

Outdoor/Posters/ Transit Shelters/
Mail Posters/ Airport Posters
Comb - Canadian Outdoor
Measurement Bureau
  1300 Yonge Street Suite 302
  Toronto, Ontario M4T 2W4
	It verifies traffic circulation for most outdoor media. Reports are produced quarterly detailing gross and in-market daily average circulation for all exterior outdoor media.

Television Research Currently Available

Research Method	*Frequency*	*Research Method*	*Frequency*
Nielsen People Meter Network	Weekly for 52 weeks	BBM Diary Spot Market	Same as Nielsen Diary
Nielsen Diary Spot Market	2-5 reports annually		

Advertising Regulations

By Product

Beverages/Alcohol
Alcoholic beverages, excluding beer, wine and coolers, are not permitted in commercials on radio or television. These commercials must be approved prior to air-date by the Canadian Radio and Television and Telecommunications Commission (C.R.T.C.), and must be individually approved by provincial boards.

Food/Restaurants
All food scripts (for broadcast) must be approved by the C.R.T.C. and remain valid for twelve months.

Cigarettes
Effective January 1, 1991 cigarette advertising is not permitted.

Advertising Regulations, continued

Pharmaceuticals/Drugs

All drugs and cosmetic scripts (for broadcast) must be approved by the C.R.T.C. and remain valid for twelve months.

Advertising To Children

Child directed advertising is not permitted in the Province of Quebec.

Child directed advertising in all provinces (excluding Quebec) must be approved by the Advertising Standards Council and C.R.T.C. and renewed annually.

Commercials featuring characters of a program cannot be broadcast within the program.

Feminine Hygiene

Feminine hygiene ads for broadcast are subject to approval of the Advertising Standards Council, Telecaster, and CBC clearance.

Tampons require a CCAC number from the Health and Welfare Department, as well as Advertising Standards Council, Telecaster, and CBC numbers.

Approval numbers are valid for one year, except CBC, which is valid for life.

By Medium

Print

Restrictions are enforced by each of the Canadian Provinces in the print medium. These generally relate to total lineage and frequency. Prince Edward Island still prohibits all print.

Outdoor

Outdoor advertising restrictions and regulations are enforced by each of the Canadian Provinces. These generally relate to a 200M radium from schools and churches. Some provinces are more strictly governed, and permit advertising of the corporate name only for cultural and sporting activities (i.e., P.E.I., Nfld) or as educational or Public Service message only (i.e., B.C., Sask.).

Text of Alcoholic Beverages Code

This Code applies to radio and television commercial messages, as the case may be, for alcoholic beverages ("product").

For the purpose of this Code, "portray" means "depict or refer to, visually or in sound".

Such messages shall not

(a)   attempt to influence non-drinkers to drink;

(b)   portray an unrealistic or excessive number of cases or containers, i.e., only one serving per person portrayed;

(c)   show or use language that suggests, in any way, product misuse or product dependency;

(d)   refer to the feeling and effect caused by alcohol consumption or show or convey the impression that the people involved are under the influence of alcohol;

(e)   portray persons with any such product in situations in which the consumption of alcohol is prohibited;

(f)   associate the consumption of any such product with the operation of any motorized vehicle, e.g., by suggesting or implying that any such product is or should be consumed prior to or during the operation of a motor vehicle;

(g)   associate the consumption of any such product with any activity requiring a significant degree of skill, care or mental alertness or involving an obvious element of danger until such activity has been clearly completed, e.g., by suggesting or implying that any such product is or should be consumed prior to or during any such activity; - a flat label or symbol associated with a brand or brand name reference, used for brand identification, will not in itself be considered to suggest consumption of that brand.

United States

Area	9,372,610 km²
Population (1992)	254,521,000
Population growth rate (1992)	0.8%
GDP	US$ 5,673 billion
GDP/per capita	US$ 22,470
Real growth rate (1991)	0.7%
Capital	Washington D.C.

Population Breakdown

By Sex		*By Age Group*		*By Socio-Economic Status*	
Male	49%	0-17	26%	A, US$ 0-19,999	30%
Female	51%	18-24	10%	B, US$ 20-34,999	25%
		25-34	17%	C, US$ 35-49,999	19%
		35-49	21%	D, US$ 50+	26%
		50+	26%		

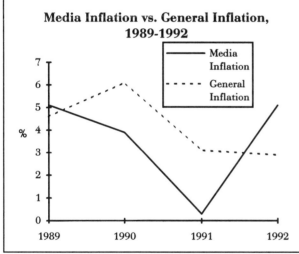

Media Inflation vs. General Inflation, 1989-1992

Number of Households	93,677,200

Ownership of household durables
- Car 89.1%
- Phone 93.7%
- Washers 76.0%
  (purchasing power equivalent)

GNP distribution by industry
- Agriculture .... N/A
- Industry .... N/A
- Services .... N/A

Exchange rates (US$ to local currency)
- 1991 .... 1.0
- 1992 .... 1.0

Source: Donnelly Marketing Information Services, U. S. Department of Commerce in Washington, D.C.

National Holidays

Holiday	*1993 Date*
New Year's Day	January 1
President's Day	February 15
Memorial Day	May 31
Independence Day	July 4
Labor Day	September 6
Thanksgiving	November 25
Christmas	December 25

School Holidays

Holiday	*1993 Date*
Christmas	December 17 - January 1
Spring Break	March (1-2 weeks)
Summer Vacation	June 1 - September 1
Martin Luther King Day	January 18
Good Friday	April 9
Columbus Day	October 11
Veteran's Day	November 11

Major Influences and Trends

Leaner budgets and an increasingly fragmented media marketplace have continued to focus attention on targeted media. Television, for example, continues to split into finer audience segments. Since 1985, the overall average number of hours of television viewed by a U.S. household has hovered around 50 hours per week. At the same time, the average number of channels receivable in those households has grown from about 19 to nearly 38.

This expansion in viewing options is due in large part to continued expansion of cable. Although growth in U.S. cable penetration is slowing, the number of cable channels continues to increase. Technological advances in digitization, signal compression and fiber optics bring the potential for a 500-channel medium. Already in place are tests to use expanded channel capacity to explore personalized, interactive services through which people can use their televisions for program viewing on demand, shopping, banking, etc.

Beyond television, other media continue to become more personalized. In print, the number of general consumer magazines still is shrinking. However, there is increased interest in custom-tailored print media. Many publications offer opportunities for insertion of personalized advertising messages in specific copies using subscriber databases. Others offer the opportunity to segment custom publishing, whereby a single advertiser creates a fully-sponsored magazine relevant to its product/service and its consumers. This type of publication becomes a vehicle for direct, personal communication with the customer.

On the whole, all forms of direct communication continue to be of keen interest to advertisers. Traditional direct mail has remained relatively strong. Television and magazines are receiving increased attention as vehicles to carry messages asking for initial consumer response via reply cards or toll-free telephone numbers.
Net, mass media vehicles, which once were directed to large undifferentiated audiences, continue to transform themselves into media types programmed for specific segments of viewers and readers.

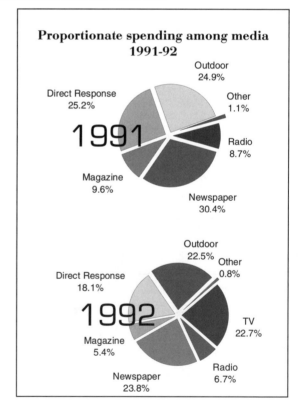

Proportionate spending among media 1991-92

Spending Analysis

National advertising spending by medium
based on appropriate year's exchange rate

	1989 US$ MM	1990 US$ MM	1991 US$ MM	1992 US$ MM
TV	26,891	28,405	27,402	29,400
Radio	8,323	8,726	8,746	8,654
Newspaper	32,368	32,281	30,400	30,737
Magazine	9,691	9,893	9,621	7,000
Direct Response	21,945	23,600	24,500	23,391
Outdoor	1,111	1,084	1,077	29,086
Other	23,601	24,651	24,915	1,031
Total	**123,930**	**128,640**	**126,661**	**129,299**

Source: Advertising Age, May 1, 1990-1993.

Media Buying

All television, magazine, radio and outdoor rates are negotiable. In newspapers, straight line rates are usually not negotiable, but special package rates and value added programs can be negotiated. Media negotiations are handled by advertising agencies rather than directly by the client. Buying services have always existed in the U.S., mainly to serve small agencies. Buying services do exist but they have never been a significant factor for larger agencies. There is no monopoly ownership of media in the U.S.

Buying Service	1992 Billings (US$)
Action Media, Inc.	1,500,000
Active Media Services	N/A
Advanswers	420,000,000
AKA Communications	N/A
American Media Services	N/A
ASI Media Inc.	N/A
Atwood Richards, Inc.	N/A
Baker Hill Media Services	N/A
Bohbot Communications, Inc.	350,000,000
Botway Group	N/A
Bray Media	4,950,000
Broadcast Time, Inc.	24,800,000
Camelot Communications	82,000,000
Casey Media	N/A
Cash Plus	120,000,000
Charney/Palacios & Co., Inc.	7,750,000
Cherokee Communications, Inc.	2,850,000
Colsky Media, Inc.	20,000,000
Corinthian Media, Inc.	300,000,000
CPM Media Managment	N/A
Creative Media Inc.	N/A
CSI International Corp.	85,000,000
Deerfield Communications Corp.	50,000,000
Dewitt Media Inc.	404,000,000
Farrell CMA	5,000,000
Ferris Marketing, inc.	N/A
Flying A	6,000,000
F/S Reilly Media	10,000,00
Gaynor Media Corp.	N/A
General Media Services	11,200,000
Greenstripe Media, Inc.	20,000,000
Neil Faber Media Inc.	67,300,000
Allan R. Hackel Organization	40,000,000
Harris & Drutt Inc.	11,115,000
Hawk Media, Inc.	N/A
Haworth Group inc.	92,000,000
Horizon Media Inc.	150,000,000
Independent Meida	N/A
Inter/Media Time Buying Corp.	67,075,000
International Communications Group	227,700,000
J.L.P. Media Inc.	N/A
Janik & Associates, Inc.	20,000,000
KJD Advertising	250,000,000

Buying Service	1992 Billings (US$)
KSL Media	N/A
KSM Inc.	N/A
Kelly Media Assoc.	N/A
Kingsbridge Media & Marketing Inc	11,000,000
Lamarca Group	N/A
Lee Corp.	3,450,000
MJP Carat Int'l	57,000,000
Media Buying Services	2,250,000
MBS International	150,000,000
The Media Department Inc.	N/A
Media Headquarters	N/A
Media/Marketing Service Center	N/A
Media Plus	10,500,000
Media Power	13,889,000
Media Services Inc.	N/A
Media Solutions	9,850,000
Media Specialists	6,800,000
Media Store, Inc.	38,500,000
Media That Works	125,000,000
Mercury Markets, Inc.	1,500,000
Molesphini & Tobin Inc.	23,500,000
Multi-Media Services	10,000,000
National Communications Concepts	N/A
National Media Mail	9,000,000
National Out-of-Home Media/Metro 8	15,000,000
Newspaper Advertising Specialists	12,000,000
Northwest Media Services	1,580,000
R. J. Palmer Inc.	80,000,000
Pacific Media Exchange	7,000,000
Perry Enterprises	500,000
Pro Media Inc.	40,000,000
RDR Associates, Inc.	N/A
RNF Media Corporation	45,000,000
Agric. Adv. & Research Div., RHP	189,338
Dewees, Bridge & Mottert	N/A
JL Media, Inc.	N/A
Katz Marketing & Media, Inc.	14,060,000
Magma Media's Technology, Inc.	8,000,000
Market/Media Analysis	N/A
Martin & Benedict Inc.	15,000,000
Media Corporate Inventory (MCI)	N/A
Media Directions Advertising, Inc.	3,000,000
Media First International, Inc.	75,000,000

Buying Service	1992 Billings (US$)
Media Rare	N/A
Mediacomm Marketing Group	350,000
Mediapower, Inc.	N/A
Military Ads, U.S.A.	1,200,000
National Media Consultants	34,000,000
National Media Services, Inc.	13,000,000
Northeast Advertising	3,000,000
Out-of-Home Media Services, Inc.	35,000,000
Perkins Nichols Media	5,000,000
Sansoni West Media Co.	1,420,000
Senior Ads, USA	1,200,000
SFM Media Corporation	724,000,000
SKR Resources	23,000,000
Slade Creative Marketing	800,000
SMY Media	N/A
Sound Communications	7,000,000
Specialized Media Services, Inc.	11,000,000
Standard Out of Home Media	6,500,000
Target Enterprises	28,500,000
Taylor-Brivic	32,000,000
The Davis Media Group	N/A
The Target Group, Inc.	2,000,000
Time Buying Services	250,000,000
Total Communications Group	10,000,000
Trade Media Intl. Corp.	2,000,000
Tradewell	N/A
TV Magazine Network	2,000,000
TVRC	N/A
Urban Media	6,000,000
Venet Media Services, Inc.	N/A
Vernon Sassos McGill, Inc.	75,000,000
Vitt Media International	441,650,000
Ward Communications, Inc.	30,000,000
WF of R, Inc.	N/A
Dick Warren Advertising	1,955,500
Media Plus International, Inc.	350,000
The Media Place, Inc.	2,000,000
Western International Media	1,100,000,000
Wilkins Outdoor Network	16,000,000
Williams Television Time, Inc.	50,000,000
Winner Communications	75,000,000

Source: Standard Directory of Advertisers, 1993

Top Advertisers (1992 Spending)

By Company

Parent Company	Product Categories	US$ MM
Procter & Gamble	Household Products/Toiletries & Cosmetics	2,149.0
Philip Morris Cos.	Food/Beer & Wine/Cigarettes	2,045.6
General Motors Corp.	Automotive	1,422.1
Sears, Roebuck & Co.	Retail	1,179.4
Pepsi Co.	Soft Drinks	903.4
Grand Metropolitan	Food	744.7
Johnson & Johnson	Toiletries & Cosmetics	733.0
McDonald's Corp.	Food	694.8
Ford Motor Co.	Automotive	676.6
Eastman Kodak Co.	Electronics	661.4

By Product

Product Category	Advertiser	US$ MM
Automotive	General Motors Corp.	5,259.1
Retail	Sears, Roebuck & Co.	5,125.9
Business, Consumer Services	AT&T Co.	3,582.8
Food	Philip Morris Cos.	3,551.9
Entertainment	Warner-Lambert Co.	2,913.2
Toiletries/Cosmetics	Procter & Gamble	2,249.3
Travel & Hotels	Walt Disney Co.	2,123.2
Drugs & Remedies	American Home Products Corp.	1,807.9
Direct Response		1,192.9
Candy, Snacks, Soft Drinks	Pepsi Co.	1,146.2

Television

TV HH Penetration				Adult Reach	
1989	*1990*	*1991*	*1992*	at 250 GRPs	72%
98%	98%	98%	98%	at 500 GRPs	78%
92,100,000	93,100,000	92,100,000	93,100,000	at 1000 GRPs	85%

Source (TV Household Penetration): Nielsen Media Research

Source (Adult Reach): Leo Burnett Reach & Frequency Tables, 1989.

Overview

63% of U.S. households can receive over 30 channels of programming. This is largely due to the continued increase of cable households. (*Source: Nielsen TV Audience*)

- HUT levels for all dayparts have remained steady over the last year.
- Primetime network HUT levels have been falling over the last few years due to pressure from cable and other sources.
- Hispanic media have become increasingly important over the last few years because Hispanics are the fastest-growing minority in the U.S. and because Hispanics primarily live in urban areas with high Hispanic concentration, where they are able to retain their language and culture. Television was the medium of choice among Hispanic marketers in 1992, accounting for 46% of total Hispanic market ad expenditures.
- In 1992, there were 3,589 advertisers/brands advertising on network TV, 11,046 advertising on National Spot TV, and 11,046 advertising on Retail Local TV.

Opportunities

Network	Number of Stations	Ownership	Station Profile	Commercial Minutes/Day	Coverage	Broadcast Hours (Sign-On/Off)
ABC	220	Private	General	120.7	99%	6am-2am
CBS	209	Private	General	136.1	99%	6am-2am
NBC	209	Private	General	138.3	99%	6am-2am
FOX	140	Private	General	145.4	92%	6am-2am

Sources: (Number of stations, coverage, broadcast hours) Networks themselves ; (Commercial minutes/day) Mediawatch

Hispanic Television

Network	Number of Stations	Ownership	Station Profile	Commercial Minutes/Day	Coverage (% Hisp TV HH)	Broadcast Hours (Sign-On/Off)
Telemundo	41 (376 Cable)	Private	Hispanic	125-150	85%	M-Th 7a-2a Fr 8a-2:30a Sa-Su 8a-3a
Univision	36 (609 Cable)	Private	Hispanic	144	91%	24 hours

Source: Networks themselves

Costs

Prime Time TV Costs for :30 in US$			
1989	*1990*	*1991*	*1992*
112,600	121,600	106,100	94,000

Source: Nielsen Media Research

Television Cost Changes Between Years

'88   5.5%   '89   8.3%   '90   -11%   '91   -11%   '92

Source: Nielsen Media Research

Audiences/CPM's

Average Cost, Audience, and CPMs by Daypart
(Top 3 Stations, :30, national audience, Target=Adults 18+)

Hours	Morning 07:00-10:00	Daytime 10:00-16:30	Prime Time M-Sa 20:00-23:00 Su 19:00-23:00	Late Night 23:00-01:00	Weekend 07:00-23:00 Sa-Sun 13:00-19:00	Children Sa 08:00-13:00
Station: ABC						
US$	$17,756	$12,724	$102,428	$38,720	$35,424	$28,939
Avg. Aud. (000)	4,395	4,341	11,095	4,920	4,417	2,929
CPM	4.04	2.93	9.23	7.87	8.02	9.88
Station: CBS						
US$	$6,984	$12,647	$10,5648	$11,970	$80,784	$23,574
Avg.Aud. (000)	2910	5361	11844	2660	8966	3034
CPM	2.40	2.36	8.92	4.50	9.01	7.77
Station: NBC						
US$	$17,389	$11,857	$64,931	$28,471	$48,238	$16,932
Avg. Aud. (000)	4,190	2731	8739	3528	6083	2955
CPM	4.15	4.34	7.43	8.07	7.93	5.73

All programming 19:00-21:00 for FOX

*Note: Special programming not included (except in weekend daypart)

Source (Household and persons cost per thousands): Nielsen Media Research

Audiences/Rating by Daypart (Target=Adults 18+)

Daypart	Hours	Household				Adult		
		Universe (000)	Hut Levels	Household Rating	Impressions (000)	Universe (000)	Adult Rating	Impressions (000)
Morning	07:00-14:00	3,166	18	6	190	6,122	3	184
Daytime	14:00-19:00	3,166	46	9	285	6,122	7	429
Primetime	19:00-23:00	3,166	63	23	728	6,122	15	918
Late Night	23:00-07:00	3,166	10	15	475	6,122	8	490
Weekend	07:00-23:00	3,166	43	13	412	6,122	6	367
Children's	14:00-21:00	3,166	53	12	380	6,122	10	612

Source: Nielsen Media Research

Scheduling/Regional/Languages

LANGUAGES	Programming		Commercials	
Primary	English	100%	English	100%
Secondary	Spanish	100%	Spanish	100%

- All programs and commercials on ABC, CBS, NBC and FOX TV networks are in English, while the Telemundo and Univision networks primarily broadcast in Spanish.
- The most common commercial length is :30. They make up 63% of network and 83.3% of spot commercials. Other available lengths are :10, :45, :60, :90 and :120+. (*Source: Leo Burnett Applebook Internal Arbitration Report.*)
- Commercials are aired throughout the day both at the beginning and end and within programs.
- Regional commericals are available through a network satellite feed system and local commercials are available through individual market buys on all stations in all markets. The costs of regional/local advertising varies by the market.

Children's Advertising

Network policies exist which limit children's advertising to certain formats and programs. Advertisements for children's toys and premiums during adult programming hours are acceptable provided the commercial is designed to appeal to a family or adult audience and not primarily to children 12 and under. Advertisements which are designed to appeal specifically to children are prohibited from airing during adult programming hours, including special programs for children.

All children's programming accepts advertising targeted at children. However, network policies prohibit advertising for children's toys and premiums which is designed to appeal to a family or adult audience from being scheduled in, or adjacent to, programs designed for children. (*Source: Network representatives*)

Programming which accepts advertising directed to children

CHILDREN'S PROGRAMMING				Kids'	
Station	Hours	Days	Universe (000)	Ratings	Impressions (000)
ABC	08:00-13:00	Saturday	36,870	*5.3	1,954.1
CBS	08:00-13:00	Saturday	36,870	*5.6	2,064.7
NBC	10:00-12:00	Saturday	36,870	*3.1	1,143.0
FOX	08:00-12:00	Saturday	36,870	*5.4	1,991.0
FOX	15:00-17:00	Mon-Fri	36,870	**5.5	2,027.9

Note: Although Saturday mornings are traditionally reserved for children's programming, NBC presently runs a schedule which is targeted toward 12-17 year-old females. NBC's rating in the 12-17 year-old female demographic group is 5.1.

*Ratings for 'Weekend daytime 6:00-18:00' for each network, respectively
**Rating for 'Weekday afternoon 13:00-18:00 Children's'
Source: Nielsen Media Research

Radio

- The penetration level of radio in the U.S. is at 95.1%; broadcasting reaches about 207,026,400 households.
- There are 12,822 radio stations; 10,939 are commercial. The number of stations in main cities are: New York-49, Los Angeles-52, Chicago-42, San Francisco-58 and Philadelphia-31. (*Source: Leo Burnett Applebook*)
- English is the primary broadcasting language; Spanish is secondary.
- The most popular program types are Country, Adult Contemporary and Classic Rock.
- Premiums are high (800% or more) for regional/local commercial air time. Commercial time is available in :30, :60, etc.

Radio Cost Changes Between Years

'88		'89		'90		'91		'92
	25%		60%		35%		53%	

Daypart Costs

Daypart	Local Time	Avg. Cost :60 US$	Avg. Audience (000)	CPM (US$)
AM Drive	06:00-10:00	510	175	2.91
Daytime	10:00-15:00	405	155	2.61
PM Drive	15:00-19:00	470	135	3.48
Evening	19:00-24:00	235	65	3.62

Ratings

Daypart	Adult Rating	Adult (000)
AM Drive	22.5	46,319
Daytime	19.6	40,425
PM Drive	16.9	34,780
Evening	8.1	16,626
Weekend	9.4	19,320

Source: Radar, Fall 1991, Volume I.

Cable

- There has been an increasing value in cable television as its programming appeal and media effectiveness continue to grow. Basic cable viewing shares and ratings have made steady gains as broadcast audiences decline.
- Cable's growing acceptance (among advertisers) is expected to continue in the years ahead. Local, regional and national cable advertising revenues will climb to 3.9 billion in 1993—14% more than the year before and the greatest rate of growth among all major media.

Cable HH Penetration			
1989	1990	1991	1992
57.1%	58.9%	60.6%	61.5%
52,600,000	54,800,000	55,800,000	57,612,000

Source: CAB 1992

- The cable penetration level is at 61.5% and is expected to reach 65% within the next 5 years.
- There are a total of 63 cable networks, 57 are commercial and all are privately owned.
- The primary broadcasting language is English; Spanish is secondary (primarily on Telemundo, Univision and Galavision.)

Top Cable Channels	Avg. :30 Cost in US$	Avg. HH Rating	Commercial Min/Hr
CNN	1,300	.7	13
ESPN	2,400	.9	10
WTBS	1,800	.8	10
USA Network	1,700	1.3	10
The Discovery Channel	1,600	.8	10

Cable Networks	Subscriber HH (000)	Cable Systems	Programming
Superstations			
TBS	60,425	11,807	General
WGN	38,100	14,354	General
WWOR	13,500	2,100	General
WPIX	9,500	638	General
Pay Cable			
Home Box Office	19,900	9,100	Movies/Sports/General
Showtime	7,300	6,000	Movies/Sports/General
The Disney Channel	7,080	7,000	Family Programs
Cinemax	6,100	5,700	Movies
Encore	3,900	1,100	Movies
The Movie Channel	2,600	3,250	Movies
Basic Cable			
Cable News Network	61,738	11,636	News
ESPN	61,600	26,116	Sports
USA Network	60,046	12,000	General
The Discovery Channel	59,533	9,756	Documentaries
TNT (Turner Network TV)	58,950	9,069	General
Nickelodeon	58,900	9,616	Children's Programs
The Family Channel	57,688	9,876	Movies, Family Programs
The Nashville Network	57,300	13,396	Country Music, Variety
MTV	57,285	8,141	Music Videos, Specials
C-SPAN	57,200	4,218	U.S. House of Representatives Cover
Lifetime	57,000	5,865	Women's Interests
Arts & Entertainment	56,088	8,400	General, Movies
The Weather Channel	53,381	4,925	Weather news
Headline News	51,632	5,763	News 24-hours
Nick-at-Nite	51,250	4,036	Classic American Programs
CNBC	48,300	4,000	Business & Consumer news
VH-1 (Video Hits One)	47,400	5,296	Music videos, Specials
QVC Network	45,000	4,071	Home Shopping
American Movie Classics	43,000	3,300	Classic Movies
Black Entertainment Television	35,300	2,661	General, Black Interests
EWIN (Eternal World TV Network)	31,000	1,025	Family/Spiritual
Comedy Central	28,000	2,004	Comedy Programming
C-SPAN II	27,900	914	U.S. Senate Coverage
Mind Extension University	23,000	798	Educational
E! Entertainment Television	21,560	950	Celebrity and Entertainment
Home Shopping Network	20,800	1,474	Home Shopping
VISN/ACTS (Vision Interfaith Satellite)	20,000	1,249	Religious

Continued on following page

Cable, continued

Cable Networks	Subscriber HH (000)	Cable Systems	Programming
The Learning Channel	19,874	1,558	Education
Country Music Television	18,900	4,800	Music, Videos, Entertainment
The Travel Channel	17,500	735	Travel News, Documentaries
Trinity Broadcasting Network	16,000	1,400	Religious
Silent Network	15,000	164	Programs for Disabled
America's Disability Channel	15,000	164	Programs for Disabled
Nostalgia Television	14,700	740	Classic American Programs
Video Jukebox Network/ The Box	13,000	104	Music Videos, interactive
Telemundo	12,400	470	Spanish-language, General
Home Shopping Network II	11,200	471	Home Shopping
Univision	11,063	609	Spanish-language, General
The Sci-Fi Channel	11,060	786	Science-Fiction Programs
Bravo	10,500	475	Cultural, Foreign Programs
Courtroom Television Network	8,000	600	Live U.S. Court Trials
QVC Fashion Channel	7,500	450	Home Shopping/Fashions
The Inspirational Network	5,500	750	Religious
The Cartoon Network	5,013	426	Animated Children's Programs
ValueVision	5,000	55	Home Shopping
KTLA	4,800	292	General
International Channel	4,000	135	Multi-language Programs
SCOLA/News of All Nations	2,800	36	International News
Sports Channel America	2,409	63	Sports
Galavision	2,300	325	Spanish-language, General
KTVT	2,200	481	General
Z Music	2,000	100	Music
WSBK	1,600	250	General

Source: Nielsen Media Research

Satellite

- Direct-to-home satellite is not common in the U.S. Today, satellites are used to deliver cable television where in-ground cables are not available. Some homes use satellite dishes to receive better transmission and a broader range of channels.
- Satellite penetration is currently at 2%; reaching about 1,873,000 households. Direct broadcast satellite (DBS) service is expected to begin in the U.S. in 1994. It will offer nationwide coverage, up to 150 channels of programming, and reach over 100 million households.

Video Cassettes

Approximately 75.1% of all TV households have video cassette recorders (VCRs), which is 73.8% of all U.S. households. VCR usage is measured by the A.C. Nielsen Company. Pre-recorded tapes do carry an average of 1 or 2 sponsors; costs vary. (*Source: A.C. Nielsen*)

Cinema

Based of a survey of 6,500 cinemas the potential 4 week reach is 47 million people (41 million: Screenvision and 6 million: Cineplex Odeon). 37.5% of U.S. theaters offer commercial time in spots from :30 to 3 minutes. The average CPM of a 4 week cinema schedule for a :60 is US$ 20. A national :30 spot is US$ 533,000, with a CPM of :30 US$ 13 for A national :60 spot is US$ 800,000.

Source: Screenvision, Anne-Marie Marc

Newspapers

There are 1,586 national daily newspapers that accept advertising with a combined circulation of 60,687,100. The literacy rate in English is 87%.

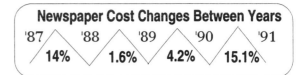

Newspaper Cost Changes Between Years

'87		'88		'89		'90		'91
	14%		1.6%		4.2%		15.1%	

Newspaper	Market	Size	Circulation (000)	Avg. Daily Aud. (000)	1 page B&W Cost (US)	Accept Color?
National						
Christian Science Monitor		Tabloid	108.6	197.7	4,275	Yes
USA Today		Standard	1,506.7 (M-Th)	1,923.2	57,505	Yes
Wall Street Journal		Standard	1,795.2	3,267.3	114,605	1-Color
Daily						
New York News	New York	Tabloid	777.1	1,414.3	22,090	Yes
New York Times	New York	Standard	1,145.9	2,085.5	53,298	No
New York Post	New York	Tabloid	438.0	797.2	20,230	Yes
Los Angeles Times	Los Angeles	Standard	1,146.6	2,086.8	55,631	Yes
Orange Country Register	Los Angeles	Standard	332.2	604.6	18,447	Yes
Chicago Tribune	Chicago	Standard	724.3	1,318.2	43,470	Yes
Chicago Sun-Times	Chicago	Tabloid	558.7	1,016.8	19,460	Yes
Philadelphia Enquirer News	Philadelphia	Standard	694.5	1,265.6	18,525	Yes
San Francisco Chronicle	San Francisco	Standard	556.8	1,013.4	32,766	Yes
San Francisco Examiner	San Francisco	Standard	134.9	245.5	17,415	Yes
Boston Globe	Boston	Standard	508.9	926.2	29,358	Yes
Boston Herald	Boston	Tabloid	330.6	601.7	12,828	Yes
The Detroit News & Free Press	Detroit	Standard	979.0	1,781.8	48,384	Yes
Dallas Morning News	Dallas	Standard	479.2	872.1	24,292	Yes
Ft.Worth Star Telegram	Dallas	Standard	256.2	466.3	17,419	Yes
The Washington Post	Wash. DC	Standard	802.1	1,460.0	47,018	Yes
he Washington Times	Wash. DC	Standard	97.1	176.7	5,670	Yes
Cleveland Plain Dealer	Cleveland	Standard	410.2	746.6	23,200	Yes

Source (Circulation and cost B/W): SRDS

Magazines

3,335 consumer magazines and 7,015 trade and technical magazines are published in the US.

Magazine Cost Changes Between Years

'88		'89		'90		'91		'92
	4.7%		3.9%		5.7%		4.3%	

Magazine	Type	Frequency	Circ. (000)	Audited?	Avg. Issue Aud. (000)	1 page 4/C Cost (US$)
Consumer's Digest	General Editorial	Bi-monthly	957.1	Yes	3,742	25,885
Ebony	General Editorial	Monthly	1,889.3	Yes	9,749	38,103
Life	General Editorial	Monthly	1,823.7	Yes	11,927	49,500
National Enquirer	General Editorial	Weekly	3,401.3	Yes	18,394	49,800
National Geographic	General Editorial	Monthly	9,787.1	Yes	24,403	142,915
New York Magazine	General Editorial	50x/Year	431.2	Yes	1,518	32,100
The New Yorker	General Editorial	Weekly	658.9	Yes	2,483	41,060
Parade	General Editorial	Weekly	36,071.0	Yes		514,500
People	General Editorial	Weekly	3,444.1	Yes	29,505	102,915
Psychology Today	General Editorial	Bi-monthly	200.0	No		7,420
Reader's Digest	General Editorial	Monthly	16,257.9	Yes	39,833	153,600
Rolling Stone	General Editorial	Bi-weekly	1,202.1	Yes	6,288	48,930
Scientific American	General Editorial	Monthly	637.3	Yes	1,907	31,300
Smithsonian	General Editorial	Monthly	2,211.6	Yes	5,851	59,500
Travel & Leisure	General Editorial	Monthly	1,103.5	Yes	2,060	48,865
Vanity Fair	General Editorial	Montly	1,151.9	Yes	2,886	52,490
Yankee	General Editorial	Monthly	722.1	Yes	1,782	17,925
Total	Entertainment	Monthly	6,812.6	Yes	8,630	75,560

Continued on next page

Magazines, continued

Magazine	Type	Frequency	Circ. (000)	Audited?	Avg. Issue Aud. (000)	1 page 4/C Cost (US$)
TV Guide	Entertainment	Weekly	14,919.9	Yes	40,180	119,500
Barron's	News & Business	Weekly	258.7	Yes	1,083	16,374
Business Week	News & Business	Weekly	886.2	Yes	6,530	61,600
Forbes	News & Business	Bi-weekly	740.5	Yes	3,386	51,440
Fortune	News & Business	Bi-weekly	732.0	Yes	3,451	56,260
INC.	News & Buslness	Monthly	646.8	Yes	1,155	56,916
Jet	General Editorial	Weekly	993.8	Yes	9,745	19,928
Money	News & Business	Monthly	2,077.0	Yes	6,587	83,200
Newsweek	News & Business	Weekly	3,232.1	Yes	20,318	120,835
Time	News & Business	Weekly	4,159.5	Yes	23,251	142,500
U.S. News & World Report	News & Business	Weekly	2,307.6	Yes	12,395	80,900
Wall St. Journal	News & Business	Daily	1,795.2	Yes		114,605
Kiplinger's Personal Finance	News & Business	Monthly	1,134.4	Yes	1,718	34,395
Bon Appetit	Women's	Monthly	1,231.3	Yes	3,802	41,335
Cosmopolitan	Women's	Monthly	2,705.2	Yes	11,702	75,260
Elle	Women's	Monthly	901.6	Yes	2,437	44,425
Essence	Women's	Monthly	900.4	Yes	5,020	30,730
Family Circle	Women's	17x/Year	5,283.7	Yes	17,533	105,000
Good Housekeeping	Women's	Monthly	5,101.2	Yes	18,685	133,875
Ladies Home Journal	Women's	Monthly	5,003.1	Yes	4,363	99,900
McCall's	Women's	Monthly	4,704.8	Yes	12,693	89,980
Parents	Women's	Monthly	1,749.3	Yes	6,554	55,210
Redbook	Women's	Monthly	3,356.1	Yes	10,530	76,525
Self	Women's	Monthly	1,409.0	Yes	2,972	47,310
Shape	Women's	Monthly	800.6	Yes	2,266	23,240
Woman's Day	Women's	17x/Year	4,810.4	Yes	15,372	92,500
Working Mother	Women's	Monthly	860.5	Yes	2,227	32,570
Working Woman	Women's	Monthly	866.8	Yes	2,624	37,500
Architectural Digest	Home Service	Monthly	653.6	Yes	2,804	44,880
Better Homes/Gardens	Home Service	Monthly	8,002.6	Yes	23,552	143,000
Colonial Homes	Home Service	Bi-monthly	632.6	Yes	1,801	34,140
Country Homes	Home Service	Bi-monthly	1,095.7	Yes	3,550	53,600
Country Living	Home Service	Monthly	1,839.4	Yes	8,033	52,295
House Beautiful	Home Service	Monthly	1,022.5	Yes	4,132	55,135
Metropolitan Home	Home Service	Monthly	726.3	Yes		37,200
Southern Living	Home Service	Monthly	2,374.5	Yes	7,450	67,300
Sunset	Home Service	Monthly	1,452.1	Yes	4,110	43,510
Soap Opera Digest	Romance & Movies	Bi-weekly	1,396.3	Yes	6,306	27,260
Bride's	Fashion	Bi-monthly	305.0	Yes	2,415	32,450
Glamour	Fashion	Monthly	2,083.8	Yes	7,857	67,730
Harper's Bazaar	Fashion	Monthly	772.7	Yes	2,425	39,610
Mademoisell	Fashion	Monthly	1,219.1	Yes	5,015	44,540
Vogue	Fashion	Monthly	1,284.2	Yes	5,561	52,680
Esquire	Men's	Monthly	730.2	Yes	2,235	41,440
Gentlemen's Quarterly	Men's	Monthly	650.3	Yes	3,617	39,200
Car & Driver	Sports & Auto	Monthly	1,019.6	Yes	5,265	65,710
Field & Stream	Sprots & Auto	Monthly	3,509.8	Yes	9,908	110,725
Golf Digest	Sports & Auto	Monthly	1,421.9	Yes	4,092	74,610
Road & Track	Sports & Auto	Monthly	758.3	Yes	4,155	48,775
Sports Illustrated	Sports & Auto	Weekly	3,432.0	Yes	21,591	134,620
Tennis	Sports & Auto	Monthly	759.0	Yes	1,612	43,470
Discover	Mech./Sci./Tech.	Monthly	1,014.2	Yes		32,995
Home Mechanix	Mech./Sci./Tech.	Monthly	1,014.0	Yes	2,000	27,560
Omni	Mech./Sci./Tech.	Monthly	702.8	Yes	2,015	30,165
Popular Mechanics	Mech./Sci./Tech.	Monthly	1,642.1	Yes	5,331	63,060
Popular Science	Mech./Sci./Tech.	Monthly	1,812.0	Yes	4,205	52,000

Source: Consumer and agency magazines, SRDS

Outdoor/Transit

Billboard	**Transit**

Sites available .... 60,000+
Lead Time to reserve .... 60-90 days adv.
 	
Exposure 84%
	Boards available (Common sizes)
	       11" x 28" interior bus or subway
	       30" x 144" exterior bus
	Exposure (metro)
	    Depends on showing level and market.

Costs
 	
Average, 1 billboard/month
  12 ft x 25 ft .... US$ 567
  14 ft x 48 ft .... US$ 2,315
     (Based on top 50 markets)
	Costs
	
	Average, 1 board/month
	Rates vary depending on poster size, number of markets, and number of displays per market.

Billboard Cost Changes Between Years

'88	'89	'90	'91	'92
	6%	6%	6%	5%

Transit Board Cost Changes Between Years

'88	'89	'90	'91	'92
	6%	6%	6%	5%

Sizes	**Sizes**

8-Sheet: 6 ft x 12 ft, 30-Sheet: 12 ft x25 ft
Bulletins: 14 ft x 48 ft,
            19 ft
            6 ft x 48 ft,
            20 ft x 60 ft
	King Size Poster 30 ft x144 ft,
	Tail light Display 21 ft x72 ft
	Interior Display 11 ft x 28 ft,
	One-Sheet: 46 ft x 30 ft
	Two-Sheet: 46 ft x 30 ft,
	Car Card: 22 ft x 21 ft *or* 33 ft x 21ft
	Standard Diorama 43 ft x 62 ft,
	Taxi Top 14 ft x 48 ft
	Telephone Kiosk 50 ft x 26 ft

Source: LNA, SMRB

Product/Category Restrictions for Outdoor Advertisements:
The State of Utah prohibits cigarette and liquor advertisements.
The States of Maine and Vermont prohibit outdoor advertisements.
Tobacco and liquor restrictions within 500 feet of churches, playgrounds, schools and hospitals.

Direct Marketing

Direct marketing continues to grow at a steady pace. It is a marketing tool used by almost every major company, and one which can be found in every possible medium.

List Broker	*Information Provided*
American List Council	Mailing Lists/Insert Programs - All Targets
Direct Media	Mailing Lists/Insert Programs - All Targets
Media Horizons	Insert Programs - All Targets
The Specialists	Mailing Lists/Insert Programs - All Targets
RMI Direct Marketing	Mailing Lists/Insert Programs - All Targets

Direct Marketing, continued

Top Telemarketing Companies	Direct Marketing Associations
WATS Marketing - Live Operator Inbound/Outbound	Direct Marketing Association
West Telemarketing - Live Operator Inbound/Outbound and Interactive	Electronic Media Marketing Association
Matrixx Marketing - Live Operator Inbound/Outbound and Interactive	List Council
Idelman Telemarketing - Live Operator Inbound/Outbound	Telemarketing Council
Call Interactive - High Volume Interactive	

Non-Traditional Media

There is a proliferation of interactive and multi-media techniques, including space marketing. Types available include Prodigy (electronic conferencing/shopping system), transaction receipts, statement stuffers, sky techniques (blimps, airplane banners), in-store, etc. The cost of this type of advertising varies.
Source: Leo Burnett Research Department

Research Sources

Media Covered	Research Company	Information
Television	A.C. Nielsen Company 299 Park Avenue New York, NY 10171	Demographic data Daypart usage Households and viewer ratings by 1000s Program performance by market
	Broadcast Advertisers Report (BAR) 142 W. 57th Street New York, NY 10019	Competitive Data
	Arbitron Ratings Company 1350 Avenue of the Americas New York, NY 10019	Same information as Nielsen
	Standard Rates & Data Services (SRDS) 866 Third Avenue New York, NY 10022	Station Index Sales Firm Representation
Radio	RADAR Statistical Research, Inc. 111 Prospect Street Westfield, NJ 07090	Demographic data Daypart usage Households and viewer ratings by 1000s Program performances by market
	Birch Radio Colonial Plaza, Suite 2D 44 Sylvan Avenue Englewood Cliffs, NJ 07632	*Same as above*
	Arbitron *(See Television Listing)*	*Same as above*
	SRDS *(See Television Listing)*	Station Index Sales Firm Representation See Television Listing

Continued on next page

Research Sources, continued

Media Covered	Research Company	Information
	Radio Expenditures Report (RER) 740 W. Boston Post Road Mamaroneck, NY 10543	Competitive Data
Newspaper	Audit Bureau of Circulation (ABC) 900 N. Meacham Road Schaumburg, IL 60173-4968	Circulation Analysis
	Leading National Advertiser (LNA) 136 Madison Avenue New York, NY 10016	Competitive Data
	SRDS *See Television Listing*	Cost Information Circulation Analysis Mechanical Information
Magazine	Media Mark Research, Inc. (MRI) 341 Madison Avenue New York, NY 10017	Detailed Readership Data
	Simmons Market Research Bureau (SMRB) 219 E. 42nd Street New York, NY 10017	See above
	Lloyd Hall's Magazine Report 544 Old Post Road #3 Greenwich, CT 06830	Analysis of magazine editorial content
	LNA *See Newspaper Listing*	Competitive Data
	SRDS *See Television Listing*	Cost information Circulation Analysis Mechanical Information
Outdoor	LNA *See Newspaper Listing*	Competitive Data
Multimedia	LNA *See Newspaper Listing*	Competitive Data
Cable/Satellite	A.C. Nielsen *See Television Listing*	*See Television Listing*

Television Research Currently Available

Research Method	Frequency
Diary (Spot TV)	Quarterly
People Meter (Network)	Weekly
(Limited Spot Markets)	Daily

Advertising Regulations

The following provides a very brief and general overview of regulations pertaining to advertising in the Untied States. For more detailed regulations, specifcially pertaining to certain prodcuts, product categories, targets and media, please consult a lawyer or the Leo Burnett, USA Legal Department.

By Product

Beverages/Alcohol
- Legislation pending that would restrict alcohol advertising.

- Advertising for beverage of 14% or more alcohol prohibited on broadcast.

- Mandatory statement designating advertiser and class/type of beverage.
- Models must be and *appear* to be of legal drinking age.
- Ad cannot claim curative or therapeutic effects.
- Flags, seals, and coat of arms prohibited.
- Product advertising may not use athletes as endorsers or spokespersons.
- Warning labels stating danger of drinking and driving, using equipment and drinking during pregnancy required on alcoholic beverage labels.
- Drinking scenarios prohibited.
- Legislation pending that would require rotating warnings in all alcohol beverage advertising.

Food/Restaurants

- Food and Drug Administration (FDA) controls package labelling: list of ingredients in descending order of prominence, name and address of parent company.
- Federal Trade Commission (FTC) handles advertising claims which must be truthful.
- Legislation pending that would require label information to appear in advertising.
- FDS proposed regulations tht would restrict health claims on packaging.

Cigarettes

- Legislation pending that would restrict cigarette advertising.
- All ads must display one of four rotating Surgeion General Warnings.
- Industry regulated self; for example, advertisers do not use models under 25, clelbrities, athletes (Cigarette Advertising Code).
- Advertising does not encourage smoking, merely brand switching.

Pharmaceuticals/Drugs

- FDA regulates labelling for over-the-counter (OTC) drugs.
- FDA regulates and restricts efficacy claims on label, FTC controls advertising.
- OTC drugs ads must state product to be used 'only as directed.'
- Models may not be shown taking medicine.

Advertising To Children

- Network policies exist that limit children's advertising to certain formats and time constraints
- Legislation that limits amount of children's advertising per show.
- Limited comparative claims allowed if clear; no exhortative language, no product endorsers, no anti-social behavior per industry code and network standards

Industry self-regulates through the Children's Advertising Review Unit (CARU).

Commercial Production:

No restrictions regarding airing internationally produced commercials. Some restrictions and immigration issues regarding out-of-country talent used in USA.

By Medium

Regulations vary be medium and vehicle. While individual broadcasters and publishers reserve the right to set their own standards, they must comply, at the very least, with FCC and BBB guidelines. In general, ads must be thoughful and nondeceptive, represent legal products or services, and, accurately describe competitors and substantiate any claims against them.
Some specific media relevant lmitations are highlighted below:

Television

Will not accept advertisements for cigarettes, hard liquor (14%+), contraceptives or abortion services.

Print

Cigarette, hard liquor and contraceptive advertising is allowed, but not accepted by all publications.

Outdoor

Tobacco and liquor advertising is restricted within 500 feet of churches, hospitals, schools and playgrounds; it is completely prohibited in the state of Utah. Outdoor advertising is completely prohibited in Maine and Vermont.

Non-traditional

Advertising copy for alcohol beverages must be self-regulated. Consumer promotions must be cleared by the Secretary of Commerce. The Secretary of Public Education supervises the correct use of language. Alcoholic beverage advertising must have a health warning phrase in the copy.

Leo Burnett Offices

Due to the inevitability of changes and because this book is issued only once a year, contact our International Media Department for accuracy.

The following office telephone numbers list the country, city, and local numbers. When dialing direct, an international access code must be inserted before the country code number. This number differs from country to country, therefore, check with the local operator for the country's international access code or refer to page 4 in the Leo Burnett International Directory. If dialing from the U.S.A., the international access code is 011.

Regional Headquarters

Asia

Leo Burnett Ltd.
Gary Brown, Regional Media Director
6th Floor, Cityplaza 3
14 Taikoo Wan Road
Hong Kong
Phone: 852-5674333
Fax: 852-885-3209
Media: 853-567-4552

Australia/New Zealand

Leo Burnett/Connaghan & May Pty. Ltd.
John Lambert, National Media Director
Leo Burnett House
Levels 3 & 4
73 Miller Street
North Sydney, N. S. W. 2060
Australia
Phone: 61-2-925-3555
Fax: 61-2-957-2152

Europe/Middle East

Leo Burnett Ltd.
Richard Zobel, Regional Chairman/CEO
48 St. Martin's Lane
London WC2N 4EJ
England
Phone: 44-71-836-2424
Fax: 44-71-829-7143
Direct Fax: 44-71-829-7169

Latin America

Leo Burnett Inernational
Daniel Moure, Regional Managing Director
550 Biltmore, Suite 870
Coral Gables, Florida 33134
U.S.A.
Phone: 305-448-5959
Fax: 305-443-6834
Direct Fax: 305-446-8571

Canada

Leo Burnett Company, Ltd.
Terry Sheehy, Sr. V.P., Media Services
Director
175 Bloor Street East
North Tower
Toronto, Ontario, Canada M4W 3R9
Phone: 1-416-925-5997
Fax: 1-416-925-3447
Media 1-416-925-3360

United States

Leo Burnett Company, Inc.
Brian Jacobs, Sr. VP, International Media
Director
35 West Wacker Drive
Chicago, Illinois 60601
U.S.A.
Phone: 312-220-5959
Fax: 312-220-6516

Offices Within Regions
Asia/Pacific

Australia

Leo Burnett/Connaghan & May Pty. Ltd.
John Lambert, Regional Media Director
Leo Burnett House, Levels 3 & 4
73 Miller Street
North Sydney, N. S. W. 2060, Australia
Phone: 61-2-925-3555
Fax: 61-2-925-2152

Leo Burnett/Connaghan & May S. A. Pty. Ltd.
Anthony Coles, Media Director
225 Greenhill Road, 2nd Floor
Dulwich, Adelaide,
South Australia 5065, Australia
Phone: 61-8-364-0066
Fax: 61-8-3640054

Leo Burnett/Connaghan & May Qld Pty. Ltd.
Mark Lacy, Media Director
33 Park Road
Milton, Queensland 4064
Australia
Phone: 61-7-368-1222
Fax: 61-7-3695365
Media: 852-567-4552

Leo Burnett/Connaghan & May Vic Pty. Ltd.
Lisa Thompson, Media Director
464 St. Kilda Road, 5th floor
Melbourne, Victoria 3004,
Australia
Phone: 61-3-867-1166
Fax: 61-3-867-4952
Media: 61-3-867-8282

China

Leo Burnett (China) Ltd.
Joe Kong, Media Director
Guangzhou Representative Office
Room 1510-1511, GITIC Plaza
339 Huanshi Dong Lu, Guangzhou
Peoples Republic of China
Phone: 86-20-331-1182/1183/1163
Fax: 86-20-331-1123

Hong Kong

Leo Burnett Ltd.
Gary Brown, Regional Media Director
6th Floor, Cityplaza 3
14 Tailoo Wan Road
Hong Kong
Phone: 852-567-4333
Fax: 852-885-3209
Media: 852-567-4552

India

Chaitra Leo Burnett Advertising Private Ltd.
R. S. Naman, Media Director
9/11 N. S. Patkar Marg
Ardeshir B Godrej Chowk
Bombay 400 036, India
Phone: 91-22-363-0373
Fax: 91-22-262-2027

Indonesia

Aim Communications
*Peggy Malik, Media Coordinator
Prince Centre Building, 15th Floor
Jalan Jenderal, Sudirman 3-4
Jakarta, 10220, Indonesia
Phone: 62-21-575279/5700415
Fax: 62-21-5703255

Japan

Leo Burnett - Kyodo Co., Ltd.
Toshio Kanda, Media Director
Akasaka Twin Tower
17-22 Akasaka 2 - chome
Minato-ku, Tokyo 107, Japan
Phone: 81-3-3584-2331
Fax: 81-3-3584-2330

Korea

Leo Burnett Sonyon, Inc.
Chul Hong Kim, Media Director
9th Floor, Youone Building
75-95, Seosomun-dong
Chung-Ku, Seoul, 100-11-0, Korea
Phone: 82-2-774-8222
Fax: 82-2-774-2226

*Affiliate

Malaysia

Leo Burnett Sdn. Bhd.
Annie Ng, Media Director
10th Floor, MCB Plaza, 6 Changkat
Raja Chulan, 50200 Kuala Lumpur
Malaysia
Phone: 60-3-201-0998
Fax: 60-3-201-0972

New Zealand

Goldsack Harris
Thompson Advertising
Christopher Sharp
Level 2, Korea House, 29 Tory Street
P.O. Box 3219, Wellington
New Zealand
Phone: 64-4-384-6488
Fax: 64-4-384-6575

Phillipines

Hemisphere - Leo Burnett, Inc.
Martiner Ventaga
2nd Floor, Planters Products Bldg
Esteban St., Legaspi Village
Makati
Metro Manila, Phillipines
Phone: 63-2-818-6056
Fax: 63-2-8153629
Media: 63-2-312-2575

Singapore

Leo Burnett Pte. Ltd.
Jaswinder Kaur
677 Rangoon Rd., #03-00
Singapore 0821
Phone: 65-2999300
Fax: 65-2999377

Taiwan

Leo Burnett Company, Ltd.–Taiwan Branch
Ivy Wong, Media Director
7th Floor, Chung Hsin Textile Bldg.
123 Chung Hsiao East Road
Section 2
Taipei, Taiwan
Phone: 886-2-396-1222
Fax: 886-2-397-3046

Thailand

Leo Burnett Limited Thailand
Triluj Navamarat, Media Director
2nd Floor, USOM Bldg.
37 Soi Somprasong 3
Petchburi Road
Bangkok 10400, Thailand
Phone: 662-255-2356
Fax: 662-253-9189
Media 662-254-1743

Europe

Belgium

Leo Burnett Worldwide Inc.
Xavier Stinglhamber, Media Director
Chaussee De Wavre 1789
B- 1160 Brussels
Belgium
Phone: 32-2-675-4900
Fax: 32-2-675-2046
Media 32-2-672-4533

Czechoslovakia

Leo Burnett Prague
Petra Vaitova, Media Director
Ceskomalinska 41,
16000 Prague 6-Bubenec
Czech Republic
Phone: 42-2-323-029
Fax: 42-2-322-981

Denmark

Leo Burnett Denmark
Peter Sevel, Nordic Media Director
Vesterbrogade 2B
1620 Copenhagen V
Denmark
Phone: 45-33-14-99-66
Fax: 45-33-14-11-55
Media 45-33-131-784

France

Bordelais, Lemeunier & Leo Burnett
Arnaud de Saint Roman, Media Director
"Espace Clichy", 6 allee Jean Prouve
92587 Clichy Cedex
France
Phone: 33-1-4968-7300
Fax: 33-1-4737-6664

Germany

Michael Conrad & Leo Burnett GmbH
Jorn Lutkat, Media Director
Alexanderstr. 65
D-60489 Frankfurt/Main
Germany
Phone: 49-69-780770
Fax: 49-69-78077700

Kastner & Partner GmbH
Johannes Kastner
Werbeagentur, Kennedyallee 94
D-60596 Frankfurt/Main
Germany
Phone: 49-69-639011
Fax: 49-69-639-016

Greece

Leo Burnett
Dimitri Batayas, Exec. VP, Media and Research
371 Sigrou Avenue
17564 Athens, Greece
Phone: 30-1-941-39-66
Fax: 30-1-9430432

Hungary

Leo Burnett Budapest Ltd. K.F.T.
Andrea Mikita, Media Manager
Suba Trade Center
Nagymezo utca 44—7th Floor
H-1065 Budapest, Hungary
Phone: 36-1-269-0555/0556
Fax: 36-1-269-0557

Italy

Leo Burnett Co., S.R.L.
Ada Ferrari, Media Director
Via Fatebenefratelli 14
20121 Milan,
Italy
Phone: 39-2-63-541
Fax: 39-2-2900-5229
Media: 39-2-281-01156

Leo Burnett Turin
Jenny Evangelisti
Corso Vittori Emanuele II 100
10121 Torino
Italy
Phone: 39-11-562-0201
Fax: 39-11-561-7566

Netherlands

Noordervliet & Winninghoff/Leo Burnett B.V.
Maarten Albarda, Media Director
Buitenveldertselaan 106
1081 AB Amsterdam
The Netherlands
Phone: 31-20-504-6161
Fax: 31-20-504-6151

Norway

Leo Burnett A/S
Lars Gronseth, Media Director
Drammensveien 130
0277 Oslo, Norway
Phone: 47-22-92600
Fax: 47-22-926999

Poland

Leo Burnett Sp.z.o.o.
Ed Russell Managing Director
ul. Zwyciezcow 18
P-03-912 Warszawa, Poland
Phone: 48-2-617-2413
Fax: 48-2-617-1462

Portugal

Cineponto/Leo Burnett Ltd.
Pedro Castel–Branco, Media Director
Rue de Santa Marta, 43E 5
1100 Lisbon
Portugal
Phone: 351-1-526243/5/6/7
Fax: 351-1-579457

Spain

Vitruvio/Leo Burnett
Jose-Enrique Gonzalez-Quijano, Media
 Director
Torre Picasso, Planta 27
Plaza de Pablo Ruiz Picasso
S/N, 28020 Madrid, Spain
Phone: 34-1-556-1120
Fax: 34-1-556-5705

Vitruvio/Leo Burnett
Elias Chahin, Account Director
Diagonal 593
08014 Barcelona, Spain
Phone: 34-3-419-3277
Fax: 34-3-419-5680

Sweden

Leo Burnett Sweden A.B.
Klaus Hahn, Client Service Director
Kungsgatan 38
11135 Stockholm,
Sweden
Phone: 46-8-200-940
Fax: 46-8-203-707

Switzerland

Matter Galbucci Leo Burnett
Karl Heinz Muller, Media Director
Ausstellungsstrasse 80
Ch-8005 Zurich,
Switzerland
Phone: 411-272-7300
Fax: 411-272-7360 (main fax)
Media: 411-383-5148

Turkey

Markom/Leo Burnett A.S.
Muharrem Ayin, Media Director
Perihan Sokak No. 126
Sisli
Istanbul, Turkey
Phone: 90-212-234-27-28
Fax: 90-212-246-0842
Media: 90-212-234-3109

United Kingdom

Leo Burnett Limited
Nick Brien, Executive Media Director
48 St. Martin's Lane
London, WC2N 4EJ,
England
Phone: 44-71-836-2424
Fax: 44-71-829-7027
Media: 44-71-829-7099

Middle East

Bahrain

Radius Leo Burnett
See U.A.E.

Egypt

AMA, Leo Burnett
Abdel Fattah Mahmoud, Media Manager
21, Ahmed Orabi Street
El Nahda Tower, 7th Floor
El Sahafeyein
Giza, Egypt
Phone: 202-346-2201/347-4377
Fax: 202-346-0662

Kuwait

Radius Leo Burnett
See U.A.E.

Lebanon

H & C, Leo Burnett
Randa Moussali, Media Director
Sofil Center, 5th Floor
Achrafiel
P.O. Box 55369
Beirut, Lebanon
Phone: 961-1-602532/201093
Fax: 961-1-602531

Oman

Radius Leo Burnett
See U.A.E.

Qatar

Radius Leo Burnett
See U.A.E.

Saudi Arabia

Targets Advertising
Gary Makdessian, Media Director
Shinkar Commercial Center, 2nd Floor
Medina Road, P.O. Box 6093
Jeddah – 21442, Saudi Arabia
Phone: 966-2-651-1272
Fax: 966-2-651-3166

U.A.E.

Radius Advertising
Raja Sowan, Regional Media Director
The Blue Building
2nd Floor
Dubai, Sharjah Road
Dubai, U.A.E.
Phone: 971-4-620431
Fax: 971-4-696109

Latin America

Argentina

Leo Burnett Co., Inc.–
  Sucursal Argentina
Edyardi Neccia, Media Director
Carlos Pellegrini 1363, 12th Floor
1011 Buenos Aires, Argentina
Phone: 54-1-394-5066/62/33
Fax:54-1-112049

Brazil

Leo Burnett Publicidade, Ltda.
Paulo Afonso Gregoraci, Media Director
Avenida Cidade Jardim 400
3rd and 4th Floors
Sao Paulo, SP CEP 01454
Brazil
Phone: 55-11-815-3611
Fax: 55-11-2119037

Chile

Leo Burnett Chile
Martin Osorio, Media Director
Eliodoro Yanez 2376, Providencia
Santiago, Chile
Phone: 56-2-2239649
Fax: 56-2-2049436
Media: 56-2-223-3375

Colombia

Leo Burnett Colombia, S.A.
Martha Marin, Media Director
Carrera 13 No. 89-59
Bogota, D.C., Colombia
Phone:57-1-218-6900
Fax: 57-1-218-9073
Media: 56-2-256-0155

Costa Rica

Comunica Leo Burnett-Costa Rica
Tatiana Murillo H. Rodriguez,
Media Director
De Pollos Kentucky
100 Metros al Este y 250 metros al Sur
Barrio Francisco Peralta
Costa Rica
Phone: 506-34-0606
Fax: 506-342424

Dominican Republic

Leo Burnett, Inc.
Doris Reyes, Media Director
Prolongacion Arabia No. 13
Arroyo Hondo
Santo Domingo, Dominican Republic
Phone: 1-809-565-0558
Fax: 1-809-566-6634

Ecuador

Valencia & Asociados
Fernando Valencia, Managing Director
Av. Coruna 1311 y San Ignacio
Quito, Ecuador
Phone: 593-222-2273
Fax: 593-256-8895
Temp: 593-222-2273

El Salvador

Comunica Leo Burnett Publicidad
See Guatemala

Guatemala

Comunica Leo Burnett Publicidad
Lucia de Ochoa, Media Director
5Ta Avenida 6-39
Zona 14, Colonia El Campo
Guatemala City 01014, Guatemala
Phone: 502-2-373-142 thru 46
Fax: 502-2-373150

Honduras

Comunica Leo Burnett Publicidad
See Guatemala

Mexico

Leo Burnett, S.A. de C.V.
Miguel Angel Ruiz Gonzalez, V.P.,
Media Director
Bosque de Duraznos 65-8 P
Bosques de Las Lomas
11700 Mexico, D.F. Mexico
Phone: 525-596-61-88
Fax: 525-596-6248
Media: 525-596-6241

Nicaragua

Comunica Leo Burnett Publicidad
See Guatemala

Panama

Comunica Leo Burnett Publicidad, S.A.
Maria I. Mantovani, Media Director
Calle Venezuela No. 5 Bella Vista
Apartado 2181, Panama 1
Republic of Panama
Phone: 507-23-15-60
Fax: 507-23-16-09

Peru

Causa Publicidad
Marcelino Ceron, Media Director
Parque Armendariz 159
Miraflores, Lima 18,
Peru
Phone: 51-14-44-0505
Fax: 51-14-440887

Puerto Rico

Leo Burnett Inc.
Cecilia Carvajal Mitja, Media Director
Banco de Ponce Building, Suite 2200
Hato Rey, San Juan
Puerto Rico 00918
Phone: (809) 754-7761 thru 67
Fax: (809) 766-1765

Uruguay

Nucleo Publicidad
Raul Yafe, General Manager
Jose Enrique Rodo 1668
Montevideo
Uruguay
Phone: 59-82-417-602
Fax: 59-82-499-064

Venezuela

Leo Burnett Venezuela, C.A.
Javier Salas, V.P. Business Development,
Director of Communication
Centro Plaza, Torre B. Niveles 7 y 8
Avenida Francisco de Miranda
Los Palos Grandes
Caracas 1062, Venezuela
Phone: 58-2-283-7066
Fax: 58-2-2850667
J. Salas: 582-283-9486